What They Said
in 1982

What They Said
In 1982

The Yearbook Of World Opinion

Compiled and Edited by

ALAN F. PATER

and

JASON R. PATER

MONITOR BOOK COMPANY, INC.

FOURTEENTH ANNUAL EDITION

Printed in the United States of America

Library of Congress catalogue card number 74-111080

ISBN number: 0-917734-08-4

WHAT THEY SAID is published annually by Monitor Book
Company, Inc., Beverly Hills, California. The title, "WHAT THEY
SAID," is a trademark owned exclusively by Monitor Book
Company, Inc., and has been duly registered with the United
States Patent Office. Any unauthorized use is prohibited.

To

The Newsmakers of the World . . .

May they never be at a loss for words

Preface to the First Edition (1969)

Words can be powerful or subtle, humorous or maddening. They can be vigorous or feeble, lucid or obscure, inspiring or despairing, wise or foolish, hopeful or pessimistic . . . they can be fearful or confident, timid or articulate, persuasive or perverse, honest or deceitful. As tools at a speaker's command, words can be used to reason, argue, discuss, cajole, plead, debate, declaim, threaten, infuriate, or appease; they can harangue, flourish, recite, preach, discourse, stab to the quick, or gently sermonize.

When casually spoken by a stage or film star, words can go beyond the press-agentry and make-up facade and reveal the inner man or woman. When purposefully uttered in the considered phrasing of a head of state, words can determine the destiny of millions of people, resolve peace or war, or chart the course of a nation on whose direction the fate of the entire world may depend.

Until now, the *copia verborum* of well-known and renowned public figures—the doctors and diplomats, the governors and generals, the potentates and presidents, the entertainers and educators, the bishops and baseball players, the jurists and journalists, the authors and attorneys, the congressmen and chairmen-of-the-board—whether enunciated in speeches, lectures, interviews, radio and television addresses, news conferences, forums, symposiums, town meetings, committee hearings, random remarks to the press, or delivered on the floors of the United States Senate and House of Representatives or in the parliaments and palaces of the world—have been dutifully reported in the media, then filed away and, for the most part, forgotten.

The editors of *WHAT THEY SAID* believe that consigning such a wealth of thoughts, ideas, doctrines, opinions and philosophies to interment in the morgues and archives of the Fourth Estate is lamentable and unnecessary. Yet the media, in all their forms, are constantly engulfing us in a profusion of endless and increasingly voluminous news reports. One is easily disposed to disregard or forget the stimulating discussion of critical issues embodied in so many of the utterances of those who make the news and, in their respective fields, shape the events throughout the world. The conclusion is therefore a natural and compelling one: the educator, the public official, the business executive, the statesman, the philosopher—everyone who has a stake in the complex, often confusing trends of our times—should have material of this kind readily available.

These, then, are the circumstances under which *WHAT THEY SAID* was conceived. It is the culmination of a year of listening to the people in the public eye; a year of scrutinizing, monitoring, reviewing, judging, deciding—a year during which the editors resurrected from almost certain oblivion those quintessential elements of the year's *spoken* opinion which, in their judgment, demanded preservation in book form.

WHAT THEY SAID is a pioneer in its field. Its *raison d'etre* is the firm conviction that presenting, each year, the highlights of vital and interesting views from the lips of prominent people on virtually every aspect of contemporary civilization fulfills the need to give the *spoken* word the permanence and lasting value of the *written* word. For, if it is true that a picture is worth 10,000 words, it is equally true that a verbal conclusion, an apt quote or a candid comment by a person of fame or influence can have more significance and can provide more understanding than an entire page of summary in a standard work of reference.

The editors of *WHAT THEY SAID* did not, however, design their book for researchers and scholars alone. One of the failings of the conventional reference work is that it is blandly written and referred to primarily for facts and figures, lacking inherent "interest value." *WHAT THEY SAID*, on the other hand, was planned for sheer enjoyment and pleasure, for searching glimpses into the lives and thoughts of the world's celebrities, as well as for serious study, intellectual reflection and the philosophical contemplation of our multifaceted life and mores. Furthermore, those pressed for time, yet anxious to know what the newsmakers have been saying, will welcome the short excerpts which will make for quick, intermittent reading—and rereading. And, of course, the topical classifications, the speakers' index, the subject index, the place and date information—documented and authenticated and easily located—will supply a rich fund of hitherto not readily obtainable reference and statistical material.

Finally, the reader will find that the editors have eschewed trite comments and cliches, tedious and boring. The selected quotations, each standing on its own, are pertinent, significant, stimulating—above all, relevant to today's world, expressed in the speakers' own words. And they will, the editors feel, be even more relevant tomorrow. They will be re-examined and reflected upon in the future by men and women eager to learn from the past. The prophecies, the promises, the "golden dreams," the boastings and rantings, the bluster, the bravado, the pleadings and representations of those whose voices echo in these pages (and in those to come) should provide a rare and unique history lesson. The positions held by these luminaries, in their respective callings, are such that what they say today may profoundly affect the future as well as the present, and so will be of lasting importance and meaning.

Beverly Hills, California

ALAN F. PATER
JASON R. PATER

Table of Contents

PART THREE: GENERAL

Editorial Treatment

ORGANIZATION OF MATERIAL

Special attention has been given to the arrangement of the book—from the major divisions down to the individual categories and speakers—the objective being a logical progression of related material, as follows:

(A) The categories are arranged alphabetically within each of three major sections:

Part One:	"National Affairs"
Part Two:	"International Affairs"
Part Three:	"General"

In this manner, the reader can quickly locate quotations pertaining to particular fields of interest (see also *Indexing*). It should be noted that some quotations contain a number of thoughts or ideas—sometimes on different subjects—while some are vague as to exact subject matter and thus do not fit clearly into a specific topic classification. In such cases, the judgment of the Editors has determined the most appropriate category.

(B) Within each category the speakers are in alphabetical order by surname, following alphabetization practices used in the speaker's country of origin.

(C) Where there are two or more quotations by one speaker within the same category, they appear chronologically by date spoken or date of source.

SPEAKER IDENTIFICATION

(A) The occupation, profession, rank, position or title of the speaker is given as it was *at the time the statement was made* (except when the speaker's relevant identification is in the past, in which case he is shown as "former"). Thus, due to possible changes in status during the year, a speaker may be shown with different identifications in various parts of the book, or even within the same category.

(B) In the case of a speaker who holds more than one position simultaneously, the judgment of the Editors has determined the most appropriate identification to use with a specific quotation.

(C) Nationality of the speakers is given only when it is relevant to the specific quotation.

THE QUOTATIONS

The quoted material selected for inclusion in this book is shown as it appeared in the source, except as follows:

(A) *Ellipses* have been inserted wherever the Editors have deleted extraneous words or overly long passages within the quoted material used. In no way has the meaning or intention of the quotations been altered. *Ellipses* are also used where they appeared in the source.

(B) *Punctuation and spelling* have been altered by the Editors where they were obviously incorrect in the source, or to make the quotations more intelligible, or to conform to the general style used throughout this book. Again, meaning and intention of the quotations have not been changed.

(C) *Brackets* ([]) indicate material inserted by the Editors or by the source to either correct obvious errors or to explain or clarify what the speaker is saying. In some instances, bracketed material may replace quoted material for the sake of clarity.

(D) *Italics* either appeared in the original source or were added by the Editors where emphasis is clearly desirable.

Except for the above instances, the quoted material used has been printed verbatim, as reported by the source (even if the speaker made factual errors or was awkward in his choice of words).

Special care has been exercised to make certain that each quotation stands on its own and is not taken "out of context." The Editors, however, cannot be responsible for errors made by the original source, i.e., incorrect reporting, mis-quotations, or errors in interpretation.

DOCUMENTATION AND SOURCES

Documentation (circumstance, place, date) of each quotation is provided as fully as could be obtained, and the sources are furnished for all quotations. In some instances, no documentation details were available; in those cases, only the source is given. Following are the sequence and style used for this information:

Circumstance of quotation, place, date/Name of source, date:section (if applicable), page number.

Example: *Before the Senate, Washington, Dec. 4/The Washington Post, 12-5:(A)13.*

The above example indicates that the quotation was delivered before the Senate in Washington on December 4. It was taken for *WHAT THEY SAID* from *The Washington Post*, issue of December 5, section A, page 13. (When a newspaper publishes more than one edition on the same date, it should be noted that page numbers may vary from edition to edition.)

(A) When the source is a television or radio broadcast, the name of the network or local station is indicated, along with the date of the broadcast (obviously, page and section information does not apply).

(B) An asterisk (*) before the (/) in the documentation indicates that the quoted material was written rather than spoken. Although the basic policy of *WHAT THEY SAID* is to use only *spoken* statements, there are occasions when written statements are considered by the Editors to be important enough to be included. These occasions are rare and usually involve Presidential messages and statements released to the press and other such documents attributed to persons in high government office.

INDEXING

(A) The *Index to Speakers* is keyed to the page number. (For alphabetization practices, see

Organization of Material, paragraph B.)

(B) The *Index to Subjects* is keyed to both the page number and the quotation number on the page (thus 210:3 indicates quotation number 3 on page 210); the quotation number appears at the right corner of each quotation.

(C) To locate quotations on a particular subject, regardless of the speaker, turn to the appropriate category (see *Table of Contents*) or use the detailed *Index to Subjects*.

(D) To locate all quotations by a particular speaker, regardless of subject, use the *Index to Speakers*.

(E) To locate quotations by a particular speaker on a particular subject, turn to the appropriate category and then to that person's quotations within the category.

(F) The reader will find that the basic categorization format of *WHAT THEY SAID* is itself a useful subject index, inasmuch as related quotations are grouped together by their respective categories. All aspects of journalism, for example, are relevant to each other; thus, the section *Journalism* embraces all phases of the news media. Similarly, quotations pertaining to the U.S. President, Congress, etc., are in the section *Government*.

––––––––––

MISCELLANEOUS

(A) Except where otherwise indicated or obviously to the contrary, all universities, organizations and business firms mentioned in this book are in the United States; similarly, references made to "national," "Federal," "this country," "the nation," etc., refer to the United States.

(B) In most cases, organizations whose names end with "of the United States" are Federal government agencies.

––––––––––

SELECTION OF CATEGORIES

The selected categories reflect, in the Editors' opinion, the most widely discussed public-interest subjects, those which readily fall into the over-all sphere of "current events." They represent topics continuously covered by the mass media because of their inherent importance to the changing world scene. Most of the categories are permanent; they appear in each annual edition of *WHAT THEY SAID*. However, because of the transient character of some subjects, there may be categories which appear one year and may not be repeated the next.

SELECTION OF SPEAKERS

The following persons are always considered eligible for inclusion in *WHAT THEY SAID*: top-level officials of all branches of national, state and local governments (both U.S. and foreign), including all United States Senators and Representatives; top-echelon military officers; college and university presidents, chancellors and professors; chairmen and presidents of major corporations; heads of national public-oriented organizations and associations; national and internationally known diplomats; recognized celebrities from the entertainment and literary spheres and the arts generally; sports figures of national stature; commentators on the world scene who are recognized as such and who command the attention of the mass media.

The determination of what and who are "major" and "recognized" must, necessarily, be made by the Editors of WHAT THEY SAID based on objective personal judgment.

Also, some persons, while not generally recognized as prominent or newsworthy, may have nevertheless attracted an unusual amount of attention in connection with an important issue or event. These people, too, are considered for inclusion, depending upon the specific circumstance.

SELECTION OF QUOTATIONS

The quotations selected for inclusion in WHAT THEY SAID obviously represent a decided minority of the seemingly endless volume of quoted material appearing in the media each year. The process of selecting is scrupulously objective insofar as the partisan views of the Editors are concerned (see About Fairness, below). However, it is clear that the Editors must decide which quotations per se are suitable for inclusion, and in doing so look for comments that are aptly stated, offer insight into the subject being discussed, or into the speaker, and provide—for today as well as for future reference—a thought which readers will find useful for understanding the issues and the personalities that make up a year on this planet.

ABOUT FAIRNESS

The Editors of WHAT THEY SAID understand the necessity of being impartial when compiling a book of this kind. As a result, there has been no bias in the selection of the quotations, the choice of speakers or the manner of editing. Relevance of the statements and the status of the speakers are the exclusive criteria for inclusion, without any regard whatsoever to the personal beliefs and views of the Editors. Furthermore, every effort has been made to include a multiplicity of opinions and ideas from a wide cross-section of speakers on each topic. Nevertheless, should there appear to be, on some controversial issues, a majority of material favoring one point of view over another, it is simply the result of there having been more of those views expressed during the year, reported by the media and objectively considered suitable by the Editors of WHAT THEY SAID (see Selection of Quotations, above). Also, since persons in politics and government account for a large percentage of the speakers in WHAT THEY SAID, there may exist a heavier weight of opinion favoring the philosophy of those in office at the time, whether in the United States Congress, the Administration, or in foreign capitals. This is natural and to be expected and should not be construed as a reflection of agreement or disagreement with that philosophy on the part of the Editors of WHAT THEY SAID.

Abbreviations

The following are abbreviations used by the speakers in this volume. Rather than defining them each time they appear in the quotations, this list will facilitate reading and avoid unnecessary repetition.

ABA:	American Basketball Association
ABM:	antiballistic missile
ARENA:	National Republican Alliance (El Salvador)
BBC:	British Broadcasting Corporation
CBS:	CBS, Inc. (Columbia Broadcasting System)
CIA:	Central Intelligence Agency
CPA:	certified public accountant
CPSU:	Communist Party of the Soviet Union
D.A.:	District Attorney
EEC:	European Economic Community
ERA:	Equal Rights Amendment
FAA:	Federal Aviation Administration
FAO:	Food and Agriculture Organization (United Nations)
FBI:	Federal Bureau of Investigation
FCC:	Federal Communications Commission
F.D.R.:	Franklin Delano Roosevelt
FOIA:	Freedom of Information Act
FTC:	Federal Trade Commission
GATT:	General Agreement on Tariffs and Trade
GNP:	gross national product
HMS:	Her Majesty's Ship
ICBM:	intercontinental ballistic missile
IDF:	Israeli Defense Forces
ILO:	International Labor Organization
IRA:	Irish Republican Army
IRS:	Internal Revenue Service
KGB:	Soviet Commission of State Security
KPNLF:	Khmer People's National Liberation Front

MBA:	master of business administration
MIRV:	multiple independently targeted re-entry vehicle
MOR:	middle of the road
m.p.h.:	miles per hour
NAACP:	National Association for the Advancement of Colored People
NATO:	North Atlantic Treaty Organization
NBA:	National Basketball Association
NFL:	National Football League
NHL:	National Hockey League
NPR:	National Public Radio
OAS:	Organization of American States
OPEC:	Organization of Petroleum Exporting Countries
OSHA:	Occupational Safety and Health Administration
PAC:	political-action committee
PBS:	Public Broadcasting Service
PLO:	Palestine Liberation Organization
POW:	prisoner of war
p.r.:	public relations
R&D:	research & development
SALT:	Strategic Arms Limitation Talks
TV:	television
UFO:	unidentified flying object
UN:	United Nations
UNESCO:	United National Educational, Scientific and Cultural Organization
UNICEF:	United Nations International Children's Emergency Fund
U.S.:	United States
U.S.A.:	United States of America
U.S.S.R.:	Union of Soviet Socialist Republics
VA:	Veterans Administration

Party affiliation of United States Senators, Representatives and Governors—
    D: Democratic
    R: Republican

The Quote of the Year

[On war]: . . . each time that we risk man's life, we start to ride along dangerous, regressive and anti-human paths. Therefore . . . humanity should question itself once more about the absurd and always unfair phenomenon of war, on whose stage of death and pain only remain standing the negotiating table that could and should have prevented it.

POPE JOHN PAUL II
Buenos Aires, Argentina, June 11,
The New York Times, 6-12-4.

PART ONE

National Affairs

The State of the Union Address

Delivered by Ronald Reagan, President of the United States, at the Capitol, Washington, January 26, 1982.

Today marks my first State of the Union address to you, a Constitutional duty as old as our republic itself.

President Washington began this tradition in 1790 after reminding the nation that the destiny of self-government and the "preservation of the sacred fire of liberty" is finally staked on the experiment entrusted to the hands of the American people." For our friends in the press, who place a high premium on accuracy, let me say: I did not actually hear George Washington say that, but it is a matter of historic record

From this podium, Winston Churchill asked the free world to stand together against the onslaught of aggression. Franklin D. Roosevelt spoke of a day of infamy and summoned a nation to arms. Douglas MacArthur made an unforgettable farewell to a country he had loved and served so well. Dwight Eisenhower reminded us that peace was purchased only at the price of strength and John F. Kennedy spoke of the burden and glory that is freedom.

When I visited this chamber last year as a newcomer to Washington, critical of past policies which I believe had failed, I proposed a new spirit of partnership between this Congress and this Administration and between Washington and our state and local governments.

In forging this new partnership for America we could achieve the oldest hopes of our republic—prosperity for our nation, peace for the world, and the blessings of individual liberty for our children and, some day, for all of humanity.

It is my duty to report to you tonight on the progress we have made in our relations with other nations, on the foundation we have carefully laid for our economic recovery and, finally, on a bold and spirited initiative that I believe can change the face of American government and make it again the servant of the people.

Seldom have the stakes been higher for America. What we do and say here will make all the difference to auto workers in Detroit, lumberjacks in the Northwest, and steelworkers in Steubenville who are in the unemployment lines, to black teen-agers in Newark and Chicago; to hard-pressed farmers and small businessmen and to millions of everyday Americans who harbor the simple wish of a safe and financially secure future for their children.

To understand the State of the Union, we must look not only at where we are and where we are going but at where we've been. The situation at this time last year was truly ominous.

Series of Recessions

The last decade has seen a series of recessions. There was a recession in 1970, another in 1974, and again in the spring of 1980. Each time, unemployment increased and inflation soon turned up again. We coined the word "stagflation" to describe this.

Government's response to these recessions was to pump up the money supply and increase spending.

In the last six months of 1980, as an example, the money supply increased at the fastest rate in postwar history—13 percent. Inflation remained in double digits and government spending increased at an annual rate of 17 percent. Interest rates reached a staggering 21½ percent. There were eight million unemployed.

Late in 1981, we sank into the present recession—largely because continued high interest rates hurt the auto industry and construction. There was a drop in productivity and the already high unemployment rate increased.

Economic Programs' Results

This time, however, things are different. We have an economic program in place completely different from the artificial quick-fixes of the past. It calls for reduction of the rate of increase in government spending, and already that rate has been cut nearly in half. But reduced spending alone isn't enough. We've just implemented the first and smallest phase of a three-year tax-rate reduction plan designed to stimulate the economy and create jobs.

Already interest rates are down to 15¾ percent, but they must still go lower. Inflation is down from 12.4 percent to 8.9 percent, and for the month of December it was running at an annualized rate of 5.2 percent.

If we had not acted as we did, things would be far worse for all Americans than they are today. Inflation, taxes and interest rates would all be higher.

Changes in Government

A year ago, Americans' faith in their governmental process was steadily declining. Six out of ten Americans were saying they were pessimistic about their future.

A new kind of defeatism was heard. Some said our domestic problems were uncontrollable—that we had to learn to live with the seemingly endless cycles of high inflation and high unemployment.

There were also pessimistic predictions about the relationship between our Administration and this Congress. It was said we could never work together. Well, those predictions were wrong.

The record is clear, and I believe history will remember this as an era of American renewal, remember this Administration as an Administration of change and remember this Congress as a Congress of destiny.

Together, we not only cut the increase in government spending nearly in half, we brought about the largest tax reductions and the most sweeping changes in our tax structure since the beginning of this century. And because we indexed future taxes to the rate of inflation, we took away government's built-in profit on

inflation and its hidden incentive to grow larger at the expense of American workers.

Together, after 50 years of taking power away from the hands of the people in their states and local communities, we have started returning power and resource to them.

Together, we have cut the growth of new Federal regulations nearly in half. In 1982, there were 23,000 fewer pages in the Federal Register, which lists new regulations, than there were in 1980. By deregulating oil, we have come closer to achieving energy independence and helped bring down the costs of gasoline and heating fuel.

Together, we have created an effective Federal strike force to combat waste and fraud in government. In just six months it has saved the taxpayers more than $2 billion, and it's only getting started.

Together, we have begun to mobilize the private sector—not to duplicate wasteful and discredited government programs but to bring thousands of Americans into a volunteer effort to help solve many of America's social problems.

Together, we have begun to restore that margin of military safety that insures peace. Our country's uniform is being worn once again with pride.

Together, we have made a new beginning, but we have only begun.

Rough Road for Economy

No one pretends that the way ahead will be easy. In my inaugural address last year, I warned that the "ills we suffer have come upon us over several decades. They will not go away in days, weeks or months, but they will go away . . . because we as Americans have the capacity now, as we've had in the past, to do whatever needs to be done to preserve this last and greatest bastion of freedom."

The economy will face difficult moments in the months ahead. But the program for economic recovery that is in place will pull the economy out of its slump and put us on the road to prosperity and stable growth by the latter half of this year.

That is why I can report to you tonight that in the near future the State of the Union and the economy will be better—much better—if we summon the strength to continue on the course we have charted.

And so the question: If the fundamentals are in place, what now?

Two things. First, we must understand what is happening at the moment to the economy. Our current problems are not the product of the recovery program that is only just now getting under way, as some would have you believe; they are the inheritance of decades of tax and tax, spend and spend.

Second, because our economic problems are deeply rooted and will not respond to quick political fixes, we must stick to our carefully integrated plan for recovery. That plan is based on four common-sense fundamentals: continued reduction of the growth in Federal spending, preserving the individual and business tax reductions that will stimulate saving and investment, removing unnecessary Federal regulations to spark productivity, and maintaining a healthy dollar and a stable monetary policy—the latter a responsibility of the Federal Reserve System.

The only alternative being offered to this economic program is a return to the policies that gave us a trillion dollar debt, runaway inflation, runaway interest rates and unemployment.

The doubters would have us turn back the clock with tax increases that would offset the personal tax-rate reductions already passed by this Congress.

Taxes and Deficits

Raise present taxes to our future deficits, they tell us. Well, I don't believe we should buy their argument. There are too many imponderables for anyone to predict deficits or surpluses several years ahead with any degree of accuracy. The budget in place when I took office had been projected as balanced. It turned out to have one of the biggest deficits in history. Another example of the imponderables that can make deficit projections highly questionable: A change of only one percentage point in unemployment can alter a deficit up or down by some $25 billion.

As it now stands, our forecasts, which we are required by law to make, will show major deficits, starting at less than $100 billion and declining, but still too high.

More important, we are making progress with the three keys to reducing deficits: economic growth, lower interest rates and spending control. The policies we have in place will reduce the deficit steadily, surely and, in time, completely.

Higher taxes would not mean lower deficits. If they did, how would we explain that tax revenues more than doubled just since 1976, yet in the same six-year period we ran the largest series of deficits in our history. In 1980 tax revenues increased by $54 billion, and in 1980 we had one of our all-time biggest deficits.

Raising taxes won't balance the budget. It will encourage more government spending and less private investment. Raising taxes will slow economic growth, reduce production and destroy future jobs, making it more difficult for those without jobs to find them and more likely that those who now have jobs could lose them.

So I will not ask you to try to balance the budget on the backs of the American taxpayers. I will seek no tax increases this year and I have no intention of retreating from our basic program of tax relief. I promised the American people to bring their tax rates down and keep them down—to provide them incentives to rebuild our economy, to save, to invest in America's future. I will stand by my word. Tonight I am urging the American people: Seize these new opportunities to produce, save and invest, and together we will make this economy a mighty engine of freedom, hope and prosperity again.

The budget deficit this year will exceed our earlier expectations. The recession did that. It lowered revenues and increased costs. To some extent, we are also victims of our own success. We have brought inflation down faster than we thought we could and have thus deprived government of those hidden revenues that occur when inflation pushes people into higher income tax brackets. And the continued high interest rates last year cost the government about $5 billion more than anticipated.

We must cut out more nonessential government spending and root out more waste, and we will continue our efforts to reduce the number of employees in the Federal work force by 75,000.

The budget plan I submit to you on Feb. 8 will realize major savings by dismantling the Departments of Energy and Education, and by eliminating ineffective subsidies for business. We will continue to redirect our resources to our two highest budget priorities—a strong national defense to keep America free and at peace and a reliable safety net of social programs for those who have contributed and those who are in need.

Social Programs

Contrary to some of the wild charges you may have heard, this Administration has not and will not turn its back on America's elderly or America's poor. Under the new budget, funding for social insurance programs will be more than double the amount spent only six years ago.

But it would be foolish to pretend that these or any programs cannot be made more efficient and economical.

The entitlement programs that make up our safety net for the truly needy have worthy goals and many deserving recipients. We will protect them. But there is only one way to see to it that these programs really help those whom they were designed to help, and that is to bring their spiraling costs under control.

Today we face the absurd situation of a Federal budget with three-quarters of its expenditures routinely referred to as "uncontrollable," and a large part of this goes to entitlement programs.

Committee after committee of this Congress has heard witness after witness describe many of these programs as poorly administered and rife with waste and fraud. Virtually every American who shops in a local supermarket is aware of the daily abuses that take place in the

food stamp program—which has grown by 16,000 percent in the last 15 years. Another example is Medicare and Medicaid—programs with worthy goals but whose costs have increased from $11.2 billion to almost $60 billion, more than five times as much, in just 10 years.

Waste and fraud are serious problems. Back in 1980, Federal investigators testified before one of your committees that "corruption has permeated virtually every area of the Medicare and Medicaid health care industry." One official said many of the people who are cheating the system were "very confident that nothing was going to happen to them."

Well, something is going to happen. Not only the taxpayers are defrauded—the people with real dependency on these programs are deprived of what they need because available resources are going not to the needy but to the greedy.

The time has come to control the uncontrollable.

In August we made a start. I signed a bill to reduce the growth of these programs by $44 billion over the next three years, while at the same time preserving essential services for the truly needy. Shortly you will receive from me a message on further reforms we intend to install—some new, but others long recommended by your own Congressional committees. I ask you to help make these savings for the American taxpayer.

The savings we propose in entitlement programs will total some $63 billion over four years and will, without affecting Social Security, go a long way toward bringing Federal spending under control.

But don't be fooled by those who proclaim that spending cuts will deprive the elderly, the needy and the helpless. The Federal Government will still subsidize 95 million meals every day. That's one out of seven of all the meals served in America. Head Start, senior nutrition programs and child welfare programs will not be cut from the levels we proposed last year. More than one-half billion dollars has been proposed for minority business assistance. And research at the National Institutes of Health will be increased by over $100 million. While meeting all these needs, we intend to plug unwarranted tax loopholes and strengthen the law which requires all large corporations to pay a minimum tax.

I am confident the economic program we have put into operation will protect the needy while it triggers a recovery that will benefit all Americans. It will stimulate the economy, result in increased savings and thus provide capital for expansion, mortgages for home building and jobs for the unemployed.

Federalism

Now that the essentials of that program are in place, our next major undertaking must be a program—just as bold, just as innovative—to make government again accountable to the people, to make our system of federalism work again.

Our citizens feel they have lost control of even the most basic decisions made about the essential services of government, such as schools, welfare, roads and even garbage collection. They are right.

A maze of interlocking jurisdictions and levels of government confronts average citizens in trying to solve even the simplest of problems. They do not know where to turn for answers, who to hold accountable, who to praise, who to blame, who to vote for or against.

The main reason for this is the overpowering growth of Federal grants-in-aid programs during the past few decades.

In 1960, the Federal Government had 132 categorical grant programs, costing $7 billion. When I took office, there were approximately 500, costing nearly $100 billion—13 programs for energy conservation, 36 for pollution control, 66 for social services and 90 for education. The list goes on and on. Here in the Congress, it takes at least 166 committees just to try to keep track of them.

You know and I know that neither the President nor the Congress can properly oversee this jungle of grants-in-aid; indeed, the growth of these grants has led to a distortion in the vital functions of government. As one Democratic Governor put it recently: "The national Government should be worrying about arms control, not potholes."

The growth in these Federal programs has—in the words of one intergovernmental commission—made the Federal Government "more pervasive, more intrusive, more unmanageable, more ineffective, more costly and above all more unaccountable."

Let us solve this problem with a single, bold stroke—the return of some $47 billion in Federal programs to state and local government, together with the means to finance them and a transition period of nearly 10 years to avoid unnecessary disruption.

I will shortly send the Congress a message describing this program. I want to emphasize, however, that its full details will have been worked out only after close consultation with Congressional, state and local officials.

Starting in fiscal 1984, the Federal Government will assume full responsibility for the cost of the rapidly growing Medicaid program to go along with its existing responsibility for Medicare. As part of a financially equal swap, the states will simultaneously take full responsibility for Aid to Families With Dependent Children and food stamps. This will make welfare less costly and more responsive to genuine need because it will be designed and administered closer to the grass roots and the people it serves.

In 1984, the Federal Government will apply the full proceeds from certain excise taxes to a grass-roots trust fund that will belong, in fair shares, to the 50 states. The total amount flowing into this fund will be $28 billion a year.

Over the next four years, the states can use this money in either of two ways. If they want to continue receiving Federal grants in such areas as transportation, education and social services, they can use their trust fund money to pay for the grants or, to the extent they choose to forego the Federal grant programs, they can use their trust fund money on their own, for those or other purposes. There will be a mandatory pass-through of part of these funds to local governments.

By 1988, the states will be in complete control of over 40 Federal grant programs. The trust fund will start to phase out, eventually to disappear, and the excise taxes will be turned over to the states. They can then preserve,

7

RONALD REAGAN

lower or raise taxes on their own and fund and manage these programs as they see fit.

In a single stroke, we will be accomplishing a realignment that will end cumbersome administration and spiraling costs at the Federal level while we insure these programs will be more responsive to both the people they are meant to help and the people who pay for them.

Hand in hand with this program to strengthen the discretion and flexibility of state and local government, we are proposing legislation for an experimental effort to improve and develop our depressed urban areas in the 1980's and 1990's. This legislation will permit states and localities to apply to the Federal Government for designation as urban enterprise zones. A broad range of special economic incentives in the zones will help attract new business, new jobs and new opportunity to America's inner cities and rural towns. Some will say our mission is to save free enterprise. I say we must free enterprise so that, together, we can save America.

Some will also say our states and local communities are not up to the challenge of a new and creative partnership. That might have been true 20 years ago before reforms like reapportionment and the Voting Rights Act, the 10-year extension of which I strongly support. It is no longer true today. This Administration has faith in state and local governments and the constitutional balance envisioned by the Founding Fathers. We also believe in the integrity, decency and sound good sense of grass-roots Americans.

Private Volunteerism

Our faith in the American people is reflected in another major endeavor. Our private sector initiative task force is seeking out successful community models of school, church, business, union, foundation and civic programs that help community needs. Such groups are almost invariably far more efficient than government in running social programs.

We are not asking them to replace discarded and often discredited government programs dollar for dollar, service for service. We just

want to help them perform the good works they choose, and help others to profit by their example. Three hundred eighty-five thousand corporations and private foundations are already working on social programs ranging from drug rehabilitation to job training, and thousands more Americans have written us asking how they can help. The volunteer spirit is still alive and well in America.

Civil Rights / Women's Rights

Our nation's long journey towards civil rights for all our citizens—once a source of discord, now a source of pride—must continue with no backsliding or slowing down. We must and shall see that those basic laws that guarantee equal rights are preserved and, when necessary, strengthened. Our concern for equal rights for women is firm and unshakable.

We launched a new Task Force on Legal Equity for Women, and a 50-states project that will examine state laws for discriminatory language. And for the first time in our history a woman sits on the highest court in the land.

So, too, the problem of crime—one as real and deadly serious as any in America today—demands that we seek transformation of our legal system, which overly protects the rights of criminals while it leaves society and the innocent victims of crime without justice.

We look forward to the enactment of a responsible Clean Air Act to increase jobs while continuing to improve the quality of our air. We are encouraged by the bipartisan initiative of the House and are hopeful of further progress as the Senate continues its deliberations.

So far I have concentrated largely on domestic matters. To view the State of the Union in perspective, we must not ignore the rest of the world. There isn't time tonight for a lengthy treatment of foreign policy—a subject I intend to address in detail in the near future. A few words, however, are in order on the progress we have made over the past year re-establishing respect for our nation around the globe and some of the challenges and goals we will approach in the year ahead.

8

The Americas

At Ottawa and Cancun, I met with leaders of the major industrial powers and developing nations. Some of those I met were a little surprised that I didn't apologize for America's wealth. Instead, I spoke of the strength of the free marketplace system and how it could help them realize their aspirations for economic development and political freedom. I believe lasting friendships were made and the foundation was laid for future cooperation.

In the vital region of the Caribbean Basin, we are developing a program of aid, trade and investment incentives to promote self-sustaining growth and a better, more secure life for our neighbors to the south. Toward those who would export terrorism and subversion in the Caribbean and elsewhere, especially Cuba and Libya, we will act with firmness.

Our foreign policy is a policy of strength, fairness and balance. By restoring America's military credibility, by pursuing peace at the negotiating table wherever both sides are willing to sit down in good faith, and by regaining the respect of America's allies and adversaries alike, we have strengthened our country's position as a force for peace and progress in the world.

Poland

When action is called for, we are taking it. Our sanctions against the military dictatorship that has attempted to crush human rights in Poland—and against the Soviet regime behind that military dictatorship—clearly demonstrated to the world that America will not conduct "business as usual" with the forces of oppression.

If the events in Poland continue to deteriorate, further measures will follow.

Let me also note that private American groups have taken the lead in making Jan. 30 a day of solidarity with the people of Poland—so, too, the European Parliament has called for March 21 to be an international day of support for Afghanistan. I urge all peace-loving peoples to join together on those days, to raise their voices, to speak and pray for freedom.

Arms Control

Meanwhile, we are working for reduction of arms and military activities. As I announced in my address to the nation last Nov. 18, we have proposed to the Soviet Union a far-reaching agenda for mutual reduction of military forces and have already initiated negotiations with them in Geneva on intermediate range nuclear forces.

In those talks it is essential that we negotiate from a position of strength. There must be a real incentive for the Soviets to take these talks seriously. This requires that we rebuild our defenses.

In the last decade, while we sought the moderation of Soviet power through a process of restraint and accommodation, the Soviets engage in an unrelenting buildup of their military forces.

The protection of our national security has required that we undertake a substantial program to enhance our military forces.

We have not neglected to strengthen our traditional alliances in Europe and Asia, or to develop key relationships with our partners in the Middle East and other countries.

Foreign Assistance

Building a more peaceful world requires a sound strategy and the national resolve to back it up. When radical forces threaten our friends, when economic misfortune creates conditions of instability, when strategically vital parts of the world fall under the shadow of Soviet power, our response can make the difference between peaceful change or disorder and violence. That is why we have laid such stress not only on our own defense, but on our vital foreign assistance program. Your recent passage of the foreign assistance act sent a signal to the world that America would not shrink from making the investments necessary for both peace and security. Our foreign policy must be rooted in realism, not naivete or self-delusion.

A recognition of what the Soviet empire is about is the starting point. Winston Churchill,

9

in negotiating with the Soviets, observed that they respect only strength and resolve in their dealings with other nations.

That is why we have moved to reconstruct our national defenses. We intend to keep the peace—we will also keep our freedom.

We have made pledges of a new frankness in our public statements and worldwide broadcasts. In the face of a climate of falsehood and misinformation, we have promised the world a season of truth—the truth of our great civilized ideas: individual liberty, representative government, the rule of law under God.

We have never needed walls, mine fields and barbwire to keep our people in. Nor do we declare martial law to prevent our people from voting for the kind of government they want.

Yes, we have our problems; yes, we are in a time of recession. And it's true, there is no quick fix to instantly end the tragic pain of unemployment. But we will end it—the process has already begun and we'll see its effect as this year goes on.

Heroes

We speak with pride and admiration of that little band of Americans who overcame insuperable odds to set this nation on course 200 years ago. But our glory didn't end with them—Americans ever since have emulated their deeds.

We don't have to turn to our history books for heroes. They are all around us. One who sits among you here tonight epitomized that heroism at the end of the longest imprisonment ever inflicted on men of our armed forces. Who can ever forget that night when we waited for television to bring us the scene of that first plane landing at Clark Field in the Philippines—bringing our P.O.W.'s home. The plane door opened and Jeremiah Denton came slowly down the ramp. He caught sight of our flag, saluted, and said, "God bless America," then thanked us for bringing him home.

Just two weeks ago, in the midst of a terrible tragedy on the Potomac, we saw again the spirit of American heroism at its finest—the heroism of dedicated rescue workers saving crash victims from icy waters. We saw the heroism of one of our young government employees, Lenny Skutnik, who, when he saw a woman lose her grip on the helicopter line, dived into the water and dragged her to safety.

And then there are countless quiet, everyday heroes of American life—parents who sacrifice long and hard so their children will know a better life than they have known; church and civic volunteers who help to feed, clothe, nurse and teach the needy; millions who have made our nation, and our nation's destiny, so very special—unsung heroes who may not have realized their dreams themselves but who then reinvest those dreams in their children.

Don't let anyone tell you that America's best days are behind her—that the American spirit has been vanquished. We've seen it triumph too often in our lives to stop believing in it now.

One hundred and twenty years ago, the greatest of all our Presidents delivered his second State of the Union Message in this chamber. "We cannot escape history," Abraham Lincoln warned. "We of this Congress and this Administration will be remembered in spite of ourselves." The "trial through which we pass will light us down in honor or dishonor to the latest generation."

That President and that Congress did not fail the American people. Together, they weathered the storm and preserved the union.

Let it be said of us that we, too, did not fail; that we, too, worked together to bring America through difficult times. Let us so conduct ourselves that two centuries from now, another Congress and another President, meeting in this chamber as we are meeting, will speak of us with pride, saying that we met the test and preserved for them in their day the sacred flame of liberty—this last, best hope of man on Earth.

The American Scene

Luigi Barzini
Author, Journalist;
Former member of
Italian Parliament   *1*

America must always try to improve the world. She fights, if fight she must, for liberty and a more just society, for peace. "Making the world safe for democracy" was not merely a catch phrase, an empty slogan; it's the very soul of America, the force of America.

Interview, Rome/
U.S. News & World Report, 6-7:27.

Daniel Bell
Professor of social science,
Harvard University   *2*

The opportunity principle has become the crucial one in American life; it's based upon some notion of a meritocracy. However, it's quite clear that even though people start out equally, they end up unequally, and sometimes the outcomes are quite disparate, and therefore themselves become intolerable. I do believe—since I'm not one who believes in absolutizing any principle—that when the outcomes become highly disparate, there ought to be an effort to redress it. But I don't believe in surrendering the first principle. What I think has been happening, unfortunately, is that there's been too much of a shift—until the Reagan Administration, anyway—to substitute equality of outcome for equality of opportunity, as a principle.

Panel discussion/
The New York Times, 1-3:(4)5.

Barber B. Conable
United States Representative,
R—New York   *3*

We [Americans] love to live from crisis to crisis. If we don't have a crisis, we find one. The job is to keep hope alive and accept the idea that we cannot solve everything, that we cannot still all the voices of hostility.

Time, 1-11:21.

Mario M. Cuomo
Governor-elect of New York (D)   *4*

[On his becoming Governor]: What do I think of a process that allows you to go from a grocery store, not being able to speak the language until you are 8—no money, no influence, no rich friends, not even a first cousin in the country—that allows you to become Governor? . . . It's quite a miracle. What an incredible commentary on this whole country. We don't appreciate how good this system is. It has imperfections, of course, but it is a marvelous process over-all.

Interview, New York, December/
Los Angeles Times, 12-17:(I-C)3.

Ralph Ellison
Author   *5*

[W. H.] Auden once said, and I love this, "A democracy is a collection of individuals." And individualism in the broader American sense means to be constantly aware of who you are. Only in that way are you able to fulfill the responsibilities of consciousness that living in a democracy requires. Ultimately, all Americans have to discover themselves.

Interview, New York/San Francisco
Examiner & Chronicle, 4-11:(Scene)4.

Eric F. Goldman
Professor of history,
Princeton University   *6*

The protest movement of the 1960s has died out on the surface, but it has not died in any fundamental sense. It is breaking forth in the creation of what might be called the "upper

WHAT THEY SAID IN 1982

(ERIC F. GOLDMAN)

American," who is quite different from anything we have seen before. This upper American is largely an outgrowth of the '60s protest against a middle-class, middle-American society. Upper Americans are not defined by income; although few are poor, they range through all the middle and wealthier classes. They are people with certain attitudes, with a strong sense of being distinct from the "middle American." They deplore food that smacks of meat and potatoes, brush aside beer and bourbon for vodka and wine. They shudder at movie heroes, advice columnists and TV evangelists, unabashed patriotism, fussy clothes, the woman who thinks a family is everything and the man who is a straight arrow. They are basically college graduates in their 20s, 30s and early 40s, especially people who have gone to school on the two coasts. The top schools have become vast homogenizers, and they turn out upper Americans. You take the rich kid, the poor kid and the middle-class kid, put him in these schools, and they come out pretty much the same. Upper Americans have respect for intellectuals but don't think of themselves as particularly intellectual. They account for about 15 per cent of the population and work in many occupations. They are often the lead group in society; they determine what's most successful in everything from clothes to food.

Interview/U.S. News & World Report,
8-16:57.

Alexander M. Haig, Jr.
Secretary of State of the United States

1

When one compares the problems of the Soviet Union with those of Western democracies, and the United States in particular—the assets available to the two—one could not help but be optimistic, provided we have the wisdom and the fortitude to conduct our affairs with a sense of self-confidence, patience, prudence and moderation, and with a conviction that we know the values and the principles that we espouse are the essential ingredients of a successful world order.

Interview/Los Angeles Herald Examiner, 1-3:(B)10.

Clare Boothe Luce
Member, President's Foreign
Intelligence Advisory Board;
Former diplomat and playwright

2

I was wondering today what the religion of the country is—and all I could come up with was sex. When I grew up we knew about romance and a little about sex. I guess we knew about sex, but not in this . . . genitalized sense. I think I was 35 years old before I knew what a homosexual was. Sex and money—those are the two dominant things in American life today.

Interview, Washington/
The Washington Post, 4-9:(D)2.

Robert S. McNamara
Former President, International Bank
for Reconstruction and Development
(World Bank); Former Secretary
of Defense of the United States

3

We [in the U.S.] exaggerate our weaknesses and our enemies' strengths. We are rich, intellectually and technologically. I feel very secure in predicting that we are headed toward superiority in the next 10 or 20 years. So many of our problems, like unemployment, are temporary conditions that we can change—if we want to.

Time, 1-11:21.

Laurence J. Peter
Author

4

America is now the greatest consumer of humor. That doesn't necessarily mean that Americans have a good sense of humor about themselves. People in the U.S. tend to take themselves too seriously. They think that if they have an idea it is, by definition, important. If they had a good sense of humor, that view would not last very long. People with a sense of humor are more likely to listen to somebody else's point of view. Rather than seeing humor in their own situation, Americans tend to be passive consumers of humor—they want to turn on the television and be entertained.

Interview/U.S. News & World Report,
10-18:66.

Ronald Reagan
President of the United States

1

I prefer to look upon this time in our history as an era of national renewal in which Americans are rediscovering the basic principles upon which our nation was founded. That means greater economic freedom, which can only come about by reducing tax rates and unnecessary regulation. It means trimming the scope of government and returning power and prerogatives to the state and local governments, and to the people themselves. It means love of family, devotion to community and faith in God. We Americans have never lost these principles, but some government policies have given them quite a beating over the last several years. I can think of no period, at least since the 1930s, when the challenges facing us have been so widespread. But then, we also have some unique opportunities to turn things around, and I'm convinced that, working together, we will be able to do this.

Interview/Nation's Business, May:30.

2

[Calling for a revival of voluntarism in the U.S.]: All of us are aware of the reservoir of goodness which lies waiting to be tapped. Let's make it our job—everyone's job—to encourage our fellow citizens to do those good works which need to be done. We think it will be good for the soul of this country to encourage people to help one another, to get involved, to take personal responsibility for the well-being of their community and neighbors instead of always leaving this to the bureaucracy. Americans have always been ready to help those in need, whatever country they come from . . . Fundamentals like this, which have played such a significant role, cannot be replaced whole-horse by Federal programs and paid bureaucracy. It won't be easy. It will take commitment, hard work and perseverance. But how great the results can be!

Before Metropolitan Chicago YMCA, May 10/
Chicago Tribune, 5-11:(1)1.

3

. . . as Lincoln said it then and it's truer even today, this [the U.S.] is the last best hope of man on earth. We are freer than any other people. We have achieved more than any other people. And if you looked around this room, I thought the other day, when we have all those representatives from all over the world, all those representatives in this room who were here to look at our election, to learn how they could spread the word about that kind of freedom in their own countries on the rest, the other continents, I thought that we could have a meeting of Americans in this room and the ethnic heritage of the Americans in this room would be as diverse and there would be as many representatives as there were in those hundreds of people who have come from foreign lands here today. And here we all live together proudly as Americans, in spite of that difference in birth. There just isn't any comparison with what we have and what we have to be thankful for.

News conference, Washington, Nov. 11/
The New York Times, 11-12:12.

Felix G. Rohatyn
Chairman, Municipal Assistance
Corporation of New York

4

A deep-seated American conviction that our children's future would be brighter than ours, that our ability to produce and create wealth knew no limits, and that all Americans would ultimately share in this cornucopia, has given way to doubt. Neither we nor our children believe that they will be better off than we were. We are now extremely conscious of the limit of our resources and for the need to cut back on some activities. The opportunities open to many Americans are being sharply curtailed.

At Middlebury (Vt.) College commencement/
U.S. News & World Report, 6-7:66.

R. Sargent Shriver
Lawyer; Former United States
Ambassador to France

5

I do believe that we the people of the United States must recapture our belief that "national survival," not national security, depends on a communal, a common, united effort in which each one of us participates with and helps others, a community to which we pledge our

(R. SARGENT SHRIVER)

lives, our fortunes and our sacred honor. National security without national community is a will-o'-the-wisp, a fatuous dream of the military mind.

At George Washington University
National Law Center/
The Washington Post, 6-4:(A)18.

James C. Wright, Jr.
United States Representative, D—Texas

1

[On what was accomplished over the past 50 years when Democrats were mostly in control of Congress]:   In those 50 years, we have indemnified 36 million Americans now against the ravages of old age through Social Security. In those 50 years, we have changed the percentage of people who own their own homes from fewer than 30 per cent to more than 70 per cent. In those 50 years, we have turned around a situation in which only 4 per cent of college-age youngsters were finishing college to a point where now 21 per cent are finishing college. Fifty years ago, fewer than 30 per cent of the non-white Americans were able to finish high school. Today, it's more than 80 per cent. Still not enough, but my, what progress has been made. The average American lives better, lives longer, is healthier, worries less, has better housing, better clothing, and is more secure in his and her person than 50 years ago. I think we've made more progress in the last 50 years than any civilized nation ever made in every like period in the history of the world. And so I reject the theory that it has been 50 years of wasted effort and that no problems have been solved.

Broadcast interview/"Meet the Press,"
NBC-TV, 11-7.

Civil Rights • Women's Rights

Thomas I. Atkins
General counsel,
National Association for the
Advancement of Colored People
1

We have made a decision at the national level to move more aggressively and more frequently to use boycotts [against those who discriminate against blacks]. We serve notice to those against whom we may use [boycotts] ... This economy has tightened up, and, as a result, people have taken that as a license to engage in racially restrictive practices that they might have been afraid to engage in some years ago. There's a belief that the Federal government under this [Reagan] Administration will not enforce the civil-rights laws. The Federal government may not, but the NAACP damned well will. Ronald Reagan cannot buy protection for the bigots in this country.

At NAACP convention.
Boston, June 29/
The Washington Post,
6-30:(A)2.

Margaret Atwood
Author
2

Of course I'm a feminist. But on the other hand, do I think that all men should be herded up and shoved off the cliff? The answer is no. So I think I'm one of those people in-between the two extremes. I don't think women should be made to feel incompetent, subservient or inferior, nor do I think they should be put down for choosing to be married, mothers or flower arrangers. I think that if feminism is defined too narrowly, we're going to lose a lot of women.

Interview, New York/The New York
Times, 3-28:(1)21.

John Baker
General counsel, Baptist Joint
Committee on Public Affairs
3

[Supporting Reagan Administration efforts to grant tax-exempt status to religious schools that practice segregation]: If you allow the IRS to force you to choose between your tax exemption and your theology, they would have the power to destroy many churches ... If public policy determines that there shall be no discrimination on the basis of sex [for example], will the theological seminaries of denominations that refuse to ordain women be denied tax-exempt status? If the law of the land is universal military service, a case could be made for taxing the schools of pacifist churches because they challenge public policy.

Interview/The New York Times, 1-23:28.

Julius Becton
Lieutenant General, United States Army
4

[On his being the highest-ranking active black officer in the Army]: If we go back in modern times, just to World War II, we had just one black flag officer, Benjamin O. Davis, Sr. We had a segregated Army, few role models; we certainly didn't perceive the opportunity to do many things other than what other "colored" troops did. [The progress of blacks in the Army today] represents the growth in the country, the opportunities that are there. It represents the fact that no longer can a person say, "I have busted my back, I work very hard and I can't get anywhere." In the services, if you are that professional, if you do your thing, and you do it well, you get recognized ... I seriously did not consider when I accepted ... [command of the] Seventh Corps that a *black* man was taking command. I felt I took it in light of the fact that someone thought I was qualified to do the

15

(JULIUS BECTON)

job. When you put the race up in front of you—"I am doing it for my race"—then I think it's wrong. You are supposed to do it for all the things we are supposed to be standing for. I think I am a soldier and I try to think like one. I use the fact that I am black to try to understand more people.

Interview, Feb. 26/The Washington Post,
2-27:(C)1,8.

Daniel Bell
Professor of social science,
Harvard University
1

... I do believe in affirmative action. However, there's been a movement in many places toward goals, which in some sense are commensurate with what you regard as the fair pool of applicants in a situation. But then goals become converted into quotas. It's at that point, it seems to me, that a shift takes place which has not really been debated. I think it goes back to a distinction that you either treat people equally or you try to make them equal. If you treat people equally, you're treating them under the law. If you try to *make* them equal, you're making administrative determinations. And the effort to intervene creates more and more high-handed bureaucratic distortions, which in the end become as bad as the effort to redress the situation in the first place.

Panel discussion/
The New York Times, 1-3:(4)5.

Richard N. Bond
Deputy chairman,
Republican National Committee
2

[On Democratic Party criticism of the Republican Party for not adopting a pro-ERA stand at its 1980 convention]: If you claim that the Republican Party stand as far as its platform is concerned on ERA manifested itself to a negative [on equal rights for women] in 1980, then I ask you why the four women who were elected to Congress in 1980 all happen to be Republicans? I ask you why the only two women members of the Senate happen to be Republicans? I further submit that it was the Democratic Party that defeated ERA. Look at

the [state] legislatures one by one and examine who was in control [when they defeated ERA]. There are a hell of a lot more legislative bodies under the control of the Democrats than are run by Republicans.

Panel discussion/
The New York Times, 7-18:(4)5.

Melvin Bradley
Special Assistant to the President
of the United States
3

I don't believe that all the subsidy and poverty programs instituted by the Democrats will continue to satisfy blacks. Historically, Democrats have been effective in using quick-fix, short-term programs. Those programs are politically attractive but economically unsound. Once you cut through the emotional rhetoric and get to the bottom line, many blacks can see they are as bad off or worse now than they were a decade and a half ago. Once they come to that conclusion, they may be prepared to make the big jump from Democrat to Republican in voting habits.

Interview/U.S. News & World Report, 4-26:66.

Ronald H. Brown
Deputy chairman,
Democratic National Committee
4

I would be the last to say that blacks should blindly follow the Democratic Party. We shouldn't let Democrats take us for granted or let the Republicans ignore us. On balance, though, any rational person would have to conclude that the Democratic Party has been much more sensitive to interests of minorities than the Republicans.

Interview/U.S. News & World Report, 4-26:66.

Shirley Chisholm
United States Representative,
D—New York
5

For far too many blacks, this country is still a land of mirage where shimmering lakes of equality and opportunity turn out to be dry, bitter sands of discrimination.

At Spelman College commencement/
Time, 6-21:82.

(SHIRLEY CHISHOLM)

1

[In race relations,] we still have to engage in compromise, the highest of all arts. Blacks can't do things on their own, nor can whites. When you have black racists and white racists, it is very difficult to build bridges between communities. People say: "Get whitey!" Oh, it's so frightening.

Interview, Washington/Chicago Tribune, 10-17:(2)5.

Mary Cunningham
Vice president for strategic planning,
Joseph E. Seagram & Sons, Inc.

2

Women must *earn* the respect of their [business] colleagues, both male and female. That means everything–how they dress, how they speak, how they present themselves professionally. It means consistency and fairness of judgment. It means not flying off the handle with a reaction to a particular comment. It means not playing into some of the stereotypes that we must be aware are out there. We must expect a certain amount of controversy over a woman's role, but we must take care not to be overly militant. Above all, we should strive to be extremely competent in whatever it is we are doing. Unfortunately, since there are still relatively few of us in top-management positions, what will be remembered too often are those who fail and not those who succeed.

Interview/U.S. News & World Report, 11-29:56.

Eugene Eidenberg
Director, Democratic National Committee

3

Two years ago at its national convention in Detroit, the Republican Party walked away from a commitment to an equal-rights amendment [for women] that it had had for decades. The Democratic Party has consistently . . . reaffirmed its commitments to equal rights and to getting that amendment adopted. It didn't matter who was speaking on the subject, or what region of the country or what delegation was involved. The point is that in walking away from this commitment, the Republican Party sent a signal on a range of issues that women care about. I think the Republican signal was: Wait a minute, the Republican Party is not

there at the line on the question of equal rights . . .

Panel discussion/
The New York Times, 7-18:(4)5.

Ralph Ellison
Author

4

What has happened in recent years as [racial] discrimination has lessened, Afro-Americans and women have become more competitive, and a lot of people don't like that. There are tensions between Negroes and Jews, tension about [educational and job] quotas. It strikes me as hypocritical, because I've been part of an excluded quota [blacks] since the beginning of the country. And a hell of a lot of people were able to start a little higher up on the rungs of American social hierarchy. I don't hold anything against them for that–it's the way history dealt it out–but I don't want them to pretend that my mother or grandfather had it as easy as they did.

Interview, New York/
The Washington Post, 4-21:(B)15.

Walter E. Fauntroy
Delegate to the United States House of
Representatives, D–District of Columbia;
Chairman, Congressional Black Caucus

5

[On the difficulty of blacks in government to have impact on national issues]: If you want to play baseball or basketball, sing or tap dance, you're fine. But if you want to deal with the most important issues facing the nation, you will not be heard.

Chicago Tribune, 3-28:(2)1.

Arthur S. Flemming
Former Chairman, United States
Commission on Civil Rights

6

We are at an important crossroads in civil rights. We have reasonably good laws and very good court decisions on civil rights, but we need to implement them. That requires disturbing the status quo, and defenders of the status quo have adopted a well-defined strategy of weakening methods for implementation.

The New York Times, 7-12:10.

Earl C. Graves
Editor and publisher,
"Black Enterprise" magazine

1

We know by now that as black Americans we cannot depend solely on government. We cannot depend on anyone or anything outside ourselves to provide real economic opportunity and justice. When we look back to those days . . . when we moved the heart and soul of this nation in our quest to achieve civil rights, and when we look at the way things are today, we realize that we have been standing in the same station waiting for economic opportunity, watching train after train pass us by. We have been waiting for the next budget . . . the next election . . . We have been waiting and waiting in the station at the end of the economic line for too many generations. We are here today because . . . we realize that we are going to have to move the train of equal opportunity out of here ourselves.

At NAACP convention, Boston, June 29/
The Washington Post, 6-30:(A)2.

Elizabeth Hardwick
Author

2

[On the employment of women]: I certainly don't think the clock will be turned back, not because of any kindness on the part of society, but because it does not suit society for women to be in the home. It is not economically possible, it is not convenient, and it's not practical. The wife economy is as obsolete as the slave economy.

Time, 7-12:23.

Gary W. Hart
United States Senator, D—Colorado

3

[Criticizing President Reagan's decision to grant tax-exempt status to church-run schools that discriminate against blacks]: Racial discrimination has no place in American society. The Federal government has a moral obligation to use whatever sanctions are available to condemn it. At a minimum, the government should not financially subsidize it through the tax code.

Jan. 9/San Francisco Examiner
& Chronicle, 1-10:(A)1.

Gordon B. Hinckley
Counsellor in the First Presidency
of the Church of Jesus Christ of
Latter-day Saints (Mormons)

4

[On his church's opposition to the ERA]: We don't need a Constitutional amendment to provide what women ought to have. They have it under the 14th Amendment. It's there. And as far as I'm concerned, I want legal provisions concerning women and their equality to come of their peers who were elected in their legislatures and not be mandated by the courts, who happen to interpret Constitutional amendments . . . Nobody has emphasized the equality of women more than we have. Our position with reference to women traditionally has been that a woman neither walks behind her husband nor ahead of him, but at his side. They are companions, sons and daughters of God, each with a divinely given responsibility and birthright to be enlarged and enhanced.

Interview/The Christian Science
Monitor, 4-28:(B)6.

Carl Holman
President, National Urban Coalition

5

[On black Los Angeles Mayor Tom Bradley's defeat in the California gubernatorial election]: Tom Bradley's defeat is profoundly disappointing. Even after all other factors have been weighed in the balance, it will be hard for young minority citizens of this country to be persuaded that, regardless of the quality of the candidate, race does not continue to be a potent negative political factor—whether in California or Mississippi.

Nov. 3/The New York Times, 11-4:13.

Benjamin L. Hooks
Executive director, National
Association for the Advancement
of Colored People

6

[The Reagan Administration's position on the Voting Rights Act] signals black people that civil rights is not a high priority. We have agitated, we have lobbied . . . talked to the President, the Vice President, members of the Cabinet. It is the main item on the agenda of

(BENJAMIN L. HOOKS)

black America . . . They [the Administration] listen but don't hear.

Before Senate Judiciary subcommittee,
Washington, Jan. 27/The Washington Post,
1-28:(A)4.

1

Nobody wants to talk about the racism that is still ingrained in America. The great majority of us still live in a segregated society as far as our social and private lives are concerned. Everything the Reagan Administration has done has been a backward step. There's no other way to describe it . . . And it has created a feeling among people out there with a cynical, defeatist attitude, and eventually some of them may turn to violence and destruction.

Los Angeles Times, 4-22:(I)12.

2

[President] Reagan has told us to vote with our feet. Well, we're [blacks] going to vote with our feet by not utilizing those industries that have refused to treat us with respect and dignity. I am not going to spend another dime as long as I live anywhere that folks don't respect me. We're insisting that every company in this country have some blacks on its board of directors.

At NAACP convention, Boston, June 30/
The Washington Post, 7-1:(A)3.

Jesse L. Jackson
Civil-rights leader; President,
Operation PUSH (People
United to Save Humanity)   *3*

Our [black] race is threatened within the country, within the law. We have the right to vote without the right of our vote to count. Today we have equal protection under the law, but we do not have equal protection within the law. Thus we do not have our share of power and our share of decision-making authority. Today, at-large elections, annexations and gerrymandering deny the impact of our vote. And thus there are 600,000 elected officials in America today and fewer than 6,000 are black—or less than 1 per cent.

At Jackson and Clark College commencement/
Time, 6-21:83.

[On the threat of a black boycott of companies that do not do enough business with black firms] : We [blacks] bought $12-billion to $14-billion worth of automobiles last year. Chrysler has used our labor, our purchasing power and [through Federally backed loans] our tax dollars. They had $7.5-billion in sales and $3-billion in procurement contracts alone. Less than $20-million of that trade was with blacks . . . I don't think [in terms of] a boycott. I prefer to think of it as a legitimate tool to keep corporate America from boycotting black executive talent, black attorneys, black CPAs . . . and black trade . . . Employment is inherent in development. The Marshall Plan was not a plan of full employment, but it produced full employment. Full employment [for blacks] is not enough. We already had that on the slave plantations.

Interview/The Washington Post, 7-21:(A)23.

John E. Jacob
President, National Urban League   *5*

The new reality is . . . the reality of black progress. In the midst of deepening hardship for many blacks, some of us have managed to acquire the skills, education and opportunity to forge careers in fields formerly closed to black people. The number of black college graduates has doubled in the past decade. The numbers of black managers and corporate executives have grown swiftly. Black Mayors run major cities like Atlanta and Los Angeles. Black sheriffs wear badges once worn by men who clubbed civil-rights organizers. Changes have come slowly and are too close, far too close, to the surface in many areas of life. But change has come. It has touched every black community and many black families. We must acknowledge that change and also celebrate it. So the new reality of the 1980s is a black population burdened by expanding poverty, but also bolstered by a depth of talent and skills unprecedented in our history.

Before National Urban League, Greenville,
S.C., chapter/Chicago Tribune, 3-12:(1)11.

E. Pendleton James
Special Assistant to the President
of the United States for Personnel

1

[On the Reagan Administration's record of hiring women for government posts]: I think our Administration has done exceptionally well on that point. We have been accused of doing less than the Carter Administration. [But] we counted all the Carter appointments of the first 17 months of his Administration and the first 17 months of the Reagan Administration. In the full-time number of women receiving Presidential appointments, Carter had 65, Reagan has 71. In terms of part-time Presidential appointments, Carter had 100, Ronald Reagan has 243.

Interview, Washington, June/
The New York Times, 6-17:16.

J. Bennett Johnston, Jr.
United States Senator, D—Louisiana

2

[On an amendment he is sponsoring that would curb the busing of schoolchildren for racial integration): There is a reason my opponents don't defend busing. There is no evidence to support it. Long-distance busing is a leech on the educational system of this country. Public support for education is gone with long-distance busing.

Before the Senate, Washington, Feb. 4/
The Washington Post, 2-5:(A)6.

Bob Jones III
President, Bob Jones University

3

[On proposals to rescind the tax-exempt status of schools such as his because of their racial policies]: Why are we being singled out? That's not America. That's Russia. It is a betrayal of everything our forefathers had to gain in coming here. Theirs was a religious motivation in the first place. The government is saying your religious rights are less important than the public policy. If public policy becomes supreme, we don't have America any more. We have the will of the bureaucrats.

Interview, Greenville, S.C./
The New York Times, 1-14:7.

Vernon E. Jordan, Jr.
Former president, National Urban League

4

We as a nation won't get very far if the barriers of race remain high and if the color of a man's skin is allowed to determine the size of his paycheck or the chances he gets in life. Our only chance to construct a viable society is for the white and black people of America to come together in full recognition of each other's humanity and equality . . . It means whites and blacks working together to build a better state and nation. And that again comes down to power. For moral appeals and common sense will only take us so far. The rest of the way is traveled through the power of the ballot, and the intelligent use of political pressures backed up with voting strength.

Montgomery, Alabama, Dec. 4/
The Washington Post, 12-8:(A)30.

Nicholas deB. Katzenbach
General counsel, International
Business Machines Corp.; Former
Attorney General of the United States

5

[Arguing against a proposed bill that would curtail the busing of schoolchildren for racial balance]: We all have to recognize that decisions of courts are not always popular. I don't think the decisions of the courts are always right . . . But I think the system has served us well, and this [the bill] is an effort to tamper with that system. This is an effort to get rid of busing whether or not busing is essential to the realization of a Constitutional right.

Washington, July 15/The Washington Post,
7-16:(A)2.

Edward M. Kennedy
United States Senator, D—Massachusetts

6

[Criticizing the tax-exempt status of religious-based colleges that racially discriminate, such as Bob Jones University]: Bigotry is not the message of Jesus Christ . . . In reality, Bob Jones University is nothing more than Jim Crow University . . . and tax exemptions must not be granted for racial prejudice in segregated schools or colleges.

At NAACP convention, Boston, June 28/
The Washington Post, 6-29:(A)3.

Clare Boothe Luce
Member, President's Foreign
Intelligence Advisory Board;
Former diplomat and playwright

1

Women simply don't have the passion for power that men do. The only change in my lifetime is that women no longer want to be objects of male power, slaves, because the object of power is to reduce people to slaves, to push them around. Women are interested in achievement, excellence, ambition, but not in raw power ...

Interview, Washington/The New York
Times, 2-7:(1)24.

Catharine MacKinnon
Assistant professor, Stanford
University School of Law

2

Feminism is not liberalism applied to women. [To feminists,] equality means the eradication not of gender differentiation but of what I call gender hierarchy ... Feminists do not seek sameness with men. We do not seek dominance over men. To us it is a male notion that someone must dominate.

At women's rights debate, Claremont (Calif.)
School of Theology, March 16/
Los Angeles Times, 3-19:(V)20.

James D. McGhee
Director of research,
National Urban League

3

[Saying blacks are more affected by unemployment than whites]: These are alarming developments, for if the black middle-income family, which has traditionally been the most stabilizing force in the black community, is endangered, then the future of all blacks is endangered. The extremely conservative political climate and the record-breaking recession combine to blunt the hopes and dash the dreams of millions of the poor, and they seriously threaten the existence of an emerging, still fragile, black middle class as well ... Under the union system, those who have less seniority are the first fired. Because blacks were the last hired because of previous discrimination, they are the first fired. I'm not talking about people

who just started. We're talking about people with 10 and 15 years' experience.

Los Angeles, Aug. 3/
Los Angeles Times, 8-4:(1)3,23.

Walter F. Mondale
Former Vice President
of the United States

4

Our history tells us justice without prosperity is unattainable, but it also tells us that prosperity without justice is unacceptable. This [Reagan] Administration doesn't understand that a ravaged environment imperils our economy, unfairness in our budget and tax code undermines public trust, that voting rights anchors our democracy, civil rights sustains our stability, women's rights affirms equality and Social Security redeems our social contract.

At National Press Club, Washington, March 9/
The New York Times, 3-10:11.

5

One helpful word from this President [Reagan] and the Equal Rights Amendment [for women] would today be part of the Constitution. It offends me that this Administration is so quick to disfigure the Constitution to restrict our rights but fights hard against this amendment to expand our rights. Mr. President: History is against you. Most Americans want the ERA. Not once in our nation's past has a movement to secure human rights been deterred by a setback. The fight for women's rights is not ending. It is only just beginning.

At Democratic Party conference, Philadelphia,
June 25/The New York Times, 6-26:11.

Richard M. Nixon
Former President of the United States

6

My views [on women] are a bit old-fashioned, I must admit. But on the other hand, [they are] very respectful. You see, I don't happen to think like the little ditty from the song, "Why can't a woman be more like a man?" I don't think that really serves the interests of women. I want women to be like women; I want men to be like men. And there's a place for both—and there's particularly a place for women in the law. I would have a

(RICHARD M. NIXON)

woman justice of the Supreme Court. Before the end of this century, there will certainly be a woman Vice President, possibly a woman President—and that's good. But they're going to be there not because they are like men, but because they are like women.

Interview, Saddle River, N.J./
Los Angeles Herald Examiner, 6-5:(B)3.

Clarence M. Pendleton, Jr.
Chairman, United States Commission
on Civil Rights

1

I'm against [racial] quotas, proportional representation or the setting aside of government contracts for minority businesses. In many cases, affirmative action takes away from legitimate minority success. People look at the black banker downtown who has made it on his own and say, "He got his job because of affirmative action." Or, an employer hires a few talented minority people who would have succeeded anyway and says, "Those are my affirmative-action hires."

Interview/U.S. News & World Report, 9-27:42.

2

The future for civil rights is very bright. If blacks stopped listening to so-called civil-rights leaders, it would be much brighter. Black people have been wards of the government much too long. We have to become much more self-sufficient than in the past.

Broadcast interview/"Nightwatch,"
CBS-TV, 10-7.

Samuel R. Pierce, Jr.
Secretary of Housing and Urban
Development of the United States

3

[On criticism of the Reagan Administration's civil-rights record]: I may not agree with [the criticism], but I can understand it. I can understand why blacks are hesitant and say, "The Administration is not doing well." But I can tell you this: that the President, I believe, is real straight on the race and civil-rights questions. In time, I do believe he will come through and the people will see that. The

Administration has not been making wild leaps into the area of civil rights. It hasn't been pushing ahead in civil rights up to this point . . . Not enough time has expired for it to disappoint me. It depends on what we do in the long run.

Interview, Washington/The New York Times, 1-18:9.

Ronald Reagan
President of the United States

4

[On his signing into law] an extension of the Voting Rights Act of 1965]: . . . the right to vote is the crown jewel of American liberties, and we will not see its luster diminished . . . This legislation proves our unbending commitment to voting rights . . . To so many of our people—our Americans of Mexican descent, our black Americans—this measure is as important symbolically as it is practically. It says to every individual, "Your vote is equal, your vote is meaningful, your vote is Constitutional."

At signing ceremony, Washington, June 29/
The New York Times, 6-30:12.

5

Usually I try to ignore personal attacks, but one charge, I will have to admit, strikes at my heart every time I hear it. That's the suggestion that we Republicans are taking a less active approach to protecting the civil rights of all Americans. No matter how you slice it, that's just plain baloney. There is no room in the Republican Party for bigots, and the record shows that we have been firm in protecting civil liberties since entering office nearly 20 months ago.

Before National Black Republican
Council, Washington, Sept. 15/
Los Angeles Times, 9-16:(I)14.

6

As the Governor of California, I appointed more minority members to executive and policy-making positions in the state government than all the previous Governors in the history of California put together. Here [in Washington]—and we haven't been here two years yet—we have 130 members of the black community in top executive positions . . . [and] we're doing the same thing with regard to

(RONALD REAGAN)

women, and we're doing the same thing with regard to Hispanics ... Also, if you look at the Justice Department and [Equal] Employment Opportunities Commission, you will find that we've broken all records in the history of the national government with regards to hearings on violations of civil rights, on trials and on successful convictions of violations of civil rights. And incidentally, just yesterday I signed a paper with a group of minority small-business people that is going to increase the amount of procurement that the Federal government buys from minority-owned businesses.

Interview, Washington, Dec. 18/
The New York Times, 12-19:(1)18.

William Bradford Reynolds
Assistant Attorney General, Civil
Rights Division, Department of
Justice of the United States   *1*

Stated succinctly, we have concluded that involuntary busing [of schoolchildren to achieve racial integration] has largely failed in two major respects: (1) It has failed to elicit public support, and (2) It has failed to advance the overriding goal of equal education opportunity. Adherence to an experiment that has not withstood the test of experience obviously makes little sense .... we recognize that no single desegregation technique provides an answer. Nor does any particular combination of techniques offer the perfect remedial formula for all cases. But some desegregation approaches that seem to hold promise for success include: voluntary student transfer programs; magnet schools; enhanced curriculum requirements; faculty incentives; in-service training programs for teachers and administrators; school closings in systems with excess capacity and new construction in systems that are over-crowded; and modest adjustments to attendance zones. The overarching principle guiding the selection of any or all of these remedial techniques—or indeed resorting to others that may be developed—is equal education opportunity ... Deliberately providing a lower level of educational services to identifiably black schools is as insidious as deliberate racial segregation.

Senate testimony/The Christian
Science Monitor, 1-20:22.

Phyllis Schlafly
President, Eagle Forum   *2*

When [people] ask me what I want for my children—for my daughters I hope for a happy marriage and a successful career; for my sons I hope for a successful career and a happy marriage. That's based on my understanding of the difference between male and female priorities. I know my husband could have had a perfectly happy, successful, fulfilled life if I had never come along ... He would have been content, happy, successful, satisfied, fulfilled. But what happens to these young women, you see, they who have rejected motherhood, and then they get a job, they get a nice affirmative-action job, they get nice promotions and they're making good money, and then they get to be about thirty, thirty-two, and then they panic. And then they realize they've only got a few more years to have a baby, and they're missing something, and then they add up how much it's going to cost financially, and they're not willing to pay the price at this point. Then they get bitter. Then they get cold and mad. And it becomes a hopeless case ... And then they look at me and they find out that I have all these beautiful children, and I'm all liberated and everything, and they just can't stand it.

Interview/Ms., January:91.

   3

[Those in the women's-lib movement] think that all men are part of an oppressive group. They think that there are no rules unique to women or unique to men ... that men and women are interchangeable ... It's not a world of women against men. [I reject] the notion of group guilt .... there are millions of men who are wonderful husbands and employers and fathers. There are certain roles that men can do better. When we look out of the third story of a burning building, we want a man to carry us down the ladder and not a woman.

At women's-rights debate, Claremont
(Calif.) School of Theology, March 16/
Los Angeles Times, 3-19:(V)20.

(PHYLLIS SCHLAFLY)

1

[Applauding the defeat of the Equal Rights Amendment for women]: This is the end of ERA. They just lost. The American public won't buy their product. They didn't have a product to sell. Their product wouldn't do any good for anyone. You could spend $1-million a day and not sell the proposition that women should be drafted.

The Washington Post, 6-30:(A)3.

Donna Shalala
President, Hunter College

2

I'm very disappointed that ERA didn't pass. Most of the critical breaks in my career would not have happened if it wasn't for the women's movement. It's going to be tough. The problems of the future are going to be more sophisticated. But I rarely meet a young woman who isn't more militant about control over her own future, as well as her own body.

Time, 7-12:20.

Eleanor Smeal
President,
National Organization for Women

3

Frankly, the Republicans by and large have deserted women's rights. President Reagan's Administration and his programs have been so extremely against the principles of women's equality and equal opportunity across the board that it is hard to single out one as being worse.

August/Los Angeles Times, 9-3:(V)2.

4

[On the defeat of the Equal Rights Amendment]: You can't look at what we've done and say we've lost. The fact that we have to spend more of our lives fighting for what should have been our birthright is a tragedy. But we turned a disgraceful defeat that should never have occurred into a base of political activity ... The miracle is we have done so much with so few people. We have become a majority movement intellectually. We did not start out that way.

Interview, Washington, November/
The New York Times, 11-30:28.

William French Smith
Attorney General of the United States

5

We have made two changes in civil-rights policy. Other than those two changes, we are enforcing the civil-rights laws in the same way they have been enforced in the past ... [The first change has] to do with mandatory busing [of schoolchildren for integration]. We don't believe it has been a success. We think it has been counter-productive. We think that if the money that had been spent on busing had been spent on trying to improve the quality of education, we would be much farther on down the road than now. And we are looking for alternate, more successful approaches, and we think those approaches are already showing signs of success. The second change has to do with what are referred to as [racial] quotas. We don't think they have been successful or effective. We think they are demeaning. We think they tend to set ceilings, not foundations. Quotas were the original basis for discrimination rather than for the elimination of discrimination ... On such matters as criminal civil-rights actions: We have filed more than any prior Administration.

Interview, Washington/The Christian
Science Monitor, 12-2:9.

Clarence Thomas
Assistant Secretary for Civil Rights,
Department of Education of the
United States; Chairman-designate,
Equal Employment Opportunity
Commission of the United States

6

I will state as a bottom line that I am tremendously in favor of equal opportunity, and I will not deny that we [blacks] have suffered adverse effects from racial discrimination. I know what it is to be scorned and not be able to go to movies and parks and drink out of water fountains. But my point is that we have gotten into a position where we believe that prescribing proportional representation is a solution to the problems that we have, and I don't agree with that. To the extent that a rigid quota system is "affirmative action," I disagree with that. [As for busing of schoolchildren for racial integration,] the problem is educating

(CLARENCE THOMAS)

our kids, not which school they go to. That is not to say they should go to all-black schools or we should resegregate our schools. We're spending an enormous amount of energy on busing. You wind up busing a kid from Roxbury to South Boston, but what have you got? You're busing a kid from a bad school to a bad school.

Feb. 12/The Washington Post, 2-13:(A)12.

Clarence Thomas
*Chairman, Equal Employment Opportunity
Commission of the United States*

1

We are simply in the habit of saying that, if a company has not hired minorities in numbers commensurate with their presence in the population, then discrimination has taken place. But discrimination does not account for all of the differential. Employment is typically based on skills. To become a news reporter, you must be able to write. Simple as that. We must deal with opportunities. To say we are protecting their rights, when in fact they are unqualified, is to create a false hope. It's like protecting my right to become a concert pianist when I cannot play the piano. I will not deny that discrimination counts for a lot, but I do not believe that the National Basketball Association, the National Football League or professional baseball are any less discriminatory than other parts of society, and yet you see blacks in these sports according to the numbers of them who are prepared.

*Interview, Washington/
The New York Times, 7-3:6.*

George C. Wallace
*Former Governor, and current
candidate for Governor, of Alabama (D)*

2

[On his segregationist beliefs in the 1960s]: I was raised that way; I believed segregation was in the best interest of both races, black and white. But, of course, we all now know that system was wrong. It's long gone, over with; and it *should* be over with, there's no question. But my wrath, if that's what you want to call it, never was aimed at black people. I tried to tell people in this country—but I was young and

not quite able to put it across—that we were against big government giving us schedules and timetables [for integration]. If I had been what the media said I was, no self-respecting black person would ever have voted for me. But in 1974, for instance, in Green County—a county in Alabama that is about 80 per cent black—I received 97.2 per cent of the vote. I used to say that God made us all and loves us all, and anybody who'd despise anyone because of their race or background despises the handiwork of God. So we Southerners believed that segregation was in the best interest. We were mistaken, and that's gone and over with.

Interview/Los Angeles Herald Examiner, 6-1:(A)12.

Lowell P. Weicker, Jr.
*United States Senator,
R—Connecticut*

3

[Saying blacks should hold Democrats as well as Republicans responsible when they vote against such measures as school busing for integration and for such things as tuition tax credits for racially segregated private schools]: Why didn't you [blacks] draw the line? Having people walk all over you is the price to pay for not drawing the line. Politicians figure that if you don't care enough to fight for racially integrated schools, then you won't mind subsidizing segregated academies with your hard-earned tax dollars. If you think you can count on the Democrats in Congress to serve your backsides on these issues any more than they did on busing, you're selling yourself short.

*At NAACP convention, Boston, July 2/
The Washington Post, 7-3:(A)2.*

Theodore H. White
Author, Historian

4

In the 1960s . . . blacks, who had been denied equality, rightfully demanded it. We could afford it, and we should have done what we did [in presenting civil rights]. But we have ended up pushing equality and other ideas to absurd limits as we sought perfect equality rather than the most realistic equality of opportunity.

Interview/U.S. News & World Report, 7-5:59.

WHAT THEY SAID IN 1982

Kathy Wilson
Chairman, National
Women's Political Caucus

1

I think the notion that there is only one pro-women party [the Democratic Party] is shortsighted and politically naive. It is exactly those women who are deserting the Republican Party who are hurting our chances the most. What we have to learn is that women haven't gotten what we should from either party. After all, all but one of the [ERA's] unratified states are headed by Democrats. It was a Republican who introduced the ERA and the Republicans who first put ERA on their platform. And in 1978, 63 of the 68 legislative seats picked up by women across the country were picked up by Republicans.

Interview, Washington/
The Christian Science Monitor, 6-22:18.

2

[On the defeat of the Equal Rights Amendment for women]: I'm mad and a little bitter. I think we all need a little rest. I think it's the beginning of the politicization of the women's movement. We've all decided it's time to quit trying to change hearts and minds and start changing faces [in Congress and state legislatures].

June 29/The Washington Post, 6-30:(A)3.

Andrew Young
Mayor of Atlanta

3

[On his being black and elected Mayor of Atlanta]: The former minority is now the majority. Those of us who know the tragedy of being ignored or taken for granted cannot allow ourselves to forget the bitter fruits of alienation which we experienced when we were invisible men and women.

Inaugural address, Atlanta, Jan. 4/
Chicago Tribune, 1-6:(1)2.

4

This is not a time [for blacks] to bemoan and despair and wallow in our frustrations. Black buying power annually is $125-billion. Indeed, we can make the difference between profit and loss in almost any industry. Whether we can organize that buying power, I think, still remains to be proved.

At National Summit Conference on Black
Economic Development and Survival, Gary, Ind.,
July 24/The Washington Post, 7-26:(Business)3.

Commerce . Industry . Finance

Joseph F. Alibrandi
President, Whittaker Corporation

1

Instead of spending so much time telling ourselves how great we all are, we in business ought to concentrate more on reinforcing a work ethic so that people take pride in what they do. It may sound corny, but maybe when I'm gone, somebody will say, "I remember Joe as a guy who was really trying to keep the free-enterprise system going for one more generation." If I can get that much, I'll be happy.

Interview/Nation's Business, March:81.

Naohiro Amaya
*Special Adviser to the Minister
of Trade and Industry of Japan*

2

If Washington approved any bills to limit Japanese trade in the United States, it would be almost unbelievable. Such legislation would be a direct violation of the GATT principles, and I can't believe the U.S. would take such an extraordinary measure against Japan, which is the most friendly country to the U.S. . . . We are very much concerned about the rising protectionist sentiment over trade in the U.S. But the sentiment is partly the result of the depressed U.S. economy. We hope the U.S. economy is revitalized as soon as possible, and once that happens the protectionist sentiment will disappear. During the transition period until that happens, we are urging Japanese exporters to be prudent and the Japanese government to open up the Japanese market as wide as possible to U.S. imports.

*Chicago, March 10/
Chicago Tribune, 3-12:(1)4.*

Rand V. Araskog
*Chairman, International Telephone
& Telegraph Corporation*

3

This [Reagan] Administration has really not faced up to aiding U.S. firms in world trade. Our Congress, our Commerce Department and our State Department need a new framework for helping American business get the same kind of support that we see given to businesses in Japan and Europe. It's ludicrous for American business to bid on a great job against a Japanese company that has a 3 per cent loan or a French company that pays no interest on loans because it's nationalized. Here [in the U.S.], firms have to fight with banks for money at 10 per cent and up. No one seems to understand that what's at stake in the end is jobs.

Interview/U.S. News & World Report, 12-6:39.

Malcolm Baldrige
Secretary of Commerce of the United States

4

It's very easy for so-called reciprocal [trade] legislation to spill over into protectionist legislation. We in no way, shape or form want to erect tariff barriers in the United States against imports. That would be most counter-productive. What we do want is equal access [to foreign markets, such as Japan], and to get equal access I would much rather, if it can be done in a reasonably speedy time, negotiate reciprocity than I would legislate reciprocity. I think we'll be far ahead if we can, and I think we have a very good chance of being able to do that.

Broadcast interview/"Meet the Press," NBC-TV, 2-14.

5

There are 4 billion potential customers [for U.S. products] outside the United States. We

(MALCOLM BALDRIGE)

can't just yield them to our trading competitors automatically. We [in the U.S.] have not been as hungry to compete in world markets as our trading partners because of our large domestic markets. To win world markets, we've got to manage the fundamentals better than the Japanese, the Germans or anyone else. This may seem obvious, but the fact is that we haven't been doing it.

At conference on international trade, New York, April 28/Chicago Tribune, 4-30:(2)4.

William Baxter
Assistant Attorney General,
Antitrust Division, Department of
Justice of the United States

1

[On why AT&T agreed, in a landmark case, to divest itself of its local phone-company subsidiaries]: First of all, the case was not going well for them. Secondly, as the year wore on, they became more and more painfully aware of the layer of regulation that was going to come out of the Congress, or indeed out of the court, if the court itself did not take the divestiture route. They came to see what I have been saying around this town all year long, that without divestiture, this is going to be the most heavily regulated industry in the world. They liked that prospect less and less. They began thinking about the unthinkable, which I had been saying again and again: "You know, fellows, there's a lot easier way to do this." Finally, they started thinking about it seriously and decided that, by golly, it *was* the best way to go.

Interview, Washington, Jan. 9/
The New York Times, 1-11:29.

2

During the 1960s, in its general hostility to conglomerate mergers, the Supreme Court cooked up a variety of esoteric and totally baseless theories about the harm caused by conglomerate mergers. [For example, by barring] entrenchment [of a dominant competitor by merging with an even larger firm, the Court] fundamentally presupposed that a company

with a lot of assets can do everything more efficiently and at a lower cost than a company without so many assets, a proposition that is ludicrous on its face and entirely without empirical support of any kind. [The Court] presupposed it had intuitive abilities to come up with propositions about commercial behavior that were entirely unrooted in the only academic discipline that addresses itself to such matters: economics.

Interview/The Wall Street Journal, 3-4:26.

3

I quite agree that we should not be nanny to the world at the Antitrust Division. We have a particular statutory mission. The statutes talk in terms of competition and restraints on trade—which I take to mean restraints on output and therefore a reference to the economists' concept of efficiency—and that's a challenging undertaking in itself. I feel no compulsion to expand it.

Panel discussion/The New York Times, 11-21:(4)5.

Bob Bergland
Former Secretary of Agriculture
of the United States

4

Some of my friends would like to believe that the world is a free marketplace. It is not. I am completely convinced that, as time goes on, at least half of the factor which determines American grain prices will be political consideration, and the other half will be marketplace.

Chicago Tribune, 5-5:(1)8.

John R. Block
Secretary of Agriculture
of the United States

5

[On the Agriculture Department]: I don't say it's a farmers' department. I think it's an agricultural department. An agricultural department deals with food and production of agriculture all across the board. And you have to start with the basics, and the basics is the production, plant and agriculture, the distribution, the handling, all the way to the consumer. I would not accept the assumption that we're not interested in all the people, but I do feel that it's in the interest of all the people that we have

(JOHN R. BLOCK)

health and prosperity in agriculture. American agriculture, wherever you travel in the world, is the envy of the world . . . American agriculture, in my opinion, is our greatest single asset in this country today. And over the next 20 years, it will become more apparent.

Broadcast interview/"Meet the Press," NBC-TV, 10-10.

William E. Brock
Special Trade Representative for the President of the United States

1

[On efforts to pass trade protectionist legislation in the U.S.] : I think people will see that the long-term consequences [of such legislation] could be disastrous. It could begin a chain reaction of retaliations that could cause a major decline in world trade. Over $200-billion worth of U.S. exports and millions of jobs would be in jeopardy if that sort of process started. Employment in our export industries is growing four times as rapidly as in industries that produce for domestic consumption. The rest of the world is very nervous about the current debate in the U.S. They're afraid it means the U.S. is falling into a protectionist shell. Unless we take the lead in liberalizing world trade, nobody else is capable of doing it.

Interview, Washington/U.S. News & World Report, 4-26:70.

2

Trade internationally is so big now that it can really make a difference [in the economy]. The world trading system now does $4-trillion worth of business yearly. That is an incredible amount of business and we're just touching the tip of the iceberg. We can do so much more. So what we're trying to say to the world is: "Let's look outward, let's look up and see what the opportunity is, if we open up the trading system." All of us have some form of protectionism. The question is—do we have the political will not to make it worse, but rather to go in the opposite direction and open up our system . . . With countries that are competitive with us—and Japan certainly is—we expect them to adopt the same rules as we do. We have said: "If you want to do business with the United States, it should be on an equivalent basis. We should have the same opportunity to compete in your markets as you do in ours." We don't make that request of smaller, poorer countries. We know they have to have time to grow and to become competitive. But Japan, Europe, the U.S. and Canada—these countries are competitive and should all work by the same rules.

Interview, Washington/The Christian Science Monitor, 11-18:3.

Philip Caldwell
Chairman, Ford Motor Company

3

What I would like to see more thought given to is the relationship between the value of the [Japanese] yen and the value of the [U.S.] dollar. When you produce in one country and sell in another country and use exchange rates as one of the key factors in determining your competitiveness, you play a totally different ball game than when all producers are operating within a common border. In other words, American auto companies would be more competitive if our currency were more competitive, and that will require more frugality by government, lower inflation rates and an improved balance of payments in international trade.

Interview/U.S. News & World Report, 5-3:77.

Daniel Carroll
Management consultant

4

I'm sure that Chrysler and General Motors and Ford will all come out of this [economic] period with far lower break-even points. But that may not mean they will be in a better position to make money and to sustain market share and growth. They may have pared expenses, but they may not be capable of creativity and innovation, of bringing out new designs that people want. Another element is that some companies that have really been through the mill probably will become more risk-averse, and that may mean they won't take any gambles. Growing a business does require taking some risk.

The New York Times, 8-8:(3)22.

Allan Cox
Management consultant

1

American business executives are quite narrow intellectually. Though not limited in intelligence, they tend to have tunnel vision because they spend up to 80 hours a week focusing on their specialized job in the corporation. They are committed to doing practical things, not to playing with ideas. You won't find them reading novels or plays; their reading tends to be technical. A lot of enormously bright executives do run around corporations with fantastic ideas, but they're not always heard, despite the fact that in the current rapidly changing environment firms must quickly come up with ideas that translate into new products. If a firm doesn't welcome new ideas, it is going to get into a great deal of trouble. When we see companies going broke now, it's not because things have been going badly through this recession; it's because they stopped putting money and effort into the development of ideas a long time ago, and that's now catching up with them.

Interview/U.S. News & World Report, 12-13:89.

John C. Danforth
United States Senator, R—Missouri

2

The problem that we have gotten into now is that the United States is practicing free trade, period—we are the exclusive practitioner of this ideal. As a result, this country has comparatively few import barriers, while foreign markets are widely protected. This has put us in a weak position to bargain for mutual concessions by other countries because there are few American import restrictions left to trade away. The Japanese definition of free trade is that they're free to ship their cars to the United States. They are free to ship their television sets to the United States. They are free to ship their Sony Walkmans to the United States. At the same time, they are free to exclude our beef, citrus, leather, semiconductors and high-technology products. It's becoming a one-way street.

Interview/U.S. News & World Report, 7-19:54.

James Dale Davidson
Chairman, National Taxpayers Union

3

[On organized business lobbies in Washington]: Frankly, these are the most feckless people you will ever find. They spend their time worrying about which of their turkey industries should get a bailout, and they never get around to taking on the structural problems. It may be bad business for me to say it, but they're more trouble than they're worth.

The Washington Post, 7-20:(A)6.

Thomas R. Donahue
Secretary-treasurer, American Federation of Labor-Congress of Industrial Organizations

4

[Arguing against "enterprise zones," areas giving special advantages to businesses moving into them]: [The zones] would not create any new jobs, and therefore no new customers and no incentive to expand production ... The tax breaks and the giveaways held out as bait would indeed encourage movement. But it would be the movement of only footloose, low-investment, labor-intensive industry, such as the apparel industry, in which companies can move with relative ease from one depressed area to another depressed area, and from one underpaid minority group to another ... Wages in the [American apparel] industry average $5 to $5.50 an hour and, with benefits, the total comes to about $6.75 an hour. That is, of course, a controllable cost, and no doubt could be reduced further. But it can't be reduced to the $1 an hour paid in Hong Kong, to the 40 cents an hour in Taiwan, the 20 cents in India, and the even lower amounts in Sri Lanka or the People's Republic of China. Yet the [enterprise-zone] proposal is to subsidize such industries by relieving them of tax obligations and of health, sanitation and labor standards to make them the parasites of another community, all the time ignoring the flood of dirt-cheap imports.

At conference on the future of cities, Providence, R.I./The Washington Post, 12-10:(A)23.

Thomas Donaldson
Professor of philosophy,
Loyola University, Chicago

1

Corporations today are meeting their social responsibilities considerably better than they were 15 years ago. But, at the same time, public estimation of the ethical character of business has slipped. To me, that is proof of a changing mandate from the public. Society has raised its standards; it expects more from a corporation ... Whereas in the past we saw the mission of the corporation essentially as maximizing profit and providing us with goods and services, we now see it as an important part of the over-all social fabric that relates to our quality of life. We feel that it has a moral responsibility to enhance the welfare of society and that society ought to have some input into the corporation. Otherwise, our quality of life will suffer.
Interview/U.S. News & World Report, 9-6:30.

Herbert P. Dooskin
Assistant managing partner, Alexander
Grant & Company, accountants

2

[On the practice of dumping—the selling in the U.S. of foreign-made products at unfairly low prices]: It's very serious. Steel and high-technology products have been the headline-grabbers, but many mundane industries are affected because ours is the largest and freest economy, and many foreign companies want to be in the United States market ... I don't consider [special duties and other measures that U.S. firms can take against dumping] protectionism, if we're acting within our rights and obligations on the basis of international treaties.
Interview/The New York Times, 8-3:30.

Peter F. Drucker
Professor of social science and
management, Clarement (Calif.)
College Graduate School

3

Management is not being brilliant. Management is being conscientious. Beware the genius manager. Management is doing a very few simple things and doing them well. You put brilliant people into staff roles. But for criss sakes don't let them ever make decisions, because the secret of management is never to make a decision which ordinary human beings can't carry out ... Work is craftsmanship. Management is craftsmanship. Most of the time it is hard work to get a very few simple things across so that ordinary people can do it.
Interview, Chicago, April/Chicago Tribune, 5-2:(5)1.

Billy Lee Evans
United States Representative, D–Georgia

4

I am deeply troubled by the number of debtors who appear to be taking advantage of the bankruptcy process. Today it is fashionable for these debtors to take straight bankruptcy—not as a matter of need, but as a matter of convenience ... It's a definite pattern in our society. Payment of one's debts is no longer important.
Nation's Business, May:46.

Thomas S. Foley
United States Representative,
D–Washington

5

[On trade protectionism]: When times get hard and large numbers of people are unemployed, there's a tremendous feeling that we ought to take care of our own first. The benefits of a free trading system are long term, diffuse and general. But the pain people feel now in particular industries is immediate, specific and acute.
The New York Times, 12-14:10.

Milton Friedman
Economist; Senior fellow, Hoover
Institution, Stanford University

6

[Corporate] mergers promote efficiency by enabling managements that are not using their resources effectively to be replaced. The economy would be far better off in a system where there were fewer restrictions and regulations against the purchase of controlling interests.
The New York Times Magazine, 7-18:56.

Robert W. Galvin
Chairman, Motorola, Inc.

7

[Saying Japan uses unfair practices in its trade with the U.S.]: In our society, if a group

31

WHAT THEY SAID IN 1982

of companies collectively decide that they are going to dominate a particular market, we consider it illegal. For the Japanese to intend to succeed is one thing; to intend to dominate is another. And to take this collective action under government guidance, as they do, is also anathema to the American private-enterprise system. I object to the Japanese using techniques that, if employed in our society, would be illegal.

Interview/Nation's Business, November:47.

Tom Gray
Chief Economist, Small Business
Administration of the United States

1

Three years of hard times means that businesses which have survived are like a marine who has just finished basic training. He is lean and mean and ready to go. When the economy turns up, they will have good profits.

The Christian Science Monitor, 10-18:3.

Barrie Sanford Greiff
Psychiatrist, Harvard Business School

2

[On executives who are fired]: It doesn't matter what you call it—fired, axed, sacked, canned, kicked upstairs or allowed to resign—they all feel the same. The only certainty about being fired is that it hurts. It threatens everyone—family, peers, even the executive who has to do the firing. It may even hurt the organization, especially if the fired executive has long standing and deeply rooted associations. But most of all, it hurts the executive who gets fired. Whatever the cause, no one wants to be told they're through.

Los Angeles Times, 6-5:(I)15.

John W. Hanley
Chairman, Monsanto Company

3

I subscribe to the thought that most people have a finite reservoir of intellectual material to add to an enterprise and that when it's gone, it's gone. Then you have to put somebody else's reservoir to work.

Interview/Nation's Business, October:76.

Don Hewitt
Executive producer, "60 Minutes"
program, CBS-TV

4

[Saying business considers the press an adversary]: And for a very special reason. The businessman only wants two things said about his company—what he pays his public-relations people to say and what he pays his advertising people to say. He doesn't like anybody ever to look above, beyond or over that.

At seminar sponsored by CBS News and Columbia University School of Journalism, Princeton, N.J., November/"Eye on the Media: Business and the Press," CBS-TV, 12-25.

Michael J. Horowitz
Special Counsel for Policy
Analysis and Law, Federal
Office of Management and Budget

5

The only people who in recent years have exuded moral self-confidence are those least entitled to it—the ones who, indifferent to inflation and private-sector productivity, have pushed for and controlled the Federal income-redistribution apparatus. Those who produce what is later redistributed have tended to apologize for their profits, for their failings, for themselves. A national sense of the moral worth of the business community and a deeply enhanced moral self-confidence on its part are critical to America's future.

At forum sponsored by Manhattan Institute for Policy Research/ The Wall Street Journal, 5-14:24.

Lee A. Iacocca
Chairman, Chrysler Corporation

6

[Calling for government incentives for Americans to buy U.S.-made cars]: Our automotive imbalance of trade with Japan is over $13-billion a year. That's the price of a [U.S.] government policy which says we don't care what it costs in unemployment, in welfare, in lost taxes, in trade deficits—we are going to be the only country in the world that says one-way free trade is the principle on which we stand ... I don't see anything un-American about giving American workers an even break at competing for the American market.

Chicago Tribune, 2-7:(1)4.

Llewellyn Jenkins
Vice chairman, Manufacturers
Hanover Bank, New York; President,
American Bankers Association

1

If anybody said they were asking us [bankers] here to lower interest rates, they didn't quite understand how interest rates are handled. Banks do not raise or lower interest rates depending upon how they feel about it. A bank buys money like a grocer buys bananas—and then adds on salaries and rent and sells the product.

To reporters after meeting with
President Reagan, Washington, May 13/
Los Angeles Times, 5-14:(IV)1.

Donald Johnston
Chairman, J. Walter Thompson
Company, advertising

2

It's hardly a secret that all advertising is based on trust. Advertising is essentially a promise of a benefit. If you don't believe the promise, you're not likely to buy the product.

Before American Association of
Advertising Agencies/The Christian
Science Monitor, 7-20:2.

Henry Kaufman
Managing director, Salomon
Brothers, investment bankers

3

The sector that this time around faces very serious problems is the business corporation. Now there is every need for everyone to be concerned about the dilemma of the American business corporations. Corporate profits are falling very, very rapidly. In the first quarter of this year, we had, against a backdrop of economic contraction, a huge volume of corporate borrowings, short-term. Liquidity of corporations is diminishing. And the risk is that if by some chance here the American corporation continues to experience lack of profits, inability to recapture liquidity, it will derail the one thing that all of us want to have, and that is a large increase in capital outlays. That is the decision that sits in front of business corporations in the second half of the year. Further squeezes on profits, further squeezes on the

ability to finance, will derail capital outlays, and the very thing that we have been trying to nurture, an investment boom, will then capsize as we go into 1983, and with it we will again face a stagnant economy and higher financial risks.

Broadcast interview/"Meet
the Press," NBC-TV, 5-9.

George A. Keyworth II
Director, Federal Office of
Science and Technology Policy

4

Many of us have been concerned for some time that we [in the U.S.] do a relatively poor job of converting our wonderful new knowledge into processes and products. How many times have we watched dumbfounded as foreign competitors—notably the Japanese—took basic research produced in American universities or our Federal laboratories and converted it into a new product better than the one we already manufactured? To me this suggests that we are probably doing a reasonably good job of maintaining our research base in this country but that it's time for more attention to the problem of moving knowledge into the marketplace.

At Rensselaer Polytechnic Institute
commencement/U.S. News & World Report, 6-7:66.

5

Our lost momentum in the world's marketplaces is largely our own fault. Back when we were basking in the dreams of an economic never-never land, Numbers 2 and 3 and on down the line were gearing up for just what we've always said American society thrived on—competition. We thought they could never catch up, but they tried harder, and here we are—to paraphrase an old American slogan, a Sony in every house and two Toyotas in every garage.

At Rensselaer Polytechnic Institute
commencement/Time, 6-21:82.

Austin Kiplinger
Editor, "Kiplinger Washington Letter"

6

The ethics of business should be the same principles that apply to the rest of human

WHAT THEY SAID IN 1982

activity. Honesty, candor and fairness are called for in all of our daily dealings, whether personal or professional. Daring, vigor and determination are as appropriate in business affairs as in personal ones ... Like most things human, business gives some pleasures in the doing of it, some in the results that flow from it, and it is always best when conducted according to the highest rules of human behavior.

At Bryant College commencement/The
Christian Science Monitor, 6-11:15.

Lane Kirkland
President, American
Federation of Labor-Congress
of Industrial Organizations

1

What has hurt the auto industry are not the union agreements but piratical marketing practices of the Japanese, extraordinary increases in gasoline prices over the past few years, the consequent drastic change in the nature of the market and, above all, interest rates. As long as these problems persist, the auto industry will be in trouble. The United Auto Workers' concessions only give the companies a bit of breathing time to try and take steps that will enable them to survive the other problems.

Interview/U.S. News & World Report, 5-17:71.

2

... the business and financial community of this country is the soft underbelly of freedom. Whenever there's been a choice between their own purse and the national interest, the business and financial community in this country has always voted for their own purse.

Interview/U.S. News & World Report, 5-17:72.

Virginia H. Knauer
Director, Federal Office
of Consumer Affairs

3

Consumer affairs is not the same in the 1980s as it was in the 1970s and 1960s. It is becoming increasingly apparent that when government supervision or control intrudes ... it restricts choices, limits values and, very simply, increases costs.

April 27/Los Angeles Times, 4-28:(I)19.

Arthur Laffer
Professor of business economics,
University of Southern California

4

[Supporting a gold standard] : The monetary system is bananas. We know very well that you never can maintain low inflation and low interest rates without having a convertible currency. With the gold standard, you are making gold worthless by making the dollar as good as gold .... if you know the dollar is as good as gold, would you bury gold? No! Everyone would dump the gold out of their basement. The price of gold would tumble sharply; we'd stop subsidizing South Africa and Russia; and we'd have a stable monetary system with low interest rates. What you really want to do is find that time in our history that had the objective criteria of all the things you really like in a society—low inflation, low unemployment, rapid growth, free trade in the world economy. I think we should try to recreate Bretton Woods, with the anchor to gold that we had and yet with the financial system that doesn't tie us inextricably to gold.

Interview/Los Angeles Herald Examiner, 3-18:(A)16.

Robert Lekachman
Professor of economics, Lehman College,
City University of New York

5

A [corporate] merger is an example of the timidity of American managers when faced with the choice between the adventure of capital investment and acquiring another company.

The New York Times Magazine, 7-18:54.

J. Paul Lyet
Chairman, President's Export Council

6

The problem of trade world-wide right now is one of barriers. Protectionism is gaining favor all over the world—indeed, even in our own country. Some of it, unfortunately, has assumed demagogic overtones ... No one's hands are clean. The European Community directly subsidizes farm exports. The Canadians have all kinds of restrictions on foreign investments. And the stories of Japanese protectionism are legion. They have quotas that limit

(J. PAUL LYET)

beef and orange imports. They have a monopoly on tobacco and salt. Some of their amateur baseball leagues keep out American-made aluminum bats. The problem isn't really high tariffs as much as it is non-tariff barriers. The Japanese have a complicated system of inspection, for example, on many products that come in. I've heard that, if we were to use the inspection techniques that they require on some products, we would be taking Toyotas off the ship one at a time at our ports and the ships would be backed up for miles.

Interview/U.S. News & World Report, 11-29:59.

Stanley Marcus
Former president, Neiman-Marcus stores   *1*

[On future shopping at home by computer]: Why wouldn't a customer prefer a computer to a store where he can't find the salesperson, or where the salesperson doesn't know anything about the merchandise? The computer catalogue can tell them exactly what they want to know about the product, and it doesn't have bad breath.

Before Fashion Island Merchants Association/
Los Angeles Times, 5-21:(IV)2.

J. Willard Marriott, Jr.
Chief executive officer,
Marriott Corporation   *2*

Despite the state of the world's economy, and the economy of our nation, it is my opinion that there is more opportunity for success in the 1980s than ever before. There are more open doors awaiting those who have the determination and self-reliance, and who have prepared to move forward, than we've ever known. There are new products to be discovered, new services to be performed that are unknown today. Human wants are never satisfied.

At George Washington University's School
of Government and Business Administration
commencement/U.S. News & World Report, 6-7:66.

William M. McCormick
President of consumer financial
service, American Express Company   *3*

Not until we all come to view corporations as full-fledged citizens of their communities

rather than just as residents; not until corporate managers view philanthropy as a necessary ingredient in successful marketing and community relations in the 1980s; and not until we as a society see corporate contributions not only in terms of the 10 per cent of income the government allows as deductible, but as 10 per cent of the corporation's manpower working to bring the communities of America to their fullest potential; only then will we have a fair chance to create the second renaissance we need so desperately in America.

Before Kansas City Arts Council/
Chicago Tribune, 6-1:(1)11.

George W. McKinney
Senior vice president, Irving
Trust Company, New York   *4*

[On whether people should blame banks for today's high interest rates]: They should not, for the same reason they don't blame the gas-station operator for the price' of gasoline or the butcher who sells you hamburger. Both have to pay for their goods. Banks have to pay for the money they lend out, and they are paying high rates right now. That is the main factor behind the level of interest rates now ... Believe me, if it were profitable to move to lower rates, banks would. But that's not the way it works. Today, you make loans at a rate that you think is reasonable, and then you fight like the dickens to finance those loans in the markets. If you make. a bad decision on the financing, you go down the tubes. Some banks are in trouble. Remember, too, we are in competition with foreign banks that undercut our prices. We are in competition with the commercial-paper market. We're in competition with the largest single lender in the United States: the Federal government. From time to time, the spread gets awfully narrow—that is, the difference between what we pay for money and what we charge borrowers.

Interview/U.S. News & World Report, 3-15:63,64.

James C. Miller III
Chairman, Federal Trade Commission   *5*

Business in America should not be the captive handmaiden of government. It should

WHAT THEY SAID IN 1982

be an institution responding efficiently to consumers in a free market.

U.S. News & World Report, 5-17:65.

1

The [Federal Trade] Commission has extraordinarily broad powers and ill-defined guidance for what it should be doing. The FTC has been characterized as the second-most-important legislative body in America. I don't believe, quite frankly, that five unelected commissioners should be that powerful. So I have asked Congress to define "unfairness" and also "deception." The legislation we're operating under only says that unfair or deceptive acts or practices are unlawful. That's all the guidance that Congress gives the Commission. Similarly, the Supreme Court has said that unfairness means pretty much what the FTC commissioners say it means. Now, that's extraordinarily broad power and, in my opinion, that wide discretion is a major reason why the Commission has gotten itself into such hot water in the past several years. Without question, there is a wellspring of hatred and mistrust toward the FTC over its prior performance, which is very difficult to overcome.

Interview/U.S. News & World Report, 8-2:62.

2

[On his policy of reducing the FTC's rules and regulations]: We have made strong progress in getting away from the notion of national nannyism and Star-Trek law enforcement where the bold go where no man has dared to go before ... [We place] more emphasis on the prosecution of cases, and less on the development of new rules.

Washington, Oct. 19/The Washington Post, 10-20:(A)21.

Henry Mintzberg
Professor of management policy,
McGill University, Montreal

3

[On the proliferation of vice presidents and other titles in the corporate structure]: The more layers you put between the chief executive and the operating people, the more you insulate the chief executive from what's going on. Many organizations are over-managed. There is too much emphasis on management technique, as opposed to knowing and seeing what the heck is happening.

Los Angeles Times, 2-12:(I)10.

J. Richard Munro
President, Time, Inc.

4

... President Reagan has promised good times ahead—with business picking up where government leaves off. Last year he said, "I believe that we will soon see a torrent of private initiative that will astound the advocates of big government." That's a tall order, and if we [in business] don't do our part, I can foresee a massive public reaction against the Reagan approach and the business community that cheered him on. Another reason for [business] being socially responsible is that it's good business—and not just for improving employee morale or your public image. We should understand the long-term benefits that business gains by being in a society that offers a better future to its people ... I don't suggest that business alone can solve our social ills. In fact, I think that the chief flaw in the Reagan approach is its over-reliance on private solutions ... [But] corporate managers lead just about the most privileged lives in our society. We should give something back in return.

At Columbia University Graduate
School of Business/
The Washington Post, 2-11:(A)22.

John Naisbitt
Business analyst

5

[Saying "smokestack industries" are on the way out in the U.S.]: Without question. We are in the process of transitioning out of automobiles—and steel and appliances and textiles and apparel and shoes and all of those industrial tasks that we used to do. As Third World countries take up those tasks, we let them go and we move on to new tasks. It's occurring globally. All the developed countries are deindustrializing—absolutely all of them. It's very clear when we look at the United Kingdom. Japan is today moving out of cars, moving out of steel, because South Korea is way under-

(JOHN NAISBITT)

selling Japan. She's moving out of shipbuilding, and Brazil and Spain and, until recently, Poland are becoming the shipbuilders. What's happening is that the whole globe is in a process of sorting out who's going to make what. It's a redistribution of labor and production. For example, after World War II, we [in the U.S.] produced 50 per cent of the world's steel; now that's down to about 12 or 13 per cent, and it will go lower. We certainly will move out of cars, too.

Interview/U.S. News & World Report, 12-27:49.

John J. Nevin
Chairman and president,
Firestone Tire & Rubber Company *1*

Protectionist sentiment has reached landslide proportions in the United States, in large part because Americans are convinced their country has been taken advantage of in foreign trade. Unless this country responds quickly to its trade difficulties, protectionist sentiment is likely to produce a reaction that will severely damage the entire world trade system ... If there were free trade in the world, the United States would be struggling to control huge trade surpluses, not huge deficits. The fact is the world does not have a free trade system. It has an administered trade system. To minimize unemployment at home and generate dollars needed to pay for imported oil, other industrialized nations have sought to rigidly limit imports and aggressively promote exports even when those efforts abrogated the letter and spirit of world trade agreements. No country in the developed world has been more successful limiting imports than has Japan.

Chicago Tribune, 7-12:(1)11.

John J. Phelan, Jr.
President, New York Stock Exchange *2*

We at the New York Stock Exchange feel that the market for stocks is definitely broadening—especially with the increased emphasis being put on savings and investment. Our planning assumes that while institutional activity will grow, the role of the individual will grow at an even faster rate. One factor that's

favorable for expanded stock ownership is growing acceptance that individuals will have to make a greater contribution toward certain financial needs, such as their retirement. So there will be a greater need for them to save and to invest some of those savings. A certain portion of those investments should flow into securities.

Interview/U.S. News & World Report, 12-13:33.

Almarin Phillips
Professor of public management,
economics and law,
University of Pennsylvania *3*

The role of an antitrust policy is quite restricted. It is supposed to be directed at achieving efficiency through the market mechanism, where that's appropriate. If one attempts to put into the guise of antitrust the attainment of other goals, make it the paramount regulator where regulation is more efficient, or make it the enforcer of OSHA-type rules or some other distributional goals, then it becomes a social agency with no clear mission ... If there are no obvious anti-competitive aspects, to try to push the Sherman Act or the Clayton Act to accomplish social goals other than promoting competition is a mistake.

Panel discussion/The New York Times, 11-21:(4)5.

Ronald Reagan
President of the United States *4*

[Criticizing trade protectionism] : The aim of these actions may be to protect jobs, but the practical result, as we know from historical experience, is the destruction of jobs. Protectionism induces more protectionism and this leads only to economic contraction and, eventually, dangerous instability.

Before business leaders, Sao Paulo, Brazil,
Dec. 2/Los Angeles Times, 12-3:(I)1.

Hyman G. Rickover
Admiral, United States Navy *5*

A preoccupation with the so-called bottom line of profit-and-loss statement, coupled with a lust for expansion, is creating an environment in which few. businessmen honor traditional values; where responsibility is increasingly disas-

(HYMAN G. RICKOVER)

sociated from the exercise of power; where skill in financial manipulation is valued more than actual knowledge and experience in the business; where attention and effort is directed mostly to short-term considerations, regardless of longer-range consequences. Political and economic power is increasingly being concentrated among a few large corporations and their officers—power they can apply against society, government and individuals. Through their control of vast resources, these large corporations have become, in effect, another branch of government. They often exercise the power of government, but without the checks and balances inherent in our democratic system.

Before Congressional Joint Economic Committee, Washington, Jan. 28/The Christian Science Monitor, 2-9:22.

David M. Roderick
Chairman, United States Steel Corporation

1

[On stiff competition for U.S. industry from foreign companies]: We have been shocked out of our complacency and smugness. We now realize that American industry has no manifest destiny to be always first, always right, always best. A world economy includes us, but we are no longer the majority stockholder.

The Washington Post, 8-10:(A)12.

Aanon Michael Rosholt
Chairman, Barlow Rand, Ltd. (South Africa)

2

[On his treatment of employees]: I'm not a humanitarian, you know. I believe that people should be treated well, but I also believe it's the way to run a business. It's the only way you're going to provide yourself with contented, trained people in the future.

Interview, Johannesburg/The New York Times, 4-11:(3)4.

Donald H. Rumsfeld
President, G. D. Searle & Company; Former Secretary of Defense of the United States

3

At the present time, a negative attitude

toward business is prevalent in the media, in academic institutions and in the political world. I don't know that I can explain how this came about, but my guess is that it happened sometime in the late 1950s and early 1960s. It didn't change fast. There was no major catalytic event. It was an incremental process that occurred over time. It's crazy for the society to be unfriendly to enterprise. It's damaging to the country and has contributed in a major way to today's economic difficulties. Yet the fundamental truth is that the relationship between enterprise and major segments of the society is not a constructive one.

Interview/U.S. News & World Report, 7-12:55.

Fernand St. Germain
United States Representative, D–Rhode Island

4

[On the current fiscal difficulties of savings and loan associations]: There's no doubt that we [Congress] created the savings and loans. We said to them, your purpose, your mission in life, is to provide home mortgage financing. And they did that for many years, successfully. We assisted them with Regulation Q and we assisted them with the differential. And yes, we said to them you can't engage in commercial lending. All you can do is lend long. In hindsight, some might say everything we did was wrong. But who could have conceived of, who could have dreamed of the fact that concurrently we'd have the Gray Panthers movement and the saver saying, "Hey, wait a second, I want a larger return on my money; I don't any longer want to subsidize the borrower"? That wouldn't have been bad had interest rates stayed at 8, 9, 10 per cent. They could have weathered that storm. However, in conjunction with that we got this sudden, right-straight-up change in interest rates. Sure, there are some instances in which we could say it's poor management and lack of foresight, but I think that's minimal. They did what we asked them to do. We want to protect the home mortgage lending industry on behalf of the home purchaser.

The New York Times, 2-28:(3)6.

Frederick H. Schultz
Vice Chairman, Federal Reserve Board

1

[On corporate mergers]: [Take-overs may well] strengthen management, generate resources for increased investment in improved facilities, produce economies of integration or scale, and, especially in the case of small enterprises, provide for orderly transfer of ownership from one generation to another.
Nation's Business, March:14.

Louis B. Schwartz
Professor of law, University of Pennsylvania

2

[Criticizing Assistant Attorney General William Baxter for being too soft in antitrust enforcement]: Economics is clearly the god of the new regression. It is downhill all the way from [former antitrust chief Thurman] Arnold to Baxter. Whither antitrust? Baxter would say, "Let it wither away."
At Columbia University Law Symposium, March/The New York Times, 3-29:14.

Joan Seidman
Senior copywriter, Batten, Barton, Durstine & Osborn, advertising

3

Honesty in advertising is a matter of pragmatics as well as morality. You can use advertising to get people to buy a product once, but if it doesn't live up to expectation or its advertising claims, who's going to buy it a second time? I can't think of a faster way to ruin a product than with advertising that's not truthful.
The Christian Science Monitor, 7-20:2.

John S. R. Shad
Chairman, Securities and Exchange Commission of the United States

4

[On "insider" stock trading]: Inside trading impugns the integrity of our securities markets. In that sense, it hurts every market participant and the capital-formation process. Some individuals are overcome by greed, are willing to risk their jobs, fines and prison terms to take advantage of inside facts ... Of course, insiders

are not always right. Speculative expectations often fail to materialize.
Interview/The Washington Post, 5-2:(L)13.

Irving S. Shapiro
Lawyer; Former chairman, E. I. du Pont de Nemours & Co.

5

The fact is that we [in business] were getting tied up by government regulations, strike suits, takeovers and protracted litigation. Everything from what fuse you use at the boiler to which people you hire was subject to regulation. I've made this speech a hundred times before. I was making the same arguments to President Carter that I'm making now. The [Federal] Occupational Safety and Health Administration has been a disaster. You don't create a safe environment for workers by having inspectors going around and fining factories. By the time he left office, I had the Secretary of Labor pretty well convinced that he was on the wrong track. I wouldn't quarrel with a suitable government program that focused on education, not penalties.
Interview, Wilmington, Del./ The New York Times, 8-8:(3)15.

Sanford Sherizen
Professor of criminology and sociology, Boston University

6

The marketplace for stolen ideas or [even] half-developed ideas is enormous ... [In some cases,] the law is not very clear in terms of what is proprietary information and what employees can and cannot take with them when they leave a job. Some of these attempts [to obtain information] skirt the line of legality. Sometimes they go over the line. I know of companies that are very competitive in the computer marketplace that take the stance that if anyone supplied them with ... information that they knew was stolen or that somehow they should not have, they would fire that individual ... Other companies take the position, "If we get it, and it helps us, we won't ask any questions." And in fact, in some cases, people who have gotten this information where no questions were asked are rewarded for it, because they helped their company.
Boston/The Christian Science Monitor, 7-21:6.

Albert T. Sommers
Chief executive,
The Conference Board

1

By cutting into capital investment now, we are bending our country's long-term growth trend down. A very prolonged deferral of investment will cost the country hundreds of billions of dollars in lost output, compared to what we would have had under conditions of reasonably normal growth. It will take a long time to make this up.

The New York Times, 8-8:(3)1.

Stuart M. Statler
Commissioner, Consumer Product Safety
Commission of the United States

2

It's an embarrassment that this agency keeps data about frivolous incidents which are only faintly associated with consumer products—which do not even approach an unreasonable risk—and then uses those incidents in projecting national injury estimates. Why bother? Who cares? Such figures are as meaningless as they are useless. To collect, code, classify and then calculate national injury estimates for over 1,000 product categories is a tragic waste of taxpayers' monies. Why, for example, do we need to collect voluminous data on drinking fountains, sewage pipes and covers, tie racks or toothpicks? Why laundry baskets, drinking straws, phonograph records or telephone accessories? Why clothespins, seeds, combs, music boxes, tombstones, or books and magazines?

May 5/The Wall Street Journal, 8-6:14.

J. Paul Sticht
Chairman, Reynolds Industries

3

Over the long run, the most efficient allocation and management of the world's resources can best be performed by those enterprises large enough, and with sufficient resources and technology, to quickly respond to changes in consumer tastes and needs. During the past 15 or 20 years, multinational companies have demonstrated remarkable ability to shift capital, resources and technology to areas of the world that have low costs of production and good market growth potential. Free competi-

tion among such companies, unencumbered by artificial national restraints on trade and investment, make needed goods available to *more* people at *lower* costs. And, equally important, these efforts by multinationals bring employment, which in turn becomes the foundation for further economic progress.

Before London Chamber of Commerce and Industry/
The Christian Science Monitor, 2-17.

Pierre Elliott Trudeau
Prime Minister of Canada

4

[On investment in various countries by multinational corporations] : I think most sovereign nations, at least until now, seem to . . . feel that their instruments of sovereignty permit them to assert whatever degree of political control is necessary over their domestic economic environment, and it is up to these governments to decide how much or how little is necessary in each circumstance. We all have the means to defend ourselves against foreign investments. The question or the problem is that we also *want* foreign investment and therefore we have to strike a balance between how much we allow and how much we disallow.

Interview, Ottawa/The New York
Times Magazine, 10-3:40.

Henry C. Wallich
Governor, Federal Reserve Board

5

We may have ahead of us a time when some of the old hypotheses about international lending may be tested. One such theory . . . says that losses in international lending have historically been lower than at home and will, therefore, continue that way. But one reason for this seemingly favorable experience may be that it is harder to recognize a loss on a sovereign loan than on a commercial loan. On a loan to a business firm, the loss is final when the borrower goes out of business. That kind of tap on the head with a two-by-four usually does not happen in the international field.

At Euromarkets Conference/
The Wall Street Journal, 4-2:22.

Lew Wasserman
Chairman, MCA, Inc.

1

Preserving our management group has been the most important part of my career, as opposed to any particular decision. I place the highest conceivable value on them. None of us is irreplaceable. None of us walks on water. As an executive, I've always tried to delegate responsibility. That's how you build an organization.

Interview, Beverly Hills, Calif./
"W": a Fairchild publication, 10-8:18.

Yoshiki Yamasaki
President, Toyo Kogyo (Japan),
makers of Mazda automobiles

2

To me, the most important element in management is the human being. You can have the best plans in the world, you can have the most marvelous equipment. But it is people that carry out the plans and use the equipment. Without willing workers, you have nothing. So the first essential is to treat people with consideration.

Interview, Hiroshima, Japan/
The Christian Science Monitor, 12-28:15.

Crime . Law Enforcement

Pete Adams
*President, Louisiana District
Attorneys Association*
1

[On the trend to impose longer prison sentences on repeat offenders] : One reason for the increase in the use of the habitual-criminal statute is that there was a realization that a 20-year sentence didn't mean 20 years. It's a better bet to put them away, these people who are constantly costing the taxpayers money. People are realizing rehabilitation is not working. The answer is long sentences.

*The New York Times,
4-25:(1)38.*

David L. Bazelon
*Senior Judge,
United States Court
of Appeals for the
District of Columbia*
2

[Saying poverty is a major cause of violent crime] : Only the blind or the willful can deny the clear association of this kind of crime with the culture of poverty and discrimination still tolerated in every American city. From my experience, I would warrant that more than 90 per cent of the defendants in prosecutions for violent street crimes come from the bottom of the socio-economic ladder. They are invariably born into families struggling to survive, if they have families at all. They are raised in deteriorating, over-crowded housing. They are subjected to prejudice and educated in unresponsive schools. With nothing to preserve and nothing to lose, they turn to crime for economic survival, a sense of excitement and accomplishment, and an outlet for frustration, desperation and rage.

*At Vanderbilt University, Feb. 12/
The New York Times, 2-14:18.*

Jerry J. Berman
*Legislative counsel, American
Civil Liberties Union*
3

[Criticizing the FBI's Abscam operation which resulted in convictions of 12 of 27 public officials on bribe charges): This is a 60 per cent success rate, but it is also a 40 per cent failure rate using a highly intrusive technique with damaging consequences. [The 27 public officials were targeted] solely on the basis of representations from middlemen who were less than reliable and outside any effective government control . . . Instead of targeting politicians merely on the allegations of middlemen, the FBI should be required to show that particular persons on the basis of reliable information or allegations are likely to engage in corrupt transactions if offered opportunities to commit crimes.

*Before Senate committee, Washington, Sept. 28/
Los Angeles Times, 9-29:(I)12.*

Alvin J. Bronstein
*Executive director, National Prison Project,
American Civil Liberties Union*
4

[Prison] overcrowding leads to a breakdown in a whole variety of things. There's an increase in violence, an increase in idleness, a decrease in services, and that increases the problem. The harsher the conditions, the more dangerous they [inmates] are when they come out. They're going to come out and make society pay for that treatment.

Los Angeles Times, 6-15:(I)18.

Richard Brzeczek
Superintendent of Police of Chicago
5

People in any community get the kind of law enforcement that they'll tolerate, and what they'll tolerate is what they deserve. If [the community] puts tremendous demands upon the [police] department, the department

(RICHARD BRZECZEK)

should . . . respond. But if the community doesn't care, there's no stimulus for the department to move forward.

Interview/Los Angeles Times, 5-24:(I)8.

Warren E. Burger
Chief Justice of the United States

1

I doubt that anyone can make the case that we [in the U.S.] are . . . too lenient with criminals. I said to the American Bar Association a year ago, as I did 25 years earlier in a lecture at a university, that a society that cannot provide its citizens with safe streets, safe homes and safe schools is not redeemed by the fact that it has the widest protections for persons accused of criminal conduct. The two ought to be brought into balance. The first function of government is to protect its people.

*Interview/U.S. News &
World Report, 2-22:39.*

Hugh L. Carey
Governor of New York (D)

2

The revitalization of our economic life will be for naught if our citizens are not safe to walk the streets. The random street crime that terrorizes neighborhoods and communities is rooted in poverty, in unemployment and in a lack of education and opportunity. The criminal-justice system is our primary means to deal with those who break the law, and that system's ability to provide swift and certain justice is itself a deterrent to crime . . . The greatest threat to our society is posed by the small percentage of the criminal population which commits a disproportionately large number of violent crimes. The effect of successfully incapacitating this core of repeat offenders cannot be overemphasized.

*State of the State address/
The New York Times, 3-7:(4)3.*

Mario M. Cuomo
Governor-elect of New York (D)

3

[During the election campaign,] I was unhappy to have to talk so much about criminal justice. It is a shame we have to spend so much just protecting ourselves from injury. But we do. It is a bad time in the streets, very bad . . . You have to deal with balancing the budget . . . but you have to, at the same time, find a way to do something about the criminal-justice system that's terribly inefficient.

*Interview, New York, December/
Los Angeles Times, 12-17:(I-C)2.*

Jeremiah Denton
United States Senator, R—Alabama

4

[Saying Americans should relinquish some of their civil rights in order to help law-enforcement deal with terrorism]: Whether we like it or not, there are elements in our society who are committed to violence, subversion and terrorism. Now, we can either sit back and hope that they will go away or we can wait until events occur before responding . . . [Law-enforcement] intelligence collection is all the more important in a highly mobile and open society such as ours in order to ensure that it remains open and free and is not subtly destroyed because of governmental inaction borne out of a narrowly focused concern for individual civil rights. These are important, but at times other considerations such as national security must not be overlooked. In some cases, circumstances dictate that the national good is best served by a limited relinquishment of some individual rights.

*At Senate Security and Terrorism
Subcommittee hearing, Washington, Aug. 11/
The Washington Post, 8-12:(A)2.*

A. C. Germann
*Professor of criminal justice,
California State University, Long Beach*

5

The public has generally been misled in terms of what a police department can do about reducing crime. Television and the newspapers and magazines suggest that something can really be done about crime. The answers to

(A. C. GERMANN)

crime and disorder do not lie in more police or more police equipment or stricter laws or longer jail terms or more police facilities, but in ameliorating the social conditions in which crime breeds. Until the citizens come to understand that the environment in which certain people live is very conducive to crime, and that when employment opportunity is available for all citizens and housing and medical care and education is available for people, only then will we find a substantial amount of crime and disorder beginning to drop.

Interview/Los Angeles Herald Examiner, 5-18:(A)8.

Diana Gordon
*President, National Council
on Crime and Delinquency*

1

For many offenders, a period of community service or a probation sentence would protect the safety of the public just as well as a prison term, and would be a great deal less costly in both social and economic terms. That, of course, is not true for all offenders—I want to be clear on that. I am not advocating community service for truly violent people. On the other hand, we often define as a violent personality someone who perhaps committed one violent crime, and I think that doesn't hold water. Those are not necessarily truly violent people because they have committed one aggravated assault. I think we have to look at informal social controls as ways of preventing behavior from escalating to the point where it becomes violent.

*Interview/Los Angeles Herald
Examiner, 4-21:(A)2.*

Gary Hayes
*Executive director, Police
Executive Research Forum*

2

I think the most important influence on [the behavior of] the officer in the street is the police leadership and the tone it sets. If he knows that the police chief means what he says about the need for restraint and an abiding concern for individual Constitutional rights, that can do more than anything to control his

behavior. The officer usually knows better than anybody whether that message is sincere or whether the leadership is just saying it to look good.

*The Christian Science Monitor,
1-19:8.*

Brian Jenkins
*Director, program on political
violence, Rand Corporation*

3

Governments are almost always at a disadvantage in dealing with terrorism. Terrorists create dramas in which they and their victims are the central figures. Except for the occasional successful commando rescue, governments seldom get to play the roles of heroes. More often, governments are seen as reactive, incompetent, impotent.

*The Christian Science Monitor,
1-12:1.*

Edward I. Koch
Mayor of New York

4

Crime is producing an enormous [anti-black] backlash by the white middle class because they perceive crime as a black issue. I believe you prevent that backlash by speaking out and pointing out that the black community is very tough-minded when it comes to criminal activity committed by blacks or whites because the *decent* black community is overwhelmingly the victim. It is the white, liberal ideologues who say, "Ah, NO! NO! NO! No, we mustn't punish people! They commit crimes because of poverty!" That's baloney! . . . People commit crimes because it's easier to make a living that way than to work. Listen, the chance of getting caught is very small. And if you are caught, the chance of getting punished is even smaller. And *that's* why they do it. The easier you treat the criminal, the softer you make the punishment, the greater the recidivism rate. We got to get tough!

Interview, New York/Parade, 8-1:10.

Patrick V. Murphy
President, Police Foundation; Former
Police Commissioner of New York City   1

There's a certain advantage that smaller [police] departments have ... In a small town where everybody knows everybody, the police tend to be in very tight with the community and get a lot of good information. In many smaller counties, the prosecutor's office may consist of three or four people, and every police officer knows every assistant D.A. What always used to frustrate me in New York City was that the system was so enormous and so centralized —maybe over-centralized, because efficiency pokes you in that direction—that it was very difficult for people to coordinate and work with one another. A detective who made 20 felony arrests would probably never deal with the same assistant district attorney.

Panel discussion,
October/
The New York Times,
10-10:6.

James F. Neal
Lawyer; Counsel to Senate
Abscam Committee   2

[On undercover law-enforcement operations] : There is such a difficult line to walk between catching the corrupt and overpowering the corruptible. I'm thinking of the type of undercover operation referred to as an "opportunity" for criminal activity, providing the opportunity to commit a crime ... An undercover operation, like a trial, is not perfect. A defendant is not entitled to a perfect trial, and there is no such thing as a perfect undercover investigation. One of the costs is that innocent people may suffer. Frequently, there's nothing fair about law enforcement. For example, a businessman who is indicted and later acquitted has suffered irreparable harm. On the other hand, no one would say a person shouldn't be prosecuted unless there's a 100 per cent chance of conviction.

Interview, Washington/
The New York Times, 6-14:18.

William O'Sullivan
Deputy Director, Illinois Division
of Criminal Investigation   3

[On the use of videotape in obtaining criminal evidence] : You can't beat pictures and recorded conversations. The use of video recordings makes for strong prosecution. Without visual and audio evidence, lawmen are faced with a one-on-one situation that raises the issue of credibility. Who is telling the truth—the accused or the undercover officer? But this [videotape] approach overcomes that obstacle. Videotaped evidence is the best evidence. It is the wave of the future in law enforcement. You see and hear the crime in progress.

Chicago Tribune, 5-2:(1)12.

Ronald Reagan
President of the United States   4

For many years, we have tolerated in America ... a syndicate of organized criminals whose power is now reaching unparalleled heights ... Today the power of organized crime reaches into every segment of our society. It is estimated that the syndicate has millions of dollars in assets in legitimate businesses; it controls corrupt union locals; it runs burglary rings, fences for stolen goods, holds a virtual monopoly in the heroin trade; it thrives on illegal gambling, pornography, gun-running, car theft, arson and a host of other illegal activities. The existence of this nation-wide criminal network and its willingness—and too often its success—in corrupting and gaining protection from those in high places is an affront to every law-abiding American and an encouragement to every street punk or two-bit criminal who hopes someday to make it to the big time ... It comes down in the end to a simple question we must ask ourselves: What kind of people are we if we continue to tolerate in our midst an invisible, lawless empire? Can we honestly say that America is a land "with justice for all" if we do not now exert every effort to eliminate this confederation of professional criminals, this dark, evil enemy within? You know the answer to that question. The American people want the mob and its associates brought to justice and their power broken. Not out of a sense of

WHAT THEY SAID IN 1982

(RONALD REAGAN)

vengeance but out of a sense of justice. Not just from an obligation to punish the guilty but from an ever-stronger obligation to protect the innocent. Not simply for the sake of legalities, but for the sake of the law that is the protection of liberty.

At U.S. Dept. of Justice, Washington,
Oct. 14/The New York Times, 10-15:11.

Stephen Sachs
Attorney General of Maryland
1

I trust that most of us in law enforcement are principled enough to avoid violating the clear Constitutional rights of suspects. But in the heat of the chase, and in the absence of effective sanction, I believe that we would define those rights, to put it mildly, somewhat narrowly. Questions of adequate identification, "staleness" of information and the need for a warrant will be answered differently by unchecked law enforcers than by judges. We are, after all, hunters stalking crime. It is simply too much to ask for objectivity in the midst of the hunt, especially when the quarry is in sight. This is precisely what the warrant requirement of the Fourth Amendment is about.

Before House subcommittee, Washington/
The Washington Post, 7-16:(A)14.

Charles E. Schumer
United States Representative,
D–New York
2

Crime is the hidden social issue of the '80s—not abortion or busing. Ten years ago, crime was a Brooklyn issue. Five years ago, it was a metropolitan New York issue. Now it's a national issue . . . This is a challenge to the Democratic Party. One reason so many blue-collar and middle-class voters went for [President] Reagan is that we [Democrats] had no effective answer to the crime issue. The Republicans don't, either, but they talk tough.

The New York Times, 3-16:10.

Ronald Scott
Assistant professor, department
of administration of justice,
University of Missouri
3

What we don't need are more places to lock people up. But judges operate almost independently of the prison system—they're responding to the social and political climate. And as long as everybody thinks of probation as easy and a slap on the wrist, rather than a legal status with conditions and supervision, we'll never be able to treat it as punishment.

The Christian Science Monitor, 1-6:14.

Nelson T. Shields
Chairman, Handgun Control, Inc.
4

I think I understand the reason that most people have that handgun in that bedside table: fear. Fear of the basic crime and violence of this society. And I would not try to legislate that handgun out of that bedside table drawer. That's an educational process. I think the average person in this country sees the handgun, mistakenly or not, as his means of self-defense in a very violent world. I think when the level of crime and violence begins to be reduced in this country—and I say *when* because it *has* to be reduced—then individuals will begin to ask themselves whether it's sensible to have that gun in that bedside table, and voluntarily get rid of that gun. But we have to get some form of control that will keep the handguns out of the wrong hands . . . I'd have the toughest punishment for people who misuse guns, criminals. Also, those people through whose negligence other people are hurt by guns. I'd get rid of the Saturday night special. Because of its concealability, its cheapness, it's the weapon of the street crime. I'd have restrictive licensing rather than permissive licensing. You would have to prove a need. All we have to prove [now] is that we're not baddies.

Interview, Wilmington, Del./
Chicago Tribune, 1-23:(1)11.

William French Smith
Attorney General of the United States

1

The continual availability of the possibility of relief has turned many prisoners into writ-writers who never confront the fact of their guilt and get on with the process of rehabilitation, but view the criminal process as an ongoing game in which they are still active contestants.

At conference on the administration of justice, Williamsburg, Va., Jan. 30/San Francisco Examiner & Chronicle, 1-31:(A)2.

2

[Defending the FBI's controversial Abscam investigation of government corruption]: Nothing would do more to undermine public confidence than for Federal law enforcement to be denied the means necessary to detect, prosecute and deter crimes committed by the powerful . . . Let everyone who seeks to improve the efforts of law enforcement in these areas keep in mind that the American public itself is also indignant about the kind of criminal activity uncovered and videotaped during Abscam. After surveying the Federal effort against public corruption, I for one want to express my indignation—not at the techniques or aims of law enforcement, but at the corruption uncovered . . . By their very nature, these are clandestine crimes. Payment of a bribe is not a public event. Neither the person who pays nor the person who takes a bribe heralds that fact from the rooftops. The person who pays, even if regarded as a victim, typically makes no report to the authorities. [To root out this corruption, law enforcement in its investigation] must feign the role of corrupt participant. If it does not, we as a society, as taxpayers, as persons with respect for law, can do nothing but tolerate this particularly pernicious and costly form of crime.

Before New York City Bar Association, June 23/Los Angeles Times, 6-24:(I)14.

3

[On celebrities who use illegal drugs and say so]: That situation is particularly unfortunate because people in [the entertainment] industry and people in athletics and so on are role models for the young. And as a result, to the extent that drugs are used and publicized in those areas, it has a magnifying effect which is highly unfortunate. Ultimately the answer to this over-all problem of drug use is to eliminate demand. And that is not within [the Justice Department's] operating function. Ultimately, too, the answer has to be education. And that could be a long process. It is interesting that Japan used to have a heroin problem. It does not have a major heroin problem now. There are other areas of drug use—amphetamines—that Japanese organized crime is involved in. But I asked them over there how they have been able to substantially reduce their heroin problem. And the response I received was: "two ways." First, to impose very heavy penalties on drug use. Second was education. And what we were told was that, by the use of those two approaches, the use of heroin was greatly limited.

Interview, Washington/The Christian Science Monitor, 12-2:9.

Adlai E. Stevenson III
Democratic nominee for Governor of Illinois; Former United States Senator, D—Illinois

4

[Arguing against capital punishment]: When the state takes a life and starts debating whether people should be injected or hanged or quartered or electrocuted, we only . . . contribute to the climate of violence. The state in all its actions should be seeking to increase the value of human life.

July 7/Chicago Tribune, 7-8:(1)3.

Strom Thurmond
United States Senator, R—South Carolina

5

[Criticizing the not-guilty-by-reason-of-insanity verdict in the case of John Hinckley, who shot President Reagan and others in 1981]: It is deeply troubling to me when the criminal-justice system exonerates a defendant who obviously planned and knew exactly what

(STROM THURMOND)

he was doing. This case has demonstrated over the many weeks of conflicting "expert" testimony that there is something fundamentally wrong with the expanded modern insanity defense.

Washington, June 22/
The New York Times, 6-23:11.

Anthony Travisono
Executive director, American
Correctional Association   1

[On the growing prison population]: The numbers are staggering. And it doesn't look like there's any respite. If we continue current [hard-line] sentencing patterns, it's going to be punishment to the taxpayers, punishment to the inmates and punishment to the prison staffs. There is no solution as long as the hard-line attitude continues.

Los Angeles Times, 6-15:(I)18.

2

[On the increasing number of women sentenced to prison]: The courts have decided that sentencing women is not as bad as it used to be and they've got public support for doing so. A few years ago, it was like a father punishing his daughter, a very difficult thing to do.

The New York Times, 11-28:(1)42.

William von Raab
Commissioner, United States
Customs Service   3

The Customs Service is no longer after the negligent traveler. We're looking for real felony cases now. That's the big difference between a Republican and a Democratic Administration. In my eyes, Democratic Administrations always seem concerned about a whole range of activities, and they don't put enough emphasis on real criminal activity. Republican Administrations, I've always found, jump with both feet on serious criminal activity and go lighter on what I would call late-to-work violations.

Interview/U.S. News & World Report, 6-7:45.

William H. Webster
Director, Federal Bureau
of Investigation   4

[On the Abscam operation which led to bribery charges against members of Congress]: Our purpose is to follow leads. When we have leads that take us into allegations of public corruption, we follow them—whether it involves a state legislator, a corrupt law-enforcement officer or even members of Congress. It would be wrong for us—and the American people would disapprove—if we were to turn away from any allegation of public corruption simply because of the potential for flak. Abscam did not start as a public-corruption investigation. It started as an investigation of stolen art, and we were led by the corrupt middlemen we were dealing with to lawmakers they told us were corrupt.

Interview/U.S. News & World Report, 8-16:50.

5

[Saying Americans may have to give up some privacy if they want the fight against crime to succeed]: [Informants, electronic surveillance and undercover agents are] so necessary to combat high-impact crime that privacy interests must yield to a reasonable degree to allow their lawful use . . . We use them because they are extremely effective and often indispensable, and because we have confidence in the safeguards we have put in place. [These techniques have] helped us reach beyond the criminal on the street to those responsible for some of the most serious and often hidden or protected forms of crime—organized crime, espionage, terrorism and corruption in public officials.

At Georgetown University Law School,
Oct. 13/The Washington Post, 10-14:(A)16.

Defense . The Military

John B. Anderson
Former United States Representative,
D–Illinois; 1980 independent
candidate for President

1

I still think people are taken in by the argument that the Soviets were building, building, building [their military forces] during the '70s and that we did nothing. [But] we developed the cruise missile, we built the Trident submarine, we MIRVed 550 Minuteman III missiles, we had people working night and day to improve the defense forces of this country.

Interview, Boston/The Christian
Science Monitor, 11-23:7.

Yuri V. Andropov
General Secretary, Communist
Party of the Soviet Union

2

Mankind cannot endlessly put up with the arms race and with wars unless it wants to put its future at stake. The Communist Party of the Soviet Union does not want the dispute of ideas to grow into a confrontation between states and peoples; it does not want arms and the readiness to use them to become a gauge of the potentials of the social system. The aggressive designs of imperialism compel us, together with the fraternal socialist states, to show concern, and in earnest at that, for maintaining our defense capability at a proper level. But . . . military rivalry is not our choice. The ideal of socialism is a world without arms.

Before Soviet Communist Party Central Committee,
Moscow, Nov. 22/The New York Times, 11-23:5.

3

[If the U.S. goes ahead with deployment of new missiles,] we will be compelled to counter the challenge of the American side by deploying corresponding weapons systems of our own—an analogous missile to counter the MX missile and our own long-range cruise missile, which we are now testing, to counter the U.S. long-range cruise missile. These are not threats at all. [The Soviet Union seeks] an honest agreement that will do no damage to either side and will, at the same time, lead to a reduction of nuclear arsenals. If the people in Washington really believe that new weapons systems will be a trump for the Americans at negotiations, we want them to know that these trumps are false.

At celebration of 60th anniversary of Soviet Union,
Moscow, Dec. 21/Los Angeles Times, 12-22:(I)10.

Les Aspin
United States Representative, D–Wisconsin

4

If I were to criticize this [Reagan] Administration, it would be for the reliance on a very large military budget—not a large military force, just a large military budget—as kind of a hedge against which it conducts foreign policy . . . I don't have any idea what this Administration's defense policy is . . . To paraphrase Will Rogers, I think this Administration has never seen a weapons system that it didn't like. That posture statement conveys that it doesn't have an over-all policy. We're just buying things without any relation to the threat. The other thing that worries me very much is the idea of parallel escalation—if they hit us at a place which is disadvantageous to us, we'll go and hit them at a place where it's advantageous to us and disadvantageous to them. This is a bizarre concept.

Panel discussion/The New York Times, 3-14:(4)3.

Menachem Begin
Prime Minister of Israel

5

As long as tyranny is armed, liberty must have and develop weapons for its defense.

WHAT THEY SAID IN 1982

(MENACHEM BEGIN)

Otherwise, slavery will engulf the whole of mankind, and all the pacts and vision will be in vain.

At UN General Assembly special session on disarmament, New York, June/Newsweek, 6-28:23.

Anthony C. Beilenson
United States Representative, D–California

1

If the U.S. continues to shun strategic-arms negotiations and builds up our nuclear forces, as the [Reagan] Administration proposes, we are committing ourselves to 10 or 15 years of an unnecessary, dangerous, highly inflationary nuclear arms race in which the Soviets will keep pace with us, and we will be no more secure at the end of it than we are now. The Reagan Administration's alarming outcries about U.S. vulnerability, its constant denigrations of our defense capabilities and exaggerations of Soviet power do not reflect the over-all military balance which exists and are probably harming our security.

Before Los Angeles World Affairs Council, February/Los Angeles Times, 2-18:(IX)5.

Joseph R. Biden, Jr.
United States Senator, D–Delaware

2

[On the U.S.-Soviet arms race]: The Soviet Union has to assume the worst, since in fact we were the only nation to ever drop a nuclear weapon; since in fact *we* have been the only ones who ever demonstrated the willingness to do that. I believe we never will, but it is prudent for them to plan [for it] . . . With the MX missile, and with the D5 [Trident submarine missile], we will be in a position, if we were to choose, which we are not going to choose, to inflict serious damage, overwhelming damage upon the Soviet Union if we struck first—a first-strike capability that far exceeds what the Soviets' first-strike capability is now. Everything that I have been told leads to that conclusion. If that is true, I do not know how we can reach an arms-control agreement with

the Soviet Union if neither of those items are negotiable.

At Senate Foreign Relations Committee hearing, Washington, December/ The Washington Post, 12-27:(A)1.

Leonid I. Brezhnev
President of the Soviet Union; General Secretary, Soviet Communist Party

3

[The Soviet Union] is ready to reach agreement not only on the complete termination of all nuclear weapons tests, but also on ending their further production and on the reduction and subsequent complete elimination of their stockpiles . . . The Soviet Union is ready for this at any moment, but the American side is incessantly postponing the dialogue on this problem, which worries the whole of mankind. [We are] ready to examine without prejudice all the proposals of the other side on disarmament. I can assure you that we study carefully the positions and proposals of the other side and never reject them out of hand.

Feb. 24/The Christian Science Monitor, 2-25:2.

David Brunell
Head of anti-nuclear-arms campaign, Union of Concerned Scientists

4

To many of us, the arms race between the U.S. and Russia is like two kids standing up to their knees in a room full of gasoline. One has 10 matches, the other eight. Neither kid says he will feel safe unless he has more matches; yet each has many more than he needs to blow up the place. That's why people don't feel more secure with more missiles.

U.S. News & World Report, 3-22:26.

Zbigniew Brzezinski
Professor of government, Columbia University; Former Assistant to the President of the United States (Jimmy Carter) for National Security Affairs

5

From everything that I know—and in recent years I came to know almost all that could be known—I conclude that the true and accurate state of the military relationship [between the U.S. and the Soviet Union] is that of strategically ambiguous equivalence. [That is,] the

(ZBIGNIEW BRZEZINSKI)

U.S. is clearly ahead of the Soviet Union in some key systems, and the Soviet Union is clearly ahead in others. It all adds up to the simple proposition that neither side can be very certain about the consequences of a military engagement, and even less so about the consequences of quick pre-emption.

Helsinki, Finland, Oct. 6/The Washington Post, 10-6:(A)18.

George Bush
Vice President of the United States

1

... we must seek [military] parity with the Soviets, so that any negotiated [arms] freeze will not result in a U.S. or Western European disadvantage. Some argue that any increase of U.S. nuclear weapons or delivery systems will only motivate the Soviets to produce more and more of their own weapons and delivery systems. I don't accept that. Recent history proves the opposite. In the late 1960s and early 1970s, the Soviets flatly rejected any attempts to limit the development of antiballistic-missile systems. Only after [U.S.] President Nixon won Congressional approval of a U.S. ABM system did the Soviets see the merit of an ABM treaty.

At Annual Public Radio Conference, Washington, April 21/The New York Times, 4-26:12.

2

This President [Reagan] really wants a reduction in arms. Most people don't know that. Because you've got that freeze thing out there. And people out there say,"If you really want an absolute reduction in arms, you go for the freeze." And those of us who aren't for the freeze are automatically categorized as not for a reduction in arms. It's an argument I take great offense with, incidentally. I find it intellectually offensive to suggest that, given the history of the ABM treaty and everything else. So there is this whole kind of feeling out there. And those of us who know the President's position so well probably haven't been as articulate as we might have been in trying to make people understand that this President is absolutely convinced that we must achieve a reduction, a real demon-strable, visible, verifiable reduction in nuclear weapons.

Interview, Washington, December/San Francisco Examiner & Chronicle, 12-26:(B)11.

Jimmy Carter
Former President of the United States

3

[President Reagan] has over-supplied the military with funding for the kinds.of weapons they have been requesting for 15 or 20 years and other Presidents have refused. Not only is it unnecessary, it is an improper allocation of priorities. The B-1 bomber is a waste of money. The dense-pack MX missile system seems ridiculous to me. I am concerned too that the [nuclear] non-proliferation effort has fairly well been abandoned.

Interview, Plains, Ga./Time, 10-11:63.

John T. Chain, Jr.
Lieutenant General, and Deputy Chief of Staff for Plans and Operations, United States Air Force

4

[On quality vs. quantity in arms procurement]: The Soviets are producing, plus or minus, 1,300 fighters a year. Next year we have in our budget 180 fighters [for the Air Force]. If we get into real numbers of what I need to go get the Soviets, it is a lot more. [But] it doesn't do, just because the Soviets have 100 airplanes, for me to build 100 inferior airplanes. I can't just fix the quantity problem without matching it with quality. If I have a choice between the two; I have got to err on the side of quality—but not take it to extremes.

Interview/The New York Times, 10-24:(1)18.

Nikolai Chervov
Chief, Department of the General Staff, Armed Forces of the Soviet Union

5

In the U.S.A., they probably entertain illusions that they are invulnerable, separated [from the U.S.S.R.] by two oceans. At present, however, distances must be evaluated differently; differently in the sense that, by moving a threat closer to others [such as updating the nuclear arsenals of Western Europe], the U.S.A. is in the same manner bringing it closer to itself.

(NIKOLAI·CHERVOV)

This important thesis follows from a law-governed pattern. Each side must measure the security of the other side by the yardstick it applies to its own security. This is an objective reality. This can be brushed aside, but it cannot be changed.

Soviet television broadcast, March 27/
San Francisco Examiner & Chronicle, 3-28:(A)2.

Norman Cousins
Adjunct professor of psychiatry and behavioral sciences, University of California, Los Angeles; Former editor, "Saturday Review"

1

We live with the illusion of protection. We throw vast billions at a concept called national defense and think all we have to do is spend more money than the Russians. Security is measured quantitatively. But we will not protect the American people just with nuclear exchange. What we will be doing is saying to the Russians, "We can kill many more of you than you can kill of us." We're relying on a psychological ploy to try to persuade them not to do something . . . The fact of the matter is this has reduced the efficacy of the threats. We're not influenced by the Soviet threat— quite to the contrary, we've just become more belligerent. The same is true of the other side.

Interview/Los Angeles Herald Examiner, 6-5:(A)2.

Alan Cranston
United States Senator, D–California

2

[A nuclear-weapons freeze and reduction] will have to come by an act of leadership from both the U.S. and U.S.S.R., a willingness to engage in negotiations like there have never been before. We have to cut out the diplomatic dance. This madness can only be broken by leaders of the U.S. and U.S.S.R. sitting down and agreeing that this must stop. We cannot let infinite detail get in the way, as in other arms talks. There should be no agenda worked out by staff in advance. We should just sit down and talk about it. The Soviets don't want to be blown up in a nuclear war; they know the danger.

Interview/Time, 3-29:16.

William J. Crowe, Jr.
Admiral, United States Navy; Commander, NATO forces in Mediterranean and southern Europe

3

The whole picture has changed in the last 25 years as the Soviet Union has transformed its Navy into what we call a blue-water fleet. At the time all of this has been happening, there has been a steady drawdown in the NATO navies and, of course, in the U.S. Navy. The balance is less now than it has been since World War II. [In the 1950s and '60s,] we were the only power here.

Interview, Naples, Italy/
Los Angeles Times, 4-29:(I-B)3.

B. L. Davis
General, United States Air Force; Commander, Strategic Air Command

4

[Saying the Soviets will use space for military purposes]: The Soviets will eventually be able to deny us use of space as a support medium and use it as a high ground to launch attacks on U.S. targets. If they should achieve superiority in space, they could well attain a decisive war-winning edge.

Before House Armed Services Committee,
Washington/The Washington Post, 3-3:(A)6.

Richard Delauer
Under Secretary for Research and Engineering, Department of Defense of the United States

5

Based on the evidence available to us, it is clear that the Soviets have a massive military space program . . . The use of space by the [U.S.] Department of Defense should not be interpreted to mean that the U.S. is "militarizing" space, as some claim. Yet . . . given the alarming rate of Soviet spending for space activities, it would be imprudent for us not to be prepared to defend our interests there, as anywhere else.

The Christian Science Monitor, 9-27:1,8.

Richard Falk
*Professor of international law,
Princeton University; Former
associate editor, "Foreign
Affairs" magazine*   1

Even if the Soviets have more throw-weight [total missile payload] than we, that doesn't go to the deeper question: What is a *sufficient* force to discourage them from using nuclear weapons in pursuit of their political goals? People today—even our leaders—haven't really absorbed fully the changed nature of warfare. The whole logic of warfare in the nuclear age means that even if you are not exactly equal, that is irrelevant once each side reaches a certain level of strength. What is needed is a level of *sufficiency*—a position taken by many prior U.S. defense officials. Even if you grant the worst possible case of the Soviets making a devastating first strike and knocking out the majority—even 90 per cent—of our land-based missiles, it still leaves them exposed to unbelievable retaliation. One American nuclear submarine alone can knock out 160 major cities. One sub can produce more damage than all the damage done in all the wars in human history. And even if we had three times as many warheads as we now have, we couldn't do more damage than we can already do, for there is a limit to how much you can destroy.

*Interview, Princeton University/
The Christian Science Monitor, 2-4:(B)19.*

Martin Feldstein
*Chairman, Council of Economic
Advisers to the President
of the United States*   2

In 1960, long before the Vietnam war, the United States was spending 9.1 per cent of GNP on defense, nearly 50 per cent higher than the 6.2 per cent share of GNP spent on defense in 1982. If defense spending today accounted for as large a share of GNP as it did in 1960 or even 1970, the deficit would be significantly larger than it is today . . . I do not want to minimize the share of defense in the national budget nor to imply that defense spending does not require careful scrutiny to find ways in which existing costs can be reduced. But I do want to emphasize that, viewed in the perspective of the past two decades, the current and projected levels of defense outlays are not responsible for our budget deficits. The real reason for large and persistent budget deficits has been the rapid growth of non-defense spending.

The Washington Post, 11-29:(A)8.

Milton Friedman
*Economist; Senior fellow,
Hoover Institution,
Stanford University*   3

I'm not opposed to the reduction of growth in military spending on strictly military grounds. I am opposed to the reduction of growth in military spending on budgetary grounds. This nation can afford to have a strong defense. Military spending is scheduled to be something like 5 or 6 per cent of our GNP. Fifteen years ago it was 8 or 9 per cent. We can afford that. On the other hand, I have no doubt that there is waste in the military area. I have no doubt that we ought to be able to get the same amount of strength for less. So if you can find ways in which we can achieve the same military defense for less money, of course we ought to do that.

*Broadcast interview/
"Meet the Press," NBC-TV, 3-21.*

Robert Fuller
*Former president,
Oberlin College;
Former professor of physics,
Columbia University*   4

The other day I was running around the track and realized no matter how fast I ran, my shadow kept up with me. That's the arms race, a race with one's own shadow. No matter how fast you go, the other guy's going to keep up with you and stay connected to you. In fact, he *is* you, the shadow side of yourself you don't like. The Russians are our shadow. We project on them all the stuff we fear in ourselves, and vice versa.

*Interview, Paris/The Christian
Science Monitor, 12-16:(B)10.*

Noel A. M. Gayler
Admiral, United States Navy (Ret.);
Former Commander,
U.S. forces in the Pacific

1

[Proposing that the U.S. and Soviet Union each turn in their nuclear weapons as a means of arms reduction]: Let each country turn in an equal, very large number of explosive nuclear-fission devices to a single conversion site offshore. Under supervision, convert the devices to power-plant fuel for generation of electricity. Let each side choose the devices it turns in. Each device counts as one. That's fair, because each [country] makes its own choice, and that clears up any argument about classification. A device is a device. Let Soviet and American teams, and perhaps a third party as referee, identify and count each device. They are uniquely identifiable by scientific means. That's verification, without intrusive inspection in either country.

News conference, Washington, April 29/
Los Angeles Times, 4-30:(I)11.

Louis O. Giuffrida
Director, Federal Emergency
Management Agency

2

[On his agency's planning a civil-defense program in the event of nuclear war and on his critics who say such planning would be ineffective and would encourage such a war by making it seem survivable]: You think I would participate in something that was a hoax? I resent that. You think we want nuclear war? My God! . . . Sure, it'll be a hell of a mess. You'll use anything at your disposal [to evacuate cities]—trains, planes, cars, shoes. It'll be terrible. It boggles the mind. But do we just throw up our hands and say, "Forget it, the job's too big"? Do we give up?

Interview, Washington/The New York Times, 4-8:15.

John Glenn
United States Senator, D—Ohio

3

[Supporting the building of large aircraft carriers]: The Nimitz carriers can stand up to far more punishment than can smaller ships. The size of the Nimitz carrier and the extra power provided by its nuclear plant have enabled designers to better protect the sensitive heart of any warship, the ammunition magazines and flammable fuel storage cells. The large carriers are also equipped with massive armor plating, extensive firefighting facilities, and more than 2,000 watertight compartments, making them far less vulnerable to conventional torpedo or missile attacks. Over its long service life, the larger carrier also will be less expensive to maintain and operate.

Senate debate, Washington/
The New York Times, 7-7:11.

Andrei A. Gromyko
Foreign Minister of the Soviet Union

4

Each day brings new evidence that U.S. foreign policy is becoming pervaded more and more with a spirit of militarism. A first nuclear strike is being talked about as if it were something casual or routine . . . The idea is being impressed on peoples' minds: If you want peace, go all out in preparing for war. Dig in, hide yourselves wherever you can, but prepare.

At United Nations disarmament
conference, New York, June 15/
Los Angeles Times, 6-16:(I)22.

Alexander M. Haig, Jr.
Secretary of State of the United States

5

Much of the argumentation for nuclear [weapons] freeze revolves around the question of how much is enough. Each side [the U.S. and Soviet Union] possesses thousands of deliverable nuclear weapons. Does it then really make any difference who is ahead? The question itself is misleading, as it assumes that deterrence is simply a matter of numbers of weapons or numbers of casualties which could be inflicted. It is not. Let us remember, first and foremost, that we are trying to deter the Soviet Union, not ourselves. The dynamic nature of the Soviet nuclear buildup demonstrates that the Soviet leaders do not believe in the concept of "sufficiency." They are not likely to be deterred by a force based upon it . . . Deterrence thus does not rest on a static comparison of the number or size of nuclear weapons. Rather, deterrence depends upon our capability, even after suffering a massive nuclear blow, to prevent an aggressor from

(ALEXANDER M. HAIG, JR.)

securing a military advantage and prevailing in a conflict. Only if we can maintain such a capability can we deter such a blow. Deterrence, in consequence, rests upon a military balance measured not in warhead numbers but in a complex interaction of capabilities and vulnerabilities.

Before Georgetown University Center for
Strategic and International Studies,
April 6/The New York Times, 4-7:6.

1

More than any other single defense or political initiative, the President's [Reagan] strategic modernization program and the Congress' support for the modernization program will make or break our attempt to negotiate a reasonable arms-control agreement [with the Soviets] ... We consider SALT II to be dead. We have so informed the Soviet Union, and they ... understand it, even if they may not like it. The worst thing we could do now would be to attempt to resurrect an agreement that could only generate massive controversy, confuse our allies, confuse the Soviets and confuse public opinion.

Before Senate Foreign Relations Committee,
Washington, May 11/Los Angeles Times, 5-12:(I)5.

2

[Arguing against a U.S.-Soviet freeze of nuclear weapons] ... merely to freeze at existing levels of forces would codify existing Soviet advantages, especially in the nuclear threat facing our allies here in Western Europe, but also among certain elements of the strategic equation. Secondly, were we to accept this approach to agree to a freeze, it is clear that the Soviet Union would then be relieved of any incentive to make rapid progress for substantive reductions. And it is reductions that constitute the main objective of President Reagan's arms-control policy.

News conference, Luxembourg, May 18/
Chicago Tribune, 5-19:(1)5.

Gary W. Hart
United States Senator, D–Colorado

3

[On the current nuclear-weapons-freeze movement in the U.S.] : It's been there all the time ... What brought it to the surface, obviously, were the policies of this [Reagan] Administration, of not going forward with [arms-control] negotiations [with the Soviets] in a meaningful way, of building up the nuclear arsenal on an almost mindless basis across the board, of believing that there was such a thing as nuclear superiority, of having policies of limited nuclear war or at least discussing those [policies] .

Interview/Newsweek, 4-26:29.

4

The Democratic [Party] vision must include a national defense that meets the demands of the 1980s–a defense that is the most effective and not merely the most expensive. If the President [Reagan] believes money alone will not solve social problems, then surely money alone will not solve military problems. Democrats know that the real choice is neither how much we spend or how little we spend, but how wisely we spend. And we know that more spending on a military that doesn't work just buys a bigger military that doesn't work.

At Democratic Party conference, Philadelphia,
June 25/The New York Times, 6-26:11.

5

[Arguing against the building of large aircraft carriers] : You do not have to sink an aircraft carrier to defeat it. All you have to do is to disable it ... A nuclear aircraft carrier, or any aircraft carrier for that matter, is a floating gasoline station. All you have to do is start a fire on board and that carrier is out of commission. That is what one missile or one torpedo will do.

Senate debate, Washington/
The New York Times, 7-7:11.

Mark O. Hatfield
United States Senator, R–Oregon

6

... the U.S. has had superiority in nuclear weapons ever since World War II, when the

(MARK O. HATFIELD)

Soviets didn't even have the bomb, and yet it is evident that the more nuclear weapons we build, the more they will build. And the result is less security in the world. Nuclear superiority is not only a meaningless term in the age of multiple overkill, it is a hindrance at the bargaining table. Now not only do the Soviets have the bomb, but by the end of this century an estimated 60 nations will be capable of building nuclear weapons. We must halt this kind of madness.

Interview/U.S. News & World Report, 4-5:55.

1

There is to me a direct ratio between the increase of our arsenals and the diminishing sense of national security. In my opinion, the only President in modern history who had any comprehension of national security was Dwight David Eisenhower, who happened to be a five-star general . . . He said that there comes a time in a nation's life when additional money spent for rockets and bombs, far from strengthening national security, will actually weaken national security—when there are people who are hungry and not fed, people who are cold and not clothed. For in the ultimate sense, that expenditure becomes a theft from those people, from those needs of those people.

Interview, Washington/The Christian Science Monitor, 6-17:(B)3.

Thomas B. Hayward
Admiral and Chief of Operations,
United States Navy

2

We are a Navy stretched thin around the globe. We are a one-and-a-half ocean Navy with a three-ocean commitment.

Congressional testimony/
The New York Times, 4-11:(1)4.

Charles Hernu
Minister of Defense of France

3

[On his country's plans to strengthen its nuclear capability rather than build up its conventional forces]: Anyone who tells me he prefers one more division of soldiers to a missile-launching submarine is living in the wrong age.

The Christian Science Monitor, 11-17:11.

Lord Hill-Norton
Retired Admiral of the British Fleet   4

[On the destruction of the British destroyer *Sheffield* by an Argentine missile in the war over the Falkland Islands]: What the *Sheffield* disaster proved is that modern weapons do what most of us have said all along they would do: They hit instead of missing. Gone are the days when you could hang about waiting to see what the other fellow was doing. If you do that, you'll get hit.

May/Newsweek, 5-17:32.

Ernest F. Hollings
United States Senator,
D–South Carolina   5

We need the draft in order to field a credible fighting force, and we need it in order to remain true to the ideals which built this country. Early in the 1970s, with America's morale sapped by our involvement in Vietnam, we bought the idea there was an easy way for the U.S. to defend itself without personal sacrifice. The disproportionate numbers of minorities in the services, and their over-representation in infantry and other combat outfits, raise the specter of death by income and social class.

San Francisco Examiner & Chronicle, 1-3:(A)8.

6

[Addressing President Reagan]: You may prefer to buy MX missiles with red ink rather than school lunches with red ink, but the ink is just as red. I know you didn't set out to become the biggest spender of all time, Mr. President. But your blind stubbornness—trying to have it all at once—has brought you there . . . While ripping [social] programs, you have launched a totally undisciplined program of weapons purchases that is busting the budget and breaking the economy upon which national security depends.

Broadcast address to the nation,
Washington, Dec. 11/San Francisco
Examiner & Chronicle, 12-12:(A)3.

Fred C. Ikle
*Under Secretary for Policy, Department
of Defense of the United States*

1

First and foremost, we want to strengthen nuclear deterrence by having forces the aggressor knows are guaranteed to survive his attack. This may mean investments in things such as command, control and communications, which aren't all that visible and glamorous for statistical tables of red and blue comparisons. But this does not mean, contrary to what has been said, an increase in the emphasis on nuclear war, and particularly not limited nuclear war. There is increasing emphasis on being prepared for a multiplicity of different types of possible conflicts involving conventional forces—not only on increased sustainability, but on our ability to have an industrial mobilization. We are presently not prepared for that sufficiently.

Panel discussion/The New York Times, 3-14:(4)3.

Bobby R. Inman
*Former Deputy Director of Central
Intelligence of the United States*

2

We have tried over the last decade to improve the nation's ability to verify arms-control treaties. There was valid criticism in Congress that the resulting capability was thin. The requirements for verification with regard to the SALT I and SALT II treaties were substantial but not overwhelming. A more complex treaty will place substantial additional burdens on verification. There are several ways to deal with that. There are, for instance, forms of on-site inspection that would increase verification capabilities. But if you insist on absolute certainty, if you insist on the capacity to detect every violation, you'll never have an arms-control process. You have to take some risks. The key is being confident that you will detect any serious cheating.

Interview, Washington/The New York Times, 7-5:8.

Henry M. Jackson
*United States Senator,
D—Washington*

3

[On public protests over nuclear weapons]: We are hearing from Main Street now. People

there are far more sophisticated than many of us think. They can understand an issue like nuclear weapons. They do not want us to follow a rigid policy. They are saying that at some point before we blow ourselves up, we are going to have to get rid of these nuclear devices. They are not crazies, and we need to listen to them.

Interview, Washington, April/Time, 4-12:19.

William J. Janklow
Governor of South Dakota (R)

4

I'm not excited about the thought of a nuclear holocaust. I'm absolutely not. But I can tell you this: I think maybe it's because there are people in America, like South Dakotans, who have been willing to live with Minuteman missile silos, who've been willing to do our fair share in national defense—just maybe that's one of the reasons we continue to live in freedom today.

The New York Times, 10-22:12.

David C. Jones
*General, United States Air Force;
Chairman, Joint Chiefs of Staff*

5

The more we talk about refusing to use nuclear weapons, the greater the danger that we may create incentives for conventional aggression and even pre-emptive nuclear attack ... Our goal is security—the avoidance of war, immunity from intimidation through the threat of force, and the strength necessary to defend ourselves and our allies should deterrence fail.

*Before American Newspaper Publishers
Association, San Francisco, April 28/
The Washington Post, 4-29:(A)2.*

6

The Joint Chiefs have been supporters of arms control. I wouldn't want to have arms control for arms-control sake, where Washington strives to achieve some treaty regardless of its merits. But truly equitable and verifiable arms-control measures can add to our security. The best way to achieve these agreements is to convince the Soviets that a continued arms buildup is not in their best interest—that they won't obtain an advantage and that it will be a

(DAVID C. JONES)

terrible strain on their economy. We're more likely to have a successful arms-control negotiation if they see we are prepared to match their efforts rather than if we exercise unilateral restraints with or without arms-control. The latter, unfortunately, has been our tendency for the last 20 years.

Interview/U.S. News & World Report, 5-24:30.

1

We've been comfortable through the years by sort of being [militarily] unprepared, always kind of expecting things to work out. We had a great industrial base, we had allies to save us time, the advantage of geography protecting us, and therefore we could be the Minutemen who don't have much capability. But we could always get organized. We had time to do something. Well, [in today's nuclear age, and with Soviet military expansion,] that's no longer true.

Interview, Washington, June 14/
Los Angeles·Times, 6-16:(I)19.

David C. Jones
General, United States Air
Force (Ret.); Former Chairman,
Joint Chiefs of Staff

2

Admiral Gorshkov, the head of the Soviet Navy, once said that the job of senior people in defense is to try to make the total capability greater than the sum of individual parts. The way we have developed over many years, in the Pentagon and in Congress, we have just the opposite. Our total capability is less than the sum of the individual parts . . . I have never used the word inferiority. That is too absolute in the implication that some Soviet advantages can be meaningful. They can be meaningful only if we allow them to be so . . . I have no doubt that we can deter the Soviets. You can hold all kinds of war games that show some difference in outcome, but in any calculation [there is] unprecedented devastation on both sides. Certainly we need to do some modernization of our strategic forces, but I'm not one to believe we've got a lot of catching up to do.

Interview/The Washington Post, 11-30:(A)18.

58

Thomas K. Jones
Deputy Under Secretary of Defense
of the United States for Strategic
Theatre Nuclear Forces

3

[Supporting civil defense against a nuclear attack]: Dig a hole, cover it with a couple of doors, and then throw three feet of dirt on top. Everyone's going to make it if there are enough shovels to go around.

Interview/Time, 3-29:24.

Al Keller, Jr.
National commander, American Legion

4

[On the memorial in Washington honoring those Americans who died in the Vietnam war]: There are those who say the war in Vietnam brought shame on America. There are those who say this memorial would bring shame on those who fought the war. But there is no shame in answering the nation's call. There is no shame in serving with honor and courage in difficult times. And there is no shame in enshrining the names of fallen comrades in immutable stone for generations to recall.

Washington, Nov. 13/
The New York Times, 11-14:(1)17.

George F. Kennan
Former United States Ambassador
to the Soviet Union

5

In the early 1970s, we put multiple warheads on our missiles in hopes of winning nuclear superiority that would force Russia to negotiate [arms control] on our terms. But the Soviets simply built up their own weaponry. The result is we're worse off today for our efforts. Besides, who is refusing to negotiate— the Soviet Union or us? We've delayed for over a year, saying that we are still studying the [arms-control] issue. We could sit down with them today, and they would not be all that unreasonable. They recognize as clearly as we do that the arms race is nearing the edge of absurdity.

Interview/U.S. News & World Report, 4-26:17.

Edward M. Kennedy
United States Senator,
D—Massachusetts

1

... the United States, having 9,000 nuclear warheads, the Soviet Union 7,000, that [means] each of us has the capability to destroy each other. Effectively, what we have is substantial equivalency. And since we have substantial equivalency with the Soviet Union, we should put in place now a freeze that would be negotiated, that would be verifiable by the United States as well as the Soviet Union, and then move toward the longer kind of negotiation, toward serious reductions in the nuclear-arms stockpile of both nations. The [U.S. Reagan] Administration believes that we have to build more now, so that we can reduce later. That doesn't make any common sense, and it is what I have stated to be basically voodoo arms control.

Broadcast interview/"Meet the Press," NBC-TV, 4-18.

Lane Kirkland
President, American Federation
of Labor-Congress of
Industrial Organizations

2

[In the past,] our working assumption has been that it is safer to err on the side of adequacy in a defense budget, so we have always tended to approach these issues with the view that unless there are overriding arguments or proofs to show these defense expenditures are imprudent, they ought to be supported. If we guessed wrong in terms of higher outlays, all we did was waste money. But if we guessed wrong in the other direction, we might lose everything ... [But now, the Reagan] Administration is taking it [defense costs] out of the hide of the poor and exempting the rich ... [Because of the] intolerable trade-off [in defense and social spending, the Administration is creating a] new, anti-defense constituency among working Americans and those who look to the government to promote the general welfare; and nothing could be more threatening to our national security.

Bal Harbour, Fla., Feb. 15/
Los Angeles Times, 2-16:(IV)1.

Frederick J. Kroesen
General, and Commander-in-Chief/
Europe, United States Army

3

[On the all-volunteer Army]: It's the highest-quality peacetime force we've put into the field in my memory. We've recruited it well, and we've trained it well. Eighty-three per cent of the soldiers in the American Army over here have high-school diplomas of some kind. We have smart people—that's a fact—and we keep only those who truly want to be United States Army soldiers. The Army's been criticized for enlisting poor-quality people. It's pointed out that roughly one third can't make it through a three-year enlistment. That's because we have high standards. We're pretty demanding. We discharge one third because they can't meet those standards, then make our Army out of the two thirds who can.

Interview/U.S. News & World Report, 8-9:24.

Gene R. LaRocque
Rear Admiral, United States
Navy (Ret.); Director, Center
for Defense Information

4

[On the controversy over the deployment of the MX missile system]: We can't find the answer because there isn't one ... There's no way you can hide a missile this big. But it's a bit like the Navy moving from the age of sail to steam; that took 40 years. You're fighting now against the old Air Force generals and the defense industry which has a vested interest in land-based missiles.

Los Angeles Times, 9-23:(I)15.

John F. Lehman, Jr.
Secretary of the Navy
of the United States

5

Clear maritime superiority must be reacquired [by the U.S.]. This is not a debatable strategy. It is a national objective, a security imperative. It must then be clearly recognized that withdrawal is the only alternative to a major naval force expansion.

Congressional testimony/
The New York Times, 4-11:(I)14.

59

(JOHN F. LEHMAN, JR.)

1

[On critics of high military spending]: There's nothing more expensive than an outbreak of war; and the perception of weakness, as we've seen in the Falkland Islands [conflict between Argentina and Britain], brings on war ... If the taxpayers are going to be so shortsighted—and their representatives—to mortgage the future and destroy the investment in reestablishing a common-sense ability to defend ourselves, then they're inviting war. It's as simple as that.

Interview, Washington/The Christian
Science Monitor, 4-12:13.

2

I believe that Allied navies have given insufficient attention to the fact that 75 per cent of the anti-ship cruise missiles in the world are not in Warsaw Pact navies; they're in free-world navies. We face a very difficult task in countering our own free-world missiles in the hands of navies that may become unfriendly. That was demonstrated when Argentina sank the British destroyer *Sheffield* with the French-made Exocet missile. I think that we have a good handle on the Soviet cruise-missile threat. We do not have as good a handle on free-world missiles. With the proliferation of foreign military sales, we have to concentrate on defeating our own weapons—the Exocet coming at the *Sheffield,* or perhaps sometime in the future the American-made Harpoon coming at the [U.S.] *Nimitz* [aircraft carrier].

Interview/U.S. News & World Report, 8-2:24.

Carl Levin
United States Senator, D–Michigan

3

It's a lot safer to vote against an MX [missile] now than it was when sentiment was running the other way. The polls are saying that we won't be called anti-defense if we vote for a spending cut or against an MX, a B-1 bomber or a nuclear carrier. It's a little easier because the public doesn't connect military spending with strength—it connects it with waste. After the Falkland Islands war, people have to wonder why we want to build a multi-billion-dollar

[aircraft] carrier that can be knocked out by a $50,000 missile. They are questioning the waste in the Pentagon and they wonder why our allies are not doing their fair share.

The Washington Post, 12-2:(A)16.

John L. Loeb, Jr.
United States Ambassador to Denmark

4

It is an illusion to think that any of us, on a national basis, can avoid the risks of this dangerous world. Nuclear weapons will not go away simply because we are horrified to deal with them ... The question of nuclear weapons is an issue which torments us all. It is a topic of public controversy in all our countries, and the Soviet Union shamelessly attempts to exploit it. The so-called peace marchers are in fact endangering the peace when they call for unilaterally dismantling the strategy of deterrence which has made it possible for their generation to grow up in conditions of peace and security.

Before Danish-American Chamber of
Commerce, New York, March 26/
The New York Times, 3-27:12.

Edward N. Luttwak
United States Defense
Department consultant

5

Roughly 10 years ago ... we were ahead [of the Soviet Union] in every single index [of nuclear weaponry] except one—gross megatonnage. Today ... we are only ahead in one—number of warheads. How important that difference is depends on whether you believe in limited nuclear war or not. If you think everybody is going to throw everything at each other, including the kitchen sink, then the difference in the over-all total hardly counts. However, if nuclear weapons are going to be used ... in controlled doses, it makes a very big difference.

Interview/Newsweek, 4-26:26.

6

[On the current nuclear-weapons-freeze movement in the U.S.]: Until the military buildup began with the Reagan Administration, we were like a patient very comfortably drifting into a coma. If we had continued with the

(EDWARD N. LUTTWAK)

pre-Reagan defense strength, we would not have woken up ... But with the Reagan defense program, the patient ... is asked to get out and to recover. And now, all the wounds hurt.

Interview/Newsweek, 4-26:29.

1

We [the U.S.] have forced our military into an obsessive concern with management of resources and with proceduralizing tactics and with environmental impacts. We don't tolerate eccentrics in our military. We demand that our military be safe. The British and Israelis train realistically and sometimes accidentally kill people in training. When we have accidents like that, there is tremendous pressure to play it safe. As a result, we have a safe military, one which doesn't take risks.

Los Angeles Times, 8-4:(I)8.

Edward J. Markey
United States Representative,
D–Massachusetts

2

[Arguing against plans for civil defense to protect the population during a nuclear war]: You cannot run from nuclear war. There is no escape for either side. We're talking about public pacification, surviving the unsurvivable, winning the unwinnable war.

Los Angeles Times, 7-30:(I)17.

Robert S. McNamara
Former Secretary of Defense
of the United States

3

There's a real question in my mind as to whether the all-volunteer [armed] force will provide sufficient manpower in conditions other than the high unemployment of today. When 47 per cent of black teen-agers are unemployed, you have what we have today, a substantial number of black teen-agers entering the military forces. Hopefully, that will be cut in half, at least, within the next three or four years. Hopefully, the 9 per cent unemployment will go down to 6 per cent or 5 per cent. When it does, I believe we'll have difficulty in filling

the manpower requirements. We are having it today. The reserve forces today, which are absolutely essential to the use of our entire forces, are short well over 100,000 personnel, and this is a very serious deficiency.

Broadcast interview/"Meet the Press," NBC-TV, 4-11.

4

Soviet conventional strength is not as great as many state it to be, and the NATO conventional weakness is not as great as it is frequently said to be. Therefore, the conventional balance is not as favorable to the Soviets as it is often assumed ... In this country [the U.S.], we commonly exaggerate the imbalance of Warsaw Pact and NATO conventional forces. In my opinion, NATO conventional forces are very strong indeed. They are not as strong as I would like to see them, not as strong as they ought to be, not as strong as they can be by applying modern technology within realistic budget constraints. But still, they are a much greater deterrent to Soviet aggression than we commonly recognize ... We overstate the Soviets' force and we understate ours, and we therefore greatly overstate the imbalance. This is not something that is new; it has been going on for years.

Interview/The Washington Post, 8-1:(B)3.

Robert H. Michel
United States Representative, R–Illinois

5

The major issue confronting the world today is not the possession of nuclear arms by the U.S., but the defense and preservation of freedom. If freedom cannot be defended through any other means but the possession of a nuclear deterrent by the U.S., the possession of such a deterrent is a political and moral imperative.

Before the House, Washington,
April/Time, 4-12:13.

Jacques Mitterrand
President, Aerospatiale (France)

6

[On the destruction of the British destroyer *Sheffield* by an Argentine Exocet missile made by his firm in the current war over the Falkland Islands]: The significance of the *HMS Sheffield*

WHAT THEY SAID IN 1982

(JACQUES MITTERRAND)

attack is that it will make these navies realize once more the importance of smaller vessels. The traditional thinking has been: the bigger the boats, the happier the Admirals. But small boats, and even helicopters, fitted with this type of missile, can have the same overwhelming punch of the battleships of 1919, or the carriers of 1943.

Newsweek, 5-17:39.

Toby Moffett
*United States Representative,
D–Connecticut*

1

[Disagreeing with President Reagan's assessment of Soviet military strength compared with that of the U.S.]: We Democrats ... don't agree that the Soviet Union is 10 feet tall. We don't believe they are stronger than America, and it serves no useful purpose for a President to keep suggesting that they are.

*Broadcast rebuttal to President's
radio address, April 17/San Francisco
Examiner & Chronicle, 4-18:(A)12.*

Roger C. Molander
*Executive director, Ground Zero
(anti-nuclear war organization);
Former nuclear strategist,
National Security Council
of the United States*

2

[On a nuclear war civil-defense program]: U.S. civil-defense programs which plan for crisis evacuation of cities could, if successful, save American lives in the short run—if one had the five to seven days of warning that would be necessary to implement such a plan and if people went where they were told to go. It's quite clear that many of [those] people ... would [eventually] suffer and die in that struggle for food, shelter and medical services—even uncontaminated water ... It comes down to ... whether saving some lives in the short run is worth $4.8-billion.

Interview/Newsweek, 4-26:29.

62

Walter F. Mondale
*Former Vice President
of the United States*

3

[Criticizing those who propose a U.S. statement that it will not be first to use nuclear weapons]: They do not answer what they would do until that day when conventional deterrence is strong enough, and I think that is very important. The reality is that if war breaks out between the United States and the Soviet Union ... the likelihood of the use of nuclear weapons is very great ... What I'm worried about now is that if we drop the so-called flexible-response doctrine, while it's generally believed our conventional deterrent is in doubt, then it might encourage the Soviet Union to believe they could be successful in a conventional attack ... And thus, the one thing that will most likely cause the use of nuclear weapons—namely, a U.S.-Soviet war—could occur.

*Interview, Washington, April 9/
The Washington Post, 4-10:(A)4.*

4

[On President Reagan's strategic-arms reduction plan]: [The proposal] must be measured by the standard that it enhances the national security of both sides. If our proposal concentrates on reducing the things the Soviets have that worry us—and not the things we have that worry them—the proposal is unrealistic.

May 10/Los Angeles Times, 5-11:(I)11.

5

This [Reagan] Administration says it is for arms control, and I'd like to believe them. But I am not persuaded. When President Kennedy proposed the test-ban treaty, Ronald Reagan opposed it. When Lyndon Johnson pushed for non-proliferation, when Nixon began SALT I, when Ford restricted weapons-grade material, when Carter negotiated SALT II—for 20 years Reagan has opposed every step toward arms control by every President of both political parties.

*At Democratic Party conference,
Philadelphia,
June 25/The New York Times, 6-26:11.*

Thomas H. Moorer
Admiral (Ret.) and former Chief of
Operations, United States Navy;
Former Chairman, Joint Chiefs of Staff   *1*

[Arguing against the theory of using many smaller ships instead of fewer but larger vessels]: That's like telling [Chicago] Mayor [Jane] Byrne to sell all her fire engines and use that money to buy Volkswagens and paint them all red and have more fire engines than anyone in the world. She would have only one problem: They couldn't fight fires.

Chicago Tribune, 7-24:(1)11.

Jan Mortenson
Assistant Secretary General of the
United Nations for Disarmament   *2*

We have to be realistic. We cannot get disarmament overnight. We cannot, through a disarmament session at the UN, arrive at final conclusions in all these problems which have tormented humankind through centuries ... I believe a viable way is to halt the arms race, to bring it down, gradually, reducing on a mutually balanced and verifiable basis. Instead of, statistically, having the capacity to destroy our civilization 10 times, why not 9 times, 8 times, 7 times, etc., to simplify it?

Interview, Washington/Los Angeles Times, 5-30:(I)4.

Edmund S. Muskie
Former Secretary of State
of the United States   *3*

It is clear from the statements of several second-level officials in the [Reagan] Administration that they do not believe in the constructive possibilities of arms-control negotiations in this historical period. The arms-control agency is only half-facetiously referred to as "the present danger," while the Joint Chiefs Chairman continues to point to SALT II's contribution to national security. I put these blunt questions to the current Administration: Just how long do you think you can sustain a huge military buildup, if you cannot assure us we will be better off at the end of the cycle, if in fact you foresee us still holding "the short end of the stick"? Have you got a better way to check and reduce the Soviet arsenal than through strategic-arms limitation talks?

March 18/The Washington Post, 3-19:(A)22.

Charles H. Percy
United States Senator, R–Illinois   *4*

[Saying he opposes using "linkage" in arms-control negotiations with the Soviets]: I have urged that we not wait for the Soviets to be acting every place in the world in accordance with our code of conduct and ethics. Nuclear warfare and the horror of it and the possibility of miscalculation is so great that it transcends all other problems. Starting talks should not be a reward for good behavior. We have ... an arms-control agency set up by law for that purpose, and it shouldn't be subject to every election and every event that occurs in the world.

Interview/The Washington Post, 4-24:(A)4.

Javier Perez de Cuellar
Secretary General of the United Nations   *5*

Today it is ironic that the accumulation of arms is one of the few expanding industries in a period of economic depression. An appalling proportion of human and material resources that should be directed to better ends continues to be wasted on this endless and illusory search for security through arms.

At UN General Assembly special
session on disarmament, New York,
June 7/The New York Times, 6-8:3.

Richard N. Perle
Assistant Secretary of Defense
of the United States   *6*

[On the Reagan Administration's plans for civil defense in the event of nuclear war]: We do not seek, nor do we believe that it is possible to obtain, levels of protection from the effects of all-out nuclear war that would reduce significantly the unspeakable horror of such an event ... The modest measures we are proposing for civil defense represent little more than insurance—insurance that in circumstances short of a central strategic exchange [all-out war], some lives must be saved that would otherwise be lost.

Before Senate Arms Control
Subcommittee, Washington, March 31/
The Washington Post, 4-1:(A)5.

Richard Pipes
*Director, East European and Soviet
Affairs, National Security Council*

1

We must adopt the attitude of saying, "Nuclear war is indeed a nightmare, but prudence requires that we face the possibility." I compare it to cancer, which used to be a taboo word. People were afraid to mention it lest they bring it about. Of course, cancer is a horror, but it exists all around us, as do nuclear weapons. Now we face cancer. And we cure a lot of cancer because of that. Nuclear weapons are a kind of international cancer. We can't pretend they don't exist. The Soviets decided 20 years ago that nuclear weapons would be decisive in an extreme situation. They concluded that if they ever had to go to war—which they do hope to avoid—they would have to make serious preparations for effective use of nuclear weapons. If they view the problem that way, we have little choice. If we insist on looking the other way and simply saying over and over again that these weapons are unusable and nuclear war is unthinkable, then we will have a defense unsuited to an adversary's offense, and that could get us into deep trouble. The objective is to formulate a strategy and proceed with deployments that will make a first strike against us not so much "unthinkable"—since the Soviet leadership considers it quite thinkable—as really unwinnable.

Interview/Time, 3-1:17.

William Proxmire
United States Senator, D—Wisconsin

2

In the area of defense, we're spending an enormous amount of money, but we're not really strengthening our military forces. We're permitting technology to become so complex and so costly that we simply can't afford to buy enough of these planes and tanks to do the job. We can build cheaper planes and tanks.

Interview/U.S. News & World Report, 3-8:52.

3

[Arguing against the revival of the battleship]: The key thing is that with each battleship you would need air defenses, maybe a couple of cruisers, picket ships and a submarine—a whole task force. And that's precisely what I'm trying to get the Navy away from. My philosophy is that we need vessels designed so that they can operate independently rather than in task forces.

The New York Times Magazine, 4-4:82.

David Pryor
United States Senator, D—Arkansas

4

Most Senators don't enjoy talking about nerve gas. It is repugnant and it goes against our basic grain of what is humane, because it kills civilians, not soldiers . . . I want to ensure that defense dollars are spent in those areas that will make this nation stronger, and simply adding to the stockpile of nerve gas will not make this country or its defenses one iota stronger . . . I don't think that our going back into the production of chemical warfare is going to scare the Russians one bit.

Interview/Chicago Tribune, 3-28:(1)20.

Dan Quayle
United States Senator, R—Indiana

5

I'm getting letters from home now; people are saying, "cut defense [spending]." It was only a year ago that everyone was supporting a buildup in defense. Now in one year, one year, the [Reagan] Administration has given the impression that the Pentagon is sacrosanct from budget cuts, and people don't like it. They say that the Pentagon is getting a blank check and everyone else has to sacrifice. To my mind, the pro-defense coalition that is emerging in Congress and in the country has been ruined . . . The Republicans have the same problem that the Democrats have. The Republicans are now giving the impression that the only way of solving national-security problems is throwing money at it. The Democrats have given the impression that the way of dealing with social problems is throwing money at it. Neither works.

The New York Times, 4-19:10.

Ronald Reagan
President of the United States   *1*

[Supporting compulsory registration for the draft] : Make no mistake: The continuation of peacetime registration does not foreshadow a return to the draft. I remain firm in my conviction, stated in 1980, that "only in the most severe national emergency does the government have a claim to the mandatory service of its young people." No such emergency now exists, and registration is in no way a proxy for conscription. However, we live in a dangerous world. In the event of a future threat to national safety, registration could save the United States as much as six weeks in mobilizing emergency manpower.

Washington, Jan. 7*/
The New York Times, 1-8:10.

2

We dare not reduce our defense budget. The bulk of the increase is not going for fancy new planes or elaborate weapons systems. Most of the money is for basic essentials now in dangerously short supply. It's going to go for manpower, maintenance and readiness. If we eliminated all the major weapons programs that are scheduled, it would only reduce next year's deficit by $6.5-billion in our $3-trillion economy. I don't think Americans want their armed forces held together with chewing gum and baling wire, unable to move for want of spare parts. We must not resign ourselves to life as a second-rate power, tempting aggression with our weakness.

At political fund-raising
event, Cheyenne, Wyo., March 2/
The Washington Post, 3-3:(A)5.

3

America's national-security policy is based on enduring principles. Our leaders and our allies have long understood that the objective of our defense efforts has always been to deter conflict and reduce the risk of war, conventional or nuclear. Together with our partners in the Atlantic Alliance, every President in the postwar period has followed this strategy, and it's worked. It has earned the overwhelming bipartisan support of the Congress and the country at large, and it has kept world peace.

News conference, Washington, March 31/
The New York Times, 4-1:18.

4

On balance, the Soviet Union does have a definite margin of [strategic] superiority [over the U.S.]. I think that a [mutual] freeze would not only be disadvantageous—in fact even dangerous—to us with them in that position, but I believe it would also militate against any [arms-reduction] negotiations . . . The Soviets' great edge is one in which they could absorb our retaliatory blow and hit us again.

News conference, Washington, April/Time, 4-12:12.

5

This stretch of 37 years since World War II has been the result of our maintaining a balance of power between the United States and the Soviet Union and between the strategic capabilities of either side. As long as this balance has been maintained, both sides have been given an overwhelming incentive for peace. In the 1970s, the United States altered that balance by, in effect, unilaterally restraining our own military defenses while the Soviet Union engaged in an unprecedented buildup of both the conventional and nuclear forces. As a result, the military balance which permitted us to maintain the peace is now threatened. If steps are not taken to modernize our defense, the United States will progressively lose the ability to deter the Soviet Union from employing force or threats of force against us and against our allies. It would be wonderful if we could restore our balance with the Soviet Union without increasing our own military power. And, ideally, it would be a long step in insuring peace if we could have significant and verifiable reductions of arms on both sides. But let's not fool ourselves. The Soviet Union will not come to any conference table bearing gifts. Soviet negotiators will not make unilateral concessions. To achieve parity, we must make it plain that we have the will to achieve parity by our own effort.

Radio address to the nation, Camp David, Md.,
April 17/The New York Times, 4-18:(1)16.

6

[On anti-nuclear-weapons and peace demonstrators] : I know of no Western leader who doesn't sympathize with that earnest plea. To those who march for peace, my heart is with

(RONALD REAGAN)

you. I would be at the head of your parade if I believed marching alone could bring about a more secure world . . . [But] those who advocate that we unilaterally forgo the modernization of our forces must prove that this will enhance our security and lead to moderation by the other side—in short, that it will advance, rather than undermine, the preservation of the peace. The weight of recent history does not support this notion.

Before West German Bundestag, Bonn, June 9/Los Angeles Times, 6-10:(I)7.

1

[On the Soviet vow not to be the first to use nuclear weapons]: We need deeds, not words, to convince us of Soviet sincerity . . . Agreements genuinely reinforce peace only when they are kept. Otherwise, we are building a paper castle that will be blown away by the winds of war.

At United Nations disarmament conference, New York, June 17/ U.S. News & World Report, 6-28:6.

2

Our deployed nuclear forces were built before the age of microcircuits. It is not right to ask our young men and women in uniform to maintain and operate such antiques. Many have already given lives in missile explosions and aircraft accidents caused by the old age of their equipment. We must replace and modernize our forces and that is why I have decided to proceed with the introduction of the new ICBM known as the MX.

Broadcast address to the nation, Washington, Nov. 22/The Washington Post, 11-23:(A)8.

3

[Criticizing the House vote against the MX missile program]: Today's vote by the House of Representatives was a grave mistake. Unless reversed in coming days, it will seriously set back our efforts to protect the nation's security and could handcuff our negotiators at the same table. I had hoped that most of the members in the House had awakened to the threat facing the United States. That hope was apparently

unfounded. A majority chose to go sleepwalking into the future . . . Unless we act soon, the Soviets can not only discount our land defenses, but they can also concentrate their new research on defeating us at sea and in the air. We should know from experience that the Soviets will not negotiate with us when we disarm ourselves . . . It would be tragically ironic if this of all days—December 7 [the anniversary of the World War II Japanese attack on Pearl Harbor]—once again marked a time when America was unprepared to keep the peace.

Washington, Dec. 7/ Los Angeles Times, 12-8:(I)1,12.*

4

To have your eye on the [Federal budget] deficit with regard to defense is to ignore, as some predecessors have, that the primary objective of government must be the protection of the liberties of our people. The Number 1 priority of the Federal government is national security. Therefore, defense cannot be looked at as a part of a budgetary solution. Defense must be looked at as to what needs to be done to ensure our national security. This doesn't mean that if you can find places . . . where without reducing the rebuilding that we think has to be done, if we can find savings, fine. We will find them. We don't want to waste money, and we wouldn't do that. We shouldn't do that, even if there is no recession. But national security cannot be used, turned on or off, just to suit some problem of a deficit or balancing of a budget.

Interview, Washington/Time, 12-13:19.

5

[On the recommissioning of the battleship *U.S.S. New Jersey*]: We have been questioned for bringing back this battleship, yet I would challenge anyone who has been aboard or even seen the *New Jersey* to argue its value. It seems odd and a little ironic to me that some of the same critics who accuse us of chasing technology and gold-plating on weapons systems have led the charge against a superbly cost-effective and maintainable *New Jersey.*

At recommissioning of the ship, Long Beach, Calif., Dec. 28/The Washington Post, 12-29:(A)5.

Hyman G. Rickover
Admiral, United States Navy

1

The Defense Department, on the military side—they change jobs every two years—the top people. On the civilian side, they generally come in without experience. So you have sort of two groups constantly rotating, and nobody ever gets time to find out what's really going on. Therefore, it has to depend on its supporters. I think considerable money could be saved in the Defense Department. I think there are areas to cut down . . . For example, take the number of nuclear submarines. I'll hit right close to home: I see no reason why we have to have just as many as the Russians do. At a certain point you get where it's sufficient. What's the difference whether we have 100 nuclear submarines or 200? I don't see what difference it makes. You can sink everything on the oceans several times over with the number we have, and so can they.

Before Congressional Joint Economic
Committee, Washington, Jan. 28/
The New York Times, 1-30:8.

Robert A. Rosenberg
Assistant Chief of Staff, Studies and
Analysis, United States Air Force

2

[On those who criticize the growing complexity of military equipment] : There is a place for simplicity and a place for complexity. We don't go after the complex weapons for the sake of it. I can't go out and fight against an enemy with a simple low-cost fighter plane when the threat coming from the other side is a night-all-weather attack aircraft. The Soviets are not building simple weapons, are they?

The New York Times, 4-8:12.

Eugene V. Rostow
Director, Arms Control and Disarmament
Agency of the United States

3

We've tended to think of arms control and disarmament negotiations as if they were a kind of magic that could produce peace if only we were intelligent or persuasive enough and could bring the Soviet Union to see the logic of our position. It hasn't happened that way; that system of world public order has been disintegrating. The reason for the eclipse of arms-control efforts in recent years is not the arms race but the process of Soviet expansion. The arms race is the symptom, not the cause.

Before Association of the
Bar of the City of New York,
March/The New York Times,
3-21:(4)5.

4

The first principle of [U.S.] President Reagan's approach to arms control and disarmament has been to insist that arms control be viewed as an integral part of our foreign and defense policy as a whole. Arms control is not a magical activity, which can produce peace by incantation, without pain and tears . . . Arms-control negotiations can be a useful element in a strategy for achieving peace. But they are not a substitute for such a strategy, nor, equally, are they a substitute for programs designed to restore the military balance with the Soviet Union. I must stress once more that nuclear arms do not exist in a vacuum. The secret is out of the laboratory, and there is no way to put it back.

Before American Institute of
Astronautics and Aeronautics,
Baltimore, May 25/
The New York Times, 6-15:14.

Donald H. Rumsfeld
Former Secretary of Defense
of the United States

5

Given the facts of Soviet power and policy of expansion, the first thing that we must do is to insure absolutely that we have the military power sufficient to enable us to contribute effectively to peace and stability in the world. Without that, we would have no policy other than accommodation to Soviet preferences, and that is not a policy but rather the inevitable result of weakness. An absence of adequate deterrent capability on the part of the United States would inject a fundamental instability into the world equation.

Interview/U.S. News & World Report, 9-6:34.

67

James R. Schlesinger
*Former Secretary of Defense
of the United States*

1

The United States has and will continue to have, in my judgment, sufficient surviving and deliverable [nuclear] weapons to destroy the urban-industrial base of the Soviet Union—even after absorbing a Soviet strike . . . If the present discussions of "superiority" and "inferiority" are taken to suggest that the Soviet Union can deny the United States that capability, then the suggestion that the Soviet Union has superiority is invalid.

*Before Senate Foreign
Relations Committee,
Washington, April 30/
The New York Times,
5-1:3.*

Helmut Schmidt
Chancellor of West Germany

2

. . . in many countries we have been witnessing in the past few days and weeks gatherings of young and older people who are voicing their fears of a terrible and excessive arms buildup and an "overkill" that can no longer be rationally comprehended . . . . we should not underestimate the great and positive moral force which emerges in the movement for effective disarmament. We should not simply push aside those who support that movement, dismissing them as amateurs who lack sufficient insight. Instead, the driving force that has become apparent in the unrest of many of our fellow citizens must be regarded as a motivation and moral obligation for us . . . Today it is not only idealistic pacifists and starry-eyed utopians who are protesting against such concepts. More and more urgently, doubts are being raised as to the wisdom of the strategic thinkers, the diplomats and statesmen, and the capability finally to break out of the vicious circle of armament and still more armament.

*At United Nations
session on disarmament,
New York, June 14/
Chicago Tribune, 6-15:(1)1.8.*

Glenn T. Seaborg
*Professor of chemistry, University
of California, Berkeley; Former
Director, Atomic Energy Commission
of the United States*

3

At the moment, the focus is on achieving an arms-limitation accord with the Soviets. But I think a comprehensive [nuclear] test-ban treaty might be easier to achieve. It is a concrete step that is feasible, and it would impede further qualitative improvements in nuclear arsenals and hence could prevent the development of dangerously destabilizing new weapons systems. Though both sides could still add to their arsenals, a test ban would at least make it very difficult for one side to get far ahead of the other. I am not suggesting that an arms-limitation accord is not worth pursuing, but some of the steps involved are so complicated that they are going to require long and tedious negotiations. In the end, we might not wind up at a level of arms limitation that is very meaningful.

Interview/U.S. News & World Report, 3-29:58.

Albert Shanker
President, American Federation of Teachers

4

As a nation, we cannot afford to accept the "guns and no butter" economics of [President] Reagan. Imagine what would happen if we had asked for a 37 per cent increase in expenditures for social programs and then said we'd figure out later how we wanted to spend it. Well, that is exactly what the Reagan Administration is doing with its proposed defense expenditures. We must stop giving our blank checks to the military.

*Bal Harbour, Fla., Feb. 15/
Los Angeles Times, 2-16:(IV)1.*

John Shattuck
*Director, national office,
American Civil Liberties Union*

5

Everyone is flailing around to find a response to crime that doesn't cost anything. Unfortunately, that often comes down to something that infringes on Constitutional rights and liberties.

The New York Times, 6-24:17.

George P. Shultz
*Former Secretary of the Treasury
of the United States*

1

[On Defense Secretary Casper Weinberger]:
Cap is a very stand-up type of guy. He'll have a
view, and it's clear-cut. And he has a backbone
of steel. He's not a trimmer ... It's never a
surprise to me that Cap speaks out ... He's
something of a renaissance man. He has views
on a lot of things. It's hard for him to learn to
bite his tongue.

Interview, April/The Washington Post, 7-4:(A)7.

George P. Shultz
*Secretary of State-designate
of the United States*

2

Today most Americans are uncomfortable
with the fact that we must spend so much of
our substance on defense—and rightly so. Yet
most Americans also recognize that we must
deal with reality as we find it. And that reality,
in its simplest terms, is an uncertain world in
which peace and security can be assured only if
we have the strength and will to preserve them.

*At Senate Foreign Relations Committee hearing
on his confirmation, Washington, July 13/
The Washington Post, 7-14:(A)20.*

3

[On the movement in the U.S. for a nuclear
freeze agreement with the Soviets]: It seems to
me that a freeze is a bad idea, fundamentally,
because a freeze is the enemy of a [nuclear-
arms] reduction. And what the President
[Reagan] has proposed is a reduction ... If we
agree to a freeze of the current situation, we
take away any incentive that the Soviet Union
has to engage in negotiations.

*At Senate Foreign Relations Committee
hearing on his confirmation, Washington,
July/U.S. News & World Report, 7-26:25.*

Adele Simmons
President, Hampshire College

4

[On the growing academic concern with
nuclear weapons]: It's a subject that lends itself
perfectly to the basic goals of education. It's an
important subject and one that students are

deeply interested in. It lends itself to interdis-
ciplinary thinking. You can also use it to force
students to figure out how two organizations—
the Pentagon and the American Federation of
Scientists—can take the same data and use it to
reach totally different conclusions about
defense policy.

The New York Times, 11-30:19.

Arlen Specter
*United States Senator,
R—Pennsylvania*

5

... although we have to be strong militarily
to prevent Soviet adventurism and nuclear
blackmail, there is a great deal beyond waste
and fraud in the military that requires a very
tough look. There isn't anything magical about
the triad—the idea of having nuclear capabilities
by land, air and sea. The triad concept is worth
re-examining to see if we have to spend such
large amounts in all three areas for an effective
deterrent.

Interview/U.S. News & World Report, 3-8:51.

Samuel S. Stratton
United States Representative, D—New York

6

[Criticizing calls for cuts in funding of Air
Force buildup plans]: The money is needed.
My fear is that we're going to have some cuts
that we shouldn't have. Even certified hawks
are talking about cutting hell out of the defense
budget. If the big [buildup] momentum generated last year is now interrupted, I fear it'll
never rise again. Suddenly everyone wants to
take money out of defense and that's a mistake,
a big mistake.

The New York Times, 4-8:12.

Edward Teller
Nuclear physicist

7

I hope [the nuclear-weapons-freeze movement in the West] will not become an important force. I hope more sense will prevail. If the
nuclear freeze goes through, this country [the
U.S.] won't exist in 1990. The Soviet Union is
a country that has had totalitarian rule for
many hundreds of years, and what a relatively

(EDWARD TELLER)

small ruling class there might do can be very different from what a democratic country can decide to do. The rulers in the Kremlin are as eager as Hitler was to get power over the whole world. But, unlike Hitler, they are not gamblers. If we can put up a missile defense that makes their attack dubious, chances are they will never try the attack. We can avoid a third world war, but only if strength is in the hands of those who want peace more than they want power.

Interview/Time, 3-29:16.

James R. Thompson
Governor of Illinois (R)

1

. . . with current defense spending estimated at $200-billion a year and projected to go to $230-billion next year, I have asked the President and the Secretary of Defense why a relatively modest amount—say, three to four per cent—could not be shifted to "down home" defense measures. That money, invested in domestic spending, would quickly aid economic recovery, e.g., in transportation and housing, or permanently strengthen our economy, e.g., aid to older cities with infrastructures in place and paid for. It is just as important to our national defense as military hardware. For the question to be answered by "defense" spending must always be: Spending for what, to protect against what, for the defense of what? . . . And what kind of country is it that we need to defend? Our "down home" defenses, our internal defenses against unequal economic opportunity, must not be ignored in calculations of total "defense" spending. For some of our citizens, it is not a question of "guns and butter," but a question of "guns and bread."

State of the State address/
The New York Times, 3-7:(4)3.

Malcolm Toon
Former United States Ambassador
to the Soviet Union

2

[Arguing against linking U.S.-Soviet arms talks with Soviet behavior elsewhere]: We

should not carry linkage to the extent of denying ourselves the opportunity to participate in negotiations which we think are in our genuine long-term interests. The arms-control talks that we're engaged in now in Geneva, and the negotiations on strategic arms that we hope to start relatively soon, are in our interest. Therefore, I would not tie those to Soviet misbehavior.

Interview/U.S. News & World Report, 3-15:45.

John G. Tower
United States Senator, R–Texas

3

Notwithstanding America's remarkable and unparalleled military record . . . the tradition of the American people is anti-militaristic. This anti-military attitude in the American mind is based, at least in part, on the deep-rooted American view that men are rational and that peaceful solutions to disputes should be achievable. Only when unambiguous challenges to America's valued ideals and personal security arise do Americans mobilize to fight. We are inclined to wait for a crisis before gathering our military potential. In today's world, absent the will to prepare, the time to fight for a cause may well have come and gone before we are ready.

At U.S. Military Academy commencement,
West Point, N.Y., May 26/The
Christian Science Monitor, 6-11:16.

4

I don't believe that a ballistic-missile defense system would be totally and 100 per cent effective. However, it could, I think, enhance the survivability of a certain number of your systems. I think, too, that you could go to deceptive-basing mode for your ballistic-missile defense system, which would complicate the problem for Soviet planners a great deal. Obviously, the more force you make them expend in an effort to overwhelm your inter-continental-ballistic-missile system, the closer they come to an unfavorable force-exchange ratio. And complicating the work of the Soviet is important. It's one of the reasons we have a triad in the first place, to make it less likely that they will consider nuclear war to be

(JOHN G. TOWER)

winnable. We do not have a first-strike policy. Therefore, we must have enough survivable systems to deter the Soviets from launching the first attack.

Panel discussion/The New York Times, 11-28:(4)3.

Harry D. Train II
Admiral, United States Navy; Commander, U.S. and allied naval forces in the Atlantic

1

It will do [the U.S.] little good to win the first few battles [in a war] if the Soviets can simply outlast us. The possible outcomes of a short war are, first, that our opponents give up—which is unlikely; second, that we surrender—which is unthinkable; third, that we go nuclear—which is catastrophic; or fourth, that we control hostilities with conventional forces. This last option gives our leaders the chance to replace conflict by negotiation—and is the only acceptable option. [For that to happen,] we must have sufficient residual forces, munitions and supplies to continue fighting a credible campaign.

Congressional testimony/ The New York Times, 4-11:(1)14.

Thomas K. Turnage
Director, Selective Service System of the United States

2

[On those who say a jail sentence or heavy fine is harsh treatment for those who refuse to register with Selective Service]: We have an army sitting in Europe now and more than a division sitting in Korea. If there were a national emergency where those people were engaged in combat, the time it would take to get replacements to them would be absolutely vital. To them, it's a matter of life and death. So it's also harsh if a young man tries to avoid fulfilling his obligation to the nation. If you look at it from the standpoint of the interests of the nation, from the interests of the young man who must remain in combat because there's no replacement for him, I don't think it's overly harsh to prosecute those who refuse to register.

Interview/U.S. News & World Report, 7-12:32.

Stansfield Turner
Former Director of Central Intelligence of the United States

3

The Soviets have progressed remarkably in recent years in being able to project power into the Third World. I believe it is here that the U.S. is most deficient in its military power and the challenge is most probable. That is what we should be emphasizing, not the MX [missile], B-1 [bomber], theatre nuclear forces, tanks and large aircraft carriers. We must return to the concept of the military as an expeditionary force that can get us wherever the U.S. has a problem.

To reporters/The Christian Science Monitor, 1-29:13.

4

One ought to broaden one's outlook on what is national security . . . Bringing down the [Federal budget] deficit is part of national security, not just economic well-being; and if it takes cuts [in defense] to achieve it, then I'm in favor of it.

To reporters, Washington/ The Christian Science Monitor, 7-2:4.

Paul C. Warnke
Chairman, Committee for National Security; Former Director, Arms Control and Disarmament Agency of the United States

5

When we talk about nuclear arms, the basic difficulty is that we still think of them as something of military utility. They aren't . . . What are nuclear weapons good for anyway? Will they give us greater freedom to use our conventional force to enforce the rule of law? Can we win a nuclear war by tinkering with our strategic arsenal? Will this advance our national security? My answer is an emphatic no. The most they can do is prevent the Soviet Union from using *their* nuclear weapons—the most important objective. We have roughly 10,000 strategic nuclear warheads [plus] four base systems in Europe that can destroy Soviet targets. The Soviets have 7,000. We're way ahead; it doesn't make a damn bit of difference. In megatonnage, the Soviets are way ahead; it doesn't make a bit of difference. The fact that they might have a two-megaton

(PAUL C. WARNKE)

warhead compared to our modest ones of something like 400,000 tons of TNT, only makes one difference: How big is the hole going to be where the high school used to be?

Before Association of the Bar of the City of New York, March/ The New York Times, 3-21:(4)5.

1

The Soviets ... have something like 80 per cent of their strategic nuclear resources in their land-based ICBMs. We have less than 30 per cent ... But if you look at 100 per cent of both forces, the respects in which we have the edge more than balance the respects in which the Soviets have the edge. [And] we have the edge in the most important respect, which is survivability, because ... over 50 per cent of our strategic warheads [are] on the least vulnerable part of the nuclear-deterrent triad ... ballistic-missile submarines ... There is no way in which either side can gain strategic superiority ever again unless the other side gives up. Now, we know we're not going to give up, and we have no reason to believe they will, so that all you will do is preserve the present nuclear stalemate at higher levels of risk [if the buildup continues].

Interview/Newsweek, 4-26:26.

Thomas J. Watson, Jr.
Former United States Ambassador to the Soviet Union

2

Politicians in Administration after Administration, heavily influenced by experts treating nuclear devices as simply upgraded conventional weapons, have been convinced that superiority in nuclear weapons is possible. Only rarely and briefly have some realized that all that really counts on either side is sufficiency. If I have a gun at your forehead, and you have a gun at mine, it makes little difference how many or what kind of guns either you or I have in reserve.

At St. Michael's College commencement, Winooski, Vt./U.S. News & World Report, 6-7:66.

Murray L. Weidenbaum
Former Chairman, Council of Economic Advisers to the President of the United States (Ronald Reagan)

3

I advocate a strong, continued buildup in our defense establishment—period. I advocate many civilian programs as well. None of that precludes a hard-nosed review of each budget. I'll put it another way. I support the maximum required defense effort that's feasible. But I worry that we might be going faster, on a bigger scale, than our economy can sustain. In our reviews, we've been far tougher on the civilian-agency budgets than on the military.

Interview/U.S. News & World Report, 11-22:61.

Caspar W. Weinberger
Secretary of Defense of the United States

4

Why must the defense budget be increased as much as we propose? First, because we must now pay the bill for our collective failure to preserve an adequate balance of military strength during the past decade or two ... Second, because we cannot, in good conscience, increase our reliance on the threat of nuclear weapons to evade the need for restoring our conventional military strength across the board. Finally, because we cannot offer the American people and our allies a mere facade of security by deploying forces that lack the necessary material and training and are not backed up by an adequate mobilization potential ... It is the Soviet military effort, its direction and its nature, that drives our defense budget.

Statement accompanying 1983 Federal budget/San Francisco Examiner & Chronicle, 2-7:(A)A.*

5

[On reports that the Soviet Union has used chemical weapons in such places as Laos, Cambodia and Afghanistan]: This accumulation of evidence from many different sources and witnesses raises a wrenching question for the future of arms-control agreements. Our past approach to [arms-control] verification often relied on the theory that the Soviets would not risk violating isolated arms-control provisions

(CASPAR W. WEINBERGER)

that were hard to verify, since there would always be some risk of detection, and to be caught would have damaging political consequences for them. In particular, this theory assumes there would be vigorous condemnation by world opinion and a strong response by many governments. What is now left of the validity of this theory?

Annual defense report*/
Los Angeles Times, 2-8:(I)8.

1

[The U.S. has] great strategic strength if all you are going to do is to count warheads. We have a lot of warheads. But you have to look at total capability, and the Soviet missiles are now more accurate than ours, much more accurate than they used to be ... There is a degree of superiority and strategic edge on the Soviet side that is necessarily a matter of great concern. It is a period which we can call by any name, including window of vulnerability, and it will last for some years through the decade even if we pursue all of the programs the President [Reagan] has sought.

To reporters, Washington, April 14/
Chicago Tribune, 4-16:(I)1.

2

[On his defense policies since taking office]: Our first strategy was to get well ... to get the armed forces in some kind of condition that they could deal with whatever crisis might arise ... Rightly or wrongly, [military spending is] the index by which the resolution and the will of America is judged. And in this case, because it meant the acquisition of things we urgently needed, and doing it at a time of economic difficulty when we were reducing all of the other departments, practically speaking ... All of these things at the same time conveyed to the world a picture of a total change in the United States and an astonishing dedication to the idea of regaining strength in the face of what all of the people interested in normal politics would tell you was an impossible set of conditions.

Interview/The Washington Post, 4-18:(B)4.

3

A nuclear [-weapons] freeze would not reduce the probability of war. It would go against the first and foremost aim of arms control because it would back the United States and our allies into a position of permanent military disadvantage ... The greatest paradox of all is that military strength is most successful if it is never used. But if we are never to use force, we must be prepared to use it and use it successfully.

At U.S. Naval Academy commencement,
May 26/The New York Times, 5-27:4.

4

Nowhere ... do we mean to imply that nuclear war is winnable. This notion has no place in our strategy. We see nuclear weapons only as a way of discouraging the Soviets from thinking that they could ever resort to them. That is exactly why we must have the capability for a "protracted" response–to demonstrate that our strategic forces could survive Soviet strikes over an extended, that is to say protracted, period. Our entire strategic program, including the development of a protracted response capability that has been so maligned in the press recently, has been developed with the express intention of assuring that nuclear war will never be fought.

At Army War College, June 3/
The Washington Post, 6-4:(A)4.

5

Our first priority is to deter an attack upon us. Then we aim at resisting conventional attacks on the central front in Europe, on the oil fields of the Middle East and on South Korea. We also maintain heavy naval forces to protect Japan and the Pacific islands. We must do that because the Soviets, no matter how many years of good feeling or detente, never stopped adding offensive military strength for activities in different parts of the globe at once. We must also consider that they'll become an energy-importing nation before too long, that their economy is in terrible condition, and that they may feel that more territory, more resources, will be needed to sustain their economy.

Interview/San Francisco Examiner
& Chronicle, 8-4:(A)14.

73

WHAT THEY SAID IN 1982

(CASPAR W. WEINBERGER)

1

When people challenge the [defense] strategy we are using and the means we are using to catch up [with the Soviets], I always ask what is it that we should give up. Should we give up Korea, Japan, the oil fields, Europe, the Caribbean, the protection of the United States? So, no one has suggested what we should give up ... When you look at a map of available Soviet air and naval access to materials and facilities now compared with 10 or 15 years ago ... all you see are red blotches .... it looks like the whole place has caught the measles.

Interview/The Washington Post, 11-30:(A)18.

Francis J. West
Assistant Secretary for International Security Affairs, Department of Defense of the United States

2

[On sales of U.S. arms to foreign countries]: It's much better to have countries do it [defend themselves with U.S.-supplied arms] than to get into using U.S. forces in some of these situations ... Basically, there is a risk inherent in having arms in the hands of nations that can do things contrary to your interests. However, our track record since World War II has been pretty good. Arms sales are one of the most sound investments we can make for our own security.

Los Angeles Times, 7-16:(I)8,9.

G. William Whitehurst
United States Representative, R–Virginia

3

We are worried that our military can no longer win, and we have doubts as to whether the American people will continue to support high and increasing budgets for a non-winning military. We believe that this situation can be reversed, but only if some fundamental changes are made in how the defenders of our country utilize its people, strategy and tactics, and hardware ...Our centralized command structures and ponderous organizations lead directly to low agility, that is, the inability to react, swift, and move faster than the enemy. And of course, centralization stifles the initiative of junior commanders, further impeding our ability to react and innovate.

The Christian Science Monitor, 1-29:13.

Paul Wolfowitz
Director, Policy Planning Staff, Department of State of the United States

4

The hostility [of the public] to new military technology is understandable. After all, it is technology that brought us nuclear weapons. But not all technological developments have increased our peril. Technological changes have actually made nuclear weapons less prone to accident, less vulnerable to terrorists and less susceptible to unauthorized use. By making nuclear delivery systems less vulnerable, new technology can reduce the danger of hair-trigger responses or surprise attacks ... In fact, changes in our nuclear forces have made it possible to reduce the total megatonnage of our strategic nuclear forces by almost 30 per cent in the last 10 years and by roughly 60 per cent from the peak levels of 1960.

The Washington Post, 7-8:(A)14.

Leonard M. Zamyatin
Director, International Information Department, Soviet Communist Party Central Committee

5

It is primitive for people to claim that the Soviet Union has surpassed the U.S. [in strategic military power]. In some areas we are ahead, and in others you [the U.S.] are. In the aggregate, both sides have accumulated so much weaponry that there is no need to develop new systems. The stockpiles are so great that they can already destroy all life on earth. We are not going into [arms-control] negotiations from a position of weakness, but from a position of equality. If that equality is upset [by a U.S. strategic buildup], then we will not be able to negotiate, because one side will think it can impose its will on the other.

Interview, Moscow, June/Time, 6-21:35.

74

The Economy . Labor

Les Aspin
United States Representative,
D–Wisconsin 1

[Criticizing a proposed Constitutional amendment to require a balanced Federal budget]: The amendment is typical of the current mood. You take a complex issue and you find a simple solution, like the nuclear freeze, or the tax cut. [We Democrats] never bothered to educate our constituents. We've always ducked the issue and said, "I'm for a balanced budget, too." All those chickens are now coming home to roost.

The New York Times, 7-16:9.

Malcolm Baldrige
Secretary of Commerce
of the United States 2

[On President Reagan's current tax-increase proposal after decreasing taxes last year]: In the way the budget deficits came out this year, the mere fact that we're asking for a tax increase, part of that back, certainly implies that if we had to do this all over again, we would have asked for less of a tax decrease last year ... [With the current $100-billion tax-increase proposal,] instead of a $350-billion tax reduction for three years, we have a $250-billion reduction. And I would submit that if we had started out with $250-billion, so that there was no change this year, there would have been the same joy and dancing in the streets and the same laudatory statements from the supply-side economists ... It's still the largest tax decrease in history.

Broadcast interview, Aug. 8/
Chicago Tribune, 8-9:(1)1,4.

William M. Batten
Chairman, New York Stock Exchange 3

Despite the rising crescendo of criticism and disagreement dinning our ears today, I still believe we have a stronger bipartisan agreement on our fundamental economic goals, including economic growth, than we have had for decades ... Both parties have agreed on the need to encourage savings, risk-taking and investment in order to create productive jobs in the private sector. Evidence of this consensus can be found in the last two tax bills. There is, of course, a difference of opinion about details—about the best policies to achieve the goals—and that is normal in the political process. But the encouraging fact is the level of agreement on the basic goals of economic policy.

Before Commonwealth Club, San Francisco/
The Wall Street Journal, 1-11:21.

William J. Baumol
Professor of economics, Princeton and
New York Universities; Former
president, American Economic Association 4

The entrepreneurial spirit was very much with us in the 1940s and early 1950s. But it has been 20 years since I have heard anyone say, "The impossible takes a little longer" ... If the reason for the lower savings rate is the disappearance of the Protestant ethic, there is no way we can deal with that problem. Sure, we could help subsidize churches and synagogues, with the admonition that every fifth sermon be about saving. But if psychologists thought that might work, at best it would take a very long time. Instead, we might try to increase savings through tax policy and interest rates ... Growth is not something you achieve without cost. There are environmental costs, and people would have to work harder. But the payoff would be a higher standard of living ... People have chosen more leisure and less pressure on the job, management as much as anyone. Much of the antitrust action we see is business trying to protect itself from the pressures of the marketplace—opting for the easy life.

Interview, Washington/The New York Times, 1-3:(3)6.

Barry Bluestone
Professor of economics, Boston College

1

If the recession comes to an end, it is not clear that there will be much recovery in terms of over-all employment in the United States. Companies will have moved more of their production out of this country, and will have begun to automate more rapidly. And those who do find jobs will move disproportionately into lower-wage industries, leading to a lower average standard of living and a significant loss in productivity.

The New York Times, 8-8:(3)22.

Richard Bolling
United States Representative,
D—Missouri

2

The condition of the economy is a direct result of the failure to understand that you can't do everything at once in a very, very quick way . . . But what the President [Reagan] tried to do is too much too quickly. He ended up with such a drain on revenue, by the enormous tax cut going into the third year, that there was no possibility, with the enormous increase in defense—the biggest of all time and the tax cut the biggest of all time in any country ever—there was no way in which we could get a reasonable balance and reduce the deficit.

Broadcast address to the
nation, Washington, April 29/
The New York Times, 4-30:12.

David E. Bonoir
United States Representative,
D—Michigan

3

[On the "trickle-down" aspect of President Reagan's economic program]: Where is the trickle-down, Mr. President? Despite mammoth concessions to corporations, our unemployed number 10 million, the business rate of investment is a meager 0.3 per cent. Where is the trickle-down? These are real people, Mr. President—the unemployed. They laugh and cry, they hope, and right now they hurt. It is time that this Administration spent less time with the blue-blooded and more time with the blue-collar. Less time with black-tie and more time with black unemployment. Less time talking with people in reception lines and more time talking with people in unemployment lines.

Before the House, Washington, Feb. 9/
The New York Times, 3-8:10.

Michael Boskin
Economist, Stanford University

4

The [Reagan] Administration's program of cutting tax rates at the margin and trying to bring inflation down through a relatively tight monetary policy is quite sensible. It is the best policy structure one can come up with to try to insure that our standard of living will be higher on average over the next 20 years. The problem is no one wants to go through the pain.

The New York Times, 6-30:29.

Bill Bradley
United States Senator, D—New Jersey

5

I have suggested that the income-tax rate be dramatically lowered to a uniform 14 per cent for 75 per cent of the taxpayers, with a progressive surtax of up to 14 per cent for the highest-income groups. Then the top rate would be no more than 28 per cent. The bulk of the tax expenditures, or deductions, would simultaneously be eliminated. It would be a much fairer system. People with the same real income would pay the same tax. It also would help the economy. When individuals make investments, they could make decisions based on real value in the marketplace—not on the impact of various provisions of the tax code. That would allow our economy to adapt quickly to a changing world environment and be more competitive internationally.

Interview/U.S. News & World Report, 6-21:34.

M. Harvey Brenner
Professor of operations research,
Johns Hopkins University

6

The most important difference between this recession and most others is that it reflects structural changes in the economy. Many workers in the extractive and manufacturing sectors

(M. HARVEY BRENNER)

are not going to find re-employment at their old jobs, nor are their sons and daughters or younger brothers and sisters going to find work careers in these stable and contracting industries. Training for services and communications-sector jobs, and for lighter industrial work, is necessary to bring these displaced workers back into productive roles.

Before House Domestic Monetary Policy Subcommittee, Washington, Aug. 12/ The New York Times, 8-13:9.

Edmund G. Brown, Jr.
Governor of California (D)

1

It is time for the President [Reagan] and the Congress to take decisive action to halt this downward spiral of recession. It is dragging this nation deeper and deeper into a black hole of unemployment, bankruptcies and economic weakness ... The hard truth is that the President's economic game-plan is not working. Wall Street knows it. Main Street feels it. The long unemployment lines prove it.

Announcing his candidacy for the California Democratic U.S. Senatorial nomination, Los Angeles, March 10/ Los Angeles Times, 3-11:(I)24.

Willard C. Butcher
Chairman, Chase Manhattan Bank

2

Interest rates are too high and unnecessarily high in view of the way inflation has come down ... I am hopeful it will be considerably lower by the end of the year. I'm emphasizing the word "hopeful." It is imperative that interest rates come down. If they are lower, the economy will be stronger. Clearly, the recovery will be delayed the longer that interest rates hang up ... This is the time for a balanced and pragmatic policy [by the Federal Reserve]. I recognize that the monetary aggregates are indeed important, but we must also recognize that the level of short-term interest rates is not unimportant.

Interview, Chicago/Chicago Tribune, 3-11:(3)1.

John H. Chafee
United States Senator, R–Rhode Island

3

[Criticizing a proposed Constitutional amendment requiring a balanced Federal budget]: A Constitutional amendment based on the premise that deficits are bad, accompanied by procedures requiring extraordinary majorities to allow them, could further confuse and complicate Congressional processes. It could seriously damage the economy by reinforcing recessions rather than counteracting them. It is in my view simply unworkable.

The Washington Post, 8-10:(A)14.

A. W. Clausen
President, International Bank for Reconstruction and Development (World Bank)

4

Countries are making [economic] adjustments by tightening up on spending. Mexico is making adjustments; Brazil is making adjustments; Argentina is making adjustments; and Poland may be. Even the United States is making adjustments. At the World Bank's annual meeting in Toronto in September, you could discern the beat—the drumbeat, the rhythm, the cacophony. The overwhelming convergence of views is that countries must adjust their economic policies—no exceptions, developed and developing [countries].

Interview/U.S. News & World Report, 11-15:64.

Alan Cranston
United States Senator, D–California

5

[On the Federal Reserve Board]: It's inconsistent with representative democracy—and contrary to consistent fiscal and monetary policy—to have seven people appointed to 14-year terms with vast, sweeping powers over the lives and fortunes of the American people, who are accountable to no one, not the President, not the Congress, not the people.

News conference, San Diego, Feb. 15/ Los Angeles Times, 2-16:(IV)2.

6

The crisis in our economy is not some temporary recession, some transient decline to

WHAT THEY SAID IN 1982

be followed automatically by new growth and progress. It is a depression. We Democrats got business working before. And we can do it now. Someday, business will learn that we Democrats are the best friends the American economy has ever had.

At Democratic Party conference, Philadelphia,
June 25/The New York Times, 6-26:11.

James Dale Davidson
Chairman, National Taxpayers Union

1

[Supporting a Constitutional amendment requiring a balanced Federal budget]: If [President] Ronald Reagan couldn't succeed in cutting outlays, who can? The likely answer is no one can. The job is undoable. The only way spending growth can ever be curtailed is by Constitutional amendment.

Chicago Tribune, 3-14:(1)4.

Robert Dederick
Assistant Secretary for Economic
Affairs, Department of Commerce
of the United States

2

My basic view is that there are a number of routes to heaven and most strands of economic theory have truth in them. But no one strand has all the truth, and what is true at one time is less important at another time. Supply-side is very important. The demand side is very important. The financial side is important. And the institutional side is important . . . I know the economy is tremendously complicated and forecasting is fraught with difficulty. A young fellow can be confident because he hasn't been wrong many times. But when you have been doing this for 25 years, you realize your fallibility.

Interview, Washington/
The New York Times, 5-3:14.

Thierry de Montbrial
Director, French Institute
of International Relations

3

Today's economic policies draw upon two schools of thought, the neo-Keynesian and the monetarist. The neo-Keynesians believe it is possible to avoid spiraling inflation by a wage and price policy and other measures that encourage worker mobility and training, flexibility of supply and demand. But this is based on the questionable assumption that one can influence the relationship between reduced unemployment and rising wages. A second false assumption is that it is possible to limit the effects of this policy on external and public debt. Modern monetarism, for which Milton Friedman has become the spokesman, asserts that if we want full employment and stable prices it is enough to give free rein to the market and carefully regulate the money supply. This theory also rests on two frail assumptions—that the monetary authorities have the power to control the money supply, and that market laws alone will eliminate unemployment. But growing unemployment in today's world is linked to other phenomena, such as accelerating technological change and the shortcomings of educational systems.

Interview/World Press Review, June:28.

Raymond J. Donovan
Secretary of Labor of the United States

4

We have to continue to control inflation. The American people are too smart and too mature to listen to those who say that our [economic] program has failed . . . Sure, we think about [using anti-recession measures to fight unemployment and the economic slump]. It's a tremendous temptation to say, "Let's take a little bit of the hair of the dog that bit us and spend our way back to economic health" . . . But that's unwise when we're at the goal line . . . We're in this fight for this generation and the next.

Interview/Los Angeles Times, 9-16:(I)10.

Byron L. Dorgan
United States Representative,
D–North Dakota

5

The banking structure in this country, led by the Federal Reserve Board, is creating high interest rates as a matter of monetary policy. That policy is designed to allocate credit through price. Those who can pay the price get

(BYRON L. DORGAN)

credit. If the Federal Reserve Board, in concert with the larger banks in America—Citibank, Chase Manhattan and their friends—want to dry up the credit supply, they let the price of credit rise to 17 or 20 per cent. That means only the Mobil Oils and their big corporate friends can afford to borrow. The little guy is frozen out . . . The Federal Reserve *is part of* the banking system. The Fed has always been dominated by big-city, Eastern bankers. Its policies reflect the policies desired by large banking institutions. Today the policy of the Federal Reserve Board, working through the banking industry, is tight credit through high interest rates. There is absolutely no economic justification for the level of interest rates today.

Interview/
U.S. News & World Report,
3-15:63.

Robert W. Edgar
United States Representative,
D—Pennsylvania

1

In an over-all sense, we are concerned that the President's [Reagan] budget focuses solely on broad-brushed economic trends, and fails to recognize the fact that ours no longer is a nation—and perhaps never was—where national unemployment rates, national inflation rates and gross national product tell the whole economic story. The national economy has devolved into several separate and distinct regional economies, each with its own strengths and weaknesses and its own claim on Federal resources. America is no longer a nation where all boats rise and fall on the same tide. Levels of economic growth and levels of investment mean something quite different in our inner cities than in some of our more affluent and growing communities.

Before
House Budget Committee,
Washington,
March 22/
The New York Times,
4-20:15.

Martin Feldstein
Chairman-designate, Council
of Economic Advisers to the
President of the United States

2

I think it is most unfortunate . . . that this idea of stimulating supply rather than demand got a bad name when the label "supply-side economics" was attached to some extreme rhetoric about self-financing tax cuts and euphoric forecasts of a painless transition to rapid but inflation-free growth. Although I reject such extremes, I do believe that it is very important to revise government policies to stimulate supply by creating capacity and by reducing disincentives and barriers to individual effort.

At Senate Banking Committee hearing
on his confirmation, Washington, Sept. 22/
Chicago Tribune, 9-23:(1)1.

3

The two reasons for the large [Federal budget] deficits I see most frequently in the newspapers are the reduction in taxes and the growth in defense spending. In fact, neither of these is a satisfactory explanation . . . The real reason for large and persistent budget deficits has been the rapid growth of non-defense spending. In 1960, non-defense spending was 9½ per cent of GNP. By 1970 it had increased to 12.3 per cent of GNP. The next 12 years saw a further increase to 17.9 per cent of the GNP in 1982 . . . In short, then, the primary cause of our current and projected budget deficits is that non-defense outlays have grown more rapidly and GNP has grown more slowly than was anticipated in the 1960s and 1970s when new programs were enacted and old programs enlarged. We have deficits because we made decisions on the basis of economic assumptions that have turned out to be wrong. We have deficits because as a nation we are not as rich as we thought we would be at this time. I believe that if we had known what we know now, we would never have enacted the programs and enlarged their benefits in the way that we did.

Before Economic Club of Boston/
Los Angeles Time,
11-15:(IV)2.

79

Martin Feldstein
*Chairman, Council of Economic
Advisers to the President
of the United States*

1

[Supporting the indexing of taxes] : I think it's critical. I think that it may be the most significant, long-lasting part of the over-all tax package. Now that we've got [tax] rates down, we've got to lock them in so that we don't have inflation continually pushing people into higher brackets. And of course, if we don't have the indexing, then there's a very strong temptation for those who want a bigger government and more tax revenue to also be in favor of more inflation. More inflation pushes people into higher brackets to generate more revenue to advance more spending. So indexing removes the temptation to inflate as a backdoor way of getting tax revenue.

Interview/U.S. News & World Report, 12-6:64.

2

High unemployment does result in considerable human suffering. But if you go back a hundred years, you'll find that every time a protracted period of inflation has been broken, there has been a reduction in economic activity and an increase in unemployment. That is the terrible price we're paying now for not getting inflation under control sooner. And that is the price we'll have to pay again if we don't keep inflation under control.

Interview/U.S. News & World Report, 12-6:64.

Nicholas Fidandis
*Director, Federal Mediation
and Conciliation Service*

3

We've never seen anything like this, so few [labor] strikes, unions so wary of going out. In years past, we had a pass-through economy, with the customer getting the bill. But now employers are being held more accountable for their costs and they have to take a stronger stand at the bargaining table. And the unions are recognizing the reality of this.

The New York Times, 7-27:10.

Gerald R. Ford
Former President of the United States

4

[On President Reagan's "supply-side" economic program] : Don't use that term with me! I don't associate myself with supply-side. Economic recovery is achievable with a pragmatic economic policy. We did it during my years in the White House. [President Reagan's] program is a gamble. It may not work. I hope it does. And I strongly support his basic thrust to correct the economy he inherited. As the recession expands and accelerates, there is no question in my mind that the Administration will have to expand and extend certain social safety-net programs. The President has to deal with the world as it is now, as opposed to some theory. For example, you have to help people get jobs who have lost them, and help those people while they seek work. The Reagan Administration, despite its firm stand on reducing government expenditures, in certain areas they'll have to face the real world. The supply-side theory has to bend to reality.

Interview, New York/Parade, 4-4:7.

Douglas A. Fraser
*President, United Automobile
Workers of America*

5

Many of the politicians in Washington don't really understand unemployment, the frustration it brings. You have to either experience unemployment to really understand it or be close enough to feel it, to touch it. It's a horrible experience—being ready and willing and able and anxious to work to support yourself and your family and unable to find a job. It's an absolute tragedy, and it is because we've been through such horrible times that job security is most prominent in the minds of our members.

Interview/U.S. News & World Report, 5-3:78.

John Kenneth Galbraith
*Professor emeritus of economics,
Harvard University*

6

It's very important not to be caught up in this—what shall one call it?—propaganda of my profession. Economists, my fellow econo-

(JOHN KENNETH GALBRAITH)

mists ... some of them have a very great investment in what is somewhat elaborately called the free market. That is what they teach, that's what's in the textbooks, that's what they're brought up with, and they are never accommodated to the age of large corporations and large trade unions. This, I say, is a minority, because I think at the present time probably a majority of economists would say that an incomes and price policy is necessary.

Broadcast interview/
"Meet the Press,"
NBC-TV, 7-25.

1

[On proposals for a flat-rate income-tax system]: Oh, I would be opposed to that. The tax system could and should be simplified, and we've worked into it an enormous number of loopholes, but I would not back away from the idea of higher percentage rates for the affluent than for the poor. This is one of the civilizing steps that the tax system has introduced, one of the reasons the system itself is tolerable. We should always remember that we promote social tranquility by having a few screams of anguish from the very rich. It's very good to have people think that *they're* complaining, too.

Broadcast interview/
"Meet the Press,"
NBC-TV, 7-25.

2

Reagonomics consists of two main elements: tax cuts to spark growth, and monetary policy to hold down inflation. But these two things cannot work together; for monetary policy slows growth as well as inflation. It drives up interest rates, prevents businesses from investing and cancels out the influence of tax reductions. The results are growing budget deficits, rising interest rates and higher unemployment. One cannot swim upstream and downstream at the same time.

Interview/Chicago Tribune,
8-12:(1)11.

Robert Georgine
President, building trades department,
American Federation of Labor-Congress
of Industrial Organizations

3

Our members are in an angry mood—angry about the lack of work, angry about being denied unemployment-compensation benefits, angry about being denied food stamps when they need them, angry about being taken for granted by the Democrats and being shunned by the Republicans.

At Building and Construction Trades
legislative conference, Washington,
April 5/Los Angeles Times, 4-6:(I)10.

Robert G. Gibson
President, Illinois division,
American Federation of Labor-Congress
of Industrial Organizations

4

[On concessions made by labor in its negotiations with management during the current recession]: It seems to me that once you begin giving back things [to management] it becomes a vicious cycle and the only losers are the workers. A perfect example is the steel companies. You make concessions and they have a good year and instead of building or improving steel mills they go out and try to buy an oil company.

Chicago Tribune, 1-3:(1)12.

Barry M. Goldwater
United States Senator, R—Arizona

5

The President of the United States [Reagan] has been traveling across the broad reaches of our West and saying on TV that we need a vast increase in taxes. In Washington, his lieutenants, captains and generals are pleading, begging and now downright threatening members of the Republican Party that unless they vote for this tax increase, they will no longer receive favors from the President. Now, I have been a Republican all my adult life, much longer, in fact, than the President of the United States has been a Republican. I intend to vote against the tax increase. I intend to vote against it because I have been living under a concept of fiscal

(BARRY M. GOLDWATER)

stability for a long, long time, and I'm not going to change at this late date.

Before the Senate, Washington, Aug. 18/
The New York Times, 8-19:12.

Alan Greenspan

Former Chairman, Council of Economic
Advisers to the President of the
United States (Gerald R. Ford)

1

This is the first time in my memory when the outlook for the international economy is forcing analysts to scale back their short-term domestic projections here in the United States. The international picture is impinging very seriously on the domestic outlook and creating a clear fear that is beginning to spill over into domestic decision-making.

At economic symposium, New York,
September/Time, 9-27:44.

Walter W. Heller

Professor of economics, University
of Minnesota; Former Chairman,
Council of Economic Advisers to
the President of the United
States (John F. Kennedy)

2

[On President Reagan's program of income-tax cuts for individuals] : It has not delivered anything it promised to deliver. That is not to say that tax cuts won't stimulate more investment. It is just the notion that cutting the gizzards out of income taxes will produce torrents of work effort and savings—that is what is just nonsensical.

The New York Times, 6-30:1,29.

3

I'm not blaming labor for inflation, but labor is the engine that perpetuates it. I mean the wage process perpetuates it once it gets going. You've got to cut back on wages, and eventually, not too long [after that], price inflation will slow down, too. That's a very bitter pill for the Democrats to swallow. But the economic logic is impeccable, and the political dangers [of failing to act] are patent.

Interview, Washington/
The Washington Post, 7-25:(G)18.

Luther Hodges, Jr.

Chairman, National Bank
of Washington (D.C.)

4

Interest rates are not unlike energy prices. Prices of both energy and money are at new levels, reflecting the economic realities of today. We have finally become accustomed to high energy prices, but it has taken some eight to 10 years of quite painful adjustment to do so. By the same token, we will have to make a similar adjustment to higher interest rates. My concern is that while we successfully adjusted over time to a new energy environment, we are being asked to adjust to the new interest-rate scenario in some 24 months. This could be more than we are prepared to handle.

Before National Bank of Washington
shareholders, Washington, March 16/
The Washington Post, 3-17:(D)8.

Andrew Jacobs, Jr.

United States Representative,
D—Indiana

5

For this [Reagan] Administration to brag about reduction in inflation is like saying that the patient died but the good news is that he's eating less.

The Washington Post, 6-6:(H)5.

James R. Jones

United States Representative,
D—Oklahoma

6

We have an [Reagan] Administration that denies responsibility for the conditions of today. It alleges that the [Federal] deficits are the creations of past Administrations and of Congress. And because the President says it over and over again, the American people believe it is so. The sources of the increased deficit are plain: defense spending, interest on a ballooning debt and the Reagan tax cut ... The 1982 Reagan Administration program created those deficits. The 1983 Administration-backed budget left those deficits untreated, to grow like a malignant tumor, spreading into and destroying healthy sectors of our economy as well as weak ones.

At National Governors Conference, Afton,
Okla., Aug. 8/Chicago Tribune, 8-9:(1)4.

(JAMES R. JONES)

1

[Arguing against President Reagan's proposed Constitutional amendment that would require a balanced Federal budget]: Rather than face reality, the President calls for and the Senate passes an amendment which, if it is effective, could throw economic policy into the Federal courts and plunge the nation into recession. The Senate has approved it. The House may well do the same, even though the overwhelming majority of members fully recognize the hypocrisy and folly of the proposal. The members know, and I believe the public knows, that the amendment is as bogus as a $3 bill. But if the President leads a full-scale charge, it may pass.

At National Governors Conference,
Afton, Okla., Aug. 8/
The Washington Post, 8-9:(A)9.

2

Sensible tax policy does not dictate that you automatically reduce taxes in the face of a larger national economic need. Consequently, we should modify or defer the third installment of the [forthcoming Federal income-] tax cut—which costs about $30-billion per year in revenues—until we don't have to borrow to pay for it.

Washington, Dec. 9/Los Angeles Times, 12-10:(1)6.

Henry Kaufman
Managing director, Salomon
Brothers, investment bankers   *3*

[On how to control the Federal budget deficit and fight inflation]: We should cut the tax reduction of 10 per cent scheduled for this July to 5 per cent. We should also rescind the tax cut scheduled for 1983 as well as indexing of the tax structure that is to take place in 1985. To go along with that, I would do away with all indexing of government programs, including Social Security. We ought to create a budgetary process where we are all at stake in the inflationary process. If the taxpayer or the recipient of government checks gets hurt by inflation, then he will be against inflation. If we index either taxes or benefits, then we are accepting inflation rather than fighting it.

Interview/U.S. News & World Report, 4-12:35.

David T. Kearns
President, Xerox Corporation

4

There's a lot of talk these days about unemployment which, I'll concede, is way above acceptable levels. But it bothers me that nobody is saying much about the other side of the coin—and that is employment. I wonder how many people know that our economy is generating jobs for a near-record number of working-age Americans. Today, the employment rate is 57 per cent. That's only two percentage points below the all-time high we had in 1979. What's more, 30 years ago—when the unemployment rate was only 2.5 per cent—the employment rate was actually lower than it is today. So there's more than enough work to do in this country. The problem is matching the workers with the work.

Before American Business Press, Boca Raton,
Fla./The Christian Science Monitor, 7-20:23.

Jack Kemp
United States Representative,
R–New York

5

I'm firm on keeping in place the tax restructuring we passed in Congress last year. In fact, I wish we had cut the tax rates on capital and labor earlier and deeper. I also wish we would move up the rate reduction on individuals to January, or even April, rather than July of 1982 and 1983. In other words, we should aim our policies at expanding the economy and lowering interest rates. The deficit is a manifestation of a sick economy, and you can't balance the budget without health in the economy. I want to disassociate myself from the idea that you can fight inflation by slowing down the economy.

Interview/U.S. News & World Report, 4-5:39.

6

[Criticizing President Reagan's tax-increase program]: As long as you ... don't use the telephone, don't have big medical expenses, don't pay medical insurance premiums, don't suffer losses due to theft or casualty, don't smoke, don't ride in airplanes, don't have a savings account ... you won't be affected.

The Washington Post, 8-18:(A)4.

83

Donald M. Kendall
*Chairman, PepsiCo, Inc.; Chairman,
Chamber of Commerce of the United States*

1

It's a mistake to focus on the short-run outlook for the economy. The basic fundamentals are already in place for a recovery. President Reagan and his Administration have been looking at the long term. All we have to do is be patient and keep Congress from doing some foolish things that will have absolutely no impact now but are apt to cause higher inflation later. For instance, this talk of postponing the next several phases of the tax cuts is ridiculous. When the economy is down, you don't increase taxes. Furthermore, while I want to see the deficit reduced, you don't do it by increasing taxes. The way to reduce the deficit is to cut spending, and the only way to do that is to send less money to Washington in the form of taxes. We haven't begun to do all the things that could be done to decrease spending. It really gets me that members of Congress are making all this noise about a big deficit, yet they go merrily on their way, increasing spending over what the President has recommended. Why do we have to have these unjustified agriculture subsidies? Why do we have to have land-bank programs? Members of Congress continue to do things to increase the deficit, yet publicly complain about the Reagan deficit.

Interview/U.S. News & World Report, 4-5:36.

Edward M. Kennedy
*United States Senator,
D–Massachusetts*

2

You can't equate President Reagan's tax cut last year with President Kennedy's tax cut of the 1960s ... The answers for the 1960s are not the answers for the 1980s. Second, when my brother's tax cut was passed, interest rates were only 4 per cent, there was hardly any inflation at all, and the Federal deficit was close to zero. Today, as a result of the [Reagan] Administration's economic plan, we have seen record interest rates and a new recession. And now we face the prospect of enormous, endless deficits. Finally, President Kennedy's tax cut was fair to the middle class and the working

families. But the Reagan tax cut gives the most to the very wealthiest individuals and corporations, including $33-billion in new tax subsidies for the oil industry.

*Broadcast rebuttal to President Reagan's
State of the Union address, January/
U.S. News & World Report, 2-8:76.*

Lane Kirkland
*President, American Federation of
Labor-Congress of Industrial Organizations*

3

There has been more nonsense talked about productivity than any other issue. Historically, productivity has been increased by adding energy and tools to human effort. If it were only a matter of how much more effort can be extracted from workers, then productivity would have peaked with the building of the pyramids. The real sources of productivity gains have been cheap and abundant energy and cheap and abundant capital. I know of no better way to destroy productivity than reversing these elements as we are seeing today. There is an almost perfect correlation between the level of economic activity and productivity.

Interview, Washington/The New York Times, 1-30:8.

4

The characteristic of this recession that sets it apart from all others in modern history is that the White House has no plan, no ideas and apparently no interest in trying to reverse the economy's downward plunge. Instead, the [Reagan] Administration has reduced unemployment-insurance benefits, training programs and welfare programs at the same time that it has put more people on the streets in search of such help. One has to look back 50 years to see such a heartless official reaction to the hardship and suffering of millions of unemployed Americans.

Interview/The Washington Post, 1-31:(D)6.

5

The evolution of trade unionism in my lifetime has brought about the democratization of privilege—that is to say, of education, leisure, travel, good health care and housing and other advantages for centuries reserved to the few—to an extent previously unknown in history. That

(LANE KIRKLAND)

process, in turn, has created new industries, services, markets and opportunities for enterprise. Can anyone reasonably hold that these advances, these revolutions of our time, have impaired rather than enhanced the capacity of man and woman to stand free and independent before the state or any other stronghold of power?

The Washington Post, 10-28:(A)22.

Edward I. Koch
Mayor of New York

1

I never understood the idea that work is demeaning. I mean, blacks and whites who grew up in the '60s say, "I can't take this job; it's beneath me." I never understood that. Be a *dishwasher?* Listen, I was a busboy, and I became Mayor of New York. If you ask a kid today to be a busboy, he'll say, "Oh, that's a dead-end job!" Am I right? I mean, some of the recent leaders of this country—the academics, the elitists—have sold us a bill of goods. Now if you get a job, you have to come out a professor or a lawyer. Or the kid's got to go to college. Why does everybody have to go to college? Why?

Interview, New York/Parade, 8-1:11.

Helmut Kohl
Chancellor of West Germany

2

We have lived beyond our means. And some people, including some political leaders, have kept believing that you can live better and better while at the same time working less and less. We now have to face the most challenging economic situation since the end of the war. There has been too much public spending, and there are more debts than ever before. Here again we come back to a moral question: Does our generation have a right to burden the following generations with debts to the extent that they no longer have a future?

Interview, Bonn, November/Time, 11-15:54.

Otto Lambsdorff
Minister of Economics of West Germany

3

Even optimists should not have, over all, any illusions that the interest [-rate] level in the United States could go down quickly, fundamentally and permanently. For it seems to me that in U.S. economic policy, there is a fundamental conflict between monetary and finance policy.

The New York Times, 3-14:(4)4.

Jim Leach
United States Representative, R–Iowa

4

One of the great problems over the last decade has been substantial Federal deficits. I don't think they're accidental. A lot of Democratic candidates get elected by isolating every interest group and promising whatever the maximum that group wants. On the Republican side, more and more are obligated to everyone seeking every conceivable tax cut. If you have a Congress wedded to extremism in spending and extremism in tax cuts, you lose discipline, so it's no accident we have inflation; it's not unrelated to the campaign issue.

Interview/The New York Times, 10-12:12.

Rene Levesque
Premier of Quebec, Canada

5

One is not a bad social democrat if he realizes that it is no panacea to try to solve all economic problems by spending more money from the public budget.

*At Parti Quebecois congress, Montreal,
Feb. 14/Los Angeles Times, 2-15:(I)9.*

Sar A. Levitan
*Professor of economics and director,
Center for Social Policy Studies,
George Washington University*

6

Even if this [Reagan] Administration's economic plan works, there is still the question of equity. Why should the lower segments of the income distribution be the group that in effect finances this program? ... This segment of society is being told, "Pay now and you *may* fly later—if any seats remain and after all the others get their goodies first."

Newsweek, 4-5:19.

Russell B. Long
United States Senator, D—Louisiana

1

Until we get the [Federal] budget under control we have no right promising continued tax cuts. The reason that tax cuts are not working is that we gave the people an overdose ... There's only one way to balance it; that's to raise enough revenue to pay it. Now, you can cut spending, sure. But after you've cut it as much as you can cut it and you're still running a deficit of over $100-billion [as now], how else are you going to balance the budget?

The New York Times, 3-29:12.

2

Many persons have asked what I think of proposals to replace our progressive-rate income-tax system with a so-called flat-rate income tax. My answer to them is simple: "If you're rich, you'll love it; if you're not rich, look out."

Before the Senate, Washington, Sept. 16/
The New York Times, 9-27:12.

Trent Lott
United States Representative,
R—Mississippi

3

[On criticism of President Reagan's economic program]: ... you cannot, and the American people I don't believe expect us to, turn this Ship of State around in one year that has been headed in the wrong direction for many years. [House Speaker, Democrat] Tip O'Neill was in Congress when I was in junior high school and Ronald Reagan was an actor, and you come right on through the process. He was Speaker when I was still in college, and when Ronald Reagan was doing *Death Valley Days* [on TV]. I mean, we [Republicans] have just gotten here. Now, we've turned the rudder of the Ship of State, but the bow of a ship turns very slowly, and as I grew up in my home town of Pascagoula watching those ships come out of the channel, I knew it's a slow process. We're going to work toward that goal, and in a period of time, we'll have to shoulder responsibility; but give us a chance.

Broadcast interview/"Meet the Press," NBC-TV, 5-16.

Richard G. Lugar
United States Senator, R—Indiana

4

[On the current recession]: The facts of life are, ladies and gentlemen, that we [Republicans] now are the party that's responsible. We can't, at this Lincoln Day, point to the Democrats with alarm and say, "Those folks have done this to us; kick the rascals out and if we were there, something else would happen." Ronald Reagan is our President. Republicans are in charge of the Senate.

At Republican banquet, Franklin, Ind., April/
The Washington Post, 4-27:(A)2.

Marc L. Marks
United States Representative,
R—Pennsylvania

5

[Criticizing Reagan Administration economic policies and the effects they have had on the country]: The time has come to stop this massacre ... The time is now to call out to thinking women and men everywhere to raise their voices against this murderous mandate that is being carried out. [We have] a President and his cronies whose belief in Hooverism has blinded them to the wretchedness and to the suffering they are inflicting. [Victims include] the sick, the poor, the handicapped, the blue-collar and white-collar workers, the small-business person, the black community, women of all economic and social backgrounds, men and women who desperately need job training, families that deserve and desire the right to send their children to college; in fact, anyone and everyone, other than those who have been fortunate enough to insulate themselves in a corporate suit of armor.

Before the House, Washington,
March/Time, 3-22:35.

Roger J. Marzulla
President, Mountain States
Legal Foundation

6

... civil liberties in this nation are dependent upon economic liberties, and the only economic system which is consistent with democracy is the free-market system. If the government controls the means of production,

(ROGER J. MARZULLA)

if it controls the way in which you make your living, then you cannot expect the government to avoid controlling freedom of speech, freedom of religion and so on.

Interview/The New York Times, 7-20:30.

James A. McClure
United States Senator, R–Idaho

1

[On the inability of the President and Congress to agree on a budget] : The country is hurting. The economy is fragile. Well-managed companies and well-managed farms are right on the edge of bankruptcy. They can't wait for a more refined solution while we haggle over the terms. Something has to be done, and done now. We've got to get our act together. There's no doubt the economy is going over the cliff if we don't produce a budget document soon.

Addressing President Reagan, Washington, May 3/Los Angeles Times, 5-7:(I)1.

Paul W. McCracken
Professor of business administration, University of Michigan; Former Chairman, Council of Economic Advisers to the President of the United States (Richard M. Nixon)

2

Nations fundamentally get the performance of economic progress for which they ask by the social and economic policies they pursue. If what they get is not what they want, it is national policy and bad luck that is at fault . . . The economic success stories in contemporary history have been societies that have placed basic reliance on a liberal, market-organized economic order. This is the system that can take advantage of the knowledge and creativity that inhere in people generally, and this . . . is the critical "natural resource" for any nation.

At International Monetary Conference, Vancouver, B.C., May/The Christian Science Monitor, 5-28:11.

Francois Mitterrand
President of France

3

It's important to fight inflation, but if the fight against inflation amounts to lethargy,

what does that mean? Remember that when you are dead you cannot catch cold.

To reporters, Paris, May 28/ The Washington Post, 5-29:(A)16.

Walter F. Mondale
Former Vice President of the United States

4

All across the American economic scene, there is suffering, rising unemployment, bankruptcies, now threats of bankruptcies of major industries . . . and the rest. I am not predicting a depression, but there is great fear in America.

March 7/Los Angeles Times, 3-8:(I)1.

5

Everyone is pleading with the President [Reagan] to abandon his [economic] program . . . But the President won't budge. He's seen too many Westerns, the ones where the Lone Ranger toughs it out on his own until the cavalry comes to his rescue. What the President doesn't realize is that it's already high-noon for our economy. The hands at the O-K Corral have all been laid off. Tonto's unemployment benefits have just run out.

At AFL-CIO Building and Construction Trades Department conference, Washington, April 6/The Washington Post, 4-7:(D)7.

Donald A. Nichols
Former Deputy Assistant Secretary of Labor of the United States

6

. . . the enormous redistribution of income that will be caused by the recent [Reagan Administration] tax [-cut] and budget [-cut] decisions may polarize society and politics in a way that will make economic policy difficult to execute for years . . . Current policy may reflect an over-reaction to some dissatisfaction with the previous distribution of the pie. To the extent that the new distribution is not broadly supported, however, we may have seen only the first of a series of swings in distribution. They are dangerous not only in themselves, but because they underscore existing divisions and inequalities that separate us as a people.

At National Policy Exchange/ The Washington Post, 2-5:(A)26.

WHAT THEY SAID IN 1982

Thomas P. O'Neill, Jr.
United States Representative,
D–Massachusetts

1

The President [Reagan] offered a raw deal to the Democrats and to the American people. He advocated that we continue his economic program, which has brought hardship to millions and brought historic rates of unemployment and business bankruptcy. [In the budget battle,] the President offered more of the same: an economic program that is not working; soft treatment for the well-to-do; and another brutal cut at those who have already been hurt the most by the Reagan program.

U.S. News & World Report, 5-10:21.

Rudy Oswald
Chief economist, American Federation of
Labor-Congress of Industrial Organizations

2

I would not be surprised if unemployment [during the current recession] tops 10 per cent, and it is possible that it will rise as high as 12 per cent. In every other recession, the government was willing to really try to turn the economy around with new jobs programs and other projects. I see this [Reagan] Administration trying to immobilize any such action because of the [budget] deficit . . . There really is not a basic trade-off between the current inflation rate and unemployment, except over a very long term and with unemployment at very severe levels. Most of the inflationary forces of recent years, such as energy, food and interest rates, were not particularly related to changes in employment and unemployment. And the cooling off of inflation over the last few months has not been brought about by unemployment either.

The New York Times, 1-10:(1)10.

William Proxmire
United States Senator, D–Wisconsin

3

The Number 1 necessity for this Congress is to cut the deficit by 30 billion to 50 billion dollars below the 91 billion in the President's budget recommendation for fiscal 1983. Unless we do that, we are throwing in the towel in the anti-inflation and anti-high-interest-rate fight. I

would raise revenues by, among other things, repealing the expensing of oil and gas drilling, repealing the business entertainment allowance and imposing a tax on effluent emissions into the air and water. On the expenditure side, we have to cut everywhere, including entitlement programs. One of the biggest explosions in spending has been in health. So I favor putting some kind of cap on Medicaid costs, for example. I feel very strongly that we have to eliminate revenue-sharing. We don't have any revenue to share. In the area of defense, we're spending an enormous amount of money, but we're not really strengthening our military forces.

Interview/U.S. News & World Report, 3-8:52.

Jane Bryant Quinn
Economics writer

4

Where our country is in trouble, it is where people have refused to change . . . in the auto industry, where they kept on building big cars; in the savings-and-loan industry, where they kept on offering low-interest savings accounts. We are in trouble wherever people predicted that past trends would always continue.

At Ithaca (N.Y.) College commencement/
U.S. News & World Report, 6-7:66.

Ronald Reagan
President of the United States

5

We believe, as did Thomas Jefferson, that what people earn belongs to them. Government shall not take from the mouth of labor what bread it has earned. Despite massive resistance from tax spenders, we put together the greatest collection of incentives in 50 years to help working Americans rebuild their financial security. In the months ahead, if they work or save more than they did before, their reward will be greater for it—and greater than it was. These incentives are just beginning. More will follow and people will take advantage of them. Dollar-by-dollar, one day at a time, they'll start saving for their future again. And as they do, they're going to save America's future . . . Surprisingly, it won't take much. If America can increase its savings rate by just 2 percentage points, we can add nearly $60-billion a year to our capital pool

(RONALD REAGAN)

to fight high interest rates, finance new investments, new mortgages and new jobs. I believe a country that licked the Great Depression and turned the tide in World War II can increase its savings rate by 2 percentage points—and will.

Before New York Partnership, New York,
Jan. 14/The New York Times, 1-15:9.

1

[On the beginning of his Administration's second year]: As a team, we are about to launch our second season, and it's going to be a tough one. Only our best will be good enough. As the old saying goes, when you're up to your armpits in alligators, it's sometimes hard to remember that you're here to drain the swamp. But that is why you're here and I'm here: to cut back on waste and mismanagement; to eliminate unnecessary, restrictive regulations that make it harder for the American economy to compete and harder for Americans to find jobs; to drain the swamp of over-taxation, over-regulation and runaway inflation that has dangerously eroded our free way of life.

To Administration officials, Washington,
Jan. 20/The New York Times, 1-21:43.

2

For years, out on the mashed-potato circuit, long before I ever thought I'd be a part of government—never had any ambition to be that—I called attention to the fact that years ago the Democratic majority . . . had adopted deliberately a policy of planned inflation, and . . . they said that a little inflation was necessary to create prosperity, and they claimed that it could be controlled. And I used to proclaim in my mashed-potato appearances that it was like radioactivity—that it was cumulative and you could not continue it without it one day getting out of control. And one day it got out of control.

Interview, Washington, Jan. 20/
Los Angeles Times, 1-21:(I)2.

3

[On political pressures to alter his economic program]: We will not play hop-scotch economics, jumping here and jumping there as the daily situation changes. To the paid political complainers, let me say as politely as I can: Put up or shut up. We have a solid plan already in place. What do they have?

Before Indiana Legislature, Indianapolis,
Feb. 9/Los Angeles Times, 2-10:(I)1.

4

. . . I have little time for parade walkers who march out to denounce the projected [Federal budget] deficit on television, but then slip back behind closed doors to bust the budget in their committees. A propaganda campaign would have us believe we have high deficits because Americans are not taxed enough. Well, taxes doubled between 1976 and 1981, and the deficits grew and grew.

Before Tennessee Legislature, Nashville,
March 15/The New York Times, 3-16:11.

5

[Saying TV news coverage contributes to the delay in economic recovery]: You can't turn on [the] evening news without seeing that they're going to interview someone else who has lost his job, or they're outside the factory that has laid off workers and so forth—the constant downbeat that can contribute to slowing down a new recovery that is in the offing . . . [TV is] an entertainment medium . . . looking for the eye-catching and spectacular. Is it news that some fellow out in South Succotash someplace has just been laid off, that he should be interviewed nation-wide?

Interview/The Washington Post, 3-18:(A)1.

6

. . . perhaps at last we have learned . . . that you can't drink yourself sober or spend yourself rich, that you can't prime the pump without pumping the prime, that you can't give government all the running room it asks for without stampeding the money supply and running up inflation and unemployment. Our Administration has been reminding the American people that the economic mess we inherited last year—and the recession we're in now—is the legacy of years of misguided policy . . . In spite of this, our [economic] proposals weren't even enacted into law before certain voices—the same voices that in the past had recommended

(RONALD REAGAN)

the easy solutions of tax and tax, spend and spend—came up with more easy solutions. Rather than come to grips with the problem of excessive Federal spending, they urged us to once again make government bigger by increasing its revenue. There were suggestions that we rescind individual tax cuts or eliminate that truly historic reform of tax indexing ... I believe in a speech to your organization some years ago I said: "Government doesn't tax to get the money it needs—government always finds a need for the money it gets." Increasing taxes only encourages government to continue its irresponsible spending habits. We can lecture it about extravagance until we're blue in the face, or we can discipline it by cutting its allowance.

Before National Association of Manufacturers,
Washington, March 18/The New York Times, 3-19:13.

1

[Criticizing the "underground economy," where sales and wages go unreported for tax purposes]: The people in this economy are, I'm sure, honest people in most of their activities. They just have a double standard where taxes are concerned ... They can be the friendly neighborhood fixit man, a mechanic, craftsman or member of the professions. They have one thing in common—they prefer to be paid in cash ... As we struggle to trim the [Federal budget] deficit, it's hard not to think about how close that unpaid tax could come to wiping out the deficit. Breathes there a man with soul so dead who never of himself has said, "I owe it to my country and my fellow citizens to quit being a freeloader"?

Radio address to the nation,
Washington, April 24/San Francisco
Examiner & Chronicle, 4-25:(A)1.

2

[Calling for a Constitutional amendment requiring a balanced Federal budget]: Most Americans understand the need for a balanced budget, and most Americans have seen how difficult it is for the Congress to withstand the pressures for more spending. This amendment will force the government to stay within the

limit of its revenues. The government will have to do what each of us does with our own family budgets—spend no more than we can afford. Only a Constitutional amendment will do the job. We've tried the carrot and it failed. With the stick of a balanced-budget amendment, we can stop the government's squandering, over-taxing ways and save our economy.

Broadcast address to the nation, Washington,
April 29/The New York Times, 4-30:10.

3

[On his plan to increase taxes that he says will fall mainly on those who are now under-paying taxes]: The bottom line is this: Would you rather reduce deficits and interest rates by raising revenue from those who are not now paying their fair share, or would you rather accept larger budget deficits, higher interest rates and higher unemployment? ... We warned you in the beginning there would be no instant miracles. If I could correct four decades of fiscal irresponsibility in one year, I'd go back to show business as a magician. You know, that might be more fun—pulling rabbits out of a hat than jackasses out of the way in Washington.

At Billings, Mont., centennial celebration,
Aug. 11/Los Angeles Times, 8-12:(I)1,9.

4

We are not proposing a "quick fix"—an artificial stimulant to the economy, such as we have seen in the several recessions in recent years. The present recession is bottoming out without resorting to quick fixes. There will not be a sudden boom or upsurge. But slowly and surely we will have a sound and lasting recovery based on solid values and increased productivity and an end to deficit spending. It may not be easy, but it is the best way—the only way—to real and lasting prosperity for all our people. Think of it: We have only had one balanced budget in the last 20 years. Let's look forward to the day when we begin making payments to reduce the national debt instead of turning it all over to our children.

Broadcast address to the nation, Washington,
Aug. 16/The New York Times, 8-17:42.

5

[On Labor Day]: This occasion brings deserved attention to those who have toiled to

(RONALD REAGAN)

build our nation and to share a prosperous life out of the dreams of early immigrants. Today we recognize the honor and value of all work and the great distinction that flows from a job well done. As champions of collective bargaining, our workers have furthered a process that has played a major role in America's economic miracle. The legal and proper use of collective bargaining is of primary importance to the continuing development of our nation and the quest for human dignity.

Labor Day message, Santa Barbara, Calif.,
Sept. 5/Los Angeles Times, 9-6:(I)16.

1

To my liberal friends I say: You can't create a desert, hand a person a cup of water and call that compassion. You can't pour billions of dollars into dead-end, make-work jobs and call that opportunity. You can't build up years and years of degrading dependence by our citizens on the government and then dare to call that hope. And believe me, you can't drive our people to despair with prices that wipe them out or taxes which sap their energies, and then boast that you have given them fairness.

Richmond, Va./The New York Times, 10-5:10.

2

[On critics of his economic policy]: [Before 1981, the Democrats] controlled the Presidency, the Senate, the House of Representatives, all the committees of Congress, the entire Executive Branch, the hundreds of departments and agencies responsible for running the Federal establishment. They had the whole enchilada. They controlled everything—everything except inflation, taxes, interest rates and a worsening economy ... There are times when I think some of our critics have been hit by meteors or something because they certainly have developed some interesting cases of amnesia. They have no recollection of the severe economic problems this nation faced prior to the day I took the oath of office. Never in political history have so many know-it-alls been stricken with such severe amnesia.

At University of Nevada, Reno, Oct. 7/
Chicago Tribune, 10-8:(1)4.

3

The leading indicators which measure the vital life-signs of our economy ... were up in September. That is the fifth increase in the last six months. Pretty soon, even the die-hard doom-peddlers will have to admit it: America is on her way back, and we will lead the way out of this world-wide recession. We are not out of the woods yet, but I think we can see daylight beyond the trees. We must stick to our course.

At Republican rally, Salt Lake City,
Oct. 30/Los Angeles Times, 10-31:(I)1.

4

The weakness in this country for too many years has been our insistence on carving an ever-increasing number of slices from a shrinking economic pie. Our policies have concentrated on rationing scarcity rather than creating plenty. As a result, our economy has stagnated. But these days are ending.

At National League of Cities
convention, Los Angeles, Nov. 29/
Los Angeles Times, 11-30:(I)6.

5

[Supporting the next tax reduction due in 1983]: Think back. When was the last time this country enjoyed real growth? When was the last period of boom, when unemployment dropped low, personal savings piled high, real wages grew, investment steadily increased, our industries were pumping at nearly full speed, and our gross national product was climbing? The last great period of American economic growth [and] low inflation rates was in the 1960s, following enactment of the tax-rate cut proposed by President John F. Kennedy. President Kennedy knew, as we know today: All the government boondoggles in the world won't fix what's ailing us. The only way to cure our problems is to get the economy moving again. And one of the best ways to stimulate the economy is to give the American worker a break and cut his or her tax rates.

At National League of Cities
convention, Los Angeles, Nov. 29/
The Washington Post, 11-30:(A)2.

91

(RONALD REAGAN)

1

The solution for unemployed auto workers and steelworkers is not a giant public-works program financed by higher taxes or increased borrowing. America's challenge for the '80s is to invest more and to invest wisely, to make our workers and products more competitive in world markets, to unleash our pioneer spirit of innovation and get this nation back on the cutting edge of growth. Compared to other industrialized countries, our rate of net private investment has been pathetically low. We've been eating our seed corn for more than a decade ... The new tax and spending increase proposed by the opposition won't stimulate the economy; they certainly won't reduce the deficit; and yet, that's all the other side has to offer.

At Republican Senatorial Dinner, Washington,
Dec. 9/The Washington Post, 12-10:(A)8.

Donald T. Regan
Secretary of the Treasury
of the United States

2

[Criticizing the Federal Reserve's handling of the monetary system]: The erratic pattern of money growth that occurred in 1980 and in 1981 ... contributed to the onset of the [current] recession. Such volatile money growth has very damaging effects on the economy. It destroys the credibility of long-run monetary controls, adds to uncertainty and risk and thereby helps keep interest rates high as lenders seek to protect their principal.

Before Congressional Joint Economic
Committee, Washington, Jan. 27/
Los Angeles Times, 1-28:(I)14.

3

Each of us could probably come up with a quick solution [to current economic problems] that might temporarily ease our pain. But quick-and-dirty fixes, no matter how tempting, will only force us deeper into the economic quagmire in which we now find ourselves. We must have the courage to stay with policies that will provide for lasting stable growth and a

permanent departure from the "stagflation" of the last decade. It will not be easy, but we really have no other choice.

Before Organization of Economic
Cooperation and Development, Paris,
May 10/Los Angeles Times, 5-11:(IV)2.

4

I don't think that Reagan economics actually [has gotten] a true test. The recession came on too fast. Officially it was here July 1 [1981]; you could see signs of it in April and May, in hindsight. We didn't see it then, but we see it now in hindsight .... most economists were also caught by how quickly it came after the Reagan programs were announced. After all, they were only announced in mid-February and then, by April, we were into the recession. They [Reagan's economic programs] literally didn't get much of an incubation period before the recession came about .... the recession came from past experiences. I'm not blaming the Carter Administration for this, but what I'm talking about here is what happened in the economy leading up to that. After all, a recession doesn't come on because of something you do 30, 60 or 90 days before the recession starts. The recession comes because of what you have done six months, 12 months beforehand.

Interview/The Washington Post, 6-1:(D)7,8.

Henry S. Reuss
United States Representative,
D—Wisconsin

5

The country is in trouble. The sources of our difficulties are the excesses of the [economic] program proposed by the President [Reagan] and enacted by the Congress last year. The tax cuts were too large. The defense buildup is vast, extravagant and wasteful. Monetary policy too tight. If the President refuses to acknowledge this, then the realistic leaders of Congress on this committee must simply sweep the President out of your way.

Before Senate Budget Committee, March 15/
Los Angeles Times, 3-16:(I)12.

Richard Richards
Chairman, Republican National Committee
1

I go into the farm area, I go into the area with realtors, and they say, "Hey, I'm hurting. I can barely hang on by my fingernails. I hope I can survive, but you're [Republicans] doing what you have to do [with the economy] and I hope it works—and I hope it works before I'm bankrupt" ... The guy who's unemployed, he isn't even going to give us till [the elections of] November of 1982 ... but those who are not unemployed, who are worried about inflation, who are trying to buy a home and can't get the interest rates down, they may give us a little bit more time. But obviously the day of reckoning is coming. One of these days, everyone's going to mark [President] Ronald Reagan's report card where he did well.
Interview, Washington, Aug. 19/
Los Angeles Times, 8-20:(I)9.

Donald W. Riegle, Jr.
United States Senator, D–Michigan
2

[Criticizing the Reagan Administration's economic program]: Why would the Administration want to stay this course? Maybe because so many of the top officials in this Administration are millionaires who have no understanding of what life is like for most Americans. Maybe it's because they have their eyes so fixed on the ticker tape on Wall Street that they don't see the growing pile of pink slips and foreclosure notices shutting down Main Street. The truth is that this Administration has created two courses: one of them a very fast economic track for a few, the other filled with potholes and roadblocks for the rest of us. That's why staying the course makes sense for them—because they're not paying the price. You are.
Broadcast address to the nation,
Washington, Oct. 13/The New York Times, 10-14:16.

Felix G. Rohatyn
Chairman, Municipal Assistance
Corporation of New York
3

Behind the dry statistics so beloved of the economists, one finds growing misery and despair among millions who cannot find work and untold others who have given up trying. [The current falling inflation rate has been achieved] at the price of high and rising unemployment and dangerously deteriorating financial structures. Violence is the handmaiden of despair. It does not take a soothsayer or an alarmist to predict that, if this process continues into the summer, it may be a very hot summer indeed.
Before The Conference Board, New York,
March 16/The Washington Post, 3-17:(D)8.

Charles L. Schultze
Former Chairman, Council of
Economic Advisers to the President
of the United States (Jimmy Carter)
4

A point about tight money: There's no question very tight money does have a payoff in reducing inflation. Secondly, like all good things, there can be too much of it. Tight money is a little like fertilizer. Enough will make the grass grow green and too much will kill it. The question is not whether you have easy or tight money, but whether today's high interest rates and the combination of today's high deficits aren't too much for the economy.
Panel discussion, July/
The New York Times, 8-1:(4)5.

George P. Shultz
Secretary of State of the United States
5

It is by now very apparent that the Communist type of command economy simply doesn't work very well. Look at countries that have taken on that kind of system and look at their economic performances. Compare them with those economies where the people can operate with a little more freedom, where the market system is permitted to function. The comparisons are quite dramatic and quite unpleasant for anyone with a Communist economy.
Interview/U.S. News & World Report, 11-8:28.

Antony Speller
Member of British Parliament
6

[Urging patience to allow U.S. President Reagan's economic program to work]: Stick it

(ANTONY SPELLER)

out. I give you [Americans] a message of good heart: It's the first two years that are the most painful. It's like an operation. An operation isn't much fun and neither is recovering from one. But you'll feel better for it afterwards.

At Republican fund-raising dinner, Dearborn, Mich., April 20/The New York Times, 4-22:14.

Beryl W. Sprinkel
Under Secretary for Monetary Affairs, Department of the Treasury of the United States

1

There is, on the one hand, an argument to keep the [Federal Reserve] independent to avoid the problem of an Administration running away on an inflationary policy. But, on the other hand, the President is elected by all the people, and he has a right to put his policies into being and to be held accountable for them. And since we [the Reagan Administration] have been down here, we have not gotten the kind of monetary policy [from the Fed] that we asked for.

June 19/The New York Times, 6-20:(1)1.

Herbert Stein
Senior fellow, American Enterprise Institute; Former Chairman, Council of Economic Advisers to the President of the United States (Richard M. Nixon)

2

There are some people who think [Federal budget-balancing] was always the right answer in the past and will always be the right answer in the future, but do not think it is the right answer now—meaning while they are in office. There are others who never thought it was the right answer in the past, but are sure it is the right answer now—while the *other* fellows are in office.

Before House Budget Committee, Washington/ The Christian Science Monitor, 3-11:11.

3

The problem with big [Federal] deficits is that too much of the private savings pool is absorbed in financing them, and investment and economic growth are slowed. Furthermore, the fear of deficits that are unlimited in size and time has caused a loss of confidence in the financial markets and is a danger to the recovery. The confidence problem causes interest rates to be even higher than could be rationally explained by the expected Federal borrowing, and that has effects on financial institutions, which could have strong psychological effects on the entire country. There is a danger, though it's not at all probable, that this [current] recession could turn into a depression if the great uncertainty in the financial markets persists and we get some dramatic business failures.

Interview/U.S. News & World Report, 4-5:35.

David A. Stockman
Director, Federal Office of Management and Budget

4

We have a recession under way that suddenly has become deeper and more prolonged than anyone imagined even four or five months ago ... The high interest rates, the unacceptable levels of current unemployment, the lost output ... the financial strains, the rising bankruptcies in the economy, the huge budget deficit that we are dealing with—none of these things are pleasant facts of life. They are all temporary and not permanent. They are all part of the cure, not the problem. They are all a prelude to the recovery, not evidence that the policies should be changed in some fundamental way.

Before Chamber of Commerce of the United States, Washington, March 4/ Chicago Tribune, 3-5:(1)1.

John J. Sweeney
President, Service Employees International Union

5

What [President] Reagan and his supporters have done is bring us to the brink of bankruptcy and then tell us we can no longer *afford* the functions of government that make us a civilized society. He manufactures a fiscal crisis, then tells us we cannot *afford* affirmative action for women and minorities. He creates a

(JOHN J. SWEENEY)

deficit so he can tell us we cannot *afford* an OSHA to guarantee workers' safety on the job. Suddenly we are told we cannot *afford* apprenticeship programs. Or adequate Social Security. We cannot *afford* to feed our hungry . . . And through his words and actions, he is telling the American public that we cannot *afford* the "inflationary" impact of collective bargaining. Is "Reaganomics" anything new? Of course not. It is a slickly packaged recycling of the conservative agenda that has been robbing working people since the dawn of the Industrial Revolution.

The Washington Post, 8-13:(A)18.

D. Garth Taylor
Assistant professor of political science, University of Chicago

1

People are really interested in understanding a lot of ideas that are behind this new set of [Reagan] budget priorities. I can't think of any reasonable systematic challenge that can be mounted to this thing; I think the Democratic programs are still pretty unsystematic and still pretty much discredited. We're in a time where it's not just policies that are changing. There is some new set of ideas that are on the agenda, and people are waiting to see how they will work . . . I don't know that this will still be the attitude a year from now, and I don't know what kind of circumstance it would take to build up a lot of frustration, but people would have to be convinced that things are worse now than they would have been under some other Administration.

Interview/Los Angeles Times, 1-19:(I)11.

Lester C. Thurow
Professor of economics, Massachusetts Institute of Technology

2

I think the real problem with Reaganomics at the moment is that it's sitting around waiting for a spontaneous combustion; the private economy is just supposed to take off on its own. But what we learned, or I think we learned, back in the Great Depression, was,

when the whole world is shut down—and that's really what we've got at the moment; you cannot exaggerate that fact—when the whole world is shut down, you don't get spontaneous combustion. You've got idle capacity everywhere, which means investment is going to continue to fall. The consumer is scared. You've got government spending falling, partly because of demography and the falling school enrollments. And in that circumstance, spontaneous combustion is just not going to occur.

Broadcast interview/"Meet the Press," NBC-TV, 10-3.

James Tobin
Professor of economics, Yale University; Former president, American Economic Association

3

The problem with "Reaganomics" is that it never was a consistent policy from the start. The Federal Reserve Board's restrictive monetary policy to fight inflation is at odds with the President's expansionary fiscal policy to promote economic growth. It's like attaching to a train in New Haven station a locomotive at one end headed east and another one at the other end headed west. The stationmaster announces that the train will leave for both Boston and New York. But, under the circumstances, it's doubtful the train will reach either destination. That's what happened to Reaganomics. One locomotive was Mr. Reagan's tax-reduction bill; the other locomotive was the Fed's tight-money policy. The result of this tug of war was that the President's train stalled, interest rates rose, and we ended up with the deep recession we now have.

Interview/U.S. News & World Report, 2-1:46.

4

[Criticizing the Federal Reserve's tight-money policy]: Monetary policy brought the high interest rates. Those rates crowded out investment and all kinds of interest-sensitive demand for goods and services. This collapse produced the recession, and the recession ballooned the [Federal] deficit for this fiscal year. The only sense in which this year's fiscal policy, including the first two installments of tax reduction, is responsible for today's interest

(JAMES TOBIN)

rates is that by keeping the economy from being even weaker, it prevents interest rates from going a bit lower. In short, it is not that monetary policy is colliding with the economy. Monetary policy would block full recovery whether the demand fuel for recovery were government spending for defense, private spending or tax cuts or entitlements, or spontaneously buoyant private investment or consumption.

At conference sponsored by The
Conference Board, New York, Feb. 24/
The New York Times, 2-25:29.

Bernard Vernier-Palliez
French Ambassador to the United States
1

. . . in the rough times the world economy is experiencing, you cannot be very dogmatic as an economist—you must be very pragmatic. I think everybody comes to power with some dogmas. [French] President Mitterrand and [U.S.] President Reagan, for instance, are applying the program they had promised to apply, which in my opinion is a good way for a politician to act. But of course, they have to adapt this program to the world-wide economic situation. You must have those pragmatisms. Nowadays, no economist can say, "We are right on that question and the other side is wrong"—because there are a lot of question marks.

Interview, Los Angeles/Los Angeles
Herald Examiner, 4-8:(A)5.

Paul A. Volcker
Chairman, Federal Reserve Board
2

[Arguing against a looser money policy in order to lower interest rates] : We cannot . . . give up the fight on inflation by declaring the battle won before it is. The reactions in financial markets and other sectors of the economy would, in the end, aggravate our problems, not eliminate them. It would strike me as the cruelest blow of all to the millions who have felt the pain of recession directly to suggest, in effect, [that] it was all in vain . . . If I could dictate that interest rates would be 8

per cent and everything would be fine, I'd do it. I don't have that power.

Before Senate Banking Committee, Washington,
July 20/Los Angeles Times, 7-21:(I)9.
3

. . . I grew up and was educated in the period when advanced thinkers said a little bit of inflation was a good thing. People thought they were a little richer each year, the profits were always a little higher than expected, it's nice to have the price of your house going up—and, the argument ran, all that will lead to a good economy. In fact, I think there is some truth to that, but it's got a big catch: There's only some truth to it so long as people are "surprised," implicitly or explicitly, by the inflation. Once they begin getting the sense that it's a game, and they're just trying to keep ahead of it but can't, then you've got an entirely different set of circumstances. I think that is the watershed we passed in the '70s.

Interview/The New York Times Magazine, 9-19:77.

Friedrich A. von Hayek
Economist
4

If the concern [of those advocating reflation] is unemployment, reflation will not help anyway. The kind of reflation which they seem to advocate will have no tangible effect. But it will be devastating on the inflation front. Inflationary expectations, which are now beginning to be subdued, would soar and inflationary habits would be resumed. Interest rates are then more likely to rise, the exchange rate reflecting inflation could fall, wage demands will increase, hopes for productivity may suffer. It is very difficult indeed to believe that they don't understand these implications. What are the motives of these reflationists, who urge what will be distinctly inflationary consequences? If it is wrongly conceived compassion, reflation now will not help the disadvantaged.

Interview/The Wall Street Journal, 8-31:22.

Murray L. Weidenbaum
Chairman, Council of Economic
Advisers to the President
of the United States
5

We are carrying out a historic supply-side tax policy. Our determination to put into effect a

(MURRAY L. WEIDENBAUM)

10 per cent tax cut this July followed by another 10 per cent cut next July should be heartening to the truest, bluest supply-sider. Let's face it, conventional Republican economics would have said: Cut spending first and hold off on the tax cuts until you balance the budget. Instead, we're cutting both taxes and spending, which is supply-side economics, as I understand it.

Interview/U.S. News & World Report, 5-10:25.

Murray L. Weidenbaum
Former Chairman, Council of Economic Advisers to the President of the United States

1

[On the Reagan Administration's attempts to cut Federal spending] : On balance, we really haven't cut the budget ... When you add [the increase in defense spending] to the big tax cuts, you get such horrendous deficits. What worries me [about the defense buildup] is that these crash efforts rarely increase national security. They strain resources, create bottlenecks ... We've shifted priorities ... We've cut non-defense spending substantially. But for the first two years, have we on balance cut the budget, not ignoring defense? No. It's a wash.

Interview, Washington/Los Angeles Times, 8-27:(I)27.

2

Over the years, the [Federal Reserve's] independence from the Executive Branch has proven to be useful. It should be preserved. There are enough times in enough different Administrations when officials want easy answers that ignore the inflationary consequences of loose-money policy. Someone is needed to play Hans at the dike—someone to take the flak, who isn't up for re-election. The Chairman of the Fed fills the bill very well.

Interview/U.S. News & World Report, 11-22:62.

Johannes Witteveen
Former president, International Monetary Fund

3

I'm less optimistic about a solution to these American government deficits ... Interest rates will stay high—indeed, they could go even higher. This means that investment will be low. The dollar will stay high and your [America's] exports will be less competitive. Therefore, the recovery [from the recession] in the United States will be postponed in the short term ... After some time, something will have to change. Events will force it. If there is less recovery and if unemployment continues, this growing deficit will have to be reduced—if not this year, then next year ... We [in Europe] very much need a reduction in [U.S.] interest rates. They are a strong brake on the European recovery. But the Europeans have seen that the [U.S.] Reagan Administration is not to be moved on this issue. It doesn't consider the international effects of its policies. That's one of the worrying things.

Interview, Chicago, Jan. 27/Chicago Tribune, 1-28:(3)1.

Albert Wojnilower
Chief economist, First Boston Corporation

4

[On whether the government should continue with current economic policy until inflation is zero] : Absolutely not. That's a form of cultism and is carrying things much too far. It seems to me that we are headed now for an inflation rate of 4 or 5 per cent. If it were up to me, I would stop and declare a victory. It's like going on a diet: You stop eating or you eat much less. But if you diet beyond a certain point of no return, you will never enjoy those new clothes. I think that analogy is quite apt.

Interview/U.S. News & World Report, 10-18:76.

James C. Wright, Jr.
United States Representative, D–Texas

5

[Criticizing Federal Reserve Chairman Paul Volcker for keeping interest rates high] : He is very pleasant; he smiles, puffs on that cigar and looks at you like a benign Buddha. But the decision of Congress and the President to stimulate economic growth has been nullified by the decision, effectively, of one man. If I were President, I would ask for Mr. Volcker's resignation. I'd have someone more responsive to the economic needs of the people.

To reporters, Washington, June 8/ Los Angeles Times, 6-9:(IV)1.

WHAT THEY SAID IN 1982

(JAMES C. WRIGHT, JR.)

1

[Criticizing the personal income-tax cut last year and the similar cut due in 1983]: The average citizen gets practically nothing out of it anyway. It has not stimulated consumer purchases, nor has it stimulated investment and those things in the business community that would create jobs, as it was intended to do. That cut has been in effect now for 21 months. It was retroactive to January of last year. It isn't working. It isn't performing the function that the President [Reagan] had in mind for it. Therefore, it is robbing the treasury of some $96-billion in this fiscal year, which adds that much, of course, to the deficit.

Broadcast interview/"Meet the Press," NBC-TV, 11-7.

Walter B. Wriston
Chairman, Citicorp

2

When you have high interest rates, as we do today, corporations can earn more by investing in financial assets, such as jumbo certificates of deposit, than they can by investing in plant and equipment. They won't step up their capital investments appreciably until they believe the recession has ended and interest rates come down.

Interview/
U.S. News & World Report,
5-31:27.

Coleman A. Young
Mayor of Detroit

3

[President Reagan] really believes that what he is doing for the economy is in the best interests of everyone ... The problem is that Reagan is a barber when it comes to the economy—and what we need is a surgeon.

To reporters/
The Christian Science Monitor,
7-16:4.

Education

Alberta Arthurs
Former president, Chatham College

1

[Saying business should contribute more to higher education]: Government and business today believe they do not need the liberal arts. What tragedies ensue from that misunderstanding! . . . My middle son, Daniel, came home one day and said, "You know what a college president is? A person who lives in a big house and begs."

At Washington College, October/
The New York Times, 10-18:8.

Bruce Babbitt
Governor of Arizona (D)

2

There are some things that states have historically done very well; for example, education. We have the finest education system in the world. It's been a creation and a creature of state and local government. Federal involvement in education has been counter-productive. I believe that it's responsible for some of the decline in quality.

Broadcast interview/"Meet the Press," NBC-TV, 1-31.

William Bentley Ball
Constitutional lawyer

3

[Favoring allowing Federal tax exemptions for private schools, even if those schools practice racial discrimination due to religious beliefs]: It is very clear under the Constitution that a citizen may not be required to recant a religious belief or practice because it conflicts with some kind of governmental idea of what is orthodox. Suppose that sex discrimination violates Federal public policy and that a Catholic seminary refuses to admit women. To deny that institution a tax exemption would be denying it its religious liberty.

Interview/U.S. News & World Report, 2-8:55.

William S. Banowsky
President, University of Oklahoma

4

This is perhaps the most materialistic generation we have seen in this century. They are majoring in the subjects where the bottom line is bucks. Ten years ago nobody wanted to major in business. That was for money-grubbing bigots who polluted the environment and ripped off consumers. Today the hottest degree in the country is the MBA degree, and those who are not majoring in business are majoring in engineering and medicine and law. I am concerned that the pendulum has swung too far. It is alarming when majors in philosophy have decreased by 65 per cent in the last decade, history majors by 50 per cent, English majors by 45 per cent. Perhaps because of our economic climate, we are forcing high-school graduates to decide what they want to be for the rest of their lives when they are 18 years old, and then we force them down some narrow tunnel of specialization. We should be requiring every college student to get a broad liberal-arts education and postpone specialization until graduate school.

Interview/Los Angeles Times, 7-26:(V)1.

Richard E. Berendzen
President, American University

5

The 1980s will be a remarkably transitional time in higher education. We have never been worse off. We've got everything going against us. On the other hand, we've never had greater opportunities before us. We now realize that there is no "right" age to go to school. We have opened higher education to all races. We have learned to blend theory with the practical, incorporating methods such as internships and non-classroom instruction. It's an enormous maturing process.

Interview/Los Angeles Herald Examiner, 9-8:(B)6.

William G. Bowen
President, Princeton University

1

[Saying more top students are opting for lucrative careers in business, medicine, engineering, etc., and fewer are going for Ph.D.s and becoming professors] : The essence of the problem is this paradox: There are too many Ph.D. candidates and not enough quality. Over the long term, we may face the possibility that the quality of teaching and research will diminish and entire fields of knowledge may be weakened. It would be tragic if we were to go through a period when the ablest candidates were discouraged from getting a Ph.D. when, over all, the number of Ph.D.s is still too large for the available jobs.

The New York Times, 3-16:1.

2

In the present economic climate, I worry that students may be less inclined to value knowledge for its own sake and more prone to focus on subjects of immediate practical use. I believe strongly in learning pursued for its own sake, and I believe that this kind of learning also has very substantial vocational benefits—providing individuals with the capacity to think, to write and to reason. Recently, I talked to an alumnus who exemplifies the value of this concept of education. He had majored in chemistry and has been very successful in his career. But he remembers most vividly a course in art history, and the professor who made an indelible impression on him taught Chinese painting. It isn't a matter of either/or. It is possible to study both chemistry and art—and, in fact, I believe that more people should.

Interview/U.S. News & World Report, 5-24:65.

Ernest L. Boyer
President, Carnegie Foundation
for the Advancement of Teaching;
Former Commissioner of Education
of the United States

3

Whether we like it or not, at the age of 15 or 16 people have ideas of their own about what's legitimate and what's Mickey Mouse [about school instruction]. Most kids go to school because the law says they have to or because they have their own personal reasons. We can either just sock it to them—we can crack down on truants and put more guards in the hall—or we can develop institutions that can engage kids in ways that are authentic.

The Washington Post, 1-2:(A)6.

4

[The quality of the nation's schools] can rise no higher than the quality of teaching. If public support continues to decline and if teaching standards continue to go down, the intellectual and economic future of this nation will be threatened ... The teaching profession is caught in a vicious cycle, spiraling downward. Rewards are few, morale is low, the best teachers are bailing out and the supply of good recruits is drying up.

At Yale University, Jan. 20/
Chicago Tribune, 1-21:(1)1.

5

The current folklore says that young people are largely undisciplined and self-indulgent. The larger truth appears to be that we have forced this life upon them. Young people are denied the responsibility of growing up. Since the 1900s, they are biologically more mature and more worldly wise, and yet the rigid lockstep (of schooling and entrance to society) has not changed ... A student who has [via TV] gone with Jacques Cousteau to the bottom of the sea or has traveled with an astronaut to outer space ... or met Leonard Bernstein with the Vienna Philharmonic or listened to the creationism debate on MacNeil-Lehrer—such a student has seen and heard far more than classroom can provide.

Before North Central Association
of Colleges and Schools,
March 28/Chicago Tribune, 3-29:(1)8.

Harold Brown
Former Secretary of Defense
of the United States

6

In domestic economic terms, productivity depends substantially, though by no means entirely, on education. There is no doubt that secondary education is better in Japan and Germany than it is in the United States; and indeed, the bulk of their industrial workers are

(HAROLD BROWN)

more literate than those in the United States. Not being able to read is a great handicap in a technological society.

At Claremont (Calif.) McKenna College commencement/U.S. News & World Report, 6-7:66.

Lois DeBakey
Professor of scientific communication, Baylor University College of Medicine

1

What we are creating is a kind of semi-literacy—a breakdown in the way we communicate with one another. Our regard for language has become so debased that it is destroying the ability even of educated people to evaluate ideas rationally.

U.S. News & World Report, 5-17:53.

John A. DiBiaggio
President, University of Connecticut

2

[Saying more students are applying to public universities since aid reductions make private institutions too expensive]: We have found, as have a number of other public institutions, that students are being driven from the private to the public sector. My fear is that such a trend will tend to modify the character of public institutions by increasing the number of affluent students enrolled and by diminishing access to students from more disadvantaged backgrounds.

The New York Times, 2-7:(1)20.

Peter F. Drucker
Professor of social science and management, Claremont (Calif.) College Graduate School

3

Of every 100 people reaching retirement age today, 80 did not even complete a junior-high-school education; and of 100 entering the labor force today, 50-plus have sat on their rear ends beyond the natural life span of man; and whether they have learned anything remains to be seen, except they are totally disqualified for

honest work. The one reason why one always goes to school was that if you sat long enough you never had to get your hands dirty.

Interview, Chicago, April/Chicago Tribune, 5-2:(5)1.

William Dunifon
Dean, College of Education, Illinois State University

4

In the current labor market, if we are going to attract absolutely the first-rate person to teaching, then we will have to pay salaries that are competitive. And we're going to have to pay teachers on a differentiated salary base—we will probably have to pay an excellent math teacher, physics teacher or chemistry teacher more money than an excellent social-science teacher.

Chicago Tribune, 10-17:(1)4.

Edward T. Foote II
President, University of Miami

5

The whole college-sports system is in danger because we have been giving young men and women athletes the message that we want them only because they can generate money or attention to the university—that we do not want them because they are students.

U.S. News & World Report, 4-5:61.

Ellen V. Futter
President, Barnard College

6

The definition of a women's college has changed. The old, Victorian notion is past. Today, being a women's college doesn't mean being cloistered. At Barnard, we offer the benefits of a women's college and a coeducational environment. And the notion of a women's college as anachronistic would be tantamount to saying that women have completely come of age. I think there are very few today who would say that.

Interview/The New York Times, 5-11:20.

John Kenneth Galbraith
Professor emeritus of economics, Harvard University

7

Many have looked at the world and seen one highly obtrusive fact: There is no country with

101

WHAT THEY SAID IN 1982

(JOHN KENNETH GALBRAITH)

a uniformly literate population that does not have a relatively high and progressive living standard. There is no country with a generally illiterate population that does.

Lecture, New Delhi, India, March/
The Christian Science Monitor, 4-20:12.

John W. Gardner
Chairman, Independent Sector; Former Secretary of Health, Education and Welfare of the United States

1

Somewhere in the '60s, the capacity of the public to remain interested in education seeped away. For 17 years it has been off the public agenda . . . The people who are ideologically at odds with the public schools are modest in number. They sound louder than they are actually influential . . . [But] there are still a lot of negatives in the public mind. We've got to counter the feeling that education is a kind of running sore. When President [Lyndon] Johnson made education a top priority issue, few in Congress dared to vote against it.

Interview, Aspen, Colo./
The New York Times, 8-3:17,20.

John I. Goodlad
Dean, Graduate School of Education, University of California, Los Angeles

2

What our society beyond schools does not do well is to provide sustained cultivation of the higher literacies: sensitivity to phenomena and stimuli, compassion, an inquiring mode of life, an ability to synthesize related events. This is the education that our schools must provide. This is the education most easily squeezed out.

The Washington Post, 1-2:(A)7.

George H. Hanford
President, College Board

3

The fact is that whether from frustration, disillusionment, boredom or impatience, American society in recent years has shown a strong tendency to devalue education. We must do everything to restore education to its place in the hierarchy of national values that we as

educators know it deserves if the other values of the nation are to be preserved, revitalized and transmitted to future generations.

Before College Board, New York, Oct. 26/
The New York Times, 10-27:15.

Caspa L. Harris
Vice president and treasurer, Howard University

4

[On the reduction in Federal aid to students and higher education]: I really feel we're going to come out of this stronger, certainly much wiser. Some institutions are not going to survive—those weaker than others, or in the wrong location, some who have almost priced themselves out of the market. First and foremost, the lesson that has been learned is that education is, first, a business. Prior to this downturn, it was a big ivory tower think tank and nobody paid attention to the fact that somebody had to pay the utility bill.

Interview/Los Angeles Times, 7-26:(V)3.

Gary W. Hart
United States Senator, D—Colorado

5

[Criticizing the Reagan Administration for cutbacks in Federal aid to education]: Our vision demands the best education system in the world. A nation that does not develop the minds of its youth is not a wealthy nation. And if this Administration thinks education is too expensive, wait till they find out how much ignorance costs.

At Democratic Party conference, Philadelphia,
June 25/The New York Times, 6-26:11.

S. I. Hayakawa
United States Senator, R—California

6

We all grew up with the concept of the American melting pot, that is the merging of a multiple of foreign cultures into one. This melting pot has succeeded in creating a vibrant new culture among peoples of many different cultural backgrounds largely because of the widespread use of a common language, English. The issue of English as our official language and bi-lingual education for immigrants is especially timely in light of the 1980 Census Bureau

(S. I. HAYAKAWA)

figures. They show that 23 million people in the United States aged 5 or older speak a language other than English at home. We as Americans must reassess our commitment to the preservation of English as our common language. Learning English has been the primary task of every immigrant group for two centuries. Participation in the common language has rapidly made the political and economic benefits of American society available to each new group. Those who have mastered English have overcome the major hurdle to participation in our democracy.

Before Senate Education, Arts and Humanities Subcommittee, Washington/ Chicago Tribune, 7-30:(1)11.

Jesse A. Helms
United States Senator, R—South Carolina
1

... much of what passes for education in our time is not education at all but indoctrination; and the aim of it is to reconcile the individual with the destruction or repudiation of the moral and ethical patrimony that has sustained the West for thousands of years.

At Grove City (Pa.) College commencement/ Time, 6-21:82.

Ernest F. Hollings
United States Senator, D—South Carolina
2

[Criticizing President Reagan's call for tuition tax credits for private-school education]: The tuition tax-cut proposal would turn our nation's educational policy on its head, benefit the few at the expense of the many, proliferate substandard segregationist academies, add a sea of red ink to the Federal deficit, violate the clear meaning of the First Amendment of the Constitution, and destroy the genius and diversity of our system of public education.

Washington, April 15/The New York Times, 4-16:9.

Robert A. Huttenback
Chancellor, University of California, Santa Barbara
3

I think the time for [faculty] tenure has really passed. The good people don't need it.

What we are most often left with are bums who got tenure when they were young and are now really stealing us blind. It's a rotten system.

Interview, Santa Barbara, Calif./ Los Angeles Times, 9-1:(I)26.

Sheppard Kellam
Psychiatrist; Chairman, department of mental hygiene, Johns Hopkins University
4

The final report card [of a child's first school year] can be a major predictor of success or failure in later life. Starting school is one of life's biggest challenges. It may be tougher than choosing a career and landing the first job, because in first grade there are no choices available. Everybody goes. The first-grade classroom is society, where the child has to survive.

Interview/The Washington Post, 11-17:(B)5.

Mary Ann Leveridge
President, National Parent-Teacher Association
5

It is more complex today and harder for parents to be involved [with their children's school]. The first thing to get involved is to open the door to the schoolhouse. If the school administration wants parents, then parents can get involved, and this makes a difference in achievement. Unfortunately, there are places where parents are not welcome. To get involved means to help, by the way, not to attack the school. Some parents only go to school when they are mad ... What goes on in kindergarten to grade 12 is not the same as 85 years ago. A person who was literate in 1898 would not be considered literate today. Reading, writing and arithmetic have changed. What I learned in physics does not apply today. This expansion of the body of knowledge and its changing nature pushed education beyond memorizing facts. Today, it is important to learn to look up or locate information and know how to use it.

Interview/Los Angeles Times, 6-10:(V)2.

Mitchell Livingston
Dean of student life, Ohio State University
6

[On the current trend of students saying that making more money is an important

(MITCHELL LIVINGSTON)

reason to go to college] : I get a sense of quiet desperation. It's something that's been growing for 10 years but, with the economy, it's getting worse. The students are constantly up, striving to succeed, wondering if there will be a job when they finish. If there is not an immediate benefit, there is less likelihood they will pick a course or go out for an activity. They have become more intense and narrow, with tunnel vision. It's the opposite of what we're trying to do in the university, to broaden them.

The New York Times, 3-7:19.

Thomas L. Martin, Jr.
President, Illinois Institute of Technology

1

I would still say the best preparation [for life] is still the kind we had 35 or 40 years ago. Reading, writing, arithmetic, science, history—the ingredients of a good general education. I don't care whether you are going to be a carpenter, a bricklayer, a steelworker or a college professor, that is where you must start.

Interview, Chicago/Chicago Tribune, 11-29:(1)8.

Charles McC. Mathias, Jr.
United States Senator, R—Maryland

2

[Arguing against Federal tax exemptions for private schools that practice racial discrimination] : . . . we do not use public funds to pay the bills for segregated education. A tax exemption is an indirect use of public funds because, in effect, funds that would otherwise be paid in taxes are allocated for a particular purpose. We simply are not funding segregation in this country any more. There is also a basic question of equity: If you allow some taxpayers to escape taxation on money used for prohibited purposes, then you increase the burden on all other taxpayers for supporting the permissible purposes.

Interview/U.S. News & World Report, 2-8:55.

Willard McGuire
President, National Education Association

3

[Criticizing President Reagan's proposal to grant tuition tax credits for students in private schools] : There can be no justification for spending billions of dollars for private and church-related schools at a time when the Administration says it can't afford to support public schools. That's just plain hypocritical.

Washington, June 22/Los Angeles Times, 6-23:(I)14.

Floretta D. McKenzie
Superintendent of Schools of the District of Columbia

4

. . . parents are the children's first teachers . . . I would like probably for parents to be a little bit more conscious of their teaching role, [even] if it's no more than making sure that the homework is done . . . You can at least find out if there was homework, what the kid is working on presently. Listen, listen to children talk about the school and about what they care about and the teachers and . . . their day. That will add a lot to what we're trying to do at school.

Interview/The Washington Post, 9-1:(DC)1.

Larry Mikulecky
Professor, School of Education, Indiana University

5

Illiterate high-school graduates are only the tip of an iceberg that includes auto mechanics unable to comprehend repair manuals, bureaucrats unable to follow written policy changes, technicians unable to read and understand safety precautions for oil pipelines or nuclear power plants, and anyone else who has found the literacy demands of a job outstripping his or her abilities.

U.S. News & World Report, 5-17:54.

Walter F. Mondale
Former Vice President of the United States

6

We have already entered an economic revolution every bit as profound as the Industrial

(WALTER F. MONDALE)

Revolution. It is the era of high technology—the computer, telecommunications, lasers, biotechnology and much more. It has always been true that most wealth in our nation is the product of the trained mind—but it will be more true than ever in the lives of our children and their children. Our defense, our economy, our jobs and our prosperity, more than ever before, depend upon the trained mind and the skilled hand.

At University of Alabama-Tuscaloosa commencement/
U.S. News & World Report, 6-7:66.

Vincent J. O'Leary
President, State University
of New York, Albany

1

[Saying there are important but less popular education programs that are in jeopardy because of the tight economic condition of many colleges]: There is a strain between things easily measured and those not so easily measured. What is the value of a classics department which teaches Latin and Greek and talks about the sources of thought, against that of a computer-science department where hundreds of students are trying to enroll?

Interview/The New York Times, 3-8:9.

James O'Toole
Associate professor of management,
Graduate School of Business,
University of Southern California

2

In the current system, general, basic, liberal education is provided to the children of the privileged, who then are able to pursue advanced, specialized education in preparation for good jobs. In contrast, narrow vocational education is given to the children of the disadvantaged who then enter the kinds of jobs that technology is eliminating . . . Soon there will only be work for those who have the skills of speaking, listening, observing and measuring, and the confidence to use their minds to analyze and solve problems. [Success will come to those who have] learned how to learn . . . Either America must begin now to educate the disadvantaged in the manner it educates the privileged, or expect a nightmare future.

At Aspen (Colo.) Institute for Humanistic
Studies/The New York Times, 8-10:24.

Clarence M. Pendleton, Jr.
Chairman, United States Commission
on Civil Rights

3

. . . I believe in freedom of choice in education. It's up to the educational system to provide those choices, such as "magnet" schools that offer special programs in the arts or sciences. We can't afford to let another generation of children be pushed through school to graduate as illiterates. Kids need to be challenged, and if the public schools aren't doing the job, parents should be able to use vouchers, tuition tax credits or other means [toward a private schooling] for a better education.

Interview/U.S. News & World Report, 9-27:42.

Robert M. Price
President, Control Data Corporation

4

It's clear enough that the shortage of trained engineers and qualified engineering educators is a root problem with regard to this country's productivity and its international competitiveness . . . . there is an urgent need for a comprehensive national program to increase the number and quality of high-school students seeking an engineering education—particularly among the disadvantaged. An effective community outreach program must involve cooperation by a local college or university, local industry, and the local school system. The second challenge is to improve the productivity of engineering education itself. Our country has a desperate need for improved growth in productivity. What an ironic and tragic thing it would be if that need went unfulfilled because the engineering profession did not apply advanced technology to its own education process.

Before American Society of Engineering
Education, Texas A&M University/
The Christian Science Monitor, 7-21:23.

WHAT THEY SAID IN 1982

Diane Ravitch
Educational historian, Columbia University

1

What we have is an inexorable push toward lower and lower requirements to remain in college, because the colleges have gotten themselves tied into a pork-barrel approach to education, just to keep the seats filled.

U.S. News & World Report, 5-17:55.

Ronald Reagan
President of the United States

2

[On critics of his proposed cuts in Federal aid for college students]: We haven't cut loans. We've cut the cost to taxpayers of making these loans available. [On many campuses,] the students are being told they might not be able to return to school next year. In some instances, they've even been incited to stage protest demonstrations against what have been called Draconian cuts in student aid. Well, a lot of people have simply been misled .... not one dime of the money being cut has ever gone directly for loans to students.

Radio address, Barbados, April 10/
San Francisco Examiner & Chronicle, 4-11:(A)11.

3

[Calling for tuition tax credits for private-school education]: Private education is no divisive threat to our system of education. It is an important part of it ... Excellence demands competition among students and among schools ... Let's remember, without a race there can be no champion, no records broken, no excellence—in education or any other walk of life .... as competition has lessened, so has quality.

Chicago, April 15/The Washington Post, 4-16:(A)7.

4

[Defending his proposal of tuition tax credits for private education]: How high would ... taxes for everyone go if those parents [with children in private schools] decided to send

their children to public schools? I think they're entitled to some kind of relief, since they're supporting two school systems and using one.

Radio address to the nation,
Washington, April 24/San Francisco
Examiner & Chronicle, 4-25:(A)24.

Carl Sagan
Director, Laboratory for Planetary Studies, Cornell University

5

[On his celebrity status resulting from his TV series *Cosmos*]: I think people are much smarter than they're generally given credit for ... And the school system and media and societal conventions don't encourage them. But humans are smart and curious and creative and they hunger for such challenges. So when by luck somebody can present things of this sort, people are grateful. In many cases, people didn't even know that they hungered for it till they came upon it. And suddenly there's a response ... So people personalize it because there's a face and a voice that presents it; but anybody can present that kind of intellectual satisfaction to people every day. So I don't think it's anything deeply personal about me.

Interview, Washington/
The Christian Science Monitor, 7-1:(B)14.

Paul B. Salmon
Executive director, American Association of School Administrators

6

At the very time that President Reagan is advocating severe cutbacks in funds for education, the Department of Defense is demonstrating that it understands we cannot have a strong military force without a well-educated populace ... The need of this country for a viable defense and the behavior of the White House are incompatible. On the one hand, you have the President, who is proposing a cut of more than 50 per cent in Title I [education] funds, and on the other hand you have a study from the Pentagon showing we must do a better job educating disadvantaged students ... When you neglect education it has a delayed effect. For example, if you neglect the education of a 12-year-old today, you may not notice the full

(PAUL B. SALMON)

effect until that student emerges at age 18 as a worker, potential college student or military recruit.

Feb. 21/The Washington Post, 2-24:(A)23.

1

We are making [schooling] decisions today that will affect the people who will chart our country's history between 1993 and 2047. We are a future-oriented society. It is our responsibility to provide education for the group of young people who will be guiding this nation over that period of time. We need to talk about that. We need to let people know that when we cut a budget today, when we cut Title I today, we're having an effect on this country that will begin in 1993 and that will extend to 2047. If you fail to educate those young people, they'll be on your relief rolls. If you fail to educate them, they will be in your jails. If you fail to educate them, they may become rocks around our necks ... We need to teach them to transfer knowledge from books and other sources into their heads ... to integrate that knowledge so that it will become a databank for solving problems. We must teach them how to learn and they will learn and learn and learn. If they do, our future will more than likely be secure.

At American Association of School
Administrators convention, New Orleans,
March/Los Angeles Times, 3-12:(V)17.

John Paul Schaefer
President, University of Arizona

2

Now, in an age when technology has become a dominant force in our society, we cannot afford to waste any of our intellectual human capital. We need to renew our commitment to provide equal educational opportunity to all segments of our society. We need to develop the kind of school systems throughout the country that are color blind, that will push each student to learn and achieve to the limits of individual ability, and that will provide the learning environment where the special magic of the educational process can flourish. That kind of educational environment is within our grasp. We only need demand of our educational

leaders, our legislators and school boards that it be set in place. It won't cost us any extra money, but it will require that parents, teachers and students care enough about education to get involved in the process.

At University of Arizona commencement/
The Christian Science Monitor, 6-11:15.

Harold T. Shapiro
President, University of Michigan

3

The individual states simply do not have the same incentive to ensure—through their tax revenues—an appropriate level of *national* investment in higher education. Why should, for example, the state of North Dakota invest $15,000 or $20,000 per year in a medical student if that doctor may choose to practice in South Dakota or Florida? Mobility of labor is an important strength of our economy and society and, in this context, it seems to me that it is essential for the Federal government to be a partner in financing certain aspects of higher education.

The Washington Post, 7-21:(A)22.

Otis A. Singletary
President, University of Kentucky

4

By its very nature, a university cannot be immediately relevant like the morning newspaper. One underlying assumption of all scholarship is that things look very different after systematic analysis than they do on the surface. Students in a good university are simply not allowed to dismiss a topic as irrelevant because they happen not to understand it or because they are unwilling to study it. Nor is a worthwhile university taken in by the natural tendency of the young to over-simplify the problems of man and society.

At University of Texas at Austin commencement/
The Christian Science Monitor, 6-11:16.

Donnis Thompson
Superintendent of Schools of Hawaii

5

Quality education is taking children to their fullest potential. For the 1980s, several things stick out in my mind. Option, or choice; along with that, quality and total involvement. For

107

(DONNIS THOMPSON)

example, every high school ought not to be the same thing. We've developed a model to prepare children for college. But I don't know that that's the only proper preparation. In some cases a diploma ought to be terminal and we ought to accept that. I don't mean the usual vocational schools. But say a student is . . . interested in communications. Why not prepare him for that? Say an art model with lots of communications courses instead of so many study halls. And besides teachers, we [need] to bring other creative people in to teach. Disc jockeys, artists, for communication. Perhaps businesses could adopt a school.

Interview, Los Angeles/Los Angeles Times, 5-7:(V)2.

Scott D. Thomson
Executive director, National Association of Secondary School Principals

1

We really are confused as a nation about what we want our schools to do, and how. We need some very clear thinking about what we want our schools to accomplish in the new information age. For this we must have a [U.S.] Department of Education . . . [as] a platform, a place to articulate the [education-al] needs of the nation. But it should not be a watchdog agency, an agency that's looking backward. It has to look forward. The U.S. has always had the advantage of being the only nation in the world with universal education through high school, and with [a] strong college college system on board. That no longer is the case. During the '70s, major new investments were made in the school systems of all the other industrialized countries, with the possible exception of Great Britain. We have the kind of competition we've never faced before. We are in a world market where the human resources of other nations are equal or superior to ours. They've learned to take the best of their old systems and the best of ours and challenge us.

Interview, San Francisco/The Christian Science Monitor, 4-9:14.

Stephen J. Trachtenberg
President, University of Hartford

2

The University of Hartford has the organis-mic quality of a corporation—a not-for-profit corporation to be sure, but a corporation nonetheless. It is, among other things, a collec-tive reasoning process—one that cannot depend on taxpayers' money to bail it out if the collective process fails and a really serious error is made. That, I believe, is an atmosphere, a set of assumptions, that rubs off on our students. It may be especially valuable for those who go into business. But it is good for anyone who faces the difficult task of making his or her way through a world in which major "bailouts" are available to very few people.

Lecture, Rockford (Ill.) College/ The Wall Street Journal, 7-27:24.

Barbara Uehling
Chancellor, University of Missouri, Columbia

3

We [in higher education] need an honest willingness to be smaller and to not continue to justify our existence on the basis of how large the budget is, but on accomplishments. It is time to do things smaller and better. The pressures were on us to grow and we did that. We've reached the point where we're spread as thin as we're going to be able to be spread effectively. I think it can be a good time for public universities, but it is a time for them to examine their purposes, do some trimming and come through as better organizations.

Interview/Los Angeles Times, 7-26:(V)2.

Richard Warch
President, Lawrence University

4

There has been an alarming rise in incidents of cheating, plagiarism and other forms of academic dishonesty in American colleges and universities in recent years. Students have rationalized this behavior by referring to the pressures of a tight job market, tough graduate-school admissions standards, and family expec-tations of achievement. Because students view these pressures, standards and expectations as

(RICHARD WARCH)

compelling, actions which seem to serve them are deemed acceptable. As a result, we face a situation in which academic honesty is seen not as absolute but as relative. This situation perhaps should distress us more than it surprises us. For the extent to which intellectual activity is perceived to have no intrinsic worth, to the extent to which higher education is viewed simply as a path to some job, the values embedded in intellectual activity and academic inquiry will be ignored or denigrated. The issue is not that students do not understand the provisions of honor codes, but that they have not been led to appreciate higher education's fundamental demands for integrity and the allegiance to truth.

Convocation address/The Christian Science Monitor, 12-28:23.

James J. Whalen
President, Ithaca College

1

[On the tight economic condition of many colleges]: [College] administrators used to wait for someone to throw a bag of money over the wall, and then they would spend it as they saw fit without anyone really asking what had been done with it. Now there is concern about finding college presidents with a track record in management.

Interview/The New York Times, 3-8:9.

James C. Wright, Jr.
United States Representative, D–Texas

2

Education ... costs money. You may call it big spending, but it doesn't cost nearly as much as ignorance. I think the best investment this country ever made—or with the single possible exception of the Louisiana Purchase—was the G.I. Bill of Rights immediately following World War II, in which we made it possible for an entire generation, my generation, to get higher education. That has paid the government back. It not only has paid the country back in an enriched social fabric and a wealthier economy, but it has paid the government back 12 or 14 times over in the increased taxes that these people were able to pay by reason of their higher earning capacities. Now, it seems to me that what we must do is again to make this nation first in education, first in people. We aren't going to be first in defense, however sophisticated our weaponry, by ignoring education, unless we have the educated manpower and womanpower to do those things that are necessary to keep us first. We only graduated 34,000 in the engineering and scientific and mathematical disciplines this last year. Japan, with half our population, graduated 77,000. Russia graduated 330,000. That alarms me. I think we must do those things that may cost money, but that are investments in America's future.

Broadcast interview/"Meet the Press," NBC-TV, 11-7.

The Environment . Energy

Benjamin M. Alexander
President, University of the
District of Columbia

1

So far . . . Americans have been blessed with a seemingly abundant supply of water, available at the turn of the tap. But there are no guarantees for the future. Perhaps we need a Madison Avenue approach to alert the public and the policy-makers to the need for continuous action, rather than crisis action, on the water problems that lie ahead. It is easy to think of water in terms of daily individual use for drinking and cooking, laundry and dish-washing—forgetting that it takes about 120 gallons to bring eggs to your breakfast table, close to 15,000 gallons to grow a bushel of wheat and 60,000 gallons to produce a ton of steel . . . Although water is plentiful—so far—so are the wide-ranging problems of ensuring a continuous supply of clean water. In this country, preventing and controlling water pollution from toxic substances is still a major issue. As many as two-thirds of the nation's lakes are considered to have serious pollution-related problems. Equally critical is the condition of the aging water systems of our cities.

The Washington Post, 11-24:(A)16.

Zachariah Allen
Vice president, F. R. Schwab and
Associates, energy consultants

2

The government seems to have the opinion that coal is a supply-constrained industry and the only thing preventing it from coming on big is the Federal government sitting on its reserves. That opinion has been shown to be incorrect. Coal, in fact, is a demand-constrained industry. The problem companies are having is lining up customers for the coal they already have.

Los Angeles Times, 7-28:(I)21.

Dean Amadon
Lamont curator emeritus of birds,
American Museum of Natural History

3

We can get intense emotional satisfaction from the sight of a great bird of prey performing . . . in its natural haunts. So when someone asks: "What good is an eagle?" he should be asked, "What good is a Mozart concerto?"

Interview, New York/The New York Times, 6-8:22.

George E. Brown, Jr.
United States Representative, D–California

4

In California alone, assessments of crop losses due to air pollution on all crops are estimated at about $1-billion . . . Some say that having to spend scarce capital on pollution-control technologies is hurting this nation's productivity. But relaxing our efforts to control air pollution will only transfer costs to the farmer.

Los Angeles Times, 2-18:(I)13.

Jimmy Carter
Former President of the United States

5

. . . during the last year and a half there has been such a radical change in environmental policy emanating from the Oval Office [of the President] that our nation has been shocked and deeply troubled. Environmental laws designed to protect the quality of the air, water and land are being circumvented or ignored. Many of our longstanding programs are being eliminated or subverted by executive order or budget policy. Formerly inviolate professional staffs are being summarily dismissed. Public lands, forests and mineral resources are being squandered or sold at giveaway prices . . . This must [now] be our goal: to modify and shape public policy to conform with the ancient bipartisan commitment to a cleaner and more beautiful America. If, in the process, some

(JIMMY CARTER)

political heads roll and some tough battles must be fought and won—so be it.

*Upon acceptance of Wilderness Society's
Ansel Adams Conservation Award, Atlanta/
The Christian Science Monitor, 8-27:23.

Bruce Chapman
Director, Federal Bureau of the Census
1

It has been assumed by a lot of people that more population is better than less—that growth is a sign of health. I'm not sure that's always true. For Phoenix, growing fast also meant sewer-and-water, crime, land-use and taxation problems. In a sense, then, we are going to have the problems of change, as well as the politics of change, all over the country.

Interview/U.S. News & World Report, 3-22:51.

John D. Dingell
United States Representative,
D–Michigan
2

[Saying the Reagan Administration is lax in enforcing environmental laws]: This Administration is short-changing the American people by failing to enforce aggressively those laws which were specifically put in place to protect their interests. The Administration must recognize that the "new Federalism" is not an excuse for undermining the basic foundation of our environmental laws.

Washington, Oct. 10/The New York Times, 10-11:8.

John Dyson
Chairman, New York State
Power Authority
3

[On public objections to power-generating facilities]: You don't want a nuclear plant because it's unsafe. You don't want coal plants because of acid rain. You don't want a garbage plant because you don't want trucks coming in. And you don't want hydropower because the line coming in is unsightly. Nobody wants it in their back yard, but they want to keep using their toaster.

The New York Times, 8-15:(4)6.

James B. Edwards
Secretary of Energy
of the United States
4

[Supporting Reagan Administration plans to dismantle the Department of Energy]: There is only one thing that produces energy, and that's the private sector, which government has hamstrung. Government has interfered with the marketplace, and consumers are paying for it in the long run.

Nation's Business, February:50.

5

[On suggestions of a special tax on imported oil]: I'm absolutely, unalterably opposed. Hardly has the consumer begun to appreciate the blessings of this lull in high oil prices when from all directions come attempts to impose oil import fees and higher Federal and state taxes ... An import fee would distort our demand patterns, create an artificial distinction between domestic and foreign oil and set the stage for a whole new regulatory apparatus that would "entitle" some refiners to special treatment if their oil costs more than somebody else's.

The New York Times, 3-21:(3)4.

6

[On Reagan Administration plans to end the Department of Energy]: I want to close down the Department, bury it once and for all, and salt the earth over it so it won't spring up again ... Every politician has his ego, and I have mine. Mine is that I want to take the Department keys over to the White House, hand them to the President and tell him I'm going home. I want to be the first Cabinet member in the history of the United States to close down a department.

Before Atomic Industrial Forum, New Orleans,
April 6/Chicago Tribune, 4-8:(1)4.

7

The energy crisis is not permanent. We do not subscribe to the theory that the government's role is to sustain a high level of tension and anxiety. Twenty-one months ago, energy was one of our most serious national problems. That era is behind us. We are not yet out of the

(JAMES B. EDWARDS)

woods . . . but the American people now know that our energy problems are being controlled.

Before National Press Club, Washington, Oct. 28/Chicago Tribune, 10-30:(1)4.

John Glenn
United States Senator, D—Ohio

1

[On Reagan Administration plans to dismantle the Department of Energy]: The Administration's proposal may be penny-wise in the short run, but it's as pound-stupid as anything I've seen in Washington in recent years.

Nation's Business, February:50.

Anne M. Gorsuch
Administrator, Environmental Protection Agency of the United States

2

[Calling for a reversion to the 1980 standards for auto emissions rather than using the more stringent 1981 standards as a way of keeping car prices more affordable]: There is no reason why a worker in Detroit, Michigan, can't have his bread and butter, and clean air. And it would be a shame if we were to seriously compromise his chances of having a job simply because of a poorly formulated environmental policy . . . [If the 1981 standards are adhered to,] more and more dollars will be spent to remove smaller and smaller amounts of pollutants to bring about undetectable differences [in air quality. The 1980 standards provide] a proven, cost-effective formula for improved air quality that we know can be practically met— one that will allow most urban areas to meet applicable standards.

Before Economic Club of Detroit, Feb. 11/ Los Angeles Times, 2-12:(I)14.

Robert Graham
Governor of Florida (D)

3

The thing that's uncontrollable in Florida is growth, growth. As long as citizens of the United States have the right to live anywhere they want to, and as long as places like Florida are qualitatively superior, they will continue to

112

receive an influx of migration. I don't believe it is very constructive to engage in arguments of growth or no-growth. The challenge is how to direct and accommodate that growth in ways that won't degrade the very quality that generated that growth.

The New York Times, 7-7:10.

Jay Hair
Vice president, National Wildlife Federation

4

We have not inherited the earth from our fathers, but we are borrowing it from our children. We are people of the land, forest and water who should harvest its abundance, but we should not be the despoilers and abusers. I fear now that we are not just borrowing, but stealing from our children.

San Francisco Examiner & Chronicle, 7-25:(C)1.

Steve H. Hanke
Senior economist, Council of Economic Advisers to the President of the United States

5

The only way to improve productivity and efficiency of public lands is to privatize them. Until we begin to privatize the public lands, we will not have accomplished anything of real economic value.

Los Angeles Times, 5-25:(I)1.

Denis Hayes
Former director, Solar Energy Research Institute

6

. . . [President] Reagan and his advisers have launched a brutal, comprehensive assault on the environment. Most environmentalists could have made peace with an honest conservative government. As a group, we tend to distrust Washington. We fear huge, faceless bureaucracies as much as we fear huge, irresponsible companies. But this is not a conservative government. Rather, in Disraeli's phrase, it is "an organized hypocrisy." Under the aegis of budget-trimming, it is seeking to "trim" the solar [energy] budget by 87 per cent and the conservation budget by 97 per cent. It would

(DENIS HAYES)

abolish every last shred of protection for low- and middle-income people from the whims of OPEC. Yet the same Administration is simultaneously pouring billions of dollars into technological black holes that the private sector would never touch. Thirty years after the launching of Atoms for Peace, the nuclear [power] industry has proved itself to be the moral equivalent of Soviet agriculture.

News conference/The Washington Post, 4-1:(A)28.

Ernest F. Hollings
United States Senator,
D–South Carolina

1

In 1790, Edmund Burke explained the basis of government and the society it governs as a "partnership not only between those who are living, but between those who are dead, and those who are to be born." It cannot have escaped your notice how applicable these words are to the stewardship of our public lands. If we are to maintain our fiduciary relationship to the generations to come, then we must maintain our lands, and their lands, in perpetual trust. These last remnants of our great natural heritage are not ours to destroy for short-term profits. What the [Reagan] Administration is proposing to do with lands held in the public trust is pursue a course of so-called "privatization." It means selling off chunks of the public's lands.

Before National Wildlife Federation,
Dec. 8/The New York Times, 12-22:14.

Leonard S. Hyman
Vice president, Merrill
Lynch, Pierce, Fenner &
Smith, investment brokers

2

The future of nuclear power will be decided by what constitutes a prudent business decision for the board of directors of a utility. In the final analysis, it is academic whether nuclear power is a blessing or a peril if those who would build the plants chose not to do so.

Nation's Business, September:39.

T. Destry Jarvis
Director of Federal programs,
National Parks and Conservation
Association

3

[Criticizing Interior Secretary James Watt for concentrating too much on fixing and improving current national parks rather than protecting wilderness areas]: There are rundown water, sewer systems and roads in parks, but ... by and large [the parks] were not in as shameful condition as Watt says. Watt has basically tried to scuttle every other program and put the need and emphasis on only those things that are visitor-use oriented. He's neglected the resource base.

The Washington Post, 11-24:(A)15.

James A. Lee
Director of Environmental Affairs,
International Bank for Reconstruction
and Development (World Bank)

4

There is around the world today still a complacency about the state of the environment. Despite the heightened awareness over the past decade, environmental concerns somehow are not regarded as serious enough or the consequences seem too far removed in time. Also, environmental concerns have been preempted by the changes in the internal and international economic situation over the past half decade—for example, skewed balance of payments, growing debt service in many countries, the cost of energy and the high cost of technology. Then there are all the tensions in the international political scene. So many countries of necessity are not able to put money and effort into addressing environmental problems.

The New York Times, 5-3:8.

Richard L. Lesher
President, Chamber of Commerce
of the United States

5

[On Reagan Administration plans to dismantle the Department of Energy]: We are far from home-free on energy. Whether it is embodied in a Cabinet department, an agency or some other governmental entity, a Federal monitoring and policy-making function, proper-

WHAT THEY SAID IN 1982

(RICHARD L. LESHER)

ly designed, is necessary and desirable.

Nation's Business, February: 52.

Roger J. Marzulla
President, Mountain States
Legal Foundation

1

The Western United States is actually more than 50 per cent owned by the Federal government. Most of the mineral and energy resources of this nation are located in precisely that same area, and the government has not been a good steward of those lands in terms of utilizing those natural resources . . . Ultimately I would like to see privatization of a substantial portion of those lands. I believe those lands would be better taken care of in the hands of a rancher or an individual utilizing them for housing or for mineral development. Obviously, I'm not talking about the areas that have significant wilderness potential.

Interview/The New York Times, 7-20:30.

Robert S. McNamara
Former President, International
Bank for Reconstruction and
Development (World Bank)

2

Short of nuclear war itself, population growth is the gravest issue that the world faces during the next decade. The threat of unmanageable population pressures is very much like the threat of nuclear war. Both can and will have catastrophic consequences. If we do not act, the problem will be solved by famine, riot, insurrection, war. The population problem must be faced up to for what it is—the greatest single obstacle to the economic and social advancement of peoples in the developing world. It is the population explosion, more than anything else, which, by holding back the advancement of the poor, is blowing apart the rich and poor and widening the already dangerous gap between them.

Chicago Tribune, 9-19:(2)1.

Guy V. Molinari
United States Representative,
R—New York

3

[Criticizing the burying of toxic chemical wastes]: Even as we meet here, the trucks are rolling to 900 landfills all over America—carrying a deadly legacy that our children and grandchildren have no choice but to accept. [The temporary lifting of the ban on such disposal is the] equivalent of opening all jails for a period of 90 days, to determine if the criminals within could possibly pose a threat to the public on the outside.

At hearing sponsored by Environmental
Protection Agency, Washington, March 11/
The Washington Post, 3-12:(A)27.

Prince Philip
Duke of Edinburgh; President,
World Wildlife Fund International

4

The difficulty with this conservation thing is that it is a slippery slope, in the sense that for every step you take forward, you're going to slide one back. You have a success here, and you suddenly uncover a can of worms over there. You think everything's going fairly well, and suddenly it blows up in your face. [Take for example the saving of Indian tigers.] Everybody was going around congratulating himself on it, and what happens? We suddenly get a spate of man-eating tiger stories going around. I got a letter from an Indian threatening to sue World Wildlife for the damage it was doing for having saved the tiger, because it was killing so many people.

Interview, Los Angeles, Sept. 21/
Los Angeles Times, 9-22:(II)1.

William K. Reilly
President, Conservation Foundation

5

When the Reagan Administration came in, we [environmentalists] were worried that our corporate participants might no longer be interested in participating, so we conducted an informal poll. We found our concern was unfounded. As one prominent official of a major corporation put it, "We read the polls [which show public support for environmental

(WILLIAM K. REILLY)

regulations]. We know environmentalists have access to the courts. After Reagan is gone we will still have these problems, which don't lend themselves to ideological solutions. We still need the dialogue."

The Christian Science Monitor, 8-3:12.

Hyman G. Rickover
Admiral, United States Navy

1

I think that ultimately we will need nuclear power, because we are exhausting our non-renewable resources; that is, coal and oil. I think they will go far more rapidly than we think they will and the cost is already going up. I believe that nuclear power for commercial purposes shows itself to be more economic, but that's a fake line of reasoning because we do not take into account the potential damage the release of radiation may do to future genera-tions .... every time you produce radiation, you produce something that has life, in some cases for billions of years; and I think there the human race is going to wreck itself. And it's far more important that we get control of this horrible force and try to eliminate it. I do not believe that nuclear power is worth it if it creates radiation. Then, you might ask me, why do I have nuclear-powered ships? That's a necessary evil. I would sink them all.

Before Congressional Joint
Economic Committee, Washington,
Jan. 28/The New York Times, 1-30:8.

Marcus Rowden
Former Chairman, Nuclear Regulatory
Commission of the United States

2

The sound use of nuclear energy has been frustrated. The reasons for this are complex and varied, but high on the list are the shackles placed on sound industry planning and sensible government decision-making by the present licensing and regulatory process ... Nuclear energy has amassed a remarkable safety record, far superior to that of virtually any other major industry.

Washington, March 30/Chicago Tribune, 4-1:(1)4.

Russell E. Train
Former Chairman, Federal Council
on Environmental Quality

3

I think that global trends in resources, including fisheries depletion, soil erosion, loss of farmland, loss of tropical forests and the extinction of species, are very disturbing. It seems to me that these are the subjects that should engage the principal attention of the international community in foreign affairs for the foreseeable future.

The New York Times, 5-3:8.

James G. Watt
Secretary of the Interior
of the United States

4

If I acquire $200-million of additional land, I haven't created one job for America. If I acquire $200-million to restore and to rebuild and to refurbish the parks and make them acceptable for your children and your families, we're creating jobs for plumbers and truck drivers and carpenters and grocery-store opera-tors—and America is revitalized. That's our thrust—not just acquiring more land and gob-bling it up for the Federal government, but to let people enjoy what we have.

Broadcast interview/
"Meet the Press," NBC-TV, 2-21.

5

The Secretary of Interior is sitting on a department filled with conflict. I am the chief environmental officer for the nation; I'm also the chief coal miner. I'm the chief protector of the parks; I'm [also] the chief oil and gas driller. I'm the chief protector of the wildlife; I'm also chief dam builder, too. I took a statutory commitment to do all those things. So there's conflict riddled in the department, and I live with it.

Broadcast interview/"Meet the Press," NBC-TV, 2-21.

6

[Supporting leases for mineral exploration and other land development]: There are no unemployment problems in areas ... where energy is the source of industry ...We can be a nation of environmentalists only if our citizens

115

(JAMES G. WATT)

have jobs and incomes to support wise conservation. If you suffer economically to the point where you can no longer hunt, fish, hike—or even travel to the forests and streams—then your burning desire to conserve is going to dim quickly, and understandably so.

Before Izaak Walton League, March/
The Washington Post, 3-12:(A)27.

1

[On critics of his environmental policies]: This is not a struggle over the environment. It is not about resources. This battle is over the form of government we will have in America. We are battling over the future of America ... The critics I contend with seek a form of government that would centralize the allocation of resources, and thus our well being. I feel strongly that is wrong, and if we are to improve our military strength, create jobs and improve environmental qualities, we have to improve, over the long haul, the freedom that comes with the marketplace and a limited form of government.

Interview, Washington/The New York Times, 4-15:14.

2

There's tremendous wealth in America's resources. The mineral and energy potential in Alaska and other states is evidence that we don't need to go on a program of sharing scarcity. Exploration and production in Wyoming, Utah, Idaho and Montana indicate that the dimensions of oil and gas can significantly reduce our dependency on foreign nations. If we release the private sector to proceed in an orderly and phased program, we can have the economic development that is needed for national security, and creating jobs as well as protecting the nation's environment.

Interview/U.S. News & World Report, 6-14:43.

H. E. Wright
Chairman, Natural Gas
Supply Association

3

[Criticizing the House vote to ban oil and mineral leasing in Federally protected wilderness areas]: This vote sends a clear signal to the oil-exporting countries of the world that the United States is not serious about developing its own energy sources. And [this country] is thus willing to remain the potential victim of an oil cutoff from politically unstable regions of the world.

Aug. 12/Los Angeles Times, 8-13:(I)1.

Daniel Yergin
Chairman, International Energy
Security Seminar, Harvard University

4

... people would love a "miracle" solution [to the U.S. energy problem], but there are no miracle solutions. The three things we ought to do are the diversification of oil supplies; substitution, and that does mean alternatives to oil; and the third element, which has proved to be the most important, although people tended to scoff at it a few years ago, is energy efficiency ... The energy question is not just a question of whether gasoline is 70 cents a gallon or $1.40 or $2 a gallon. It is a question of the possibilities of renewed economic growth, about the durability of democratic institutions and, ultimately, about war and peace. And as long as we remember that it's about those questions, and focus on it, I think we can deal with this without going from panic to complacency and again find ourselves in hot water.

Interview/San Francisco Examiner
& Chronicle, 8-8:(D)9.

Foreign Affairs

Elliott Abrams
*Assistant Secretary for Human Rights
and Humanitarian Affairs, Department
of State of the United States*   *1*

[On the human-rights policies of the Reagan and Carter Administrations]: There is less difference than a lot of people expected. The goals are essentially similar, but the tactics vary. The Carter Administration was more given to public criticisms of friendly governments than we are. Another difference is that we say it is not enough to ask who is in power and what is he like. We also have to ask the likely prospects for improvement. Look at Vietnam and Iran. Bad situations can and do get worse.

Interview, Washington/The New York Times, 10-19:8.

Yuri V. Andropov
*General Secretary, Communist
Party of the Soviet Union*   *2*

We know full well that it is useless to beg peace from the imperialists. It can be upheld only by resting upon the invincible might of the Soviet armed forces.

*Upon his being named General Secretary, Moscow,
Nov. 12/The Washington Post, 11-13:(A)1.*

3

We are deeply convinced that the '70s, characterized by detente, were not—as is asserted today by certain imperialist leaders—a chance episode in the difficult history of mankind. No, the policy of detente is by no means a past stage. The future belongs to this policy.

*Before Soviet Communist Party Central Committee,
Moscow, Nov. 22/The New York Times, 11-23:5.*

Georgi A. Arbatov
*Director, Soviet Institute.of
U.S.A. and Canadian Affairs*   *4*

You have actually an extremist government in your country [the U.S.] ... Their intent is at least to try to transform our country from the outside, and if it doesn't work, to destroy it, and we have to be ready for it. We look for any positive signal. We look for every good signal coming from the United States, if there will be a positive attitude. If this positive attitude will prevail, [we] will meet more than halfway the Americans.

Interview/The Washington Post, 11-30:(A)22.

Michael Barone
Public-opinion analyst   *5*

The public is writing two contrary prescriptions. They want an assertive, aggressive-sounding foreign policy. But they don't want to risk American involvement. It's the opposite of "speak softly, but carry a big stick." The public doesn't think this through. It caused problems for [former President] Carter. It'll cause problems for [President] Reagan and whoever follows him.

Interview/The Christian Science Monitor, 1-19:4.

Beatrix
Queen of the Netherlands   *6*

We must accept the fact that developing countries are not primarily seeking Western solutions to their problems; they want to go their own way and find their own answers. What we must constantly bear in mind is that in our relations with the Third World we are principally concerned with combatting poverty, illiteracy, disease, and even prejudice against ourselves. The West has the technological capacity to aid developing countries. We must provide that aid with patience and persistence, without pretension or arrogance, in the knowledge that other cultures have a right to their own identity.

*Before National Press Club, Washington,
April 20/Chicago Tribune, 4-21:(1)5.*

Anthony C. Beilenson
United States Representative,
D–California

1

Beyond their borders, [the Soviet Union is] losing, rather than gaining, strength and influence. In Europe, Spain and Portugal are succeeding with their democratic governments, and both are firmly in the Western camp. West European armed forces are stronger and better prepared than they were a few years ago. In Africa, after years of economic and diplomatic efforts, the Russians have influence in about three countries—three countries that I can think of out of 53 . . . In Asia, the world's most populous nation, China, has moved closer to the United States. Soviet-Japanese relations are extremely poor. The Russians are being isolated in a world that is hostile to them politically and close to them geographically. We have Canada and Mexico as neighbors. They [the Soviets] have a 5,000-mile border with China, whom they are terribly afraid of, plus Iran and Afghanistan, the NATO countries, Japan and the Warsaw Pact nations whose support in a time of hostilities they cannot count on. As someone has said, fortunately it is the Soviet Union and not the United States that is surrounded by hostile Communist countries. When you get right down to it, Russia is very much alone in the world, while we have strong and powerful allies.

Before Los Angeles World Affairs Council/
Los Angeles Times, 2-18:(IX)5.

Radomir Bogdanov
Deputy director, Soviet Institute
for the U.S.A. and Canada

2

The 1950s and 1960s were a time of American nuclear superiority. Now things are on an absolutely different qualitative level. For us, there is no more talk of American superiority. But this [U.S. Reagan] Administration behaves as if American superiority were still there, and they can force anything, not only on us but on the whole world. These people think that if they do not succeed in shaping the world the way they want, they should go back to Fortress America and become strong against the

whole hostile world. What worries us is they look at the world as a hostile place, which is not true. If you base everything on that, your reactions become irrational.

Interview, Moscow/Chicago Tribune, 2-22:(1)8.

Rudolph E. Boschwitz
United States Senator, R–Minnesota

3

It's my belief that you should sell the Russians anything they can't shoot back at you. If they buy our grain, they'll have less money to do mischief with.

U.S. News & World Report, 8-23:65.

Leonid I. Brezhnev
President of the Soviet Union; General
Secretary, Soviet Communist Party

4

Diplomacy calls for the unraveling, not the linking, of issues. The tangled knot of conflict situations and disputed problems in today's world cannot be cut by a sword. The only way is to engage in patient, constructive talks . . .

At reception for Socialist International,
Moscow, Feb. 3/The New York Times, 2-4:4.

5

One could probably say that international relations as a whole have now come to a distinctly visible crossroads. On the one hand lies the path of strengthening peace and extending peaceful cooperation among all states, cooperation based on unfailing respect for the independence, rights and interests of each country, on non-interference in internal affairs and on joint efforts to strengthen world security and mutual confidence . . . On the other hand lies the path onto which the world is being intensively pushed by the newly fledged devotees of cold war and dangerous balancing on the brink of a real war. They would like nothing better than to tear up the legal and ethical norms of relations between states that have taken shape over the centuries and to cancel their independence and sovereignty. They are trying to re-tailor the political map of the world, and have declared large regions on all continents as zones of their "vital interests." They have arrogated the "right" to command

(LEONID I. BREZHNEV)

some countries, and to judge and "punish" others. Unembarrassed, they publicly announce and try to carry out plans for economic and political "destabilization" of governments and states that are not to their liking . . . It is simply astonishing to see it all, and you cannot help asking yourself: What is there more of in this policy—thoughtlessness and lack of experience in international affairs or irresponsibility and, to say it bluntly, an adventurist approach to problems crucial to the destiny of humankind?

Before Congress of Soviet Trade Unions, Moscow, March 16/The Washington Post, 3-17:(A)24.

1

Israel's aggression in Lebanon should . . . be regarded as a consequence of the political course taken by the Americans. It is clear that this is, in the final count, the doing of the U.S.A. The situation in a number of regions of Africa, Asia and Central America is very complicated. The reason is the same: attempts to impose American diktat on them. The masses of people on all continents angrily protest against Washington's aggressive policy, which is threatening to push the world into the flames of a nuclear war. The adventurism, rudeness and undisguised egoism of this policy arouse growing indignation in many countries, including those allied with the U.S.A.

The New York Times, 10-28:8.

2

The world now lives in no easy times. The broad offensive on socialism and the national-liberation movements, unleashed by imperialism in all directions, complicated the international situation. But it is not the tradition of our party, of our people, to retreat before the difficulties. We shall do the utmost to see to it that those who like military adventures should never take the land of the Soviets unawares, that the potential aggressor should know [that] a crushing retaliatory strike will inevitably be for him. Our might and vigilance will cool, I think, the hot heads of some imperialist politicians. The Soviet Union will continue persistently fighting for detente, for disarmament.

We shall be building up efforts to avert the threat of a nuclear war. The essence of our policy is peaceableness, the sincere striving for equitable and fruitful cooperation with all who want such cooperation. Our profound belief is that exactly such a way will lead mankind to peace for the living and would-be generations.

At celebration of 65th anniversary of Bolshevik revolution, Moscow, Nov. 7/The New York Times, 11-8:6.

Harold Brown
Former Secretary of Defense of the United States   *3*

I'm against all-out economic warfare against the Soviets. In the first place, it won't work because they are autarkic—that is, independent of the outside world—except for feed grains. Naturally, they'll do better if they get infusions of capital and technology from outside. But you're not going to cause them to collapse even if you adopt all-out economic warfare. All-out economic warfare is more likely by far to disrupt our alliances than it is to destroy the Soviet system. In saying this, I do not rule out the use of economic sanctions, such as the grain embargo that the [U.S.] Carter Administration invoked. But such sanctions should be applied only in situations where military action by the U.S. is either infeasible or too dangerous but where something more than mere moral outrage is required. [The Soviet invasion of] Afghanistan was such a case. Furthermore, when applied, sanctions should be limited in time because they become ineffective after a limited time because of leakage—even if they're effective at the beginning . . . In short, we ought to use economic levers, but we should not engage in economic warfare. There is a distinction: Economic warfare is aimed at trying to collapse or destabilize the system. That is not going to work, and it is very dangerous.

Interview/U.S. News & World Report, 9-6:33.

Zbigniew Brzezinski
Professor of government, Columbia University; Former Assistant to the President of the United States (Jimmy Carter) for National Security Affairs   *4*

. . . by and large since World War II, we've had two systems [for handling foreign policy].

119

(ZBIGNIEW BRZEZINSKI)

One is the Presidential, which approximates what I described as the best system, though in varying degrees, and that was characteristic of [Presidents] Carter, Nixon and Kennedy. But, secondly, we had the Secretarial system, in which a relatively passive, disengaged President deliberately permitted his Secretary of State to be dominant. And that was used by Truman with Acheson, Eisenhower with Dulles, and Ford with Kissinger. I expected that with [current President] Reagan you would have the second system. And it is, I repeat, a perfectly respectable system. [But] what amazes me is that [today] we have neither the Presidential nor the Secretarial system . . . . chaos and confusion might be functional but uncharitable descriptions . . . We have a Vice President in charge of a crisis committee, which means that he is in charge of a crisis in an area regarding which he'll have no ongoing policy involvement until the crisis appears; and no ongoing policy continuity once the crisis is terminated. A bureaucratic absurdity. We have a National Security Adviser reporting to a domestic adviser with no foreign-policy experience. And a Secretary of State who is very able and who is *the* outstanding member of the team but who is deliberately checkmated.

Interview/The New York Times, 1-6:25.

1

. . . the general thrust of history is toward greater independence for smaller states. We are accepting that in Central America, though painfully. We have evolved a much more equitable relationship with Latin America. The French and British colonial empires have been terminated. The Soviet empire eventually will have to be terminated as well. The key question is: Can it be done peacefully and gradually, or will it be violent and dangerous? Movements such as Solidarity [the independent Polish trade union] offer hope of peaceful evolution. Soviet suppression makes eruptions and dangerous consequences more likely.

Interview/U.S. News & World Report, 1-11:18.

2

In my judgment, we are at one of those stages similar to the immediate post-World War II period—and then later in the '50s—when basic and long-term historical commitments may be in the process of being shaped. The first phase produced the prolonged Cold War; the second produced a prolonged and rather uncertain detente. I believe we are at a stage in which we may be faced with acute intensification of the already unstable American-Soviet rivalry. But it is still possible that the present conditions of uncertainty could be exploited to start again stabilizing the relationship and developing what should become a genuinely more comprehensive and reciprocal detente.

Before Executive Club, Helsinki, Finland, Oct. 6/The New York Times, 10-12:12.

3

[On the new head of the Soviet Communist Party, Yuri Andropov]: The choice in the Soviet Union is not between doves or hawks or conservatives or liberals, which is the way I think the [Western] mass media misrepresent the problem, but between different types of tough guys. There is the rigid, ignorant, parochial tough guy—I think Chernenko fits that mold—and there is the more sophisticated, skilled, experienced tough guy: Andropov fits that mold. For us the question is, is it preferable to have an ignorant tough guy in charge who might produce an explosion in Eastern Europe and probably fail to renovate the Soviet system? Or is it preferable to have an intelligent rival who might defuse some of the tensions in Eastern Europe while [still] skillfully retaining control and even liquidating dissent? That is the choice. In the nuclear age, probably the second is less dangerous than the first.

Interview, November/Newsweek, 11-22:41.

Arthur F. Burns
United States Ambassador to West Germany

4

You're called a diplomat if you confront facts vaguely or obliquely. That has become the meaning of the word, and I think it's awful . . . What's the use of being in government unless you. address problems directly instead of sweeping them under the rug?

Interview, Bonn/The Washington Post, 7-22:(A)29.

Jimmy Carter
Former President of the United States

1

[On U.S. foreign policy since President Reagan assumed office]: It is hard to think of any nation that has a closer relationship with us now than a year and a half ago, except for two or three countries ruled by right-wing regimes. Deteriorating relationships in Latin America, Asia, Europe and Africa all grieve me.

Interview, Plains, Ga./Time, 10-11:63.

Konstantin U. Chernenko
*Member, Politburo, Communist
Party of the Soviet Union*

2

The Soviet Union is opposed to a further growth of tensions in Soviet-American relations. We stand for their normalization and improvement and are prepared to engage in businesslike and detailed negotiations which must of necessity take account of the interests of both sides. If, however, Washington proves unable to rise above primitive anti-Communism, if it persists in its policy of threats and diktat, well, then, we are sufficiently strong and we can wait. Neither sanctions nor bellicose posturing frighten us. We believe in reason, and we believe that sooner or later—and the earlier the better—reason will triumph and the military threat will be averted.

Moscow, Oct. 29/The New York Times, 10-30:1.

Ray S. Cline
*Senior fellow, Center for Strategic
and International Studies, Georgetown
University; Former Deputy Director of
Central Intelligence of the United States*

3

The weakness of America in world affairs in the last 10 years or so has been not a weakness of our military system, but a lack of a coherent national will to carry out our strategic objectives.

Los Angeles Times, 9-12:(I)24.

Thierry de Montbrial
*Director, French Institute
of International Relations*

4

If detente means the need for dialogue, cooperation and moderation, then it continues despite ups and downs. If by detente we mean what [for U.S. Secretary of State] Henry Kissinger probably meant—a set of ground rules covering all the world's problems including North-South relations and arms control—then it has failed. One mistake has been to forge too strong a link between detente and Third World crises, and between detente and arms control.

Interview/World Press Review, June:27.

Patricia M. Derian
*Former Assistant Secretary
for Human Rights, Department
of State of the United States*

5

[Criticizing the Reagan Administration's record on human rights in foreign affairs]: The policy is disastrous. It's catastrophic. They have essentially abandoned human-rights policy and then continued this incredible courtship with the sleaziest of the world's leaders. Falling all over [Philippine President] Marcos. The guy from South Korea. You pick a seedy dictator and you've got a great friend in the Reagan Administration.

The New York Times, 10-19:8.

Edward J. Derwinski
*United States Representative,
R—Illinois*

6

[On foreign aid]: Too often aid has been used as a crutch for diplomacy. The ambassador says it makes life easier if he has a goody to parcel out.

U.S. News & World Report, 12-13:57.

Milovan Djilas
*Author; Former Vice President
of Yugoslavia*

7

Generally, I think the [U.S.] Reagan Administration's foreign policy is better than [former President] Carter's. Carter was good only on human rights. Present U.S. policy is more practical, more realistic, more critical of the U.S.S.R. Carter underestimated the Soviet danger; even [former President] Nixon did.

Inteview, Belgrade/The New York Times, 6-20:(4)4.

Charles F. Doran
Foreign-policy authority,
Johns Hopkins University

1

[On President Reagan's handling of foreign affairs]: ... one has a President who is not concerned about the details of policy at all. He delegates these matters, is willing to tolerate a lot of inefficiency and incompetence on the part of others, and in fact only deals with issues when they become either a crisis or are so central to the whole program that he in fact has gotten involved. The problem in foreign policy is inconsistency, and this creates enormous unease among those expected to implement policy, because they don't get the signals they need from the President.

Interview/The Christian Science Monitor, 1-6:6.

Lawrence S. Eagleburger
Assistant Secretary for European
Affairs, Department of State
of the United States

2

In foreign policy you don't buy a company, you don't make a merger. Instead, you are always faced with another challenge. You seldom win a victory; more often, you avoid disasters. I can say I was "successful" [as U.S. Ambassador to Yugoslavia]. But what the hell does that mean? I improved relations between the two countries—but that's not a final status. It's an ongoing thing.

The New York Times Magazine, 9-19:11.

Richard Falk
Professor of international law,
Princeton University; Former
associate editor, "Foreign
Policy" magazine

3

The application of American force ends up radicalizing liberation movements, confirming their claims that we are the enemy of change, getting us stuck in support of leaderships that are isolated from their people, and even putting us in a position where we are acting against our own democratic values, since an incentive arises in our government to keep things secret and mislead our own people ... The nationalist movements are like volcanoes. If we are going

122

to reduce global tensions in the long run, we need to realize these kinds of political eruptions cannot be contained militarily, and the effort to do so only intensifies the explosions when they occur. If we followed this line of thinking, our opportunities for relating successfully to developing countries would be much better.

Interview, Princeton University/The
Christian Science Monitor, 2-4:(B)4.

Hans-Dietrich Genscher
Foreign Minister of West Germany

4

I personally am an optimist. I think we [in the West] have reason for being optimistic. I'm confident that we have the cards in our hand; but we must make use of [the] cards we have with a sense of self-confidence and trust in one another, and we must not let ourselves become defeated and close our eyes to what is going on in the Soviet sphere, and engage ourselves in self-tormenting faults with our own problems, confusing real problems with artificial problems.

To reporters, Washington/
The New York Times, 3-10:27.

Rudolph W. Giuliani
Associate Attorney General,
Department of Justice
of the United States

5

With the unemployment that we have, with our own cultural and economic problems, we have to enforce the immigration law. We allow more people into our society than any other country in the world ...Each one ... has to be decided upon the basis of an evaluation of ... the country from whence they came. Otherwise, nobody could come into the U.S.... Most people who flee from the Soviet Union claim political asylum [because] they either were persecuted in their home country or, if they were returned, they would be singled out for oppressive treatment. That's why we have asylum ... [But] there's no civil strife going on in Haiti that I know of. Haiti may be poorer than some of the other Latin American countries ... but it is not a situation of tremendous political foment ... I fear that if you open the political-asylum process to those with only an

(RUDOLPH W. GIULIANI)

economic claim, you're going to swallow up political asylum—because two thirds of the world have a valid economic claim to come to this country.

Interview/The Washington Post, 7-24:(A)3.

Allan E. Gottlieb
Canadian Ambassador to the United States

1

Ambassadors today are increasingly being drawn into public debate over U.S. domestic policy. And this seems to violate one of the cardinal rules of international diplomacy— namely, thou shalt not interfere in the internal affairs of the host country. If you believe, as I do, that this is a good rule which serves an important purpose, then you might well wonder what has changed which warrants its contravention . . . [In economic matters,] it is a primary responsibility of today's Ambassador to point out the ties of interdependence, to remind audiences that "quick fix" protectionist measures are not without costs.

Before Harvard Law School Association,
June 16/The New York Times, 6-25:12.

Andrei A. Gromyko
Foreign Minister of the Soviet Union

2

The Soviet Union is prepared already today to come to the negotiating table in order to formalize strict obligations not to use force in settling disputes and differences which exist between states. It has to be noted, however, that the United States of America has chosen a different policy for itself. The essence of this policy is the desire to impose its will on other states and peoples. That desire underlies all plans of production of weapons and foreign policy.

At United Nations, New York, Oct. 1/
The New York Times, 10-2:6.

Alexander M. Haig, Jr.
Secretary of State of the United States

3

No matter how much Communist repression, no matter how many Soviet nuclear missiles, no matter how many Afghanistans and Polands,

some would still put pressure on the West to improve relations with the Soviet Union—rather than to demand from Moscow the moderation of its behavior . . . Isn't it time that our Western critics stop their double standard, and isn't it time to give greater weight to the precious freedoms and values with all their failings and stop this masochistic tearing down of our values? The question itself reflects a double standard that boggles my mind.

At International Press Center, Brussels,
Jan. 12/The New York Times, 1-13:5.

4

Critics of American foreign policy must view our actions in historic perspective. We have re-established that we will not be passive in the face of unacceptable Soviet behavior worldwide. We have dedicated ourselves to the strengthening of our alliances—and I do not believe the Atlantic Alliance is weaker today than at any time in its history. We have shown clearly to friend and foe that the United States does stand for values which it intends to pursue vigorously. Finally, we have reaffirmed that we do have obligations that go beyond our shores and that in a changing world those obligations can best be met by a concert of collective action by those who have equal stakes in the outcome.

Interview/U.S. News & World Report, 2-1:26.

5

[Saying the government should not publicly state what it will or will not do in specific foreign situations]: . . . as a matter of principle, the sterility of drawing lines around America's potential options constitutes the promulgation of roadways for those who are seeking to move against America's vital interests. It is the most self-defeating kind of contemporary public-relations manipulation that I can conceive. Sovereign states never indulge in it if they are prudent about their public statements.

Interview, Washington, Feb. 5/
The New York Times, 2-8:4.

WHAT THEY SAID IN 1982

(ALEXANDER M. HAIG, JR.)

1

[On the use of economic sanctions in foreign policy]: I think the basic question in the area of economic sanctions has always got to be: Will it be effective? In other words, will we accomplish the objective that the action was undertaken to achieve? Nothing could be more foolhardy than to unilaterally punish all or segments of American industry or agriculture with meaningless sanctions... There is another, unquantifiable, aspect of the judgment calculus involved in the sanctions, and that is, we also have the ephemeral obligation of not pursuing business as usual and not pursuing policies which reflect an endorsement or a contribution to the suppression [by the object country] that is under way. It cannot be a steely-eyed calculus of "is it going to be 100 per cent successful?" It has to go beyond that, and that is where the delicate judgment factor is applied.

Interview/The New York Times, 2-7:(1)6.

2

[Calling for U.S.-Soviet talks on the major issues dividing them]: We cannot claim that we are too weak to negotiate and at the same time insist that we are strong enough for a policy of all-out confrontation. Nothing is gained by appearing to fear diplomatic discussions—neither leverage over the Soviets nor the respect and confidence of our allies.

Before Chamber of Commerce of the United States, Washington, April 27/Los Angeles Times, 4-28:(I)1.

3

Do I think U.S. foreign policy is inept? No more so than in 200 some years of American history. At times it is. At times it's not. At times it's even brilliant. At times it's rather stupid. It would be very hard to ask me to label it.

News conference, London, June 8/ The New York Times, 6-9:7.

4

[Reading his resignation letter]: Dear Mr. President [Reagan]: Your accession to office on January 20, 1981, brought an opportunity for a new and forward-looking foreign policy

resting on the cornerstones of strength and compassion. I believe that we shared a view of America's role in the world as the leader of free men and an inspiration to all. We agreed that consistency, clarity and steadiness of purpose were essential to success. It was in this spirit that I undertook to serve you as Secretary of State. In recent months it has become clear to me that the foreign policy on which we embarked together was shifting from that careful course which we laid out. Under these circumstances I feel it necessary to request that you accept my resignation.

Washington, June 25/The New York Times, 6-26:4.

Walter E. Hoadley
Senior fellow, Hoover Institution, Stanford University; Former executive vice president and chief economist, Bank of America

5

A new surge of American home-grown confidence, based on a more realistic appraisal of our capability and resources relative to all others, could touch off a wave of new expansion of enormous value to our people. Almost certainly it would be followed by a similar wave in other parts of the world, helping to ease many political and economic tensions... In stark reality, actual or perceived weakness of the U.S. now constitutes one of the most destabilizing forces across continents as well as within our own national boundaries. In contrast, any new global perception and conviction of more U.S. will and power to compete internationally will constitute an exceedingly strong force to accelerate national and global economic growth, as well as contribute to peace for ourselves and others.

Before Conference Board, New York/ The Wall Street Journal, 3-15:26.

Richard C. Holbrooke
Former Assistant Secretary for East Asia and Pacific Affairs, Department of State of the United States

6

[On the resignation of U.S. Secretary of State Alexander Haig]: All his life he had been the hardest-line man in government, in bureaucratic disputes. In this [Reagan] Administra-

(RICHARD C. HOLBROOKE)

tion, without changing his position he became a moderate in an Administration more hard-line than he had anticipated.

Interview/The New York Times, 6-26:5.

John Hughes
Associate Director,
International Communication
Agency of the United States

1

[On Voice of America broadcasts]: The feeling has been that facts, fairly presented, speak for themselves. The worst thing we can do is present a distorted view. It would cost us the most precious thing we have—credibility.

U.S. News & World Report, 1-11:29.

Arthur Hummel, Jr.
United States Ambassador to China

2

[On his dealings with former Secretary of State Henry Kissinger]: To this day, Henry likes to tell people that I'm mean to him. I'm proud of the fact that I'm one of the few Kissinger subordinates who, after one of his statements, looked him in the eye and said, "Bullshit." Four or five times he directed me to do things I just thought were wrong. In shouting matches, I insisted that at least he listen to me. Sometimes, Kissinger would listen, but I ended up doing what he wanted anyway. Frankly, I believe that's the only way to deal with one of these mad geniuses, which is what he is. There was a daily sense of tension whether you were going to have your job the next day.

Interview, Peking/The Washington Post, 8-25:(A)19.

Bobby R. Inman
Former Deputy Director of Central
Intelligence of the United States

3

[On foreign covert activities of the U.S.]: When the Soviets use armed forces outside their own borders or when they use proxy troops outside their own borders, covert action can raise the cost for them and may discourage them from expanding. And where Russia mounts a major propaganda campaign to shape the attitudes of other countries, covert action to counter them can be useful. At that point, I've run the gamut of where I believe covert action can be truly useful to the United States. This is the single most divisive issue in trying to create a consensus on intelligence policy. In the public perception, covert action is our major function. In reality, it is a minuscule part of our total effort.

Interview/U.S. News & World Report, 12-20:37.

Harold K. Johnson
General (Ret.) and former Chief
of Staff, United States Army

4

I have felt for a long time . . . that we're much too paternalistic. We [the U.S.] seem to have a feeling that we enjoy all the wisdom and that our allies should blindly follow where we lead. I don't happen to share that view. I think that there has got to be a great deal more consultation with the allies than there has been and a consideration of the viewpoints that they hold.

Interview/U.S. News & World Report, 1-18:25.

John Paul II
Pope

5

Among public opinion all over the world, the conviction is strengthened day by day that peoples must be able to choose freely the social organization to which they aspire for their own country and that this organization must conform with justice, respect for liberty, religious faith and the rights of man in general. It is a commonly shared conviction that no people should be treated by another people as a subordinate being or an instrument, to the detriment of the equality which is inscribed in human conscience and recognized by the norms of international law. In the same way that in relations between persons it is not permitted for one person to make use of another as if he were an object, so in international life, everything that attacks the freedom of expression of the will of nations should be denounced.

To diplomatic corps, Vatican City,
Jan. 16/The New York Times, 1-17:(1)8.

WHAT THEY SAID IN 1982

David C. Jones
General, United States Air Force;
Chairman, Joint Chiefs of Staff

1

Part of deterrence is uncertainty—making the Soviets nervous about how we may respond. They are then forced to consider these uncertainties in their strategic calculations. Nothing could be worse than for them to know that there would be no penalty for an aggressive act somewhere in the world. They should know there would be a penalty but have no certain knowledge about what it may be. That may not prevent them from moving, but they are likely to consider the risks before they act.

Interview/U.S. News & World Report, 5-24:30.

Max M. Kampelman
Chief United States delegate to
the Madrid conference on the 1975
Helsinki human-rights accords

2

The Helsinki Final Act has been pummeled to near death by the Soviet Union. Yet we hear the chirping "Let's go back to work" by those who have been demonstrating by their actions their utter contempt for the Final Act and for our process ... The only work I have seen is work represented by the [Soviet] invasion of Afghanistan, or the work of putting people in jail at psychiatric institutions [for criticizing Soviet policy]. Are [the Soviets] offering more talk, more words on paper they will disregard? More promises they will not keep? Their words are useless in the face of their deeds against the Final Act. They are wrecking the Final Act.

At Madrid conference, Feb. 24/
The New York Times, 2-25:4.

Edward M. Kennedy
United States Senator,
D—Massachusetts

3

In general, the Senate and House prefer to cooperate with the President on foreign policy, but the Constitution gives us [in Congress] a legitimate role to play. Congress will never be a rubber stamp for policies with which it profoundly disagrees.

The Washington Post, 1-23:(A)2.

George F. Kennan
Former United States Ambassador
to the Soviet Union

4

[Calling for an end to Western economic sanctions against the Soviet Union]: We must immediately and completely stop every type of economic warfare. The attempt to prevent or set back the entire economic development of another people has no place in the politics of a democratic state in times of peace. These are means for preparing a new war, not the means for preventing one ... We must put an end to this destructive militarization of the public discussion of relationships between East and West, an end to this constant talk about the horrible things the Russians could do to us and we to them in a supposedly imminent war. And we must also stop making the intentions and military preparations of a possible opponent always appear to the public in a threatening and alarming light. Indeed, we have to put an end to the often systematic condemnation of another great people and its government—a condemnation which, if not stopped, will really make war inevitable by making it seem inevitable.

Accepting Frankfurt Book Fair Peace Prize,
Oct. 10/The New York Times, 10-11:6.

Lane Kirkland
President, American Federation of
Labor-Congress of Industrial Organizations

5

[Calling for economic sanctions against the Soviet bloc because of actions such as martial law in Poland and other Soviet transgressions]: Some say that sanctions would sacrifice "detente." Yet the most cogent argument for detente was that expanded commercial relations with and financial concessions to the Soviet bloc would give the West the strings with which to restrain Soviet lawlessness ... It is time we saw the backside of detente. If we are not prepared to do that, then it is we who have become ensnared and the East that has us in its net. If it be said that termination of trade and credits would be expensive to Western interests, then all the more reason to do it now, before the cost surpasses tolerance.

The Washington Post, 4-23:(A)28.

Jeane J. Kirkpatrick
*United States Ambassador/Permanent
Representative to the United Nations*

1

[On the U.S. at the UN]: We are in a situation in which on almost every issue we lose. The biggest question becomes how we are going to lose. How long is it going to take ... will we lose big or small? That's a very frustrating situation to be in.

Interview/The Washington Post, 1-28:(A)14.

2

The truth is that most of the governments of the world are, by our standards, bad governments. Corrupt, inefficient. Sometimes we are going to have to support and associate with governments that do not meet our standards.

*Before American Legion/The
Christian Science Monitor, 3-30:24.*

3

The decline of U.S. influence in the UN is part and parcel of the decline of U.S. influence in the world ... and that is a direct reflection of what has been persisting U.S. ineptitude in international relations ...We have not been effective in projecting a conception of international programs; we have not been good at the politics of the United Nations. It is a political arena ... We have treated it as though it were something other than a political arena ... a strange thing, really.

*At Union League Club, New York, June 7/
The Washington Post, 6-8:(A)14.*

4

[On the distinction she makes between "authoritarian" and "totalitarian" governments]: It's not a new or original concept. Political scientists have been using it for years to draw the distinction between traditional dictatorships and ideological phenomena like Nazi Germany. I never said I was a defender of authoritarian regimes. What I said is that some are worse than others. And I criticized the Carter human-rights policy for only one thing— that it didn't work. I believe the United States should have a human-rights [foreign] policy. But I also believe it should be realistic and capable of achieving its aims.

*Interview, United Nations, New York/
The Washington Post, 11-25:(A)35.*

5

Rational behavior indicates that if you're a small country in the UN and you know there's going to be a price for opposing the Soviet bloc or the Cuban-dominated non-aligned bloc, and no price for opposing the U.S., you will oppose the U.S., obviously. Look: Plain old logrolling and horse trading goes on in the UN. You have to do this. You trade votes from time to time. There's nothing corrupt about it. It's a question of building cooperative relationships. For whatever reason, we [the U.S.] haven't been astute about the politics of the UN. There are three possible reasons: One, we haven't understood the game; two, we haven't cared to win; or, three, we haven't cared to engage in the politics because we are too genteel.

Interview/U.S. News & World Report, 12-27:30.

6

Rather frequently, what goes on in the UN actually exacerbates conflicts rather than tending to resolve them. That is certainly true in the case of the Arab-Israeli conflict. It's probably true with regard to southern Africa. It's no coincidence that some of the most successful recent examples of peace-making have taken place entirely outside the UN structure. The peaceful transformation of white-minority-ruled Rhodesia into black-majority-ruled Zimbabwe was done wholly outside the UN. The same is true of the Camp David accords between Israel and Egypt. And now much of the negotiation for a Namibia settlement is taking place outside the UN framework . . In the UN, conflict is extended. All kinds of countries that don't have any direct interest in a conflict get involved in it. As a result, you might say all conflict is globalized. States in Africa get involved in the Arab-Israeli conflict or the Iran-Iraq war. All of Latin America and all of Europe become involved in the Falklands issue. This happens repeatedly. Secondly, conflicts are polarized to the utmost. This comes from the "bloc" structure at the UN. Every issue is washed through the political blocs, and in the process it becomes ideological. Specific, concrete debate is transformed into a big, global ideological debate. There's no kind of debate that is more difficult to resolve.

Interview/U.S. News & World Report, 12-27:29.

WHAT THEY SAID IN 1982

Henry A. Kissinger
*Former Secretary of State
of the United States*

1

I think it is a failure of Western leadership that we have not been able to define for ourselves what it is we want from the Soviet Union in the political field or that we have not been able to agree with each other on credit policies and pricing policies that are in the common interest. Lenin is supposed to have said 60 years ago that the day would come when the capitalists would fight with each other for the privilege of selling the rope with which to hang them. What he didn't know is that they would also offer credits to buy the rope.

*At Georgetown University Center for
Strategic and International Studies/
The Christian Science Monitor, 10-13:22.*

Helmut Kohl
Chancellor of West Germany

2

If the question of human rights is concerned or involved, I am not blind either on the right eye or on the left eye. So it doesn't make any difference whether it's a Fascist dictator or a Communist dictator who violates human rights. Our sympathy must be with those whose rights are hurt and offended and violated and who are being enslaved. This is the fundamental question.

Interview, Bonn, Nov. 9/The New York Times, 11-11:6.

Andrew Kohut
*President, Gallup Organization,
public-opinion analysts*

3

In the strong current support for defense spending, something can be described as a "fortress America" outlook. But other opinion indicators—the willingness to use those arms or troops—went the other way in 1981. There is less support for the draft. [President] Reagan got low support from the public for arms for El Salvador, terrible things on El Salvador when his ratings for everything else were terrific. It's almost as if Americans think they can *buy* themselves world strength.

Interview/The Christian Science Monitor, 1-19:4.

Ernest W. Lefever
*Former nominee for Assistant Secretary
for Human Rights, Department of
State of the United States*

4

Misguided U.S. policies have helped deliver the people of Iran and Nicaragua into the hands of regimes that show less respect for basic human rights than their less-than-perfect predecessors. Human experience demonstrates that the best is often the enemy of the good. A fastidious opposition [by the U.S.] to an authoritarian regime may hasten the advent of a totalitarian one. To withhold economic or military aid to a besieged ally whose human-rights record is not blameless may help assure a far more repressive successor ... We should never condone the violation of basic rights anywhere, but we should recognize the severe limitations of public preaching and punitive measures directed against our friends and allies. An attitude of mutual respect supported by material assistance provides a more favorable atmosphere for encouraging them to correct abuses ...

*Before Pittsburgh World Affairs Council/
Chicago Tribune, 4-20:(1)11.*

John F. Lehman, Jr.
Secretary of the Navy of the United States

5

What are we prepared to do to defend against seizures or blockades or infringements against our vital interests and those of our allies that we are bound to by treaty? We see that the most likely contingencies in the world—in the real world—are largely unpredictable. Second, they are likely to take place at the conventional level where conventional forces—particularly naval forces—are the determinant of the outcome even though the nuclear balance provides the environment in which that kind of threat can be carried out.

*Interview, Washington/
The Christian Science Monitor, 4-12:13.*

Clare Boothe Luce
*Member, President's Foreign Intelligence
Advisory Board; Former diplomat
and playwright*

6

We talk our heads off about the diversity of ethnic groups in America and the importance of

(CLARE BOOTHE LUCE)

ethnic groups' trying to maintain some of their own culture, but this tolerance to diversity at home is not shown in foreign relations. Everyone has to be like us. We are practically every day of our lives insulting some nation.

Interview, Washington/
The New York Times, 2-7:(1)24.

1

Soon there will probably be as many Mexicans in Texas, New Mexico, lower California and Arizona—and as many Cubans and Latin Americans in Florida—as there are natives . . . Sure, in the 19th century the United States absorbed something like 40 million immigrants. But the vast majority of them were of a fundamental culture, and they were all white. They were not black or brown or yellow . . . Today, we have this curious idea that we must tolerate to the maximum all diversities. I am not sure we are not heading for the fate of ancient Rome, which in its later days had far fewer Romans than immigrants from all the conquered provinces around the Mediterranean basin. Rome became a city of pollution and noise and foreigners, and it collapsed under the weight of the barbarians. But in truth, Rome collapsed because the people within lost all desire to coalesce and defend it. It just fell apart.

Interview/The Washington Post, 9-15:(A)25.

Ferdinand E. Marcos
President of the Philippines

2

I have always found that the predatory powers have found the export of war, subversion and destabilization to be profitable . . . [Subversion] is just like malaria. It increases in intensity depending on the resistance, the economic development, the morale, the strength of the political leadership in government. And when that is low, then the infection builds up.

Interview/Newsweek, 9-20:52.

Carl Marcy
Co-director, American Committee
on East-West Accord

3

[On economic sanctions against the Soviet Union]: Economic sanctions generally do not

work. Take, for example, the Arab oil boycott of the U.S. a few years ago. What did it accomplish? Did it make the United States do what the Arabs wanted? No, it forced us to increase fuel reserves and probably had the effect of changing our entire automobile industry from building large cars to building small, fuel-efficient cars. Or take the case of Germany during World War II. We blockaded the Germans, cut off their rubber supplies, cut off their fuel supplies, and what happened? Germany developed synthetic rubber and synthetic fuels. In short, sanctions have unintended effects.

Interview/U.S. News & World Report, 10-11:27.

Jose Maria Marin
Governor of Sao Paulo, Brazil

4

I'm not one of those who blame the United States for all the evils in this world. Neither do I expect salvation to come from the United States. However, if the developed nations show no understanding for the problems faced by developing countries, the path ahead of us all will be more arduous.

Before business leaders, Sao Paulo,
Dec. 2/Los Angeles Times, 12-3:(I)10.

Walter F. Mondale
Former Vice President
of the United States

5

We're seeing a [Reagan Administration] foreign policy that is badly coordinated. You can't manage without an effective and sophisticated National Security Council, and we do not have one. The Administration has resorted to very loose talk about nuclear weaponry—such things as winning limited nuclear wars and firing warning shots—that has just driven our European allies up the wall. They have abandoned efforts of the Carter and Ford Administrations to put a crimp on nuclear proliferation. I think that is a serious mistake. I also believe the Administration is guilty of converting human rights from a principle to a tactic. They are right in criticizing the abuse of liberties in Poland. But credibility is diminished by our cozying up to the South Africans, the Argentines and the Chileans.

Interview/U.S. News & World Report, 3-1:20.

Christopher A. Nascimento
Former Minister of
Information of Guyana

1

The power to inform is one of the keys to power as such. The communications industry, the development of "transnational" news agencies, the evolution of electronic information systems, the billions expended on pioneering the advancement of space and computer technology, all serve and continue to serve as a means of political, commercial, social and cultural dominance of the world by the developed nations.

At UNESCO meeting, Paris, November/
The New York Times, 11-28:(1)3.

Richard M. Nixon
Former President of the United States

2

It disturbs me—and I'm a hawk on the Soviet Union—that the hawks always want [a trade] embargo [against the Soviets]. Our trade with the Russians amounts to $2-billion; Europe's with the Russians is $40-billion ... I'm not among those who say the Russians are repressive, and they are; expansionary, and they are; that they lie, although they do; and that their agriculture is in horrible shape, although it is. Those who do say these things say we must have nothing to do with the Russians; that if we isolate them, they'll collapse. These people won't say we must deal with them. But we *must,* with a carrot or a stick ... I'm for *trade* but not for *aid* to the Soviet Union. Their trade with us should not be subsidized [by us], [and] there should be restraints on the trade of military technology, direct or indirect ... We and the Russians must get to the *causes* of our difficulties. I'm not suggesting we should be soft on the Russians. God knows, I've never been that. But it is vitally important that the leaders know each other *not* by hotline but face-to-face.

Interview/The New York Times, 11-23:23.

3

You can't hold an alliance, or a country, together just with fear. Fear alone won't allow a free nation to sustain the support necessary for high defense budgets and an intelligent foreign policy that avoids the pitfalls of isola-

tionism and protectionism. Our leaders have got to provide what is the missing ingredient at the moment, and that is hope. There's got to be some hope that relations can get better and that equitable deals can be made. We've got to get over our disillusionment with detente and put aside the idea that the Soviets will always get two of everything for our one and the notion that the Soviet Union is an outlaw nation and must be so treated.

Interview, New York, December/Time, 12-27:18.

Anthony Parsons
British Ambassador/Permanent
Representative to the United Nations

4

All negotiations are the same, in one sense. You make progress quickly as you work your way through the peripheral issues. The closer you get to the heart of the matter, the more difficult it is and the greater the chance of failure.

Interview, London, May 13/
The New York Times, 5-14:6.

Javier Perez de Cuellar
Secretary General of the United Nations

5

[On his being the new Secretary General]: I don't intend ... to be anyone's puppet, nor to act as a bull in a china shop. I am fully aware of the fact that I am not some kind of president of the world and that the UN is at the service of its member states. Some of those who clamor for moral leadership are the first to shout "Don't meddle in my affairs" when the UN objects to some of their own misdeeds. By resorting to persuasion, by exerting moral pressure, by using diplomatic imagination, I hope to be able to contribute to bring about some movement on such delicate problems as Afghanistan, Cambodia, Cyprus, Namibia, the Middle East, to name but a few which involve the UN.

Interview, United Nations, New York, Jan. 7/
The Christian Science Monitor, 1-11:4.

Richard Pipes
Director of East European and Soviet
Affairs, National Security Council

6

Sanctions [against the Soviet Union], to be effective, must involve commodities over which

(RICHARD PIPES)

you have control. When we embargo large rotors, there is no other place else the Soviets can easily get them. But the world is awash with grain. If we embargoed grain, all we would be doing is robbing our own farmers and benefiting foreign farmers. The Carter Administration tried an embargo on grain three years ago. Nobody [else in the world] followed suit. I won't say it was totally ineffective—it cost the Soviet Union something. But in all these cases, the question is: Will it work? If it doesn't work, why should we punish ourselves?

Interview/U.S. News & World Report, 10-11:28.

Norman Podhoretz
Editor, "Commentary" magazine

1

My view generally is that the Soviet Union is similar in character to Nazi Germany: a revolutionary, totalitarian power bent on establishing a new international order in which it would enjoy political hegemony .... we now have a chance to do more than merely contain Soviet expansionism. We can also exploit the forces of disintegration that now seem to be exploding within the Soviet empire. These forces consist not only of the political discontent we have witnessed in Poland; they also include the severe economic problems that exist throughout the empire and within the Soviet Union itself. Instead of letting them suffer the consequences of their own failures and their own crimes, we have been helping them stabilize their empire. At the very minimum, we ought to stop doing this, particularly at the moment in Poland. That's the minimum.

Interview/U.S. News & World Report, 9-6:35.

Michel Poniatowski
Member, European Parliament; Former Minister of the Interior of France

2

I do not believe that one country can master the world. The superpowers, with their combined population of 480 million, cannot control a world of 7 billion. And they have no stake in trying, because that would disperse their strength. Imagine a country trying to take

charge of Pakistan or Bangladesh; it would sap its resources. The superpowers are trying to get strategic footholds and strike a balance in their relations. At this point the game consists of destabilizing the other side by acquiring influence or using terrorism. Even the Soviet Union would pay with its soul for trying to occupy Western Europe.

Interview/World Press Review, October:25.

Dan Quayle
United States Senator, R—Indiana

3

There is so little cohesion in defense and foreign policy now. You have a real problem with [Defense Secretary] Weinberger and [Secretary of State] Haig. They don't get along. It almost seems like whoever's out front on one issue, the other will come along and take the other side. Haig was much tougher on the Caribbean than Weinberger. Haig says you have to consider China more than Taiwan. Weinberger goes the other way. There's no consistency.

The New York Times, 4-19:10.

Ronald Reagan
President of the United States

4

[On foreign aid to Third World countries]: We must design a program, including direct aid, to meet the problem of each country, to help them eliminate social and economic inequities that make them targets for imported revolution. We suggest to the developing countries that government can do only so much, and that there's vast power in private enterprise to help development. Show us a Marxist system that has produced anything but poverty and misery. On the other hand, look at South Korea, Singapore, Taiwan, the Philippines, Hong Kong, where they have turned to the marketplace—their standard of living is approaching ours.

Interview/Los Angeles Times, 1-15:(II)12.

5

[On the possibility of using farm-product embargoes as an instrument of U.S. foreign policy]: There may come a day when our national security is threatened, and the issue of an embargo is raised again. In that case, I would not hesitate to declare such an embargo, [but

WHAT THEY SAID IN 1982

only] if it was part of a complete boycott, and if we could have the cooperation of other nations so that we wouldn't end up hurting ourselves with no harm done to those we are trying to influence ... Agricultural commodities are fungible; that is, they are easily interchanged for the same commodity from other nations. For this reason, the [grain] embargo of 1980 [against the Soviet Union] was almost totally ineffective; yet it caused great economic hardship to United States agriculture. We will not repeat such action.

To editors of farm publications, Washington, March 22/The New York Times, 3-23:39.

1

I don't need to recite the list of diplomatic efforts, spanning all Administrations, in which we've [the U.S.] been instrumental in ending war and restoring peace. Yet there are some who still ask which nation is the true peacemaker, the United States or the Soviet Union. Well, let us ask them which country has nearly 100,000 troops trying to occupy the once non-aligned nation of Afghanistan; which country has tried to crush a spontaneous workers movement in Poland; and what country has engaged in the most massive arms buildup in history? Or, let's put the question another way. What country helped its World War II enemies back on their feet? What country is employing trade, aid and technology to help the developing peoples of the world, and actively seeking to bring peace to the Middle East, the South Atlantic and to southern Africa? The answer is clear and it should give us both pride and hope in America.

Radio address to the nation, Camp David, Md., April 17/The New York Times, 4-18:(1)16.

2

I believe the unity of the West is the foundation for any successful relationship with the East. Without Western unity, we will squander our energies in bickering while the Soviets continue as they please. With unity, we have the strength to moderate Soviet behavior. We have done so in the past and we can do so again.

At Eureka (Ill.) College commencement, May 9/The Washington Post, 5-10 (A)12.

I know there are some who question the value of the (Western) alliance, who view it as cumbersome and at times unresponsive to the need for action. And there are those people still, in our land, who yearn for the isolationist shell. But because we've rejected those other courses back over the recent decades, there has been peace for almost 40 years on the Western front.

Before embarking on European trip, Washington, June 2/Time, 6-14:19.

4

Wherever the comparisons have been made between free and closed societies—West Germany and East Germany, Austria and Czechoslovakia, Malaysia and Vietnam—it is the democratic countries that are prosperous and responsive to the needs of their people. And one of the simple but overwhelming facts of our time is this: Of all the millions of refugees we have seen in the modern world, their flight is always away from, not toward, the Communist world. Today on the NATO line, our military forces face east—to prevent a possible invasion. On the other side of the line, the Soviet forces also face east—to prevent their people from leaving.

Before Parliament, London, June 8/ U.S. News & World Report, 6-21:73.

5

Some argue that we should encourage democratic change in right-wing dictatorships, but not in Communist regimes. To accept this preposterous notion—some well-meaning people have—is to invite the argument that, once countries [such as the Soviet Union] achieve a nuclear capability, they should be allowed an undisturbed reign of terror over their own citizens. We reject this course. As for the Soviet view, Chairman Brezhnev repeatedly has stressed that the competition of ideas and systems must continue and that this is entirely consistent with relaxation of tensions and peace. We ask only that these systems begin by living up to their own constitutions, abiding by their own laws, and complying with the international obligations they have undertaken. We ask only for a process, a direction, a basic code of decency—not for instant transformation.

Before Parliament, London, June 8/ The Washington Post, 6-9:(A)11.

(RONALD REAGAN)

1

America has no territorial ambitions. We occupy no countries and we have built no walls to lock our people in. Our commitment to self-determination, freedom and peace is the very soul of America. That commitment is as strong today as it ever was. The United States has fought four wars in my lifetime. In each, we struggled to defend freedom and democracy. We were never the aggressors. America's strength, and yes, her military power, have been a force for peace, not conquest; for democracy, not despotism; for freedom, not tyranny.

At United Nations special session on disarmament, New York, June 17/The Washington Post, 6-18:(A)12.

2

Soviet-sponsored guerrillas and terrorists are at work in Central and South America, in Africa, the Middle East, in the Caribbean and in Europe, violating human rights and unnerving the world with violence. Communist atrocities in Southeast Asia, Afghanistan and elsewhere continue to shock the free world as refugees escape to tell of their horror. The decade of so-called detente witnessed the most massive Soviet buildup of military power in history. They increased their defense spending by 40 per cent while American defense spending actually declined in the same real terms. Soviet aggression and support for violence around the world have eroded the confidence needed for arms negotiations.

At UN General Assembly conference on disarmament, New York, June 17/ The Washington Post, 6-18:(A)13.

3

[Addressing CIA employees] : Whether you work in Langley [CIA headquarters] or a faraway nation . . . it is upon your wit and intuition that the fate of freedom rests for millions of your countrymen and for many millions more, all around the globe. You are the tripwire across which the forces of aggression and tyranny must stumble in their quest for global domination.

At CIA headquarters, Langley, Va., June 23/ Los Angeles Times, 6-24:(I)27.

4

It is precisely when totalitarian regimes begin to decay from within— . . . when they feel the first real stirrings of domestic unrest— that they seek to reassure their own people of their vast and unchallengeable power through imperialist expansion or foreign adventure.

At Central Intelligence Agency headquarters, Langley, Va., June 23/Los Angeles Times, 6-24:(I)27.

5

[On critics of his policy of selling U.S. grain to the Soviets] : We're asking the Soviets to give us cash on the line for the food they buy. We're not providing them with any subsidies or pumping any Western currencies into Soviet pockets. It's always seemed ironic to me that many people who are so quick to sacrifice the interest of farmers in an effort to seem tough [with the Soviets] are unwilling to do the real things we need to send a signal of national will and strength [such as a military buildup to match the Soviets]. We [in the Administration] have our priorities right.

Radio broadcast to farm states, Washington, Oct. 15/The Washington Post, 10-16:(A)7.

6

The balance between the United States and the Soviet Union cannot be measured in weapons and bombers alone. To a large degree, the strength of each nation is also based on economic strength. Unfortunately, the West's economic relations with the U.S.S.R. have not always served the national-security goals of the [Western] alliance. The Soviet Union faces serious economic problems, but we, and I mean all of the nations of the free world, have helped the Soviets avoid some hard economic choices by providing preferential terms of trade, by allowing them to acquire militarily relevant technology and by providing them a market for their energy resources, even though this creates an excessive [Western] dependence on them. By giving such preferential treatment we've added to our own problems, creating a situation where we have to spend more money on our own defense to keep up with Soviet capabilities which we helped create.

Radio address to the nation, Nov. 13/The New York Times, 11-14:(1)9.

Donald T. Regan
Secretary of the Treasury
of the United States

1

[On President Reagan's urging curbs on trade concessions to the Soviet Union]: If you extend too much in the way of credit to your adversary, aren't you indeed propping up your adversary to your own disadvantage? If you loan too much, pretty soon your debtor becomes the master and you're the slave because you have to keep the debtor going. What President Reagan is trying to do is to point out the dangers of such a course to the Western nations. If that's an obsession, so be it.

To reporters, Versailles, France,
June 4/Los Angeles Times, 6-5:(I)12.

David Rockefeller
Head of international advisory
committee, and former chairman,
Chase Manhattan Bank

2

Americans tend to assume that because a particular country has accepted support from a Communist state and has used Marxist rhetoric, we should never deal with them. Cutting off all contact—even with the Sandinistas in Nicaragua—may be a mistake. I'm not saying we should support them, but we need to be concerned about them. I think we need in our foreign policy more sophistication and flexibility.

Interview/U.S. News & World Report, 10-11:72.

Carlos P. Romulo
Foreign Minister of the Philippines

3

There are two United Nations: the specialized agencies and the political body. The specialized agencies—UNESCO, UNICEF, ILO, FAO and others—have in a large measure assisted the world and not just the Third World. They have fed the hungry, educated children, given hope to the distressed, upheld the dignity of men. The political body has been less successful ... Member states must come to recognize that the common interest of humanity takes precedence over their narrow national interests. In this country [the U.S.], the states of the union eventually recognized the authority of the Federal government. One hundred

fifty nations must understand that their individual interests must be submerged in the larger interest of peace and order.

Interview, New York/The
Christian Science Monitor, 12-28:8.

Edward L. Rowny
Special Representative for Arms
Control and Disarmament for the
President of the United States

4

[On the current arms-control talks with the Soviet Union]: We [Americans] tend to think that this is an NFL football-type negotiation or a labor-versus-management type negotiation. But these are different cultures. Unfortunately, we don't study that, we don't understand that. We get frustrated, and we end up negotiating among ourselves. The Soviets have been trained under authority, and they don't understand democracy. To the extent that they understand it, they think it's a weakness. Compromise is seen as weakness. But the essence of Western negotiations is compromise ... In the spirit of Greek rationalism, we believe that problems are there to be solved. The Soviet attitude is that they may be there to be solved, or they may not be.

Interview, Washington/The
Christian Science Monitor, 10-4:17.

Donald H. Rumsfeld
Former Secretary of Defense
of the United States

5

In framing U.S. policy, it is important to keep in mind that the Soviet Union is not just another nation or even just another big nation. It is a nation that rejects our basic values of respect for individual freedom and self-determination for nations. Its approach is diametrically opposed to ours. It is expansionist in nature. And, at the same time, it is the only nation on earth that has the power to threaten our values—indeed, to threaten Western civilization. The threat it poses to the West derives entirely from its accumulation of raw military power.

Interview/U.S. News & World Report, 9-6:34.

Helmut Schmidt
Chancellor of West Germany

1

[On criticism of Western trade with the Soviet Union]: Trade is not a weapon for East or West. It's a ridiculous, preposterous idea that you have a handle to a pan if you have influence on just 1 per cent of their GNP. All their Western trade is on that order. On the other hand, I think it's normal that countries that neighbor each other should have some trade with each other, and we will not easily cut this off. We are a free-trade country. We have to sell about 30 per cent of our GNP on the world market. Our sales to the Soviet Union are not half our sales to a small country like Austria or Switzerland. But altogether it counts.

Interview, New York/Newsweek, 6-28:51.

Patricia Schroeder
United States Representative,
D–Colorado

2

[Saying the U.S. should reduce its troops overseas]: We're saying we're no longer interested in being the Wyatt Earp of this earth. We are only 3 per cent of the population of this planet and we cannot keep the whole world free by ourselves.

Los Angeles Times, 7-30:(I)1.

Jerome Shestack
President, International League
for Human Rights

3

A nation with human rights is less likely to be aggressive. Human rights is the drumbeat to which the masters of the world march.

At American Bar Association
convention, San Francisco, August/
The Christian Science Monitor, 8-9:4.

George P. Shultz
Secretary of State-designate
of the United States

4

It is critical to the over-all success of our foreign policy that we persevere in the restoration of our strength. But it is also true that the willingness to negotiate from that strength is a fundamental element of strength itself.

At Senate Foreign Relations Committee
hearing on his confirmation, Washington,
July 13/Los Angeles Times, 7-14:(I)8.

5

Today, most Americans recognize that a steady and coherent involvement by the U.S. in the affairs of the world is a necessary condition for peace and prosperity. Over and over again since the close of the Second World War, the U.S. has been the global power to whom others have turned for help, whether it be to assist in the process of economic development or in finding peaceful solutions to conflicts ... If we are strong, we buttress our allies and friends and leave our adversaries in no doubt about the consequences of aggression. If we provide assistance to help others to be strong, our own strength can be husbanded and brought to bear more effectively. If we are confident, we give confidence to those who seek to resolve disputes peacefully. If we are engaged, we give hope to those who would otherwise have no hope. If we live by our ideals, we can argue their merit to others with confidence and conviction.

At Senate Foreign Relations Committee
hearing on his confirmation, Washington/
The Christian Science Monitor, 8-2:23.

George P. Shultz
Secretary of State of the United States

6

[On being a mediator]: Sometimes a mediator has to carry messages faithfully back and forth. Sometimes a mediator needs to go to one party and the other and really talk about the point of view and the problems of the other side. Sometimes the role of the mediator is to develop some proposals and put them forward to the parties privately. Sometimes the role of the mediator is to put forward certain kinds of proposals publicly.

Before House Foreign Affairs Committee,
Washington, Sept. 9/The New York Times, 9-10:6.

7

[On the U.S. message to the new Russian leadership now that Soviet leader Leonid Brezhnev is dead]: I don't think this message is complicated, and that's what makes it a good one. It's a simple message: We are realists, and we'll stay that way. We are strong, and we'll stay that way. We're constructive and ready to solve problems, and we'll continue to be ready

(GEORGE P. SHULTZ)

to do so. And if this takes place, the world will be a better place for everyone.

To reporters, Moscow, Nov. 14/
Los Angeles Times, 11-15:(I)1.

Alexander I. Solzhenitsyn
Exiled Soviet author

1

It seems to be fashionable in the West to demand from all who stand in the forefront of defense, under machine-gun fire, to demand the widest democracy, and not just simple, but absolute democracy, bordering on total dissoluteness, on state treason, on the right to destroy their own state and country—such freedom as Western countries tolerate. Such is the price the West demands from each menaced country . . .

Broadcast address, Taipei, Taiwan/
The Wall Street Journal, 12-15:28.

Susan Sontag
Author

2

There are many lessons to be learned from the Polish events [the martial-law crackdown on the Solidarity union movement]. But, I would maintain, the principal lesson . . . is the . . . failure of Communism, the utter villainy of the Communist system. It has been a hard lesson to learn. And I am struck by how long it has taken us to learn it . . . We had identified the enemy as Fascism. We heard the demonic language of Fascism. We believed in, or at least applied a double standard to, the angelic language of Communism . . . The emigres from Communist countries we didn't listen to, who found it far easier to get published in the *Reader's Digest* than in *The Nation* or the *New Statesman,* were telling the truth. Now we hear them. Why didn't we hear them before? . . . The result was that many of us, and I include myself, did not understand the nature of the Communist tyranny . . . What the recent Polish events illustrate is something more than that Fascist rule is possible within the framework of a Communist society . . . What they illustrate is a truth that we should have understood a very long time ago: that Communism *is* Fascism . . . Not only is Fascism the probable destiny of all Communist societies . . . but Communism is in

itself a variant . . . of Fascism. Fascism with a human face.

Before audience gathered to
support Polish Solidarity union,
New York, February/Newsweek, 2-22:28.

Harold B. Steele
President, Illinois Farm Bureau

3

[Criticizing the possibility of a U.S. grain embargo against the Soviet Union because of the martial-law crackdown in Poland]: Even the threat of an embargo over the Polish crisis is depressing grain prices as much as if an embargo were declared. Moreover, there is no support for an embargo from our free-world allies, which indicates it would be hard to make one effective. No doubt stopping trade with our enemies is an idea which has great popular appeal, but it would hurt our farmers more than it would the Soviets. We need a strong, determined foreign policy to deal with world problems, but a grain embargo is neither strong nor determined.

News conference, Bloomington, Ill.,
Feb. 2/Chicago Tribune, 2-3:(1)1.

Robert Teeter
Public-opinion analyst

4

[The public's attitude on foreign policy is] not isolationism. It's a return to normalcy. From World War II, the prevailing view was that it was in America's interest to have a strong national defense and involvement in world affairs. Vietnam interrupted that. The return to normalcy after Vietnam was accelerated by [the Soviet invasion of] Afghanistan and [the overthrow of the Shah of] Iran. There is still no stomach for sending troops anywhere. And there is a strong nationalist feeling—that American interests should be pressed. But that's not isolationism.

Interview/The Christian Science Monitor, 1-19:4.

Margaret Thatcher
Prime Minister of the United Kingdom

5

In the weeks and months ahead we shall watch the new Soviet leadership [put in place after the death of Leonid Brezhnev] earnestly

136

(MARGARET THATCHER)

for solid evidence of a willingness to work for genuine multilateral disarmament ... But I cannot forget that over the past years, where the Soviet Union has advanced, it has done so not by force of ideas but by force pure and simple.

At Guildhall, London, November/Time, 11-29:35.

Malcolm Toon
Former United States Ambassador
to the Soviet Union   *1*

... with respect to the Soviet Union, I am concerned about the tendency of [U.S. President] Reagan and some people around him to hold the Soviets responsible for every instance of unpleasantness that happens around the world. I am the first to blame the Soviets for misbehavior. But it's a bit simplistic for us to assume that everything that happens that has an anti-American tinge is directly attributable to the Soviet evil genius.

Interview/U.S. News & World Report, 3-15:45.

2

[Criticizing President Reagan's Ambassadorial appointments]: We do not have to accept the poor sort of talent we have seen over the last year. We have an actor [as Ambassador] in Mexico City, a political post, the most sensitive spot in the hemisphere. We have a man in London who owes his place in life to the fact that his parents founded a furniture-polish dynasty. His only qualification for the job is that he speaks English. We have a man in Paris, a highly proficient banker, whose main qualification for his job is that he speaks French and is a friend of [former French President Valery] Giscard d'Estaing, who is out of power and is considered the archenemy of the man who is running the country [President Francois Mitterrand]. In Italy, we have an equally eminent lawyer who speaks no Italian in a country where the Ambassador must speak the language to have an impact.

Interview/The New York Times, 4-1:8.

Pierre Elliott Trudeau
Prime Minister of Canada   *3*

The U.S. has a special role to play in this dangerously disturbed and divided world, a role

based on power and the responsible use of power—superpower to be more precise—and the super responsibilities that go with it. The burden that this places upon Americans is enormous, and it is not surprising that you have known moments of self-doubt and withdrawal. The health and vitality of our system and way of life are, ultimately, in your hands.

At University of Notre Dame
commencement/Time, 6-21:82.

Brian E. Urquhart
Under Secretary General for
Special Political Affairs
of the United Nations   *4*

[On U.S. criticism of the UN]: The UN is the only place the U.S. can turn to in time of crisis, when there's the risk of a serious confrontation between the nuclear powers. It makes no sense to throw away the key to the shelter.

The New York Times Magazine, 12-19:44.

Cyrus R. Vance
Former Secretary of State
of the United States

5

The [Reagan] Administration doesn't seem to have recognized that for dealing with the Soviets, you have to have a plan. If they have a plan, it's certainly not been articulated. I don't think they recognize that any strategy for managing the relationship with the Soviets must have both carrots and sticks. It cannot have only sticks.

Interview, Mt. Kisco, N.Y./
The Christian Science Monitor, 3-10:9.

Gore Vidal
Author; Candidate for California
Democratic U.S. Senatorial nomination

6

One of the most ancient stories of our race is how Prometheus stormed the ramparts of heaven in order to seize fire. In the 5,000 years since Prometheus, we have laid constant siege to heaven ... But there is a dark side to our divinity. At heart we are still frightened. Stone-Age savages clustering together in tribes in order to fight off enemies and gain new territories ... We must now transcend those

(GORE VIDAL)

loyalties that we associate with the nation-state, because the fire we stole from heaven last time was nuclear fire ... So let us begin to make connections with one another so that we can send the military-political complex that governs this country the unmistakable message that we no longer believe a word that they have to say about invented dangers in the jungles of other countries, that we will no longer waste a third of our wealth on the mindless making of armaments and that if they do not change their ways, we will remove them from power.

Campaigning at University of San Francisco,
April 14/Los Angeles Times, 4-15:(I)22.

Caspar W. Weinberger
Secretary of Defense of the United States

1

[When the Reagan Administration took office,] it was vital to change the perception of the United States in the world, and that perception was very bad–very unreliable ally, no willingness to fight, no willingness to stay with a tough course. A lot of very vague perceptions that all we were really interested in [in foreign policy] was human rights and what is generally viewed as the equivalent of unilateral disarmament. A lot of pious hopes and hand-wringing but not willingness to insert any muscle into the process. And a whole raft of perceptions about the country that weren't all that wrong, unfortunately, but had urgently to be changed ...

Interview/The Washington Post, 4-18:(B)4.

2

Soviet leaders have learned they can obtain Western technology through both legal and illegal channels. Where they have failed to get what they want openly, they have resorted to a well-coordinated illegal acquisitions program. Using agents, co-opting citizens, taking advantage of unsuspecting businessmen, moving goods through neutral and Third World countries, they are gaining access to Western technology on an unprecedented and alarming scale ... We have been selling them the rope to hang us.

Before Foreign Policy Association, New York,
May 21/Los Angeles Times, 5-23:(I)1.

William C. Westmoreland
General, United States Army; Former
Commander, U.S. forces in Vietnam

3

Intelligence is at best an imprecise science. It is not like counting beans; it is more like estimating cockroaches.

News conference, Washington, Jan. 26/
The Christian Science Monitor, 1-27:3.

Charles Z. Wick
Director, International Communication
Agency of the United States

4

[On the Voice of America, which his agency oversees] : The role [of the Voice of America] essentially is still to tell the world about America in a credible way. [But] we place a new priority on our awareness that the sophistication of Soviet disinformation is hurting our [national] interests ... by painting us as war-mongers while [the Soviets] shout "peace, peace, peace" and go on pursuing territorial expansionism .... and we certainly do want the [Voice of America] commentary to be more attuned to [correcting] Soviet disinformation.

Interview, Washington/Los Angeles Times, 6-17:(I-B)6.

Gary Wills
Professor of American culture
and public policy,
Northwestern University

5

As a nation, we have a rather childish sense of our power. We think that if we have military and economic might, others will do our will. But the truly powerful do not boss others around; they elicit their cooperation. Clausewitz, the Prussian military strategist, says that victory is getting others to do your will ... In exercising power, America has traditionally been contemptuous of world opinion. We want other countries–even if they cooperate with us–to subordinate their goals to ours. We don't think of ourselves as having strength in union, as being part of the non-Communist world, which in its aggregate, is much stronger than the Communist world. Yet our real strength has largely been the widespread nature of our alliances, though we have endangered that over

(GARY WILLS)

and over in the name of what we erroneously thought of as strength.

Interview/
U.S. News & World Report, 7-26:46.

Howard E. Wolpe
United States Representative,
D–Michigan

1

The President [Reagan] needs to understand that the world is a much more complicated place than suggested by the simplistic East-West labeling of his Administration's foreign policy. He must understand that, generally, the underlying bases of conflicts in the Third World are social and economic and that efforts to impose military solutions are counter-productive. We play into the hands of the Soviets or their surrogates when we become identified with repressive regimes and appear to be resisting revolutionary movements struggling for more-just social and political systems.

Interview/
U.S. News & World Report, 4-19:39.

Leonid M. Zamyatin
Director, International Information
Department, Soviet Communist Party
Central Committee

2

If the Soviet Union and the U.S. want to conduct negotiations on a whole complex of questions that concern, literally, the fate of the earth, then this process has to be based on a certain amount of mutual trust. Speeches like [U.S. President] Reagan's [criticizing the Soviet Union] undermine that trust and create new tensions between our nations. We are not suggesting that we should love each other. We are not expecting Reagan to turn sentimental about us. We are not going to turn him into a friend of the Soviet Union any more than he is going to make capitalists out of us. But since he is the head of the U.S. government, with which we have relations and must conduct negotiations, we put aside emotions and propaganda and try to get down to business. Reagan talks about using force in the ideological struggle. We do not include within the framework of the ideological struggle an attempt to impose our ideas on the U.S. by force or the threat of force. That is the difference between Reagan's concept and our own.

Interview, Moscow, June/Time, 6-21:35.

Government

Martin Anderson
*Former Assistant to the President
of the United States (Ronald
Reagan) for Domestic Affairs*

1

In any new Administration, 80 to 90 per cent of what you will accomplish comes in the first year, and from then on you are making adjustments. There also comes a point where you have to decide if you want to be a public bureaucrat or an academician. I had one of the best government jobs—but it was still a government job.

*The Washington Post,
7-4:(A)16.*

William L. Armstrong
United States Senator, R—Colorado

2

[On the use of the appropriations process to push an amendment or change the law]: In my judgment, if somebody has an issue that they want to raise and the rules permit it to be raised through use of an appropriations bill, I don't criticize them for doing so. If somebody wants to filibuster to prevent an amendment from passing, you'll never hear me criticize that either. The rules exist in order to establish a framework under which decisions may be made, and there's nothing inherently right or wrong about any particular procedure. I do think it lends credibility to a proposed amendment, for example, if it has been the subject of hearings and study in the committee that has jurisdiction over it. But that doesn't make it wrong to raise it on an appropriations bill—particularly where a limitation on funding is the issue . . .

*Interview/
The New York Times,
2-7:(4)5.*

Thorne O. Auchter
*Assistant Secretary for Occupational
Safety and Health, Department of
Labor of the United States*

3

[On working in the Federal government]: It's not the long hours of hard work, which can actually be fun. The tough part is getting used to the criticism. If you make a mistake in private industry, only a handful ever know about it. If you make one here, the whole country soon knows, and you soon know that they know.

Interview, Washington/The New York Times, 10-29:8.

Howard H. Baker, Jr.
*United States Senator,
R—Tennessee*

4

[Advocating the televising of Senate sessions]: The whole concept of representative government is based on the idea that the public should have access to that process. Otherwise, there would be no public galleries in the Senate and House. I'm convinced that had we had television at the time the Constitution was adopted, we'd have had television in Congress then as a simple extension of the public's right to see, to hear and to understand what these trustees were doing on their behalf and in their name. So I feel that television is overdue. It is a logical extension of the public gallery.

Interview/U.S. News & World Report, 3-8:53.

5

The one great fault of the Senate, in my judgment, is that, over the years, we have squandered our prime resource, and that is our character as a great forum for the discussion of public issues. I would like to see, once again, briefer periods in which the full Senate was in

(HOWARD H. BAKER, JR.)

session and more Senators participating in debate with less reserve and caution .... we might restore the character of the Senate to the time of its greatest grandeur in the decades just before the Civil War. Then it was the center of the decision-making process.

Interview/U.S. News & World Report, 3-8:54.

James A. Baker III
*Chief of Staff to the President
of the United States*

1

... all Presidents get frustrated with leaks [of confidential and classified information]. And this President [Reagan] is just as concerned about them as other Presidents have been. It's a very difficult problem. We recognize that it is. And we also recognize that there's no easy answer or easy solution. The recent directive put out with respect to classified information will make it a little easier to determine what public official has access to classified information. And disclosure of classified information is a crime.

*Interview, Washington/The
Christian Science Monitor, 2-9:10.*

Richard Bolling
*United States Representative,
D—Missouri*

2

[Arguing in favor of a Congressional pay raise in the face of strong opposition]: I believe the inability of this institution to deal with our salaries makes the institution ridiculous. It grossly skews the ability to get qualified people [into both Congress and the Executive Branch].

Los Angeles Times, 12-14:(I)5.

Helen Boosalis
*Mayor of Lincoln, Neb.; President,
United States Conference of Mayors*

3

[The Reagan Administration's "new Federalism" plan has] gone a long way toward dismantling the system of government programs that counteract the hardships of economic downturns and help the people of this country when they most need help ... I wonder if we are moving toward a time when the only imperatives of our national government are the manufacturing of money, stamps and missiles.

*At U.S. Conference of Mayors meeting,
Washington, Jan. 28/
Chicago Tribune, 1-29:(1)1.*

William M. Brodhead
*United States Representative,
D—Michigan*

4

[On why he has decided not to run for re-election]: I've had it ... I ask myself, what kind of life do I have? I'm tired of being tired all the time. I'm tired of being broke. I'm tired of being lonely. You can't make friends in this town [Washington]. First, because there's not much time for it. Second, I've never been to a social occasion in this town, ever, where somebody wasn't trying to hustle me to vote for or against some piece of legislation.

U.S. News & World Report, 10-11:51.

Jack Brooks
*United States Representative,
D—Texas*

5

[On President Reagan's proposals to stop the Federal government from interfering in state and local affairs]: Mr. Reagan makes it sound as if there were some big power grab by Washington. But it's been the other way around, at least in the 30 years I've been in Congress. The states and cities have been back here [in Washington] asking for highway money, for airport money and flood-control money and money for schools and hospitals. And not just asking. They beat on us. They clogged the halls and filled the committee rooms demanding money. They watched every vote. They played real tough. And I must say I haven't seen any of them lately coming around and asking us to stop giving them the money ... If public money is going to be handed out [by the Federal government], you better have some strings someplace.

*Interview, Washington/The
Wall Street Journal, 2-23:29.*

141

Clair W. Burgener
United States Representative,
R–California

1

[Supporting a pay raise for members of Congress]: Good pay is essential to good government ... and bad pay is leading to bad government. [The alternative to adequate pay is a Congress filled with] a bunch of millionaires [or] ne'er-do-wells, and once in a while you'll get them [both] in the same package.

Washington, Dec. 14/The
Washington Post, 12-15:(A)6.

George Bush
Vice President of
the United States

2

[On the Vice Presidency]: It's a funny role, because you can't make it into something it's not. You shouldn't worry about whether other people understand. I don't spend any time worrying about it. If somebody comes to me and says, "Well, prove you've got influence; give me some examples of where you've got influence," I'm very sorry–I can't do it. If the price of that is obscurity, or anonymity or allegations that you don't have any clout, fine. But I want confidence from the President so I can go in and say, "I feel very strongly about this, Mr. President," or "I disagree on that." And he'd know he could discuss it with me and know for a fact certain that I wouldn't discuss it with his staff, my staff, the press, my family or anyone else.

Interview/The New York Times, 2-28:(1)18.

3

[On being Vice President]: You gotta know what it is. And you gotta know what it's not. You gotta know what you can do; and you gotta know what you ought not try to do. And you gotta get these dimensions at least clear in your own mind and in a way that is compatible with whoever the President happens to be ... I have more access to information in this job than anyone in the United States except for one, the President. And that of itself is a luxury. That of itself makes you better able to do what the Constitution provides–take over if you have to. And I have access to the President–which I

don't talk about publicly a lot, but which is there ... But I just don't understand the cynics who say it's a nothing job. It was in the old days, when you sat up there in the Senate and couldn't vote and had no connection with the Executive Branch whatsoever. Indeed, the job has evolved just in the last 10 years. But the real key to it is the relationship between the Vice President and the President.

Interview, Washington, June/The
Christian Science Monitor, 6-28:22.

Frank C. Carlucci
Deputy Secretary of Defense
of the United States

4

[Saying he is leaving government to make more money in the private sector]: Nobody joins the government to get rich. But I got to the point where I had to borrow money to keep my son in college, and there are two more coming after him. I am a little sad that the government can't pay enough to keep people once they've gained the experience they need.

Interview/Los Angeles Times, 12-27:(I)4.

Richard B. Cheney
United States Representative,
R–Wyoming; Former Chief of Staff
to the President of the United
States (Gerald R. Ford)

5

The White House staff jobs give you a broader opportunity to influence a variety of events, but you're ultimately a hired gun. When you serve in the House [of Representatives], you may cast only one of 435 votes, but it's your decision to make. The House is where the action is. It's no longer a place where you have to be quiet for 10 years before you have an impact.

Interview, Washington/The New York Times, 4-6:14.

William S. Cohen
United States Senator, R–Maine

6

[On the misuse of the filibuster]: I recall that during the impeachment proceedings a few years ago I read a quote from a high-court

(WILLIAM S. COHEN)

justice who said that this sort of impeachment ought to be kept in a temple and withdrawn only on great occasions. And that had some meaning for me at the time. And it seems to me that the same sort of principle applies to filibusters. It's being withdrawn on too many occasions. So what we've done is to trivialize the process itself. And what we need to do is to change the rules when we go back into session next year and eliminate, as much as we can, the post-cloture debate . . . I think the filibuster should be reserved for great moral issues, very significant policy issues . . . I've always believed that freedom of speech under the First Amendment doesn't mean you have the right to strangle democracy with a single set of vocal chords.

To reporters, Washington, December/
The Christian Science Monitor, 12-27:7.

Barber B. Conable
United States Representative,
R–New York

1

[On members of Congress who change their votes on issues]: Peer-group pressure is of considerably greater significance than Presidential blandishments. There are very few people who look neither to the left or right, and just vote and walk out. Power and influence in Congress is the power to cause some people to question whether they have voted correctly.

The New York Times, 9-22:14.

Mario M. Cuomo
Governor-elect of New York (D)

2

If all I did was balance the budget without finding ways to improve the conditions of people's lives—the middle class, the poor, the disadvantaged—then a balanced budget would become the emblem of hypocrisy. Government has to do more than make the books come out.

Interview, New York, December/
Los Angeles Times, 12-17:(I-C)1.

John C. Danforth
United States Senator, R–Missouri

3

[Arguing against televising Senate sessions]: What is our justification for existence? Is it to

debate great issues of public policy or to dream up "one-liners" suitable for 60-second slots on the evening television news shows?

Before the Senate, Washington, Feb. 2/
The Washington Post, 2-3:(A)4.

4

Rules and regulations that entangle the Federal procurement system do more than simply aggravate the people who try to do business with the Federal government. They cost the taxpayer money. The complexities of the procurement system discourage people from doing business with the government. That means less competition for government work and higher prices. And the government's propensity for writing detailed specifications for government work, telling businesses how to build products instead of just telling businesses what it wants to buy—that costs money, too, driving up costs as businesses strive to customize products to government specifications. It also keeps the government from taking advantage of new product innovations, new technologies.

Nation's Business, October: 73.

Samuel Dash
Professor, Georgetown University
Law School; Former chief counsel,
Senate Watergate Committee

5

The President of the United States is still the most powerful chief executive in the free world. But we had seen a drift toward an imperial Presidency, going all the way back to [Franklin D.] Roosevelt. [Richard] Nixon took it to the extreme of believing he was an absolute monarch. Watergate stopped that trend and brought back to reality the doctrine of separation of powers.

Los Angeles Times, 6-17:(I)7.

Cleta Deatherage
Oklahoma state legislator

6

People say we [in state legislatures] should be more like [the U.S.] Congress and meet all the time. I think Congress should be more like us. I think it should adjourn on September 30 every year, except in the case of a national

(CLETA DEATHERAGE)

emergency . . . All I know is, I learn a lot more about what's going on at the cottage-cheese counter at the supermarket than anywhere else. Who has time to go to the supermarket during the session?

At National Conference of State
Legislators, Nashville, Tenn., March/
The Washington Post, 3-22:(A)5.

Robert J. Donovan
Journalist

1

. . . the arrival of the big jets—that changed the Presidency more than people realized. There was Eisenhower's great trip to India in 1959—which I covered and which I think was the great spectacle of my life. But the jets made the great difference. Theretofore, Presidents couldn't travel. They couldn't leave this country. There were very rare cases when they did; Woodrow Wilson to Paris was a notable one. But Presidents couldn't leave, because traveling by ship meant they had to be gone too long. The jet planes just opened the world to Presidents. And they loved it. And they couldn't stay off them. And I think it has made a great difference in the Presidency, in the coverage of the Presidency, and in diplomacy.

Interview, Washington/The
Christian Science Monitor, 9-15:3.

Robert K. Dornan
United States Representative,
R—California

2

[On members of Congress who use illegal drugs]: The full force of the law should come down like an anvil on the head of any Congressman who uses illegal drugs. It is the personification of the most arrogant boast of Lenin, that we're going to rot from within. And the last thing we need on Capitol Hill is a flaky, cocaine-snorting Congressman pumping money into organized crime.

U.S. News & World Report, 7-19:28.

144

David F. Durenberger
United States Senator, R—Minnesota

3

[Criticizing Reagan Administration ideas on a "new Federalism"]: Does this Administration—does my party—care about the poor? Is the "new Federalism" a smoke screen for a repeal of the New Deal? Is private-sector initiatives a fig leaf to cover a lack of compassion? . . . That the national government usurped its powers from its creators, the states, is, of course, baloney. We shouldn't sacrifice programs that have worked, to some simple notion of wrongful usurpation that is blind to the needs of our counties and cities.

Before National Association
of Counties, Baltimore, July 12/
The Washington Post, 7-13:(A)4.

Glenn English
United States Representative,
D—Oklahoma

4

[Criticizing Reagan Administration plans to limit the Freedom of Information Act]: . . . I think the changes would jeopardize the atmosphere of open government fostered by the Act, which gives the public wide access to unclassified government documents. The law embodies the very essence of our type of government: openness, public involvement, the right to know what your government is doing. The Reagan Administration wants to make wholesale changes that would make it much more difficult, if not impossible, for the public to discover the errors of government. This seems to be every Administration's approach, whether it is Democratic or Republican, liberal or conservative. We find that those who are out of power are the most enthusiastic supporters of the Act. It is only when they get into power that they begin to voice their concerns about it. And the bureaucracy itself, of course, doesn't want to have to bother with the requirements of the law. It is an inconvenience.

Interview/U.S. News & World Report, 1-18:69.

J. James Exon
United States Senator, D—Nebraska

5

[Criticizing the tax break for members of Congress that allows greater deductions for

(J. JAMES EXON)

living expenses in Washington]: The Congressional tax deduction is one of the most devastating blots on the credibility of Congress under present economic circumstances. It will be virtually impossible for Congress to exercise any type of leadership calling upon the American people to sacrifice for the good of the country unless we eliminate this abomination.

U.S. News & World Report, 4-12:14.

Dean Fischer
*Spokesman, Department of State
of the United States*

1

A government that does not keep secrets does not receive them.

*Washington, March 20/
The New York Times, 3-21:(1)11.*

Lee Fritschler
*President, American Society
for Public Administration*

2

We have moved from a time when people looked on their government as a problem-solver, even a helper, to a period of distrust and outrage ... Ask any person on the street, and here is what they will tell you about government: "Welfare is the largest Federal program, perhaps second only to defense"; in fact, spending for all Federal social services—very broadly defined—is no more than 8 per cent of the Federal budget. "The number of people on the Federal payroll is growing at an exponential rate, out of control"; in truth, it has remained constant at about 2.7 million civilians for the last 20 years ... "Waste and fraud are rampant in the Federal system" ... The General Accounting Office in a recent 24-agency, three-year study found that $187-million was lost due to fraud. And the agencies they studied were some of the largest in government ... A $187-million loss out of a 3½-year Federal expenditure of at least a couple of trillion dollars is a remarkable testament to honesty and efficiency ... Every public-sector failure story can be matched with a private fable about the "free market" left to its own devices—

Kepone in the James River, the Love Canal in upstate New York, PCBs in Michigan, the decline of the auto industry ... It has to be acknowledged—any reading of history confirms it—that it was the mix of business and government activity in this country that made our economy sing in the past.

The Washington Post, 4-28:(A)24.

J. William Fulbright
*Former United States Senator,
D—Arkansas*

3

When I came to Washington there was a feeling of continuity. There was the principle of seniority, and we had a number of experienced people in government. That's been changed. Everything is new, all the people are new. It strikes me there's no leadership—I'm speaking about the Congress now. There used to be that system of seniority, which meant really a form of hierarchy in which there was an acknowledged leader. And in the Executive, in the State Department, you had people at the higher levels who had been there for a while, who had been functioning in those areas. Today, I have a feeling that everybody's new, and nobody has had any experience, and it's all a great game of amateurs.

Interview/The Washington Post, 7-18:(B)3.

J. Joseph Garrahy
Governor of Rhode Island (D)

4

Being Governor of Rhode Island is different because the state is so small. The demands on my time are unbelievable. I'm invited to attend practically every christening, bar mitzvah and wedding in the state, to functions of just about every organization, the ethnic picnics, small-town political rallies—you name it. And they all expect me to show up. Not long ago I went to 25 different affairs one Sunday afternoon. In other states, most citizens never meet their Governor. I bet I've met just about everyone in Rhode Island.

*Interview, Providence/
Los Angeles Times, 5-3:(I)12.*

Harrison J. Goldin
Comptroller of New York City

1

Our historic belief in the role of government, imperfect though it be—to help fashion a better society, to help protect the disadvantaged and the powerless, to avoid chaos not only in the streets but in the job place and marketplace as well—is mocked by a new breed of elected officials who would use the powers of government to diminish and dismantle its protective role.

At his swearing-in ceremony, New York, Jan. 1/The New York Times, 1-2:10.

Richard C. Halverson
Chaplain of the United States Senate

2

No one who does not work here can possibly comprehend the unforgiving pressure under which the Senate operates: pressures from constituents, from lobbyists, from diverse self-interest groups; corrupting, seductive, destructive pressures of power, position and prestige; the pressure of having to live in two cities, with the travel demands. The awesome pressure of decisions involving the nation and world and affecting millions. The relentless pressure of responsibility that will not go away and from which there is never an escape; financial pressure, family pressure, peer pressure.

Prayer at opening of Senate session, Washington, Sept. 22/ The New York Times, 10-14:14.

Bryce N. Harlow
Former Counsellor to the President of the United States (Richard M. Nixon)

3

Every President has three circles around him—the inner circle, the outer and the far-outer. The far-outers try to get into the middle-outer and the middle-outers try to get into the inner, and the inners try to keep them all out. The President is their pet, their own private property. They don't want him defiled; they don't want their clutch weakened. Well, in about two years, normally, the inners collapse; they just sort of wear out. And about the same time, the President starts getting claustrophobia

and he breaks up that inner circle. By the end of his third or fourth year, the President starts breathing again.

Interview, Washington/The New York Times, 4-27:14.

S. I. Hayakawa
United States Senator, R—California

4

In the Senate, the right to speak at length is protected with almost a holy zeal. But the right to speak doesn't mean anything unless it's accompanied by listeners. What happens when a filibuster goes on? All the Senators leave.

Interview/The Christian Science Monitor, 11-3:1.

Howell Heflin
United States Senator, D–Alabama

5

[Criticizing Congress for voting itself a tax reduction last year]: Two hundred years ago, American patriots rose up in revolution against the basic evil of taxation without representation. But now that most members of Congress have taken their own names off the taxpayer rolls, there could very well be another revolution in this country—against what is being widely perceived as representation without taxation.

January/Chicago Tribune, 2-2:(1)4.

Nicholas Henderson
British Ambassador to the United States

6

You don't have a system of government [in the U.S.]. You have a maze of government. In France or Germany, if you want to persuade the government of a particular point of view, or find out their point of view on something, it's quite clear where the power resides. It resides with the government. Here [in Washington], there's a whole maze of different corridors of power and influence. There's the Administration. There's the Congress. There are the staffers. There's the press. There are the institutions. There's the judiciary. The lawyers in this town . . . So that makes life in Washington for a foreigner very much more exciting, difficult, varied than anywhere else. A familiar sight of Washington is to see some bemused diplomat pacing the corridors of the Capitol, trying to

(NICHOLAS HENDERSON)

find out where decisions are being taken. And when he's found that out, he may find it isn't on [Capitol] Hill at all. It's somewhere else . . . No, I don't think I understand it. I promise I don't.

Interview, Washington/The New York Times, 4-21:14.

Ken Holland
United States Representative,
D–South Carolina

1

If something doesn't change, this institution [Congress] will be made up of two classes of members–the wealthy and the ne'er-do-well. Middle people like me are not going to be able to come here until they've accumulated a lot of money to see them through.

U.S. News & World Report, 10-11:52.

Harry Hughes
Governor of Maryland (D)

2

[On the Reagan Administration's plan for a "new Federalism"]: This concept, of course, envisions the shifting of the decision-making responsibility . . . from Federal to state and local governments, a process I embrace with alacrity. We have seen the beginnings of the implementation of that philosophy through the folding of numerous categorical grants into block grants. Unfortunately, at the same time, we have seen sharp reductions in the funding of domestic programs far beyond what was originally envisioned. There are legitimate concerns to be wary of in the implementation of new Federalism . . . There are those of us who fear that an increasingly larger financial burden will be placed on state governments to maintain vital programs as the White House considers reducing its obligations under entitlement programs, as the Administration continues to consider the paring down of appropriations for future block grants . . . Lacking the resources to substitute state dollars for Federal funds, the only viable alternative is a steady reduction in state services. As this trend continues, it will be incumbent upon all of us to demonstrate both ingenuity and courage in spending tax dollars

and to use whatever resources we have available to use to discourage policies at the national level that balance budgets on the backs of the weaker amongst us.

State of the State address/
The Washington Post, 12-7:(A)20.

Thomas L. Hughes
President, Carnegie Endowment
for International Peace

3

Those [in Washington] who talk about power are those who lack it themselves. Lack of power is actually more interesting than power–it's more universal. Power corrupts and lack of power corrupts absolutely.

Interview, Washington/The New York Times, 4-16:10.

E. Pendleton James
Special Assistant to the President
of the United States for Personnel

4

[On his job of supervising Presidential personnel appointments]: You don't bat 1.000 in this business. Not everyone you appoint turns out to be a superstar; [and] some who you thought were mediocre appointments turn out to be stars. We ought to correct our mistakes. On the appointees that didn't turn out as well, we ought to ask them to go home. We can find the real achievers and move them up. I'm constantly harassed daily by people who are conniving, scheming, jockeying for government jobs. Now, that's not necessarily the way you should staff an Administration.

Interview, Washington, June/
The New York Times, 6-17:16.

Lady Bird Johnson
Widow of the late President of the
United States Lyndon B. Johnson

5

[On her experiences as First Lady]: You get a cram course in the United States of America–the history, the geography, the people that make it up and what they do for a living, the different racial and cultural strains in its history. It enlarges you, makes you a more understanding person. It was yeasty, hopeful, charging forward against the troubles of the time.

Interview, Washington/The New York Times, 3-22:24.

WHAT THEY SAID IN 1982

John J. LaFalce
United States Representative,
D–New York

1

During our history, good and respectable men, public servants from a multitude of backgrounds and political persuasions, have openly, honestly and fairly debated the merits of Jefferson's admonition that "the government which governs least, governs best." Today that debate has taken an ugly turn for the worse, a turn which has been dominated by slogans suggesting that government is inherently bad, inherently ineffective, inherently evil. That is a most dangerous turn of events. The notion of "government as Klutz," as conservative columnist George Will has termed it, is a very dangerous notion. It is unfortunate that it has become the battle cry for those who wish to reduce the size of government, for it reduces the platform for debate on the myriad number of specific issues to a mere shouting match over "getting government off our backs."

Lecture, Canisius College/
Chicago Tribune, 2-17:(1)11.

Richard Lamm
Governor of Colorado (D)

2

I favor the proposal to shift some Federal programs to the states *if* we get the corresponding revenues to help finance them. I want Washington thinking about El Salvador and the Middle East and inflation—not about potholes and how many calories are in a school-lunch program.

U.S. News & World Report, 3-8:50.

Paul Laxalt
United States Senator, R–Nevada

3

Federalism means to me, and I think it means to the President [Reagan] that we peel back those programs that can more efficiently and compassionately be handled at the local level. We were both local officials, both Governors, and we both experienced the frustration any Governor or Mayor has in feeling very quickly you are a messenger boy for Washington in carrying out very inefficient programs. If you simply had the responsibility for admin-

istering the program, you feel you could do a better job.

Interview/Forbes, 3-1:109.

Patrick J. Leahy
United States Senator, D–Vermont

4

I sense in the current [Reagan] Administration a consistent bias against openness in government. I see an effort to gag bureaucrats; I see attempts to weaken the Freedom of Information Act; I see an excessive use of Executive privilege to withhold documents that have nothing to do with national security.

At symposium on Freedom of
Information Act, Washington, May 4/
The Washington Post, 5-5:(A)5.

Russell B. Long
United States Senator, D–Louisiana

5

[Arguing against the televising of Senate sessions]: ... it would drastically change the nature of the Senate, and not for the best. It would impede the Senate's work and prevent us from doing what the people have the right to expect us to do—defeat some bad bills even though they may be politically popular at the moment ... The Senate is expected to give stability and statesmanship to our government to a degree that is not expected of the House. A lot of unwise proposals sailed right through the House but were defeated in the Senate because the Senate has unlimited debate that can continue for days or months. Issues can be considered in a much more careful manner. That character of the Senate would not survive live television coverage.

Interview/U.S. News & World Report, 3-8:53.

Paul N. McCloskey, Jr.
United States Representative,
R–California

6

[On Washington]: Nobody should fall in love with this town. Nobody should have to be here to be happy. Most of the common sense is somewhere outside of Washington.

Interview, Washington/
The Washington Post, 6-12:(A)2.

Dan Clinton McKinnon
*Chairman, Civil Aeronautics Board
of the United States*
1

As a businessman, I have always believed the bottom line was results. In Washington, I found that the bottom line is talk, and you could see that by the way offices are organized—desks shoved over in the corner, and clusters of couches and chairs in the middle forming a conversation pit.
Interview/The New York Times, 9-28:12.

James C. Miller III
Chairman, Federal Trade Commission
2

The Postal Service should be required to produce a detailed empirical study of the economic justification for continuing its monopoly over first-class mail. If that justification does not exist, I would urge an end to the monopoly. This would likely have a substantial, beneficial effect on the market for first-class mail. In a competitive market, private firms would vie with the Postal Service in reducing costs and improving services for customers. Private firms normally perform better than government enterprises, and competitive markets usually perform better than monopolized ones.
Interview/U.S. News & World Report, 8-2:63.

William G. Milliken
Governor of Michigan (R)
3

In a personal sense, there is an enormous commitment that one in public life makes. You live in a goldfish bowl and you live by schedules ... You live by the building of budgets and by the writing of state-of-the-state addresses and policy decisions that have to, like clockwork, come every year. You're not free to do anything.
Interview/Los Angeles Times, 3-8:(I)8.
4

Fourteen years ago, there was relatively little [state] contact with the Federal or with regional governments. Today, no Governor can function without a clear understanding of the position of the Federal government. The same thing is true in the region. We have the Upper Great Lakes Council of Governors. We work closely on environmental and other matters. We even work closely with the provinces of Ontario and Quebec. There is commonality of interest.
Interview/The New York Times, 8-15:(4)5.

Walter F. Mondale
Former Vice President of the United States
5

I believe the debate over Federalism is warranted. I have no objection to that at all. But I don't think we can strengthen our country if we say the national government is no longer a central forum for discussion of our problems.
Interview/U.S. News & World Report, 3-1:20.

Lyn Nofziger
*Former Special Assistant to the
President of the United States (Ronald
Reagan) for Political Affairs*
6

To a certain extent, people who are on the President's staff are always reluctant to bring him bad news. In addition, it's a little difficult to find out what's going on outside. So it's very helpful to the President to have someone he trusts, someone who's not grinding his own ax.
The New York Times Magazine, 3-21:26.

Sandra Day O'Connor
*Associate Justice, Supreme
Court of the United States*
7

My experience in the Executive, Legislative and Judicial branches of government and my position on the Supreme Court all point to this conclusion: An informed, reasoned effort by one citizen can have dramatic impact on how someone, like a legislator, will vote and act. When I was in the legislature, one person, sometimes with a direct interest in the matter, sometimes without one, would on occasion persuade me by the facts, by the clarity of the explanation and by the reasoning, to do something which I never would otherwise have done. I have been at caucuses when a group of legislators was trying to decide what to do, and, time and time again, my fellow legislators would refer to the logic or fairness of what some plain, unknown citizen has said. I have had an opportunity to view this same basic

(SANDRA DAY O'CONNOR)

phenomenon from a different perspective in my role as a Supreme Court Justice. A majority of litigants who come before us are people who are essentially unknown, not only to us but even within their own community. We resolve their problems and, in the process, resolve the problems of thousands or millions similarly situated.

At Stanford University commencement/
The Christian Science Monitor, 7-16:23.

William A. O'Neill
Governor of Connecticut (D)

1

If we don't have a strong national government, the country will start to disintegrate. Holding the line and walking away from responsibilities in Washington would weaken, not strengthen, this country. In the modern world, we cannot go back to the days of 50 individual states, all doing their own thing. Too many responsibilities are intertwined, whether it's the highway and rail systems or whether it's jobs, health and welfare. These are not local problems. They're Federal problems, and they can only be solved on a Federal level.

Interview/U.S. News & World Report, 8-30:63.

Roger B. Porter
Special Assistant to the
President of the United
States for Policy Development

2

. . . a successful [Presidential] decision-making process requires skillful management. Someone must be in charge—calling meetings, setting agendas, developing papers . . . He must exhibit two crucial qualities of an honest broker. On the one hand he must ensure due process, making certain that the views of interested departments and agencies are reflected fairly and faithfully. But he must also promote a genuine competition of ideas, identifying viewpoints not adequately represented or that require qualifications, and sometimes augmenting the resources of one side or the other so that a balanced presentation results.

Before American Economic Association/
The Christian Science Monitor, 2-4:10.

William Proxmire
United States Senator,   D—Wisconsin

3

[Criticizing recent tax breaks voted itself by Congress] : It's outrageous at a time when ordinary citizens are paying taxes through the nose that members of the House and Senate will get a big tax break denied to all other taxpayers . . . When Congress returns January 25, I will introduce a bill to repeal the sweet expense account tax bonanza Congress voted itself in December. It's a sneaky, back-door way for members of the House and Senate to vote themselves a pay raise. It's worth at least $10,000 a year and probably much more . . . Not only did Congress vote itself this largess, but made it fail-safe. The IRS cannot audit or challenge it.

Interview, January/Chicago Tribune, 1-19:(1)1,8.

Robert Ray
Governor of Iowa (R)

4

[On his advice to his successors as Governor] : I know the advice I gave myself. I was just absolutely overwhelmed when I had to put together a staff, a budget for the legislature, a whole legislative program, had 30,000 applications for notary public, four-and-a-half pages, legal-size paper single spaces of names of people waiting to see me. And I, lying back in that big chair, said, Look, I don't have to have the job. I can make more money practicing law as I was doing before. There's only one way to run this office and that is to listen to the people that you can hear from and learn all that you can, know what the options are, select the one that you think is the right one, and then stay with it and take the flak. And if they don't like you, why, let them get another Governor.

Panel discussion/The New York Times, 8-15:(4)5.

Ronald Reagan
President of the United States

5

Unauthorized disclosure of classified information under the jurisdiction of the National Security Council and of classified intelligence reports is a problem of major proportions with

(RONALD REAGAN)

the U.S. government. The Constitution of the United States provides for the protection of individual rights and liberties, including freedom of speech and freedom of the press, but it also requires that government functions be discharged efficiently and effectively, especially where the national security is involved. As President of the United States, I am responsible for honoring both Constitutional requirements, and I intend to do so in a balanced and careful manner. I do not believe, however, that the Constitution entitles government employees, entrusted with confidential information critical to the functioning and effectiveness of the government, to disclose such information with impunity. Yet this is precisely the situation we have. It must not be allowed to continue.

Washington, Jan. 12*/
The New York Times, 1-13:12.

1

[On his "new Federalism" plan for turning over more responsibilities to states and localities]: Those who still advocate far-removed Federal solutions are dinosaurs, mindlessly carrying on as they always have, unaware that times have changed. We are attempting to improve the Federal system so that government can meet the needs of today instead of deepening the mistakes of the past.

To TV reporters and executives, Washington,
Jan. 27/The Washington Post, 1-28:(A)8.

2

Washington, D.C., has no corner on compassion or wisdom or morality. If we do nothing else in this Administration we're going to convince that city that the power, the money and the responsibility of this country begin and end with the people, and not in some puzzle palace on the Potomac.

Before Iowa Legislature, Des Moines,
Feb. 9/Los Angeles Times, 2-10:(I)6.

3

Whoever said the worst place to get a perspective on America is Washington, D.C., was absolutely right. You don't have to spend much time in Washington to appreciate the

prophetic vision of the man who designed all the streets; they go in circles.

At rally, Cheyenne, Wyo., March 2/
The New York Times, 3-3:11.

4

. . . feeding more dollars to government is like feeding a stray pup. It just follows you home and sits on your doorstep asking for more.

Before National Association of Manufacturers,
Washington, March 18/Los Angeles Times, 3-19:(I)1.

5

Forcing the American people to accept the dictates of a swollen government in Washington has been one of the more serious mistakes of this century. Either you believe in democracy, or you don't. Like you, I believe. Our founding fathers knew the value of diversity in America; they understood the need to control the size of government and to hold it accountable to our people . . . Traditionally, we have been able to adapt well to change and meet our challenges because we could reach across a vast and varied continent for ideas and experience. In the recent past, as the Federal government has pushed each city, county and state to be more like every other, we have begun to lose one of our greatest strengths: our diversity as a people. If we are to renew our country, we must stop trying to homogenize America.

Before National Association of Counties,
Baltimore, July 13/The New York Times, 7-14:13.

6

When the tough but necessary decisions to cut back on [Federal] spending are made, they are described [by some] in negative terms—how much less government will spend, how much fewer benefits will be given away, how many fewer programs will survive. But cutting back on the runaway growth of government can be a profoundly positive step, like performing necessary surgery on a patient to save his life. This Federal government of ours, by trying to do too much, has undercut the ability of individual people, communities, churches and businesses to meet the real needs of our society, as Americans always have in the past.

At Kansas State University, Sept. 9/
Los Angeles Times, 9-10:(I)11.

151

WHAT THEY SAID IN 1982

(RONALD REAGAN)

1

[On criticism that he doesn't put in enough hours as he should as President] : The thing the critics go by are the hours you sit at your desk. I don't know of a single evening that goes by that I don't carry a load under my arm up to that second floor of the White House. It's my bedtime reading. During the evening it's become kind of a laughing matter between one of the ushers and myself because as fast as I'm reading it, folders keep being sent up. And I keep telling him, "Go down and tell those people to go home."

Interview, aboard Air Force One/
U.S. News & World Report,
10-25:96.

2

[On being President] : . . . frankly, I have enjoyed the opportunity of dealing with the problems that are before us . . . [But] it has its drawbacks, of course. You . . . live like a bird in a gilded cage, and sometimes I look out the window at Pennsylvania Avenue and wonder what it would be like to be able to just walk down the street to the corner drugstore and look at the magazines. I can't do that any more.

Interview, Washington/
The New York Times,
12-19:(1)18.

John J. Rhodes
United States Representative,
R—Arizona

3

[On new Congressmen entering office] : A lot of these kids come in nine feet tall. They come here to do a job and they don't consult anybody else about what the job is. But after they've been here a while, they settle down pretty well and become cognizant that they are part of the team. They finally see their role to be part of the institution rather than the star halfback.

Interview,
Washington, December/
The New York Times,
12-18:8.

Hyman G. Rickover
Admiral, United States Navy (Ret.)

4

Trying to make things work in government is sometimes like trying to sew a button on a custard pie . . . Government is not a religion; it should not be treated as such; it is not God. It consists of humans, of fallible people who are nest-builders and bird-hatchers much of the time. Our government is the welfare state gone wild. The system maximizes the rights of the citizen and minimizes his obligations. What about over-regulation? Does Xerox ever complain about over-regulation? Not while all the regulations are being Xeroxed.

At Multi-Unit Food Service
Operators Conference, Washington,
Oct. 26/The New York Times, 11-4:12.

Felix G. Rohatyn
Chairman, Municipal Assistance
Corporation of New York

5

Today's conservative experiment [in government] will fail because it has no relevance to the world we live in, just as yesterday's liberalism failed for somewhat different reasons. The appropriate role of government remains the major unanswered question, and we are soon going to run out of time for experiments.

Before U.S. Conference of Mayors, Minneapolis,
June 23/The New York Times, 6-24:16.

E. S. Savas
Assistant Secretary of Housing and Urban
Development of the United States

6

Government should do those things it does best, like national defense, and the private sector should do those things *it* does best, including the delivery of many municipal services . . . Take Veterans Administration nursing homes. Studies show that the cost per person-day is 83 per cent higher than when the VA places patients in private nursing homes, because of higher productivity in the latter. On the city level, Detroit discovered that it cost $26 to process a $15 parking ticket, so it contracted out the processing to a clerical firm which can do the job for $1.80 a ticket. Is that less or better government? This kind of privatization is sweeping the country. In Newark, for

(E. S. SAVAS)

example, [Mayor] Ken Gibson is doing it with refuse collection, street sweeping and building demolition; and in Kansas City, Phoenix and New Orleans, private firms are now handling services in some city areas.

Interview, Washington/
The New York Times, 7-13:12.

Antonin Scalia
Professor of law,
University of Chicago

1

[On the Freedom of Information Act]: In this country, we have a tradition of respecting the autonomy and privacy of non-governmental organizations—whether they're churches or corporations or labor unions or universities. We have specified, law by law, certain institutions and certain activities that must be public. All the rest have, of course, been subject to *investigation* by the government as needed—but not to a requirement of public disclosure. The effect of the 1974 FOIA amendments was to say that whenever the government investigates an organization—which it must do increasingly these days, to insure compliance with an increasing number of laws—all of the information swept up in the course of that investigation, with very limited exceptions, becomes public. I don't believe such a wholesale elimination of what might be called institutional privacy is compatible with our free traditions . . . Where there are categories of private information that are quite likely to be useful to the public, we should—as we have done in the past—require public disclosure for those categories. But the judgment that all private information that happens to come into the government's hands falls into those categories is simply not reasonable.

Interview/U.S. News & World Report, 1-18:70.

Bob Schieffer
Correspondent, CBS News

2

[Criticizing Reagan Administration proposals to broaden government powers to classify material]: The proposed order would foster a new torrent of over-classification. The public does not need a new way for the government to hide or compound its mistakes under the banner of national security.

At House Government Operations Subcommittee
on Information hearing, Washington, March 10/
The New York Times, 3-11:15.

John E. Simonds
Executive editor,
"Honolulu Star-Bulletin"

3

Half of Congress is running on a treadmill. The other half is waiting to see if it's safe to get on.

U.S. News & World Report, 5-10:41.

Richard A. Snelling
Governor of Vermont (R)

4

Most Vermonters will applaud a restoration of the original design of our Federal government if the responsibilities and burdens of the Federal, state and local governments can be sorted out to provide a reasonable correlation between responsibility and capacity. For such a change to work and for a revised Federal system to retain the support of the American people, it is important that major responsibilities are not handed off by the Federal government at a rate faster than they can be reasonably assumed [by state and local governments].

State of the State address/
The New York Times, 3-7:(4)3.

Frank J. Sorauf
Professor of political science,
University of Minnesota

5

. . . Presidential power—and our reliance on it—has its limits and its dangers. Watergate revealed a good deal about the dangers of an imperial Presidency—an isolated, imperious Presidency, surrounded by courtiers and very powerful, insulating individuals who recognize no limits. I'm not sure we learned those lessons, however. In fact, one of the more striking things to me about the 10 years after Watergate was how quickly we forgot everything.

Interview/U.S. News & World Report, 6-14:54.

153

Ted Stevens
United States Senator, R—Alaska

1

God forbid that anyone will ever tell me that the city of Washington is my home; it is not. I detest it. I really do. I cannot think of another place to have a nation's capital in the world that is a worse place to live . . . We shorten our life span by coming to this town. As far as I am concerned, I know of no town—no town—that has a worse crime standard, a worse set of schools, a worse circumstance to live in and work in than the city of Washington. I do not care who knows it. I will tell everyone.

At Senate debate, Washington/
The Washington Post, 4-18:(B)2.

I. F. Sunia
Delegate to the United States House of Representatives from American Samoa

2

[Washington is] the top of the world . . . the source of just about everything, but primarily financial support. Back in the territory we used to have a saying that "all blessings come from Heaven, but via Washington."

Interview, Washington/
The Washington Post, 4-26:(C)1.

Franklin A. Thomas
President, Ford Foundation

3

There is a fairly big cloud on the horizon which I think needs to be addressed head on. And that is the appropriate role for government to play in insuring that the basic needs of citizens are met. My view is that the government's role is large and pervasive, although it may choose to execute its role through a variety of forms. Some of these may be wholly private, where it is simply a matter of providing some funds or incentives. It may execute a part of its role through government-private mixes, and some ought to be executed wholly by the government because it is best suited to discharge them.

Interview/The New York Times Magazine, 10-10:83.

Lewis Uhler
President, National Tax Limitation Committee; Former Chairman, then-California Governor Ronald Reagan's Tax Reduction Task Force (1973)

4

There is no internal mechanism by which Congress can discipline itself—that goes against the essential nature of Congress, or any legislative body. We have a tendency to think that legislative bodies are like corporate enterprises—take General Motors—where there's one end product, and the focus of everybody in the management structure is to get the best thing you can and sell it effectively. But Congress has no corporate objective. It's 535 guys, each of whom have a single personal objective—re-election. There is no unity or integration of their objectives. So unless we direct those bodies with a set of external constraints, we don't get the result we want.

Interview/Los Angeles Herald Examiner, 6-8:(A)2.

Ted Weiss
United States Representative, D—New York

5

Recent history has proven that a government shrouded in secrecy becomes not only unaccountable but eventually irresponsible.

The New York Times, 11-16:2.

Fred Wertheimer
President, Common Cause

6

[On President Reagan's "new Federalism" plan of giving states and localities responsibilities now handled by the Federal government]: Government has been our civilizing and unifying force. I may be sympathetic to the argument that it is not working well on the details, but while it is legitimate to look at the performance of programs, we should do it while trying to understand what is the role of government, whether it's Federal, state or local. That's at the heart of the discussion on which we are about to embark.

San Francisco Examiner & Chronicle, 1-31:(A)13.

Theodore H. White
Author, Historian

1

If you ask me what the public wants, it wants a sense of control. When the people vote for the President, they want a strong leader who can cope. They'll grumble if their privileges are cut down, but they'll accept an awful lot of sacrifices if they sense that the leader is strong and moving for the greater good of the country. The public is you, it's me, it's the guy driving the bus, it's the old lady watching TV who is lonesome. All want a sense of a decent and strong President. But a good deal of faith in the Presidency has been wasted in the past 15 years. You put a country through Vietnam and Watergate, and the people lose faith. That faith in Presidential leadership will not be restored in the next six months or the next 18 months. It will take time, lots of time.

Interview/U.S. News & World Report, 7-5:60.

Charles Z. Wick
Director, International Communication Agency of the United States

2

I think the cancer we have in our govern-ment today are those leaks [of private or classified information]. To think that responsible individuals, no matter what their political persuasion in government, would seek to take these candid aspects and utterances that help formulate our national policy, I think is nothing short of seditious. And it is very troubling. It chills comment. It chills the ferment and formulation of policy. I don't think it's in our national interest.

Before Los Angeles World Affairs Council, March 5/Los Angeles Times, 3-6:(I)30.

James C. Wright, Jr.
United States Representative, D—Texas

3

[Addressing former members of Congress] : I look out among these faces and I think, "How young they look." So many of you look better, more rested, more relaxed and more refreshed. It is almost tempting enough to make a fellow want to join you, and I do aspire to join you. But it is a little like St. Augustine when he prayed, "Lord, make me holy, but not just yet."

May 17/The New York Times, 5-20:14.

Law . The Judiciary

Howard H. Baker, Jr.
United States Senator,
R–Tennessee

1

[On the verdict of not-guilty-by-reason-of-insanity in the trial of John Hinckley, accused of shooting President Reagan and others last year]: I think the insanity plea does have a place in the American system of jurisprudence, but I think we sort of turn the whole thing upside down when we require the prosecutor to prove that a person was sane, instead of the defendant to prove that he was insane.

Washington, June 22/Los Angeles Times, 6-23:(I)19.

William Baxter
Assistant Attorney General,
Antitrust Division, Department
of Justice of the United States

2

When one is engaged in litigation for a long time, one undergoes a kind of psychological conditioning that commits oneself to the enterprise in which he is engaged . . . I have never met a litigator who did not think he was winning the case right up to the moment when the guillotine came down.

News conference, January/
The Washington Post, 4-18:(B)3.

Melvin Belli
Lawyer

3

Lawsuits help insure that Americans have a good life. We protect our rights by litigating if anyone attempts to trample on them. We have always been like that. One of the colonial flags included a rattlesnake with the legend "Don't Tread on Me." That's the American mind of today as expressed by lawyers: We don't let anybody tread on us. In this scheme of things, the courts play an important role. We ought to be glad that courts get into all the areas that they do, from school desegregation to worker rights. If we had cases that the courts couldn't scrutinize, we'd really be in trouble. The law should be able to examine everything, even the question of when life begins. If the courts see a clear and present danger, they should act without waiting for the legislature.

Interview/U.S. News & World Report, 9-20:64.

4

In determining the outcome of a given case, a lawyer's flamboyance plays a part. His or her performance in the courtroom is responsible for about 25 per cent of the outcome; the remaining 75 per cent depends on the facts. The facts and the law tell whether you've got a good case, but a lawyer's presentation is important, just as an architect's is in selling a building or a salesman's in selling a suit. Those who criticize flamboyant trial lawyers are just envious.

Interview/U.S. News & World Report, 9-20:64.

Rose E. Bird
Chief Justice, Supreme
Court of California

5

I think the Supreme Court can never be particularly popular because the umpire is not popular. The umpire is not popular in baseball or football; it's not popular in any other endeavor in which you have an umpire. We are the ones who have to call the close calls; we're the one that has to make the decisions. One side succeeds and the other side doesn't. So you're always going to have one side disgruntled, no matter what you do. And, also, the courts are a very easy target. In an age when nobody reads, we speak through the written word; we don't interpret what we say; we don't give you a little two-minute analysis that can go on the evening news. We don't talk back when people attack us.

Interview, San Francisco/
San Francisco Examiner & Chronicle, 2-14:(A)1.

(ROSE E. BIRD)

1

We must use our courage to ensure a judiciary not governed by the daily polls but by the rules of law, serving not the special interest of the few but the best interest of all, devoted not to self-preservation but to the preservation of those great Constitutional principles which history has bequeathed to us.

Before California Labor Federation, Anaheim, Calif., July 19/Los Angeles Times, 7-20:(I)18.

2

The courts are an easy scapegoat because, at a time when everything has to be boiled down to easy slogans, we speak in subtleties.

Newsweek, 8-9:10.

Robert Bork
Judge, United States Court of Appeals for the District of Columbia

3

The [U.S. Supreme] Court responds to the press and law-school faculties. The personnel of the media are heavily left-liberal. Their values are quite egalitarian and permissive. Law-school faculties tend to have the same politics and values. So if there are new Constitutional values, they will be the values of that class.

At symposium of Yale Federalist Society, New Haven, Conn., April 24/ The New York Times, 4-26:15.

William J. Brennan, Jr.
Associate Justice, Supreme Court of the United States

4

Even the premise that state courts can be trusted to safeguard individual rights cannot justify either the [U.S. Supreme] Court or Congress in limiting the role of the Federal judiciary. For to do so overlooks one of the strengths of our Federal system—that it provides a double source of protection for the rights of our citizens. Federalism is not served when the Federal half of that protection is crippled.

At New York University Law School, April 15/The New York Times, 5-19:10.

Warren E. Burger
Chief Justice of the United States

5

If the courts are to retain public confidence, we cannot let disputes wait two, three or five years to be disposed of, as is often the situation. It is now clear that neither the Federal nor the state court systems are capable of handling all the burdens placed upon them. Even when an acceptable result is finally achieved in a civil case, that result is often drained of much of its value because of the time lapse, the expense and the emotional stress inescapable in the litigation process.

State of the Judiciary address, Chicago, Jan. 24/Los Angeles Times, 1-25:(I)5.

6

Arbitration is a very ancient mechanism for resolving disputes. It has been neglected in this country. Arbitration began at least as far back as Homer, was used by the Phoenicians and later by the Hanseatic League. In my travels, I have found in many other countries that something in the nature of arbitration is the dominant method of settling disputes. It is generally cheaper and speedier than a trial, causes less wear and tear on the participants and will very likely produce a more satisfactory result. Unless the experience of all these other societies for hundreds of years is wrong—and I don't believe it is wrong—we have been neglecting a very valuable tool.

Interview/U.S. News & World Report, 2-22:36.

Jose A. Cabranes
Judge, United States District Court for the District of Connecticut

7

Alone among our national public institutions, the Federal courts have retained their legitimacy. The people by and large believe in them ... Why? Because the Federal courts have given citizens what they expect and what they want—greater protection for their individual rights. As our politics have collapsed or proved unwieldy—the parties, the Congress, the post-Roosevelt Presidency are widely believed to be in disarray—our least democratic branch of

(JOSE A. CABRANES)

government [the judiciary] has become the chief mechanism for serving democratic ends ... The implications of all this seem clear enough. The current attack on the Federal courts is dangerous, not because it seeks to take power from the Federal courts, but because it delegitimates the one national institution that people seem to believe in ... If state courts are to play a greater role in protecting individual rights, they must demonstrate over time ... that they can and do provide a sympathetic forum. If they do not, and access to the Federal courts is barred, and national institutions otherwise fail to meet widespread needs, the demand for rights will surely find some other ... form of expression.

At symposium on individual rights, Hartford, Conn., April 17/The Washington Post, 6-6:(C)6.

Gerhard Casper
Dean, University of Chicago Law School

1

There can be no question that law schools must train advocates. This, however, is not an all-permeating function. The most rigorous standards of professional education are satisfied only when we teach the *substance* of law, and when lawyers state it as precisely as they can, being fair and clear about where their own preferences come into play. Neither law nor its history can be infinitely manipulated to suit our own views. Those who believe otherwise will simply be bad lawyers, in every sense of the word.

At John Marshall Law School commencement, Chicago/The Wall Street Journal, 4-13:24.

Lee Coleman
Director, Center for the Study of Psychiatric Testimony, Berkeley, Calif.

2

The insanity defense is based on a bunch of lies. The idea is that if the defense is successful, the person won't be punished. But the truth is the person gets locked up anyway—in a mental hospital rather than a prison. The final hooker in the total hypocrisy is this: When a person is

found insane and put in a mental hospital, how long he is kept there depends on the opinion of a psychiatrist. Yet psychiatrists for years have been telling us they don't know how to tell who is dangerous and who isn't. Also, since the psychiatrist determines when a person will be released, instead of confiding in the psychiatrist, the person sets out to gather what I call mental-health brownie points to convince the doctor he is well. It means a lot of games and manipulation, not real treatment. What he should do is give a person a fixed number of years for his crime and then, once that person is incarcerated, give him whatever psychiatric care he needs.

Interview/U.S. News & World Report, 6-7:58.

Archibald Cox
Professor of law, Harvard University; Chairman, Common Cause

3

One of the greatest dangers facing the country at the present time is the effort of Senator Jesse Helms, Senator Orrin Hatch and others to subject the [U.S.] Supreme Court to reversal by Congress. That would upset the balance of the whole political system. It's not really a new problem—it's almost as old as our country's history—and the country has always rejected these attempts to alter the Constitutional system. The extraordinary thing is that here are men who call themselves conservative, and who are proposing to overturn one of the most fundamental things that has kept the government going for 200 years. They're not conservatives, they're radicals!

Interview/Los Angeles Herald Examiner, 2-1:(A)7.

4

A great many college graduates come here [to Harvard Law School] thinking of lawyers as social engineers arguing the great Constitutional issues. But as they go through here, some of these idealistic aspirations get tempered by the desire to become established, by ambition, by families and marriage. There's a certain temptation to say that the law school brings this about, when it really is an accommodation to living in society.

San Francisco Examiner & Chronicle, 6-6:(This World)23.

Norman Davis
Vice president, WPLG-TV, Miami
1

[On TV broadcasting of court trials]: The less experience courts have with TV, the more they fear it. There's this standard litany of fears that you hear in every state where cameras are still banned: TV will scare witnesses, bring out the worst showoff instincts in judges and lawyers, disrupt everything. People are *sure* of this. But as soon as they try it, the fears start to die away. We've had courtroom TV in Florida for longer than almost anybody, and I can't over-stress how ordinary it seems now. There simply is no issue any more in this state.
Interview/TV Guide, 8-14:9.

Alan M. Dershowitz
Lawyer; Professor of law,
Harvard University
2

I am not interested in my clients' innocence or guilt; I'm not interested in seeing that justice is done when I'm the defense attorney. I am interested in seeing them acquitted. It's not the defense attorney's job to do justice. His job is to defend vigorously his client ... It's not a happy experience to get people off who are guilty. I don't expect any prizes or plaudits for it. Defense attorneys don't win Nobel Prizes. What we do is a necessary evil—a *very* necessary evil.
Interview, Boston/Los Angeles Herald Examiner, 5-26:(A)5.

3

There should be only one major criteria to being a judge in the United States—and that is a strong commitment to the Constitution's safeguards. By that criteria, most of the current Supreme Court would be disqualified. [Chief Justice] Warren Burger and [Associate Justice] William Rehnquist just don't give a damn about the Bill of Rights. Well, they *do* give a damn—they'd like to see it abolished.
Interview, Boston/Los Angeles Herald Examiner, 5-26:(A)5.

4

Plea-bargaining is an evil. It may be a necessary evil, but it's an evil. Consider what would happen if we went into a courtroom today and saw a sign hanging up that said, "Reward: For waiving your right to trial, $1,000." We'd say, "That's outrageous. You can't buy people's rights." But that sign is there, in invisible ink. It says, "Reward: For giving up your right to trial by jury, a year less in prison." That's what plea-bargaining is all about. You're selling your Constitutional rights for time on the street. It doesn't benefit anybody. I'd rather see more cases go to trial, though we might have to stop prosecuting gambling offenses and drug offenses and other kinds of victimless crimes. I just don't want to see our court system turned into a Persian bazaar, which is what it's becoming.
Interview/Chicago Tribune, 6-14:(1)14.

5

... all sides in a trial want to hide at least some of the truth. The defendant wants to hide the truth because he's generally guilty. The defense attorney's job is to make sure the jury does not arrive at *that* truth. The prosecution is perfectly happy to have the truth of guilt come out, but it, too, has a truth to hide: It wants to make sure that the process by which the evidence was obtained is not truthfully presented, because, as often as not, that process will raise questions. The judge also has a truth to hide: He often hasn't been completely candid in describing the facts or the law. Truth suffers enormously in the adversary system of justice. Despite this, the system generally produces accurate results. The system is the best we can get. As Churchill said about democracy: It's the worst system except for all the others.
Interview/U.S. News & World Report, 8-9:62.

Bernard L. Diamond
Professor of law and psychiatry,
University of California, Berkeley
6

[On the insanity defense]: Many people think the criminal law should be based on what works best. If it works better to send people to prison, you send people to prison; if it works better to execute them, you execute them; if it works better to send them to a mental hospital, you send them there. They are omitting a very important consideration—justice. Traditionally,

(BERNARD L. DIAMOND)

when an individual commits a criminal offense in which the criminal behavior was a result of mental illness and was not under the voluntary control of the offender, he is not blameworthy. He has to be treated differently. And psychiatrists can be very helpful to juries who must make these determinations.

Interview/U.S. News & World Report, 6-7:58.

Charles G. Douglas III
Justice, Supreme Court
of New Hampshire

1

[On the relationship between state courts and the U.S. Supreme Court]: Why should we always be the tail being wagged by the Federal dog? As a Federalist, I feel it's safer in the long run to have an independent state judiciary. No matter what happens 200 years from now in Washington, maybe some things can be prevented at the state level.

The New York Times, 5-19:10.

Albert Gore, Jr.
United States Representative,
D–Tennessee

2

Among attorneys in Tennessee the saying is: When you have the facts on your side, argue the facts. When you have the law on your side, argue the law. When you have neither, holler.

At House hearing on Environmental Protection Agency performance, Washington/ The Washington Post, 7-23:(A)17.

Harold H. Greene
Judge, United States District Court
for the District of Columbia

3

...the courts themselves have recognized that the Constitution is a living document, to be interpreted in light of changing conditions. But such evolution comes about naturally and deliberately, following over-all societal change. This kind of natural growth differs sharply from change effected as a consequence of a particular election or a different composition of the Congress. Abrupt departures based directly on political considerations disrupt the sense of

continuity and legitimacy ... We cannot know today what passions will be aroused tomorrow and what measures our legislative representatives will feel they should adopt to satisfy the demands made upon them. Even those who now regard the independent judiciary as an inconvenience or worse might be quite uncomfortable with their own doctrine should the electorate at some future date decide to vote into office a government that was completely out of sympathy with their most cherished interests and concerns.

The Washington Post, 6-23:(A)26.

Charles R. Halpern
Dean, City University of
New York School of Law

4

To be a lawyer, you have to learn to work off of precedents and to explore statutory ambiguities. But you should also understand that the law is not a disciplined set of rules. The landscape in which the law exists is changing, and so should the law-school curriculum.

The New York Times, 9-14:19.

A. E. Howard
Professor of law,
University of Virginia

5

[On the growing caseload of the U.S. Supreme Court]: The vast majority [of the filings] are from lawyers who have never been there. They have no intuitive sense of what's worthy [for Supreme Court review], and no one to tell them. So they go to the big court ... There's also an ego factor. A lawyer wants a moment of glory. And there are breast-beating promises to clients: "I'll take your case all the way," and that sort of thing.

The Washington Post, 9-24:(A)3.

James Jenner
Public defender, Alameda
County, Calif.

6

I'm skeptical of hypnosis-aided testimony—in fact, I'm terrified of it. People think that somehow with hypnosis the truth will emerge like phoenix from the ashes ... Everybody's looking for a "scientific tool" to find

(JAMES JENNER)

the truth—polygraphs, voiceprints and now the modern thing, hypnosis. The problem is that witnesses are "suggestable" to hypnosis. They feel they have a duty to come through [with more information] ... Hypnosis-aided testimony may help corroborate independently obtained evidence—but when it's used just by itself, therein lies the danger.

Los Angeles Times, 3-19:(I)3.

Gideon Kanner
Professor, Loyola University
Law School, Los Angeles

1

I think there comes a point when a legitimate question comes up in a democratic society. That is, has the judiciary's perception of right and wrong gone so far out of the mainstream of that society that people are concerned and alarmed? If they are, they [should be able to] express it through the ballot box. They [justices] cannot become some kind of priesthood beyond the reach of people in a democratic society.

The Christian Science Monitor, 10-13:2.

Nicholas deB. Katzenbach
General counsel, International
Business Machines Corp.; Former
Attorney General of the United States

2

In many of our [legal] cases, there are highly complicated business and technological points of view that require a great deal of organization. In a long trial, you don't get any jurors who have better than a high-school education, and many of them don't have that. Now, how in hell do you communicate? We're not talking about abolishing juries in a massive sort of way. But when you have a protracted case, we can't get a jury of peers.

Los Angeles Times, 1-5:(I)20.

Hans A. Linde
Justice, Supreme Court of Oregon

3

[Saying state courts are becoming more independent of the U.S. Supreme Court]: A lot of [U.S.] Supreme Court doctrines are no longer persuasive, but filled with fuzzy, soft terminology which has no cutting edge. When the Court's doctrinal cogency and coherence begins to fall apart, we have state courts saying, in effect, "We don't have to do it that way."

The New York Times, 5-19:10.

Edwin Meese III
Counsellor to the President
of the United States

4

There shouldn't be a Legal Services Corporation, and I think that it is very clear that if you did away with the Legal Services Corporation and turned it over to the professional bar associations of the country, who could do it far better with far greater coverage of poor people and far less cost, the whole country would be better off ... The message we are trying to get over is that we ought to be providing legal services to the poor not at taxpayers' expense. This is something that is a professional responsibility, and when taxpayers' money is used up for any reason in overhead expense, this is a bad thing as far as legal services is concerned. That's why you shouldn't have a corporation.

To reporters, Washington, Dec. 23/
The Washington Post, 12-24:(A)2.

Norval Morris
Professor of law and criminology,
University of Chicago

5

[On the insanity defense]: Clearly, mental illness should be admissible on the question of whether a person intended a prohibited harm; for example, whether a person intended to kill somebody. But the insanity defense has gone astray. We now find defendants not guilty of acts they, in fact, intended on the grounds that they were swayed by mental illness. We ask juries to decide whether a defendant had a "substantial capacity" to know right from wrong or had a "substantial capacity" to control himself. Those concepts are manifestly ambiguous. They turn some cases into circuses which have no moral validity.

Interview/
U.S. News & World Report, 7-5:15.

Stanley Mosk
Justice, Supreme Court of California

1

[Saying state courts are growing more independent of the U.S. Supreme Court]: Today a new body of constitutional law is emerging, based not on the Constitution of the United States but on the constitutions of the several states. Liberal state courts have taken the doctrines of Federalism and states' rights, heretofore associated with people like [former Alabama Governor] George C. Wallace, and adapted them to give citizens more rights under their state constitutions than to oppress them.

The New York Times, 5-19:10.

Bruce Allen Murphy
Assistant professor of
political science, Pennsylvania
State University

2

Whether [U.S. Supreme Court] Justices should be involved politically is a decision that the public and political leaders have to make. In doing so, they need to be aware of the trade-offs involved. If we decide to allow such activity, we have to realize that Justices might use their power and influence to act for their own personal gain ... But if we decide not to have Justices involved in politics at all, we eliminate the possibility of people serving on the Court who may have answers for America's problems. In addition, if we bar political activity by Supreme Court Justices, how will we enforce that rule? Finally, do we want to pick for the Court somebody who has absolutely no contact with the real world and maintains that posture, yet is constantly called upon to decide real-world issues? One way or another, we need to establish standards of some kind, either stating that political activity should continue—and in an open way—or making clear that the Court should stay out of politics.

Interview/U.S. News & World Report, 4-19:101.

James Noe
Judge; Chairman, National
Conference of State Trial Judges

3

Whatever method is used, the [U.S.] Supreme Court must assume full responsibility to choose the cases it hears, because I think the people expect the highest court in the land to decide the most important cases in the land to hear. To allow some other court to decide what cases the Court will hear would dilute that responsibility.

Before American Bar Association, San Francisco,
Aug. 7/San Francisco Examiner & Chronicle, 8-8:(A)4.

Lewis F. Powell, Jr.
Associate Justice, Supreme
Court of the United States

4

The sheer volume [of cases] ... may prevent the same degree of judicial care in selecting cases for full review [by the Supreme Court] that probably existed a decade or more ago .... unlike some high officials in the other branches of government, [Supreme Court Justices] do their own work. And although the assistance of able law clerks is essential, the decisions and opinions are those of the Justices. [When a case is first filed with the Court,] I rely initially on memoranda prepared by law clerks to help me identify petitions that need plenary consideration in our regular Friday conferences. [However,] each of us [Justices] still makes a personal judgment with respect to each petition.

Before American Bar Association, San Francisco,
Aug. 9/Los Angeles Times, 8-10:(I)5.

Ronald Reagan
President of the United States

5

[Most Americans] respect and abide by the decisions of the judiciary as a matter of course. Now, this isn't to say, of course, that we'll always agree on the important issues that are presented to you for decision. But we frequently take a little comfort in the fact that the [U.S. Supreme] Court, itself, is frequently of more than one mind about such matters. And it's neither surprising nor disturbing that our citizens may at times side with the dissenters. It's even rumored that Presidents sometimes disagree with particular Supreme Court decisions. It's inevitable that the Court's decisions become the focus of popular attention and debate, and certainly, our founding fathers expected nothing different.

At luncheon for U.S. Supreme Court justices,
Washington, Oct. 1/The New York Times, 10-2:10.

(RONALD REAGAN)

1

[On the Legal Services Corp.]: This idea that our opposition to the legal service as an autonomous and outside corporation is because we don't want legal help for the poor—that's not true. We want to provide, and are ready to provide, $100-million block grants to the states for legal help to the poor. [The Legal Services Corp. wasn't] really doing the things for individuals who had a legal problem and were too poor to have legal help. They were busying themselves out there under the guise of class-action suits trying to get what belongs in the legislative process—trying to get it through court decisions and with the taxpayers' money.

Interview, Washington, Dec. 16/
The Washington Post, 12-17:(A)2.

Martin Reiser
Director, behavioral science services,
Los Angeles Police Department

2

[Criticizing a California Supreme Court decision barring testimony from witnesses who had been hypnotized to restore their memory]: The decision is very unfortunate and ill-advised. Hypnosis has been particularly effective in cases with a single eyewitness and victim—like rape—where the crime is so traumatic the victim will forget or repress a lot of details. [Hypnosis] is not the magical "Svengali" thing that it's been portrayed to be.

Los Angeles Times, 3-19:(I)3.

Stanley M. Roden
District Attorney, Santa
Barbara County, Calif.

3

We start jury selection, and in walks an army of psychologists—including one to study the "body language" of the jurors and another to feed questions to defense counsel. Jurors were asked: "Are you in a union? Have you served in the military? Belong to a church? What are your beliefs? Who's your favorite novelist?

What's the last movie you saw? When you first looked at the defendant, what was the first thing you thought?" We want to remove bias and prejudice, of course. But what I saw was a hell of a lot of time wasted. The questioning was very personal. I sensed some of the jurors have resented it.

Los Angeles Times, 2-9:(I)1.

Stephen Sachs
Attorney General of Maryland

4

[Criticizing Reagan Administration attempts to cut or end Federal legal services to the poor]: To cripple or destroy programs which feed and house and educate and heal the nation's poor is bad enough. But this Administration, by seeking to ration justice as well, would strip its critics of the means to fight back. That tactic is familiar, and terribly unfair. In sporting arenas it is called hitting and holding. On the streets it's called mugging.

Before Senate Appropriations subcommittee,
Washington, April 28/The Washington Post, 4-29:(A)5.

R. Sargent Shriver
Lawyer; Former United States
Ambassador to France

5

... I do believe our government, my government and my profession have a positive moral and legal duty to make sure that legal services are available to the poor on an accessible, affordable, regular, dignified basis and, if necessary, free of charge. Which means that I, as a lawyer, as a professional, believe that some significant part of my money, time, thought and energy belongs—I don't give it, it *belongs*—to others, not just to me. Which means that I believe I am not wholly "independent," not a creature whose self-interest is paramount.

At George Washington University National
Law Center/The Washington Post, 6-4:(A)18.

William French Smith
Attorney General of the United States

6

The courts themselves engage in politics if they exceed their Constitutional role and intrude upon the policy-making responsibilities of the political branches. The promotion of judicial restraint is thus an effort to secure the independence of the judiciary, not undermine it ... The inclination of lawyers as a group to turn every social issue into a legal question requiring judicial resolution can only exacerbate the public's suspicion of the legal profession.

Before American Bar Association House of Delegates, Chicago, Jan. 25/The New York Times, 1-26:8.

1

The Department of Justice, by virtue of its functions, is bound to have a certain tension, not only with the White House but also with other government agencies. We are in a position where we have to say no a lot. Certain people don't like that ... But we have to enforce the law ... That's one of our basic functions here.

Interview, Washington/ The Washington Post, 5-31:(A)11.

2

I'm the President's lawyer. I'm not the President's lawyer in the sense I used to be, not his personal lawyer any more. But one of the functions of the Attorney General is to advise the President and other members of the Cabinet on legal matters. We're in a position here [at the Justice Department], just by the nature of our job, where we have to say "no" to a lot of people. I suppose in one sense you could say we're sort of a business, that sooner or later we're going to make everybody mad at least once. Even among the Administration, there are those who think that all the laws they didn't like were repealed on Election Day, and don't understand what to us is pretty elemental; namely, that our function is to enforce the law as it is, whether we like it or not. And those who don't like it, of course, have to change the law. We never can and never would not enforce the law to meet some philosophical or political position or need.

Interview, Washington/The New York Times, 6-8:14.

3

[On the verdict of not-guilty-by-reason-of-insanity in the case of John Hinckley, accused of shooting President Reagan and others last

year]: There must be an end to the doctrine that allows so many persons to commit crimes of violence, to use confusing procedures to their own advantage, and then to have the door opened for them to return to the society which they victimized.

June 22/Los Angeles Times, 6-23:(I)19.

4

The criminal-justice system has tilted too decidedly in favor of the rights of criminals and against the rights of society. [We should] effectively eliminate the insanity defense except in those rare cases in which the defendant lacked the state of mind required as an element of the offense. A mental disease or defect would be no defense if a defendant knew he was shooting at a human being to kill him. Mental disease or defect would constitute a defense only if the defendant did not even know he had a gun in his hand or thought, for example, that he was shooting at a tree.

Before Senate Judiciary Committee, Washington, July 19/Chicago Tribune, 7-20:(1)4.

Arlen Specter
United States Senator,
R—Pennsylvania

5

If the Congress exercises power to take away ... [court] jurisdiction in matters involving [racial school] busing because it is unpopular with the majority, then the precedent is established that whenever the majority disfavors an individual's legal rights, court jurisdiction to enforce such basic rights as freedom of speech, of the press and of religion as well as equal protection, due process and the entire Constitution itself may be removed ... Rights that cannot be enforced because resort to the courts has been blocked are really not rights at all.

U.S. News & World Report, 3-22:96.

John Paul Stevens
Associate Justice, Supreme
Court of the United States

6

I believe that an independent tribunal that did not have responsibility for deciding the merits of any case would do a far better job of

(JOHN PAUL STEVENS)

selecting those relatively few cases that should be decided by the Supreme Court of the United States. The present Court . . . grants too many cases, and far too often we are guilty of voting to grant simply because we believe error has been committed rather than because question presented is both sufficiently important for decision on a national level and also ripe for decision.

Before American Bar Association, San Francisco, Aug. 6/San Francisco Examiner & Chronicle, 8-8:(A)4.

Laurence H. Tribe
Professor of law, Harvard University

1

There is a reciprocal relationship between the U.S. Supreme Court and the state courts. As the Supreme Court's own energy flags or it reaches the limits of appropriate Federal judi-

cial activity, it may nonetheless have marked the path that creative state jurists will want to follow. In the long view of history, most of the truly creative developments in the American law have come from the states.

The New York Times, 5-19:10.

Elyce Zenoff
Professor of law, George Washington University

2

The insanity defense is a key part of our criminal-justice system, which is founded on the belief that people normally choose whether or not to obey the law. Certain people, we have said historically, cannot make that choice, however, either because they are too young or because of severe mental retardation or mental illness. The insanity defense exists in practically every civilized country. It is not some kind of aberration, as some seem to be suggesting . . .

Interview/U.S. News & World Report, 7-5:15.

Politics

William W. Abbot
Professor of history,
University of Virginia   *1*

Today, America seems to lack political leaders of the caliber of [George] Washington and others who founded this nation. Probably that is because in the latter part of the 18th century, people of genius—of political talent—found themselves in a position to really go as far as their talents would permit. Many of the gifted men who founded this nation looked to independence as a way of opening up things at the top for themselves as men of character and talent. It was not so much a chance to get wealth or to get power but to gain honor. The way the country is constituted now, the road to political authority and influence is less open to those of political genius. Opportunities to move up are somehow clogged by institutions. We need to try to figure out ways to bring into political action those people who, like Washington, have so much to contribute.
Interview/U.S. News & World Report, 2-22:58.

Ed Asner
Actor   *2*

[On actors who speak out on controversial subjects such as politics]: Years ago, I'd see an actor talking on television about some issue and I'd wish there'd be a subtitle saying, "Remember, folks, it's just an actor." I don't feel that way now. I don't think actors give up their citizenship the day they become actors. Hell, we have an actor [Ronald Reagan] in the White House now, and he didn't get there by keeping his mouth shut. Maybe now they should have a caption that says, "Remember, folks, it's just a politician." Sure, it's unfair to use your celebrity to speak out. But if it's unfair in a good cause, then maybe it's worth all the heat.
Interview, Los Angeles/San Francisco
Examiner & Chronicle, 3-28:(Calendar)44.

Joseph R. Biden, Jr.
United States Senator, D–Delaware   *3*

I'd say [to President Reagan]: Expand the group of people with whom you speak, listen to the mainstream of the Republican Party and shed the ideologues of the far right. The President always quotes Franklin D. Roosevelt. I'd tell him that I don't expect him to have F.D.R.'s philosophy but that he should at least adopt the same style—that is, be an idealist in principle, but a pragmatist in practice.
Interview/U.S. News & World Report, 4-19:40.

Edmund G. Brown
Former Governor of California (D)   *4*

[On today's political campaigning]: The issues—the budget, the fiscal policies, the question of crime and punishment, the question of natural resources—haven't changed at all. But the attacks are more virulent. People don't talk about the issues so much; they talk about the weakness of their opponent instead of what *they're* going to do. The worst thing in the world are those [political TV] spot advertisements—30 seconds. They're very expensive, they don't tell anything about the candidate at all, they're based upon the greatness of the p.r. guy writing them. Most of them are negative against the other guy. I think they should be absolutely barred. To put them on, you've got to raise money from an awful lot of sources, and that's bad in and of itself.
Interview/Los Angeles Herald Examiner, 11-3:(A)2.

Jimmy Carter
Former President of the United States   *5*

I like politics, but it is not all good. The tedium of repetitive public appearances, dashing madly from one community to another, receiving lines, receptions, begging for contributions—none of those things are attractive or

(JIMMY CARTER)

enjoyable to me. Dealing with issues and making decisions, planning a campaign, the direct relation with voters—those elements of politics I enjoy.

Interview, Plains, Ga./Time, 10-11:63.

1

There is no way for me to express adequately my concern about the detrimental impact of special interests in Washington. In many cases, members of Congress can be induced to vote against the interests of the country—bought legitimately, with political threats on one hand and financial rewards on the other. The situation is getting worse. You have not only the financial payoffs with contributions and honorariums, but a tendency by Congress and the Administration to weaken ethics restraints. There are also those right-wing political-action committees that can spend hundreds of thousands to promote or defeat a candidate. Their scruples are sometimes nonexistent.

Interview, Plains, Ga./Time, 10-11:64.

2

I have to say in complete candor ... that the way the Democratic National Committee has been structured in recent years, it has been of very little help, either to an incumbent President or to the nominee of our Party ... The Democratic National Committee or national party quite often is more of a burden on a nominee than it is an asset to him.

Broadcast interview/"Today" show, NBC-TV, 10-27.

Bruce Chapman
Director, Federal Bureau of the Census

3

The baby-boom generation's voting participation is lower than its predecessors' was at the same age ... Turnout for 25-34-year-olds in the 1964 elections was 64.7 per cent, for example, while 25-34-year-olds in 1980 turned out to vote at a rate of only 54.6 per cent. Later baby-boom-generation adults, I expect, will have even lower turnout records ... I personally attribute a large part of the change to the elimination or diminution of school instruction in what used to be called "civics."

U.S. News & World Report, 5-31:76.

Alan Cranston
United States Senator,
D—California

4

[On Senator Harrison Williams, who was convicted in the FBI's Abscam operation]: I believe that there has been the grossest abuse of power and misconduct by the Executive Branch of the government of the United States in the investigation and subsequent prosecution of Senator Williams. It took the government a long time, and constant prodding and pressure, to manufacture a crime which it could induce Senator Williams to commit—if he did. Somewhere along the way, Senator Williams *may* have yielded, in terms of criminal activity, to the persistent, pernicious pressure of the government and its hired con man, Mel Weinberg. Without regard to the criminality, I am convinced that Senator Williams *did* succumb to this pressure and engage in clearly improper conduct. Senator Williams faced what, in my opinion, was a cruel, unreasonable, unwarranted, improper test. But, even conceding the interpretation of events most favorable to him, I conclude that his conduct fell short of what must be the high standard for every Senator here.

Before the Senate, Washington, March 9/
The New York Times, 3-10:17.

Robert J. Dole
United States Senator, R—Kansas

5

[On Senators accepting honorariums, payments for outside speech-making]: I'm not certain there ever should have been a limit [on speaking fees]. I remember the old days when [the late Senator] Hubert Humphrey used to go out and pile up the money, $70,000, $80,000 ... As long as you have to report your honoraria and let the public know, people will make their judgment at election time.

The Washington Post, 2-28:(A)8.

6

There is a perception in this country, rightly or wrongly, that [the Reagan] Administration tilts everything to the upper-middle class and higher, and there is not enough concern about low-income people ... I really believe that if

167

WHAT THEY SAID IN 1982

(ROBERT J. DOLE)

we [Republicans] are going to have a party, we are going to have to focus more on women, blacks, Hispanics, middle income. I'm talking about the lower end of the middle income and below, working people who supported the President. But there are a lot of people out there who firmly believe Republicans are a sort of heartless group, and we are going to balance the budget by cutting every program that affects people on welfare.

The Washington Post, 4-25:(G)7.

Hugh Downs
Host, "20/20" program, ABC-TV

1

I realized long ago that the world is not thirsting for my opinion. I don't think anyone watching me on television would know whether I'm a Republican or a Democrat—and that's the way I want it. It was once suggested to me that I run for Governor of Arizona. I turned them down and I'll tell you why. I've spent my whole life trying to ingratiate myself with 100 per cent of the people. When you go into politics, the mere act of party affiliation alienates half of them.

Interview, New York/TV Guide, 9-4:23.

Eugene Eidenberg
Director, Democratic
National Committee

2

Over the last decade or so, the Democratic Party has been less and less able institutionally to raise funds and to communicate its message and build the infrastructure of a party that is effective and viable on a national basis. We've been a party that gathered every four years, in effect, in convention and hoped that the American people would understand this is a national political party. The thing simply evaporated after the national campaign and election until the next one. The Republican Party ... has demonstrated most impressively how effectively a political party organization can be used.

Panel discussion/The New York Times, 7-18:(4)5.

Glenn English
United States Representative,
D–Oklahoma

3

All Administrations try to control information for their own political purposes. The difference with the Reagan team is the degree of effort being put into reaching this goal. Mr. Reagan's people want to provide the American people with less information about their activities so they cannot be held accountable.

The New York Times, 11-15:14.

Orval Faubus
Former Governor of Arkansas (D)

4

We've got bogus liberals today. Big ideas but no details. It's like Will Rogers' plan to get U-boats out of the ocean during the war. He said just heat all the water up to boiling, and they would soon come up. Someone asked him how to do that, and he said, "Well, the detail people can handle that. I'm an idea man." That's what liberals are like today.

Interview, Little Rock, Ark./
Chicago Tribune, 1-3:(2)9.

Mervin Field
Public-opinion analyst

5

[On the forthcoming state-wide elections]: The largest single effect on Republican state-wide races will be how the public views [President] Ronald Reagan. A year ago it appeared that Republicans would have the edge. All they had to do was wrap themselves in the mantle of Ronald Reagan. Now that mantle may be a smothering blanket ... The single biggest delicate problem for Republican campaign managers will be how to get succor from Ronald Reagan being President, but not be crushed by it.

The Christian Science Monitor, 6-4:10.

Gerald R. Ford
Former President of the United States

6

The Republican Party that I'm part of never has been anti-Negro, anti-Semitic, anti-minorities or anti-women's rights. And I believe, as a matter of record, during *my* Administration

(GERALD R. FORD)

particularly, we welcomed people from all segments of our society. I'm proud of that. No major political party can succeed in this country if it closes the door on broad-based participation.

Interview, New York/Parade, 4-4:5.

J. William Fulbright
Former United States Senator,
D—Arkansas

1

One of the most discouraging things in the news—little things—I saw recently was that the White House had taken on a third pollster. If there's anything inimical to the exercise of good judgment it's a pollster. That means you might as well have a computer as your leader. It means that they're not even thinking on their own about what ought to be done. They're only trying to find out what the majority says. And this popularity of poll-taking strikes me as inimical to good government. I mean, that's the ultimate, going out and finding out what the great mass—people who have no particular understanding or real direct interest—think.

Interview/The Washington Post, 7-18:(B)3.

Francois Furet
French historian

2

The French never understood why the Americans got so upset over Watergate. The French in particular and Europeans in general do not have a moral conception of politics.

June/Time, 6-14:26.

A. Bartlett Giamatti
President, Yale University

3

In choosing between ideologues of the Right and of the Left, I choose to eschew both because they are finally, in their desire to control and exclude, not different. If you believe they are, if you believe that an ideologue of the Left is less authoritarian in impulses and acts than one of the Right, look again.

At Yale University commencement/
The Christian Science Monitor, 6-11:16.

Henry B. Gonzalez
United States Representative,
D—Texas

4

[Political-action committees] have to be one of the most alarming developments in my 20 years here. PACs have donated campaign funds by the millions of dollars, and the full impact of it didn't show up right away. But it did show up—in tax bills. There is a direct relationship between those massive donations and their representatives' votes on tax legislation.

U.S. News & World Report, 7-19:29.

Edward A. Grefe
Political and public-affairs
consultant

5

[On political action committees]: The real power in the long term is to use the corporate PAC to educate employees on the political process, motivating them to become involved to help people get elected. The unions learned that basic principle a long time ago. The future belongs to those who stress political education and participation, rather than just fund-raising. The old political education and saying about the "Four I's" is still appropriate: Get them interested, informed and involved—then get them to invest.

Nation's Business, May:35.

Howell Heflin
United States Senator, D—Alabama

6

[Calling for the expulsion from the Senate of Harrison Williams, convicted in the Abscam influence-peddling case]: If a member of this body really knows right from wrong . . . then that member would not hesitate for a moment to get up and walk—walk away from sleazy characters swearing like sailors; walk away from talk about sheiks and deals and hiding interests and protection and concealment . . . ; walk away, in other words, from obvious impropriety . . . But he didn't. He stayed. He discussed. He agreed. He promised. He pledged—to abuse his office, his public trust, for which now he must be expelled.

At Senate hearing, Washington, March 4/
U.S. News & World Report, 3-15:8.

WHAT THEY SAID IN 1982

Charlton Heston
Actor

1

[On actors becoming politicians] : Historically, politicians have always been required to be effective performers. Of course, they don't like to have it pointed out. You're not supposed to be an actor unless you're getting paid for it. But a leader has to communicate, inspire, exhort, persuade; that's precisely how you do it. Marc Antony was a remarkable example. In this country [the U.S.], acting as a profession has come late to the ranks of respectability. A half-century ago, no one would have thought to invite actors to a prestigious university, much less elect them to national office. But it's not unreasonable to suppose that actors would go into politics. Only a certain amount of social pressure has prevented more actors from involving themselves in politics.

Discussion with students, University of
Chicago/Chicago Tribune, 11-29:(1)13.

Philip B. Heymann
Professor, Harvard Law School;
Former Assistant Attorney General,
Criminal Division, Department
of Justice of the United States

2

[On the FBI's Abscam investigation which resulted in convictions of several Congressmen for taking bribes] : No one felt they were out testing the corruptibility of Congressmen or Senators. The sense was that the Bureau was discovering what were the practices among a handful of corrupt politicians . . . . there is out there surrounding the Congress a world full of foreign representatives and private parties ready and willing to offer bribes to protect their vast stakes in what the Congress does.

Before House Judiciary subcommittee, Washington,
June 3/The Washington Post, 6-4:(A)3.

Ernest F. Hollings
United States Senator,.
D—South Carolina

3

[On his liberal colleagues] : They've thrown

money at enough problems, God knows. Safe cars, safe streets, safe this, safe that, truth in lending, truth in packaging, the right to this, the right to that. The average guy out there paying taxes is totally frustrated. It was the Democrats who elected [President] Ronald Reagan.

The New York Times, 3-3:12.

Irving Howe
Author; Political activist

4

I think the thing that hurt me the most, in a personal sense, was the virulence of the attacks that we of the Old Left suffered at the hands of the New Left. We had always been able to handle attacks from the right wing, even relished them. But when all these kids in the early 1960s decided that we old fuddy-duddies had never done anything right and that history had to be written all over again—which is what all young people have always believed—but then proceeded to get so vicious and personal, I confess it hurt. I think they were savaging the wrong targets, and it got so very coarse and brutal that I think much of the general malaise and self-centeredness of the present decade is a perhaps natural reaction, or over-reaction, to the excesses of the 1960s.

Thomas H. Kean
Governor of New Jersey (R)

5

I was appalled, as I'm sure most of you were, by the corruption exposed in our own state and elsewhere by the FBI's Abscam operation and by the recent indictments and convictions of a number of our [government] officials. But I find much more dangerous and equally appalling the attitude held by many that this is just "politics as usual" and that the best thing to do is to drop out and turn away from public affairs. Such an attitude will eventually lead to the death of democracy, not by ambush or assassination but slowly through apathy, indifference and under-nourishment.

At Rutgers University commencement,
May 26/The New York Times, 5-27:18.

Edward M. Kennedy
United States Senator,
D—Massachusetts

1

We can be true Democrats without becoming the party of the bleeding heart or the party whose heart has turned to stone.

At Democratic Party meeting, Philadelphia, June/U.S. News & World Report, 7-5:65.

Ann F. Lewis
Political director, Democratic
National Committee

2

Third-party efforts, from what I can tell, are irrelevant in national politics. The purpose of a political party is to win, to gain power and then to govern. We have something in this country that people die for every day in other parts of the world—the ability to govern ourselves. The system we have depends on two large parties which are at varying times responsive and then sometimes need to be reminded and get more responsive. The number of people in that system who are going to choose voluntarily to deprive themselves of power by acting through a third party is always going to be small.

Interview/The New York Times, 11-7:(4)3.

Trent Lott
United States Representative,
R—Mississippi

3

Americans think of themselves as conservatives; they want government reduced. But in their hearts they're liberals; they want money for sewers and libraries and all the goodies coming in. It's a fact.

The New York Times, 11-18:14.

Michael Maccoby
Director, Project on Technology,
Work and Character, Washington

4

In politics, our wish for *the leader*—for someone who would solve everything—goes back to our fantasizing of the perfect parent. We tend to put an aura of greatness around those leading us because we wish they were great. But leadership is so difficult—just as being a great parent is difficult—that nobody is ever going to measure up to the need we have.

That's why, in this day and age—particularly with the growth of the self-oriented character—we must begin to demystify leadership. We should see the leader as a valued resource and also realize that all of us have to improve our leadership ability. We're not going to have a highly productive society unless more people take responsibility for leadership and don't look for *the leader.* Those in politics who are in tune with the new leadership model may be less charismatic than those the media are normally attracted to. That's one of the problems in getting the leaders we need. It takes more active work by the media to find them than to discover those who dazzle but who may not be adequate for the times.

Interview/U.S. News & World Report, 3-15:81.

Thomas E. Mann
Executive director, American
Political Science Association

5

[On President Reagan's success in getting Congress to vote his way during 1981]: There was no real great disruption of voting patterns. Voting patterns are stable over time. There was less high drama, less ideological change, and more traditional politics than generally thought. It was really retail politics in the new Congress—trading with fence-sitters. The most important change in the House was the simple replacement of 33 Democrats by Republicans. In close votes, such marginal shifts are crucial.

The Christian Science Monitor, 2-3:1.

Eugene J. McCarthy
Former United States Senator,
D—Minnesota

6

Politicians should be reasonably detached. So if you lost [an election] or were defeated, it wouldn't be the end of all things.

Interview, March 30/Chicago Tribune, 5-5:(1)11.

Paul N. McCloskey, Jr.
United States Representative,
R—California

7

I've never been a good politician and I never will be. I believe in speaking out and stating my beliefs. Politicians prosper by saying what polls tell them people want to hear. I've never been able to do that.

Interview, Washington, August/San Francisco Examiner & Chronicle, 8-15:(A)5.

Toby Moffett
United States Representative,
D–Connecticut

1

There's something inherent in politics and that is the feeling that you've got to try to move on to so-called higher office. It's something that pushes you. The fact is that your political stock is never standing still in this business. It's either going up or going down.

The Washington Post Magazine, 5-9:13.

Walter F. Mondale
Former Vice President
of the United States

2

I have never, ever seen the kind of special-interest money that's slopping around this country today [during the current national election campaign] ... There is going to be a scandal with big money in politics as sure as the sun rises in the morning. You cannot have $80-million, $90-million, $100-million slopping around this country today, like it is, and not sooner or later have a little smell.

Campaigning for Democratic candidates, October/Los Angeles Times, 10-31:(I)33.

Ronald M. Mottl
United States Representative, D–Ohio

3

Politics is very analogous to sports. When you're a winner, you're a hero, and when you lose you're a bum.

Interview, Washington/The New York Times, 6-14:18.

Bill Moyers
Commentator, CBS News

4

[On the news media's various evaluations of President Reagan's first year in office]: The Reagan Administration is not even at mid-semester yet and it's too early to give them even a tentative grade ... We reporters don't

have any business giving overnight ratings to Presidential decisions. You can only judge a President by the consequences of his decisions. Do they add up to a country that is better off or worse off—and you cannot determine that in the hot glare of the moment. We must wait and assess the impact. We're all caught up with style and smile and very little with substance and sequence.

Interview/San Francisco Examiner & Chronicle, 1-10:(TV Week)3.

Ralph Nader
Lawyer; Consumer-rights advocate

5

Almost 30 of the top officials [in the Reagan Administration] are millionaires, and many are multi-millionaires who view the Federal government as an instrument for the powerful and wealthy, unaccountable to the public. It is a government of extraordinary broad wealth, narrow vision and little compassion.

News conference, Washington, Aug. 30/ The New York Times, 8-31:11.

Richard M. Nixon
Former President of the United States

6

I think that it's understandable that with the morbid fascination that Watergate has, particularly for people in the media, who feel that they played a great part, as they did, in not only Watergate but the Vietnam war and everything else where they opposed me; that under the circumstances, they think that I, therefore, must be like they are, and that every year I've got to look back and wring my hands and say, "Why did this happen? Why did this happen?" and so forth. My attitude is somewhat different from that. I think, well one of my favorite expressions was, when we made some of the tough decisions that helped bring the war in Vietnam to an end—like going into Cambodia, which of course saved thousands of American lives by destroying the Communist supplies in that area; the bombing and mining of Haiphong ... which of course set the stage for ending the war and getting back our POWs. And after it happened, there'd be demonstrations in the streets [of the U.S. against those

(RICHARD M. NIXON)

actions], and all that sort of thing; and people would come to the office wringing their hands and saying, "My God, couldn't we have done it a different way, or maybe we shouldn't have done it." And I always said this: "Remember Lot's wife. Never look back." Now, I don't mind others looking back, and being critical. "Why was this done. Why was that done?" and all that sort of thing. If they think that's going to serve the interests of the country, let them do so. I don't think it is, but maybe it'll do their own Narcissus complexes some good; and if it does, that doesn't bother me a bit. But as far as my participating with them in it, no way. I'm looking to the future. They can look back.

Broadcast interview/
"CBS Morning News," CBS-TV, 6-3.

1

[There is] a very fine line [between not being candid and] lying in an immoral sense. There's a lot of hypocrisy and cant and so forth in political life. It's necessary in order to get into office, in order to retain office.

Broadcast interview/
"Good Morning America," ABC-TV, 10-27.

2

[On the recent election in which the Democratic Party increased its hold on the House, and the effects of this on the way the Reagan Administration will operate]: [President Reagan] is a man of great principle, but also one who likes to be effective. He's not stupid. He'll look at the election results and see he does not have as much support in the House as he had in the last two years. He will then recognize those realities and continue on his course but do so in a way that is effective. He isn't going to just dig his feet in and be remembered as the veto President.

Broadcast interview/"Today" show, NBC-TV, 11-4.

Thomas P. O'Neill, Jr.
United States Representative,
D—Massachusetts

3

[On the forthcoming Congressional elections]: Self-preservation is the first law of

politics. Congress is going to be a different body, an entirely different body. They will center on the elections. They will follow the whims of their constituents more than the whims of their party.

Washington, Jan. 5/The New York Times, 1-6:11.

4

The old liberals are concerned about the poor, the senior citizens and the indigent—people. [The] new liberals are concerned about clean air, clean water—issues.

Time, 4-26:13.

Bob Packwood
United States Senator, R—Oregon

5

I really think the President [Reagan] has an idealized concept of America. And maybe many Americans wish we were like that. Maybe many Americans wish we all looked alike, went to the same middle-of-the-road Protestant church, and we'd all be better off. I don't think we would be better off ... The Republican Party has just about written off those women who work for wages; we are losing them in droves. You cannot write them off and the blacks off and the Hispanics off and the Jews off and assume you're going to build a party on white Anglo-Saxon males over 40. There aren't enough of us left ... What I want is when people go down the [ballot] list and finally come to the office they've never heard of and candidates they've never heard of, that they vote Republican because they have an intuitive feeling that the Republican Party is watching out for their interests.

Interview, February/The New York Times, 3-2:9.

Charles Peters
Editor, "The Washington Monthly"

6

... the liberal movement has to change and reject the liberal cliches and automatic responses of the past—for instance, pro-government and pro-union, anti-defense and anti-business—for what we like to call "compassionate realism." The conventional liberal position has been to spit on business. I've come to treasure the entrepreneur. I want to help the sick and needy, but somebody out there has to be

(CHARLES PETERS)

making the money to pay the taxes to help support those programs.

Interview, Washington/The New York Times, 4-22:16.

Kevin Phillips
Political commentator

1

The 1980s are going to be a decade of confusion, fragmentation and ideological transformation in American politics. There will be continued weakness of the party system, the emergence of new parties and confusion of ideology in the sense that nobody is going to be quite sure what's conservative and what's not, what's liberal and what's not. One reason for this: A large element of the country has lost its party moorings. A frustrated middle-class electorate composed in part of blue-collar workers and rural Southerners has broken its long-term relationship with the Democratic Party. At the same time, these people haven't developed a relationship with the Republican Party. They start to do so and then seem disillusioned by Republican economics. The question is: Will they find a niche in the party system, or will they continue to be volatile and, with each passing four- or eight-year period, more frustrated?

Interview/U.S. News & World Report, 10-11:41.

Ronald Reagan
President of the United States

2

What are the Democrats going to run on [in the next election]? Raising taxes? Bargain basement defense when our planes won't fly? Where the hell have they been for the last 40 years? They have been in charge and look at the mess they've created. That's why I say draw sabers and charge.

To Republican leaders, Washington,
March/Time, 3-22:34.

3

The other side [the Democrats] believes the solutions to our nation's problems lie in the psychiatrist's notes or in the social worker's file or in the bureaucrat's budget. We [Republicans] believe in the workingman's toil, the

businessman's enterprise, the clergyman's counsel.

Campaigning for upcoming elections, Columbus,
Ohio, Oct. 4/The New York Times, 10-5:12.

4

At my age, I didn't come to Washington to play politics as usual. I didn't come here to reward pressure groups by spending other people's money. And, most of all, I didn't come here to further mortgage the future of the American people just to buy a little short-term political popularity. I came to Washington to try to solve problems—not to sweep them under the rug and leave them for those who will come later.

Broadcast address to the nation, Washington,
Oct. 13/The New York Times, 10-14:16.

5

I have no reason to make decisions based on a political future. As a matter of fact, I don't let my Cabinet talk to me about the political ramifications of any issue. Oh, perhaps the strategy that must be used to try to get what we're trying to get. But as to whether we adopt a policy or not, I ask only: Is it good for the people? Is it right, morally right?

Interview, aboard Air Force One/
U.S. News & World Report, 11-1:92.

George E. Reedy
Professor of journalism, Marquette
University; Former Press Secretary
to the President of the United
States (Lyndon B. Johnson)

6

Lyndon Johnson had an uncanny knack for changing history as he went along, to justify what he was doing at any given time. It wasn't lying; he did very little lying. What happened was he first convinced himself that something happened in a certain way. Then, because he had such a compelling personality, he was able to convince others it happened that way, too. Thus, all testimony about him is suspect . . . He didn't alter the record just to fool others. He convinced himself that that was the way the record was. This enabled him to convince others of things that weren't so. The problem is, once he reached the White House there was no one there to pull him back to reality, like there had been when he was in Congress.

Interview, Milwaukee/Chicago Tribune, 2-1:(1)13,14.

Edward V. Regan
Comptroller of New York State

1

We're not going to accomplish much, if anything, if our Congress continues to be paralyzed by the demands of special-interest groups concerned solely with single issues benefiting themselves. Somehow, Congress is going to have to face up to the job of representing the best interests of the country over the vested interests of single-issue groups. An example of what I mean is the story told about Neville Chamberlain at the time of Munich just before World War II. Chamberlain rose in the House of Commons to speak, he said, for the Conservative Party. From a back-bencher came the cry: "Never mind the party. Speak now for England!" That's what we need in Washington—men and women who speak for America.

At observance of National Affairs Week, Chautauqua, N.Y./Chicago Tribune, 10-22:(1)11.

Abraham A. Ribicoff
Former United States Senator, D—Connecticut

2

[On his voluntary decision not to seek re-election in 1980]: I can't tell you the number of Senators who have talked to me about this. I've told them that there is a time to stay and a time to go. You tip your hat when you're on top, and say goodbye. There's no greater tragedy for a person of ability, character and prestige than to try to stay that one extra term. You forget that you don't have a lock on anything forever... Once you are out of office, don't try to second guess. Be an observer and not a participant. Forget the power that you had. Be available for advice and friendship, but don't try to run the show any more.

Interview, New York/The New York Times, 1-28:12.

Burns Roper
President, Roper Organization, public-opinion analysts

3

[For a President] to have a negative rating [in public-opinion polls] is not hopeless. We're getting into the situation where the yardstick is perfection, rather than "What's the alterna-

tive?" It's now "Reagan vs. what-I'd like-to-see-as-the-President," not "Reagan vs. Kennedy," or "Reagan vs. Carter," or "Reagan vs. Mondale." Reagan's going to be increasingly in this situation until [the election] two years from now, when he will again be measured not against the ideal, but against the alternative.

The Christian Science Monitor, 3-3:6.

Benjamin S. Rosenthal
United States Representative, D—New York

4

[On Congressmen's behavior during an election year]: Everything you do is geared toward the election. Objectivity and statesmanship are at a minimum. Everybody's Number 1 priority is re-election, and that will temper legislation, stimulate hearings and have a multitude of effects.

The New York Times, 1-6:11.

Patricia Schroeder
United States Representative, D—Colorado

5

I wish only individual [political campaign] contributions could be accepted [by candidates] and political-action committees were outlawed. We are becoming the finest Congress money can buy.

U.S. News & World Report, 3-15:24.

Leon Shull
Executive director, Americans for Democratic Action

6

The economic issue now is jobs. And jobs is our [liberals'] issue—a good old-fashioned liberal issue. The other big issue is the military. The country is not enthusiastic for a big military buildup, and fears of nuclear war are building. These are liberal issues, too. The big Democratic [Party] weakness so far is they haven't convinced the public they have alternative programs—new or old. [Senator Edward] Kennedy [who just announced he will not run for President in 1984] stood for something. That's going to be a loss for liberals... Unless [former Vice President Walter] Mondale makes people feel he has a program, has a passion,

WHAT THEY SAID IN 1982

(LEON SHULL)

convinces people he can make it on his own, he's not going to make it [as a Presidential candidate in 1984]. He's got to come out with a clear and decisive program—something people will love or hate.

The Christian Science Monitor, 12-7:5.

Nancy Sinnott
Executive director, National
Republican Congressional Committee

1

The Republican Party—Republican institutions—has perfected certain things over the years—small-giver fund raising; candidate improvement and training; the whole range of direct candidate services. The Democratic Party has perfected [voter] turnout .... clearly their forte is mobilizing bodies in the last three weeks [before an election]. And they proved again this time [in the recent election] that they do that very well. That is a mandate for our party.

Interview/The New York Times, 11-7:(4)3.

Maurice H. Stans
Former Secretary of Commerce
of the United States

2

Watergate dragged into the web an awful lot of innocent people—who got hurt by the extremes of investigation, by the extremes of prosecution and by the extremes of politics. John Connally was found innocent; Bebe Rebozo, investigated ad infinitum, but they found nothing wrong; the President's [Nixon] brothers, who were targets of attack all along; the President's secretary; my own secretary not only threatened by prosecutors, but couldn't get a job for two years in Washington after it was all over. A lot of little people were hurt. A lot of [political financial] contributors were pursued and publicized unfairly, even though they had given their contributions perfectly legally. All of that was part of Watergate.

Interview/Los Angeles
Herald Examiner, 6-16:(A)9.

Adlai E. Stevenson III
Democratic nominee for Governor
of Illinois; Former United States
Senator, D—Illinois

3

[On a code of ethics for government officials]: I don't like the use of ethics codes. I don't think you ought to have to legislate the obvious, to legislate morality. But if it is not clear that as a public official you do not accept things of value, discounts, paid vacations, then yes, we'll have to have a code of ethics.

Radio broadcast, Chicago/
Chicago Tribune, 4-9:(1)1.

Gore Vidal
Author

4

The founding fathers would be appalled by the notion of a "professional politician." If you were an architect or a banker or—God help us—a lawyer, you were expected to give six years of your wisdom to your country toward the end of another career. Now we have 25-year-olds who come direct from law school to the House of Representatives with their blow-dry hairdos looking like anchorpersons or weather people. What do they know? What could we expect them to know?

Interview, Los Angeles, Jan. 25/
Los Angeles Herald Examiner, 1-27:(C)5.

5

[Announcing his candidacy for the California Democratic U.S. Senatorial nomination]: The founding fathers were not always wrong, and they thought that you should achieve your fame and your fortune before you went into public life. And then in middle life you would give six years of your life to government and lend what expertise you might have, or even wisdom. And then you'd go home. That is pretty much my approach. At 56, I don't need money and I don't need glory and I have a certain sense of frustration about the way the country is going ... and I find that people seem to find this approach appealing.

Interview, Los Angeles, March 8/
Los Angeles Times, 3-9:(I)3.

176

Glenn Watts
President, Communications
Workers of America   1

The labor movement has made a clear decision to be more active in party affairs. While it appears that this means exclusively the Democratic Party, that's not the intention. But it's the only place labor appears welcome right now. So it's working hard within the Democratic Party right now. Labor won't turn its back on all Republicans. But I believe labor is going to have a lot more influence on the Democratic Party than in 1980.

Interview, Washington/The New York Times, 3-20:9.

Stephen J. Wayne
Professor of political
science and public affairs,
George Washington University   2

In 1980, the elements of surprise were the Republicans winning control of the Senate, and [then-President-elect] Reagan's unanticipated [election] victory margin. It prompted Republicans in close elections to attribute their wins to Reagan, and in turn this contributed to his capacity to gain unified support in the House in his first encounters. It contributed to his ability to convince the public that he'd received in 1980 a mandate for his economic policy—when in actuality the public voted less for him than against [Jimmy] Carter.

The Christian Science Monitor, 11-1:5.

Theodore H. White
Author, Historian   3

There are plants that are called heliotropic because they turn to the sun regardless of where you plant them. All politicians today are videotropic: They turn to television.

Interview/U.S. News & World Report, 7-5:60.

Harrison A. Williams, Jr.
United States Senator, D–New Jersey
                                         4

[On his possible expulsion from the Senate for his conviction for bribery and conspiracy during the FBI's Abscam investigation]: It is in light of this Executive Branch culpability [the FBI's alleged attempt to entrap him in phony criminal activity] that we must consider this preposterous recommendation that I be expelled ... For the first time in the history of our country ... the Executive Branch has sought to create crimes here [in Congress]. I stand before you not merely in my own self-defense, but to assure that together we preserve the U.S. Senate as an institution.

Before Senators considering his expulsion,
Washington, March 4/Los Angeles Times, 3-5:(1)19.

Sam Yorty
Former Mayor of Los Angeles
                                         5

[On the use of television advertising in political campaigns]: It's really become a contest between professional TV people, instead of between the candidates. The only way people know the candidates is by these 30-second spot commercials, which I think are a real detriment to politics. The candidate ought to have to get on and face his opponent and discuss the issues. And these things [the spot ads] cost a lot of money, so the candidates have to spend most of their time raising money—and people don't put up money who are disinterested in what the candidate is going to do in office. There are a lot of good people who would like to run for office, but they don't want to do what you have to do to raise money.

Interview/Los Angeles Herald Examiner, 11-3:(A)2.

Social Welfare

Bruce Babbitt
Governor of Arizona (D)

1

...while the states do some things very well—education, roads, law enforcement, many municipal functions—welfare has never been a popular issue. It's one that has never been handled historically adequately at the state level, and it's one of those areas where I think a moral sense of what government ought to do compels you to say we ought to have a uniform minimum national standard, maybe a little less, but certainly a uniform national standard ... Because historically the state governments, mine included, have not done an adequate job of meeting the needs of the poor and the elderly and the dispossessed. That was the great discovery of the New Deal, that this particular group, if they're going to be treated equitably, must be a national responsibility. That's the reason for moving toward more Federal responsibility, rather than less ...

Broadcast interview/"Meet the Press," NBC-TV, 1-31.

Robert M. Ball
Former Commissioner, Social Security Administration of the United States

2

[Saying he would not be averse to raising the Social Security payroll tax if necessary to keep the system solvent]: It's a payment for a very important type of protection that people can't get in any other way. I really think we ought to be planning a huge celebration for this system, not wringing our hands about [its fiscal problems], as we near its 50th anniversary. Back in 1935, not more than about 15 per cent of workers were in jobs that had any kind of retirement protection. Social Security has given an independence and dignity to all generations that didn't exist before.

Interview/The New York Times, 12-26:(4)5.

Jack Brooks
United States Representative, D—Texas

3

[On Reagan Administration plans to shift social programs from the Federal to state and local governments]: The thing that bothers me most about this proposal, I guess, is that it seems to be based entirely on shifting costs. There has been no showing that the states can do a fairer, more humane job in administering welfare. And the problems won't go away just because Mr. Reagan shifts responsibility for solving them to the states. They'll still be there. And so will the costs—only it will be the property tax instead of the Federal income tax that pays for the solutions. Is that a big plus? Is that worth all the disruption and discussion and time and trouble it would take to put something like this in place? I don't think so. I'd kind of like to see us move a little more cautiously, and be a little more certain of where we're heading, before we try to alter things with "one bold stroke."

Interview, Washington/ The Wall Street Journal, 2-23:29.

Edmund G. Brown, Jr.
Governor of California (D)

4

I was once taught in grammar school that we always were to pray for the most forgotten soul in purgatory. And their number has grown. And they're becoming more forgotten. And I take it as our responsibility to try to get out and put a real net under these people, so they'll have some piece of the American dream that has not otherwise been extended to them. At a time when we need national unity more than ever before, we are experiencing a growing division because of this transfer of wealth from the working poor to the working rich and the

(EDMUND G. BROWN, JR.)

non-working rich [as a result of the Reagan Administration's economic program].

Broadcast rebuttal to President's
State of the Union address, Jan. 26/
The New York Times, 1-27:10.

Robert N. Butler
Director, National Institute on
Aging of the United States   *1*

There's still an awful lot of tension and uncertainty and fear about Social Security. If we lived in a truly primitive society, the family and village would make sure people would not have to be frantic about old age. But since we live in a very humane and sophisticated society, everybody over 60 is scared to death as to whether they're going to be able to make it.

Interview/The Washington Post, 7-28:(B)5.

Robert B. Carleson
Special Assistant to the
President of the United States
for Policy Development   *2*

[Saying income belongs to the people who earn it]: It does not belong to the state, nor does it belong by right to any other segment of the population. No threat of unrest, whether idle or not, should be permitted to cow a government into transferring income from one group of people to another when that transfer is not justified by accepted social norms.

The New York Times, 4-26:12.

Bruce Chapman
Director, Federal Bureau
of the Census   *3*

The two most rapidly growing groups in the population are the elderly and the baby-boom generation. The elderly have their Social Security indexed to inflation and the protection of medical insurance provided by the government, while the young are watching their Social Security taxes go up and up. There may come a point where there's going to be intergenerational strife over that fact as people realize the economic consequences. Social Security planners really failed to grasp what was happening to mortality rates. The rates went down sharply in the last decade—especially among the elderly. This was a real break from the immediate past. Whereas a half century ago people may have expected to live into their mid-60s, they now expect to live into their mid-70s, and soon will be expecting to live into their mid-80s. Now, that's a wonderful boon. But, at the same time, there are costs attached. Individuals and the society have planned programs on the basis of a certain length of life. All of a sudden, they realize that past assumptions are no longer valid.

Interview/U.S. News & World Report, 3-22:52.

Archibald Cox
Professor of law, Harvard University;
Chairman, Common Cause   *4*

Beginning in the 1930s there was a major change in the role of government, to prevent people with economic power from abusing people lacking economic power. To make sure people had certain minimums of food, shelter, it then became the role of government to take some measures to help those who had been denied access to the mainstream of American life to help get them access. There was enormous progress for almost everyone. That was the political philosophy that dominated for more than half a century. What was the meaning of the election of 1980, when the bulk of the people said government isn't doing its job? Does the [Reagan] Administration read the election as a means to turn back this unhealthy part of the growth, or is it saying the election means that we should carry this country back 65 years if we can, to the 1920s [by cutting government social programs]? I worry that it is trying to say the second.

Interview, Los Angeles/
Los Angeles Times, 2-5:(V)2.

Alan Cranston
United States Senator,
D—California   *5*

Millions of Americans placed false hopes in [President] Ronald Reagan. And what did they get? Cuts in the lifelines to children and to older citizens, to the poor and to all those living in cities. The American people were right to

(ALAN CRANSTON)   *3*

protest against unresponsive bureaucracy and taxes that pay for wasteful programs. But let us not turn America into a mean, narrow, selfish land—without vision, without grandeur, without grace. We have in the White House a man who seems oblivious to some of our greatest national problems, indifferent to others, and whose approach to those he's aware of is superficial and simplistic.

At Democratic Party conference, Philadelphia,
June 25/The New York Times, 6-26:11.

Mike Curb
Lieutenant Governor of California (R)

1

[Criticizing the welfare system]: What we have is a situation now where we are bringing up people not to work. It's that simple. And our welfare state happens to perpetuate that. Dignity of a job means nothing . . . So many of our American workers are on welfare and they're not willing to work on the farms any more. I grew up for eight years delivering papers in the San Fernando Valley. I was taught to work . . . Now I talk to [newspaper] publishers around the state and they say [they] can't find people to deliver our papers any more. I talked to farmers. It didn't use to be so bad for a person after school—to pick tomatoes. Now, for heaven's sake, that's beneath anyone's dignity. You don't dare to do that. Our kids wouldn't dare do that.

Before Republican women, Northridge, Calif.,
May 19/Los Angeles Times, 5-20:(I)3,21.

Robert J. Dole
United States Senator, R—Kansas

2

You can't balance the [Federal] budget on the back of one or two programs. You can make reasonable cuts in programs such as food stamps and Medicaid, but that shouldn't be the centerpiece. Our centerpiece ought to be a balanced program that cuts across the board. Republicans keep saying, "Cut more from social programs." I think they have to take their foot off that accelerator.

Interview/U.S. News & World Report, 2-22:23.

[On how to tackle the growing Social Security fund deficit]: I would not raise payroll taxes. That's one thing, as far as I'm concerned, that's not an option. We're already over-taxed in that area. In fact, many young couples pay more in Social Security tax than they pay in income tax. I do believe we have to look at the formula of how we increase benefits on an annual basis. Maybe that should be changed. Maybe we should reduce the growth of benefits and maybe change the time you retire, make it less generous if you retire early and encourage later retirement.

Broadcast interview/"Meet the Press," NBC-TV, 8-15.

Pete V. Domenici
United States Senator, R—New Mexico

4

[Favoring a cut-back in Social Security annual cost-of-living adjustments]: We owe it to the Social Security recipients, and to those millions who are paying taxes into the trust funds, to do everything we can to keep the funds solvent and to make certain the Federal government meets its basic responsibilities. I find nothing in the history of Social Security to indicate a contractual responsibility to pay the basic benefit plus automatic increases each year based on the consumer price index. After all, we only started automatic indexing of Social Security in 1975. If we keep the current schedule and do not alter the cost-of-living adjustments at all, the main trust fund will fall below acceptable reserve levels in 1983. If we don't do something, we could arrive at a point where there is not enough money to pay 100 per cent of the benefits. That has never happened in our history, and I don't want to be part of it ever happening.

Interview/U.S. News & World Report, 5-10:82.

Gary W. Hart
United States Senator,
D—Colorado

5

The Democratic Party, over the years, has believed in the idea of justice; not handouts, but justice. And the programs that we've

(GARY W. HART)

developed to help people get jobs and keep jobs and train for jobs in the future—have decent housing, have education for their children, have decent health care—have all been based upon that idea of justice. This [Reagan] Administration—and I think its party [Republican]—believes that if the wealthy are getting wealthy enough, that they'll provide some sort of kindness and generosity to people. But that's all accidental. It may or may not happen. We believe a fair and decent and just society in the 20th century ought to make that happen.

Broadcast rebuttal to President's
State of the Union address, Jan. 26/
The New York Times, 1-27:10.

Larry Jackson
President, Lander College

1

I feel very strongly there are many reasons for keeping the [government] social programs in place other than social justice. I would defend them all on the question of justice, but I think a pragmatic social stability argument is just as valid. It's not whether we can afford them. It's whether we can possibly *not* afford those programs. They are not luxuries. They have assured our own stability. We cannot enjoy a high standard of living unless we maintain stability by assuring a basic level of living for everybody. I think that is threatened. If the people who control production in this country want to keep the very ample benefits they are now receiving, they'll have to pay to keep these programs in place. I could make an equally impassioned plea because I think justice requires them, but I also think stability and our own self-interest requires us to keep them in place.

The Washington Post, 10-27:(A)7.

John E. Jacob
President, National Urban League

2

In 1981 the black community was hit by economic and political disasters of the first magnitude. For black Americans, 1981 was a year of economic depression, savage cuts in survival programs for the poor and the betrayal

of basic civil-rights protection . . . This time around, the social safety net is in shreds. Cuts in Federal social programs did not just trim the fat, they slashed deep into bone. And these cuts were concentrated in programs in which blacks were a third to a half of all beneficiaries. We must be very clear about what happened in 1981: The rich got tax cuts, the Pentagon got a blank check; but poor people lost jobs, training opportunities, food assistance, health care and much else.

News conference, Washington, Jan. 18/
Chicago Tribune, 1-20:(1)4.

3

The seductive idea of transferring programs and powers [from the Federal government] to the states is a non-starter. Those programs and powers came to Washington because of state abuses, and turning them back to the states is bound to lead to new abuses. The "new Federalism" was a mistake when it was limited to packaging various Federal health and social welfare programs into block grants to be administered by the states. The new plan to turn basic survival programs like welfare and food stamps to the states promises nothing less than a disaster . . . The conceptual flaw behind the "new Federalism" is the idea that local governments can best deal with local problems. But poverty is not a local problem: It is national. Fully Federalized welfare would acknowledge that. It would recognize that national problems require national solutions; that hunger in Michigan is the same as hunger in Mississippi; and that fairness demands poor people receive the same treatment wherever they reside.

Before Congressional Joint Economic Committee,
Washington/The Washington Post, 7-18:(B)6.

4

[Calling for a national public-works program]: The last time we were in a depression, our leaders created jobs that produced buildings, bridges and dams we still use. The last time we were in a depression, our leaders took kids off city streets and gave them jobs building playgrounds and preserving nature. Just think of the tremendous amount of work to be done

(JOHN E. JACOB)

in an America where millions are idle. Our national infrastructure is falling apart. Roads and bridges need to be repaired and replaced. Our rail system and ports need to be revitalized. We need to build homes, sewer lines and water systems. A decade of disinvestment forces us to strengthen the economic infrastructure of America if we want to grow . . . It's an investment rather than an expenditure. The return of people to working and paying taxes and buying cars would generate a return on investment very quickly.

At National Urban League conference, Los Angeles, Aug. 1/Los Angeles Times, 8-2:(I)3,16.

William J. Janklow
Governor of South Dakota (R)

1

If I was an elderly person dependent on Social Security to live, I'd be scared to death at the way this rhetoric is flying around from the Republican Party [on how to return the system to solvency]. Every day, somebody is coming up with a new screwball plan to scare the hell out of everybody.

At Republican Governors Conference, Kansas City, Nov. 15/Los Angeles Times, 11-16:(I)4.

Alan Karcher
New Jersey State Assemblyman (D)

2

The only thing that trickles down from the "new Federalism" is the agony and bitterness of cutting people off. It goes from the President to the Governor to the county executive to the guy at the local school board. He's the one with the real dirty end of the stick, the one who has to fire the teachers. You're given this block grant: Who do you pull the plug on? Do you pull it on people getting day care, drug care, or someone being treated for alcohol abuse? That's a wretched decision. It puts an unfair burden on us. If there's no money for senior-citizen lunch programs, the President ought to say that. Let him take the political heat for it.

The Washington Post, 12-27:(A)4.

Edward I. Koch
Mayor of New York

3

For years, Federal policies have encouraged the concentration of poverty and dependency in our cities. For years, we have asked Washington to assume responsibility for social programs, which are the rightful obligation of our entire country. For years, we have watched them evade responsibility for the consequences of Federal policy. And now we are seeing them not only turn their heads, but also attempt to turn back the clock [by giving more responsibilities to the cities and cutting back on funds].

Inaugural address, New York, Jan. 1/ The New York Times, 1-2:10.

Jacques Lesourne
President, French Association of Economic Sciences

4

Despite its inefficiency, its functional shortcomings and its disappointing efforts at redistribution, the welfare state remains a major stride forward in the protection of the individual. Building a developed society without it is neither possible nor desirable. Many Americans find that insecurity is a stimulus, but for others it can be demoralizing. The problem of the welfare state is a contradiction between people's needs; they want security and social protection, but also the highest possible income. During periods of slow growth, these contradictions can reach a high pitch. The demands made on the welfare state are increasingly complex, reflecting local, social and family situations of all kinds. This implies increasing taxes, so real income will grow very slowly and we should brace ourselves for some conflicts.

Interview/World Press Review, July:33.

Sar A. Levitan
Professor of economics and director, Center for Social Policy Studies, George Washington University

5

The family today is under stress and undergoing very real changes. More women are working outside the home and are economically independent. Moreover, families today have

(SAR A. LEVITAN)

fewer children, and some have none. The ability of families to decide when they are going to have children—or if they are going to have any—is a recent development. We're still not used to some women saying, "I don't want to have kids." Thirty years ago, a woman who said that would be considered strange. Now that position is perfectly respectable. The most significant and disturbing change: Millions of kids are being brought up by one parent, usually the mother. Many of these youngsters are going to be raised in poverty, in part because at least two thirds of the male parents who have left the nest do not support their children after they depart. In spite of all these things, the basic structure of the family is not endangered. History shows that the family is a very resilient institution.

Interview/U.S. News & World Report, 4-26:77.

Joseph E. Lowery
*President, Southern Christian
Leadership Conference*

1

[Criticizing President Reagan's plans to shift many Federal programs, such as welfare and food stamps, to the states]: The Federal government assumed responsibility for these programs as a result of the states' inability to provide them. We feel these functions are legitimate Federal interests and should not be left to the discretion of the states.

*To reporters, Washington, Jan. 27/
Los Angeles Times, 1-28:(I)18.*

Marc L. Marks
*United States Representative,
R—Pennsylvania*

2

[Criticizing Reagan Administration budget cuts affecting welfare and social-service programs]: The time is now to see to it that what Washington, Lincoln and Roosevelt accomplished—that is, to provide for those who for whatever reasons cannot provide for themselves—is not destroyed by a President [Reagan] and his cronies whose belief in Hooverism has blinded them to the wretched-

ness and to the suffering they are inflicting, through their policies and their refusal to re-evaluate those policies on the sick, the poor, the handicapped, the blue-collar, the white-collar workers, the small-business person, the black community, the community of minorities generally, women of all economic and social backgrounds, men and women who desperately need job training, families that deserve and desire the right to send their children to college or graduate school—in fact, anyone and everyone, other than those who have been fortunate enough to insulate themselves in a corporate suit of armor. My own experience leads me to believe that if this President knows at all about what is taking place throughout this land, then he lacks the compassion necessary to be President.

*Before the House, Washington, March 9/
The New York Times, 3-13:9.*

Jean Mayer
*President, Tufts University;
Nutritionist*

3

With the steady hacking away at [Federal] food programs, we are seeing hunger reappear in the United States. Simple economic calculations show that there is a growing number of people who literally cannot afford what nutritionists consider to be a minimal diet . . . Of all the foolish ways to save money, not to feed people—particularly at a time when we have [food] surpluses coming out of our ears—seems to be one of the most shortsighted.

*Broadcast interview/
"Face the Nation," CBS-TV, 12-26.*

Howard M. Metzenbaum
United States Senator, D—Ohio

4

[Opposing cuts in annual Social Security cost-of-living adjustments as a way of balancing the system's budget]: I believe that a contract was made with the people when they entered the Social Security System. This is their money; they had it deducted from their wages. You don't lead people down a primrose path, tell them they're going to get retirement benefits they paid for, and then suddenly tell them they aren't going to get it. I see no logical reason

(HOWARD M. METZENBAUM)

why the burden of balancing the budget should be placed upon people who are receiving Social Security. How cruel and inhumane that would be! There is no justification for this other than the fact that these recipients don't have as powerful a lobby as do some defense contractors or other special interests.

Interview/U.S. News & World Report, 5-10:81.

Walter F. Mondale
Former Vice President
of the United States

1

[Saying he disagrees with Reagan Administration plans to turn over Federal social-service programs to the states and cities]: The reason is a simple one: If it is all put on state tax burdens, each state in trying to hold and attract business will be driven to reduce taxes in order to keep a healthy economic base, and inevitable pressures will be placed on programs such as Aid to Families with Dependent Children or unemployment insurance, and those programs will be squeezed. That is why they should remain national programs so that they can be uniform nationally and not dependent on inter-state tax competition.

At Chicago Gift Show, Jan. 31/
Chicago Tribune, 2-1:(1)9.

2

In [President] Reagan's America, if you're sick, they make you pay more. If you're young, they call ketchup a vegetable. If you're poor, they fire your lawyer. And if you're hungry, they make you wait in the cold for cheese.

At Democratic Party conference, Philadelphia,
June 25/Los Angeles Times, 6-26:(I)3.

3

What this [Reagan] Administration is well on the way toward doing is creating two Americas, one for the well-to-do who aren't suffering—they are doing better all the time— and the other America for the rest of us who are getting less and less. [The wealthy are benefiting from tax cuts, while] if you're sick,

they make you pay more, if you're young, they call ketchup a vegetable, if you're poor, they fire your lawyer, and if you're hungry, they make you sit in the cold for cheese.

At NAACP convention, Boston, July 1/
The New York Times, 7-2:11.

Daniel P. Moynihan
United States Senator, D—New York

4

[Criticizing Reagan Administration proposals to shift welfare responsibilities from the Federal to state governments]: It's a radical act. If there is anything this country has agreed on for the past half-century, it is that if you are a dependent child or a mother with dependent children, you are entitled to support from the Federal government. It may not be bloody lavish, but you are not going to be left to beg.

Newsweek, 4-5:19.

J. Richard Munro
President, Time, Inc.

5

[Criticizing Reagan Administration plans to put more of the welfare and social-service burden on states rather than the Federal government]: Instead of the present national standard of assistance set by Washington, we would have a national standard set by the least-generous states, a lowest common denominator. States that already provide little direct aid would probably do even less. Other states might choose to decrease the level of aid rather than raise taxes. To hold the line would raise fears of an influx of the dependent poor from a less-generous state and an exodus of the productive skilled and their employers—voting with their feet, in other words . . . Even if there were no economic case for aiding the poor, the fact remains that the Administration's program is just plain unfair. Deficits are soaring because of contradictions in the program that were obvious from the start. Business leaders knew that, but we went along anyway. Yet who gets the blame? The poor. Who makes the sacrifices? The poor. And who has less to do with this mess than anyone else? The poor.

Before advertising executives/
Los Angeles Times, 3-18:(II)11.

Thomas P. O'Neill, Jr.
United States Representative,
D—Massachusetts

1

[Criticizing President Reagan's budget proposals which include cuts in social entitlement programs]: He [Reagan] went with the old hackneyed stories that he tells about the woman up in Westchester who makes $75,000 a year, and her child is on the student free-lunch program. I said: "Mr. President, it can't happen." I visit the schools . . . I find out that in Massachusetts 640,000 have been denied school lunches since last year and don't qualify this year—about 30 per cent of the schools. He doesn't appreciate that . . . You know, genuinely I like the fellow. He tells a great Irish story. But the truth of the matter is—yeah, I believe he has forgotten his roots and he has associated with the country-club style of people who love to say: "Social Security is wrong."

To reporters, Washington, Feb. 8/
Los Angeles Times, 2-9:(I)12.

2

I don't think [President Reagan] has an understanding, I don't think he has a care, I don't think he has a concern for those who are on the bottom rung of the ladder. It's nice to have an effervescent smile and a friendly way and a warm handshake, but you've got to have more than ice water for blood that pours to the heart. It's one thing to feel sad for them, but it's another thing to do something for them.

Broadcast interview/"Today" show, NBC-TV, 9-16.

Rudolf Penner
Authority on the Federal budget,
American Enterprise Institute

3

[President] Reagan has not cut the size of government in any substantial way. He has changed what government emphasizes, from non-defense spending to defense spending, without in any way reversing the Great Society. This so-called conservative President will probably be most famous in history for having sanctified the Great Society much as Eisenhower sanctified the New Deal by not reversing New Deal programs like Social Security. Reagan has not even proposed doing away with the really core Great Society programs— food stamps, Medicare and Medicaid. He has sliced more vigorously only the chaff of the Great Society programs, . . . things like mental-health programs which [former President] Carter had already begun to slash vigorously.

The Christian Science Monitor, 9-3:3.

Peter G. Peterson
Former Secretary of Commerce
of the United States

4

The real acid test of Congressional ability to get the budget under control is whether lawmakers really take action on the vast entitlement programs that essentially go to middle and upper-income groups. I would emphasize Social Security, but also include Federal pensions, veterans' pensions and railroad-retirement pensions. Benefits under these programs now rise at 100 per cent of the inflation rate. Contrary to popular opinion, most beneficiaries are not poor people. Benefits go to anyone who qualifies, regardless of income . . . Any reform of Social Security must preserve the solvency and credibility of the system while strongly reaffirming our commitment to the truly needy among the aged. But today many of the aged are not needy. The best approach is gradually to reduce the growth of benefits, giving everyone time to plan for retirement. But we should return to the original objective of Social Security. That is, to provide a minimum floor on retirement income for the elderly.

Interview/U.S. News & World Report, 7-26:34.

Ronald Reagan
President of the United States

5

The Reverend Billy Graham estimates that if every church and synagogue in the United States would average adopting 10 poor families beneath the poverty level, we could eliminate all government welfare in this country—Federal, state and local. Isn't it about time we all agree that we should be providing incentives to help people get off welfare so we can stop demoralizing human beings and start saving them?

Before New York City Partnership, New York,
Jan. 14/Los Angeles Times, 1-15:(I)12.

(RONALD REAGAN)

1

As to the cuts in social reforms, most of what we have done in that regard has not been a cut; there has not been a cut in the over-all spending on human resources. Actually, there is an increase over the year before and there will be an increase in '83 over '82, and on down the line. We have reduced the rate of increase in those programs, but much of the cut is aimed at trying to eliminate from the rolls those people who I think are unfairly benefiting from those programs. Nothing has happened to change the situation of the person who is totally dependent on the government for help, nor are we going to change those things.

News conference, Washington, Jan. 19/
The New York Times, 1-20:12.

2

Back in the New Deal days, many critics of Franklin Roosevelt accused him of trying to destroy the free-enterprise system. F.D.R.'s answer was simple: He wasn't out to destroy our political and economic freedom; he was out to save it at a time of severe stress. Today, I'm accused by some of trying to destroy government's commitment to compassion—and to the needy. Does this bother me? Yes! Like F.D.R., may I say I am not trying to destroy what is best in our system of humane, free government. I am doing everything I can to save it—to slow down the destructive rate of growth in taxes and spending, to prune non-essential programs so that enough resources will be left to meet the requirements of the truly needy.

Accepting Charles Evans Hughes medal, before
National Conference of Christians and Jews, New York,
March 23/Los Angeles Times, 3-24:(I)12.

3

While we've quite justly, and out of economic necessity, cut some budgets [of Federal programs], we have not, contrary to what seems to be the perception, abandoned America's commitment to the poor. We must recapture the spirit of brotherhood, however, of family and community that once was the hallmark of this country. We're trying to get people, once again, trying to help others directly. Accomplishing this is not simply a matter of raising money; it's not just reaching into our

pockets, but reaching into our hearts ... I'm not suggesting, nor have I ever suggested, that churches and other voluntary groups should pick up the dollar-for-dollar cost of reduced Federal programs. I just believe it would be a good thing for the soul of this country to encourage people to get involved and accept more direct responsibility for one another's health, happiness and well-being, rather than leaving it to the bureaucracy.

Before national religious leaders, Washington/
The Christian Science Monitor, 4-26:26.

4

Where does compassion [for the poor] start? I know where it starts; it starts for anyone that's got a problem and is in need. But, also, where do you cut it off? The Democrats tend not to cut it off until at a point when people who are not really needy are benefiting from their programs, and the people they take taxes from to fund the programs are really getting strapped. What about that guy out there who is getting up in the morning and going to work and sending the kids to school, contributing to his church and charity and paying his taxes and making the wheels go round? What compassion for him, when every month that went by during all those years we were taking another chunk of purchasing power out of his money? I keep remembering Lyndon Johnson's line when he began the Great Society, when he went nation-wide and stated, "We are going to take from those who have and give it to those who have not." Well, the "haves," in that view, was every worker in America.

Interview, aboard Air Force One/
U.S. News & World Report, 10-25:98.

5

The answer to this problem is so serious—the solvency of Social Security—that it is time that those who have frightened the senior citizens of this country the way they have, quit frightening them because I know of no one, and especially me, who is going to support any program for restoring fiscal solvency that reduces the checks below the level that the present beneficiaries are getting. And these people, poor people, have been frightened to death by charges that there were some of us out there that were

(RONALD REAGAN)

trying to take this away from them. And we're not . . . It is time for the leadership—both of us, both sides of the aisle—to come together with the knowledge that we've got to sit down around a table and work out a solution to this problem.

News conference, Washington, Nov. 11/
The New York Times, 11-12:12.

B. F. Skinner
Psychologist

1

I'm sorry society enforces retirement. There are things people could do that are rather like what they used to do . . . People who work hard think that not having to do anything would be wonderful. They don't know that it's the worst possible thing, not having to do anything. It's the problem of the leisure class, characteristically an unhappy class.

Interview, Washington/
The Washington Post, 8-24:(B)9.

John A. Svahn
Commissioner, Social Security
Administration of the United States

2

We're facing right now a situation where anywhere from two thirds to three quarters of the population does not believe Social Security will be there when they retire. As long as the United States government keeps pointing out that we've got a potential $1.5-trillion deficit in 1981 dollars over the next 75 years and people walk around saying, "I don't know how we're going to solve this," there's no reason for them to believe that it's going to be there, other than good faith. So it's a responsibility of the government to bring the system back into balance.

Interview/U.S. News & World Report, 2-15:36.

3

In the year 2015 we'll need $1.5-trillion to keep up today's [Social Security] benefit structure. Either [taxpayers are] going to have to start paying an awful lot more now . . . up to 24 per cent . . . or we're going to have to expect

less . . . Seventy per cent of the American population doesn't believe Social Security will be here when they retire. It's that same group of people we are going to have to rely upon [for payments to keep the system going].

Before American Society of Hospital
Personnel Administrators, Baltimore, July 26/
Chicago Tribune, 7-28:(1)4.

David B. Swoap
Under Secretary of Health and Human
Services of the United States

4

[On the Reagan Administration's cuts in aid to poor people]: When people see those numbers, they automatically assume that all of them are needy or that all of them are poor, and that somehow we are casting them off without any other resources. One of the fundamental premises behind what we are trying to do is that many of those people are not, in fact, needy. They have crept into the eligibility formula for the various categorical aid programs, and they do have resources of their own on which they could rely, and should . . . In most cases, [the truly needy] are people who, for one reason or another, be it their physical condition or their family circumstances or their inability to hold full-time or part-time employment, people who literally have no other resources on which to rely, other than assistance from their fellow man in the form of the Federal, state or local taxpayer.

Interview, Washington/The New York Times,
3-14:(4)2.

Franklin A. Thomas
President, Ford Foundation

5

It is not acceptable to me, as a social-development strategy, that the Federal government, which ought to be the means through which all of our collective interests are served and mediated, should withdraw from a concern for basic human welfare. The needs of housing, food, health care and education are national needs, because a nation doesn't survive as a healthy nation unless the great bulk of the people have the capacity to obtain these basic needs.

Interview/The New York Times Magazine, 10-10:83.

Lester C. Thurow
Professor of economics, Massachusetts
Institute of Technology

1

[The] Social Security [fund deficit] is a perfect example of a common problem. We have built an economy, both in the public economy and the private economy, that assumes economic growth. If you have a 3 or 4 per cent growth rate in the economy, Social Security doesn't have any financial problems until 2012. If you have a zero growth rate, it runs out of money next summer; and that leaves you with a dilemma as to what you do about it. I think what you have to do about it is recognize some fundamental facts in Social Security. The first is that life expectancy at age 65 is rising, and that means the retirement age is going to rise. The second is, I think the payroll tax has simply come to the end of the line as the vehicle for financing that system and unemployment insurance, and we're going to have to shift to something like a value-added tax. The third is that we're going to have to tie the system to something other than the Consumer Price Index. I think the right thing is the per capita GNP. If everybody is getting an increase in their income, then the elderly can have an increase. If everybody is getting a cut in their income, then the elderly are going to have to have a cut in their income. But the key problem in Social Security is not in Social Security; it's the economy.

Broadcast interview/
"Meet the Press," NBC-TV, 10-3.

Peter Townsend
Professor of social policy,
University of Bristol (England)

2

[Saying money is an inadequate measure of poverty] : . . . a measure of money does not tell you what people need. The argument about human needs has gone on for centuries. The Victorians, in looking at social welfare, looked very closely at people whose needs were food, shelter and clothing. And I think that both in the United States and in Britain the judgment as to how much money the poor need is very physically based. My whole point is to chal-

188

lenge this notion because, of course, we are first and foremost social rather than physical beings, and it is in our relations with our families, as neighbors, as workers and workmates, as citizens—that's how our needs are actually determined. And I believe quite passionately that this is a very important insight to which sociologists are contributing. We are dominated by monetized conceptions of the management of our society, and the realization that you've got to interrelate social and economic policy has not been very well developed . . . We cannot as governments take decisions about fair distribution of income or fair distribution of living standards only by looking at cash income. We've also got to take into account, well, free social services, which of course we've got in rather larger measure in this country than you [Americans] have in yours . . .

Interview/The New York Times, 4-11:(4)9.

Murray L. Weidenbaum
Former Chairman, Council of
Economic Advisers to the
President of the United
States (Ronald Reagan)

3

You don't start slashing Social Security because you have a deficit. Still, it is clear that facing up to the Social Security financing problem—and facing up to the defense question, for that matter—will simultaneously help reduce the deficit. Even if the budget were in surplus—a happy thought, but unrealistic—you still have to face up to the fact that the Social Security fund is not adequately financed, that Congress has voted more benefits than there are revenues coming in. That has to change, regardless.

Interview/U.S. News & World Report, 11-22:62.

Theodore H. White
Author, Historian

4

The Great Society is the best example of good-will being pushed too far. Each program and entitlement was good. But when you added them up, they didn't make common sense. These programs, plus OPEC's squeeze on oil, were the largest contributing factors to the

(THEODORE H. WHITE)

inflation, which is a terror. Inflation is the plague of planning and hope and the end result of going beyond our resources in the interests of good-will. I'm not willing to cut back on the good-will, but I would like to make it more manageable. Pierre Mendes-France, the former Prime Minister of France, once said, "To govern is to choose." We have to choose what we can do; we have to discipline our good-will.

Interview/U.S. News & World Report, 7-5:59.

Hosea M. Williams
Civil-rights leader

1

[To blacks who are hostile to the Reagan Administration]: Drop the welfare philosophy; stop begging. Social programs have outlived their usefulness. The war on poverty was lost because by the time it trickled down to the poor, all they received was advice.

The Christian Science Monitor, 2-8:15.

Coleman A. Young
Mayor of Detroit

2

Anyone who looks at our Constitution and our Bill of Rights knows that, among other things, American citizens are guaranteed life, liberty and the pursuit of happiness. Now, it is my contention that included in the pursuit of happiness is the right to a job; the right to eat; the right to human dignity. And that's a Federal responsibility and not to be shifted off to the states or to the cities—which is the attempt [of the Reagan Administration's "new Federalism" plan]. And it certainly can't be shifted off without any means with which to pay it. To the degree that our Federal government dodges its responsibility to all the people, it's exactly to that degree that we're in trouble. And we are in trouble.

Broadcast rebuttal to President's State of the Union address, Jan. 26/The New York Times, 1-27:10.

Transportation

Philip E. Benton, Jr.
Vice president, North American
sales division, Ford Motor Company
1

[On the possibility of more U.S. manufacturers making their cars in foreign countries]: In the final analysis, we have to make a profit. We'd have to cut the suit to fit the cloth. If the cloth gets too small, the question of foreign sourcing looms much larger. We sure don't plan to go out of business in the United States. If we have to make some cars somewhere else we're as the devil prepared to do it.
Interview/The Washington Post, 1-10:(G)3.

Edwin I. Colodny
Chairman and president, USAir
2

[On the new cut-rate airlines]: What is happening today in our industry is that the new entrants are giving it away. I have nothing against competition or new entrants. But I do have a bone to pick with those who want to give the new entrants credit for something they don't deserve. Any fool can cut the price of his product and give it away. It takes no genius, but these same folks, stimulated by deregulation, have won a lot of favor in some communities because they cut the price. What those communities don't realize is that when you give here, you've got to make it up there.
Interview/Nation's Business, December:62.

Peter F. Drucker
Professor of social science and
management, Claremont (Calif.)
College Graduate School
3

The automobile industry is in trouble everywhere. The only company that is not is Mercedes. Renault is in trouble. Peugeot is in trouble for the first time. The Japanese are essentially not making money, but they are not losing money. Is it permanent? Probably not. The industry is in transition. The auto industry in developed countries is on the replacement basis, which means that its rate of growth is tied to the number of young people who reach the age of their first driver's license. On that basis, what can you expect when there has been a drop in the birth rate?
Interview, Chicago, April/Chicago Tribune, 5-2:(5)3.

Richard J. Ferris
Chairman and president, UAL, Inc.
(United Airlines)
4

[On the continuing cutback in the air-traffic control system due to the firing of striking controllers last year]: The air-traffic control system is very definitely inhibiting the way we would like to do business. It does so in that we cannot fly our planes when we want, where we want and the time of day we want. That leads to inefficiencies in scheduling and utilization of our asset base. We are greatly desirous of the day that the government will be out of the business of controlling airlines. In essence they are still regulating in that they control the skies.
Interview/The New York Times, 11-23:30.

Douglas A. Fraser
President, United Automobile
Workers of America
5

If you look at the demographics of our nation and at the lack of a public transportation system, you cannot visualize the day when the American people will be without their automobiles. What is happening is that people hang on to their cars longer and no longer regard them so much as status symbols. The automobile is now what it should be—a means of transportation.
Interview/U.S. News & World Report, 5-3:78.

Robert D. Gallaway
President, Texas
International Airlines

1

[Airline] deregulation is a problem because a lot of airline executives were not raised in a deregulated environment. If you're not allowed to lower prices [under regulation], you don't know what happens if you do [under deregulation]. You don't know what the other airlines will do if you make a move, and you have to learn how not to do things where you know the competition will come back and hurt you.

The New York Times, 2-14:(3)6.

Michael Graves
Architect; Associate professor of
architecture and urban planning,
Princeton University

2

Why can't American car manufacturers learn from, say, BMW? That's my biggest cry. Why is Chrysler sitting there day after day taking pictures of [its chairman] Lee Iacocca when they can't design a good car? A car is a machine. It shouldn't look like a piece of architecture. Why do they put fake wood inside? Why do they have to make it look like a French whorehouse? I've never understood that. They say that's what the American public wants—and yet that's not what we're buying, is it?

Interview/TWA Ambassador, March:27.

John Heinz
United States Senator, R—Pennsylvania

3

[Saying he favors a 5-cent increase in the Federal gasoline tax]: We can't afford not to increase the gas tax. Our highways, bridges and mass-transit systems have badly deteriorated and are in disastrous shape. If we don't take care of the bridges, they will fall down. The interstate highways of the Federal highway system alone cost $800-billion to create, and they are a tremendous national asset. Were we to replace them, it would cost us $3-trillion. The 5-cent increase in the gas tax—1 cent of which would go for mass transit—would provide $5.5-billion annually for maintenance. That is a very modest increase when measured against

the potential loss of the entire Federal highway system.

Interview/U.S. News & World Report, 12-13:71.

J. Lynn Helms
Administrator, Federal
Aviation Administration

4

On a given day, about 100,000 airplanes are in the air, and we'll have the second 100,000 in the air in just nine more years. We absolutely must modernize our [air control and airport] equipment and install new automation techniques that will allow us to fly twice as many airplanes, yet reduce our [air-traffic] controller work force to 9,500. Our collective problem is not to restrain aviation, but to have to continue the outstanding safety record and its very strong leadership role for the national economy.

Interview/U.S. News & World Report, 8-9:51.

Alfred E. Kahn
Former Chairman, Civil Aeronautics
Board of the United States

5

[On the problems resulting from airline deregulation, which he favored]: I am, of course, not happy that the industry is losing so much money. But I warned the people in the industry that there was nothing that would insulate them from recessions in the economy, and I didn't foresee the doubling of fuel prices. When I look at the important economic effects, they have been essentially what we predicted—the entry of new, low-cost competitors, competition in fares and kinds of service, and pressures to become more efficient. There have been downward pressures on high wage costs and pressures on airlines to rationalize route structures, and that's healthy.

The New York Times, 2-14:(3)6.

Drew Lewis
Secretary of Transportation
of the United States

6

In urban areas, where over half of all highway travel occurs, congestion has become a constant, unwelcome and costly feature of peak-period travel, which affects nearly half of

(DREW LEWIS)

all urban Interstate [Highway] travel. Threatening to compound these congested highway conditions are growing deficiencies in public-transit performance. Transit facilities in older, larger cities, such as New York, Philadelphia, Boston and Chicago, have reached the stage of severe deterioration. Total repair needs now far exceed what can realistically be expected from the cities' own finances or currently planned Federal assistance.

Before panel of U.S. Conference of Mayors/
The New York Times, 2-14:(1)18.

1

I would support ending the 55-m.p.h. speed limit that the Federal government imposed, but there's no chance of that happening. For example, in my home state, Pennsylvania, 55 m.p.h. is fast enough because of the deteriorating road conditions. But it may not be right for every state. Senator John Tower has remarked that if you're going 55 in Texas, you'd better be driving on the shoulder.

Interview/U.S. News & World Report, 12-20:30.

2

[On his leaving office to enter private industry]: I leave here with two regrets. One is that we had to have the [1981 air-traffic] controllers' strike and it affected so many families. And the second is that I think it's very important that we rebuild the FAA so that some Secretary of Transportation in the future does not have the same problems that I had ...

We had very serious personnel problems and they're not resolved yet, and they won't be because you don't change what's existed for 25 years in six months or a year. I would say in the FAA we have a two- to three- to four-year rebuilding program in terms of personnel policies and management ... I regret I will not be here to see that happen, but even if I stayed four years it would not have happened.

News conference, Washington, Dec. 28/
The Washington Post, 12-29:(A)10.

John A. Volpe
Former Secretary of Transportation
of the United States

3

The drunk-driving toll is nearly 70 people a day. That is nearly as many people as were killed in the Air Florida crash in the Potomac River [earlier in the year]. And you repeat that 365 days a year. Now, if you went to the President and the Congress and you said that you were having one plane crash a day as bad as that one, they'd say, "How much do you want us to appropriate [to deal with the situation]? Do you want $3-billion? Or $6-billion?" And yet we do the same thing on the highways, in terms of death toll, day in and day out ... The difference is that, even though these [drunk-driving] accidents happen, only one, two or three people die at once. The only time it catches any real amount of media attention is when a van full of 10 youngsters crashes into a station-wagon ... The problem is that drinking and driving is just a way of life in our country.

Interview/Los Angeles Times, 12-14:(V)7.

Urban Affairs

Alan Beals
Executive director, National
League of Cities

1

The near-term outlook for cities is indeed bleak. It seems to be all over. Cities everywhere are suffering from extreme fiscal stress. With the recession likely to continue and the recovery expected to be weak and slow, local fiscal conditions—already strained—should worsen ... This is the first time since the 1940s that cities have been unable to act as a buffer by working to save some jobs, or at least maintain services. They are now adding to the recession by cutting out jobs and cutting out activities at a time when the economy is desperately in need of some stability—or better yet, some stimulus.

News conference, Washington, Dec. 28/
Los Angeles Times, 12-29:(I)13.

Carol Bellamy
President, New York City Council

2

We at the local level are doing much better than our colleagues at the national level at living within our means. Washington is only *talking* about fiscal austerity, but the cities are *living* it.

At National League of Cities
convention, Los Angeles, Nov. 28/
The Washington Post, 11-29:(A)3.

Wyeth Chandler
Mayor of Memphis

3

We [in the cities] deserve a lot more money [from the Federal government] than we've been getting, but we don't live for it and spend all our time lobbying for it. There's no question but that some of the most vehement critics of the President's [Reagan] urban policy have indeed become "wily stalkers of Federal

funds." I was semi-aghast at that language, but there's some truth to the allegation. Many cities have hired full-time lobbyists in Washington ... In the past, your Congressman did your lobbying ... I happen to be one of the few Mayors who believe that if the Federal government doesn't ... balance its budget, the impact on cities is going to be much worse than it is now with the budget cuts.

Interview/The Christian Science Monitor, 7-23:7.

Scott Fosler
Vice president, Committee
for Economic Development

4

[On cities' efforts to attract companies and industries]: For a long time there was smokestack chasing—any big new firms from outside were considered the plums. But now there's a growing realization that it's equally, if not more, important to pay more attention to existing businesses within the city and try to help them solve problems that might make them leave or keep them from growing.

The Christian Science Monitor, 2-3:6.

Richard G. Hatcher
Mayor of Gary, Ind.

5

When a black becomes Mayor, a new set of dynamics takes place. Whites begin the process of disinvestment—moving out as residents in rapid flight, and transplanting their businesses, often leaving downtown almost bare. And the public loses its interest in schools, public services and tax incentives.

The Christian Science Monitor, 8-23:6.

Edward I. Koch
Mayor of New York

6

[Saying it is becoming difficult to site social-service institutions in many neighbor-

(EDWARD I. KOCH)

hoods]: Communities raise their hands not to volunteer but to point somewhere else. Build it over there, not here ... Every community would like another police station, another school, another firehouse. The problem comes when it's time to build a waste-disposal facility or a prison or find a place to shelter the homeless ... How do we explain this outbreak of selfishness? I'm not sure. President Reagan has initiated a regressive philosophy of government in which the concept of Federal burden-sharing is being eliminated. And people are told to watch out for themselves.

Before City Club, New York, Dec. 17/
The New York Times, 12-18:10.

1

[On New York City's new budget]: Make no mistake about it, this is a tough program. It will not simply involve deferring planned improvements. It will reduce services. There will be fewer police than we had hoped to have. Potholes will be filled less often. Streets will be dirtier. Park maintenance will decline even further. Libraries will be open even fewer hours. The city's work force will shrink dramatically ... I am still convinced the present crisis is temporary—as long as concern for the future is not sacrificed to short-term solutions, as long as the state and Federal governments begin to recognize their responsibilities, as long as the spirit that brought us through the [fiscal] ordeal of 1975 remains alive. Today New York City is not alone. Today there is nowhere to run, nowhere to hide. Our problems are the problems of local governments everywhere.

News conference, New York, Dec. 18/
The New York Times, 12-19:(1)22.

Philip R. O'Connor
Illinois Director of Insurance

2

The insurance industry in the United States has total assets of about $600-billion. Roughly 10 per cent of that is invested in real estate. What we'd like to see is another billion dollars invested over the next five years and scattered throughout 100 cities to finance worthwhile

194

projects in neighborhoods which are hard-pressed for funds. That kind of investment could be the linchpin in turning around a declining neighborhood.

Chicago Tribune, 6-8:(1)7.

Ronald Reagan
President of the United States

3

... we are proposing legislation for an experimental effort to improve and develop our depressed urban areas in the 1980s and 1990s. This legislation will permit states and localities to apply to the Federal government for designation as urban enterprise zones. A broad range of special economic incentives in the zones will help attract new business, new jobs and new opportunity to America's inner cities and rural towns. Some will say our mission is to save free enterprise. I say we must free enterprise so that, together, we can save America.

State of the Union address, Washington,
Jan. 26/The New York Times, 1-27:8.

George Sternlieb
Director, Center for Urban Policy
Research, Rutgers University

4

The harsh reality is that cities don't face much in the way of a choice. There are no more fairy godmothers ... It's every city for itself. It can only look to its own pockets ... It's a real selling job that's needed. Politically it can be very tough, but the Mayor as merchant-in-chief has to get the message across that unless the city gets a new coat of paint [and attracts and holds businesses to it], "We're all going to rust."

The Christian Science Monitor, 2-3:6.

Coleman A. Young
Mayor of Detroit

5

[Criticizing the Reagan Administration's policy toward cities]: There is no other major country in the world today whose federal government refuses to help stabilize the economies of its large population centers. Nor is there another national government anywhere in the world which has washed its hands of its cities and its essential industries, and is standing

(COLEMAN A. YOUNG)

back on the sidelines like a disinterested party awaiting the outcome of an unimportant contest.

At his installation as president of U.S. Conference of Mayors, Minneapolis, June 23/ The New York Times, 6-24:16.

1

Unemployment is 20 per cent in Detroit. That means 40 per cent unemployment among blacks—and more than 50 per cent among teen-age blacks. But the city is still calm. There's no sign that, as some have predicted, we will have the racial explosion that we saw in the late 1960s. Instead, it's more like the Great Depression. Blacks see that everyone is out of work, the whites as well as themselves. So they accept their situation as a condition of life— that you complain about it like you would complain about the rain.

To reporters/The Christian Science Monitor, 7-16:4.

PART TWO

International Affairs

Africa

Mahmoud Abdel-Fattah
*Chief permanent representative
in Algiers of Polisario Front*

1

[On his organization's fighting Morocco over control of Western Sahara]: The prospects of a military confrontation and an internationalization of the Sahara conflict have grown. The American involvement with Morocco is prejudicial for the equilibrium of Africa. The [U.S.] Reagan Administration's military and economic assistance to Morocco is not only in support of King Hassan but directly against us. The United States, which calls itself the friend of Africa, appears to be implicated in an effort to destroy existing borders by helping Morocco swallow up the Sahara . . . If the Reagan Administration continues this kind of support to Morocco, our response will be to ask all those who can help us for more weapons—it's logical. The Soviet Union? My reply is, why not?

Interview, Algiers/The New York Times, 4-19:4.

Pieter W. Botha
Prime Minister of South Africa

2

We do not stand in the way of independence for [Namibia]. As a matter of fact, we are in a hurry because that territory has been a tremendous financial burden to us. The question is who is going to fill the vacuum when we leave. We are not going to allow Communist forces, at the point of a gun, to subject the people of Namibia. But we won't stand in the way of independence, and we hope that the Western countries will share with us the burden of developing it.

Interview/Time, 4-26:47.

Roelof F. Botha
Foreign Minister of South Africa

3

The South African government is absolutely committed to a peaceful solution in Namibia and is conscious of the benefits that would flow from an internationally acceptable solution. To achieve the latter and yet not to bring peace and stability would be a disaster . . . The Soviet Union is not interested in a peaceful solution. We are not prepared, for the rest of history, to be blamed for destroying a country. My government is not prepared to be a party to Soviet expansion in this area or anywhere else in the world and have a finger pointed at us by our own children. It is better to be destroyed in a different way than that. We cannot swallow that.

Interview, Cape Town/Time, 2-22:29.

George Bush
Vice President of the United States

4

The U.S. possesses neither troops nor proxies in [southern Africa]. We have no colonial interests, nor do we have military ambitions. On the contrary, the sole American interests in southern Africa are the interests of all men in all places—freedom and peace. The inescapable need for peaceful change is challenged by a climate of fear, distrust, foreign intervention and cross-border violence. The U.S. wants an end to South Africa's occupation of Namibia. At the same time, the U.S. wants an end to Angola's suffering and to the dangerous cycle of violence in the region. Our Number 1 strategic objective in Africa is to help establish a framework of restraint that discourages outside intervention in African conflicts,

WHAT THEY SAID IN 1982

(GEORGE BUSH)

while it encourages negotiated solutions and constructive change.

At banquet in honor of Zimbabwean Prime Minister Robert Mugabe, Harare, Zimbabwe, Nov. 16/Los Angeles Times, 11-17:(I)11.

1

The withdrawal of Cuban forces from Angola in a parallel framework with South Africa's departure from Namibia is the key to the settlement we all desire . . . My government is not ashamed to state the U.S. interest in seeing an end to the presence of Cuban forces in Angola. Their introduction seven years ago tore the fabric of reciprocal restraint between the U.S. and the Soviet Union in the developing world. Such restraint is vital if African regional security and the global balance are to be maintained.

At dinner, Nairobi, Kenya, Nov. 19/ The Washington Post, 11-20:(A)1.

Fidel Castro
President of Cuba

2

Our position, in common agreement with the Angolans, is that the purpose of the Cuban troops in Angola has to do only with the security of Angola and has nothing at all to do with the Namibian issue. We do not accept the linkage of the presence of Cuban troops to the Namibian issue. The Cuban and Angolan governments have made a joint statement. If the independence of Namibia is obtained and the South African troops withdraw to the south of Namibia and when no danger is posed to the security of Angola, then we will start again with the progressive withdrawal of our troops—for the third time. We are interested in solving these problems so that our troops can return home. Their presence in Angola implies sacrifices for our people. Many young people are there who have been absent from their homeland for a long time. We not only wish for a politically negotiated solution to take place in Central America, but we also wish for a politically negotiated solution in southern Africa.

Interview, Havana, March 26/ The Washington Post, 4-25:(C)3.

Peter Enahoro
Publisher, "Africa Today"

3

The African image of the West is that of "grabbers." Westerners do not realize that others see them as people ready to grab what they can and dump their inferior products on the Third World. By contrast, we get the feeling of dedication from the Eastern bloc, but that is deceptive. The West has the better system and we must imitate it. Because Americans are basically isolationist, we are even farther away in their minds than Eastern Europe. When I learned that Poland had been borrowing money from Western banks to the tune of $28-billion, I was shocked. The people—the Eastern bloc— who had been telling us that we should cut our coat to our size, that we should not borrow from Western capitalists, were borrowing quietly all along—and trying to prevent us from competing with them for the same funds.

Interview/World Press Review, August:25.

Alexander M. Haig, Jr.
Secretary of State of the United States

4

I've said that our objective is, after 6 years of Cuban occupation of Angola, to set in train a process which would lead to their withdrawal and to recognize that there's an empirical relationship between that withdrawal and the withdrawal of the South Africans from Namibia and the independence of Namibia. And that sounded like heresy 10 months ago, and it is now becoming rather broadly understood and accepted.

Interview, Washington, March 3/ Los Angeles Times, 3-4:(I)25.

Hassan II
King of Morocco

5

If tomorrow it became necessary to conclude a treaty with the United States to defend Morocco against hegemonism and against attacks against its sovereignty and territorial integrity, it's not just the King but all 20 million Moroccans who would be ready to sign with anyone they want . . . [But] if one day the United States asks for facilities for use in the Middle East against an Arab country, it's

(HASSAN II)

for certain that we would say no. We are committed to the democratic world and we will defend our freedoms at all cost. But we are and always will be non-aligned. There is no question that we are non-aligned. But non-alignment is not non-commitment. Morocco is an independent state, but if Morocco believes that its authenticity, its territorial integrity, its independence and its dignity are being endangered, then Morocco has the right, even the duty, to choose its friends. It is precisely its independence and its sovereignty that allow Morocco to choose its friends.

Interview, Fez, Morocco, May 14/
The New York Times, 5-17:3.

Slimane Hoffman
Chief of Foreign Policy
Commission, ruling National
Liberation Front of Algeria

1

We need more economic cooperation with the West and the United States; we are open to it. In America, however, they still put us in the Eastern bloc. Why? Aside from the weapons from the Eastern bloc, our commercial dealings are 85 per cent with the West, with only 5 per cent with the Eastern bloc, including the Soviet Union. But it seems that in the opinion of the [U.S.] Reagan Administration, the one who is not with them is against them.

Interview, Algiers, April/
The New York Times, 4-25:(1)8.

Paolo T. Jorge
Foreign Minister of Angola

2

One thing we don't understand is why the American Administration is so worried about the presence of Cuban forces in the People's Republic of Angola ... when the United States has a lot of military people in Cuban territory [at the Guantanamo naval base] ... When we see considerable evolution in the process of independence of Namibia, the withdrawal of South African forces [from Namibia] and the threat against the People's Republic of Angola considerably reduced—at [that] moment, the

Angolan and Cuban governments will set up a new program of gradual reduction of Cuban forces.

News conference, New York, Oct. 5/
Los Angeles Times, 10-6:(I)15.

Kenneth Kaunda
President of Zambia

3

I don't think we have a [historical] parallel to what is taking place in South Africa today ... We have heard of explosions or revolutions that are the result of "haves" and "have-nots" colliding ... but not where the haves and have-nots are drawn along color lines ... This one is building fast ... I can see it now—in a couple of years, three years, four years. I can see an explosion taking place in South Africa that will give no one an opportunity to quench the fire before it exhausts itself. I take no joy in saying this.

Interview, Lusaka/Newsweek, 11-15:74.

Bruno Kreisky
Chancellor of Austria

4

[On U.S. charges that Libyan leader Muammar Qaddafi promotes terrorism in the world]: There is no proof that Qaddafi pulls the strings of international terrorism. The people in Washington are talking themselves into a frenzy that is dangerous for all of us.

Interview/Newsweek, 3-22:44.

Robert S. McNamara
Former President, International Bank
for Reconstruction and Development
(World Bank); Former Secretary of
Defense of the United States

5

South Africa's racial policies warrant international concern, because I believe that unless they are fundamentally redesigned they will eventually lead to a catastrophic racial conflict that will have serious ramifications throughout the Western world. Because the South African government continues to refuse to make any fundamental change in its racial policies, a violent explosion appears inevitable.

Lecture, University of Witwatersrand, South Africa,
Oct. 21/Chicago Tribune, 10-23:(1)5.

Robert Mugabe
Prime Minister of Zimbabwe

1

Eventually we hope we can socialize the entire socioeconomic system. It will take some time to achieve [and] we will be quite judicious and cautious . . . Socialism means socialism. It doesn't mean at the final stage we are talking of capitalism. [In the end,] we must be able to say now we have achieved socialism.

News conference, Salisbury, April 17/
The Washington Post, 4-18:(A)18.

2

We strongly feel that the U.S., as a country which fought its own war of independence 200 years ago, should strongly support the principle of independence and side with Africa in the struggle to achieve independence for Namibia . . . To us there can be no conjunctive link with other issues such as the presence of Cuban troops in Angola, because the rights to independence and self-determination, being a basic and inalienable right, cannot be subjected to such an extraneous condition.

At banquet in his honor, Harare, Zimbabwe,
Nov. 16/Los Angeles Times, 11-17:(I)11.

Joshua Nkomo
Leader, Patriotic Front
Party of Zimbabwe

3

[On Prime Minister Robert Mugabe's crackdown on Nkomo's party]: This is the ZANU [Mugabe's party] way of doing things. They worked with us up to a point. Now they think they can dispense with us, just like that. It would be better to shake hands and go our separate ways. The slap [Mugabe] has given me in my face is very hard.

News conference, Salisbury, Feb. 16/
Los Angeles Times, 2-17:(I)17.

Harry F. Oppenheimer
Chairman, Anglo American
Corporation (South Africa)

4

I think there is a great resentment among the black people of South Africa against the way they're treated as inferiors. I think the resentment is translating itself more and more into a

202

positive hatred by black people for white people. I don't think it is possible, or practical, to live in a country where a majority of the people—even though still a powerless majority—feel the sense of grievance and even of hatred against the people governing the country. This is our real trouble and this is what we've got to put right . . . I believe there is time, but the thing is a great deal more urgent than it was even five years ago. I think that within another five years blacks must have a real share in political power.

Interview, Johannesburg/Los Angeles
Times, 4-26:(IV)1.

Muammar el-Qaddafi
Chief of State of Libya

5

[On U.S. President Reagan's announced ban on U.S. imports of Libyan oil]: President Reagan tries to terrorize other people. He started an economic war against Libya. Reagan is a terrorist and a destructive person . . . We are not terrorists. We love peace and work for peace . . . I think that resorting to arms is barbaric. [The U.S.] is risking a third world war by interfering in our internal affairs. Such a war would endanger the whole world, but especially Europe. A nuclear war would destroy Europe.

News conference, Vienna, March 11/
Los Angeles Times, 3-12:(II)12.

Ronald Reagan
President of the United States

6

[Announcing a cut-off of Libyan oil imports to the U.S. as well as other economic sanctions]: We are taking these measures in response to a continuing pattern of Libyan activity which violates accepted international norms of behavior. We believe that these measures will focus attention on the fact that Libya is able to threaten its neighbors and international order because of the revenues it derives from its oil trade. We will no longer be providing the dollars or technology to Libya which can be used for activities that threaten international stability.

March 10/Los Angeles Times, 3-11:(I)9.*

David Rockefeller
*Head of international advisory
committee, and former chairman,
Chase Manhattan Bank*

1

[On his just-completed trip to 10 African
nations]: My feeling is that all of the [left-
wing] ones I visited would like to see a move
away from the Soviets and toward the United
States. They feel they have much greater
opportunities in working with us than with the
Soviets. Most of them have been disillusioned
by the lack of support from the Soviet Union
and the strings attached to any kind of Soviet
aid. And therefore their wish is for more
understanding and support from the United
States . . . African socialism is no threat. I really
am convinced that socialism for most of the
African leaders I talked with meant a very
specialized thing and has little to do with
Marxism. One comes to the assessment whether
their ideology is that deep, and my impression
is that it is the other way around. I think
corruption may be more serious than ideology.

Interview, Marrakesh, Morocco/
The New York Times, 3-10:4.

Oliver Tambo
President, African National Congress

2

The most peculiar thing about South Africa
is that you have 28 or 29 million people living
in the same country—and 24 or 25 million [the
blacks] don't exist! They're virtually foreigners
in South Africa, without any rights. Immigrants
can come from Europe or Latin America and in
two years become citizens, participating in rule
over people who have been there for generations. That must end. The 25 million [blacks]
must come alive and become part of the
country, not part of the animal population—
and together with the other, take part in
running the country without racism. There
must be no discrimination. We have been the
victims of racism. We would not want anybody
else to be such a victim. Our white compatriots
have of course missed the experience of being
objects of discrimination. They might complain
they might want to know what it feels like, but
we would deny them that experience.

Interview, New York, January/
The New York Times, 2-7:(4)3.

Desmond M. Tutu
*General secretary, South African
Council of Churches*

3

. . . apartheid, a system as vicious as Nazism
and Communism, must one day bite the dust,
for as academics we are all agreed that a lie
cannot prevail forever against the truth. So
apartheid and injustice and oppression must
end and justice and goodness and love and
compassion prevail.

At University of Witwatersrand, South Africa,
Aug. 3/The New York Times, 8-4:2.

The Americas

Elliott Abrams
*Assistant Secretary for Human Rights
and Humanitarian Affairs, Department
of State of the United States*   *1*

[On the human-rights situation in El Salvador]: There is a beginning in the last six months of punishment of military officers and enlisted men who commit human-rights offenses—and policemen. That's a very important sign that you can't do this stuff any more. Progress has been slower than we would like and the human-rights situation continues to be bad. But [the U.S.] Congress wisely asked, "Is it moving in the right direction?" The answer is yes ... I said to the head of the National Police—let's talk about human-rights violations. The first thing he did was pull down a looseleaf book filled with the pictures and biographies of young National Police officers who were killed by guerrillas. He said, "Aren't those human-rights violations?" When guerrilla activity goes up, government military activity goes up. Inasmuch as the guerrillas frequently hide behind civilians and travel with civilians, civilian casualties go up, too.
Interview, July/The New York Times, 7-25:(4)2.

Gustavo Alvarez Martinez
Chief of Staff, Honduran armed forces   *2*

Our country is small and weak. Honduras now is confronting an armed aggression from the Soviet Union by way of Cuba. Because of that, if no other possibility exists to preserve peace, Honduras is in agreement that the United States, as a friendly country, intervene militarily in Central America.
*Broadcast interview, April 1/
The Washington Post, 4-2:(A)18.*

Javier Arias Stella
Foreign Minister of Peru   *3*

[Criticizing the U.S. for supporting Britain in its dispute with Argentina over the Falkland

Islands]: A country like the United States, which has been propounding the thesis of the Americas for the Americans, now appears to be propounding the thesis of the Americas for Great Britain.
Lima, April 30/The New York Times, 5-1:7.

Tony Benn
Member of British Parliament   *4*

[On what the U.S. position will be in the British conflict with Argentina over the Falkland Islands]: [U.S.] President Reagan is not only going to be neutral but bitterly hostile to any act of war against Argentina, because American power rests on the rotten military dictatorships of Latin America.
Time, 4-19:31.

James L. Buckley
*Under Secretary for Security
Assistance, Science and Technology,
Department of State of the United States*   *5*

[On the guerrilla war in El Salvador]: We are not looking at a localized conflict in El Salvador, but [at] what we can expect in Guatemala, Honduras and Costa Rica unless we give aid there. We may be finding ourselves facing a real crisis in the Caribbean that will test the will of the [U.S. Reagan] Administration and of Congress.
*Before Institute for Contemporary Studies,
Pebble Beach, Calif./Los Angeles Times, 2-15:(I)5.*

George Bush
Vice President of the United States   *6*

When we look at Cuba and what is happening in Nicaragua and Grenada, what do we see? We see economically weak, militarized, repressive countries, dependencies tied on a very

(GEORGE BUSH)

short leash to their Soviet sponsor and useful principally for creating mischief among their neighbors.

At Conference on the Caribbean, Miami,
Dec. 5/The New York Times, 12-6:6.

Leopoldo Calvo Sotelo
Prime Minister of Spain

1

[On his country's support for Argentina in its war against Britain over the Falkland Islands]: There is no contradiction between our European and Latin American calling; and I say this with deep conviction, precisely now, when a military conflict is tearing the Western World apart and threatening to open up a profound rift of extremely serious political and historic consequences. Our voice in this assembly, without prejudice to our loyalty to the [NATO] alliance, is and shall always be at the service of a formula which reduces, so far as possible, the inevitable scars already inflicted by military actions. The use of force is not a way for settling differences between nations, but some problems which most acutely offend sensibilities of peoples need careful and generous solutions in order not to become sources of international tension.

At NATO conference, Bonn, West Germany,
June 10/Los Angeles Times, 6-11:(I)20.

Rodrigo Carazo Odio
President of Costa Rica

2

Ninety per cent of Central America's problems are economic. What better candidate is there to become a guerrilla than someone who is unemployed?

Newsweek, 3-1:22.

3

One of the basic and most regrettable facts of life in Central America is that in too many countries the status quo has been maintained by military force. People who have wealth have established a relationship with the armed forces. As a result of this connection, there has been an incredible increase in the misery of the population at large.

Time, 3-22:27.

Hugo Carrillo
Chairman, Foreign Relations Committee,
Constituent Assembly of El Salvador

4

[Criticizing the U.S. Congress for proposals to cut American military aid to his country because of the policies of the newly elected government]: The United States is treating El Salvador like its own hacienda. The United States wants to manage this government the same way it has managed the [previous Christian Democrat-military] government for the last two years. Well, the United States does not yet understand us. We are not all rightists. Many of us are committed to reforms. But we are nationalists.

Interview, San Salvador, May 27/
Los Angeles Times, 5-28:(I)11.

William J. Casey
Director of Central Intelligence
of the United States

5

Nicaragua, a country of 2½ million people, has an army twice the size of El Salvador's, which has twice the population and is fighting for its life. Nicaragua is sitting there with a big army that's getting bigger, with Soviet tanks and airfields being extended and pilots being prepared for Soviet supersonic planes. When and if that happens—I think it will happen in six months—Nicaragua will have military dominance over the rest of Central America, with a population seven times theirs. If Cuba, with 10 million people, and Nicaragua, with 2½ million people, take over the rest of Central America and build up the armies on the scale of their own, you would have a very large army down there on our doorstep. Mexico is sitting there with a military force of about 150,000 today and never thought of having anything more.

Interview/U.S. News & World Report, 3-8:24.

Fidel Castro
President of Cuba

6

Cuba, without any [U.S.] Alliance for Progress, without any [U.S.] Caribbean Basin initiative, has a better social situation than any other country in Latin America. We have no drugs,

(FIDEL CASTRO)

we have no gambling, we have no prostitution, we have no beggars, we have no unemployment.

Interview, Havana, March 26/
The Washington Post, 4-25:(A)33.

1

We [Cubans] must not fool ourselves. We have [economic] difficulties and we are going to have difficulties in the coming years, and these difficulties could even be greater ... The capitalist world is going through a profound economic crisis, maybe one of the greatest in its history. This crisis affects especially the under-developed world, but it also influences the socialist countries.

At celebration of 29th anniversary of his
revolutionary career, Bayomo, Cuba, July 26/
Chicago Tribune, 7-28:(1)5.

Alfredo Cesar
President, Central Bank of Nicaragua

2

[On the Marxist government's attempt at a reconciliation with Nicaragua's business community]: If this works, then the mixed economy is a reality here, which is what we want. I don't have anything more up my sleeve to give to the private sector. I've given them credit, foreign exchange, restructured their debt on really good terms and now I'm giving them more cordobas to the dollar. I expect this year that one of two things is going to happen. Either we get an upturn—or we don't get it because of "extra-economic" measures. If that happens, I don't think there's anything more I can do. Then you've got real problems. If you've got two-thirds of the production in private hands, what do you do? Using the productive sector of the economy to press for political things is something the government simply cannot let them do.

The Washington Post, 3-12:(A)21.

Nicanor Costa Mendez
Foreign Minister of Argentina

3

[Defending his country's military takeover of the British Falkland Islands]: Argentina has borne with the situation of continued usurpa-

tion of its territory by a colonial power [Britain] for 150 years ... The events of 1833 [the seizure by Britain of the islands] were one more reflection of the imperialist policy that the European countries carried out in the 19th century at the expense of America, Africa and Asia. [The Falkland affair] is a colonial issue in the most classic meaning.

At United Nations, New York, April 3/
The New York Times, 4-4:(1)8.

4

[On his country's conflict with Britain over the Falkland Islands, which Argentina recently took over by military force]: The invader [Britain] shall learn that the Americas are not the land of vassals. The Argentine flag, which is the flag of the Americas, shall not be taken down while a drop of blood remains in the veins of the last Argentine soldier who defends the Malvinas [Falkland] Islands. To this I commit the honor of my country.

Before Organization of American States, Washington,
April 26/The Washington Post, 4-27:(A)14.

5

[Criticizing U.S. support for Britain in the current Argentine-British war over the Falkland Islands]: [U.S. support of the British is] an act of the utmost gravity, unprecedented in the history of our inter-American system. There will be many Argentine lives, American in the end, which that ominous aid will help to sacrifice.

At meeting of foreign ministers of
Organization of American States, Washington,
May 27/Los Angeles Times, 5-28:(I)2.

6

[On the British victory over Argentina in the war for the Falkland Islands]: What has occurred in no way alters Argentine sovereignty over the Malvinas [the Falklands] and does not affect the decision to continue our struggle on all fronts, opportunities and forms to gain full recognition of Argentine sovereignty over these islands.

To reporters, Buenos Aires, June 15/
Los Angeles Times, 6-16:(I)10.

Alan Cranston
United States Senator, D–California

1

[On the possibility of Argentina developing nuclear weapons] : Given the Argentine junta's contempt for international law–as evidenced by their occupation of the [British] Falklands and the massacre over the past six years by government security forces of thousands of their own citizens–there is reason to fear that the Argentines may simply breach [nuclear] safeguards agreements when they deem it desirable . . . My information is that Argentina is now pressing toward completion of the missing links in this chain. They are building a pilot heavy-water plant to complete a key facility, an unsafeguarded reprocessing plant at Ezeiza, on the outskirts of Buenos Aires. This clandestine reprocessing plant will be completed some time in the latter half of 1982, giving Argentina the potential to produce enough pure, weapons-grade plutonium for at least one atomic bomb less than six months after this plant begins operations.

Before the Senate, Washington, April 21/
Los Angeles Times, 4-22:(I)6.

Roberto d'Aubuisson
ARENA Party candidate for President
of the Constituent Assembly of
El Salvador

2

The people of El Salvador do not want the old schemes, much less the scheme of "communitarianism" [óf current Salvadoran President Jose Napoleon Duarte]. We offer a very simple human thing: peace and work. We seek a representative democracy, where the power comes from the people, and a free-market society. We believe in and respect human rights. We are totally opposed to [Cuban-style] Castro terrorism.

Interview, San Salvador/Time, 3-29:34.

Roberto d'Aubuisson
President, Constituent
Assembly of El Salvador

3

Now that we are starting on the road toward representative democracy, we will leave in the past all desires for revenge. We will use all our strength to guarantee human rights, and we will gain, step by step, that precious tranquility that we have lost.

Upon assuming his position as President of the
Assembly, San Salvador, April/Time, 5-3:36.

Miguel de la Madrid
President-elect of Mexico

4

In the case of Mexico, one should bear in mind that we have a majority political party which holds a majority, and consequently we hold a majority in the Chamber of Deputies and in the Senate. What usually occurs is that the legislative power must support the President of the republic. But that does not mean the President of the Republic may do whatever he pleases. We have a system of balance of power, we have very active public opinion, we have pressure groups, and the President has a certain leeway within that context.

Interview/Chicago Tribune, 7-10:(1)11.

5

[On Mexican-U.S. relations] : I think we know how to handle ourselves with dignity and respect even if we are not in agreement about everything. I have the feeling that the fundamental interest of the United States is to have a neighbor without problems and, if possible, prosperous. We will always live next to each other. We cannot move.

Interview, Mexico City/
U.S. News & World Report, 7-19:49.

6

[On his country's economic problems] : It is not the first time that the government finds itself with problems of this nature. Of course, now they are of a larger magnitude. The country is also larger. But Mexico is now in a superior economic position because of its oil reserves, natural resources and skilled people. In other countries under such circumstances of economic difficulty, there are changes of government and *coups d'etat*. Mexico is proving the solidness of its political system. This is a very important asset–more important than oil for solving the crisis.

Interview, Mexico City/
U.S. News & World Report, 7-19:49.

WHAT THEY SAID IN 1982

(MIGUEL DE LA MADRID)   1

The question of Cuba has been an issue on which the United States and Mexico traditionally do not agree. Mexico has maintained relations from the start with revolutionary Cuba, and my country, and I, believe that this policy is consistent with our support for the doctrine of self-determination. Mexico believes it inadvisable to isolate any American nations because of differences of ideology or political, economic or social systems ... I am a firm believer in political and economic pluralism. Peace and tolerance stem from respect for differences. And I also believe that relations between the United States and Mexico have reached a level of maturity that enables us to remain friends and continue cordial ties even though we are not in total agreement on all issues in international affairs.

*Interview, Mexico City/
U.S. News & World Report, 8-16:47.*

Miguel de la Madrid
President of Mexico
2

I cannot offer, in the immediate future, any substantial or rapid improvement in [Mexico's economic] situation ... I am aware that I assume office in difficult hours. Recovery will take time—at least two years. The first months of the government will be arduous and difficult. The situation demands it. Austerity is mandatory ... Social equality is the original demand of the Mexican Revolution. Social inequality continues to be one of our most serious problems.

*Inaugural address, Mexico City, Dec. 1/
Los Angeles Times, 12-2:(I)1,13.*

Christopher J. Dodd
*United States Senator,
D–Connecticut*
3

[On U.S. backing of the government of El Salvador in the guerrilla war in that country]: We are engaged in the biggest diplomatic crapshoot in a long, long time. We have allowed ourselves to become everybody's bad guy. The right in El Salvador thinks we are a bunch of Communists, and the left thinks we are a bunch of right-wingers.

Interview/Los Angeles Times, 3-19:(I)1.

Jose Napoleon Duarte
President of El Salvador
4

[Criticizing U.S. news coverage of the guerrilla war in his country]: The news from El Salvador is more and more *amarillismo*—yellow journalism. Why is a guerrilla always more sympathetic than a [government] soldier? Why are all your stories the same—with the same pictures of bodies and blood all over and big headlines that say "El Salvador! Murder! Death!"? That is not a lie, but also not the whole truth. Why does only a part of the truth get told and retold? We are losing the fight with the guerrillas not only in the countryside, but in the pages of *The New York Times* and *The Washington Post.*

Interview, San Salvador, February/Newsweek, 2-15:34.

Jose Rafael Echeverria
*Costa Rican Ambassador to the United
States and chief delegate to the
Organization of American States*
5

[On the OAS' putting off action on the Falkland Islands crisis between Argentina and Britain]: It seems incredible, but it is true, that an armed [British] fleet is coming at maximum speed from Europe to the southern part of our continent in the spirit of war. To sit here with arms folded, like spectators in a bullring, will someday haunt us.

*At meeting of Organization of
American States, Washington, April 8/
The New York Times, 4-9:8.*

Elizabeth II
Queen of England
6

[Proclaiming Canada's new Constitution]: It is one of the quirks of history that over a century should have passed before Canada obtained her own Constitution, formulated by Canadians and approved by her own Parliament. But the years have not been wasted, and a great nation has grown up in this magnificent land.

*Ottawa, April 17/San Francisco Examiner
& Chronicle, 4-18:(A)24.*

Thomas O. Enders
*Assistant Secretary for Inter-
American Affairs, Department
of State of the United States*

1

[Supporting the Reagan Administration's plans to continue and increase U.S. military and economic aid to El Salvador in that government's fight against guerrilla forces]: The decisive battle for Central America is under way in El Salvador ... Americans will not permit Central America's future to be decided in Moscow or Havana. If, after Nicaragua, El Salvador is captured by a violent minority, who in Central America would not live in fear? How long would it be before major strategic interests—the [Panama] Canal, sea lanes, oil supplies—were at risk? [Cuba] is systematically expanding its capacity to project military power beyond its own shores.

*Before Senate Foreign Relations Subcommittee
on Western Hemisphere Affairs, Washington,
Feb. 1/Los Angeles Times, 2-2:(I)1.*

2

We have tried to talk with Cuba in the past and it would be wrong to rule out trying to again. But the record is daunting. In 1977 we started talking seriously to the Cubans, saying we wanted to create conditions in which the legacy of the past—the embargo and the political tension—could be overcome. We suggested a gradual withdrawal of the more than 20,000 Cuban troops from Angola; after all, the civil war [in Angola] was over. While we talked, Cuba went into Ethiopia. Conversations continued. In mid-1978, Cuba launched upon a new aggressive strategy in Central America, uniting the left parties of, first, Nicaragua, then El Salvador, then Guatemala, committing them to the destruction of their established governments. Talks went on. In 1980, [Cuban President Fidel] Castro turned the desire of many of his countrymen to flee Cuba into a hostile act against the U.S.—the Mariel boatlift.

*Before Senate Foreign Relations
Committee, Washington, March 25/
The New York Times, 3-26:7.*

3

[Criticizing the view that only negotiations with guerrilla forces in Central America could stem total left-wing victories in the area]: The argument has been, co-opt the left before it's too late. That analysis has been proven incorrect, but another has been proven right—that is, that if only given the opportunity to choose, Central Americans will choose democracy over authoritarianism, and reform over revolution.

*Before House Inter-American Affairs
Subcommittee, Washington, April 21/
The New York Times, 4-22:10.*

Francisco Fiallos Navarro
*Nicaraguan Ambassador
to the United States*

4

We [the Sandanist government of Nicaragua] are ready to talk [with the U.S.] and they don't want to talk. They say we're aiding the rebels in El Salvador. Well, let's talk about it. Let's see proof ... We're ready to talk about disarmament, to sign a non-aggression pact with our neighbors ... I don't understand why it's so difficult for the U.S. Administration to believe arms are being sent to El Salvador without Nicaragua knowing.

Interview/Los Angeles Times, 9-17:(I-A)5.

5

[On his being removed as Ambassador because of his criticism of Nicaragua's Sandinista government]: The love for my people, the reverence for my country and the most elemental sentiment of personal dignity could not allow me to go on representing a government that has forbidden me to express my ideas and my feelings to the Nicaraguan people ... We have to avoid going from a rightist dictatorship to a leftist dictatorship. To overthrow a rightist dictatorship does not give us the right to repress our people, to forbid the press to publish anything they want. We must preserve the liberties, the freedoms of the people ... [However], I think the policy of the [U.S.] Reagan Administration toward Nicaragua is wrong. The worst thing they can do is help the Somozistas [who were overthrown by the present Sandinista government]. The Nicaraguan problem should be solved between Nicaraguans and between Sandinistas. It has to be democratic. It

(FRANCISCO FIALLOS NAVARRO)

has to be pluralistic. The problem of Nicaragua should be solved by Nicaraguans.

News conference, Washington, Dec. 20/
The New York Times, 12-21:1,4.

Amadeo Frugoli
Minister of Defense of Argentina

1

[Acknowledging Britain's military advantage in the current British-Argentine war over the Falkland Islands]: I would say that [Argentina] has achieved victory by demonstrating that a country that exercises its right of sovereignty can count on the support of an entire continent [South America] and many other countries. And by having changed the situation of colonialism and injustice, Argentina has already won political objectives that make it victorious.

Radio broadcast, May 31/
The Washington Post, 6-1:(A)12.

Carlos Fuentes
Mexican author

2

Nationalism represents a profound value for Latin Americans simply because of the fact that our nationhood is still in question. In New York, Paris or London, no one loses sleep asking themselves whether the nation exists. In Latin America you can wake up and find that the nation is no longer there, usurped by a military junta, a multinational corporation or an American ambassador surrounded by a bevy of technical advisers.

At Wesleyan University commencement/Time, 6-21:83.

Leopoldo F. Galtieri
President of Argentina

3

[On his country's recent military take-over of the British Falkland Islands]: With all due respect to the English people and Britain, they have to understand that history has progressed, that centuries have passed, that the world has evolved and certain things cannot return.

Falkland Islands, April 22/
Los Angeles Times, 4-23:(I)1.

4

[On his country's military take-over of the British Falkland Islands]: Sovereignty [over the Falklands] is our objective. We are not going to renounce this objective, but we can talk to achieve it. We can talk for a reasonable period of time—as long as it is not another 149 years—to achieve this sovereignty.

To British newsmen, Buenos Aires,
May 13/Los Angeles Times, 5-14:(I)8.

5

[On his country's war with Britain over the Falkland Islands]: As I now have the blood of more than 400 Argentines on my shoulders, the Argentine people, I am sure, are willing to accept not only 400 deaths but 4,000 or 40,000 more.

Newsweek, 5-24:34.

6

[On his country's war with Britain over the Falkland Islands]: Nobody, and even less so the enemy, can doubt the outstanding efforts made by our country to prevent this war . . . during 149 years [of British rule of the islands] . . . [Argentina's] arms will continue fighting against the enemy for every Argentine portion of land, sea and sky, with growing courage and efficiency, because the soldiers' bravery is nourished by the blood of his fallen brothers and by the conscious patriotic fervor of a nation united as never before in its history, determinedly leading him to fight . . . Argentina does not need mercenaries because the world's weaponry would not be sufficient for all volunteers, both men and women, who are requesting to take part in this fight. I have no more weapons, nor cannons, nor tanks for them. We have no more ships nor planes to be manned. If we had them, we would be an armed force made up of millions ready to fight for this legitimate right to defend what is ours.

Buenos Aires, May 29/
The Washington Post, 5-30:(A)21.

7

[On his leaving office after Argentina's loss of the war with Britain over the Falkland Islands]: I am leaving because the Army did not give me the political support to continue as

(LEOPOLDO F. GALTIERI)

commander and President of the nation. I am not one of those who abandon ship in the middle of the storms, with the difficult hours such as those that the nation is living through.

Buenos Aires, June 17/
The Washington Post, 6-18:(A)1.

Jose Guillermo Garcia
Minister of Defense of El Salvador

1

[On U.S. military aid to the government of El Salvador during the current guerrilla war in that country]: This is very important for the United States because, like it or not, the battle in El Salvador will have military repercussions outside the country. It is better to give us aid now than later. Now is the moment. We warned the North Americans months ago about Nicaragua, and they paid no attention. Now we have the problem of Nicaragua.

Interview, San Salvador, Feb. 17/
Los Angeles Times, 2-18:(I)1,10.

Allan E. Gottlieb
Canadian Ambassador
to the United States

2

[Some in the U.S. business community and some members of the U.S. Reagan Administration have] a very odd misunderstanding about the nature and character of Canada—one of the greatest democratic societies of the world. They thought that we were gaga with interventionism [in Canadian business], that we are socialist, that Canada is falling apart.

To reporters/Los Angeles Times, 10-26:(I)7.

Andrei A. Gromyko
Foreign Minister of the Soviet Union

3

[There] is the region of Central America and the Caribbean, where a campaign of pressure and threats is going on unabated against Cuba and Nicaragua, whose only fault is that they want to live according to their own standards. Attempts are being made to portray them as the trouble-makers in that region. Those are

attempts in bad faith. Together with other peoples and states in the Caribbean, Cuba and Nicaragua come out for turning it into a zone of peace, independence and development; and the Soviet Union is sympathetic to this goal.

At United Nations, New York, Oct. 1/
The New York Times, 10-2:6.

Alexander M. Haig, Jr.
Secretary of State of the United States

4

Strategically, Central America is an injured area which is absolutely vital to United States' strategic interests in trade, energy sources—less so, but an important market as well. It is the source of, and could be in the period ahead a dramatic source of, a step-up of undocumented immigrants—at 1.5 million in 1989 alone, with Mexico being the main source. But just conceive of what will happen if totalitarianism swept that region and if it ever got into Mexico . . . because the great flow of refugees globally over the last 10 years has been from the excesses of the totalitarian left . . . . it's not necessarily domino. It's not a question of one black chip knocking over another. But it is a clear, self-influencing sequence of events which could sweep all of Central America into a Cuba-dominated region and put a very fundamental threat on Mexico in the very predictable future . . . . the avoidance of Big Brotherism or the Goliath of the North has got to be the style we pursue. The basic thrust of what we are trying to do is to deal with the longer-term, more difficult socio-economic crisis in the region . . . It becomes increasingly important in the light of the willingness of the Soviet Union and the Cubans to once again engage in increased interventionist activity—not only world-wide, but in this hemisphere. So the problem now is to deal with the socio-economic, recognizing that time may not be available to solve that. And it means, therefore, that we've got to deal with the security side of it, to help to the degree we can those nations that are moving in a proper direction in terms of modernization and pluralization and democratic principle.

Interview, Washington, March 3/
Los Angeles Times, 3-4:(I)25.

WHAT THEY SAID IN 1982

(ALEXANDER M. HAIG, JR.)

1

The situation [in the guerrilla war in El Salvador] is global in character. The problem is world-wide Soviet interventionism that poses an unprecedented challenge to the free world. Anyone attempting to debate the prospects for a successful outcome in El Salvador who fails to consider the Soviet menace is dealing with only the leg or the trunk of the elephant.

Before Senate Appropriations Subcommittee,
Washington, March 10/Time, 3-22:18.

2

[The guerrilla war in El Salvador] has a major global and regional as well as a local aspect. That is a fact, of theological and practical reality. Certainly the conflict has to be dealt with on the ground politically and militarily in El Salvador itself. There has never been a question of that. But the neighboring state, Nicaragua, is also deeply involved. And part of the solution, therefore, lies in Nicaragua. And the regional powers, Venezuela, Mexico, can also help in this regard. Beyond that, Cuba is a big part of the problem, because it was Cuba that unified the left-wing parties in El Salvador and did so in Havana with [Cuban President Fidel] Castro's personal involvement, trained their men, provided initial armament, arranged for other arms supply and is now involved in command and control ... And the Soviet Union is also involved, and deeply so, because that's where the resources and the arms come from for Cuba and other recipient guerrilla movements. That's where the Communist radical net is run from, without which the insurgents themselves could not exist.

News conference, New York, March 15/
The New York Times, 3-16:6.

3

[On the forthcoming elections in El Salvador and the possibility that extreme rightists might be elected, rather than the moderates the U.S. has been supporting]: If we espouse a democratic process and the people of El Salvador, in critical, credible elections, select a candidate, I think that's their business. Now, as far as the United States is concerned, we have supported

212

the current regime based on the reforms that that regime has instituted—land reform, improved pluralization, democratic reform, efforts to improve the human-rights situation, economic reform. It will be adherence to those principles that will determine the level of American support [of a newly elected Salvadoran government].

Broadcast interview/
"Meet the Press," NBC-TV, 3-28.

4

[On the just-held national elections in war-torn El Salvador]: The Salvadoran people's stunning personal commitment to the power of the democratic vision is an unanswerable repudiation of the advocates of force and violence. I would like to note that yesterday's results are a military defeat for the guerrillas quite as much as a political repudiation. Despite their undeniable repudiation by the people of El Salvador, the guerrillas still have the external support to continue their campaign of terror at levels that would be impossible if they depended on their own people ... We are confident that the constituent assembly, given the extraordinary mandate it has received from the Salvadoran people, will find ways to hold out a hand of reconciliation to those adversaries who are prepared to take part peacefully in the democratic process now so encouragingly under way in El Salvador.

At State Department briefing, Washington,
March 29/Los Angeles Times, 3-30:(I)8.

5

[On what is at stake for the U.S. in the Argentine-British war over the Falkland Islands]: There are basic issues of international law and their relationship with the fundamental objective of this [Reagan] Administration's foreign policy, and that is to insist that historic change occur through the accepted rules of law. So that's a stake of principle. Secondly, there are hemispheric interests. We have been working to enhance our relationship with the Organization of American States and its member states, and have had considerable success in getting their support for the policies that we have been pursuing in El Salvador and Nicaragua. That is also at stake. Then there are the

(ALEXANDER M. HAIG, JR.)

Atlantic-community interests. An American misstep could have lasting consequences. There are also North-South overtones of colonialism and anti-colonialism. It would be a tragic outcome if this issue were to deteriorate into that highly charged context. Finally, of course, there are East-West overtones. It is the proclivity of the Soviet Union to fish in troubled waters, and there is no reason to anticipate it could be any different in this situation.

Interview, April/Time, 5-3:13.

1

[On the current Argentine-British dispute over the British Falkland Islands which Argentina recently invaded]: Argentina's position remains that it must receive an assurance now of eventual sovereignty or an immediate *de facto* role in governing the islands which would lead to sovereignty. For its part, the British government has continued to affirm the need to respect the views of the inhabitants [of the islands] in any settlement ... A strictly military outcome cannot endure over time. In the end, there will have to be a negotiated outcome acceptable to the interested parties—otherwise, we will all face unending hostility and insecurity in the South Atlantic.

Washington, April 30/The New York Times, 5-1:8.

2

[On the Argentine-British war over the Falkland Islands and those who say British control of the islands amounts to colonialism]: It is impossible to speak of colonialism when a people [the Falklanders] is not subjugated to another and, as we all know, there was no such subjugation on the island ... There is no way in which the inter-American system ... can be interpreted as sanctioning the first use of armed force [such as Argentina's invasion of the Falklands] to settle a dispute. With full respect for the views of others, the United States' position is clear: Since the first use of force did not come from outside the hemisphere, this is not a case of extra-continental aggression against which we are all committed to rally.

At meeting of foreign ministers of Organization of American States, Washington, May 27/Los Angeles Times, 5-28:(I)2.

Morton Halperin
Director, Center for National Security Studies, American Civil Liberties Union

3

[Saying President Reagan's certification, in January of this year, that El Salvador's progress on human rights entitled it to continued U.S. aid, was unsupported by any valid research]: The Administration has not taken the process of certification seriously ... If the intelligence community was asked to do a study, it would do an honest, straightforward study, and I think that's the reason they have been asked not to do a study. It knows what everybody knows; namely, that these conditions have not been met, were not met six months ago, and will not be met now ... In order not to tell us what's going on, [the Administration is] not going to find out what's going on, and didn't find out the last time, because they didn't want to know.

Washington, July 8/The Washington Post, 7-9:(A)4.

Dietrich Hammer
European Economic Community Ambassador to Canada

4

This country [Canada] presents a schizophrenic image to the world in its attitude toward foreign investment. In the same body, it manages to combine the features of come-hither eyes and the cold shoulder.

U.S. News & World Report, 8-16:44.

Charles Hernu
Minister of Defense of France

5

[On U.S. criticism of his country's decision to sell military equipment to leftist Nicaragua]: When a country like Nicaragua applies to France, it's generally a sign that it is seeking to escape being dependent [on the superpowers]. I think our American friends should not be alarmed more than is necessary ... From a military point of view, developing countries are very aware that they have to avoid total dependence for their security on just one country, one of the two big powers. We can discuss military arrangements with countries without posing ideological conditions. We have

(CHARLES HERNU)

a liberty of action that the United States should encourage.

Interview, Washington, Jan. 7/Chicago Tribune, 1-9:(1)5; The Washington Post, 1-8:(A)18.

Deane R. Hinton
United States Ambassador to El Salvador

1

[With the upcoming elections in El Salvador,] there will be a new government, and the government will no longer be a revolutionary junta imposed after a dictator is thrown out, but will be the legitimate elected government of the people of El Salvador. Unfortunately, that does not end the [guerrilla] war. Elections could have been a political solution to the war, and they weren't because these [guerrillas] who allege they're so goddamned popular wouldn't participate and take their chances.

Interview, San Salvador, Jan. 29/ The Washington Post, 1-31:(A)1.

2

El Salvador's a crazy place. It's a mess, too much indiscriminate killing. It's a sick society, an agonizing situation. But if the other guys [the guerrillas] take over, it would be a lot worse.

The New York Times, 7-24:6.

3

[Saying the Salvadoran government must improve its human-rights policies]: Every day we receive new reports of disappearances [of people] under tragic circumstances. American citizens in El Salvador have been among the murdered, among the disappeared. Is it any wonder that much of the world is predisposed to believe the worst of a system which almost never brings to justice either those who perpetuate these acts or those who order them? The mafia must be stopped. Your [El Salvador's] survival depends on it. The gorillas of this mafia, every bit as much as the guerrillas [fighting against the government], are destroying El Salvador ... The message is simple. El

Salvador must make progress in bringing the murderers of our citizens, including those who ordered the murders, to justice; in advancing human rights; and in controlling the abuses of some elements of the security forces. If not, the United States, in spite of our interests, in spite of our commitment to the struggle against Communism, could be forced to deny assistance to El Salvador.

Before U.S.-Salvadoran Chamber of Commerce, Oct. 29/The New York Times, 11-3:8.

David C. Jones
General, United States Air Force; Chairman, Joint Chiefs of Staff

4

[On U.S. involvement in the guerrilla war in El Salvador]: In my judgment, our role for now and for the future is purely limited military assistance [to the Salvadoran government]. I do not see any circumstances under which we would intervene with American forces. I don't think that's necessary, and I don't think that would be the right course of action.

Before House Foreign Affairs Committee, Washington, March 10/The New York Times, 3-11:8.

Jeane J. Kirkpatrick
United States Ambassador/Permanent Representative to the United Nations

5

[On the guerrilla war in El Salvador]: The government of El Salvador has said it is prepared to negotiate with anybody who is willing to stop fighting and participate in elections. The United States supports the view that the [forthcoming] elections, which permit people to decide for themselves what sort of government they prefer, are the most appropriate way for a government to be formed ... [But the guerrillas want to] negotiate the composition of the government. Then they want to purge the armed forces. Then they say after six months [of being in power] they commit themselves to holding not an election but a plebiscite on the government which has been established. What they want is someone to give them a share of power which they do not think they can win through elections and apparently are doubtful they can win on the battlefield.

Interview, United Nations, N.Y./ San Francisco Examiner & Chronicle, 3-21:(A)22.

Basilio Lami Dozo
Member, ruling junta of Argentina

1

[On the current British-Argentine war over the Falkland Islands] : We already have won the political victory. Many times, people have won the military war but lost the political one . . . We have a different Argentina today, an Argentina that is considered in the international context and known in various international forums where it has been conducting itself as a country that has faith in its destiny and is capable of dealing with other countries that years ago would have never imagined such a possibility.

To reporters, Comodoro Rivadavia, Argentina, May 31/The New York Times, 6-2:9.

Gilles Lamontagne
Minister of Defense of Canada

2

[The majority of Canadians] are in favor of defense . . . until we go beyond what would be acceptable to their way of thinking. Defense is important, defense is necessary, but it should not go beyond a certain limit where you would have to cut some social benefits or lower our standard of living or something like that. I don't think Canadians are ready to do that.

Interview, Ottawa/Los Angeles Times, 6-17:(I-B)1.

Jim Leach
United States Representative, R–Iowa

3

[On Argentina's military take-over of the British Falkland Islands]: The possibility of armed conflict over the Falkland Islands is a poignant reminder of the need for caution and restraint in arms sales abroad. As Argentina and Britain prepare to square off in a 17th-century sort of crisis over control of a remote island chain, there is a real danger that arms supplied by the United States to a Latin American military dictatorship will be used against one of our most important allies. This situation has arisen at a time when there has been consideration within the [U.S. Reagan] Administration of certifying that Argentina is eligible on human-rights grounds for renewed U.S. arms sales. Argentina's reckless use of force to establish control over British territory should

make it absolutely clear that its government lacks the responsibility that we should demand of those to whom we sell arms.

Before the House, Washington, April 5/ The New York Times, 4-9:13.

Rene Levesque
Premier of Quebec, Canada

4

The political climate [in Quebec] right now . . . is a bit like a rollercoaster . . . There still is lurking in the background the uncertainty about where Quebec is going. But it's also, "Where the hell is my life going and my kids' future and what have you?" It's a sort of piling on of uncertainties . . . Over the next few years, somewhere at the turn of probably [Canadian Prime Minister Pierre Elliott] Trudeau leaving first . . . yours truly and others being replaced not long afterwards, I think at that moment something very close to 50 per cent would be there [for Quebec independence from Canada], the moment of truth . . . Four years, five years, three years, six years, I don't know. But somewhere in the '80s, I'd say for sure.

Interview, Montreal, February/ Los Angeles Times, 3-12:(I-A)2.

Sol M. Linowitz
Former United States delegate to the Organization of American States

5

Canada seems so much like us [the U.S.] that we expect Canada to be like us and do like us. And when Canada does differently by recognizing China or Cuba or struggling against us to maintain its independence, we are surprised and can overreact.

At meeting sponsored by Columbia University Graduate School of Business and Touche Ross & Co., Toronto, May/The New York Times, 5-9:(1)4.

Jose Lopez Portillo
President of Mexico

6

[Announcing the nationalization of Mexico's banks]: [A] group of Mexicans, led, counseled and supported by private banks, have taken more money out of the country than all the empires that have exploited us since the beginning of our history . . . It is now or never [for

WHAT THEY SAID IN 1982

(JOSE LOPEZ PORTILLO)

nationalizing the banks]. They are already sacking us. Mexico is not finished. They will never sack us again. The country can no longer permit the exit of dollars to pay for real estate acquired outside the country. We should make every effort so that this practice ends.

State of the Union address, Mexico City,
Sept. 1/Chicago Tribune, 9-6:(1)10, 9-2:(1)1.

1

[On Mexico's economic crisis]: A pernicious sequence of inflation, devaluations, mounting prices and wages braked our prosperity. In just three years, capital flight [from the country] was double the level of foreign investment in our country. Thus, the financial system and freedom of exchange, especially in the light of our proximity to the wealthiest country in the world [the U.S.], led to exhaustion of our reserves. [Mexico is] a living example of what occurs when that enormous, volatile and speculative mass of capital goes all over the world in search of high interest rates, tax havens and supposed political and exchange stability. It decapitalizes entire countries and leaves destruction in its wake.

At United Nations, New York, Oct. 1/
The New York Times, 10-2:5.

2

[On his impending departure from office]: I'm going to be attacked a great deal by those whom I have affected, by those whom I could not satisfy, for what I could not do. But this is the secret of our stability: that there are these cycles of regeneration and substitution that allow tensions to be released and a new epoch to be born.

The New York Times, 11-26:3.

Alvaro Magana
President of El Salvador

3

[On his being inaugurated President during the current guerrilla war in his country]: We have no room for resentment, for revenge, for hatred or for sectarianism. Only a true spirit of fraternity and solidarity on the part of all

216

Salvadorans will enable us to overcome the worst crisis in our history ... I dedicate all the days of my government to the fulfillment of peace. We have nothing to revenge, nothing to repress and nothing to negotiate ... Salvadorans are not cannon fodder for anyone's appetite, nor for any dictatorship, nor for anyone's Cold War.

Inaugural address, San Salvador,
May 2/Los Angeles Times, 5-3:(I)5.

4

[On the possibility of negotiations between the Salvadoran government and leftist guerrillas]: Words like "negotiations" and "dialogue" are emotional words. But I am convinced that everybody in this country, including any party that would be considered rightist parties, are also interested in peace. [The recent elections were] a mandate for peace. If I had taken steps to make peace that did not have the support of the main political parties, it would not get any results. So what I have been doing is organizing this political commission, which will have the support of political parties, the army and myself ... [The guerrillas] know there is no opportunity for a military solution. My impression is they have lost the support of the people. After two years [of fighting] you get desperate if you don't have results. The [Salvadoran] Army is more effective. If we need to replace 20 soldiers, we have 200 waiting to come in. They [the guerrillas] don't have that. My impression is that some of them have changed their attitude and want to go within the democratic process.

Interview, San Salvador, Sept. 22/
The New York Times, 9-24:4.

Dan Marriott
United States Representative, R—Utah

5

[On the guerrilla war in El Salvador]: A negotiated settlement would play directly into the hands of the Marxists and lead to an unrepresentative government. If we go to a negotiated settlement, it will simply give a minority interest—the Marxists—more power and probably enable them ultimately to take over the entire government. This is what happened in Nicaragua. The guerrillas cannot win

(DAN MARRIOTT)

an election. And they cannot win a military struggle either, unless Washington abandons the existing government. They simply want power any way they can get it. To give them the means to gain power, without free elections, is wrong.

Interview/U.S. News & World Report, 2-22:34.

Paul N. McCloskey, Jr.
United States Representative,
R–California

1

[On U.S. policy in Central America]: We want to promote governments that will be stable and relatively sensitive to their people's needs. But . . . a lot of those Latin American dictators I wouldn't support at all. My rule of thumb would be to follow the Monroe Doctrine to the letter: Any foreign intrusion into this hemisphere you meet. But . . . if there is a bona fide revolution against the junta in El Salvador, I wouldn't get so locked into the government of El Salvador that if they ultimately get toppled we are then tied with a situation like we were with the Shah of Iran or Somoza [in Nicaragua]. I would be much easier, I think, with the Sandinistas [now in power in Nicaragua]; I would not drive them into the Communist camp by an iron hostility. I think half these guys that claim they're Communists today may be socialists tomorrow.

Interview/The Christian Science Monitor, 2-18:7.

Julio Cesar Mesquita
Senior editor, "O Estado
de Sao Paulo" (Brazil)

2

. . . the U.S. believes that the only problem in the world is the Soviet Union. If the U.S. tried to strengthen the entire hemisphere, from Uruguay to Canada—which it has the means to do—we wouldn't have to worry about the Russians. I cannot understand why the U.S. doesn't pay more attention to its neighbors. If we had the help of the U.S. we would become the greatest continent in the world . . . I think the U.S. moves to find quick solutions for the

problem of the moment—like Nicaragua, El Salvador and Guatemala. It doesn't think of developing Brazil, Argentina or Chile for the future, but only for the present. When crisis threatens, when the U.S. thinks the Communists are going to take over, then it goes into action. That is a great mistake.

Interview/World Press Review, February:33.

Francois Mitterrand
President of France

3

[On the unrest in Central America]: Our first duty is to fight against poverty and the exploitation of human beings and the domination on the part of bloody dictatorships. We must work to find the way of furthering the cause of democratic government, and there, there is something [the U.S. and France] have in common, and that leads to a meeting of the minds between us. We should do everything that can enable the democratic powers of the West to achieve a better understanding and be better able to give more assistance to the peoples that are rebelling against their fate.

Washington, March 12/Chicago Tribune, 3-13:(1)1.

4

The peoples of Central America, too, have the right to determine their own fate and to refuse a life in misery and suppression by dictators and ruthless economic power-holders. Therefore, I support the revolt by these people. If that does not please the United States, and it clearly does not, it is just too bad. But the United States has to see that by opposing the demands of the people, they create the openings for Cuba and the Soviet Union.

Interview/The New York Times, 4-26:4.

Luis Alberto Monge
President-elect of Costa Rica

5

[On the guerrilla war in El Salvador]: The guerrillas have not been able to crush the professional army . . . and the army has not been able to crush the guerrillas . . . If the guerrillas win, there is no assurance that the

(LUIS ALBERTO MONGE)

people of El Salvador will have a democratic government. What they would be doing would be exchanging one despotic ideological side for another. On the military side, we know that there are certain negative security forces that are responsible for massacres, murders and acts of genocide.

News conference, Los Angeles, March 11/
Los Angeles Times, 3-12:(I)12.

1

It has been the tendency of the U.S. to behave toward this [Central American] region like a fire brigade. Whenever a fire breaks out, the U.S. comes down and tries to put it out. At other times, there is an attitude of neglect toward your southern neighbors.

Time, 3-22:28.

Daniel P. Moynihan
United States Senator, D–New York

2

The invasion by the Argentine military of the [British] Falkland Islands is the first occasion since the establishment of NATO in 1948 that nationals of a NATO member have been subjected to military occupation by another power .... our Secretary of State should make it absolutely clear that there is nothing to mediate between a country using force without provocation and a country resisting that use of force. This is exactly the situation that [the late French] President de Gaulle envisioned when he took France out of the military wing of NATO. This is the test of de Gaulle's hypothesis, that we would not stand by our allies. This is the test of our understanding of the alliance.

Before the Senate, Washington, April 13/
The New York Times, 4-16:10.

John Nott
Minister of Defense
of the United Kingdom

3

[On Argentina's military take-over of the British Falkland Islands]: It does not matter what we want or what the Argentinians want, but what the islanders want. It is their rights

that have been taken away by naked aggression and it is their rights that shall be restored ... We have no wish to shed blood, but we shall not acquiesce to any act of unprovoked aggression, undertaken presumably in the false belief that we lack courage and the will to respond. Let the world be under no illusion. [The Falkland Islanders] are British and we mean to defend them. We are earnest and no one should doubt our resolve.

Before Parliament, London, April 7/
The Washington Post, 4-8:(A)23.

Wallace H. Nutting
Lieutenant General, United States Army;
Commander, U.S. Southern Command

4

[The U.S.] Congress does not appreciate the historic importance of the competition in Central America. Therefore, the will is not apparent in the United States to take those steps necessary to assure an agreeable outcome in Central America. And until understanding and will increase, the guerrilla will persist ... I believe that no single government in Central America is capable of sustaining itself against the present [guerrilla] assault. They've got to have outside support [from the U.S.] because outside support is being funneled to the opposition and they [the governments] cannot cope with the problem alone. It's not a problem for each individual country to face.

Interview, Panama/
The New York Times, 8-22:(1)6.

Alejandro Orfila
Secretary General, Organization
of American States

5

There is a constant ebb and flow in the growth and progress of the hemispheric association. Its formidable strength has been proved time and time again during the course of our uneven history together. But one feature stands out in our relationship: the belief of OAS nations and peoples that, despite all their differences, they need each other. At times, this conviction is weak and clouded by harsh rhetoric. But it is nonetheless always present.

The Washington Post, 7-28:(A)20.

Daniel Ortega Saavedra
Member, ruling junta of Nicaragua

1

[On the guerrilla war in El Salvador]: The peoples of the region demand a negotiated political solution; U.S. public opinion demands a negotiated political solution; the peoples of Latin America and the worthy governments demand a negotiated political solution; the peoples and governments of the world are expecting a negotiated political solution.

At United Nations, New York, March 25/
The New York Times, 3-26:8.

2

[Saying the U.S. is hostile to his government]: The actions of the current U.S. Administration are directed at provoking the Sandinista revolution to radicalize and, because of that, to destroy the possibility of this project [the revolution]. The current U.S. Administration would find it easier to fight against a radicalized revolution than against a revolution with the characteristics that Sandinism defends. All this has to do with the fear that the U.S. Administration has of change in the Central American region ... But despite all this, we believe that the project [the revolution] continues to be viable.

Interview, July/
The Washington Post, 7-26:(A)17.

David Owen
Member of British Parliament;
Former Foreign Secretary
of the United Kingdom

3

[On U.S. attempts to mediate the Falkland Islands dispute between Argentina and Britain]: It is not possible to be neutral between the fire and the fire brigade.

In the House of Commons, London,
April 14/The New York Times, 4-17:5.

Olof Palme
Prime Minister of Sweden

4

[I am] deeply worried about developments in Central America, the mounting repression [and wars]. Some of these people being killed are old friends of mine in Guatemala, El Salvador ... I think the [U.S.] Reagan Administration is putting too much emphasis on military means and too little emphasis on talks and negotiations or economic and social reform ... When the U.S. takes responsibility for conditions in those countries, as it has, and the repression goes on, then the United States leaves itself open to criticism.

Interview, Stockholm/
The Washington Post, 12-10:(E)3.

Ruben Dario Paredes
Commander-in-Chief,
National Guard of Panama

5

The moment of great definitions is arriving [for Panama]. We had wanted to be free, a friend of the whole world, as long as nobody bothered us. But unfortunately the world today turns around two poles: traditional democracy and an open economy led by the United States; and the Communist world led by the Soviet Union, with a system we never want to see in our country. We are enemies of Russia, but we don't want them ever to fool with us here. We respect the Cuban form of government and if they think it's best for them, that's their problem and their right. But that's not what we want for Panama.

Interview, Panama City/
The Washington Post, 7-27:(A)11.

Claiborne Pell
United States Senator, D–Rhode Island

6

[On the guerrilla war in El Salvador]: [Salvadoran President Jose Napoleon] Duarte is a genuinely decent man but has virtually no power. He's not a President; he's the chairman of the board of the junta ... People that he is with in the government are military people on the right. They're not as far to the right as the military dictatorship that they threw out in 1978, but they're still to the right ... If Duarte wins [the upcoming elections], I presume he'd have more real power. He really is a weak reed on which we lean, but he is our only reed.

News conference, Feb. 18/
U.S. News & World Report, 3-1:27.

WHAT THEY SAID IN 1982

Francisco Pena Gomez
General Secretary, ruling
Dominican Revolutionary Party
of the Dominican Republic

1

We are in a worse position than any other country in the Caribbean Basin. Every other country has its godfather. The English and French islands have the European community, which helps them out with preferential markets for their exports. Puerto Rico receives more than $2-billion each year from the United States, and Cuba has the Soviet Union. The U.S. has a responsibility to act as a great power and to assist us.

The Christian Science Monitor, 2-25:4.

Carlos Andres Perez
Former President of Venezuela

2

[On his country's purchases of U.S. military equipment]: Venezuela must only buy what is necessary. If Cuba is a Russian base, then we should be careful not to become a U.S. base. We must not become an American puppet.

Chicago Tribune, 3-29:(1)5.

Jose Pedro Perez Llorca
Foreign Minister of Spain

3

[Saying Spain supports Argentina in its current war with Britain over the Falkland Islands]: As a democratic country, we will be loyal to the [NATO] alliance. Nevertheless, Spain feels a part of the Latin American community. Spain is allied to England in the context of defending democracy ... It is absolutely not allied to England in the Malvinas [Falklands]. This dual sense of belonging ... is something we will bring to the alliance, and we will make it a more positive attitude to our sister nations in Latin America.

May 31/Los Angeles Times, 6-1:(I)7.

Francis Pym
Foreign Secretary of
the United Kingdom

4

[On Argentina's military take-over of the

British Falkland Islands]: They've got to go. They began the aggressive action. They invaded the islands ... They have no right to be there, and they'll have to go from there. We want them to go back as a result of a peaceful settlement, if we can. But if not, then I'm afraid they'll go back by force.

To reporters, Washington, May 2/
Los Angeles Times, 5-3:(I)10.

George Radwanski
Editor-in-chief,
"The Toronto Star"

5

Canadians are being given a feeling that the [U.S.] Reagan Administration doesn't respect Canada's right to pursue its own interests. The Reagan Administration has already done more to imperil the traditional good feelings between Canada and the United States than certainly any other recent American government.

The Washington Post, 8-3:(A)10.

Sergio Ramirez Mercado
Member, ruling junta
of Nicaragua

6

[On U.S. charges that his country's military buildup is excessive]: When [U.S. Secretary of State Alexander] Haig is saying every day that they are going to bomb us and attack us and blockade us, how can they then turn around and ask us not to defend ourselves? ... We have more military garrisons, of course. But it is precisely because the spread of [former Nicaraguan dictator Anastasio] Somoza's national guard was not based on national defense but on internal repression. He didn't want to have any of his military units out of his reach in Managua because he feared that independent garrisons would revolt. He centered the military here in the bunker with his armored cars, tanks and elite forces all in one place in Managua. Our military organization has to do with the need to defend ourselves. We don't fear any upheaval among the troops. We have spread out our garrisons the way any regular military force in the world does.

Interview, Managua, March 9/
The New York Times, 3-10:1,7.

Ronald Reagan
President of the United States

1

I think tightening our trade embargo [against Cuba] is of help because Cuba's economy is in desperate straits. The goal should be to hope that Cuba would see that they have tied themselves to the Soviet Union in such a way that they've become a satellite, and that they would be far better off if they were one of the family of American states.

Interview/The Washington Post, 1-18:(A)2.

2

For almost two years, Nicaragua has served as a platform for covert military actions. Through Nicaragua, arms are being smuggled to guerrillas in El Salvador and Guatemala. The Nicaraguan government even admits the forced relocation of about 8,500 Miskito Indians, and we have clear evidence that since late 1981 many Indian communities have been burned to the ground and men, women and children killed. The Nicaraguan junta cabled written reassurances to the OAS in 1979 that it intended to respect human rights and hold free elections. Two years later, these commitments can be measured by the postponement of elections until 1985, by repression against free trade unions, against the media, minorities, and the defiance of all international civility by the continued export of arms and subversion to neighboring countries.

Before Organization of American States,
Washington, Feb. 24/The New York Times, 2-25:8.

3

[The government of El Salvador] has repeatedly urged the guerrillas to renounce violence, to join in the democratic process—an election in which the people of El Salvador could determine the government they prefer. Our own country and other American nations, through the OAS, have urged such a course. The guerrillas have refused. More than that, they now threaten violence and death to those who participate in such an election. Can anything make more clear the nature of those who pretend to be supporters of so-called wars of liberation? A determined propaganda campaign

has sought to mislead many in Europe, and certainly many in the United States, as to the true nature of the conflict in El Salvador. Very simply, guerrillas, armed and supported by and through Cuba, are attempting to impose a Marxist-Leninist dictatorship on the people of El Salvador as part of a larger imperialistic plan. If we do not act promptly and decisively in defense of freedom, new Cubas will arise from the ruins of today's conflicts. We will face more totalitarian regimes, tied militarily to the Soviet Union; more regimes supporting subversion; more regimes so incompetent yet so totalitarian that their citizens' only hope becomes that of one day migrating to other American nations, as in recent years they have come to the United States.

Before Organization of American States,
Washington. Feb. 24/
The New York Times, 2-25:8.

4

[Criticizing Argentina for its military takeover of the British Falkland Islands]: We must remember that the aggression was on the part of Argentina in this dispute over the sovereignty of that little ice-cold bunch of land down there, and they finally just resorted to armed aggression. I think the principle that all of us must abide by is, armed aggression of that kind must not be allowed to succeed.

Before editors and broadcasters,
Washington, April 30/
The New York Times, 5-1:8.

5

I can honestly tell you that relations between the United States and Mexico are good. The friendship between our peoples is excellent. While there are occasional differences in approach between our two countries, the honest good-will which exists between us has assured the maintenance of dialogue and created new opportunities for cooperation. After all, we strive to achieve the same goal—a free and prosperous Central America.

At U.S.-Mexico Interparliamentary
Conference, Santa Barbara, Calif.,
May 28/Chicago Tribune, 5-29:(1)5.

WHAT THEY SAID IN 1982

(RONALD REAGAN)

1

[On the U.S.' support for Britain in the current British-Argentine conflict over the Falkland Islands and its effect on U.S.-Latin American relations]: I know the bloodshed that is taking place around the Falkland Islands is of deep concern to every nation in this hemisphere. We understand and are sensitive to Latin American sympathies in this crisis, something which made our own decisions more painful and difficult. I hope you will, also, as neighbors and friends, do your utmost to understand the importance we attach to the principle that armed force [Argentina's military take-over of the Falklands] should not be used to assert claims in an international dispute ... Let's make certain that emotions don't blur the truth of how close we really are during this tragic conflict. We all did our best to prevent bloodshed. Now that hostilities have started, we are united in the desire for a negotiated settlement.

At U.S.-Mexico Interparliamentary Conference,
Santa Barbara, Calif., May 28/
Los Angeles Herald Examiner, 5-29:(A)4.

2

[In Latin America,] just as threatening as conventional armies or nuclear weapons are counterfeit revolutionaries who undermine legitimate governments and destroy sources of economic progress; insurgents who are, at great expense, armed by the surrogate of a faraway power, a power that espouses a philosophy alien to the Americas, whose goal is the destabilization of our governments and economies. This is aggression, pure and simple.

At dinner in his honor, Brasilia, Brazil,
Dec. 1/Los Angeles Times, 12-2:(I)14.

3

[On his just-completed trip to Latin America]: I didn't go down there with any plan for the Americas or anything. I went down to find out from them and their views. You'd be surprised; they're all individual countries. I think one of the greatest mistakes in the world that we've made has been ... lumping Latin America. You don't talk that way about

Europe; you recognize the differences between various countries.

To reporters, aboard Air Force One,
Dec. 4/Los Angeles Times, 12-6:(I)1.

Ptolemy A. Reid
Prime Minister of Guyana

4

[On his country's economic problems while trying to become self-sufficient and develop socialism]: Development has its pains. It takes a little time for acceptance. Unless we can appreciate the pains of development, we will all go around in the old ways and will remain with ignorance and poverty.

Interview/
The New York Times, 10-3:(1)9.

Efrain Rios Montt
Leader, ruling junta of Guatemala

5

[On the coup installing him to power]: We are striking for an honest government, a democratic one that serves the people of this nation ... by getting the military out of politics.

The Christian Science
Monitor, 4-1:12.

Carlos Rafael Rodriguez
Vice President of Cuba

6

We naturally would like it if all of Latin America were socialist. We would not be Communists if we did not think so. And we are Communists. Not only Latin America, we would like it if all of Europe were socialist. That's obvious. But wishing that Europe were socialist does not mean that we are going to start promoting upheaval, as we were accused by some of doing in France in 1968. It's ridiculous. If we see the possibility of making a socialist revolution some place [in Latin America] ... it would be very important—well, we would be happy. And we would help within our modest resources.

Interview, New York/
The Washington Post, 6-21:(A)16.

Carlos Romero Barcelo
Governor of Puerto Rico

1

Puerto Rico's current political condition *is* inferior. It is recognized as such around the world—by citizens of Latin republics, who belittle us as "lackeys of the imperialist yankees"; by the vast majority of our fellow American citizens, some of whom, when they think about us at all, regard us as a kind of "foreigners with special immigration privileges"; and by the international adversaries of the United States, who relentlessly proclaim that Puerto Rico is an "oppressed colony," being exploited for military and economic reasons. The Puerto Rican people are fully aware that our political status is inferior; every political party on the island advocates change. My party favors statehood. The principal opposition party calls for "greater autonomy." And a minority of about 6 per cent favors independence.

*At Woodrow Wilson International Center/
The Washington Post, 4-30:(A)30.*

Nestor D. Sanchez
*Deputy Assistant Secretary for
Inter-American Affairs, Department
of Defense of the United States*

2

Unless we [the U.S.] provide timely security assistance to help our friends [in Latin America] respond effectively now to the threat in the region, we are likely to have far greater future demands forced upon us wherever [Cuban President Fidel] Castro and his Soviet mentors perceive an opportunity to strike.

*Before House Foreign Affairs Committee,
Washington, July 29/The New York Times, 7-30:2.*

George P. Shultz
*Secretary of State
of the United States*

3

[Saying Congress should approve President Reagan's proposal for a $350-million aid program for the Caribbean]: Our security and credibility are at stake. The tragic war in the South Atlantic [in which the U.S. supported Britain against Argentina in the fight for the Falkland Islands] has led some hemispheric friends—mistakenly I believe—to challenge our commitment to them as a partner. We must show them that this is not so.

*Before Senate Finance Committee, Washington,
Aug. 2/The New York Times, 8-3:2.*

4

The trouble with Cuba is its behavior. When the behavior of Cuba changes, when it stops exporting revolution, when it stops sending armaments to Nicaragua, when it stops feeding guerrilla movements designed to disrupt duly constituted government processes in the area, then there's something to talk about [between Cuba and the U.S.].

*Broadcast Interview/
"Face the Nation," CBS-TV, 9-5.*

5

Clearly, no strategy for peace [in Central America] can succeed if those who take up arms against their fellow citizens and neighbors go unopposed. Peace is impossible without security . . . Fortunately, not all of the conditions for war are present in Central America. Most states still lack the major offensive weapons that would be needed for an attack on their neighbors. That may give us our opening. Why shouldn't we encourage the governments of Central America to agree, all of them, on a basis of reciprocity and strict verification, not to import major offensive weapons? Clearly, that's only part of the solution, but it would be a start . . . [As for the presence of] foreign military advisers, . . . why not go for agreement among Central American countries, again on a basis of reciprocity and verification, to reduce their numbers to some low agreed level—or to zero? The same treatment—reciprocity and verification—could be applied to practical and mutual undertakings to end any and all of the support for violent activity on the territory of others.

*Before Organization of American States,
Washington, Nov. 17/Los Angeles Times, 11-18:(I)4.*

Hernan Siles Zuazo
President of Bolivia

6

[On his country's return to civilian rule]: We have overcome dictatorship and that is what

223

(HERNAN SILES ZUAZO)

is important ... More than taking reprisals, we are interested in building the democracy for which our martyrs died for. We want a government of Bolivia for Bolivians. And furthermore, we are extending the frontiers of democracy to the south in the uncontained advance of liberty and human rights.

Inauguration address, La Paz, Oct. 10/
The New York Times, 10-11:3.

Walter J. Stoessel, Jr.
Deputy Secretary of State
of the United States

1

Today the peace and security of the Caribbean basin are deeply threatened by a web of political violence, economic collapse and Cuban support for subversion. In the Caribbean, the smallest islands are as exposed politically as they have long been to the sudden violence of tropical storms. Three years ago a tiny band of armed men, who turned out to be Marxists, took over the nation of Grenada. Other islands are equally vulnerable to small groups of many political stripes, adventurers, even gangsters. In Central America, acute economic troubles are unsettling rigid social compacts formed generations ago in Guatemala, widening distrust in El Salvador and bringing Costa Ricans to worry about the sturdy democratic compact that has served them well for more than 30 years. Timing its move to exploit these vulnerabilities, Cuba has mounted a campaign to establish Marxist-Leninist dictatorships in both Central America and the Caribbean ... Our message to Cuba is clear. We will not accept that the future of the Caribbean basin be manipulated from Havana. It must be determined by the countries themselves.

Before Senate Foreign Relations Committee,
Washington, March 25/The New York Times, 3-26:7.

Roberto Suazo Cordova
President of Honduras

2

Central America deserves to be an area of peaceful coexistence ... instead of bellicose confrontation ... I promise to make this a government of morality in which the officials are the servants of the people and not the beneficiaries of the state.

Inaugural address, Tegucigalpa, Honduras,
Jan. 27/Los Angeles Times, 1-28:(I)6.

Margaret Thatcher
Prime Minister of the United Kingdom

3

[On Argentina's military take-over of the British Falkland Islands]: We have a long and proud history of recognizing the right of others to determine their own destiny. Indeed, in that respect we have an experience unrivaled by any other nation in the world. But that right must be upheld universally and not least when it is challenged by those who are hardly conspicuous for their own devotion to democracy and liberty. The eyes of the world are now focused on the Falkland Islands; others are watching anxiously to see whether brute force or the rule of law will triumph. Wherever naked aggression occurs it must be overcome. The cost now, however high, must be set against the cost we would one day have to pay if this principle went by default. And that is why, through diplomatic, economic and if necessary through military means, we shall persevere until freedom and democracy are restored to the people of the Falkland Islands.

Before House of Commons, London, April 14/
The New York Times, 4-15:8.

4

[On Argentina's military take-over of the British Falkland Islands]: Sovereignty [over the Falklands] at the moment is ours. It has not been changed by invasion. And sovereignty must never be changed by invasion. That's point Number 1. Number 2—we believe in the right of people to democracy and therefore they [the islanders] must have an enormous say in their own future. Point Number 3—if this [Argentina] invasion succeeds, there will be very many people the world over who are at risk.

Broadcast interview, London, May 19/
Los Angeles Times, 5-20:(I)9.

(MARGARET THATCHER)

1

[On Britain's military victory over Argentina in the war for the Falkland Islands] : I hope we have restored once again the dominance of Britain and let every nation know that where there is British sovereign territory it will be well and truly defended.

Before House of Commons, London, June 15/
Los Angeles Herald Examiner, 6-16:(A)13.

2

[Criticizing the U.S. vote in the UN for negotiations between Britain and Argentina over the future of the British Falkland Islands] : We've always been true to the values which we and the United States share—values of freedom, justice and democracy. I find it incomprehensible that [the U.S.] should vote with Argentina, a totalitarian government that has invaded a democracy [Argentina's recent takeover of the Falklands, after which Britain fought and won it back]. Anger? No, disappointment. Very deep indeed ... In our system and in the United States we believe in self-determination. That's what put President Reagan where he is in the United States, and that's what put me where I am in the United Kingdom. And in the end it's the fundamental human rights that matter ... We will not change our fundamental obligation to the British people in the Falkland Islands.

BBC interview, Nov. 5/
The Washington Post, 11-6:(A)19.

Pierre Elliott Trudeau
Prime Minister of Canada

3

Within the United States the economy has slowed to a crawl, and with that decline has gone a good part of a major market for what we in Canada produce. The effect in all this has been substantial in every country, but we next door have felt it more than most ... To ensure continuing investment in Canada, to give reasonable protection to our dollar ... the government of Canada has had little choice but to let our interest rates keep pace with, indeed sometimes exceed, those set in the United States.

At economic conference, Ottawa, Feb. 2/
*Los Angeles Times, 2-3:(*V)1.*

4

[Comparing U.S. attempts to block a natural-gas pipeline from the Soviet Union to Western Europe with U.S. domination of its economic relations with Canada] : I think that suddenly the Europeans have realized how serious a situation is when a country as powerful as the United States can impose the application of its laws, especially in the economic field, on other countries. Now perhaps they will understand a bit better that a country which is economically dominated, as Canada is, has a right to attenuate the effects of that economic domination.

News conference, July 9/
The Washington Post, 8-3:(A)1.

5

Our main exports to the United States are hockey players and cold fronts. Our main imports from the United States are baseball players and acid rain.

At all-star baseball luncheon, Montreal,
July 13/The New York Times, 7-14:24.

6

Certainly since the middle '70s the trend has been all in the direction of the states' rights people [in Canada]. There has been an increasing demand on the part of the provinces for increased rights, and that increased demand met with a rather sympathetic response at provincial election time in Quebec and in other parts of the country where the question was posed directly by the running incumbent Premier. Newfoundland is the most recent example. Alberta is not a very old example either. It is the perception of that trend and a fear of where it is leading us that has caused our government and our party to stand for Canadian unity ...

Interview, Ottawa/The New York
Times Magazine, 10-3:54.

7

... I have no great quarrel with the U.S. Administration, the present one—nor indeed the previous ones. I believe, by and large, that these Presidents and this President [Reagan] have been, with varying degrees of success, embodying good-will toward Canada—which I

225

WHAT THEY SAID IN 1982

(PIERRE ELLIOTT TRUDEAU)

hope our government has reciprocated—and a willingness to understand our divergencies in foreign or domestic policies ... Since I have been interested in public life, I remember instances of the American government, either directly or through the head offices [of corporations] trying to direct how their subsidiaries in Canada would trade with China or Cuba or whatever. To me it has been and remains a problem, but it is not a running sore. It is something which we are working to correct and which, over the years, has shown some progress and some lack of progress.

Interview/Chicago Tribune, 10-9:(1)11.

Paul E. Tsongas
United States Senator,
D—Massachusetts

1

[Arguing against further U.S. aid for El Salvador]: First, more military equipment will not by itself solve the problem of political unrest in El Salvador. The problem is basically political—and military force isn't going to resolve it. And second, if the U.S. wants to supply whatever military means are required to defeat the Marxist insurgents in El Salvador, then we have to ponder the ultimate U.S. commitment: ground troops. It is obvious that the American public would not support sending soldiers into El Salvador. So the final card is not playable. We'd simply be wasting time and money. More importantly, we'd be missing an opportunity to end the civil war through a cease-fire and then negotiations.

Interview/U.S. News & World Report, 2-22:33.

Julio Cesar Turbay Ayala
President of Colombia

2

The fight in the Caribbean today is between democracy and Marxism, and not between democracies and Fascist governments. Those have mostly disappeared.

Interview, Bogota, March 17/
The New York Times, 3-18:4.

Guillermo Ungo
President, Democratic Revolutionary
Front of El Salvador

3

[Criticizing the forthcoming elections in El Salvador]: You can't talk about elections when people vote through fear, when people know that if they don't vote they'll be threatened [by the government], jailed or killed. I would like to participate in the elections, but the army has decided I cannot by publishing a hit list of 138 names of supposed subversives. My predecessor as president of the front was murdered and I don't want to end up like him.

Interview, Mexico City, Feb. 27/
The New York Times, 2-28:(1)10.

4

We are a very democratic coalition with different political forces. I am not a Communist. I don't intend to become a Communist. In El Salvador, everybody is considered to be an extremist, and that is why so much killing is going on. Even the American journalists are considered to be extremists because they are telling the truth, and the truth is subversive in El Salvador.

Broadcast interview/
"Meet the Press," NBC-TV, 2-28.

5

[Criticizing the forthcoming elections in El Salvador]: ... so long as there is no dialogue [among the parties in the Salvadoran guerrilla war], it is logical to expect the war to continue, before, during and after next Sunday's elections. The actions we see now merely reflect the growth in the revolutionary movement ... Even the United States government knows that the elections won't bring a solution in El Salvador, because they are elections by the right for the right, by a minority for a minority. After the elections, it will be more difficult to work out a negotiated settlement, but the need will be even greater. First, what we saw from Washington was a policy of war and reforms, but the reforms failed. Now we have war with elections, and that too will fail. So next, we could have war with negotiations.

News conference, Managua, Nicaragua,
March 21/The New York Times, 3-22:6.

Vernon A. Walters
United States
Ambassador-at-Large

1

[On the Argentine-British war over the Falkland Islands]: ... this is an absolutely pointless war. It's a silly war between countries which have great connections with each other, which have a great deal in common. What you really have here is a problem of two *machismos,* and the *machismo* of women [such as British Prime Minister Margaret Thatcher] is even more sensitive than the *machismo* of men. Without attributing fault to either side, I am just stating a fact.

Before American Institute
for Public Policy Studies,
Washington, May 10/
Los Angeles Times,
5-11:(I)12.

Caspar W. Weinberger
Secretary of Defense
of the United States

2

[On the guerrilla war in El Salvador]: We do have to make sure that we don't allow on the mainland ... a bastion of Communism, a foothold to be given to this kind of thing. It would make the defense of the United States infinitely more difficult. We have a lot of those problems with Cuba. They would be multiplied many times over if that situation were transferred to the mainland ... I think it's very much to our interest to have El Salvador remain as a country that is free of Marxist-Cuban-Soviet-inspired Communism. And I think that there's considerable danger of that happening if we don't assist the [Salvadoran] government in what it's trying to do.

Broadcast interview/"Today" show, NBC-TV, 2-16.

Asia and the Pacific

David L. Boren
United States Senator,
D—Oklahoma

1

[Criticizing U.S. President Reagan for allegedly backing down from a U.S. commitment to provide what Taiwan needs for its defense]: Nowhere does it appear that we held to a strong bargaining position [in negotiations with China] on behalf of the 18 million free people of Taiwan. What did we get [from China] in return for apparently bartering away their [Taiwan's] security? What guarantee did we obtain for their right to self-determination? How can we defend such callous treatment of a nation which is one of our best trading partners and one of the few that pays its bills with hard cash? Taiwan has also been our ally in the Korean conflict and in every other international and military crisis.

The Washington Post,
8-25:(A)22.

Leonid I. Brezhnev
President of the Soviet Union;
General Secretary,
Soviet Communist Party

2

[On Soviet-Chinese relations]: We have never considered normal the state of hostility and estrangement between our two countries. We are ready to come to terms, without any preliminary conditions, on measures acceptable to both sides to improve Soviet-Chinese relations on the basis of mutual respect for each other's interests, non-interference in each other's affairs and mutual benefit—certainly not to the detriment of third countries.

Tashkent, U.S.S.R., March 24/
Los Angeles Times, 3-25:(II)12.

William E. Brock
Special Trade Representative for
the President of the United States

3

Japan has an absolute quota on a number of U.S. products—beef and citrus, for example. Only so many oranges can come in in a given year. That violates the rules of the [trading] game. The Japanese are complaining vigorously about aluminum imports from the United States. They have very severe barriers to paper goods and a lot of consumer products and agricultural products in which the United States has a far superior quality at a far lower price. Almost anything you buy in a department store you can buy cheaper in the United States than you can in Japan. The list is almost endless: pharmaceuticals, cosmetics, wood products, paper products, down to the stationery that you use. In most sectors, this country is far and away the most productive and the most competitive in the world. There is just no question that Japanese workers and business people have a far, far more open opportunity to sell in this country than we do in theirs.

Interview, Washington/
U.S. News & World Report, 4-26:70.

George Bush
Vice President of the United States

4

I . . . reaffirm to the Chinese leadership the fundamental principles on which we [the U.S.] established normal relations, including the United States' position recognizing there is only one China. This position has been clearly stated by [U.S.] President Reagan. Let it be clear that we consider China an equal partner in world affairs. There are, as I see it, great issues before us—before us, not between us, and this is an important distinction.

Hangzhou, China, May 5/
Los Angeles Times, 5-6:(I)5.

(GEORGE BUSH)

1

We live in a time when the Soviet Union continues its brutal occupation of Afghanistan. It exerts unconscionable pressures on the people of Poland, suppressing their will to be free. It continues to sponsor aggression, subversion and violence in Kampuchea [Cambodia] and other places throughout the globe. In the face of such blatant expansionism, the United States and China have vital roles and responsibilities in doing all that we must to bring about and maintain global peace . . . [The U.S. and China] share not only a common interest in the face of hegemonistic expansionism, but we share a common responsibility.

At banquet in his honor, Peking, May 7/
The New York Times, 5-8:3.

2

[On U.S. involvement in the Vietnam war during the 1960s and '70s]: We're glad to see the end of the Vietnam syndrome, with all of its apologies to neutrals and our enemies and lectures to our friends. This [Reagan] Administration makes no apologies for what our country set out to do in Vietnam. [But] the President and I believe that our military forces should not be sent into a conflict unless we intend to win it.

At Armed Forces Day ceremony, Nellis Air
Force Base, Nev., May 15/San Francisco
Examiner & Chronicle, 5-16:(A)9.

3

So what if there is a reduction of tensions on the Soviet-Chinese border. I don't think that is necessarily detrimental to the interests of the United States. Now, if you say to me that the Soviets are going to take 20 divisions off the Chinese border and put them into Europe, then we would say, "Hey, that wouldn't be very good." That would be destabilizing. But just to have reductions in tensions between them—I don't think that should make us feel all uptight. Just as if *we* reduce tensions with China, that that should drive the Soviets up the wall.

Interview, Washington, December/
The Christian Science Monitor, 12-20:23.

Deng Xiaoping
Vice Chairman, Communist
Party of China

4

[Criticizing U.S. support for Taiwan]: We cannot accept the American way of dealing with the Taiwan problem. On this problem, we have no room for maneuver. If nothing can be done, then relations will retrogress. What is so extraordinary about that? I think the Chinese nation will still exist. We have explained this principle many times [but still] some people in America think Taiwan is their unsinkable aircraft carrier in the Far East. If this idea prevails, it is very difficult to build good Sino-American relations. The essence of this idea is to deny that Taiwan is a part of the People's Republic of China. Now we will wait and see. We are well-prepared for any situation that can happen.

February/The New York Times, 3-27:6.

Peter F. Drucker
Professor of social science
and management, Claremont (Calif.)
College Graduate School

5

Everybody is very bullish on Japan. I am not . . . Their government spending is getting totally out of control. And yet they have no defense spending. It won't take much to push Japan into defense spending . . . The Russians are building up more in the North Pacific than in any other area. The fundamental premise on which the Japanese economy has operated in the post-war world suddenly doesn't work any more. Before, when the Japanese economy was in any trouble, exports have pulled it out. This time, exports are not pulling the economy . . . Probably because . . . tax rates are beginning to be too heavy a brake on the economy.

Interview, San Francisco/
The Christian Science Monitor, 5-4:15.

Richard Falk
Professor of international law,
Princeton University; Former associate
editor, "Foreign Policy" magazine

6

[The Soviet invasion of] Afghanistan, I think, has . . . exposed the weakness of Soviet

(RICHARD FALK)

militarism, as much as its frightening potency. It will probably prove an inhibiting experience for them just as Vietnam was for us [the U.S.]. If all that military prowess can't succeed in a country of goats and mountains, then where can it succeed?

Interview, Princeton University/
The Christian Science Monitor, 2-4:(B)4.

Indira Gandhi
Prime Minister of India

1

Our relations with the Soviet Union are exactly what they were. They never were as close as Americans said they were. Although we are friendly with the Soviets, that friendship does not affect what decisions we take on any international or national matter. The impression is given in the U.S. that we do what the Soviets do or that we follow their advice. We haven't; we have been fiercely independent because I still belong to the generation whose whole life has been spent fighting for freedom. And I cannot conceive of an India which has any kind of shadow on its independence.

Interview, New Delhi/
U.S. News & World Report, 2-15:26.

2

Our [Indian] version of socialism is entirely different from what is practiced in the Soviet Union or the so-called socialist countries of Europe. It has to be something that grows out of the people's needs here, and it has to fit in with our tradition to some extent as well as what we want to do in the future. But the basic point is that we must give hope; not only give hope, we must do something tangible for these vast millions of poor. And we cannot do it if we leave it to big business.

Interview, New Delhi/
U.S. News & World Report, 2-15:28.

3

American perceptions have not been correct because they have been constantly trying to propagate the theory that we [India] are in the Soviet camp, which we have never been at any stage . . . the American people should have a

more realistic picture of what India is, what India stands for, what we have been trying to do and what are the tremendous obstacles and difficulties . . . I will try [to improve U.S.-India relations], whether there is a possibility of improvement or not. I believe in banging your head against the wall until some dent is made.

Interview, New Delhi, July 22/
The New York Times, 7-23:3.

4

We believe in democracy; we were brought up with those ideals. And in India, we simply cannot have another way . . . Only a democracy will allow our great diversity and allow small explosions in different parts of the country. If you have any other system and you try to stop these explosions, the steam will gather, and you will have a very large explosion, which could be a revolution.

Interview, New Delhi/Parade, 7-25:6.

5

In India, our preoccupation is with building and development. Our problem is not to influence others, but to consolidate our political and economic independence. We believe in freedom with a passion that only those who have been denied it can understand. We believe in equality, because many in our country were so long deprived of it. We believe in the worth of the human being, for that is the foundation of our democracy . . .

At ceremony welcoming her to Washington,
July 29/The New York Times, 7-30:4.

6

[On her country's relations with Pakistan] : I do not know how close they want to get. We have been anxious for friendship, not for any idealistic reason, but because it is a necessity for us. We want our neighbors to be stable and strong. Nothing is so dangerous as a weak neighbor. You just do not know what they will do.

Interview, New Delhi/Time, 8-2:33.

7

It is entirely an incorrect notion to think that here [in India] everything is nationalized or is under the government. It isn't. The private sector has by far the largest chunk [of the

230

(INDIRA GANDHI)

economy]. All agriculture is private. Everything that touches the people—like retail trade, health, education and most of industry, even big industry—all these things are in the private sector. We have only what we call the "core sector" [controlled by government] ... So in no way is the private sector getting a raw deal here. On the contrary, they have been very much pampered.

Interview, New Delhi/The
Christian Science Monitor, 9-30:13.

S. I. Hayakawa
United States Senator,
R–California

1

[On criticism of Philippine President Ferdinand Marcos' [current martial-law government]: There has been a vast increase of freedom [in the Philippines], a steadying of the political situation and a rise of the gross national product. But instead of watching the progress being made, American journalism has made a big, big thing of treating Marcos as if he is some kind of two-bit Hitler.

Before Senate Foreign Relations
Committee, Washington, Sept. 17/
Chicago Tribune, 9-18:(1)4.

James Day Hodgson
Vice chairman, U.S. chapter, Pacific
Basin Economic Council; Former
United States Ambassador to Japan

2

The now-flourishing Pacific region ... constitutes nothing less than one of the great developments in human history. A new era is indeed upon us. From now on, the words "Pacific" and "future" will be synonymous for all North Americans.

Panel discussion/The
Christian Science Monitor, 9-28:11.

Joshua B. Jeyaretnam
Leader, Worker's Party
of Singapore

3

[Criticizing Singaporan Prime Minister Lee Kuan Yew]: ... someone must say that there

are 5,000 detained people in Singapore who have not had a trial. People don't really know what is happening in Singapore. They see the clean streets and the tall buildings, and they don't know people are starving here. Eventually, people here will overthrow the government via the ballot box.

Interview, Singapore/
The New York Times, 3-13:4.

Kim Young Sam
Former leader of banned New
Democratic Party of South Korea

4

[On the restrictions placed on him by the South Korean government]: Plainly, I can give no interviews, seek out no chance to express my views on television. All they want is for me to keep my head down. I won't do that any more. My country is entering an extremely dangerous period. There's great restlessness. The government just tells lies, lies, lies about the political situation, the economy, everything. They don't trust the people ... Officially, I am a non-person; but let me tell the American people this: The first and best defense this country can have is democracy, to have the people with us.

Interview, Seoul/The New York Times, 4-16:7.

Lee Kuan Yew
Prime Minister of Singapore

5

Soviet aims [in Southeast Asia] are similar to those she has for other areas of the world of strategic importance: first to make friends, then to be the Big Brother and finally to be the arbiter. The Strait of Malacca lends this area great strategic importance. The Strait is one of the five strategic choke points of the world, besides Gibraltar, Suez, Panama and the Cape of Good Hope. They must never become "chokable" by the Soviets.

Interview, Singapore/
U.S. News & World Report, 2-8:37.

Mike Mansfield
United States
Ambassador to Japan

6

The root cause of economic friction between Japan and North America and between Japan

(MIKE MANSFIELD)

and Europe is the belief that Japan's success results in large measure from a freer and fairer access to world markets than others have to Japan's market ... This belief increases in intensity during periods of economic difficulty and large-scale imbalances ... The solution doesn't lie in protectionism—that will only harm the welfare of all of us. The solution must be found in increased opportunities for foreign access to the Japanese market ... Although both [the U.S. and Japan] are responsible for managing ourselves through the current trade friction, I must frankly say that the largest part of the decisions lie with Japan. Japan is now a mature economic power, with the obligations that accompany that status. To the rest of the world, the image of a "vulnerable" Japan is outdated ... The perceptions of the past—that Japan must limit its imports generally to raw materials, provide the highest possible level of added value in Japan and export completed manufactures—no longer have the same validity. As a mature, strong economy whose economic miracle has largely been possible because of the open international trading system, Japan must now participate fully in that system and work to strengthen it.

At Foreign Correspondents Club, Tokyo, Jan. 6/The Wall Street Journal, 1-7:22.

1

The most important bilateral relation in the world, bar none, is that between Japan and the United States ... [The Japanese] are a people who want the U.S. to succeed. If there is anyone who wishes to see the United States recover from the recession, it is the Japanese.

Interview, Tokyo/The Christian Science Monitor, 10-13:9.

Ferdinand E. Marcos
President of the Philippines

2

It is necessary that the United States now look to the Pacific as a part of its security plans, because security cannot be divided. You cannot have security in Europe without security in the Pacific. First of all, the security of the

Middle East would have to be supported from the Indian Ocean. This means that you have to protect the Pacific area. In fairness to the American planners, may I say that apparently this is what they're trying to do.

Interview, Manila/ U.S. News & World Report, 5-17:40.

3

... one must be conscious that when the economic health of a country is low, political sickness is liable to erupt. That is what would happen if at any given time the Philippines became so weak and politically unstable that the Marxists would again be able to claim they are ready to take over with the "parliament of the streets." But I think our people now have seen the effects of a leftist movement; they are aware that the leftists offer sterile slogans allegedly of salvation when, in truth, they are cruel even to their own kind.

Interview, Manila/ U.S. News & World Report, 5-17:41.

4

... a dictator is one who decides alone. Let me clarify all of this. I don't decide things alone in the Philippines. We decide this by consensus, even during martial law. There is a current belief that the military took over and I was the Commander-in-Chief, and therefore I just dictated whatever the decisions were. No. On the contrary, the military supported the decisions of the civil government. The civil government is run by a party caucus. We have a modified Presidential system, and the party in power controls the legislature.

Broadcast interview/ "Meet the Press," NBC-TV, 9-19.

5

[On the human-rights foreign policy of the U.S. during the Carter Administration, which adversely affected the Philippines because of alleged human-rights abuse there]: We have no quarrel with a policy that seeks to support human rights. In your [U.S.] financing institutions, the instructions under President Carter were either to vote against Philippine projects or to cast a neutral vote on the ground that we had violated human rights ... It's a question of

(FERDINAND E. MARCOS)

arriving at conclusions based on distorted media and embassy reports. We felt that the Philippines was entitled to more attention in the matter of really determining what was happening. These statements about torture, about alleged misuse of power and things like that insulted the Filipinos more than their leader because it was made to appear as if Filipinos would tolerate a leader who would torture his own people, who would utilize his executive prerogatives for abuses.

Interview, Manila, September/Time, 9-20:51.

Ramon H. Myers
Senior fellow, Hoover Institution, Stanford University

1

Taiwan's future can be influenced by American foreign policy. If any American Administration presses [Taiwan's] leader to confer with [mainland China's] leaders, and terminate arms sales to Taiwan, that island state will be placed in great jeopardy. Is China so important to the United States that our leaders should accede to such demands from Peking? My answer is no. For the U.S. to base its entire Asian policy upon [mainland] China's interests would be irresponsible for our Asian friends and not in our own best interests.

Before World Affairs Council, Santa Clara, Calif./Chicago Tribune, 6-17:(1)11.

Yasuhiro Nakasone
Prime Minister of Japan

2

Until now, the relationship between Japan and the U.S. has been basically very friendly and cooperative, but on trade and defense issues we have not necessarily had the fullest possible communication . . . Of course, between economic giants such as Japan and the U.S., there can always be problems. But the important issue is how to find the means for smoothly solving them. In any democratic society we need full dialogue and sincere implementation of what has been talked about, and that is what counts . . . Where we don't reach agreements, we should be able to agree to

disagree. Often the tendency of Orientals has been to be rather vague, opaque and foggy, but my style is different. I want to get rid of opaqueness and fogginess and clarify my position as much as possible. My policy is to regard the Japan-U.S. relationship as the most important relationship of all, and I want to establish a firm and very strong bond between our countries. On the basis of this strong tie we can develop our policies vis-a-vis the Communist-bloc nations or the Middle East nations or developing nations elsewhere. A strong U.S.-Japan relationship should be the basis for our diplomatic attitudes toward North-South issues, East-West issues, or whatever.

Interview, Tokyo/
The Wall Street Journal,
12-14:24.

Richard M. Nixon
Former President of the United States

3

[On U.S.-Chinese relations]: The more we develop that relationship, the better we can both achieve our objective of containing the Soviet threat. It is therefore in the strategic interest of the United States to have China strong: strong economically, strong militarily, and strong in its determination to stand firm against aggression or hegemonism.

At banquet in his honor, Peking, Sept. 7/
Los Angeles Times,
9-8:(I)15.

4

[On U.S.-Chinese relations]: There will be some huffing and puffing in certain quarters that the United States is no longer reliable and that the [Chinese] relationship should be dissolved. But the Chinese leaders aren't stupid. They know we are still the richest country in the world. They know that potentially we are the most powerful country in the world. And they know that without us they would be down the tube.

Interview, Peking, Sept. 8/
Los Angeles Times,
9-9:(I)11.

233

WHAT THEY SAID IN 1982

(RICHARD M. NIXON)

1

There's no question that the Taiwan issue has poisoned relations [between the U.S. and China] for the past two years. Some people here in the U.S. took the attitude that they could do anything they wanted with regard to Taiwan, and that forced the Chinese leaders to demonstrate that Peking can't be taken for granted, that China has other places to turn to. Let's keep that problem on the back burner and not go off on new arms sales [to Taiwan] at least so long as Peking continues down the path of "peacefully resolving" the issue. I think it will be resolved subtly. The Chinese know they need a vital, economically strong Taiwan and Hong Kong, too. Both, I think, may eventually end up in some sort of a loose federation or commonwealth with the People's Republic [China]. They don't know exactly how it will work, but it will be very clever.

Interview, New York/Time, 11-1:56.

Robert Oxnam
President, Asia Society

2

China has economic problems and problems of the spirit. But with limited resources it also feeds and provides health care to a billion people. If we can integrate the critical perceptions with an appreciation of China's considerable accomplishments, there will be a realistic basis for U.S. government, business and other dealings with the Chinese.

Newsweek, 5-24:51.

S. Rajaratnam
Second Deputy Prime Minister of Singapore

3

The theory of democracy as [political] opposition [to the government] is founded, at least as far as Singapore is concerned, on intellectual dishonesty. No opposition enters Parliament to help a government govern well ... Put bluntly, the role of an opposition is to ensure bad government.

Los Angeles Times, 7-16:(I-A)3.

234

Ronald Reagan
President of the United States

4

We are not going to abandon our long-time friends and allies on Taiwan. And I'm going to carry out the terms of the Taiwan Relations Act, and this has been made clear. We have no secret agreements of any kind [with the mainland Chinese] or anything that should cause the government of the people of Taiwan to have concern about that. It is a moral obligation that we'll keep.

*News conference, Washington, July 28/
The New York Times, 7-29:12.*

5

Building a strong and lasting relationship with China has been an important foreign-policy goal of four consecutive American Administrations. Such a relationship is vital to our long-term national-security interests and contributes to stability in East Asia. It is in the national interest of the United States that this important strategic relationship be advanced.

*Washington, Aug. 17/
The New York Times, 8-18:4.*

6

[On the Soviet invasion and occupation of Afghanistan]: The United States does not intend to forget these brave [Afghan] people and their struggle [against the Soviets]. We hope that the new leadership of the Soviet Union will take advantage of the opportunities the New Year will no doubt offer to achieve a solution for Afghanistan ... Afghanistan is important to the world because the Afghan people are resisting Soviet imperialism. Three years after the invasion, the Soviet occupation is not a success.

Washington, Dec. 26/Chicago Tribune, 12-27:(1)5.

Carlos P. Romulo
Foreign Minister of the Philippines

7

I am distressed that the West seems to be so very concerned about the Soviet military occupation of Afghanistan, but so little concerned about the Vietnamese military occupation of Cambodia. They are twin problems. Both invasions were in violation of the United Nations Charter. Furthermore, the Vietnamese invaded

(CARLOS P. ROMULO)

Cambodia with the full support of the Soviet Union, whose Pacific fleet now has the use of the great naval base that America built at Cam Ranh Bay ... If we allowed the Vietnamese invasion and occupation of Cambodia to go scot-free, it would have set a dangerous precedent. They could do the same thing to any of us.

Interview, Manila/San Francisco
Examiner & Chronicle, 4-25:(B)13.

1

[Saying the U.S. should not encourage Japan to increase its military might]: Those who ignore history tend to become its victims. I've always said the United States should be very careful about making Japan its surrogate for the defense of the Pacific ... The Japanese are a very determined people. They have brains. At the end of World War II, no one thought that Japan would become the foremost economic power in the world—but they are ... All countries see no harm if Japan has to defend itself against Communism—but do they need offensive arms? We must be careful not to encourage any aggressive designs ... Back in 1918, I told my American classmates [at Columbia University] to beware of the Japanese, and my American classmates said, "Those jokers wouldn't dare." Well, they dared, and Pearl Harbor is the witness.

Interview, Manila, Dec. 29/
Los Angeles Times, 12-30:(I)4.

Arun Shourie
Executive editor, "Indian
Express," New Delhi

2

Today, [Indian Prime Minister Indira] Gandhi maintains the illusion of government. Should something happen to her, we would have an Italian-type situation of coalition following coalition. That could lead to the urge for a man on a white horse. But until that time, press freedom will survive. Not only because of the grace of the government, but because at least a small articulate section of the country values it.

Interview/World Press Review, June:8.

Norodom Sihanouk
Exiled former Chief
of State of Cambodia

3

[On his new partnership with the Khmer Rouge against Vietnamese forces in Cambodia]: We have to choose between letting Vietnam colonize Cambodia or working with the Khmer Rouge [Communists]. The Cambodians prefer to be killed by the Khmer Rouge, because at least they are [Cambodian], than to be killed by Vietnamese and Soviets. [The Khmer Rouge] are crude, but at least they are patriotic.

News conference, Kuala Lumpur, Malaysia,
June 22/Los Angeles Times, 6-23:(I)5.

4

[On why he is now associated with the Khmer Rouge, whom he previously shunned, in trying to remove the Vietnamese occupiers from Cambodia]: In terms of humanity, the Vietnamese occupants were [originally] kinder to my people than the Khmer Rouge would have been. But now, gradually, the Vietnamese are colonizing Kampuchea [Cambodia], taking over its riches. Little by little, Kampuchea is becoming a Vietnamese province and my people are in danger of losing their very identity. The same Kampucheans, intellectuals, cadres, middle-class people, who previously had urged me never to associate with the Khmer Rouge, have recently urged me to form a coalition with all the resistance groups. Fighting the Vietnamese must be given priority over all other considerations, they say. Thus, I had to overcome my personal feelings in the interest of my country.

Interview, New York/The
Christian Science Monitor, 9-28:3.

Son Sann
Leader, Khmer People's National
Liberation Front (Cambodia)

5

It is a ridiculous situation—Pol Pot and the Khmer Rouge have lost all support of the Cambodian people, yet they are regarded [by the outside world] as the legal government. Heng Samrin and his Vietnamese masters are tolerated by the Cambodian people only

235

(SON SANN)

because they are viewed as more desirable than the murderous Khmer Rouge ... We know we cannot defeat 200,000 Vietnamese soldiers on the battlefield. But if Cambodia were allowed to have national elections supervised by the United Nations, we know the KPNLF, and not the Khmer Rouge or Heng Samrin, would be the victors.

Interview, Sroch Srang, Cambodia/
Chicago Tribune, 5-2:(1)14.

Walter J. Stoessel, Jr.
Deputy Secretary of State
of the United States
1

[Reaffirming the U.S. commitment to the defense of Taiwan in the face of Chinese criticism of that commitment] : We are hopeful we can find a solution to this problem so that we can get with the over-all efforts toward improving and strengthening the U.S.-Chinese relationship ... But I would like to reaffirm that we have very much in mind our obligation with regards to the defense of Taiwan as stated in the Taiwan Relations Act. We recognize that, we adhere to it, and we are not about to deviate from that.

Before Senate Foreign Relations
Committee, Washington, June 10/
The Washington Post, 6-11:(A)30.

Sun Yun-hsuan
Prime Minister of Taiwan
2

The Chinese Communists have attempted to use peace talks as a means of seizing Taiwan when they are unable to do so by armed force. The China problem is not a struggle for power and interest between two factions of a country but a conflict between two different systems and styles of life. The Communists' proposal for reunification is intended to make ours a "local government," and theirs the "central government." Such unification would be tantamount to selling out the future of the Chinese people. Consequently, we adhere to our position of not getting in touch or negotiating with Peking.

Interview, Taipei/The
Christian Science Monitor, 6-30:(B)6.

Zenko Suzuki
Prime Minister of Japan
3

[On U.S. desires that his country assume more of the burden of defending itself] : Japan's defense plan will be formed within the constraints of the Constitution, with the trend of public opinion in mind and in coordination with fiscal and other national policies, [not] under pressure from foreign nations.

Before Parliamentary Budget
Committee, Tokyo, April 5/
Chicago Tribune, 4-7:(1)5.

Nguyen Co Thach
Foreign Minister of Vietnam
4

[On Chinese pressure for Vietnam to leave Cambodia] : China seeks to destabilize us, by bleeding us in Kampuchea [Cambodia] through the Khmer Rouge and by threatening us with a "second lesson" on our northern border. But we have 1,000 years of experience in how to resist the Chinese. Recently, we offered China a de facto cease-fire. It has rejected it ... We have had problems with China long before the Soviet Union and even Russia existed.

Interview, New York/The
Christian Science Monitor, 9-29:3.

Malcolm Toon
Former United States Ambassador
to the Soviet Union
5

It's important for us to understand that the Soviets have a very deep—and, from their point of view, understandable—concern about China over the long term. If they felt that we [the U.S.] were developing a tight political relationship with the Chinese, with clear arms-supply overtones, I think they would be capable of doing something irrational. Therefore, our relationship with the Chinese ought to be free of any commitment on our part to supply them with arms—which the Soviets might regard as threatening to them .... we should develop a soundly based, rational relationship with China without any emotion, without any illusions about Peking's attitude toward us, and also without any blatant attempt to inject a clear anti-Soviet bias into that relationship.

Interview/U.S. News & World Report, 3-15:46.

Seiki Tozaki
President, C. Itoh & Co.,
Japan (trading house)

1

The United States and Europe are asking Japan to assume its responsibility as a member of the Western alliance. Average Americans, for example, are asking the very simple question: "With an $18-billion trade deficit with Japan, why should we assume a military burden for Japan?" To date, Japanese responses have been insufficient.

At symposium sponsored by Japanese
Federation of Economic Organizations,
Tokyo/Los Angeles Times, 5-6:(IV)2.

Caspar W. Weinberger
Secretary of Defense
of the United States

2

No one in the United States wants to see Japan become a military superpower. But Japanese forces capable of providing sea and air defense in the northwest Pacific could complement U.S. strategic and conventional forces in the area . . . The vital arteries of free commerce in the Pacific would be strongly defended. Thus Japan can, within the constraints of self-defense, contribute to her own and, indeed, to global security.

Before Japanese National Press
Club, Tokyo, March 26/The Christian
Science Monitor, 3-30:5.

Zhao Ziyang
Premier of China

3

China must never repeat the same stupidity that it once committed in pursuing excessively high growth in production to the neglect of economic results. Inflated [production] targets do us more harm than good . . . In a socialist country, efforts must be made to study in earnest the needs of society and to meet the ever-growing demands of society. Economic plans must truly reflect . . . society's demands.

At national industrial conference,
Peking, March 4/
Los Angeles Times, 3-5:(I)5.

4

As to sovereignty [over Hong Kong], of course China must regain sovereignty, but I do not think the question of sovereignty will affect Hong Kong's prosperity. If China regains sovereignty, it will certainly take a series of measures to guarantee Hong Kong's prosperity and stability . . . I don't think Hong Kong needs to be concerned about the future. What do they have to be concerned about?

To reporters, Peking, Sept. 23/
Los Angeles Times, 9-24:(I)13.

Mohammed Zia ul-Haq
President of Pakistan

5

We have a military regime in Pakistan, and this has been accepted by the people of Pakistan. We have been here in business for the last five and a half years. And if we did not have the support of the people of Pakistan, we would have been in the streets by now—because the people of Pakistan can take a lot, but they're also very volatile when they want to [be]. I do not think that a military regime—benign as it is in Pakistan—which is trying to put Pakistan's ideology on the rails, which favorably meets the people's aspirations—is in conflict with basic human rights. I think there could be no other person, or no other apparatus, more keen for human rights than the Islamic philosophy on the rights of men over men; the rights of government over the people that they govern; the rights of people over the government that they have. These are all the injunctions of Islam, which I, my colleagues, have tried to fulfill better than many of the elected governments of Pakistan. That is my concept of human rights.

Interview, Rawalpindi/The
Christian Science Monitor, 11-30:12.

6

[Criticizing the Soviet invasion and occupation of Afghanistan]: We have never laid down any preconditions for any type of [Afghan] government. We are sticking to four principles—the withdrawal of Soviet troops, return

237

WHAT THEY SAID IN 1982

(MOHAMMED ZIA UL-HAQ)

of the refugees with honor and dignity, return of the non-aligned status of Afghanistan and the right of the people of Afghanistan to select the type of government that they want. What we are very vocal about, and on which we are not prepared to compromise, is that a super-power has no right, even if it is a neighbor, to intervene with close to 100,000 troops, bring in a man [Afghan President Babrak Karmal] on its tanks and install him in a small country like Afghanistan. Aside from that, we agree in principle to the extent that the Soviet Union could even have a very pro-Soviet Afghanistan. We have no objections.

Interview/U.S. News & World Report, 12-13:41.

Europe

Yuri V. Andropov
General Secretary,
Communist Party
of the Soviet Union

1

Rallying still closer round the Party, its Leninist Central Committee and its collective leadership, the Soviet people voice their support for the policy of the Party and their boundless trust in it. The Party will continue to do everything necessary for further raising the living standards of the people, for developing the democratic mainstays of Soviet society, for strengthening the friendship of the fraternal peoples of the U.S.S.R. The CPSU Central Committee will undeviatingly translate into life the decisions of the 26th Congress of the Party and the will of the Soviet people. We shall do everything possible for further increasing cohesion of the great community of socialist states, the unity of the ranks of Communists of the whole world in the struggle for common aims and ideals. We shall guard and develop our solidarity and our cooperation with the countries that have gained freedom from colonial oppression, with the struggle of the peoples for national independence and social progress. We shall always be loyal to the cause of the struggle for peace, for the relaxation of international tension. In the complicated international situation, when the forces of imperialism are trying to push the peoples onto the road of hostility and military confrontation, the Party and the state will firmly uphold the vital interests of our homeland, and maintain great vigilance and readiness to give a crushing rebuff to any attempt at aggression. They will redouble their efforts in the struggle for the security of the peoples and strengthen cooperation with all the peace forces of the world. We are always ready for honest, equal and mutually beneficial cooperation with any state that is willing to cooperate.

At funeral of Soviet leader Leonid Brezhnev,
Moscow, Nov. 15/The New York Times, 11-16:6.

Luigi Barzini
Author, Journalist; Former
member of Italian Parliament

2

The American role at the moment is to frighten the Russians with frank remarks and vigorous explanations of future intentions. The European role is that of going to the Kremlin and telling the Russians: "Be patient. Don't do anything rash. We'll talk to the Americans." We Europeans need the Americans to make a firm, outspoken stand. And the Americans need the Europeans to go to the Kremlin and explain that things might not be as bad as they seem. To my mind, this separation of roles is proving very effective.

Interview, Rome/U.S.
News & World Report, 6-7:27.

3

Europe and the United States have a common destiny. We may love each other at times, irritate each other at times. We may differ in some points of view or lines of conduct. But we know that each must rush to the other's help when necessary, whether we like it or not. Nations are not moved by sentiment—love, fondness, enmity, hatred—but by vital interest. It is not important to discover whether we are friends or antagonists. What is important is that neither we nor the Americans could survive without the others. Incidentally, most Italians—even Communists, love, admire, imitate and envy the Americans. These feelings, however, are not the reason why Italians are among the most reliable and staunchest allies of NATO. The reason is simply that we know

239

(LUIGI BARZINI)

there's no salvation in isolation, neutrality, unilateral disarmament. There's no other choice.

Interview, Rome/U.S. News & World Report, 6-7:28.

Enrico Berlinguer
First Secretary, Communist Party of Italy

1

How many Italian workers, even among those who truly want to build a socialist society in our country and in Western Europe, aspire to a type of society and economic and political order that exists in the Soviet Union and in other countries in the East? I believe if we had a referendum, they would be in the minority.

Rome, Jan. 15/Los Angeles Times, 1-16:(I)20.

Lawrence J. Brady
Assistant Secretary of Commerce of the United States

2

[Saying the U.S. is against the planned natural-gas pipeline between the Soviet Union and Western Europe]: We are pledged to limit the direct and indirect contributions made by our resources to the Soviet military buildup, and we are pledged to substantially reduce Soviet leverage over the economies of the non-Communist world ... The West is being asked to make a huge investment in building the Soviet economy when few, if any, of the political gains from detente have materialized ... We must never forget the words of Vladimir Lenin, who prophesized that the capitalists would gladly sell the rope with which they would be hung. The Siberian pipeline represents just such a rope.

Before international trade committee of National Association of Manufacturers, San Francisco, Jan. 13/The New York Times, 1-14:4.

Leonid I. Brezhnev
President of the Soviet Union; General Secretary, Soviet Communist Party

3

[Supporting the current martial law in Poland]: It is not easy for Poland today. The waves of anarchy, chaos and terror would not roll back overnight. The imperialist powers, the United States in the first place, are increasing their pressure on Poland and in doing so trample underfoot law and morals. They would like to bring new trials and ordeals upon the heads of Poles. But let no one hope that socialism will not defend itself. It will. And with all resolution. Beyond the present complicated day, one can already see a better day coming. We helped socialist Poland the best we could and we shall continue helping it. These are not just words.

At dinner in honor of visiting Polish leader Wojciech Jaruzelski, Moscow, March 1/ The New York Times, 3-2:5.

4

[Addressing the President of Finland on relations between their two countries]: If the good fundamentals underlying our relations were more broadly applied in the world, there would be far fewer seats of tension and conflict on our planet.

At banquet for visiting Finnish President Mauno Koivisto, Moscow, March 9/ The New York Times, 3-10:4.

5

... the Soviet leadership has taken a decision to introduce, unilaterally, a moratorium on the development of medium-range nuclear armaments in the European part of the U.S.S.R. We are freezing, in both the quantitative and qualitative respects, the armaments of this kind already stationed here, and are suspending the replacement of old missiles, known as the SS-4 and SS-5, by newer SS-20 missiles. This moratorium will be in force either until an agreement is reached with the United States to reduce, on the basis of parity and equal security, the medium-range nuclear missiles designed for use in Europe, or until the time ... the U.S. leaders ... actually go over to practical preparations to deploy Pershing II missiles and cruise missiles in Europe ... If the governments of the United States and its NATO allies, in defiance of the will of the nations for peace, were actually to carry out their plan to deploy in Europe hundreds of new American missiles capable of striking targets on the territory of the Soviet Union, a different

240

(LEONID I. BREZHNEV)

strategic situation would arise in the world. There would arise a real additional threat to our country and its allies from the United States. This would compel us to take retaliatory steps that would put the other side, including the United States itself, its own territory, in an analogous position. This should not [be] forgotten.

Before Congress of Soviet
Trade Unions, Moscow, March 16/
The Washington Post, 3-17:(A)15.

Zbigniew Brzezinski
Professor of government, Columbia
University; Former Assistant to the
President of the United States
(Jimmy Carter) for National
Security Affairs   *1*

In my judgment, Soviet strategy regarding [the unrest in] Poland is based on the following three preferences: Preference Number 1 is to have Solidarity [the independent Polish trade union] and all free spirit crushed by Polish secret police. If that fails, preference Number 2 is to plunge Poland into such a catastrophe that eventual Soviet intervention is welcomed by the West—notably by West European bankers—to re-establish needed "law and order" and "prevent civil war." All else failing, the Soviets' last preference is for accommodation between the Polish [Communist] Party, the church and what still survives of Solidarity. We can try to make preference Number 3—accommodation—Moscow's first preference by increasing the costs of the present policy to the Polish Communists and to the Soviet government. We can do that by imposing sanctions, by making life more difficult for Polish Communists and Soviet authorities, and by encouraging passive resistance in Poland by offering Western moral support.

Interview/U.S. News & World Report, 1-11:17.

Arthur F. Burns
United States Ambassador
to West Germany   *2*

As yet, I see no significant change in the *Ostpolitik* being practiced in [West Germany].

And I must say there are reasons for that, which we in the United States should try to understand. Germany is a divided country. Very many German families are broken families at the present time. Nearly everyone living in West Germany has relatives or friends in East Germany. *Ostpolitik* has been helpful in making it possible for members of a family to get together with some frequency. That is one of its achievements, and this is clearly a matter of great importance to the German people. To give up *Ostpolitik* or to modify it sharply could lead to a loss of the advantages to family relationships that the Germans have been able to attain through detente.

Interview, Bonn/U.S. News &
World Report, 4-19:63.

3

[On his seminars with West German students]: They're not Communist, not anti-Americans. They have their own opinions, which I don't always agree with . . . But I have found it possible to do what people told me I couldn't. I was told these are irrational people and you couldn't reason with them. My advice is, stop blaming the Russians, stop condemning these young people in the peace movement. If you're going to criticize anyone, criticize their parents and their teachers. Look on these young people as individuals seeking truth, a better world, and help them rather than condemn them. That may just be an educator's faith, but I hold it strongly and sincerely.

Interview, Bonn/The
Washington Post, 7-22:(A)38.

Charles
Prince of Wales

4

There is no set book of rules, so to speak, as to what my job is in the scheme of things. I am heir to the throne, full stop. That's all. I could do absolutely nothing if I wanted to. I could go and play polo all over the world, I suppose . . . I can make speeches until I am blue in the face, but I believe that that's not really going to have much effect. It's the way you behave, the way you act, what things you do and how you do them, and how you are seen to be doing them

(CHARLES)

which is what ultimately is going to have an effect ... It's very interesting how if you bang your head against one bit of the wall, eventually you will dislodge a bit of the brick, or you might knock one out, and at that point you are achieving something.

Interview/The Washington Post, 8-25:(D)11.

Claude Cheysson
Foreign Minister of France
1

... we Europeans do not accept the idea of an economic war with the Soviet Union, unless, of course, new developments occur. At the point where we are now, we condemn a number of decisions taken by the Soviet Union—occupation of Afghanistan, pressure on Poland and now the piling up of armaments in Eastern Europe, which threaten Western Europe. All this we condemn. But we do not consider that it should be the reason, the justification, for an economic war. We do not think that an economic war will really have an impact on Russia, and we do not think that an economic war will serve its ultimate purpose, which is to let the Russians and their allies change progressively toward more liberty.

Interview/The Washington Post, 7-6:(A)17.

2

We Europeans and the U.S. have stopped speaking the same language. We are partners, and thus competitors. In times of recession, frictions tend to increase. Sometimes our interests collide; that is normal, even healthy; it could be managed if we consulted with each other, if we spoke the same language. But since February, 1981, the United States speaks' American only and seems to feel that it is up to itself to decide, for the allies to follow. That is not the way we view an alliance of free countries. We are not client states.

Interview, New York/The
Christian Science Monitor, 10-5:5.

Stanislaw Ciosek
Minister of Trade Union Affairs of Poland 3

[On the current economic crisis and martial law in Poland]: We need an agreement with

society at large, with conditions and understandings on both so we can go to the workers with a concrete timetable, say that after five, perhaps four, years of reduced consumption we can begin to climb back to decent standards. It sounds brutal, but it is correct and it is realistic. Martial law is no bed of roses, but we must use discipline instead of money because we have no money—it's as simple as that.

Interview, Warsaw/The
Christian Science Monitor, 6-8:9.

William P. Clark
Assistant to the President
of the United States for
National Security Affairs

4

[Supporting U.S. Reagan Administration attempts to stop construction of a natural-gas pipeline from the Soviet Union to Western Europe]: Leadership does not always mean going along, even with friends. It means doing what is right, doing what is correct. In this case, the President's defense of our pipeline decision is right, and unless there is significant progress away from oppression in Poland, the decision sticks ... How do the critics [of the U.S. position] respond to the fact that American involvement in the pipeline would be interpreted as approval of repression in Poland, an approval of the purported use of Gulag forced labor in Siberia for pipeline construction? ... At a time when Soviet troops slaughter Afghan freedom-fighters, and at a time when Soviet armament production continues unabated, it is no time to offer them a massive infusion of hard currency or ... subsidized credit so even more of their resources can be channeled to make more weapons.

Before Veterans of Foreign Wars, Los Angeles,
Aug. 16/Los Angeles Times, 8-17:(I)5.

Lord Cockfield
Secretary of Trade
of the United Kingdom

5

[Criticizing U.S. President Reagan's embargo of parts needed to construct the natural-gas pipeline from the Soviet Union to Western Europe]: The embargo in the terms in which it

(LORD COCKFIELD)

has been imposed is an attempt to interfere with existing contracts and is an unacceptable extension of American extraterritorial jurisdiction in a way which is repugnant in international law. In the absence of a mutually acceptable solution, I am determined to defend our own national interests.

Before House of Lords, London, Aug. 2/
The New York Times, 8-3:1.

Cahal Daly
Roman Catholic Bishop of
Belfast, Northern Ireland

1

[On the sectarian violence in Northern Ireland]: The paramilitaries' remedy is continued violence and continued revolution, thereby destabilizing all institutions. In Northern Ireland, they like to clad themselves in green; but they are constantly in touch with terrorists elsewhere and receive aid, indoctrination and technical advice from these international bodies. The young people who assist them don't have to understand the ideology of those who lead them. Some Irishmen in America may mouth some facile slogans about "Brits Out!" but we are not fighting for independence here. We are trying to find a peaceful political solution.

Interview, Belfast, October/
The New York Times, 10-24:(4)4.

Jacques Delors
Minister of Finance of France

2

We have some peculiar conceptual talents here in France. We start off by saying: *"Voila, reform."* Then, of course, we have to try to put it into effect. The most crowded cemetery in France is the one reserved for laws that are not applied and reforms that are not carried out.

The New York Times Magazine, 2-7:71.

Thierry de Montbrial
Director, French Institute of
International Relations

3

A psychological problem now weighs upon U.S.-European relations. Sensing that their

American ally is weakening and fearing that it will back away, Europeans can be lured into a more conciliatory stance toward the other superpower [the Soviet Union]. The U.S., irked by this attitude, threatens to let us down. That is not the reaction of a confident power seeking to reassert its role. [U.S. President] Reagan may be speaking loudly and carrying a small stick; a great American would speak softly and carry a big stick. Mr. Reagan may not be successful in restoring U.S. credibility.

Interview/World Press Review, June:26.

Gabino Diaz Merchan
President, Spanish
Episcopal Conference

4

[On the restoration of democracy in Spain embodied in the recent national election which installed the Socialist Party in control]: Spain is experiencing a renewal with what is at times the uncertainty of an adolescent taking his place in society at large. There are inflamed attitudes, and unfortunately violence and demagogy are not absent among them.

The New York Times, 10-31:(1)10.

Milovan Djilas
Author; Former Vice President
of Yugoslavia

5

I'm for abolishing all nuclear weapons, but as long as the Soviet Union has them, I think the U.S. should, too. Conventional arms are more important anyway. What would happen if the Soviet Union attacked Europe with conventional forces and at the same time warned the U.S. that it would use nuclear arms against the United States? I'm not at all sure the U.S. would come to the rescue of Europe with its own nuclear weapons. At any rate, with the [U.S.] Reagan Administration, we Yugoslavs feel more secure. If the Soviet Union intervened here, at least the U.S. would not be indifferent. [Former U.S. President] Carter would have only protested and prayed to God to save Yugoslavia.

Interview, Belgrade/The New York Times, 6-20:(4)4.

WHAT THEY SAID IN 1982

Marian Dmochowski
Deputy Foreign Minister of Poland

1

The sanctions recently introduced by the Western states against our country following the introduction of martial law here ... seem very strange to us. I would like to say that from our point of view these decisions are incomprehensible. First, because our decision to introduce martial law on 13 December [1981] is a sovereign Polish decision. It is a decision by the Polish authorities on behalf of Polish interests ... It is obvious that an attempt has been made [by the U.S.] to exploit the unstable situation in Poland to destabilize the situation in Europe. Perhaps this does not concern the whole [U.S.] Administration; perhaps it does not apply to all its governing bodies. But there surely are people and circles there—one can't overlook this here—who would go whole hog and who would exploit the situation in Poland, for instance to justify intensifying the arms race.

Polish broadcast interview, Jan. 10/
The New York Times, 1-11:9.

Lawrence S. Eagleburger
Assistant Secretary for
European Affairs, Department
of State of the United States

2

In the last analysis, what drove the Polish government ... to take the steps it took on the 13th of December 1981, [the institution of martial law to stem the independent trade-union movement] had little to do with the economic situation in Poland, and a great deal with their seeing the [Communist] Party losing all authority, Solidarity [the independent union] becoming a major popular force in Poland, and the possibility of a major change of the whole political structure in Poland ... Money, I don't care how much, would not have changed the fact that reform was going on in Poland.

Broadcast interview/"Newsmaker
Sunday," Cable News Network, 1-2.

3

[On the forthcoming NATO summit meeting during which Spain will be inducted as a member]: We [in NATO] stand for things no one else in this world stands for. The fact that these [15] guys [and a woman] are getting together in itself constitutes a very effective piece of political theatre. It is a point not lost on our adversaries. [There is] an eloquent contrast between the way the West does business and the manner in which the Communist bloc operates. How many countries are vying to join the Warsaw Pact? There will be a strong recognition that NATO is not a marriage of shared convenience but an alliance of democratic values.

To reporters/Los Angeles
Herald Examiner, 5-30:(A)6.

4

[Criticizing a bill that would limit U.S. military strength in Europe]: Passage of this legislation would be a fundamental departure from the historical bipartisan post-war U.S. approach to national security. Never has the American role in the defense of Europe been reduced through legislation. Never has the U.S. backed away from its NATO commitments. And never have the elected representatives of the American people voted not to stand by our allies and back up our defense commitments. Are we really ready now to take such a fateful step? Do we really want to greet the new Soviet leadership with a sharp deviation from the policies that have so successfully preserved Western security and American leadership in Europe? ... Proponents of this legislation may claim that our doing less would jolt our allies into doing more. I see no basis for such wishful thinking. U.S. cuts would have the opposite effect. If we do less, the Europeans will do less, and we will be less secure.

Before Senate Foreign Relations
Committee, Washington, Nov. 30/
The Washington Post, 12-1:(A)12.

Bulent Ecevit
Former Prime Minister of Turkey

5

[Criticizing martial-law conditions in his country]: In order to really defeat terrorism we must defend democracy and we must be committed to democracy, because the goal of

(BULENT ECEVIT)

terrorism is to eliminate democracy and alienate the people from democracy. Other countries in the world, like Spain and Italy, defend democracy despite terrorism.

At his trial for defying martial law,
Ankara, April 29/Los Angeles Times, 4-30:(I)5.

Murray Feshbach
Senior research scholar, Kennedy
Institute of Ethics; Professional
lecturer, department of demography,
Georgetown University

1

... 75 per cent of industrial output in the Soviet Union is concentrated in the north, primarily in the Russian Republic, where the working-age population is declining. The areas in the south where the working-age population is growing sharply are relatively undeveloped. That means enormous deformations of capital and labor. The Soviets either must devote enormous capital resources to develop the south or move labor to the industrial areas in the north, which would require a great increase in capital expenditure on housing in that area. Remember: The country's resources already are strained. From the viewpoint of Soviet planners, things are out of whack.

Interview/U.S. News & World Report, 12-6:28.

Vigdis Finnbogadottir
President of Iceland

2

[In Iceland,] intellectuals and those who do not have education are not as close to each other as they were before. The difference is that, before, everybody participated in the Icelandic heritage. But now we have a class distinction that has nothing to do with money, but that has to do with an awareness of identity. I hope that we will not lose our identity, but we have been drifting into a society of consumers, living with more material things than we need.

Interview, Reykjavik, Iceland/
The New York Times, 4-4:(1)3.

Michael Foot
Leader, British Labor Party

3

[Criticizing Prime Minister Margaret Thatcher for wanting to put more state-run industries under private ownership] : Your government was elected on a lie and is sustained by a lie, and our business is to tell the truth to the nation ... The Prime Minister and the government never seem to look on public enterprise and public industry as industries which could be used to try to deal with the over-riding unemployment problem. They just look on them as places to plunder.

In House of Commons, London, Nov. 3/
The New York Times, 11-4:3.

Hans-Dietrich Genscher
Foreign Minister of West Germany

4

... the peoples of Eastern Europe realize to an increasing extent that the very low standard of living they have to endure is due to two reasons. These are, first, to a wrong economic order that has been imposed on them by Moscow; and second, on excessive military costs that have also been imposed on Eastern Europe. And these underscore the need for disarmament. This, I feel, is going to be the central issue for many years to come, namely, whether the Soviets will be able to react adequately and inflexibly to this basic movement which is gaining momentum everywhere, and also in Eastern Europe—an urge and desire, a striving and yearning for more independence, for more self-determination, for more freedom.

To reporters, Washington/
The New York Times, 3-10:27.

5

[Saying installation of new NATO nuclear missiles in West Germany should go ahead] : Nothing should obscure the simple realization that we are not threatened by Western medium-range missiles that do not exist, but we are threatened by Soviet SS-20 missiles that already are aimed at us ... Here in Berlin, it is clear how incorrect are those who would have us believe that we must keep an equal distance between the United States and the Soviet Union. Here, one knows that American troops

(HANS-DIETRICH GENSCHER)

stand by us so that free trade unions can exist, and Soviet troops stand in Poland so that, there, no free trade unions can exist.

Before Free Democratic Party, West Berlin, Nov. 5/The Washington Post,.11-6:(A)19.

Jozef Cardinal Glemp
Roman Catholic Primate of Poland

1

[Criticizing the martial law in his country]: We want to help each other, but still we do not see a plan of action, an initiative [by the authorities] that would be and could be accepted by all. We still see a lack of something there; we hear too much about people's sufferings, we hear about more arrests, and there are such a lot of internees who wait to be released to rejoin work, activity and mutual aid. Not only those interned, but also many other groups of people suffer because they must or are persuaded to sign declarations that are contrary to their views and their conscience, and, what is more, these people are fired from their jobs. If we want cooperation in our country, we need dialogue. It is not enough to threaten people, to fire them from jobs, but it is necessary to talk to the people . . .

Sermon, Warsaw, Jan. 17/ The Washington Post, 1-18:(A)13.

Felipe Gonzalez
General secretary, Socialist Workers Party of Spain

2

[On the possibility of a military coup if the Socialists win control of Spain in the forthcoming election]: The armed forces, like everyone else, wants a government that's capable of governing. I don't believe a Socialist administration would cause a new coup. Democracy is consolidated by the alternation of power.

Television broadcast, Madrid/The Christian Science Monitor, 10-21:12.

Felipe Gonzalez
Prime Minister of Spain

3

[On the British colony of Gibraltar which Spain claims is her own territory]: Spain's

246

armed forces have the Constitutional duty to defend our territorial integrity without subordination to any outside forces. The case of Gibraltar is especially painful. It's impossible for us to accept that Spain's armed forces be dependent for the defense of this territory on a force that is, in our opinion and according to the United Nations, occupying part of our territory.

Interview, Madrid, Dec. 13/ The New York Times, 12-14:4.

Alexander M. Haig, Jr.
Secretary of State of the United States

4

[On the current martial law and trade-union suppression in Poland]: Some claim Poland is an aberration. They say we should leave it alone; it's in the sphere of post-Yalta agreements; we will forget it as quickly as Hungary and Czechoslovakia were forgotten. How comforting such justifications must be to some. But it cannot be a comfort to Americans to forget the principles of detente and the Helsinki [human-rights] accords. If that concept was a sham, we in the West have bought a very sour bill of goods.

San Francisco/The Washington Post, 1-3:(A)12.

5

[On the current martial law and suppression of the Solidarity free trade union in Poland]: Soviet responsibility for present events is clear. A Western failure to act would not only assist the repression of the Polish people but also diminish confidence about our reactions to future events in Poland and elsewhere . . . The Soviets must know that there can be negative or positive consequences [to their actions], depending on their conduct. Poland is a test case and European history teaches that the greatest mistake in dealing with heavily armed aggressors is to ignore their violations of international agreements and to act as though nothing has happened . . . Beyond the fate of Poland, beyond East-West relations, we must ultimately ask ourselves what these developments mean for our self-respect if we do not respond together. The West is often accused of being merely a collection of consumer societies.

(ALEXANDER M. HAIG, JR.)

Are we so sated or intimidated that we fear to defend the values that make life worth living?

At International Press Center, Brussels,
Jan. 12/The New York Times, 1-13:5.

1

Linking together strategic and conventional forces are theatre nuclear forces, that is, NATO's nuclear systems based in Europe. These systems are concrete evidence of the nature of the American commitment [to Europe]. They're a concrete manifestation of NATO's willingness to resort to nuclear weapons, if necessary, to preserve the freedom and independence of its members. Further, the presence of nuclear weapons in Europe insures the Soviet Union will never believe that it can divide the U.S. from its allies or wage a limited war with limited risks against any NATO member ... Twice in this century, America has been unable to remain aloof from European conflict but able to intervene in time to prevent the devastation of Western Europe. Neither we nor our allies can afford to see this pattern repeated a third time. We have, therefore, chosen a strategy which engages American power in the defense of Europe and gives substance to the principle that the security of the alliance is indivisible.

Before Georgetown University's Center
for Strategic and International Studies,
April 6/The New York Times, 4-7:6.

Ralph Harris
General director, Institute
of Economic Affairs, London

2

The perverse British combination is of high taxation on low earnings together with an array of social benefits that are high in relation to average earnings, especially for families with children. The result of this tax-benefit mangle is that the incentive for many unemployed to work, or for workers to earn more, is reduced or even obliterated. Thus a man with a wife and two children can, without working, receive from welfare benefits over 70 per cent of average manual wages after tax. If he has four

children, this proportion ... goes up to 94 per cent. For a family man earning two-thirds of average wages, the welfare bait is 90 per cent—two children—and 99 per cent—four children—of what would be his net take-home pay. How many people would welcome working eight hours a day, five days a week, for an income only 1 per cent, 10 per cent, or even 30 per cent higher than social benefits, which leave him 100 per cent leisure with the choice of cash earnings in the underground economy?

Before Mont Pelerin Society, Berlin/
The Wall Street Journal, 10-7:28.

Charles J. Haughey
Prime Minister of Ireland

3

[On Northern Ireland]: We look forward to, and will actively seek to bring closer, the day when the rights of self-determination of all the people of Ireland will again be exercised in common, and when the final withdrawal of the British military and political presence takes place.

The Christian Science Monitor, 3-15:6.

4

[On the possible reunification of Northern Ireland with Ireland]: Let me emphasize that violence, evil in itself and appalling in its consequences, can only postpone the day of Irish unity. Far from advancing, it will further delay a final British military and political withdrawal from [Northern] Ireland. Violence and the bitterness it involves only frustrate the ultimate achievement of national unity. Nobody in America should support or subscribe to policies which envisage violence and terror as the means of bringing about the unity of Ireland.

Before Irish-American leaders, New York,
June 10/The New York Times, 6-11:9.

Denis Healey
Deputy leader, British Labor Party

5

[Criticizing U.S. President Reagan's intention of imposing sanctions on British firms which supply American-licensed equipment for construction of the natural-gas pipeline between the Soviet Union and Western

(DENIS HEALEY)

Europe] : This is the sort of issue on which the European countries should stand firm and show this very muddled Reagan Administration that there are certain things we stand for and clear things we won't put up with.

Aug. 31/The Washington Post, 9-1:(A)16.

Geoffrey Howe
Chancellor of the Exchequer
of the United Kingdom

1

[On the Thatcher Administration's 1982-83 budget] : [It is] a budget for industry and, so, a budget for jobs ... a budget for people ... a budget that will strengthen the foundations of economic recovery. This is a budget that will give confidence at home that growing markets will be there for those prepared to go out and win them ... and confidence abroad that Britain stays on course to put a dismal record of performance behind us once and for all.

Before Parliament, London, March 9/
Los Angeles Times, 3-10:(I)4.

Wojciech Jaruzelski
Prime Minister of Poland; First
Secretary, Polish Communist Party

2

[On the martial law in his country instituted as a response to labor unrest] : I don't intend to claim that a better era began on December 13 [1981, when martial law was declared]. We are far away from it. Martial law has only created a chance that ought to be used in every respect. It is a kind of bridge that makes it possible to get through a critical period. The question is often asked when martial law will be lifted. My answer is: May it be lifted as soon as possible. But the duration of martial law is not dependent simply on our intentions. It is dependent on realistic conditions, on the fulfillment of conditions that would secure a permanent, safe and normal course of life, the smooth functioning of the economy. The calendar must not decide the future of our country, and above all no external pressure whatsoever must decide it.

Before Parliament, Warsaw, Jan. 25/
The New York Times, 1-26:4.

3

Poland is living through days of trial. Last year, the forces of counter-revolution backed by imperialist centers brought the country into a state of anarchy, dealing telling blows on the economy, aggravated every-day difficulties in the life of society, created a threat to the mainstays of Polish socialist statehood ... Our situation is also being significantly complicated by the economic sanctions introduced by the American Administration as well as—under its pressure—by the governments of some other capitalist countries. Against this backdrop, becoming even more evident is the tremendous importance of the irreplaceable internationalist assistance that is being given to us by the U.S.S.R. .... Poland will not abandon the road of socialism. It will not be its weak link.

At dinner, in his honor, Moscow,
March 1/The New York Times, 3-2:5.

4

The suspension of martial law means that its basic rigors will cease to function before the end of this year. Only such regulations should be binding, either in full or limited dimension, which directly protect the basic interests of the state, create the shield for the economy and strengthen the personal security of citizens. Not a single limitation more than absolutely necessary should be kept up, nor a single less ... I do not make any promises. But I do promise one thing: Anarchy will not be allowed into Poland. Let no one in Poland or outside cherish any illusions that the present decisions will allow for another round ... We have survived the [foreign] boycott, restrictions and the barrage of instigatory propaganda. The government of the United States and some of its customers can see for themselves the bankruptcy of attempts to interfere in Polish internal affairs.

Broadcast address to the nation, Warsaw,
Dec. 12/The New York Times, 12-13:6.

Michel Jobert
Minister of Foreign Trade of France

5

The United States must calculate the stakes of its policy, which consist primarily of having world-wide responsibilities and, secondly, of

(MICHEL JOBERT)

responsibilities which concern only itself, which some call selfish ... It has been said 1,001 times in past years: "Careful, don't upset the Americans because you risk them abandoning us [Europeans]." If it's in their interest to abandon us, then even if we are nice and complacent, they will leave. But I don't think it's in their interest to leave, and therefore we should incorporate that idea in our own reasoning. It's in their best interest to follow the most equitable route with Europe.

Interview/Los Angeles Times, 7-1:(IV)2.

John Paul II
Pope

1

[On the imposition last year of martial law in Poland]: Societies all over the world, particularly the nations of Europe and America, continue to demonstrate concern because of the situation in Poland in relation to the proclamation of martial law. Under the threat of losing their jobs, [Polish] citizens are forced to sign declarations that don't agree with their conscience and their convictions ... It is the most painful blow inflicted to human dignity. In a certain sense, it is worse than inflicting physical death, of killing.

Vatican City, Jan. 10/
The New York Times, 1-11:6.

2

[On martial law in Poland]: In Rome and outside Rome, I have intensely lived through the particularly difficult events which have affected my country, in particular the most recent ones. I have said this to state authorities in Poland, as well as to the leaders of other countries—that the rights of nations must be respected. This is a heritage of many years. We did not learn this from the United Nations declarations after World War II. We learned this centuries ago.

To Poles, Lagos, Nigeria, Feb. 16/
Chicago Tribune, 2-17:(1)5.

Harold K. Johnson
General (Ret.) and former Chief
of Staff, United States Army

3

NATO is still doing the job it was created to do. It was established to maintain peace in Western Europe, and it has done that for 35 years or so. There have been no overt hostilities involving Western Europe. There was a second purpose for establishing this alliance which is not talked about much in this country. It was designed to be a mechanism to keep Germany under some restraint and control. When the West Germans were allowed to rearm, they agreed that their forces would serve under NATO command. This was intended to allay fears of what a rearmed Germany might do unilaterally. This is very important to the people of the Low Countries and in Britain, who still are deeply distrustful of Germany. NATO still is essential for this purpose.

Interview/U.S. News & World Report, 1-18:25.

Juan Carlos
King of Spain

4

We were not mistaken when we chose liberty and justice as aims to build a pluralistic society and a single Spain. We were not mistaken when we decided to follow with the fullest collective responsibility the same path as the free nations of the West.

At Saragossa Military Academy, Feb. 20/
The Washington Post, 2-21:(A)20.

George F. Kennan
Former United States Ambassador
to the Soviet Union

5

I don't think there has ever been any evidence of any reason that the Soviet regime would have to launch World War III. As far as Europe is concerned, they bit off—when they accepted what you might call major political-military responsibility for all of Eastern Europe and a part of Central Europe in 1945—they bit off something that they would never be able to chew entirely. To my mind, this Soviet hegemony over this part of the world is not a permanently feasible arrangement. It has got to disappear sooner or later. They don't want to

(GEORGE F. KENNAN)

increase that problem by taking responsibility, similarly, for other countries in Western Europe. They would never be able to do it. I mean, if you let them try to occupy Western Europe today, they wouldn't be able to do it. Look what's happening in Poland. There are limits to the capabilities of great countries for ruling other countries, and the farther away these countries are, the greater the limits; and also, the higher the civilization level of those countries, the more difficult it would be to occupy and to run them.

Broadcast interview/
"Meet the Press,"
NBC-TV, 1-3.

1

[On the recent unrest in Poland and the imposition of martial law]: To me, one of the most significant things that has happened and perhaps *the* most significant is the very fact that, despite all that has occurred in Poland in the last year and one-half, the Soviet Union has not intervened actively with its own forces. This seems to me to represent a considerable change from earlier decades and to indicate that the Soviet leadership has to recognize that a new situation exists in Eastern Europe, not just in Poland, but in Eastern Europe generally, which will have to be taken into account and will have to be respected in Soviet policy. In connection with that, and of great importance to my mind also, is the fact that they have accepted, whether willingly or otherwise, for the first time, the leadership in a member state of the Communist bloc of a man [Prime Minister Wojciech Jaruzelski] who is appearing not primarily as a Party official, although he belongs to the Party, but is appearing really as the head of an army and a police establishment. These two things seem to me to be highly significant, and they mark important changes in Soviet policy.

Panel discussion,
Washington/
The New York Times,
2-14:(4)5.

Lane Kirkland
President, American Federation
of Labor-Congress of Industrial
Organizations

2

[Calling for an end to Western economic credits and other support for Eastern bloc countries]: It's the only way that I know of to stop this constant financing of the Eastern bloc, the financing of the buildup of military power and the enforcement of police-state measures. We're financing it as it stands now. Western banks are pouring credits into Eastern Europe at favorable rates of interest ... [If these measures force Eastern countries to default on their loans from Western banks,] if it hurts us now, all the more reason to do it before it hurts us even more in the future. We've put ourselves in the position where, virtually, they [the Eastern bloc] own us in terms of the banking connection. If we're going to sell them the rope with which they're going to hang us, at least we ought to make them pay cash for it.

Broadcast interview/
"Face the Nation," CBS-TV, 10-10.

Henry A. Kissinger
Former Secretary of State
of the United States

3

[On policy disagreements between the U.S. and its European NATO partners]: I don't think there is any question but that the alliance is in deep difficulty, and we do not do ourselves a favor [by pretending things are not so bad] ... How much diversity can we stand? ... If it leads to paralysis and inaction, then the alliance will gradually disintegrate because it will not be relevant to most of the issues that arise ... The long-term survival of the West depends on whether we can use the few years of margin we still have to develop a policy and strategy related to our period. [The West can] let things drift and paper over crises ... but that cannot go on forever. Something will happen somewhere along the line.

At meeting sponsored by Committee
for the Free World, Washington, Jan. 24/
The Washington Post, 1-25:(A)3.

(HENRY A. KISSINGER)

1

[On President Reagan's sanctions against Western European companies that contribute to the construction of a natural-gas pipeline from the Soviet Union to Western Europe]: I do not think that the timing and the tactics of the American decision on the pipeline will go down in history as classic examples of modern diplomacy. I do believe, however, that the questions raised by the President's pipeline decision were important. And I cannot endorse the self-righteous confrontational reaction of so many of our [European] allies who hide behind allegations that they were simply carrying out obligations, and make debating points that since *we* were selling grain [to the Soviets] they had a right to sell the pipeline. Everybody knows that if we stopped selling grain tomorrow the pipeline would still go forward. The question raised by [President Reagan] was fundamental. Incidentally, I am not a wild supporter of the grain sales, either.

At Georgetown University Center
for Strategic and International Studies/
The Christian Science Monitor, 10-13: 22.

Helmut Kohl
Chancellor of West Germany

2

The Americans are our most important partners and allies—to put it simply. Without the umbrella and protection of the United States, we wouldn't have the Federal Republic [of West Germany] as it is today. That means friendship and partnership, not dependency.

News conference, Bonn, Oct. 4/
The New York Times, 10-5:1.

3

[On his and his party's recent assumption of power]: The question for the future is not how much more the state can do for its citizens. The question for the future is how can freedom, dynamism and self-reliance blossom anew. It is upon this idea that this coalition of the middle is founded.

Before Parliament, Bonn, Oct. 13/
The New York Times, 10-14:5.

4

[On Poland's banning the Solidarity independent trade union]: The ban on the independent trade union Solidarity is not only a breach of promises made by the Polish government, not only a violation of the Helsinki [human-rights accord] Final Act, but also a cold surprise strike against the Polish people.

Before Parliament, Bonn, Oct. 13/
The Washington Post,
10-14:(A)27.

5

I believe that in the course of the past few years European-American relations have been defined too much in a military way. Of course it is important to talk about missiles. It is also important to count arms. However, NATO is in the first place a community of ideas, not a community of arms. As a matter of fact, the community of arms is there to defend the community of ideas. The important point is that we have common ideas regarding human rights, civil rights, our moral values, our moral laws. These have to be defended by the alliance. Hence it is vital that these common ideas be stressed again, in particular with a view to the younger generation.

Interview, Bonn, November/Time, 11-15:54.

6

[On the natural-gas pipeline now being constructed between the Soviet Union and Western Europe]: I find myself in a rather strange position [on the pro or con of the pipeline]. I haven't invented that deal nor have I ever been a fan supporting that thing. And again and again I asked our American friends and those to whom I had an opportunity to talk, what is your position, how do you see it? And for a long time the answer was yes and no, yes but! It was not clear. And now I am Chancellor. And what I found were treaties, contracts that have been concluded. And I want to pursue a policy which is serious. At any time a serious policy must be a calculable policy. We, the Germans, must be politicians whose actions are calculable. And our word must be valid. This must seem so in Washington and in Moscow. And that is why I am all in favor of

(HELMUT KOHL)

keeping [the pipeline] contracts that have been concluded and to honor them.

Interview, Bonn, Nov. 9/
The New York Times, 11-11:6.

1

...the majority of the Germans have not given up the idea of German reunification. I'm making this point because for years I have been ridiculed because I have been the only one who reminded of that point. Even in American newspapers you could read that this was evidence of my provincial background. On the other hand, do not forget that I'm living amidst the country, amidst the people, not above them. No nation would voluntarily give up its identity. But the great majority of the Germans know that there will be no way back to the national state created by Bismarck. Our opportunity as a nation lies under a European roof.

Interview, Bonn, Nov. 9/
The New York Times, 11-11:6.

Robert Komer
Former Under Secretary for Policy,
Department of Defense
of the United States

2

...if U.S. forces are pulled out of Europe, the world balance of power could tilt decisively against America in favor of the Soviet Union. Western Europe is the greatest prize in the East-West struggle. It has the greatest concentration of economic, technological and industrial power on earth. Its gross national product is greater than ours and far greater than Russia's. That economic strength, added to what Russia already has, would transform the Soviet Union into a *super* superpower. So we have no alternative to keeping Western Europe from falling under Soviet political or military domination... The critical question boils down to this: Is Western Europe still a vital interest of ours? If it is, the U.S. must help defend it. It's difficult to envision credible deterrence or defense against Soviet aggression without adequate U.S. forces on the ground in Europe.

Interview/U.S. News & World Report, 2-1:17.

Frederick J. Kroesen
General, and Commander-in-Chief/
Europe, United States Army

3

I would not like to see the American forces in Europe reduced in size from what we now have... we have an adequate combat force over here for us to initiate the combat operations that would provide the American contribution to the defense of NATO Europe. If we reduce it further, we reduce the capability of the Army to sustain itself long enough for reinforcements to get over here. We would run the risk that the soldiers already here would be expended rather than sustained as a fighting force, and I don't believe anyone thinks we should be [in Europe] to conduct another Bataan defense or a Dunkirk evacuation.

Interview/U.S. News & World Report, 8-9:24.

Spyros Kyprianou
President of Cyprus

4

[On Turkey's 1974 invasion of his country and its continuing occupation of much of it]: The aggression of Turkey against Cyprus is not only a present-day violation of sovereignty and territory integrity; it is also a sacrilegious trespass on one of the oldest recorded histories of the world.

At United Nations, New York, Oct. 7/
The New York Times, 10-8:4.

Otto Lambsdorff
Minister of Economics
of West Germany

5

[On U.S. President Reagan's plans for sanctions against West European companies that use U.S.-licensed technology to help build the natural-gas pipeline from the Soviet Union to Western Europe]: We are moving in a dangerous trend, from one sanction and one embargo to another. It goes on and on, and where do we end up? We end up with our system of open trade [in jeopardy] ... I can't remember when Europeans paid as much attention to any issue as they have to the pipeline. I see it as a politically dangerous situation, the way [the U.S. and Europe] are shouting at each other ... The only thing I'm sure of is what

(OTTO LAMBSDORFF)

everybody in Europe is sure of, and that is that the pipeline will be built ... I am not a betting man, but I am willing to bet that the Russians will supply gas to us on the very first day they promised. You see, the Russians are saying, "We'll show the U.S.!" So in the long run, the pipeline will be built, and the Soviet Union will have made themselves substantially more independent in the field of technology ... I can tell you that German companies are thinking through their relations with American companies. It worries me, but what they are saying is, "If we can't rely on American companies, we'd better become self-sufficient."

*To reporters, Washington, July 20/
The Washington Post, 7-21:(A)16.*

Clare Boothe Luce
*Member, President's Foreign
Intelligence Advisory Board; Former
American diplomat and playwright*

1

. . the Russians only have another five or six years to make it. After that, they may crumble. So we may be in the most dangerous decade since 1776. The U.S.S.R., you'll recall, is only 49 per cent Russian. And the other 51 per cent is beginning to feel its desire for rising.

*Interview, Washington/
The Washington Post, 4-9:(D)2.*

Charles McC. Mathias, Jr.
United States Senator, R–Maryland

2

[Criticizing U.S. Reagan Administration attempts to block construction of a natural-gas pipeline from the Soviet Union to Western Europe]: With all of the tremendous problems we've got with Europe, we should not be aggravating them by a policy that is destined to create a collision. What is being overlooked here is that this pipeline project is important to the Europeans as well as the Soviets.

The New York Times, 7-24:5.

Robert S. McNamara
*Former Secretary of Defense
of the United States*

3

The Russians are people that I would not trust to act other than in their own narrow national interest, so I am not naive. But they are not mad. They are not mad. They have suffered casualties, and their government feels responsible to their people to avoid those situations in the future. They are more sensitive to the impact of casualties on their people than we appear to be in some of our statements and analyses of fighting and winning nuclear wars which would extend over a period of months. So they are not mad. They are aggressive; they are ideological; they need to be restrained and contained by the existence of our defensive forces. But they are not mad, and I see no evidence that they would accept the risks associated with a first [nuclear] strike against the United States.

Interview/The Washington Post, 8-1:(B)3.

Milos Minic
*Former Foreign Minister
of Yugoslavia*

4

Yugoslavia stands neither with East nor West. It forms its own attitudes and judges the performance of each bloc on its merits. We have friendly relations with the United States ... but on individual questions we cannot keep silent, or approve acts of which we disapprove ... [As to] our second big friend, the Soviet Union: How can we agree with its intervention in Afghanistan?

The Christian Science Monitor, 6-29:6.

Francois Mitterrand
President of France

5

I must express *all* the desire of the nation. Ah!—this diversity, this pluralism, how I hold it dear! How I wish that France, in its depth, shall remain diverse and contrary, but not contradictory. How I love those who challenge me, when I find with them the common language of those who want to serve and love France.

*Figeac, France/The
New York Times, 10-3:(4)3.*

253

WHAT THEY SAID IN 1982

Paul H. Nitze
*United States negotiator
at strategic-arms limitation
talks with the Soviet Union;
Former Deputy Secretary of
Defense of the United States*

1

The Soviet, in addition to wishing to arrive at an [arms] agreement which substantially favors their side, have given every indication that they propose to use the issues involved in the negotiations to foster what some of them call "individualism" in NATO. They would like to see the natural tensions between European NATO and the United States grow deeper. They would like to see the natural tendencies for friction between the Continental European members of NATO and England come to the fore again. They would welcome a resumption of the historic rivalry between Germany and France and of the tendencies toward neutralism in the low countries and the Scandinavian countries to the north. But more importantly, they seek to exploit the tensions between the leading political parties in those countries and, indeed, between the moderate and more extreme wings within those parties.

The New York Times, 1-10:(4)25.

John Nott
*Minister of Defense
of the United Kingdom*

2

[On his country's decision to add the U.S.-designed Trident II missile submarine to its arsenal]: Trident expenditure over the next 15 years is a far smaller amount than our planned expenditure on equipment for our major conventional capabilities, such as anti-submarine warfare or offensive air operations. For about 3 per cent of the defense budget, we will be modernizing the British independent nuclear force that successive governments have considered to be essential for our national security over the past 30 years. To choose a system lacking in credibility to an aggressor—or still more, to abandon unilaterally a [nuclear] credibility we have now maintained for three decades—would be a futile gesture that would

254

serve to increase rather than diminish the risk of war. *Before Parliament, London, March 11/
Los Angeles Times, 3-12:(I)8.*

3

Our splendid success in the South Atlantic [the British military victory over Argentina in the war for the Falkland Islands] must not obscure the fact that the main threat to the United Kingdom is from the nuclear and conventional forces of the Soviet Union and her allies ... The speed with which we were able to dispatch a large and powerful task force to the South Atlantic [is a tribute to the British armed forces]. It is also visible evidence that our force structure is adaptable enough to permit an effective and timely response to developments outside the NATO area. But the next challenge to British interest may come elsewhere; it may require a different mix of forces.

*To reporters, London, June 22/
The New York Times, 6-23:3.*

Lionel H. Olmer
*Under Secretary for International
Trade Administration, Department
of Commerce of the United States*

4

[Supporting U.S. sanctions against European companies that supply U.S.-licensed equipment for construction of the natural-gas pipeline from the Soviet Union to Western Europe]: ... the reliability of the United States [as a commercial supplier] should also be viewed in the context of its responsibilities as a leader of the free world—its reliability as a strong national-security leader. The President's [Reagan] policy [against the pipeline] was clearly enunciated and to do other than fulfill the intent of that policy would have caused serious undermining of our reputation for reliability .... we are not telling [the European companies] to violate any law [of their own country]. We have certain laws and regulations which we believe they had an obligation to fulfill at the time they entered into contract with United States firms, that there were understandings of the limitations on the technology they purchased, and that those understandings should have enabled them to take prudent steps to avoid violating those sanctions.

*Interview, Aug. 27/
The New York Times, 8-29:(4)3.*

Olof Palme
Prime Minister-elect, and former
Prime Minister, of Sweden

1

[On his plan to use revenues from payroll and excess-profit taxes to buy shares in Swedish industry on behalf of workers]: It's a basic problem in advanced industrialized societies: How do you generate capital? You can nationalize outright and put tax money in, but that has always struck me as a conservative, old-fashioned method. You can increase profits, which is fine, but not if they all go to a few people and into bank accounts in Switzerland and Liechtenstein. This [new plan] is a reasonable way of tackling the problem, which will help to increase productive saving and to redistribute wealth. By the 1990s, I imagine the funds owning 10 to 15 per cent of industry, which does not seem excessive to me.

Interview, Stockholm, Sept. 20/
The New York Times, 9-21:3.

Andreas Papandreou
Prime Minister of Greece

2

[On the problem of Cyprus, which was divided into Greek and Turkish sectors following the 1974 Turkish invasion]: The Cyprus struggle is my struggle, too. It is said that the Cyprus problem has been forgotten by the majority of the [mainland] Greeks, but this is not true. We have started a crusade for Cyprus and shall continue it to internationalize the problem.

Larnaca, Cyprus, Feb. 27/
The Washington Post, 2-28:(A)16.

3

I don't believe socialism must be forcibly applied from above. That requires the dictatorship of the party and inhibits freedom ... I believe in a mixed economy, as long as it is compatible with personal liberty.

The New York Times Magazine, 3-21:80.

Sandro Pertini
President of Italy

4

Italian terrorism has not been defeated yet, notwithstanding the serious defeats which Italian terrorism is suffering. The terrorist hideouts which have been discovered are very important, as are the weapons which have been found. But for me, the indication that Italian terrorism is about to be defeated is another. The reason is this: The terrorists are talking. Before, they didn't. Terrorists are now talking. From what I have been told, over 300 jailed terrorists are talking. If these terrorists are talking, it means first of all that they are not guided by any true political belief. Second, it indicates that they are feeling the ground eroded out from under their feet ... If they are talking, it's because they are all puppets. They are in the hands of some puppeteer who would want to blow up this democratic bridge, which is Italy. He is not yet defeated, but we're on the right road.

At Johns Hopkins University School
of Advanced International Studies/
The New York Times, 4-3:19.

Richard Pipes
Director, East European and
Soviet Affairs, National Security
Council of the United States

5

Many Americans are wrong in thinking that the Soviet government is in the hands of relatively moderate men and that if we are not accommodating to them, we will strengthen the dreadful hawks waiting in the wings. I believe the contrary. The current leadership is dominated by parochial old Stalinists. What can be worse than that? The next generation will certainly be less parochial, and it will be post-Stalinist. The people who now run the Soviet Union are really very hawkish, and the alternative to them is not a still more hawkish group, but rather a group that is more reform-minded. These are dedicated, intelligent Russian nationalists who believe that a policy of hostility to the U.S. and confrontation abroad may have become counter-productive; they worry whether the Soviet economy can support such egregious imperialism. I think it is worth a gamble to support those latter elements, because every meaningful reform entails a certain degree of democratization, which would be good for the Soviet people as well as the rest of the world.

Interview/Time, 3-1:16.

Norman Podhoretz
Editor, "Commentary" magazine   *1*

Many of us who thought that a resurgence of American power and resolve would stiffen the European spine are now beginning to think we were wrong. We have begun to wonder how much longer the United States can go begging other people to allow it to defend them.

At meeting sponsored by Committee
for the Free World, Washington, Jan. 24/
The Washington Post, 1-25:(A)3.

James Prior
British Secretary of State
for Northern Ireland
                                                    2

What I'm trying to do is at least make it possible for the people of Northern Ireland to take some steps toward solving their own problems. If they don't wish for it, well then, we have to continue with direct [British] rule. What we're heading for, if we are successful, is a devolved government for Northern Ireland, but one which recognizes that straight majority rule would not create stability. It can be best described by recognizing that democracy is not about the rights of the majority. True democracy is about the rights which an opposition has.

The New York Times, 7-19:3.

Francis Pym
Foreign Secretary
of the United Kingdom
                                                    3

[Criticizing U.S. sanctions against European firms that use American-licensed technology in construction of a natural-gas pipeline from the Soviet Union to Western Europe]: We firmly believe that existing contracts should be fulfilled and that major decisions affecting us all should not be taken without effective consultations. American measures have caused painful strains within the [Atlantic] Alliance because the basis for them, and the purpose of them, are themselves contentious and debatable. Those European countries, which have decided to buy Soviet gas, having weighed the alternatives, will go ahead.

Before Foreign Policy Association, New York,
Sept. 27/The New York Times, 8-28:9.

Muammar el-Qaddafi
Chief of State of Libya
                                                    4

The U.S. bases in Western Europe must be dismantled as quickly as possible. That can be accomplished through the great demonstrations and protest. Instead of demonstrations on the street, they should take place at the bases, and water and supplies should be cut off. Naturally, all by peaceful means. When peaceful efforts don't lead to success, then they become military efforts. *Fedayeen* groups will be founded again in order to reach this goal. That must be made clear to the masses. Either the bases will be stopped through your peaceful efforts, or the alternative would be war and destruction. We support this peaceful program and are ready to offer the necessary means.

Before European anti-nuclear
groups, Tripoli, Libya, July/
The New York Times, 7-27:6.

Dan Quayle
United States Senator, R–Indiana
                                                    5

[On American sanctions against European companies that supply U.S.-licensed technology for construction of a natural-gas pipeline from the Soviet Union to Western Europe]: The President [Reagan] should not consider lifting the sanctions until the Europeans agree to a binding, long-term accord [on deals with the Communist bloc]. First, there must be no subsidization of financial credits on any future sales to the East. Second, there must be strict adherence and enforcement of the restrictions placed on the exportation of high-technology goods to the East ... Such a consensus could rejuvenate the Western Alliance, unravel the confusion about U.S. foreign-trade policy with the Soviets and quell the increasing calls from both sides of the Atlantic for protectionist measures.

U.S. News & World Report, 9-13:84.

Mieczyslaw Rakowski
Deputy Prime Minister of Poland
                                                    6

[Defending the martial law in his country imposed last year after labor unrest sparked by the Solidarity independent trade union]: Free-

(MIECZYSLAW RAKOWSKI)

dom, freedom, freedom! For 200 years the Poles sold nothing but freedom, Chopin, the Polonaise! What freedom is a freedom which doesn't provide anything to put in the stomach? The hotheads of Solidarity supplied those poor workers with the most unrealistic ideas about freedom, and look where we are! All right, maybe this system isn't great, maybe it is guilty of many faults, but step by step it was moving ahead. Poland was an open country in the East, a country we could travel to and from, where any kind of book could be read, where different opinions were accepted. And now all this is spoiled. Didn't they know where Poland is placed? Didn't they know how the world is divided? One has to see freedom in the framework of a situation, a reality. I repeat that blood would have flowed like rivers if we hadn't imposed martial law the 13th of December. And civil war would have followed; so the forces of the Warsaw Pact would have entered. Yes, in such cases they would have entered because a civil war would not have been a matter of Poland and the Soviet Union only. It would have affected the balance now existing in the world, with God knows what consequences. Then the world would have yelled at us: "What kind of politicians were you? Why didn't you prevent it with a martial law? Why did you drive the Warsaw Pact forces to intervene?"

Interview, Warsaw, February/
The Washington Post, 2-21:(D)4.

Ronald Reagan
President of the United States

1

[On the present government of the Soviet Union]: Can anyone say that the czar was any more repressive on the Soviet people than this regime is? Did the aristocracy, in the old days, did they have any different elevation of luxury over the peasantry than hierarchy has over the average Soviet citizen, the so-called masses, today?—beach homes on the Black Sea, private jets, helicopters, country homes outside, special stores where they can purchase the certain special kind of goods. They've created an

aristocracy. What's ever happened to that equality of man that they teach?

Interview, Washington, Jan. 20/
Los Angeles Times, 1-21:(I)13.

2

The Soviet Union is a huge empire ruled by an elite that holds all power and all privilege. They hold it tightly because—as we have seen in Poland—they fear what might happen if even the smallest amount of control slips from their grasp. They fear the infectiousness of even a little freedom, and because of this in many ways their system has failed. The Soviet empire is faltering because rigid, centralized control has destroyed incentives for innovation, efficiency and individual achievement. Spiritually, there is a sense of malaise and resentment.

At Eureka (Ill.) College commencement,
May 9/The Washington Post, 5-10:(A)12.

3

[Criticizing Western Europe's plan to build a pipeline to obtain natural gas from the Soviet Union]: There is a danger to Europe in making itself too dependent on the Soviet Union as an energy source. [The allies should consider] if they want to be that dependent on someone who has 900 nuclear warheads aimed at them.

Interview, May 21/
Los Angeles Times, 5-28:(I)18.

4

[On the Berlin Wall]: I really want to hear their [the Communists'] explanation of why that wall is there, why are they so afraid of freedom on this side of the wall. Well, the truth is they're scared to death of it because they know that freedom is catching, and they don't dare leave their people have a taste of it.

West Berlin, June 11/
Los Angeles Herald Examiner, 6-11:(A)6.

5

Yesterday, the Polish government, a military dictatorship, took another far-reaching step in their persecution of their own people. They declared Solidarity [the independent trade union], the organization of the working men

WHAT THEY SAID IN 1982

(RONALD REAGAN)

and women of Poland, their free union, illegal ... Ever since martial law was brutally imposed last December, Polish authorities have been assuring the world that they're interested in the genuine reconciliation with the Polish people. But the Polish regime's action yesterday revealed the hollowness of its promises. By outlawing Solidarity, a free trade organization to which an overwhelming majority of Polish workers and farmers belong, they have made it clear that they never had any intention of restoring one of the most elemental human rights—the right to belong to a free trade union.

Oct. 9/The New York Times,
10-10:(1)8.

1

[On the U.S. embargo of technology used to construct a natural-gas pipeline from the Soviet Union to Western Europe]: In June of this year, I extended our embargo to include not only U.S. companies and their products but subsidiaries of U.S. companies abroad and on foreign licensees of U.S. companies. Now, it's no secret that our [European] allies didn't agree with this action ... Well, I'm pleased today to announce that the industrialized democracies have this morning reached substantial agreement on a plan of action. The understanding we've reached demonstrates that the Western alliance is fundamentally united and intends to give consideration to strategic issues when making decisions on trade with the U.S.S.R. As a result, we have agreed not to engage in trade arrangements which contribute to the military or strategic advantage of the U.S.S.R. or serve to preferentially aid the heavily militarized Soviet economy .... the United States imposed sanctions against the Soviet Union in order to demonstrate that their policies of oppression would entail substantial costs. Well, now that we've achieved an agreement with our allies which provides for stronger and more effective measures, there is no further need for these sanctions and I am lifting them today.

Radio address to the nation, Nov. 13/
The New York Times, 11-14:(1)9.

Jeffrey Record
Senior fellow, Institute
for Foreign Policy Analysis

2

[Saying the U.S. should withdraw its troops from Europe]: First, this is the only realistic way for the U.S. to prevent a disastrous shift in the East-West balance of power. Allies in Western Europe must be jolted into making a far stronger military effort to defend themselves so that U.S. forces can be freed to shore up the West's weaknesses elsewhere in the world. Otherwise, Russia will quite certainly achieve political and military domination of Europe—an incalculable defeat for the United States. Second, U.S. troops are now in serious physical danger because our European allies refuse to back them with adequate defense forces. We shouldn't allow them to become cannon fodder in some future European war .... only American ground forces should be pulled out. This should be done deliberately, after careful planning over 10 or 15 years. The United States would continue to provide other means of support for the defense of Western Europe—tactical air power, naval forces, nuclear weapons, those sorts of things. This is not a punitive measure, and it is not an action that one approaches with any great enthusiasm. We are forced to apply this kind of shock treatment simply because our allies are not pulling their military weight.

Interview/U.S. News & World Report, 2-1:17.

Thomas C. Reed
Consultant to Presidential National
Security Assistant William Clark

3

There is a crisis in the Soviet Union, where the demands of the economy are colliding with those of the political order. The Soviet Union is an economic basket case, and yet the Soviet leadership continues to pour resources into its military establishment. Despite its immense size, it cannot feed its own people, and it is hard-pressed to finance the import of food and other products necessary to prop up its mismanaged and misdirected economy.

Before Armed Forces Communication
and Electronics Association,
June 16/The New York Times, 6-17:6.

John J. Rhodes
United States Representative,
R–Arizona

1

The power of Europe is infinitesimal compared to the dominant position which it occupied prior to World War I . . . Yet we [in the U.S.] continue to base much of our foreign policy and our military planning on the needs and wants of . . . Western Europe. I think it is becoming increasingly apparent that this policy needs to be re-examined.

U.S. News & World Report, 6-21:75.

Helmut Schmidt
Chancellor of West Germany

2

[On Polish Prime Minister Wojciech Jaruzelski, who declared martial law in Poland last year to counter the activities of the Solidarity independent trade union]: I consider Jaruzelski, first of all, to act out of what he believes to be in the best of interest of the Polish nation, in the first instance as a Pole. In the second instance, I think, he comes as a Communist. So his action, I think, has to be evaluated against his personal background . . . We hate the news that comes out of Poland. I said, in front of Parliament at home in a rather solemn declaration, that I am from the bottom of my heart on the side of the workers in Warsaw and in Silesia and in Gdansk. But we would find it very difficult to apply sanctions ourselves against Poland.

Interview, Sanibel Island, Fla./
The New York Times, 1-3:(1)10.

3

. . . the attempts to scare the Europeans by the threat to withdraw American military forces from Europe is a futile effort. My first discussion on that subject took place over a quarter of a century ago. Such discussions come and go and come and go. You [the U.S.] would abdicate your leadership role in the Western world and I think that the political elites in the U.S. will always be sober enough not really to consider such a fatal move.

Interview, Sanibel Island, Fla./
The New York Times, 1-3:(1)10.

4

From time to time, leaders in the West—and I myself—are deeply in despair about developments in Eastern Europe. From time to time, we get angry. But never did anybody try to intervene by force. And I hope nobody will, because that would mean war. We have tried to influence spiritually. We have tried to influence by economic exchange, by scientific exchanges. We have tried to influence by human contacts, and by financial help as well. And these are the fields in which we have to try to influence development over there also in the future. And, therefore, it is questionable whether one is doing oneself a favor in the long-run aspect if one voluntarily limits such possibilities of influence.

Interview, Sanibel Island, Fla./
The New York Times, 1-3:(1)10.

5

[On criticism in his country of the large number of foreigners living in West Germany]: There is a tendency among millions of Germans to blame foreigners for all our problems. This reminds me of the cheap excuse of the 1920s to blame the Jews for everything. For God's sake, let us not feel this way too. [But] we have to say clearly and honestly that we just cannot take any more foreigners into our country, except those who have reason to apply for political asylum. It doesn't make sense to allow people into our country who immediately make more money through welfare and unemployment aid than they would make in their home country working 45 hours a week.

Before Social Democratic Party, Hamburg/
Los Angeles Times, 3-12:(I-A)8.

6

Ronald Reagan is the fourth American President with whom I am collaborating, and altogether I have never changed my constant belief in the reliability of the U.S. as a nation. We have believed in your continuity more than you yourselves have believed in it . . . . if you look at the polls in Western Europe, especially in West Germany, you find an unequaled and unchanged commitment to friendship with the U.S. and to the [NATO] alliance. On the other

(HELMUT SCHMİDT)

hand, you also find that it does not mean that
we think the social and economic and domestic
order of the U.S. necessarily has to serve as a
model for ourselves. It does not, it has not, and
it will not.

Interview, Hamburg/Time, 5-3:33.

1

[On imposing economic sanctions against
Poland during the current martial-law crackdown there]: The old talk about sanctions is
without substance. Trade between Poland and
Western Europe is already minimal. Sanctions
make the Polish people suffer, especially in the
area of food, medicine and basic necessities, but
they do not undercut military rule in Warsaw. I
think the idea of imposing sanctions was
understandable from an emotional point of
view, but it could not weaken the grip of the
military government there.

Interview, Hamburg/Time, 5-3:35.

2

[Criticizing U.S. efforts to block construction of a natural-gas pipeline from the Soviet
Union to Western Europe]: We and our European partners will stick to the gas-pipeline deal.
We are doing this because it serves the necessary
diversification of our energy supplies. We have
made sure that no dependence will be created
by this deal. We will and must show contractual
fidelity ... This [American] action implies an
extraterritorial extension of U.S. jurisdiction
which in the circumstances is contrary to the
principles of international law, unacceptable to
the [European] community and unlikely to be
recognized in the courts of the EEC.

Before the Bundestag (Parliament),
Bonn, June 24/
Chicago Tribune,
6-25:(1)1,8.

3

If you would dismantle NATO, then you
would very quickly feel that the main danger
point would be in Europe again. If there isn't
the feeling of great danger in Europe, it is due
to the existence and the successful joint policy

260

and strategies of NATO. As regards the future, I
would, for the rest of this century, not conceive
of a situation in which you could do without
NATO. I have no doubt that it will be
maintained and that it will be persistent.

Interview, New York/
Newsweek, 6-28:51.

4

[Criticizing U.S. attempts to block construction of a natural-gas pipeline from the Soviet
Union to Western Europe]: By claiming the
right to extend American law to other territories, it is affecting not only the interests of
European trading nations but also their sovereignty. The fact that this decision was taken
without consultation does not make it easier.
The maxim among friends should be: It is
better to discuss a question without settling it
than to settle a question without discussing it.

Before Bay Area Council,
San Francisco, July 22/
Chicago Tribune,
7-24:(1)5.

George P. Shultz
Secretary of State-designate
of the United States

5

[On the possibility of a U.S. troop pull-out
from Europe]: I think it would be a devastating
blow to the NATO alliance, and therefore to
ourselves. And it does seem to me clear that the
NATO alliance must be given a great amount of
credit for the fact that, with all of the troubles,
we have managed to have peace in Europe for
quite a stretch of time now—almost 40 years.
And that's a good record and a good accomplishment for that alliance. And they are also a
strong element in the over-all deterrence as
applied to the Soviet Union. So I think a [U.S.]
pull-out would be a very bad thing.

At Senate Foreign Relations
Committee hearing
on his confirmation,
Washington, July 14/
The New York Times, 7-15:8.

George P. Shultz
Secretary of State
of the United States
1

[On the martial law in Poland]: Events in Poland ... cannot be ignored or explained away. The Polish people want to be their own master. Years of systematic tyranny could not repress this desire. And neither will martial law. But in Poland today, truth must hide in corners.

At United Nations, New York, Sept. 30/
The New York Times, 10-1:10.

Beryl W. Sprinkel
Under Secretary for Monetary
Affairs, Department of the
Treasury of the United States
2

[On European complaints that high U.S. interest rates are hurting their economies]: All the hand-wringing in the world wouldn't make it possible to insulate Europe from economic reality. [Besides,] the impact of U.S. interest rates on foreign economies has been grossly exaggerated ... If they want to opt for slower inflation and more real growth, as we're doing, we certainly would welcome it. But if they don't opt in that direction, it's understandable their exchange rates are going to decline vis-a-vis the dollar.

New York, Feb. 26/
The Wall Street Journal, 3-1:41.

David Steel
Leader, British Liberal Party
3

[British Prime Minister Margaret Thatcher] sticks to her policy, yes; but if by an election she hasn't produced the goods ... There is no evidence that [her economic policy] is working. The country's industrial base keeps shrinking. We [the Liberal and Social Democratic coalition] can say no to the unions but at the same time offer expansion and industrial partnership. The vacuum is there waiting to be filled. If we don't do it, it's our fault. Steel and [Social Democratic leader Roy] Jenkins have to come through as people who can actually offer an alternative economic policy—and run a more contented, socially generous society.

The New York Times, 7-26:19.

4

[British Prime Minister Margaret Thatcher] has presided over a shambles of incompetence in her conduct of foreign policy and defense. Yet she has set out, quite deliberately, to cover up her administration's nakedness by wrapping herself in the Falkland's bunting [the British military defeat of Argentina in the war for the Falkland Islands], by belligerence of language, by a simplistic invocation of the Falklands spirit in the totally different sphere of industrial relations.

At Liberal Party convention,
Bournemouth, England, Sept. 24/
The New York Times, 9-25:6.

Ted Stevens
United States Senator, R—Alaska
5

[On Western Europe's commercial dealings with the Soviet Union, including the proposed natural-gas pipeline from the U.S.S.R. to Western Europe]: I don't know why we have to have U.S. troops defending Europe if they [the Europeans] are going to have commerce with the Soviet Union. If they feel so secure in their relationship with the Russians, then I think it's time for us to re-examine the number of troops we have in Europe.

Washington, March 2/
The New York Times, 3-3:4.

Margaret Thatcher
Prime Minister of the United Kingdom
6

Look at the enormous increase in industry and commerce in this country during Victorian times, which brought with it a consciousness of duty to others. They built the hospitals. They built the schools. They built the prisons. They built the industries. They built the town halls. They had confidence in the future, and their success brought them the wealth and resources to build the future. [In present-day Britain,] what I can't stand are all the people who are prepared to go tap the industries making profits, for the arts or music or charity, and then, in the next breath, despise industry.

Interview, London, June 2/
The Washington Post, 6-4:(A)26.

WHAT THEY SAID IN 1982

(MARGARET THATCHER)

1

[On the IRA bombings in London's Hyde and Regent's Parks]: These callous and cowardly crimes have been committed by evil and brutal men who know nothing of democracy, and we shan't rest until they are brought to justice.

Chicago Tribune, 7-22:(1)10.

2

[Criticizing U.S. President Reagan for his sanctions on European companies that use U.S.-licensed technology for construction of a natural-gas pipeline from the Soviet Union to Western Europe]: One of the consequences of what the United States has done may well be that we may no longer incorporate American technology in our exports, as we have done previously, because they might suddenly be cut off [by the U.S.] ... We are each and every one of us in the OECD and in the summit of seven *free* countries. That means we can freely agree with other countries not to do something —but we don't like things being imposed on us.

At Japan National Press Club, Tokyo,
Sept. 21/Los Angeles Times, 9-22:(I)19.

3

[On Labor Party criticism of her economic policies]: It is no service to the unemployed to build false hopes and make false promises. It is no service to them for you to promise to spend huge sums of money you do not possess in order to create jobs whose short-lived existence would be paid for at the expense of the jobs of some of those now in work. [The Labor Party] recipe for more jobs has just three ingredients: borrow more and more again in order to spend more, pay back the lenders in the debased currency by printing money, and control nearly everything in an attempt to hide from economic reality.

In House of Commons, London, Nov. 3/
The New York Times, 11-4:3.

Gaston Thorn
President, European Economic
Community (Common Market)

4

Impressive progress has been made [by the Common Market] in 25 years, and much of what Europe has achieved is of real historic significance. However, we are forced to recognize that despite the record, Europe's achievements and Europe's institutions are frail and inadequate, faced with the challenges of today and tomorrow. Achievements are under serious threat from nationalist and protectionist tendencies. The crisis is widening the economic and social gap between member states to alarming proportion. It is sapping solidarity and undermining internal cohesion. [The challenges call for] closer European integration and increased exploitation of the European dimension before we step into the 21st century.

At ceremony marking 25th anniversary
of the Treaty of Rome, Brussels, March 29/
Los Angeles Times, 3-30:(IV)1.

Leo Tindemans
Foreign Minister of Belgium;
President, Council of Ministers,
European Common Market

5

With all our arrogance and self-importance, Europe at this moment signifies nothing. Europe has no policy. It is not involved in power politics ... I don't need a threat to plead in favor of Europe. But often governments do. The current threats are obvious enough and should be sufficient, but I don't see the Europeans reacting really.

Interview/The New York Times, 3-21:(1)6.

Malcolm Toon
Former United States Ambassador
to the Soviet Union

6

I would not be very smug if I were one of those sitting in the [Soviet] Politburo today. They have the problem of China, which is a matter of deep and continuing concern to any Soviet leadership. They have the problem of Afghanistan, where they are having greater difficulty maintaining control against rebel forces than they ever anticipated. They have continuing problems of control in Eastern Europe, as evidenced most dramatically in Poland. They have an economy which is hopelessly inefficient and which cannot be modernized without downgrading the role of the

(MALCOLM TOON)

Communist Party. And they have an agricultural system that is absolutely impossible. They also have an increasing level of discontent among their people, reflected not only in the attitude of dissidents and "refuseniks" but also in the aspirations of the people in the Central Asian republics for greater independence of expression ... I don't want to overdo it. I wouldn't want to imply that the discontent is anywhere near the point where people are going to rise up tomorrow and toss out the rascals. But in the long term, these problems are going to lead not to the downfall of any particular Soviet leadership but to a basic change in Soviet behavior. But that is a long way down the road.

Interview/U.S. News & World Report, 3-15:46.

John G. Tower
United States Senator, D–Texas
1

[Some allies] have not borne as much of the common burden of which, they are capable ... [But] while I am in sympathy with those who desire our friends to do more, we must never forget that Western Europe remains a vital interest of the United States and it is fundamentally in the U.S. national interest to help protect it.

*At Senate Armed Services Committee
hearing, Washington, March 26/
The Washington Post, 3-27:(A)20.*

Paul E. Tsongas
*United States Senator,
D–Massachusetts*
2

[Criticizing the U.S. Reagan Administration for attempting to stop construction of a natural-gas pipeline from the Soviet Union to Western Europe]: Opponents of the pipeline have argued that it will deepen European economic dependence on the Soviet Union. This may well be the outcome, but it is worth noting that our European allies are united in their support for the pipeline in spite of such dependence. In any case, Europe will pay cash for Soviet natural gas, and it is fair to say that the Soviets need hard currency as much as or

more than the Europeans need natural gas. Dependence in this case will be mutual. The U.S. pipeline sanctions are damaging our relations with Europe, and inflicting harm on the U.S. economy while the intended victim, the Soviet Union, escapes almost unscathed. Sanctions are a ponderous and costly foreign-policy lever and must be used only when the policy impact is assured and the cost to the U.S. economy is minimal. The pipeline sanctions satisfy neither requirement.

The Washington Post, 8-18:(A)22.

Adam Ulam
*Professor, and director of Russian
Research Center, Harvard University*
3

[On the death of Soviet leader Leonid Brezhnev]: Brezhnev's leadership was pretty successful from the point of view of the Party elite. He succeeded in putting the lid on dissent, in eliminating liberalization and suppressing the issues that [former Soviet leader Nikita] Khrushchev allowed to come to the surface, like the problem of Stalin and the past crimes and errors of the Party. But from the perspective of a future historian, Brezhnev could be said to have been successful because he swept major problems under the rug. He left major problems with the economy and in Soviet relations with the United States.

Interview/The New York Times, 11-12:6.

Jerzy Urban
*Official spokesman for
the government of Poland*
4

[On U.S. economic sanctions against Poland because of the martial-law crackdown following civil unrest last year]: We do not turn flour into cannons and corn into missiles ... The Poles know well that the aim of the decision of [U.S. President] Ronald Reagan's Administration is not the well-being of the Polish nation, but other goals: introducing discipline in Western Europe in accordance with the U.S. policy, using the Polish pretext as a power play against the Soviet Union. Poland is being castigated because the hopes of the U.S. President for the change of the balance in power in Europe which could have resulted from the destabilization in Poland have failed. Yet, you cannot change the results of World War II by corn pecked at by hens.

Interview/Newsweek, 2-1:47.

Valentin I. Varennikov
*General and First Deputy Chief
of Staff, Soviet armed forces*

1

[Criticizing the U.S. arms buildup] : Can the Soviet Union sit idly by under such conditions? No, it cannot. We have to react to the military threat created by the United States and, on our part, are deploying the necessary weapons. But the Soviet Union has never sought and does not seek military superiority. The Soviet Union has a big military potential. Any attempts at gaining military superiority over our country are doomed to failure.

*News conference, Moscow, Jan. 25/
The New York Times, 1-26:7.*

Helen Vlachos
Editor, "Kathimerini," Athens

2

Our people do not know exactly what NATO stands for. We cannot forget that the 1967 coup of the colonels started with NATO tanks, or that the generals from NATO came around kissing and hugging those colonels. That memory is difficult to erase. NATO also likes Turks better than it does Greeks. On the other hand, logical people say, "NATO is a lovely supermarket full of arms and tanks they sell us cheaply—sometimes even on credit—so forget about patriotism before that closes." NATO has no respect in Greece.

Interview/World Press Review, July:30.

3

[On Greek Prime Minister Andreas Papandreou] : The situation here is strangely incoherent. Papandreou is a mystery man in many ways, a kind of Jekyll and Hyde. He is a demagogue, but not only when he speaks at a rally. He will sit across from you, listen to what you have to say, tell you that he agrees with you, then go away and do the opposite.

Nobody knows if Papandreou behaves like this on purpose or whether it is a Pavlovian reaction—that is, he wants to be pleasant, promises people what they want to hear, and doesn't care if he changes his mind later. This worries everybody.

Chicago Tribune, 9-26:(1)4.

Lech Walesa
*Former national chairman,
now-banned Solidarity (independent
Polish trade union)*

4

[On his being released after 11 months in prison for Solidarity activities] : I have signed nothing, I haven't resigned from anything, I haven't declared anything, and I haven't compelled myself to anything. I was released, to my surprise, without obligations, as a really completely free man.

*News conference, Zaspa, Poland, Nov. 15/
Los Angeles Times, 11-16:(I)1.*

5

The awakening of social efforts and strengthening the position of Poland in the world is possible only through rebuilding mutual trust between society and the government. Meeting the expectations of the nation is the only way to awaken hope and contribute to social stability. [There should be] a general amnesty for those tried during martial law for [trade-] union activity and protest actions—all internees to be automatically released with the lifting of martial law; secondly, that those dismissed from work during martial law for either union activity or just for membership in the [now-banned Solidarity] union [should] be reinstated in their jobs; a breakthrough in the trade-union impasse by the return to the principle of plurality. The fact that the working class has not accepted the solutions implemented by the government is now clear to all those who do not close their eyes to reality . . . Without the acceptance of the government's position by the working class, we will not get far. These steps would open the road to a true social agreement. No one of us is doing each other a favor, and none of us has to ask for agreement on our knees, because agreement is a

(LECH WALESA)

necessity if you care about the good of the country.

Warsaw, Dec. 11*/San Francisco
Examiner & Chronicle, 12-12:(A)28.

Caspar W. Weinberger
Secretary of Defense
of the United States

1

We have to recognize that [U.S.] trade with the Soviet Union is not like trade with Britain or France or Japan. The profits that arise from trade in the Soviet Union go directly, for the most, to the [Soviet] military. In the case of a power that uses everything it can to enhance its military, you have to apply different standards and different protection rules.

Interview/Time, 3-1:14.

2

[Criticizing a natural-gas pipeline, now under construction, from the Soviet Union to Western Europe]: The pipeline does add to the dependence of Western Europe, in an undesirable way, on the Soviet Union. [The pipeline] energizes the entire Soviet industrial system [bringing needed energy to the western part of the U.S.S.R.] long before it gets to Western Europe ... Neither SALT negotiations, nor economic distress [in the civilian sector], nor detente, nor anything else has ever slowed the

[Soviet] military buildup. With that in mind, it is a little hard to see how trade of this kind, that has such an obvious military advantage in providing this much [hard Western currency to the Soviets], most of which would go into military spending, can do anything but increase the danger to all of us.

At conference sponsored by Georgetown
University Center for Strategic and
International Studies, Washington,
Sept. 21/The Washington Post, 9-22:(A)14.

Charles Z. Wick
Director, International Communication
Agency of the United States

3

[On West European youth who protest against U.S. strengthening of Western Europe defenses]: These young people seem to feel that we are the aggressors. They're blind to the Russian pattern of encroachment and the rape of Hungary, Czechoslovakia, Afghanistan ... The Soviets tend to manipulate the idealism and the fears and genuine concerns of these people. And the extent that that successor generation may inhibit the deployment of those [Western] missiles ... will be the acid test ... as to whether the [NATO] alliance can remain cohesive and resist the intimidation of the Soviets.

Interview, Washington, May 26/
Los Angeles Times, 5-27:(I)11.

265

The Middle East

James Abourezk
*Director, American-Arab Anti-Discrimination
Committee; Former United States Senator,
D—South Dakota*

1

It is probably true that the Soviets are
looking for Middle East allies and bases of
operation. But it has to be understood that the
Palestinians, like every other revolutionary
movement, get support wherever they can.
Since the U.S. has refused to support the
Palestinians, they have been forced to turn to
the Soviet Union. My knowledge of Palestinians
is that they are more pro-American than they
are pro-Russian. Most Arabs find Americans
appealing as persons, however much they dis-
like government policy. People tend to forget
that once nationalistic revolutions seize control
of a country, they tend to want to kick out all
foreign powers. They would drop the Soviets
like a hot potato.

Interview/U.S. News & World Report, 11-29:34.

Jonathan Aitken
Member of British Parliament

2

[On the Israeli invasion of Lebanon to drive
out the PLO]: The key to the situation in the
Middle East is the future of the United States-
Israel relationship. At present, Washington is
letting Israel get away with murder and has
been doing so for a considerable time.

The Washington Post, 6-27:(A)24.

Kamal Hassan Aly
Foreign Minister of Egypt

3

[On Israel's scheduled withdrawal from the
Sinai on April 25]: Israel's fears that Egypt
may adopt a different [more hostile] policy
toward it after April 25 are based on weak
arguments and in fact are groundless. The

relations with the Arabs will not be at the
expense of peace with Israel.

*Broadcast statement, Cairo/
San Francisco Examiner & Chronicle, 4-18:(A)18.*

Mustafa Amin
Egyptian journalist

4

As far as democracy goes, America had it
when its literacy rate was as [low] as Egypt's.
If we wait until every Egyptian has a Ph.D.,
we'll never have democracy.

*Interview, Cairo/Los Angeles
Times, 3-12:(I-A)6.*

Yasir Arafat
*Chairman, Palestine
Liberation Organization*

5

In my opinion, it was American policy that
killed [assassinated Egyptian President Anwar]
Sadat—the squeezing for concessions [to the
Israelis], concessions, concessions! And here is
the result: The group that killed him was not
from any other Arab country, but from his own
army . . . To give you an idea of the importance
of Palestine in the consciousness of the Egyptian people, remember that when the Israeli flag
was raised over the Israeli Embassy in Cairo,
one million Palestinian flags were raised by the
Egyptian people. You [the U.S.] are losing
your friends because of your unlimited support
for Israel. You spoil this naughty baby, and this
naughty baby will damage U.S. interests.

Interview, Beirut/Time, 2-8:46.

6

[On the Israeli invasion of Lebanon to drive
out the PLO]: The Israeli military operation
took place with the complete approval of the
U.S. Administration. The U.S. justifies this
operation by claiming that it will create a

(YASIR ARAFAT)

strong government in Lebanon. Frankly speaking, I do not see the possibility of creating a strong government in any Arab country through the use of Israeli tanks. A dangerous situation has been created in the Middle East through U.S. support of Israeli aggression against the Palestinian peoples and through the Palestinians against the Arab and Islamic peoples. Washington has struck a massive blow at its moderate Arab friends.

Interview/Time, 7-5:34.

1

[On his leaving Beirut as a result of Israeli military force]: Whatever I do, I will not be able to express in these few words the feelings of love and appreciation that I hold in my heart for all those I have known in this country who embrace our revolution with love, tenderness and sacrifice. Beirut has recorded a miracle of heroism inspired by the decision we took together to defend it against the criminal invaders [the Israelis] in the shadow of the most difficult circumstances ever lived by our Arab nations. This made Beirut a symbol which will go down in history. I am leaving this city; my heart is here—a part of my heart, a part of my conscience. This [Beirut] is a station and I am going to another station. This is a long march.

Beirut, Aug. 30/The
Christian Science Monitor, 8-31:6.

2

As I proposed at the United Nations eight years ago, we are calling for a democratic state of Palestine through peaceful means. But we will continue our struggle until the enemy forces [Israel] return to their senses . . . I come as a messenger of peace. The struggle for Palestine is not a conflict between the Jews and Arabs, who have lived together peacefully for centuries, interrupted only when the Zionists forced a Jewish state on us, ignoring the tragedy of a people condemned to exile.

Before Inter-Parliamentary Union, Rome,
Sept. 15/Los Angeles Times, 9-16:(I)7.

3

[On the massacre of Palestinians by Christian militiamen in refugee camps in Israeli-controlled Beirut]: [Israeli Prime Minister] Begin and [Defense Minister] Sharon are not Jews. The crimes they commit do not conform to Jewish morality or tradition. The real Jews are those who refuse to be associated with the attempt to annihilate the Palestinian people . . . To all of them, to all of the Israeli or Jewish pacifists and democrats, I address the esteem and gratitude of the Palestinian people who will never forget their solidarity at the time of trial.

Interview, Damascus, Syria, Sept. 19/
The New York Times, 9-21:29.

Theodore Arcand
Canadian Ambassador to Lebanon

4

[On the current Israeli invasion of Lebanon]: I always had an enormous admiration for the Israelis—their musicians, their men of science—which I try to think of despite my travels in south Lebanon. I have seen all the human misery . . . and I wonder where the Israel I knew has gone, and I am sure many Israelis are wondering, too. One is disappointed in a country that Canada has given so much support to.

Los Angeles Times, 7-29:(I)9.

Moshe Arens
Israeli Ambassador to the United States

5

[On Israel's invasion of Lebanon]: Our foremost goal—and the specific reason for the operation—was to free northern Israel from the repeated bombardments by the PLO in southern Lebanon. No government could put up with that sort of thing for any length of time. A government has the responsibility of protecting its citizens. We would like to see an end put to the PLO's use of Lebanon as a center of international terrorism. We also would like to see an evacuation of foreign troops from Lebanon, an end to the military presence of the PLO and the evacuation of the Syrian Army from Lebanon. We feel that the presence of the PLO as a military group running a quasi state in Lebanon was a destabilizing influence in the

WHAT THEY SAID IN 1982

(MOSHE ARENS)

entire area ... We are not going to stay in Lebanon. We are going to get out. But if Israel were to withdraw immediately, as the PLO and the Syrians—and the Russians—would like us to do, then no doubt there would be an almost immediate return to the situation that we had before. So our withdrawal must be phased and correlated with the building up of the authority of the Lebanese government and the rebuilding of the Lebanese Army.

Interview/U.S. News & World Report, 6-28:21.

Hafez al-Assad
President of Syria
1

[On his Administration]: We are not a one-man regime, not a military force, not a family, not a clan, but a popular force that represents the broad masses of the people.

To European correspondents/
U.S. News & World Report, 3-22:34.

Uri Avnery
Israeli journalist; Former member
of Israeli Knesset (Parliament)
2

I'm pro-Israel, and because I'm pro-Israel, I feel we'll never have security unless we have peace, and we'll only have peace if we make a settlement with the Palestinians, and we have to do that with the PLO. There's only one leadership organization that all Palestinians accept—as much as the Israelis are still trying to invent another.

Interview/The Washington Post, 7-17:(C)9.

George W. Ball
Former Under Secretary of
State of the United States
3

U.S. Middle East policy has marched to an Israeli drum far too long, as though we were powerless to pursue a course of our own. There is nothing in our Constitution that requires the American taxpayer to dole out $2.5-billion a year to a nation that repeatedly ignores our interests; in shaping our national budget, we do not treat the claims of America's poor as so sacrosanct.

Before Senate Foreign Relations
Committee, Washington, July 15/
Los Angeles Times, 7-16:(I)10.

Haim Bar-Lev
Member of Israeli Knesset
(Parliament); Former Chief
of Staff, Israeli Army
4

[Criticizing Israel's current attacks on Beirut to drive out the PLO, and Prime Minister Begin's comparing it with allied bombing of Nazi Germany]: This comparison does not solve the problem of Israel's image abroad nor does it ease the conscience of many, many people in Israel. The claim that we caused less damage to Lebanon than the PLO [did] may be true, but we expect more from ourselves than from them, and others expect us to act according to different norms.

Before the Knesset, Jerusalem, Aug. 12/
Los Angeles Times, 8-13:(I)10.

Menachem Begin
Prime Minister of Israel
5

[Criticizing Britain for urging Israel to ease its control over the West Bank, just before Argentina invaded the British Falkland Islands which Britain is now preparing to defend]: Here was [British Foreign Secretary] Lord Carrington, pleading with us to "show magnanimity" with territory which starts just 1 kilometer from the center of our capital. And a few days later, the whole of Britain was ready to go to war for the sake of a few small islands 8,000 miles from London. What do they expect us to do?

Dimona, Israel, April/
Newsweek, 4-19:48.

6

[On criticism of Israel's occupation of the West Bank, also known as Judea and Samaria]: Our nation was born in Judea and Samaria, not in Jaffa and certainly not in Tel Aviv. In Judea and Samaria our prophets prophesied; in Judea and Samaria the ancient Jewish culture, from which we are nurtured to this very day, was created. Judea and Samaria are occupied territory? Judea and Samaria were occupied territory by the Jordanians, who conquered the western part of the land of Israel. And once it

(MENACHEM BEGIN)

was occupied territory by the Egyptians when they invaded Israel. But it is not occupied territory [now]. It is the land of Israel.

Interview/The New York Times, 4-27:8.

1

[Saying the PLO may keep its small guns when it leaves Lebanon as a result of Israel's current invasion of that country]: In medieval times, the personal weapon was a sword. Knights who wished to maintain their honor kept their swords at their waists. Nowadays, the sword is called Kalashnikov [a Soviet-made rifle]. I want to say from this podium that we are willing to allow the terrorists to leave with their Kalashnikovs. We are not afraid of their Kalashnikovs... We will not humiliate them, but they must leave... Under no condition will we allow them to remain.

Before the Knesset (Parliament),
Jerusalem, June 29/Los Angeles Times, 6-30:(I)1.

2

[On Israel's invasion of Lebanon to force the PLO out of that country]: Why should I talk to a man like [PLO leader Yasir] Arafat? If he had the power and strength to destroy each one of the 3½ million Jews now living in Israel, he would do so. Now he has to look for asylum, and he is not in a good situation... Israel doesn't want to keep its troops in Lebanon a minute longer than necessary. Lebanon is not the land of Israel. It is a sovereign foreign country. We want an independent Lebanon whose borders we will respect. We want to sign a peace treaty with Lebanon on the basis of its territorial integrity. We are prepared to leave Lebanon today, tomorrow, anytime soon. We want our soldiers back home. But as [U.S.] President Reagan recently told the British Parliament, the scourge of terrorism in the Mideast must be stamped out. We will not leave Lebanon until the lives of our children are no longer threatened. We must be sure that security arrangements are so organized that no gun, no rocket will hit our towns and villages. When these arrangements are completed, we will say "goodbye" to Lebanon—but not before.

Interview/The Washington Post, 7-4:(B)2.

3

[Saying he has no intention of permitting a Palestinian state in the West Bank]: Arabs have a vast empire of more than 4.5 million square miles extending from the western coast of North Africa to the eastern shores of the Persian Gulf. They have sovereignty over 22 countries of their own. Why should we allow them to create a 23rd Arab state within our own borders that would only be a constant threat to the peace and security of Israel itself. No. Never.

Interview, Jerusalem/
Chicago Tribune, 7-18:(2)1,5.

4

[On Israel's invasion of Lebanon and Beirut to drive the PLO out of that country]: We could have gone on seeing our civilians injured in Metulla or Qiryat Shimona or Nahariya. We could have gone on counting those killed by explosive charges left in a Jerusalem supermarket, or a Petah Tikvah bus stop. All the orders to carry out these acts of murder and sabotage came from Beirut. Should we have reconciled ourselves to the ceaseless killing of [Israeli] civilians?... There are slanderers who say that a full year of quiet has passed between us and the terrorists. Nonsense. There was not even one month of quiet. The newspapers and communications media, including *The New York Times* and *The Washington Post,* did not publish even one line about our capturing the gang of murderers that crossed the Jordan in order to commandeer a bus and murder its passengers... We can already look beyond the fighting [in Lebanon]. It will soon be over, we hope, and then I believe, indeed I know, we will have a long period of peace. There is no other country around us that is capable of attacking us.

At Israeli National Defense College,
Aug. 8/The New York Times, 8-21:6.

5

[Proposing Arab autonomy in the Israeli-occupied West Bank]: Autonomy would be a very great achievement. For the first time in history they would have an administrative council elected by themselves, taking care of all

WHAT THEY SAID IN 1982

(MENACHEM BEGIN)

their daily affairs except security, which we must reserve. It's not true it's a restrictive autonomy. It's a very wide autonomy. We suggest the following functions for the autonomy: justice, agriculture, finance, civil service, education and culture, health, housing, public works, transportation, communications, labor and social welfare, municipal affairs, local police, religious affairs, industry, commerce and tourism. It's a quasi-government. Quasi, of course, pseudo, because it's not a state. It's autonomy. But this is what we suggested. This is Camp David [the Israeli-Egyptian agreement].

Interview, Jerusalem, Aug. 27/
The New York Times, 8-29:(1)8.

1

[On the PLO's leaving Lebanon as a result of Israel's invasion of that country]: They are a beaten organization. What is their future? They are dispersed in eight countries. Everybody disarms them. First those countries didn't want to receive them at all. What can they do? They can carry out several individual terrorist acts. That they can do, but that happens in London as well. But they can't fight any more. They don't have the arms; they don't have the bases; they don't have their headquarters.

Interview, Jerusalem, Aug. 27/
The New York Times, 8-29:(1)8.

2

[On the massacre of Palestinians in a refugee camp in Israeli-occupied Beirut]: There is no fault in Israel. There is no fault in the Israeli Army. There is no [Israeli] guilt. But there was a disaster. I am willing to stand before any man in Israel—with my head high and upright—and tell him the complete story of how we meant to do well. We are trying to convince the world that this is the truth, but part of the nation will not allow us to do so.

Before the Knesset (Parliament), Jerusalem,
Sept. 22/Los Angeles Times, 9-23:(I)10.

3

[On why Israeli forces allowed Lebanese militia into refugee camps in Israeli-occupied

Beirut where Palestinians were then massacred]: The picture drawn for us was of difficult fighting, that the Lebanese forces would be compelled to battle the many [Palestinian] terrorists dug in in those camps. Given this situation, it was never imagined that the Lebanese forces, who are trained and organized military units, and who were assigned the task of fighting under difficult conditions, would want to—or be able to—perpetrate a massacre [of Palestinian civilians].

Written testimony to Israeli judicial
committee investigating the massacre, Jerusalem,
Dec. 9/Los Angeles Times, 12-10:(I)14.

Eliahu Ben-Elissar
Chairman, Israeli Knesset
(Parliament) Foreign Affairs
and Defense Committee

4

[Arguing against critics of Israel's current invasion of Lebanon to oust the PLO]: The free, Christian world has still a long way to go to get used to a new type of Jew. We are a very normal people. No nation would allow its citizens to be killed [by the PLO] with impunity. But somehow, people take it for granted that Jews have always been killed throughout their history, while Americans or French or others would never let it happen. We have always been asked to behave otherwise. But we are not the Jews of the Diaspora. We will show to the nations that we are not that kind of Jew.

The New York Times, 8-8:(4)1.

Julius Berman
President, Union of Orthodox
Jewish Congregations of America;
Chairman, Conference of Presidents
of Major Jewish Organizations

5

[On the massacre of Palestinians by Christian militiamen in refugee camps in Israeli-controlled Beirut]: We join with [U.S.] President Reagan and [Israeli Prime Minister] Begin in expressing our shock and revulsion at the massacre of civilians in Beirut. We reject the idea of any participation or involvement by the Israeli Defense Forces in this terrible event. The history of the Jewish people is too full of massacres and pogroms, and the injunctions of

(JULIUS BERMAN)

Jewish laws are too powerful a force in Jewish consciences, to have permitted or even countenanced a Jewish role in this awful incident. Any suggestions that Israel took part in it or permitted it to occur must be categorically rejected.

Interview, Sept. 20/The New York Times, 9-21:7.

Leonid I. Brezhnev
President of the Soviet Union;
General Secretary, Soviet
Communist Party

1

[On Israel's invasion of Lebanon to drive out the PLO]: Why is Israel continuing its brigand aggression? Why is it disregarding the decisions of the United Nations Security Council that call for the immediate and unconditional withdrawal of the aggressor troops from Lebanon? Why does it permit itself to disregard world public opinion? This is all happening because it is backed by a power whose address is well known—the United States.

Interview/The New York Times, 7-21:10.

2

[Saying the U.S. shares responsibility with Israel for the Israeli invasion of Lebanon]: It was the United States that supplied the aggressors with their deadly weapons [and] that provided political and diplomatic cover for the aggression. Today, too, the United States is trying to deny the Palestinians their sacred right to self-determination and to establishing their own state. In this hour of trial, I confirm anew that the Soviet Union was and remains on the side of the Arab people of Palestine and their only legitimate representative—the PLO.

Sept. 14*/The Washington Post, 9-15:(A)21.

L. Dean Brown
President, Middle East Institute;
Former United States Ambassador to
Jordan and special envoy to Lebanon

3

I think it is time for Lebanon to remove itself from the world's international system—to say that its problems and its aspirations are so unique that it seeks a new and different status.

By this I mean a neutral state. Not just neutral, like Switzerland, but neutral and disarmed, like Austria. This means that Lebanon will withdraw from the League of Arab States—perhaps from the United Nations. It will no longer proclaim itself the capital of any regional group. It will seek UN guarantees. It will ask for a multinational force to back up those guarantees—at least for a stated period of years. It will pass legislation preventing the use of Lebanese facilities by any power to attack any other. In other words, it will seek true neutrality not only in what it speaks but in what it does or does not do. A neutral, disarmed Lebanon which preaches no lesson other than tolerance could be a shining beacon in the Middle East. It would also mean that no outside power—Syria, Israel, the PLO, Libya or the U.S.—could interfere with internal political working of the new system. Perhaps—some day—we will see it happen.

Before Army and Navy Club, Washington/
The Christian Science Monitor, 7-28:23.

Jimmy Carter
Former President of the United States

4

[On Israeli Prime Minister Menachem Begin]: He is a man of almost unshakable beliefs. He finds it very difficult to change his mind. It was torture for him to agree to remove the [Israeli] settlers from the Sinai. He has a single-minded commitment to annex permanently all the other [Israeli-] occupied territories. He has a tendency to treat the Palestinians with scorn; to look down on them almost as subhumans and to rationalize his abusive attitude toward them by categorizing all Palestinians as terrorists. I do not think Begin has any intention of ever removing the [Israeli] settlements from the West Bank, and that is a very serious mistake for Israel. There is no doubt Begin's purpose all the time was to cut a separate deal with Egypt. He disavowed that intention, but all his actions, all his words, indicated that. Begin was the most recalcitrant of all the Israelis at [the] Camp David [talks in 1978]. I almost never had a pleasant surprise in my dealings with him.

Interview, Plains, Ga./Time, 10-11:62.

Zev Chafets
Director, Israeli Government
Press Office   1

Democracies cannot cope with a minority which is hostile to the fundamental idea of the country, the essence of the country as it is constituted. In America, the minorities want equal shares, but they want it within the framework of what is basic to America. They believe in that framework. Israel is a Jewish state. That's basic. It's a homeland for the Jews—that's basic. The Arab citizens of Israel are a minority, but they are part of an Arab majority—a hostile regional majority at war with us. I don't think the Israeli Arabs would fight to destroy us, but if there were a button to press that would make us collectively disappear, a lot of them would press it. In a democracy, the basic assumption is that the citizens in it are loyal to it. When that assumption changes . . . well, the United States put the Japanese-Americans into concentration camps during World War II.

Interview/The New York Times Magazine, 3-7:22.

Claude Cheysson
Foreign Minister of France   2

France extends recognition to states only, and the PLO is not a state. But we say that it represents the Palestinian combatants and, therefore, must participate in any negotiations that aim at the realization of peace.

Cairo, Jan. 3/Chicago Tribune, 1-4:(1)1.

3

[Criticizing Israel's invasion of Lebanon to oust the PLO]: We certainly are disappointed that this state to which we are so attached—Israel—should go against one of the principles [of peace] and should use violence when it has a problem. We do not deny that there was a problem, that at times villages in the north of Israel were being bombed from the neighboring country. But we do not think that [Israeli] violence was the proper answer. This is our frustration, this is our disappointment, that it should come from Israel, it should come from these people that have suffered so much, so much, in their lives during the last tens of years, during the last centuries, I would even say.

Interview/The Washington Post, 7-6:(A)17.

Thomas F. Eagleton
United States Senator,
D—Missouri   4

Let's be honest about it. [U.S.] President Reagan was never all that enthusiastic about the [Egyptian-Israeli] Camp David process. After all, that was [former U.S. President] Jimmy Carter's "bag" . . . Let's be honest about it. [Egyptian] President Mubarak isn't all that hot about the Camp David process. After all, that was [the late Egyptian President] Anwar Sadat's "bag," and Mubarak realizes that Egypt's days of isolation from the rest of the world are nearing the end. Let's be honest about it. [Israeli] Prime Minister Begin was less than totally comfortable with Camp David. To him, the West Bank is still Judea and Samaria, and [Arab] "autonomy" to him is just another way of saying "Judea and Samaria." Egypt can never agree to the Begin version of "autonomy in Judea and Samaria."

Before the Senate, Washington/
The Washington Post, 3-26:(A)30.

Elias Freij
Mayor of Bethlehem,
Israeli-occupied West Bank   5

[Saying the PLO should recognize Israel]: The present stalemate in the West Bank and Gaza is enabling Israel to strengthen its presence in the [occupied Arab] territories, to build more settlements, to enlarge existing settlements. If this trend continues, in the next 10 years we will be witnessing a Jewish West Bank . . . Peaceful coexistence means, in plain language, coexistence with the state of Israel. Therefore, there is no alternative for us but to recognize the right of Israel to exist if we really expect the international community and the American government to support our demands for [Palestinian] self-determination and the withdrawal of Israel from the occupied territories . . . I think it is in our own interest that a political dialogue between the PLO and the United States government should be initiated. We should have the moral and political courage to challenge Israel on its stated desire for peace by recognizing Israel. I believe that such a move would be in the interest of the Palestinian Arabs.

Interview, Jan. 22/The New York Times, 1-23:6.

(ELIAS FREIJ)

1

The Israelis were and are determined to annex the West Bank. Their policy is to take Arab land, push us [Palestinians] into small enclaves and so make it impossible to form an independent homeland. . . . America is the key. Whether we like it or not, the U.S. is the only large power really active in the Mideast. We must now put some oil in the lock and take our case to the American public. We must convince them that we want peace with Israel—peace that includes our freedom.

U.S. News & World Report, 9-13:22,23.

Amin Gemayel
President of Lebanon

2

[Today] I shall offer no program for a new era, because a single concern grips us now. This is to stop the vicious cycle of bloody violence on Lebanon's soil. The wars in Lebanon and at Lebanon's expense must stop. The security of the nation must be guaranteed as well as that of its citizens. This will not be fulfilled except through a strong, independent, sovereign state preserving public liberties and working for the evacuation of all foreign armies from Lebanon's soil.

Inaugural address, Beirut, Sept. 23/
The Washington Post, 9-24:(A)18.

3

[On the recent Israeli-PLO warfare in his country]: In the name of the Lebanese people, I want to tell you: We have had enough—enough of bloodshed, enough of destruction, enough of dislocation and despair. We have paid the high price of war. We should not pay an additional price for peace. As a member of the United Nations, we want our rights to be restored to us. Each country enjoys internal sovereignty. So should we. Each country depends on an effective army to defend its independence. So should we. As we wish to live in peace and freedom in our land, so should the Palestinians live in peace and freedom and self-determination in their land, Palestine. And as we cherish our independence, we also cherish the hope that Palestinians and Israelis, with the support of the world community, will reach a settlement that will allow them both to enjoy the fullness of rights.

At United Nations, New York, Oct. 18/
The New York Times, 10-19:5.

4

American commitment to the sovereignty and territorial integrity of a free democracy in Lebanon has been fundamental to our survival. We see the U.S. role as the indispensable ingredient to bring peace not only to Lebanon but also to the whole region as well. We firmly believe that [U.S.] President Reagan's initiative has created unprecedented opportunities for peace.

Washington, Oct. 19/
The Washington Post, 10-20:(A)16.

Boutros Ghali
Foreign Minister of Egypt

5

If we want a future for a continuing dialogue between the Israelis and the Palestinians, we must see that the Palestinians are not weakened to the point that all that remains is a monologue . . . We in Egypt have not gotten along well with the PLO in the past. But what we must have is a valid interlocutor, and if they are eliminated there will be no peace here.

Interview, Paris, July 2/
The New York Times, 7-3:4.

Nahum Goldmann
Former president, World Jewish
Congress; Leader in the
Zionist movement

6

[Criticizing Israel's current invasion of Lebanon and its attack on Beirut]: If Israel remains as it is now, it will be a caricature of Jewish history and it will soon cause a fundamental conflict in the hearts of Jews all over the world. All Zionist leaders . . . would turn in their graves if they could see what has become of Israel.

Interview/Los Angeles Times, 8-31:(I)8.

WHAT THEY SAID IN 1982

Barry M. Goldwater
United States Senator, R—Arizona

1

[On Israel's invasion of Lebanon to drive out the PLO]: [Israeli Prime Minister Begin] had no right to invade another country. And the United States has no right to support the invasion of another country unless it's a matter of world war ... We are bound to support Israel if Israel is attacked, but we have no bind to support Israel if Israel attacks—and that's something we have to get through our head and get through rather fast.

Washington/Chicago Tribune, 7-5:(1)5.

Andrei A. Gromyko
Foreign Minister of the Soviet Union

2

[On the massacre of Palestinians in refugee camps in Israeli-occupied Beirut]: Could Israel commit aggression and perpetrate genocide against the Palestinians but for its so-called "strategic consensus" with the United States? The root cause of the Lebanese tragedy lies in Camp David. It should be clear now to every unbiased person that separate anti-Arab deals only put off the establishment of a just peace in the Middle East. Washington's recent statements, which it is serving as a Middle East settlement plan, confirm that they are still thinking there in terms of diktat and enmity with regard to the Arabs rather than in terms of peace.

At United Nations, New York, Oct. 1/
The New York Times, 10-2:6.

Alexander M. Haig, Jr.
Secretary of State
of the United States

3

[There is a] complication in the Middle East that must be viewed with increasing interest if not concern, and that is the growing alignment of Syria with Iran and the possible increase in Soviet influence on both. Now, as it's turned out, the growing alignment of Syria with Iran has resulted in a ... growing concern among moderate Arab states that this is a threat with which they have to deal, especially the Gulf states and Saudi Arabia ... It is now a fact of

life and it's going to have an increasing impact on both Arab-Israeli issues and regional issues at large.

Interview/Newsweek, 5-3:36.

4

[On Israel's invasion of Lebanon to force the PLO out of that country]: The situation in Lebanon offers a great strategic opportunity for the moderate Arab world, for the United States, and above all for the tortured people and populations of Lebanon who have been under the heel of an international terrorist organization [the PLO]—and terrorized, plagued and brutalized since the entry of the PLO into that country in the mid-1970s ... Today, the West is facing the judgment—should, or can, we insist on arrangements which will leave the Palestinian terrorist organization intact as an armed extra-territorial element within the sovereign borders of Lebanon? The answer is a resounding "No." It is vitally important for the West to keep its eye on the historic perspective of the tragedy that is Lebanon today and not reimpose the conditions which brought about this tragic situation.

Interview/The Washington Post, 7-4:(B)2.

Jesse A. Helms
United States Senator,
R—North Carolina

5

[Criticizing Israel's invasion of Lebanon and its attack on Beirut to oust the PLO]: [Israeli Prime Minister Begin] has done the impossible. He has made a palatable character out of [PLO chairman Yasir] Arafat. And, if he doesn't watch out, the public opinion in this country [the U.S.] is going to push this government much further than Mr. Begin ever imagined ... [Begin] can make all the statements he wants to, but sooner or later he's got to stop this business because the American people find repugnant the continuation of the destruction of the property of innocent people, not to mention the killing of innocent people.

Broadcast interview/"Newsmaker
Saturday," Cable News Network, 8-7.

Chaim Herzog
*Former Israeli Ambassador/Permanent
Representative to the United Nations* *1*

[On criticism of Israel's invasion and current occupation of Lebanon to force out the PLO]: We need the perspective of time and history. In December 1973, for example, you would have said that the Yom Kippur war was an unmitigated disaster. Now you see that it has led to peace with Egypt. This war has broken the logjam, just as the Yom Kippur war broke the logjam. It's broken the logjam on the Palestinian question and it's given a completely new dimension to that issue.
The New York Times, 11-14:(1)10.

Salim Hoss
Former Premier of Lebanon *2*

[On the Israeli invasion of Lebanon to oust the PLO]: I think, in a way, the crisis has damaged us a lot by way of standing and image. But, looking at it another way, it has also improved our standing and image, because if we can weather this, we can weather anything. I have always said I would worry about Lebanon. But not about the Lebanese.
Interview/Los Angeles Times, 10-25:(I)8.

Hussein I
King of Jordan *3*

[On the Iran-Iraq war]: We have supported Iraq in the war from the beginning. Iraq is our strategic depth. It has supported us whenever we were in difficulty. And we are facing a threat that is aimed not only at Iraq but at the entire Arab world. Iran is engaged in a sinister drive to create a rift between Sunni and Shiite Moslems. Its goal is the destabilization of not just Iraq but the entire Arab [Persian] Gulf and Saudi Arabia. The recent coup attempt in Bahrain was backed by Iran and was proof of Iran's ambitions. Beyond that, Israel is supporting Iran with arms and equipment and spares—and has been even through the [U.S.] hostage crisis, along with radical Arab states. The effect is a dangerous polarization of the area. What is at stake is the very future of the Arab world as we know it.
*Interview, Amman/
U.S. News & World Report, 3-15:32.*

4

So many things have happened of late [in the Middle East]. The [Israeli] annexation of the Golan Heights was but one of a series of events that have created great instability in the area—[Israel's] bombing of Beirut and the nuclear reactor in Baghdad, to name a few. These are moves against peace, and they are enhanced by Israel's tremendous arsenal. We have been told that Israel can wage war on all fronts for at least six months without need of outside support. This was [former U.S. Secretary of State Henry] Kissinger's theory: that a strong Israel would be more reasonable, responsible and secure—and more willing to make peace. The opposite has happened. Some people say it is just [Israeli] Prime Minister Begin. But his re-election after the attack on Baghdad and Lebanon indicates to me that he identifies with the people and they with him.
*Interview, Amman/
Chicago Tribune, 3-26:(1)11.*

5

[On whether Jordan could become the Palestinian homeland]: Jordan has, to its credit, always associated itself with the Palestinian hopes and aspirations, with the Arab cause, [giving Palestinians] the chance to feel at home here in Jordan as members of the Jordanian family. [But] this does not mean in any way that the issue is resolved. The issue has been, will be—until a resolution is reached—that of legitimate Palestinian rights on Palestinian soil under occupation by Israel: West Bank, Arab Jerusalem and Gaza.
*Broadcast interview, Amman/
"This Week with David
Brinkley," ABC-TV, 8-29.*

6

I've never had any idea of holding negotiations with the [current Israeli] government based on what I've seen, what we have lived through in this area, of their attitude throughout and of their actions in the occupied territories. In any event, they have made it clear time and again that in their view Jordan is Palestine and the territories under [Israeli] occupation are theirs. So there has never been any room to consider involvement in any

(HUSSEIN I)

negotiations. [As for the Camp David peace process,] it was hardly a matter of days [after the accord was signed] before [Israeli] settlements [in the West Bank] began and continued, and to every American attempt to put an end to that ... the Israeli response was to accelerate their movements in that area. Camp David may have achieved something in terms of Sinai and the Egyptian territory that was occupied. But it certainly gave Israel a chance to cause far more damage to the possibilities of peace than at any previous phase or stage.

Interview, Amman, Sept. 21/
The Washington Post, 9-22:(A)19.

1

[On his opinion of Israeli Prime Minister Menachem Begin]: What can I say? He is one of the world's foremost terrorists. I honestly can't see how negotiations are possible under the present circumstances [the Israeli occupation of Lebanon] and the present leadership. They [the Israelis] threaten not only themselves but future generations.

Broadcast interview, Amman/
"Today" show, NBC-TV, 9-21.

Saddam Hussein
President of Iraq

2

[On his country's war with Iran]: The war will continue until our enemy respects us and respects our independence. There is no other choice. We have tried every means, knocked on all the doors. We have nothing before us but to fight.

To U.S. journalists, Baghdad, Nov. 16/
Los Angeles Times, 11-17:(I)1.

Henry M. Jackson
United States Senator, D—Washington

3

...let us remember when we're talking about Israel that it's the only ally we have out there that has credibility ... as we look at the entire Middle East area. The only ally that has discounted—discounted the Soviet Union's finest conventional armor, the SAM-6s, their tanks, their aircraft, and so on. So Israel is a

very important ally, a democracy that we can rely on in the event that the situation in the Persian Gulf should blow apart. The other Arab countries have no credibility in terms of a deterrent force in that area.

Broadcast interview/"Meet the Press," NBC-TV, 11-28.

Ali Khamenei
President of Iran

4

[On the successes and failures of the revolution which ousted the Shah in 1979]: We experimented with freedom. We have freed our culture to a great extent from the dependence which our enemies, especially the Americans, imposed on us. We have been born again. On the other hand, we have many failures. We still have not built the Islamic society we envisioned. We confess many imperfections still exist ... Our greatest problem is that our people never believed that by their actions they could determine their own fate. The old regime taught us to sit and wait for everything—wheat, eggs, chickens, industrial machines, drugs, household goods—to come from abroad ... We have to convince our people completely to stand on their own feet—in what they consume and in what they produce.

Interview, Teheran, February/
Newsweek, 2-22:41.

Ruhollah Khomeini
Spiritual leader of Iran

5

[Addressing Iraqis on that country's current war with Iran]: Your Iranian brothers, in order to defend their country and push back the attacks of the enemy of Islam, have been forced to cross over into Iraq to save the oppressed Iraqi people from the dominance of the [ruling] Baath Party. Rise up and install the Islamic government that you want. Do not let the United States decide the destiny of your country.

Broadcast address, July 14/
The Washington Post, 7-15:(A)1.

Rami Khouri
Editor, "The Jordan Times"

6

The PLO is fully aware of the close links between Jordanians and Palestinians and the

(RAMI KHOURI)

logic of some kind of an association. But this linkage can only come after the PLO has acquired a sovereign state of its own. The PLO seems prepared to show some flexibility on the question of territory, but it is never going to compromise on the question of sovereignty.

The New York Times, 10-15:6.

Jeane J. Kirkpatrick
United States Ambassador/Permanent Representative to the United Nations

1

Israel is a very unpopular nation at the UN, and [the U.S.] position [of support] on Israel and the Middle East is a very unpopular one. Israel is regularly scapegoated in the UN. The Arab bloc is very well organized, sometimes linked to the Soviet bloc on one hand and the Africans on the other. The phrase, "Zionism is racism," embodies the political alliance between Arabs and Africans on Middle East as well as African questions.

Interview/The Washington Post, 1-28:(A)14.

Henry A. Kissinger
Former Secretary of State of the United States

2

[Israeli] annexation of the West Bank—overt or disguised—will sow the seeds of endless crises, one of which will eventually erupt into conflagration. It is not even in the interest of Israel however narrowly conceived. The incorporation of Gaza and the West Bank into Israel will sooner or later produce an Arab majority that will destroy the essence of the Jewish state. And if Israel seeks to escape this dilemma by expelling all the Arabs, it will lose the moral support of even its best friends. Over an historical period, Israel would not be able to withstand the crisis that would result.

Interview/The Christian Science Monitor, 11-26:24.

Francois Mitterrand
President of France

3

I feel the [Arab] inhabitants of the Gaza Strip and the West Bank should have a home-
land of their own because you can't expect a people to renounce their identity ... They [must] be permitted to decide their own fate ... The first right is the right to live, the right to exist, which is yours, ladies and gentlemen, and ... [also is the right] of the Palestinians of the Gaza Strip and West Bank and the people of Lebanon.

Before the Israeli Knesset [Parliament], Jerusalem, March 4/ Los Angeles Times, 3-5:(I)10.

Hosni Mubarak
President of Egypt

4

Egypt belongs to all the people, and so the wealth of this country should not be restricted to a privileged few, nor should the grass roots be shouldering beyond what they can endure ... We would not like any of those big leaps, but a gradual and cautious development for a maximum rate of growth. The government cannot alone perform miracles. There should be genuine mass sharing.

Broadcast address to the nation, Cairo, Jan. 26/The New York Times, 1-27:6.

5

We deal with all countries with an open heart and without complexes, as long as they respect our sovereignty and our free will in deciding what is best for us and our interests and is in keeping with our principles, the foremost of which is the philosophy of non-alignment ... We shall cooperate with all countries who extend a friendly hand, but we reject subordination. Egypt's strategic interests lie in its ties with Arab, African and Islamic nations, but that does not prevent close and deep relations with European states, the United States and others.

Broadcast address to the nation, Cairo, Jan. 26/Los Angeles Times, 1-27:(I)13.

6

Both [Israel and the Palestinians] have an inherent right to exist and function as a national entity, free from domination and fear. The exercise of the right to self-determination cannot be denied to the Palestinian people. In fact, it is the best guarantee for Israeli security. This is the lesson of history and the course of the future.

At White House, Washington, Feb. 3/ The New York Times, 2-4:4.

WHAT THEY SAID IN 1982

(HOSNI MUBARAK)

1

You [Israelis] are a very strange people. You want us to have peace with you and to have no relations with anybody else? We are a part of the Arab world, and for hundreds and hundreds of years we've had good relations with it. There is no conflict between the [Egypt-Israeli] peace process and our relations with the Arabs. I have said many times that if our relations with the Israelis are good, we can ease any tensions that might arise between you and the Arabs. That's a fact. But your people are always suspicious and they have an imagination. As [Israeli Foreign Minister] Shamir told me: "We are afraid that the Arabs are pressuring you not to visit Jerusalem." I told him I never accept pressure from any foreign power at all. You [Israelis] are suspicious by nature.

Interview/Newsweek, 3-15:34.

2

[Saying his country will not turn against Israel after the Israeli withdrawal from Sinai in April]: I remember the words we agreed on when [Israeli Prime Minister] Begin was here to attend the funeral of [the late Egyptian] President Sadat. We agreed about peace forever, and we shook hands on that. He mentioned it again in my house—that we should build peace forever. And I agree 100 per cent ... Everybody's thinking that after April we are going to drop relations with Israel, we are going to make tensions with the United States, we are going to turn back to the Soviet Union. It's for those who are living in another world, it's wild imagination, it's illusions.

Interview, Heliopolis, Egypt,
March 21/The New York Times, 3-23:4.

3

The present rate of population increase [in Egypt] obstructs economic development and shatters our hopes for securing a prosperous life for every Egyptian.

Los Angeles Times, 4-23:(IX)6.

4

[On the possible evacuation of Lebanon by the PLO as a result of the Israeli invasion of

278

that country]: Where will the Palestinians go? They will be dispersed among many countries. The distribution of the Palestinians among Arab countries is an Arab question, not an American or Israeli question. Accordingly, the Arabs must sink their differences and meet and agree on a unified policy for solving this problem ... Instead of expelling them, we must find a land where they can take refuge. We must give them the right of self-determination.

News conference, Cairo, July 15/
The New York Times, 7-16:4.

Yitzhak Navon
President of Israel

5

My criteria for judging what world leaders want to do is the following: Whatever they tell their own people in their own language over a certain period of time is their real intention. Whatever the PLO or others will say in interviews with foreign correspondents is not relevant. They can say whatever they want; it is propaganda. [But] whatever they tell their own people in Arabic for a long period of time, that is the truth.

Interview, Jerusalem/
Los Angeles Times, 1-20:(I)16.

6

[On foreign press coverage of Israel]: You build a house, lay its foundations, brick by brick. What's there to write about? You finish it in a year, it's completed, and that's it. But if the building explodes? That's dramatic, to film, to talk about. I get a little desperate sometimes. There are so many positive things [in Israel], and they have no echo in the media, in the world. What are we in the media? What picture do you make of us before the world? A nation of guns, war, conflict, crisis. Is that all there is? Just people with guns? We have 27 daily newspapers, including in Arabic; 75 weeklies. We publish about 4,000 new books a year, two-thirds of them new original works. Forty plays a year in our theatres, and going out to every town; 79 art exhibitions every year. This is not part of the world's image of Israel. Israel is now the world center of Jewish studies. Is that nothing?

Interview/The New York Times Magazine, 3-7:55.

(YITZHAK NAVON)

1

[Recommending an official commission of inquiry into the massacre of Palestinians in a refugee camp in Israeli-occupied Beirut]: After all that has happened, we must not pass on to business as usual. We have an obligation to ourselves, to our self-image, as well as to that part of the civilized world to which we feel we belong. We are an ancient people, experienced in suffering and possessing an ancient heritage of moral values of truth and justice. If we will cling to these values, I am sure that we will emerge from this far stronger.

The New York Times, 9-24:8.

Nayif ibn Abdel Aziz
Minister of the Interior
of Saudi Arabia

2

The [Iraqi] conflict with Iran is not only a war between Iran and Iraq. It is [Iran's] ambition to control the Arab side [of the Persian Gulf] beginning with Bahrain and ending with all other space by trying to install pro-Iranian regimes.

Interview/Chicago Tribune, 4-18:(1)20.

Andreas Papandreou
Prime Minister of Greece

3

[On PLO chairman Yasir Arafat's arrival in Greece after being driven out of Lebanon by Israel]: We feel honored that Yasir Arafat and his collaborators chose to land here. In their sacred struggle, they will always find us on their side ... We have assured Mr. Arafat that the Greek people and the Greek government are standing beside the struggle of the Palestinian people for full autonomy, their own homeland and their own state.

Athens, Sept. 1/Los Angeles Times, 9-2:(I)2.

Shimon Peres
Chairman, Israeli Labor Party

4

[The] Labor [Party] does not stand for the removal of [Jewish] settlements [in Israeli-occupied Arab territory], but it also opposes the addition of new settlements in densely populated Arab areas because we believe this will ... change Israel from a Jewish state into a Jewish-Arab state.

Jerusalem, April 30/The Washington Post, 5-1:(A)15.

5

[Saying Israeli forces should not go into West Beirut during their current invasion of Lebanon]: We must remember nowadays that a war is a photographed war. In the battlefield there are not only tanks and cannon but television cameras. Pictures are stronger than words; they conquer world public opinion. In addition to the moral consideration, which does exist, we must consider this factor too. For this reason, we are against entering [West] Beirut.

Before the Knesset (Parliament), Jerusalem, June 29/Los Angeles Times, 6-30:(I)6.

6

[On the massacre of Palestinians in refugee camps in Israeli-occupied Beirut]: I do not suggest for a second that anybody in Israel would knowingly lend his hand, directly or indirectly, to this shocking criminal act. And even as I come to call this government and its head to account, I must make clear that I do not accuse them of premeditated connections in any way to this heinous deed ... We are sure that the Israeli Defense Forces did not lend its hand to this spilling of blood. Nevertheless, there is no way to pass over the heavy sins of the government, which did not pay attention to the obvious state of things: grave mistakes in judgment, closing its ears to warnings; and which because of lack of ability or lack of will tries to shake off the burden of responsibility for its actions and its failures ... I want to ask, Mr. Prime Minister, Mr. Defense Minister, whose was this stupid idea, to send the [Lebanese] Phalangists [who carried out the massacre] to the refugee camps to find the [PLO] terrorists? ... You don't have to be a political genius or a decorated general; it's enough to be a village policeman, to understand ahead of time that these militias—in the wake of the [recent] murder of their leader—were more liable than ever to sow destruction, even among

279

WHAT THEY SAID IN 1982

innocent people. Is this surprising? This was something unprecedented?

Before the Knesset (Parliament), Jerusalem; Sept. 22/The New York Times, 9-23:8.

Norman Podhoretz
Editor, "Commentary" magazine

1

[On those who say the PLO is largely a social-welfare organization]: Anyone who thinks that drafting 12-year-old children into military service and hiding behind civilians so that there will be a maximum number of civilian casualties in the event of a war, anyone who thinks that such an organization is benign and beneficent and engaged in "social welfare" is perverting the language. What is more, the people in southern Lebanon [from where the Israelis recently uprooted the PLO], the Lebanese themselves—as we now know from an abundance of testimony from the area—regarded the PLO as a bunch of thugs, killers and tyrants, and are very happy to be freed from their tyrannical domination.

Interview/Los Angeles Herald Examiner, 10-4:(A)5.

Muammar el-Qaddafi
Chief of State of Libya

2

Saudi Arabia is the Number 1 enemy of Islam and the Arab nation. Saudi Arabia, with orders from the United States, has declared a war of hunger against Libya . . . Saudi Arabia has flooded the world market with its oil. It is selling its oil cheap, and by doing this it is declaring its open alliance with Israel and America against Libya and other nations who depend on oil for their livelihood . . . These nations now face an economic blockade ordered by America and executed by Saudi Arabia.

March 2/Chicago Tribune, 3-4:(1)1.

Yitzhak Rabin
Former Prime Minister of Israel

3

[Criticizing Israel's current invasion of Lebanon]: We never thought that we should go to war in order to intervene in the internal affairs

280

of a neighboring country. There is no justification for launching another military campaign in order to achieve this goal. It would be a grave mistake to endanger the lives of Israeli soldiers for this. I am doubtful as to whether even after Beirut is cleared up, the Lebanese will have the strength to overcome their sectarian strife. Regarding the ousting of the Syrians from Lebanon—if we can achieve this through negotiations, fine. If not, we must not resume the fighting in order to achieve this goal. We must not prolong the stay of the Israeli Army in Lebanon in order to achieve this goal.

Before the Knesset (Parliament), Jerusalem/Los Angeles Times, 7-4:(V)6.

Nick J. Rahall
United States Representative, D–West Virginia

4

[Criticizing Israel's invasion of Lebanon]: I submit that this country [the U.S.] has given birth to a monster. We have let that monster [Israel] grow, we have armed it, and now we can't control it.

At House subcommittee hearing, Washington, June 17/ Los Angeles Times, 6-18:(I)10.

Ronald Reagan
President of the United States

5

I know the PLO has kind of held a position that their non-recognition of Israel is a bargaining chip they could bring to the negotiating table. I think they're wrong. I don't see how you sit down to bargain with someone who has taken a position where they deny your right to exist, and that you should be destroyed. That to me is not a bargaining chip. And I am hopeful that, as we continue dealing with the more moderate Arab states, we will bring them to accept recognition that Israel is a nation that is going to continue existing.

Interview/Los Angeles Times, 1-15:(II)12.

6

Israel is a strategic treasure. In contrast to other pro-Western states like Saudi Arabia and the Gulf Emirates, Israel is strong. After the overthrow of the Shah [of Iran], Israel remains

(RONALD REAGAN)

the only reliable ally of America in the Middle East ... Israel does not depend on the existence of an autocratic ruler. It is guided by a democratic purpose, national unity. It has the technological and military foundations that make it capable of being a loyal ally of America.

Interview/Chicago Tribune, 2-8:(1)5.

1

[On Israel's imminent return of occupied Sinai to Egypt]: We fervently pray that the return of the Sinai will be accepted for what it is ... a magnificent act of faith by Israel for the sake of peace. Today we are reminded we must be sensitive to the history of a people whose country [Israel] was reborn from the ashes of the Holocaust, a country that rightfully never takes its security for granted.

At Holocaust remembrance ceremony, Washington, April 20/Los Angeles Times, 4-21:(I)10.

2

... it is clear to me that [Arab-Israeli] peace cannot be achieved by the formation of an independent Palestinian state in [the West Bank and Gaza]. Nor is it achievable on the basis of Israeli sovereignty or permanent control over the West Bank and Gaza. So the United States will not support the establishment of an independent Palestinian state in the West Bank and Gaza, and we will not support annexation or permanent control by Israel ... But it is the firm view of the United States that self-government by the Palestinians of the West Bank and Gaza in association with Jordan offers the best chance for a durable, just and lasting peace ... It is the United States' position that, in return for peace, the withdrawal provision of [UN] Resolution 242 applies to all fronts, including the West Bank and Gaza. When the border is negotiated between Jordan and Israel, our view on the extent to which Israel should be asked to give up territory will be heavily affected by the extent of true peace and normalization and the security arrangements offered in return. Finally, we remain convinced that Jerusalem must remain undivided, but its final status should be decided through negotiations ...

And make no mistake, the United States will oppose any proposal—from any party and at any point in the negotiating process—that threatens the security of Israel. America's commitment to the security of Israel is ironclad—and, I might add, mine is ironclad too.

Broadcast address to the nation, Burbank, Calif., Sept. 1/ Los Angeles Times, 9-2:(II)12.

3

[On the assassination of Lebanese President-elect Bashir Gemayel]: [It is a] heinous crime against Lebanon and against the cause of peace in the Middle East. [The] tragedy will be all the greater if men of good-will in Lebanon and in countries friendly to Lebanon permit disorder to continue in this war-torn country. This must not happen. The U.S. government stands by Lebanon with its full support in this hour of need.

Washington, Sept. 15/ Los Angeles Times, 9-16:(I)1.*

4

[On the massacre of Palestinians by Christian militiamen in refugee camps in Israeli-controlled Beirut]: The scenes that the whole world witnessed this past weekend were among the most heart-rending in the long nightmare of Lebanon's agony ... It is not enough for us to view this as some remote event in which we ourselves are not involved. For our friends in Lebanon and Israel, for our friends in Europe and elsewhere in the Middle East, and for us as Americans, this tragedy, horrible as it is, reminds us of the absolute imperative of bringing peace to that troubled country and region ... Israel must have learned that there is no way it can impose its own solutions on hatreds as deep and bitter as those that produced this tragedy. If it seeks to do so, it will only sink more deeply into the quagmire that looms before it.

Broadcast address to the nation, Washington, Sept. 20/ Los Angeles Times, 9-21:(I)8.

WHAT THEY SAID IN 1982

(RONALD REAGAN)

1

[On those who say he is trying to undermine the government of Israeli Prime Minister Menachem Begin]: We have never interfered with the internal government of a country, and we have no intention of doing so. We never have had any thought of that kind. We expect to be doing business with the government of Israel and with Prime Minister Begin if that is the decision of the Israeli people. The Israeli people are proving with their reaction to the Beirut massacre that there is no change in the spirit of Israel. They are our ally. We feel morally obligated to the preservation of Israel, and we are going to continue to be that way.

News conference, Washington, Sept. 28/
Los Angeles Times, 9-29:(I)11.

Danny Rubinstein
Chief correspondent on Arab affairs,
"Davar," newspaper of General
Confederation of Labor of Israel

2

We [Israelis] are not a tolerant people any more. The Jewish communities in New York and throughout the United States are more liberal, more tolerant, more humanistic than the Jewish community here in Israel . . . It's the pressure of continuous war, of feeling isolated, surrounded by enemies, of wondering how to keep on. This pressure creates a withdrawal from liberal values. People feel, "Leave me alone, I want to be without doubts. I want to be strong, able to defend myself—that's all that counts." The children of this country are not Jews any more. Or maybe it's that we are Jews, but not Jewish.

Interview/The New York
Times Magazine, 3-7:22.

Etienne Saqa
Leader, Guardians of the Cedars
(affiliated with Phalange Party
of Lebanon)

3

[Defending the massacre of Palestinians by Lebanese militia in refugee camps in Israeli-occupied Beirut]: We have the full right to deal with our enemies in Lebanon in a manner we

find suitable. This is our internal problem. Don't interfere in this . . . Why is the whole world upset about [the massacre] while we have been killed and persecuted for eight years by the PLO and the Syrians? It was a Lebanese reaction from the parents and relatives of our martyrs, of the 100,000 Lebanese killed. Don't think we are killers. We are civilized people.

News conference, Jerusalem, Dec. 1/
Chicago Tribune, 12-2:(1)5.

Saud al-Faisal
Foreign Minister of Saudi Arabia

4

It is time for the United States to look not to the security of Israel but to how it wants to be viewed in the international community. If the United States guarantees Israel's security with aid and military resources, it should also guarantee to Arabs that these resources should not be used against them. Israel is misusing these resources and undermining the security of the region. Making Israel more secure has led not to compromises, but to Israeli aggrandizement—and has brought destruction on the Palestinians and Lebanese, with American arms. [Israel's assault on Beirut] is a result of the Camp David process. It happened after Camp David, not before.

To reporters, Washington, July 19/
Los Angeles Times, 7-20:(I)6.

Yitzhak Shamir
Foreign Minister of Israel

5

Israel will make no [more] compromises. At Camp David we reached the final and absolute limit . . . The world had better know that we will take no more serious risks . . . We must tell the United States and others who want us to go further: "slow down."

Before youth wing of Herut Party/
Newsweek, 1-18:43.

6

We want peace, but only on conditions which will enable us to continue our existence, and this means the Golan Heights, Judea and Samaria [the West Bank] within the boundaries of the land of Israel.

At convention of Aguda/Newsweek, 1-18:43.

(YITZHAK SHAMIR)

1

Any support of the PLO in action or by declarations, directly or by implications, weakens the chances for a dialogue between us and our Arab neighbors. Calls to include the terrorist organizations in negotiations encourage their activities and disregard reality, and they make more remote the quest for peace.

May 30/The Washington Post, 5-31:(A)26.

2

[On the massacre of Palestinians in refugee camps in Israeli-occupied Beirut and on criticism of Israel for that massacre]: Everyone knows [the Phalangists] committed the crime. Lebanon knows, the Arab countries know, the PLO knows, the United States knows. Europe and everyone else knows. Yet not one word of condemnation has been uttered against those who committed this cruel massacre—all the propaganda is directed against Israel. Everyone must mobilize against this terrible false libel with which they are seeking to smear the Israeli people and nation.

To reporters, Tel Aviv, Sept. 28/
Los Angeles Times, 9-29:(I)8.

Ariel Sharon
Minister of Defense of Israel

3

[On criticism of Israeli force used in response to Arab provocations]: An Israeli diplomat is murdered in Paris, a sergeant is killed in a grenade attack in Gaza, a bomb explodes beside a kindergarten in Holon, and no one is surprised. Suddenly everybody—from around the world and inside Israel—turns to us and appeals that we shouldn't act ... A nation that wishes to live cannot act this way. A nation must defend its sons. They say that nothing that has happened justifies action, that there must be what the Americans call "clear provocation." But what is clear provocation? One amputee? One dead? Five dead? Ten dead?

At Young Herut conference, April 12/
The New York Times, 4-14:4.

4

[On Israel's ending of its occupation of Egyptian Sinai]: Today we are completing the

evacuation of Sinai in the framework of the Camp David accords and the first peace treaty that Israel has signed with the largest and most important of the Arab countries—Egypt. We have decided to give peace a full chance while assuming the full extent of the risk. For a generation, we have fought again and again in Sinai ... The sands of the Sinai Desert are soaked with the blood of our fighters.

Order of the day, April 25/*
Los Angeles Times, 4-26:(L)13.

5

[On Israel's invasion of Lebanon to drive out the PLO]: What's happening is an immense blow to the Palestinian and international terror movement. Whatever the impact of our strike, it will take them a lot of time to reorganize and start operating again. The bigger the blow is and the more we damage the PLO infrastructure, the more the Arabs in [the West Bank] and Gaza will be ready to negotiate with us and establish coexistence. I am not sure whether the destruction of these organizations will convince ransom-paying Arab governments to abandon the PLO. [But] I am convinced that the echo of this campaign is reaching into the house of every Arab family in [the West Bank] and Gaza. *Interview/Time, 6-21:19.*

6

[On criticism of Israel's invasion of Lebanon to drive out the PLO]: I remember how you [the British] totally destroyed cities in World War II. I never heard one word from you when Jews were killed by the PLO in Israel and in Europe. I never heard one word about the [PLO's] massacre of Christians in Lebanon. We [Israelis] have shown more humanity in this operation than you British have shown anywhere, at any time.

BBC interview/Time, 7-5:35.

7

As long as the PLO exists in Beirut there will be no strong and independent government in Lebanon. Our demand [during Israel's current invasion of Lebanon] means that all foreign troops down to the last man must leave the

WHAT THEY SAID IN 1982

(ARIEL SHARON)

country—the terrorists, the Syrians and ourselves.

Interview/The New York Times, 7-11:(1)6.

1

...I am not a warmonger. I had the privilege to participate in all the wars and battles of this country. I have seen the most glorious moments, felt the horror of war. I don't believe that one who has passed all this way, as I did, could be a warmonger ... I get up at 5:30; I like to see the sunrise, to see the fields in the morning. If every member of the Cabinet held the horns of a ram every day, all the problems of the government would be solved. Among the sheep, I look like a man—only among men do I look like a wolf.

Interview/Life, September:40.

2

[On the massacre of Palestinians in refugee camps in Israeli-occupied Beirut]: This is a dark day for all of us. Innocent people, old men, women and children were murdered for no crime in Beirut. In the cruelest possible way. The heart beats faster and our eyes well with tears. The human mind cannot accept that such would be the fate of innocent people. How is it possible to explain something for which there can be no explanation, no forgiving and no pardon? I did not come to explain this terrible tragedy, because it is part of a nether world, not ours, but of those who perpetrated this slaughter. I hope they get their just punishment, although this is not under our control ... [Israel is] not at war with the Palestinian people. We have declared a war of destruction on Palestinian terror. And if there are those indirectly responsible for these acts of murder—those directly responsible are Lebanese—then those indirectly responsible belong to the PLO terror organization. Therefore, I can say clearly and immediately that no soldier and no commander in the Israeli Defense Forces participated in this terrible act. The hands of the IDF are clean.

Before the Knesset (Parliament), Jerusalem, Sept. 22/The New York Times, 9-23:8.

Rashad Shawa
Former Palestinian Mayor
of Israeli-occupied Gaza

3

[On Israel's firing him as Mayor]: Dismissing me and my type is not going to help solve the Palestinian problem. This will make it more complicated. I feel that, together with our right to our own homeland and to self-determination, we [Palestinians] can live peacefully side by side with Israel. Now they [the Israelis] will have to deal with more extreme people in the future.

Interview, July 9/
Chicago Tribune, 7-10:(1)8.

George P. Shultz
Secretary of State-designate
of the United States

4

The legitimate needs and problems of the Palestinian people must be addressed and resolved—urgently, and in all their dimensions ... There are many problems in the Middle East. But ... without a satisfactory solution to this one, it's very hard to imagine the prospect of peace in the Middle East ... Right now, the issue of the Palestinians' needs, grievances and objectives is one that we must address ourselves to ... You have a very substantial number of people—who are capable, energetic people—with no place to go, and it's just an inherently explosive situation.

At Senate Foreign Relations Committee
hearing on his confirmation, Washington, July/
U.S. News & World Report, 7-26:24.

5

[Saying the U.S. should strengthen its ties to the Arab world]: It is from them that the West gets much of its oil; it is with them that we share an interest and must cooperate in resisting Soviet imperialism; it is with them, as [with] Israel, that we will be able to bring peace to the Middle East. The brilliant Arab heritage of science, culture and thought has a fresh dynamism.

At Senate Foreign Relations Committee
hearing on his confirmation, Washington,
July 13/Chicago Tribune, 7-14:(1)1.

(GEORGE P. SHULTZ)

1

[No one] should dispute the depth and durability of America's commitment to the security of Israel or of our readiness to assure that Israel has the necessary means to defend herself. I share in this deep and enduring commitment. And more, I recognize that democratic Israel shares with us a deep commitment to the security of the West.

At Senate Foreign Relations Committee hearing on his confirmation, Washington, July 13/The New York Times, 7-14:1.

George P. Shultz
Secretary of State
of the United States

2

[On the PLO having been driven out of Lebanon by Israel] : I think, as a military force, they have been reduced drastically in importance, and the support that they were getting from the Russians just was not there. And I think also—even more profoundly—that the pattern that they have represented of terror, of violence, as a way of doing something for the Palestinian cause has been shown not to work. And so I would hope that the leaders of the PLO and everyone in the area will start looking at the peace . . . process rather than the violence and the war process.

Broadcast interview/
"Face the Nation," CBS-TV, 9-5.

3

Of the peoples of the world who need and deserve a place with which they can truly identify, the Palestinian claim is undeniable. But Israel can only have permanent peace in a context in which the Palestinian people also realize their legitimate rights. Similarly, the Palestinian people will be able to achieve their legitimate rights only in a context which gives to Israel what it so clearly has a right to demand—to exist, and to exist in peace and security.

At United Nations, New York, Sept. 30/
The Christian Science Monitor, 10-1:15.

Israel Singer
Executive director,
World Jewish Congress

4

When you say Zionism is racism, you're not saying that Jews are not allowed to be in the West Bank. You're not saying that Jews are not allowed to be occupiers. You're not saying that Jews aren't doing enough for Palestinians. You're saying that the principle that Jews have a national ideology is racism. You're saying that Jews are different from every other people. That's anti-Semitism.

Interview/Los Angeles Herald Examiner, 5-25:(A)4.

Jacobo Timerman
Argentine-Israeli journalist

5

My generation was brought up with the conviction that the kibbutz and its way of life represented the moral tradition of the Jewish people, as well as the political conscience that would lead them to become a normal people in a democratic state. The ideal of Israel was rooted in the belief that the Jews were a people incapable of collectively doing harm to any other people. Normalcy was synonymous with being peaceful, enjoying freedom and friendship with everybody. But Israel is now a military power because of reasons of security. This is a betrayal of the ideas of Israel's founders. And those ideas are the best guarantee for Israel's security.

Interview, Jerusalem, December/
Los Angeles Times, 12-12:(VII)3.

Ali Avbar Velayati
Foreign Minister of Iran

6

It should be taken for granted that Iran has declared that it wants to actively participate in the task of liberating Palestine [from the Israelis]. Negotiations on humiliating terms with Israel, on vacating the Moslem [Israeli-] occupied territories, cannot solve any problem. Israel was created by force and it is indulging in expansionism. Israel understands only the language of power and strength, and this is why the Moslem countries will need to form an Islamic army. Iran can suggest the mechanism to do so, and the relevant details.

News conference, Islamabad, Pakistan/
Chicago Tribune, 4-3:(1)5.

Nicholas A. Veliotes
*Assistant Secretary for Near East
and South Asian Affairs, Department
of State of the United States*

1

[On charges that U.S. Middle East policy relies too heavily on military assistance]: Over any long period of time, clearly the accumulation of large numbers of weapons by potential adversaries has the logic of the outbreak of war ... [Arms sales] are by no means the only portion of our policy [which is designed] above all to try to move the area toward peace. The Soviet Union has used arms sales and grants as the principal if not only means of acquiring influence in the Mideast. We must be responsive to requests for arms from certain of our friends.

*Before Senate Foreign Relations
Committee, Washington, April 15/
The Washington Post,
4-16:(A)4.*

Caspar W. Weinberger
*Secretary of Defense
of the United States*

2

Our principal objectives are to assure the continued access to Persian Gulf oil and to prevent the Soviets from acquiring political military control of the oil directly or through proxies. To achieve these goals, we must allocate a disproportionately larger investment in this region, and we must upgrade our capabilities to project forces to, and operate them in, the region. We should also urgently increase and improve the capabilities of friendly indigenous forces.

*Interview, Washington, June/
The Washington Post, 6-27:(A)9.*

3

[Criticizing the Israeli invasion of Lebanon]: We understand the provocations [the Israelis faced]. We understand that there was shelling of Israeli villages [by the PLO]. We understand the worries about the PLO. But we can't really support or endorse or approve the idea of changing the status quo by the unilateral resort to military force [by the Israelis], and that's one of the things that has made the whole situation not only much more difficult, but much more vital that it be ended as quickly as possible.

*Broadcast interview/
"Meet the Press," NBC-TV, 7-11.*

Mohammed Zia ul-Haq
President of Pakistan

4

[On Israel's invasion of Lebanon to drive out the PLO]: I will not mince my words. Our people are somewhat dissatisfied and quite amazed as to why the U.S. should not take a stand against brutal acts of aggression by the Israelis. The people of Pakistan know that the U.S. has very good relationships with many of the Middle East countries—take Jordan, take Saudi Arabai and the countries of the [Persian] Gulf. Then how could it allow murder to be committed in broad daylight in Lebanon? Pakistani people are quite disappointed that a superpower like the U.S., that stands for human rights, stands for liberty and stands for freedom, is impotent when it comes to Israel. Without U.S. assistance, Israel stands nowhere. There can be no solution to the Middle East problem unless the inherent right of the Palestinians for self-determination is granted. I would then be among those who believe in the right of Israel to exist.

Interview/U.S. News & World Report, 12-13:42.

War and Peace

Harold Brown
*Former Secretary of Defense
of the United States*
1

Strategic [nuclear] war is so obviously catastrophic to all engaged in it that it is only under enormous political stress, provocation and escalation—probably from lower levels of conflict—that it has any chance of happening. A nuclear war would probably get started only by miscalculation.

Time, 3-29:25.

William F. Buckley, Jr.
*Political columnist; Editor,
"National Review"*
2

. . . some things are worth dying for. The special challenge of the time is the sophisticated proposition that although some things may be worth dying for, it cannot be worth dying for nothing, which is what would be left over in the event of a nuclear exchange. All the strategic wit at our resources must be summoned to prevent such an exchange, but the deepest reserve of that wit is the willingness to say, acquiescently, that yes, rather a nuclear exchange than the sale of our souls to the Faustian monsters who sit unsmiling behind their hydrogen missiles, seeking to mastermind the greatest act of human choreography in the history of the world . . . . if the Soviet Union opted for a massive nuclear war, our option must be to return that hell in kind. And this option we would need to choose for so simple a reason as that we would not then have died for nothing, because it is better than nothing to rid the world of such monsters as would unleash such a war.

*Before Philadelphia Society, Chicago/
The Wall Street Journal, 5-21:24.*

McGeorge Bundy
*Professor of history, New York University;
Former Assistant to the President of
the United States (John F. Kennedy
and Lyndon B. Johnson) for
National Security Affairs*
3

It is fundamentally false to suppose that weapons are good for us and limits on weapons bad. I believe that there is a nuclear danger, a Russian danger and an American danger. The short and ugly answer is that not common humanity but two great opposing governments are the primary decision-makers here . . . and these governments have found it easier to build their colossal forces than to limit them.

*Panel discussion, San Francisco/
San Francisco Examiner & Chronicle,
12-26:(Datebook)58.*

Claude Cheysson
Foreign Minister of France
4

[Criticizing current popular peace movements]: The cause of peace is not served by awakening or exploiting the psychosis of war, or by multiplying unilateral proposals of a vague and spectacular nature with the aim of manipulating public opinion. The real paths to disarmament can only be the result of a realistic and objective analysis of the factors that increase or may increase the threat of a generalized military confrontation.

*At United Nations session
on disarmament, New York, June 11/
Los Angeles Times, 6-12:(I)2.*

Alan Cranston
United States Senator, D–California
5

Traditionally, wars have been fought to defend a nation, or to conquer a nation—to

(ALAN CRANSTON)

acquire or defend territory, to defend or violate a principle. Nuclear war can serve none of those purposes, good or bad. There will be no winner; all will be losers. And there may be no survivor to know what principle has been upheld or brought down.

At Democratic Party conference,
Philadelphia, June 25/
The New York Times, 6-26:11.

Richard Falk
Professor of international law,
Princeton University; Former associate
editor, "Foreign Policy" magazine

1

. . . no political goal any country could pursue could justify risking another Hiroshima, or worse. The human race is not suited to handle—let alone survive—today's awesome nuclear weapons. There may be *some* species on *some* planet *somewhere* in the galaxy that has sufficient infallible institutions and sensibilities, but human beings are not that species. So I think we are being compelled to find ways to evolve a less militarized, more sustainable world order.

Interview, Princeton University/
The Christian Science Monitor, 2-4:(B)2.

Robert Fuller
Former president, Oberlin College;
Former professor of physics,
Columbia University

2

The question people in the peace movement should ask themselves is, "What would you do with your life tomorrow morning if God said there won't ever be another war?" Every peace-maker better have a good answer, such as "I'd go fishing or collect photographs of grasses." Chances are, they're searching for peace with a certain hidden element of belligerence, attacking somebody, some enemy, domestic or foreign. My ultimate question is, "Is there a better game than war?" War has been an activity that men and women have played and have loved, and if we're ever going to transcend war-making, it's crucial we admit our own

eternal fascination with its moments of individual exhilaration, comaraderie, nobility and glory . . . Peace is the absence of a very exciting activity: war. Nobody ever opted for nothing in place of something. Expressing peace as anti-war says only what you're *against*. You've got to figure out what it is you are actually *for*. Otherwise, peace sounds like serenity and bliss. If you look at who favors peace and quiet, it's usually the privileged. People who are hungry and oppressed never want peace and the status quo. They are willing to make revolution and war to produce food and justice.

Interview, Paris/The Christian Science
Monitor, 12-16:(B)6.

Alexander M. Haig, Jr.
Secretary of State
of the United States

3

The simple possession of nuclear weapons does not guarantee deterrence. Throughout history, societies have risked their total destruction if the prize of victory was sufficiently great or the consequences of submission sufficiently grave. War, in particular nuclear war, can be deterred, but only if we are able to deny an aggressor military advantage from his action and thus insure his awareness that he cannot prevail in any conflict with us. Deterrence, in short, requires the maintenance of a secure military balance, one which cannot be overturned through surprise attack or sudden technological breakthrough. The quality and credibility of deterrence must be measured against these criteria.

Before Georgetown University's Center
for Strategic and International Studies,
April 6/The New York Times, 4-7:6.

Mark O. Hatfield
United States Senator, R—Oregon

4

[On nuclear war]: I see all life as a part of God's creation, and I think it's rather audacious and presumptuous of humankind to consider that it has the right to destroy creation, to destroy all life. We've developed the ability to

(MARK O. HATFIELD)

destroy the planet, but that doesn't give us the *right* to destroy the planet.

Interview, Washington/The
Christian Science Monitor, 6-17:(B)2.

William G. Hyland
Former Deputy Director, National
Security Council staff   *1*

[On the public movements against nuclear arms, such as the Ground Zero organization]: I'm kind of appalled at the popularization of these subjects. I don't like the idea of a lot of people screaming and yelling that these war-mongers in Washington need to be brought under control. What happens in these Ground Zero-type operations is you get a lot of emotion stirred up, but there's no alternative program. Since it's an issue between us and the Russians, it doesn't lend itself to constant massaging.

Interview/The Washington Post, 4-16:(B)6.

Henry M. Jackson
United States Senator, D–Washington

2

[On the possibility of the U.S. and Soviet Union being accidentally drawn into a conflict between other nations]: That can always be a real danger. World War I was not premeditated and designed. It was by accident and miscalculation ... I think that is what's really worrying people, because it doesn't do any good to freeze the balance of terror; you want to eliminate it. And you want to be sure that you have the institutions in place that can avoid war by accident and miscalculation. I think that is what's really worrying the American people, that some trigger-happy episode will lead to a nuclear showdown and a nuclear conflict.

Interview, Washington, April 25/
The New York Times, 4-26:3.

John Paul II
Pope
                                                            3

The world aspires to peace, seeks peace, has devised means and organizations to protect peace. [But] when a serious controversy presents itself, men seem incapable, even with the help of willing mediators, to find a solution that would save those principles, respect those sentiments and at the same time preserve the peace. How can humanity still have faith in the possibility of peace, especially if, rather than a controversy that is grave, yes, but relatively limited, there were to present itself more grave and complex ones, which would oppose more numerous nations or blocs of countries? ... Give back to the world the hope that good-will, intelligence, magnanimity, political farsighted-ness can at all moments, even the most diffi-cult, succeed in overcoming the temptation to cut with a sword the knots that put in peril peaceful international coexistence.

Weekly blessing, Vatican City, May 2/
The New York Times, 5-3:12.

4

Our world is disfigured by war and violence. People are having to live under the shadow of the nuclear nightmare, yet people everywhere long for peace. [But peace is more than just the absence of war.] It involves mutual respect and confidence between peoples and nations. It involves collaboration and binding agreements. Like a cathedral, peace has to be constructed patiently and with unshakeable faith. War should belong to the tragic past, to history, and it should find no place on humanity's agenda for the future.

Coventry, England, May 30/
The Washington Post, 5-31:(A)18.

5

[On war]: ... each time that we risk man's life, we start to ride along dangerous, regressive and anti-human paths. Therefore ... humanity should question itself once more about the absurd and always unfair phenomenon of war, on whose stage of death and pain only remain standing the negotiating table that could and should have prevented it.

Buenos Aires, Argentina, June 11/
The New York Times, 6-12:4.

George F. Kennan
Former United States Ambassador
to the Soviet Union

6

[Saying the U.S. should publicly announce that it will not be the first to use nuclear

(GEORGE F. KENNAN)

weapons in any future war]: The number of nuclear arms in the superpowers' arsenals is so great and so horrendous that the risk has become unacceptable. To initiate atomic war, even on a small scale, would be a profound gamble. The damage that would result from escalation to an all-out nuclear exchange is difficult to assess but probably beyond belief. It would shatter Western civilization. One mustn't play with such a possibility. By clinging to a "first use" option, we are, in fact, doing precisely that. It's time to finally put this idea behind us ... Today, it is perfectly clear that neither side can initiate a nuclear attack—no matter how limited—without facing the certainty that it will be answered by a nuclear strike in retaliation. When we declared this doctrine [of possibly using battlefield nuclear weapons against a large Soviet conventional aattack in Western Europe] some three decades ago, the U.S. had overwhelming nuclear superiority. Soviet retaliation was questionable. Today, it is no longer in question. The Russians won't blink.

Interview/U.S. News & World Report, 4-26:17.

Jeane J. Kirkpatrick
United States Ambassador/
Permanent Representative
to the United Nations 1

We have war when at least one of the parties to a conflict wants something more than it wants peace.

Interview/U.S. News & World Report, 12-27:29.

John F. Lehman, Jr.
Secretary of the Navy
of the United States 2

Peace is not the result of unilateral disarmament. It never has been. And it never will be. Peace doesn't just happen; it must be forced.

At dedication of church, Philadelphia/
Los Angeles Times, 3-8:(I)2.

Fred Luchsinger
Editor-in-chief, "Neue
Zurcher Zeitung," Zurich 3

Pessimism is not a bad mood for viewing the world situation. Too much optimism often

290

means neglecting problems. We have grave problems and cause to worry. On the other hand, pessimism can be excessive. There is a tendency, for instance, to exaggerate the danger of imminent war. Today's European pacifist wave, which is a pessimistic wave, tends to overlook the basic political conditions for securing peace and may well be followed by a real crisis. In 1938-39, Europe—England, France—had a pessimistic pacifist wave that neglected the need for resistance by military equilibrium against the Nazis, and it had to pay for it.

Interview/World Press Review, September:27.

Richard W. Lyman
President, Rockefeller Foundation
4

[On nuclear war]: We are faced with an unprecedented, all-but-indescribable power of destructiveness in the hands of a species with an all-too-familiar capacity for aggressive, not to mention self-destructive, behavior. Treating nuclear war, and even the nuclear arms race, as "insanity," too readily becomes a way of over-simplifying the problems. It suggests that all that is necessary to be rid of this nightmare is to put power into the hands of people more rational than those who have been wielding it.

At symposium on nuclear war/
The Washington Post, 4-16:(C)1.

Roger C. Molander
Executive director, Ground Zero
(anti-nuclear war organization);
Former nuclear strategist, National
Security Council of the United States 5

A new [defense] triad must emerge. Weapons systems for defense and arms control agreements are necessary but not sufficient elements for preventing nuclear war. What we need is a third element: specific efforts to alter, and improve, the political relationship between the United States and the Soviet Union. Arms control can no longer carry the burden of improving that relationship. In fact, the opposite is true. We probably can't have meaningful arms-control agreements unless there is an improvement in the U.S.-Soviet relationship.

Interview, Washington/The New York Times, 4-17:8.

Daniel P. Moynihan
United States Senator, D—New York   *1*

[On conveying the horror of nuclear weapons]: Twenty Americans died at Yorktown. In the Napoleonic Wars, the British Navy lost scarcely 6,000 men. How are we to think of civilization disappearing in an hour's time? Hard and carefully, that is how.

Time, 2-1:69.

Ronald Reagan
President of the United States   *2*

Peace is not the absence of conflict, but the ability to cope with conflict by peaceful means. I believe we can cope. I believe that the West can fashion a realistic, durable policy that will protect our interests and keep the peace, not just for this generation, but for your children and grandchildren. I believe such a policy consists of five points: military balance, economic security, regional stability, arms reduction, and dialogue.

At Eureka (Ill.) College commencement, May 9/The Washington Post, 5-10:(A)12.

3

A great many of the peace demonstrators [around the world] are truly sincere ... but I'm equally sure that those who plan and promote some of the demonstrations have motives of their own, and I will believe in their sincerity when they promote or demand a peace demonstration on the other side of the Iron Curtain.

At fund-raising dinner for Texas Governor William Clements, Houston, June 15/ Los Angeles Herald Examiner, 6-16:(A)7.

4

Agreements on arms control and disarmament can be useful in reinforcing peace, but they are not magic. We should not confuse the signing of agreements with the solving of problems. Simply collecting agreements will not bring peace. Agreements genuinely reinforce peace only when they are kept. Otherwise, we are building a paper castle that will be blown away by the winds of war.

At United Nations special session on disarmament, New York, June 17/ The Washington Post, 6-18:(A)12.

5

We desire peace, but peace is a goal, not a policy. Lasting peace is what we hope for at the end of our journey; it does not describe the steps we must take, nor the paths we should follow to reach that goal. I intend to search for peace along two parallel paths—deterrence and arms reduction. I believe these are the only paths that offer any real hope for an enduring peace.

Broadcast address to the nation, Washington, Nov. 22/The New York Times, 11-23:4.

Hyman G. Rickover
Admiral, United States Navy

6

The lesson of history is: When a war starts, every nation will ultimately use whatever weapon has been available. That is the lesson learned time and again. Therefore, we must expect, if another war—a serious war—breaks out, we will use nuclear energy in some form.

Before Congressional Joint Economic Committee, Washington, Jan. 28/The Christian Science Monitor, 2-9:22.

Eugene V. Rostow
Director, Arms Control and Disarmament Agency of the United States

7

As [British] Prime Minister Thatcher said last summer during the [UN] Second Special Session on Disarmament: "It is not merely a mistaken analysis but an evasion of responsibility to suppose that we can prevent the horrors of war by focusing on its instruments. They are more often symptoms rather than causes." For too many people, the complex rituals of arms-control diplomacy have become a convenient escape from the central problem. Arms-control agreements can be useful in reinforcing a regime of peace; they can never be a substitute for the harsh and unremitting effort to sustain peace directly.

At United Nations, New York, Oct. 27/ The New York Times, 11-16:12.

Helmut Schmidt
Chancellor of West Germany   *8*

Our citizens, frightened by the terrors of a nuclear holocaust, may soon no longer be

WHAT THEY SAID IN 1982

(HELMUT SCHMIDT)

willing to understand why negotiations concerning practical steps toward disarmament go on for years and years; why, as they see it, the idea of national prestige has a greater effect on the decisions of governments than the necessities of mutual security.

At UN General Assembly special session
on disarmament, New York, June 14/
The New York Times, 6-15:6.

Margaret Thatcher
Prime Minister of the United Kingdom

1

To start a war among nuclear powers is not a rational option. [Nuclear] weapons succeed insofar as they prevent war. And for 37 years, nuclear weapons have kept the peace between East and West ... Our key need is not for promises against first use of this or that kind of military weapons. Such promises can never be dependable amid the stresses of war. We need a credible assurance, if such can ever be obtained, against starting military action at all ... Few if any of the 140 conflicts since 1945 can be traced to an arms race. Nor was the World War of 1939-1945 caused by any kind of arms race. On the contrary, it sprang from the belief of a tyrant that his neighbors lacked the means or the will to resist him effectively ... The causes which have produced war in the past have not disappeared today, as we know to our cost. The lesson is that disarmament and good intentions on their own do not insure peace.

At United Nations disarmament
conference, New York, June 23/
Los Angeles Times, 6-24:(I)6.

Paul E. Tsongas
United States Senator,
D—Massachusetts

2

We were not put on this earth and I did not watch my three children be born on this earth to have them incinerated in the pursuit of rhetoric and cold-war ideology. When you take responsibility for your future, you take some responsibility for the future of all humanity.

292

When you bring a child into the world, you promise them hope, peace and survivability. And if you love your children, there is nothing else. Limited nuclear war, winnable nuclear war, definite margins of superiority—contemplate your future, go home and look at a child.

At Emmanuel College commencement/
The Christian Science Monitor, 6-11:16.

Cyrus R. Vance
Former Secretary of State
of the United States

3

In the nuclear age, peace and security are possible if we have the necessary political will. The process of arms control takes time, and time is running out. In the 1980s, the concepts of dominant unilateral advantage and limited nuclear conflict are bankrupt. For security in the nuclear age means common security—a commitment to joint survival rather than the threat of mutual destruction.

News conference, Washington, June 1/
The New York Times, 6-2:9.

Kurt Vonnegut, Jr.
Author

4

When I was a boy, it was unusual for an American, or a person of any nationality, to know much about foreigners. Those who did were specialists—diplomats, explorers, journalists, anthropologists. And they usually knew a lot about just a few groups of foreigners ... Now look what has happened. Thanks to modern communications, we have seen sights and heard sounds from virtually every square mile of the land mass on this planet. Millions of us have actually visited more exotic places than had many explorers during my childhood. So we now know for certain that there are no potential human enemies anywhere who are anything but human beings almost exactly like ourselves. They need food. How amazing. They love their children. How amazing. They obey their leaders. How amazing. They think like their neighbors. How amazing. Thanks to modern communications, we now have something we never had before: reason to mourn

(KURT VONNEGUT, JR.)

deeply the death or wounding of any human being on any side in any war.

*At Cathedral of St. John the Divine,
New York/The New York Times,
6-13:(4)25.*

James Wade
*Under Secretary of Defense
of the United States*

1

[On civil-defense preparedness]: We don't want to fight a nuclear war, or a conventional one either, but we must be prepared to do so if such a battle is to be deterred, as we must also be prepared to carry the battle to our adversary's homeland. We must not fear war.

*Before House Defense Appropriations
Subcommittee, Washington/
The Christian Science Monitor,
2-1:8.*

Caspar W. Weinberger
Secretary of Defense of the United States   *2*

The greatest paradox of all is that military strength is most successful if it is never used. But if we are never to use force, we must be prepared to use it and to use it successfully. The greatest victory lies not in the battle which is fought and won, but in the battle which was never fought. As Milton said so simply, "Peace has her victories, no less renowned than war." The only war we want is the war which-never-was. But the war which-never-was is a war that was never fought because we were prepared to fight it, and to win it. It is on this paradox that the first principle and fundamental goal of our military lies: that as George Washington said, "To be prepared for war is one of the most effectual ways of preserving peace" ... There is nothing new about deterrence, nothing at all. It is not unique to the West, to democracies, or to the nuclear age. The only thing that has changed over the thousands of years of human history is that the stakes of deterrence have risen as the destructive power of war has grown.

*At U.S. Naval Academy commencement/
The Christian Science Monitor, 6-11:15.*

PART THREE

General

The Arts

William S. Anderson
Chairman, NCR Corporation

1

We believe that supporting the arts is one of the best investments NCR can make. There is a high level of competition throughout the industry to hire the caliber of people we need. Dayton [where NCR is based] is not in the Sun Belt. It is neither on the East Coast nor on the West Coast. In fact, whether we like it or not, many people consider this part of the country just a step or two removed from the boondocks. When we recruit new employees, they want to know what they are getting into. This inevitably leads them to ask what the Dayton area has to offer in the arts and cultural activities.

The New York Times, 3-28:(2)14.

Ingmar Bergman
Motion-picture director

2

Art can have immense therapeutic value, but the time for art to be an agent of change, a force for reform, has passed. The other media have taken over that function. I make my films so people can use them, and then, if somebody is able to understand something better, I feel I've made a good film. Art exists, you see, to console, to enlighten, to help, to shock—and it can go on doing all those things. But the assumption that art can bring us new ideas, fresh impulses—I haven't much confidence in that.

Interview, Stockholm/Saturday Review, April:38.

Leonard Bernstein
Composer, Conductor

3

The [U.S. Reagan] Administration's policy of cuts in arts support strikes me as being quite as uncivilized, un-American and, frankly, barbaric as all the other cuts in welfare, education, socio-medical services, etc., which are being made in favor of increasing the budget for military operations and weaponry. We are turning into a poor nation of immeasurable wealth, a pitiful giant—aggressive, greedy and morally passive.

At hearing of House Subcommittee on
Post-secondary Education, New York,
March 5*/The New York Times, 3-6:13.

Daniel J. Boorstin
Historian; Librarian of Congress
of the United States

4

. . . I think that we should have a national cultural policy only in the sense that it should be our policy to discover what we can do and what we can't do. There are two different aspects to cultural resources. One is the audience and the other is the creators of the works of art. What distinguishes greatness in the arts is the unexpectedness and originality and freshness of the creation. Some of the greatest works of literature came out of Czarist Russia. We would not want to create that kind of a society in the hope of creating more Tolstoys . . . One of the most interesting things about the recent events in the arts and humanities is the outcry that was produced by the reduction in the [U.S. National] Endowments' appropriations, which when added together amount to less than the annual budget of the University of Chicago. This indicates some of the dangers of [dependency on] public grants. People become dependent; also a power is given to people who give the grants. That's out of the mainstream of the development of our culture. The opportunities to try new things . . . come from diversity.

Panel discussion, Washington/
The New York Times, 4-25:(4)6.

297

WHAT THEY SAID IN 1982

Willard Boyd
President, Field Museum of
Natural History, Chicago

1

In the future, the humanities and arts must be stressed as well as the sciences. Arms do not guarantee international security. Longer life and cleaner air do not guarantee international security. Longer life and cleaner air do not assure happiness. Ideas and ideals, understanding and sensitivity give meaning to life. Because there are limits to material growth, we must concentrate on other means of development and fulfillment. Humanities and arts are essential ingredients of our future development and fulfillment.

Before House Appropriations Committee,
Washington/Chicago Tribune, 6-9:(1)11.

Francis Ford Coppola
Motion-picture director

2

American culture is not in the hands of the design class—the creative and intuitive people. It is controlled by a growing class of lawyers, agents, middlemen and marketing people who are more cynical and work for status, power and wealth ... My dream is that the artist class—people who have proven through their work that they are humanists and wish to push for what Aldous Huxley called the desirable human potentialities of intelligence, creativity and friendliness—will seize the instrument of technology and try to take humanity into a period of history in which we can reach for a utopia ... At the moment, the nation is in a fog, and we've got to put our headlights on. Artists—those who rely on their intuition—can be the nation's headlights.

Interview/U.S. News & World Report, 4-5:68.

Enzo Cucchi
Painter

3

I really don't know what to think about art today. The artist's condition is gloomy ... How could it be otherwise? We have lost iconography. The avant-garde, with all its ideas, has committed a great violence against the artist by depriving him of iconography, the essential element of his language. Now we are in a

298

situation similar to the one that existed after the invention of writing. Oral communication has lost life, and men have lost an important means of expressing themselves.

Interview/The Wall Street Journal, 9-24:25.

Peter F. Drucker
Professor of social science and
management, Claremont (Calif.)
College Graduate School

4

Politics is the art of the possible. No artist worth his salt accepts the notion of the impossible ... In our age, politics exceeds its normal limits. This is one of the most highly politicized ages we have ever gone through. Art today is threatened by the absolutism of our politics, and so we must demand more from the arts today.

At "The Arts and Politics" symposium,
Claremont (Calif.) College Graduate School,
May 14/Los Angeles Times, 5-18:(VI)9.

Arlene Goldbard
Co-director, Neighborhood
Arts Programs National
Organizing Committee

5

In terms of the smaller institutions, the creation of a "great audience" [for the arts] should be a secondary or a tertiary goal of public policy. The real issue is participation, not consumption. Those [new] technological systems have created a situation in which increasingly cultural participation is private and passive. So, for small organizations that we're working with, the question is how to confront some pretty big monsters, like television. What can we do to help people out of their houses again, to become not just consumers of culture that somebody else has created but culture builders themselves?

Panel discussion, Washington/
The New York Times, 4-25:(4)6.

Michael Graves
Architect; Associate professor of
architecture and urban planning,
Princeton University

6

I would like to see architects be better educated. And that's very threatening to a lot

(MICHAEL GRAVES)

of architects. What I mean is that people—archi-tects—have got to know the literature of archi-tecture. A lot of smart people for a very long time have made a lot of good architecture, and to throw all that out is just nonsense. That doesn't mean you build Baroque buildings or Renaissance buildings or Gothic buildings. But there's a lot of language that shouldn't have been thrown out ... People don't realize how difficult architecture is. It's like writing a novel. It's like—like anything artistic. Buildings are more than ways to keep people dry from the rain. All you need for that is pure shelter. That's easy. But architecture ... architecture is something else. It's an invention. There's an artist involved.

Interview/TWA Ambassador, March:27,32.

Francis Hodsoll
Chairman, National Endowment for the Arts of the United States

1

[Saying the arts flourished in the U.S. even before the existence of government support]: All this came about ... with little specific, or directed, help from government ... And yet, if there were not a National Endowment for the Arts, I would propose such an agency for these reasons: to recognize the importance of the arts by conferring prestige and expressing advocacy at the highest level; to insure support—as in the sciences—for new and experimental ventures that might be too risky to elicit sufficient private investment; to foster a climate for the unpredictable; to preserve art in danger of loss or deterioration; to provide some cushion for the nation's most excellent artistic institutions so that they do not stagnate; to encourage the kaleidoscope of American culture; to increase access to the arts for American citizens every-where.

Address on the first anniversary of his holding office/The Washington Post, 12-16:(A)22.

Shirley M. Hufstedler
Former Secretary of Education of the United States

2

Any society, if it is to endure, let alone flourish, must have creativity and its artists. And yet they make us very uncomfortable, for very good reason: They think to do things that haven't been done before ... And we tend to admire them as they comfort us, and be deeply disturbed when they challenge our ideas of ourselves.

At "The Arts and Politics" symposium, Claremont (Calif.) College Graduate School, May 14/Los Angeles Times, 5-18:(VI)9.

John Huston
Motion-picture director

3

Sometimes when I look at the body of my work I'll say, "Oh s----!" But even Michelangelo on his deathbed thought he'd done nothing to ennoble art. He wanted to destroy his work— the Pieta! And this from the greatest artist who ever lived. Of course, I am not comparing my work to Michelangelo's. But this eternal dis-satisfaction of the artist is what I was talking about.

Interview/Los Angeles Herald Examiner, 4-26:(A)7.

4

A work of art doesn't dare you to realize it. It germinates and gestates by itself.

At tribute to him by Directors Guild of America, Los Angeles/ Daily Variety, 5-25:9.

Yousuf Karsh
Portrait photographer

5

Great personalities do not always yield great photographs. But if genius is 98 per cent ordinary, then it is the task of the man behind the camera to bring out the glorious 2 per cent ... I have no preconceived notions of what any final portrait will be. In retrospect, you can talk about the picture objectively. But when you are actually taking the picture, it is the two of us interacting. The photographer must intuitively see and sense the past, present and future of the subject.

Interview/People, 3-1:71,72

299

William M. McCormick
*President of consumer financial
service, American Express Company*

1

Few people would dispute that without the inspiration and imagination of the performing and visual arts, the quality of life in our cities and in our country would be greatly diminished. Yet the question of the prospects for the arts is a very real one, and it takes on a new urgency in this time of decreasing activity on the part of all governments and in a time of only slowly increasing charitable contributions from the private sector. Current economic circumstances in the nation indicate that America's great corporations must take a leading role in financing a needed reawakening in art and humanities in America.

*Before Kansas City Arts Council/
Chicago Tribune,
6-1:(1)11.*

Jonathan Miller
Producer, Director, Writer

2

... if the meaning [of a book, film, play or other work of art] is whatever meaning a critic, interpreter or stage director can find in a word, then there's absolutely no standard about which meaning is the central one. There must be *a* meaning, and the idea that any work contains an infinite series of meanings leads, finally, to a chaos of interpretation. Criticism should be aware of those principle axes of meaning, and stage direction is an act of criticism ... I just believe that, in the end, works of art are not orphan objects lying around on an unattended desert, ready to be incorporated into some collage of your own making.

Interview/Opera News, June:14.

Bill Moyers
Commentator, CBS News

3

Art asks what is worth thinking. Politics asks what is worth doing and becoming ... If we drive those freest spirits among us into the wilderness, we are the poorer for it. If we allow

300

the expression of only those sentiments that please us, soon we will not be pleased with ourselves.

*At "The Arts and Politics" symposium,
Claremont (Calif.) College Graduate School,
May 14/Los Angeles Times, 5-18:(VI)9.*

Andre Previn
*Music director, Pittsburgh
Symphony Orchestra*

4

No creative artists live in a vacuum; they are affected by what goes on around them ... Yet the very greatest artists of this century seem to have been able to transcend anything horrible that has occurred around them in both the social and political areas. In the end, the handful of gigantic people in the field seem not to pay too much attention to anything but their own genius. They have always marched to their own beat—and they always will. When you are in a concert hall listening to music, it seems to me that the ever-present outside influences and anxieties that make us all frightened to pick up the morning paper disappear because the concentration is on something that will outlast transient events.

Interview/U.S. News & World Report, 1-11:59.

Leontyne Price
Opera singer

5

Traditionally, Americans have been so magnanimous to other peoples, countries and even buildings. If the English needed help to rebuild Westminster Cathedral, we could be counted on to give. Yet we neglect the best within ourselves, our own culture and pride in cultural achievement. We have the world's best opera companies, best orchestras, and the best artists. Yet to survive, artists must forever be embarrassed about our tin cup in hand.

*Interview, San Francisco/San Francisco
Examiner & Chronicle, 11-14:(Datebook)35.*

Derek Walcott
Poet

6

I'm getting more and more convinced that there really is some kind of immortality in art. There really is. It's a phrase one used as an adolescent when one thought of Keats or

(DEREK WALCOTT)

Shelley or Rimbaud. But the survival of art, the knowledge that comes with art—I believe in that. The death of the artist, however tragic—or even the life of the artist—is minimal in importance to what he's left behind.

*Interview, Trinidad/The
New York Times Magazine, 5-23:51.*

Sidney R. Yates
*United States Representative,
D–Illinois*

1

Yes, we have big deficits and we have high unemployment, but the difference I have with this [Reagan] Administration is over whether there should be any Federal assistance for the arts at all. I think the Reagan Administration would be against any Federal funds for the arts . . . The arts make an economic contribution to the prosperity of the country as well as enhancing the quality of life of the American people. That's why I think it is important to make a Federal contribution to the arts . . . Even in prosperous times, the private role was not adequate to take care of the needs of the arts and humanities, to keep theatres alive, to keep the dance alive. Operas and symphonies were strapped . . . [Presidents] Kennedy and Johnson found that the arts were a proper role for the government. Every President, including Republicans, funded the arts on higher levels until the Reagan Administration came along.

Interview/The New York Times, 12-28:12.

Journalism

Richard V. Allen
*Former Assistant to the President
of the United States (Ronald Reagan)
for National Security Affairs* 1

Competition among the Washington press for air time and space is so great that sometimes an inadequate respect for the facts takes over. Their willingness to publish leaks and the views of "anonymous" sources leads to particularly vicious situations that are grossly unfair to the object of the leak. There is also a propensity on the part of the Washington press to tear down people in high places. The standards applied to officials are so rigorous that even a hint of behavior that appears not in accordance with those standards can lead to sensational charges. The recent fabrication of news stories shows that the media are also not perfect. But their admissions of wrongheadedness generally are not featured on page 1. They appear back among the corset ads.

Interview/U.S. News & World Report, 3-22:56.

Russell Baker
Columnist, "The New York Times" 2

I never understood what good taste means in the newspaper business. By definition, a newspaper is an act of bad taste. One of the first things I did on *The Times* was on Christmas Eve. We got word that an airplane had crashed on takeoff in Ireland. We had a list of the passengers, and I had to telephone people to ask if they knew if their relative had actually boarded the plane. They would ask why, and by now it was Christmas morning and I had to tell them about the crash. That struck me as an act of egregiously bad taste. But any newspaperman who refused to do it would not be worth his salary. *Interview, New York/"W": a Fairchild publication, 10-22:10.*

3

[On writing his column]: You always begin the same way—sitting there thinking, "My God, what am I going to write about today?" I never think about it till I sit down and start. I might sit there for two hours trying things, throwing them away, getting nothing. And, as the clock moves on, I become less and less demanding, my standards go down. Often, when I get something I know is not terribly good, maybe not very good at all, I keep saying, "It's only daily journalism" . . . I've got to write three times a week, week after week, year after year, decade after decade. I look into the future as far as I can see, and I see myself doing the same thing. Now, that's maddening in one way, but in another way it makes it easier because you're really in for the long run. And the audience is not that demanding—you're never going to have this snotty reviewer say, "Mr. Baker showed so much 'potential' and his original work has gone stale." You just keep churning it out. It makes it easier, surprisingly.

*Interview, Los Angeles/
Los Angeles Herald Examiner, 10-29:(A)2.*

David Brinkley
Commentator, ABC News 4

The Washington press used to be thought of as somewhat raffish. Now they are quite well educated and prepared in their fields—often more so than the people they cover.

U.S. News & World Report, 3-22:55.

Tom Brokaw
Anchorman, NBC News 5

[Journalism] beats any occupation I can imagine. It's mind-expanding. You live well doing it. It's rewarding. Why shouldn't I be charging at every turn? Why should I be cynical? I get so aggravated when correspondents get cynical. *This* is the big adventure.

Interview/TV Guide, 4-10:32.

(TOM BROKAW)

1

[On the use of unnamed sources for news stories]: The real sloppiness I notice recently is ... this business about ... "A number of people on the Hill believe ... " That becomes a kind of convenient coatrack on which they [reporters] can hang any number of judgments that the reporter may have put together on his own.

Los Angeles Times, 11-17:(I)18.

Dan M. Burt
President, Capital Legal Foundation

2

[On the recent multi-million-dollar court verdict against *The Washington Post* in a libel case]: The healthiest thing for the First Amendment is that the people through the jury system have the opportunity to discipline rogue members of the media. It's obviously part of a whole trend; there's been a tremendous loss of confidence in the media. If the jury system and the courts don't act when the media is unfair, the Congress will, and I believe that would be horrible.

The New York Times, 8-1:(1)14.

Jimmy Carter
Former President of the United States

3

[On the treatment of President Reagan by the press]: Reagan has been treated with kid gloves. He has been given the benefit of the doubt, not only during this first year and a half, but also during the [1980 election] campaign, when his detrimental policies were never analyzed by the press. Reagan's demeanor as an "aw shucks" grandfatherly type appeals to the country and the press. Some of his characteristics, such as his not being familiar with details of issues, even arouse a sense of protection in the press. [During the Carter Administration,] there was a kind of game by the press to see if there were questions I could not answer. Part of the reason for this challenge was the aura of morality that I had wrapped around myself, and my commitment not to lie. There was a natural inclination by the press to prove this guy is not as clean and moral as he claims.

Interview, Plains, Ga./Time, 10-11:63.

John Chancellor
Commentator, NBC News

4

Walter Lippmann, the late author and columnist, once wrote that journalism should give people a picture of the world upon which they can act. It seems to me it hasn't turned out that way, in this age of omnipresent news. Journalism today does give more people a picture of the world—in greater detail and in sharper focus than Lippmann would have believed—but I see little evidence that more people are "acting" because of what they know. In the last 20 years, we have seen an enormous expansion of the knowledge of the American people about current events and current affairs—nothing like it has ever happened before. And, when I was a young man, many of us believed that if we could get more information to broad masses of people, the country would be a much better place. Well, we did get that information out, but I'm not sure the country is in that much better shape. I have come to the conclusion that we can notify, but not educate.

Lecture, University of Chicago/
Chicago Tribune, 5-17:(1)11.

5

I'm personally disturbed sometimes at the world's capacity now through TV and radio to bring horrors into your living-room. On the other hand, I can't find any ethical reason to be against it. We've always been in the business of covering conflict and change. That's what journalism is all about. That's what it *has* to be about.

Interview, New York/The Christian
Science Monitor, 11-18:(B)22.

William E. Colby
Former Director of Central
Intelligence of the United States

6

[On how Soviet disinformation is spread by the press]: It's really quite masterful. They plant a story—totally fictitious—in a leftist paper in, say, Bombay. Then it gets picked up by a Communist journal in Rio. Then in Rome. Then Tass, the Soviet news agency, lifts it from the Rome paper and runs it as a "sources say"

(WILLIAM E. COLBY)

news item. And soon the non-Communist press starts to pick up on it, using terms such as, "It is alleged that . . . " And thus an absolute lie gets into general circulation.

TV Guide, 6-12:5.

Walter Cronkite
Former anchorman, CBS News

1

[Criticizing alleged Reagan Administration restrictions on the press because of its reporting on El Salvador and other issues]: . . . we are already hearing echoes of that earlier [Vietnam] battle between press and officialdom. The reporters are "naive," "romantic," "leftist," "subversive," "anti-American." "They don't or won't understand the big picture . . . Why the hell can't they get on the team?" Yes, we've been down this road before. [Concerns about press freedom grow from] all the little restrictions and constrictions enacted and proposed on the people's right to know [by the Administration]. None of these proposals and initiatives may seem all that serious a matter in itself, but taken together they form a pattern which we should all be worrying about. It is a pattern of restriction. It is the solution of those who feel America has become too˙open a society and needs to be closed off some . . . [Journalists should defend a] fair and vigorously active media and [its] access to information a democratic public needs to know. That remains democracy's only fail-safe system against both the dangers of its own excesses and the approach of tyranny.

Before National Association of
Broadcasters, Dallas, April 7/
The Washington Post, 4-8:(B)13.

Tom DeFrank
Correspondent, "Newsweek" magazine;
President, White House
Correspondents Association

2

[On reporter Sarah McClendon's sometimes rough treatment of Presidents during Presidential news conferences]: Sarah's conduct can make you cringe sometimes, but she has every

304

right to ask a question in whatever fashion she chooses. I have never bought this ridiculous argument that Presidents must be handled with kid gloves and addressed in the most reverential terms.

The Washington Post, 7-30:(A)3.

Sam Donaldson
White House correspondent,
ABC News

3

The Washington press corps is the best in the business. Reporters do a good job and are getting better and better as they become more sophisticated and specialized. When I came to Washington 21 years ago, generalists were the rule. We covered everything. Now reporters who cover the courts often have a legal background. Those who cover economics have expertise in that field. Taken as a whole, Washington reporters are highly qualified. They write well, are intelligent and well educated. We make mistakes and have blind spots, but are often unjustly maligned by know-nothings. Bad reporters don't stay in Washington very long because of the competition for these jobs.

Interview/U.S. News & World Report, 3-22:56.

Robert J. Donovan
Journalist

4

I don't approve of all this adversary journalism. I think that public officials are sometimes treated unfairly. On the other hand, I think they got away with murder in the old days. If investigative reporters I've known around Washington had been turned loose, the way they are now, on the Roosevelt Administration, with all that money pouring out of the alphabet agencies, we would have had a field day here in town.

Interview, Washington/The Christian
Science Monitor, 9-15:3.

Charles D. Ferris
Former Chairman, Federal
Communications Commission

5

[Arguing against repeal of the Fairness Doctrine, which some say encourages broadcasters to shy away from airing controversial issues]:

(CHARLES D. FERRIS)

Remember that the Fairness Doctrine does not permit broadcasters to duck the responsibility of covering such issues. Some broadcasters tend to hedge on that obligation because granting too much time to public affairs affects their profits. There's a running battle between the broadcaster's business side, which wants to devote more time to entertainment shows that attract big audiences, and the journalistic side, which focuses on issues that may appeal to fewer people. If you eliminated the Fairness Doctrine, coverage of key issues would be significantly reduced. It's far more profitable to air an entertainment show than a talk show.

Interview/U.S. News & World Report, 8-2:31.

Mark S. Fowler
Chairman, Federal Communications Commission of the United States

1

[Criticizing the broadcast Fairness Doctrine]: The simple fact is, no newspaper and no magazine is subject to second-guessing by a government agency when it comes to fairness. No newspaper and no magazine is forced to sell the same number of column inches to all [political] candidates, with their printing presses taken away if they don't. It's one thing for stations to follow principles like fairness or equal time. I call that not only sensible but good business. It's another, when the government enforces those rules. That, I call censorship.

Before National Association of Broadcasters, Dallas, April 7/ The New York Times, 4-8:22.

2

The Fairness Doctrine, which requires broadcasters to provide time on the air for balanced presentations of controversial issues, is a disincentive to free speech because if broadcasters present one side, they have to present the contrasting viewpoint. If they can't find someone to pay for the contrasting viewpoint, they must give the time away in order to balance. So if somebody wants to buy a half hour to present, let's say, a conservative viewpoint, many television stations, fearful that they can't sell the opposing side, will deny the initial request. Viewers and listeners lose because an issue has not been ventilated.

Interview/U.S. News & World Report, 4-12:43.

Reuven Frank
President, NBC News

3

[Saying TV news staffs today regard themselves as too self-important and solemn]: In my time, you didn't go into news for that. It was not holy orders. We thought it might be fun. If you couldn't stand the idea of doing the same thing every day, this was one way you could make sure that you wouldn't. And these were the impulses that drove people into news. Now, it's so deadly. And when it is leavened, it is so self-conscious and so obvious—"Hey, folks, we got a funny one." A lot of things are interesting that are not important. A lot of things are important that are not solemn. And it's not that they cry the end of the world all the time; it is, somehow, "I am Sir Oracle, and when I speak, let no dog bark." And I don't like it. I'm as smart as those guys.

Interview, Washington/ The Washington Post, 3-5:(B)6.

4

[On the use of graphics on TV news programs]: During the Falkland Islands crisis, when we weren't getting any information you could show, we started using graphic representations of planes coming in, usually from the wrong trajectory. All of a sudden, a war I thought was kind of serious started to look like Pac-Man [a video game] on the three networks. I had to put out a note to get us to stop. There's all of this cant about using graphics in a visual medium, but in fact just the opposite is happening. The picture is now seen to have no journalistic value of its own. It merely illustrates the word or the chart. The things that pictures can do, intelligently used, are being lost sight of. Instead, we're trying to outdo each [other] with electronics.

Interview/The New York Times, 10-17:(2)33.

WHAT THEY SAID IN 1982

(REUVEN FRANK)

1

The swaying of multitudes is not the business of news. Any good that is done is usually incidental. And any evil is in the eyes of the beholder. News, I suspect, is a simpleton's business. It is only organized curiosity, people wanting to know what is new, and other people happy to find out and tell them ... Individual complaints I have seen that we are pushing people to one side of a controversial issue always come from people passionately on the other side. They see us as having the power to anoint their cause, and if we do not, it can only be because we are deliberately on the other side. News today, here [in the U.S.], in any medium, or in all the media, has no power because it is not being consciously and deliberately used to any end. There are places where it is; there have been places and times where it was. But there is no such power here now. There is potential, which may have the same root but is a different word. When the potential is used as power, it will no longer be simple, or innocent, or news. And what it will be, you won't like.

Before University of California-Los Angeles
Journalism Alumni Association,
November/Variety,
12-1:52.

Steve Friedman
Producer, "Today" show, NBC-TV

2

I think that news is going to take more and more of the networks' attention. If you can have news at 1 a.m., if you can have news at 6 a.m., why can't you have news on at other places on the schedule? Why not in prime time? I think you're going to see an explosion of news. I think you're seeing the dawn of the news revolution in television.

Interview/Los Angeles Times, 5-11:(VI)1.

Fred W. Friendly
Professor of journalism,
Columbia University; Former
president, CBS News

3

[Advocating expansion of the nightly TV network newscasts]: In 1982, television may be the most powerful, most pervasive medium, but it does not yet do an adequate job of providing a reliable picture of the world. In 22½ minutes [the current news content time of network newscasts], all you can do is an index, at best a digest ... Often, television tries to tell a story when it really doesn't have time to tell it completely, leaving people with the impression they have the full story. The tragedy is that many viewers believe they are getting all the news, so they don't bother reading a newspaper.

"Chet Huntley Memorial Lecture,"
New York University, March/
The New York Times,
3-13:15.

Katharine Graham
Chairman, Washington Post Company

4

I don't think in our lifetime we'll see again an American press content to take the government handout, publish more or less what the established order wants published and collude with it habitually and systematically to put out a version of the truth that officialdom has decided is the one fit for public consumption. That is past, dead and gone ... I am saying that there is a strong tradition of independent, irreverent journalism in our country, and that it was the fact that this had been in abeyance so long before the '60s came along that was remarkable, not its overdue resurgence.

At Massachusetts Institute of
Technology commencement, June 1/
The Washington Post,
6-2:(A)16.

Stephen Hess
Author; Senior fellow,
Brookings Institution

5

The press is now more conservative and apolitical than a decade ago. Reporters come to Washington because it is the top of the career ladder, not because they are passionately interested in political theory.

U.S. News & World Report, 3-22:55.

Don Hewitt
Executive producer, "60 Minutes"
program, CBS-TV

1

I've felt for a long time that titles like "producer" and "executive producer" are misnomers. When TV news was just starting in 1948, they didn't know what to call us, so they borrowed from theatre and movies. But I think it's caused great confusion and I think it's about time we eliminated those titles. I'm really more an executive editor than an executive producer. The man who we call a producer is really a reporter ... I know some producers who are great at finding out things but couldn't communicate their own names. I also know some guys who are good communicators but couldn't find out where the men's room is, much less report a story.

Interview/The New York Times, 6-23:18.

Gene F. Jankowski
President, CBS/Broadcast Group

2

[Advocating repeal of the broadcast Fairness Doctrine]: We live in a verbal society, not a pictorial one. As much as you can give credit to television, pictures are not as important as the words and ideas conveyed. We are not living in a country of mindless people who are very easily swayed by whatever it is they happen to see or read. If people aren't persuaded by what they read in the newspapers, which don't have to comply with the fairness and equal-time rules, then they're not going to be persuaded by what they see or hear on television.

Interview/U.S. News & World Report, 8-2:32.

William B. Ketter
Editor, "The Quincy (Mass.)
Patriot Ledger"

3

The First Amendment [of the Constitution] doesn't give anything special to the press. The people should be in the spotlight. But we [the press] are their surrogate. We're fighting for their rights. But we have to make it clear! It's not the press's rights. It's the people's rights.

Interview, Quincy, Mass./
The Christian Science Monitor, 6-3:13.

Austin H. Kiplinger
Editor, "Kiplinger
Washington Letter"

4

Editorial inventiveness can usually find a way to satisfy the information demands of any given period in history. Two generations ago, there occurred a germinal explosion of new publications, which set trends that persist even now. The *Reader's Digest*, which started in 1921, gave its readers a broader diet of the popular and up-beat reading matter. *Time* magazine, which hit the scene in 1923, gave continuity and interpretation to the news. The *Kiplinger Letter,* founded in the same year, brought big economic developments down to levels of useful judgments. All three were the products of ... talented editors, but they could not have succeeded if the times had not provided a need and an appetite for their output. What survives today, therefore, will be whatever serves the needs of the last two decades of the century.

Lecture, Dec. 1/
The Washington Post, 12-2:(A)26.

Raul Eduardo Kraiselburd
Editor, "El-Dia," La Plata, Argentina;
Chairman, committee on freedom of
the press and information,
Inter-American Press Association

5

In the United States there is a tendency among the magistrates to question freedoms of the press, and many of those cases are being tested in the courtrooms. Of course, things in this country [the U.S.] are not as bad as Latin America. At least here there is a guarantee of freedom of the press. In Latin America it is a matter of permission—more permission or less permission. There is no guarantee of freedom.

Chicago, September/Chicago Tribune, 9-27:(1)2.

Bill Leonard
Former president, CBS News

6

There are three qualities to being [a network TV news] anchorman. The first is how you appear on the screen as a broadcaster. The

WHAT THEY SAID IN 1982

(BILL LEONARD)

second is the ability to be able to be "Mr. Emergency"—the guy to whom the organization looks when the world falls apart. The third is the ability to represent [the network] to the world—to be the *presence* [of the network] : to stroke affiliates, to make promos, to be the greeter at meetings.

Interview/TV Guide, 12-4:29.

Jose Lopez Portillo
President of Mexico

1

[On the withdrawal of government advertising from a news magazine that has been critical of the government] : Does a private publication, organized as a business, have the right to obtain government publicity in order to systematically oppose the government? This, gentlemen, would be a morbid, perverse, sadomasochistic relationship. It would resemble other perversions which I won't bother to mention in deference to my audience—"I'll pay you to hit me."

*At Freedom of the Press Day
ceremony, Mexico City, June 7/
Los Angeles Times, 6-28:(I)1.*

Kurt M. Luedtke
*Former executive editor,
"Detroit Free Press"*

2

There is no such thing as the public's right-to-know. You [in the news media] make that up, taking care not to specify what it was that the public had a right to know. The public knows whatever you choose to tell it, no more, no less. If the public did have a right to know, it would then have something to say about what it is you choose to call news.

*Before American Newspaper Publishers
Association, San Francisco/
The Washington Post, 5-3:(A)10.*

Jeff MacNelly
Political cartoonist, "Chicago Tribune"

3

[Cartoonists] violate all the rules of journalism. We misquote and slander . . . and

distort . . . and everything else. [But] the interesting thing is the political cartoonist usually, if he is any good, gets a hell of a lot closer to the truth . . . than a responsible reporter.

Interview/Los Angeles Times, 3-17:(I)24.

Frank Mankiewicz
President, National Public Radio

4

[Arguing for retention of the broadcast Fairness Doctrine] : At least in theory, you can start a newspaper. You can start a magazine. You can start a newsletter. And in the whole area of print, there are some pretty good success stories over the last 15 to 20 years. But you can't start a radio station unless you get a frequency, and there aren't any left. And the same is true of television stations. Now, that is the vast difference. And that is why the government should retain the ultimate regulatory control over fairness.

Interview/Los Angeles Herald Examiner, 2-3:(A)11.

Robert Marbut
*President, Hart-Hanks Communications;
Chairman, telecommunications
committee, American Newspaper
Publishers Association*

5

I think that a likely development [in the future] in which a newspaper will continue to perform its role in a community is as an information retailer. Right now, newspapers get a lot of information from across the country: from the Associated Press satellite, press releases from the Postal Service, on the Greyhound Bus. They edit it, package it and promote it in a way that's convenient to the consumer. If you translate that to an electronic mode, then you have electronic wholesalers—the wire services, a ski report service, all kinds of databases from around the world—providing information. The local newspaper will be a storage place and a gateway for that information—an electronic window on the world. A consumer can pick up a keypad and go through a local newspaper's gateway computer for the information he wants.

*San Francisco Examiner &
Chronicle, 4-25:(D)1.*

Edward J. Markey
United States Representative,
D—Massachusetts   *1*

[Arguing in favor of retaining the broadcast Fairness Doctrine]: Repealing the Fairness Doctrine would harm information-poor segments of our society. At this time there are parts of our society that have neither the political clout nor economic prowess to make their own views heard. The First Amendment right of the public to receive information would be seriously undermined if the vehicle of enforcing the right—no matter how clumsy— were not maintained.

The Christian Science Monitor, 6-3:14.

Amadou-Mahtar M'Bow
Director General, United Nations
Educational, Scientific and
Cultural Organization   *2*

If the [news] media has the liberty to say what they like, then others have the right to judge what they say. What becomes of freedom when people claim to inform according to their own view and then refuse or seek to refuse to allow others to judge what they say? When this is the case, there is no liberty but the monopoly.

Paris/The New York Times, 12-4:3.

George Melloan
Deputy editorial-page editor,
"The Wall Street Journal"   *3*

[On charges that reporters are biased in reporting on guerrilla wars]: ... I think some reporters tend to identify with guerrilla and revolutionary movements to some degree . . . . this comes partly out of the tradition of American journalism to support the underdog, and sometimes it goes beyond that into the genuine political orientation that is Marxist in nature; but that's in very few cases, I think.

Broadcast interview/
The New York Times, 3-2:25.

Mark Monsky
News director,
Metromedia Television   *4*

[On the increasing risks to journalists in covering volatile areas of the world]: Intimida-

tion has its cycles. Right now, we're definitely on an upswing. I think the degree to which the gringo press has been subject to abuse and harassment and assault in Latin America is part of it. There's going to be more of us killed. All those kids in journalism schools across the country thinking about Pulitzers don't realize the number of gun barrels they're going to have to stare down.

Interview/TV Guide, 10-23:10.

Roger Mudd
Chief Washington
correspondent, NBC News

5

[On TV coverage of election returns]: Over the last 15 years, as competition has sharpened between the networks, none of us is content to let an event be an event. We have to fix it. We have to foreshorten the conclusions, hasten the end, predict before anyone else does who's going to win. We have to take an issue on our own terms, and we won't let the candidate lay out the issues on his terms. [As a result, TV news is] less honorable [than it was 10 years ago].

At conference on TV election
coverage, Harvard University, January/
The New York Times, 2-1:9.

6

You would think that the [news] competition between networks would produce stronger, more thoughtful reporting. But instead, the competition has resulted in a hype that's very disturbing and a tendency, as people start to switch their dials, to try to grab them with electronic tricks and "glitzy" news that really doesn't have much to do with journalism. You begin to get awfully close to changing reality. You get so absorbed in technology that you forget you're really covering news. I just think you need good, strong reporting.

Interview, Washington/The Christian
Science Monitor, 4-2:19.

7

A lot of people go into television news for the wrong reasons . . . attracted to it because it is quick and I suppose fairly easy money. In the great quest for supreme position in the ratings,

(ROGER MUDD)

the main reason for our calling—which is to get close to the truth—competes with other factors ... The best chore we can perform is to provide a believable service of disseminating news and information. If reporters allow their sense of outrage, or lack of patience, or frustration to get into their reporting, then they destroy their credibility.

Interview/TV Guide, 12-4:32.

Ron Nessen
Former Press Secretary to the President of the United States (Gerald R. Ford); Former correspondent, NBC News

1

[On journalists who cover volatile situations around the world]: Reporters are seen as the enemy. If you're a guerrilla, then the reporter is seen as an agent of the government. If you're the government, then the reporter is seen as an agent of the guerrillas.

Interview/TV Guide, 10-23:6.

Richard M. Nixon
Former President of the United States

2

Let's talk about some of the ladies of the press for a moment. We have to realize that men reporters can be tough, but women reporters think they have to be tougher. They've got to prove something. And they particularly think they have to be tough with other women. Women can be very tough in the questioning ... I want them to do that. But I don't think they have to demonstrate that they can be as crude and as ruthless and as vulgar as men are.

Broadcast interview/ "Morning News," CBS-TV, 6-2.

3

... my feeling about the press is not personal at all. I've had good relations on a personal basis with members of the press going back 35 years, because I've been around a long time ... The media generally is in an adversary position to whoever is in a top position ... I was simply not their favorite pin-up boy. Now,

I must say, speaking of President Reagan, that I admire *his* press relations. He's done extremely well. I do not believe that the press has a visceral reaction against him. They maybe did against me. Maybe it was my manner; I don't know. But it was there. And as far as I'm concerned, it's now "live and let live."

Interview, Saddle River, N.J./ Los Angeles Herald Examiner, 6-5:(B)3.

Lyn Nofziger
Former Special Assistant to the President of the United States (Ronald Reagan) for Political Affairs

4

[The press wants] something to write about, and ... they think that somewhere along the line God has given them a right to ask [the President] any silly question that comes to mind. I'm not anti-press, by the way; but I am "anti-" some things that the press tries to bring pressure to do, using the so-called "right to know." There is no "right to know." Show me any place in the Constitution that talks about a "right to know."

Interview/Los Angeles Herald Examiner, 3-4:(A)8.

Michael J. O'Neill
Editor, "New York Daily News"; President, American Society of Newspaper Editors

5

The media have ... made a considerable contribution to the disarray in government and therefore have an obligation to help set matters straight. We should begin with an editorial philosophy that is more positive, more tolerant of the frailties of human institutions and their leaders, more sensitive to the rights and feelings of individuals—officials as well as private citizens. No code of chivalry requires us to challenge every official action, either out of Pavlovian distrust of authority or on the false premise that attack is the best way to flush out the truth. Our assignment is to report and explain issues, not to decide them.

Before American Society of Newspaper Editors, Chicago, May/ The New York Times, 5-8:7.

(MICHAEL J. O'NEILL)

1

It may be foolhardy to say anything unchari-table about investigative reporting; it is in such vogue now. We have all basked in the glory of exposes and gloated while public officials have turned slowly on the spit of newspaper disclo-sures. On balance, investigative reporting has done more good than harm, though a wise member of *The New York Times* editorial board, Roger Starr, would dispute the point . . . He said that muckraking did so much damage to the cities that he hated to think what havoc modern investigative reporters might cause. Muckraking has been over-emphasized, tending to crowd out other more significant kinds of reporting. If we had not been so busy chasing corrupt officials, for instance, we might not be guilty of having missed some of the biggest stories of the last half-century: the great migra-tion of blacks from the South to the industrial cities of the North, something we didn't dis-cover until there were riots in the streets of Detroit; the first mincing steps toward war in Vietnam, which we did not begin reporting seriously until our troops were involved; the women's-liberation movement and the massive migration of women into the job market, a social revolution that we originally dismissed as an outbreak of bra burnings.

Before American Society of
Newspaper Editors, Chicago, May/
Chicago Tribune, 5-9:(2)2.

Jean Otto
Editor, "Milwaukee Journal";
Former president, Society
of Professional Journalists

2

The press suffers from arrogance. Some-times, people in the press act as if they are doing their jobs for each other and maybe God, and nobody else ought to get in the way.
U.S. News & World Report, 9-20:69.

Bob Packwood
United States Senator, R—Oregon

3

The far right finds the media licentious or unpatriotic or untrustworthy. They would inhibit freedoms through censorship and other means. The far left wants government owner-ship of the media at the extreme, or govern-ment direction of the media at a minimum. Both the right and left seek government inter-vention to solve the problems they believe confront our society, and they both feel that the media is to be used at the direction of the government to help solve those problems. We must take the regulation of freedom of expres-sion away from the government. And to whom shall we give it? Again, the answer is self-evident. The power to regulate freedom of communication must be entrusted to no group, and that can be accomplished only by the extension of First Amendment freedoms to all forms of communication.

Before National Association
of Broadcasters, Dallas/
The Wall Street Journal, 4-16:24.

Dan Rather
Anchorman, CBS News

4

[On the pressure on him to increase his news program's audience ratings]: [There's] quite a bit. I'm reluctant to say that. Everyone likes to say there's no pressure. I expected to get a lot of press attention [when he took over for the retiring Walter Cronkite] because in this busi-ness you're under the magnifying glass. But it's greater than I ever thought it would be and it manifested itself in different ways than I expected. The slightest mannerism. How your hair is cut. Whether you feel good or bad . . . Does he have a handkerchief in his pocket? Is he wearing a tweed coat? It lasted a good deal longer than I expected.

Interview, New York/
Los Angeles Times, 2-15:(V)11.

Ronald Reagan
President of the United States

5

[On .his recent criticism of the press]: Presidents . . . have moods just like everyone else, including members of the press. Some of the things we say and do regarding each other may cause a little momentary frustration or misunderstanding, but that's all it is. So I hope

311

WHAT THEY SAID IN 1982

(RONALD REAGAN)

I didn't touch a nerve with any of the press a few days ago because I think that most of the time the overwhelming majority of them are doing a fine job; and as a former reporter, columnist and commentator myself, I know just how tough their job can be.

Before National Association of
Manufacturers, Washington, March 18/
Los Angeles Times, 3-19:(I)14.

1

[Humorously speaking of the press]: I hope [Soviet President] Leonid Brezhnev can come to New York in June. I want him to see our free press in action. I want him to see that contrast between a free press and a controlled press—that's the only thing he knows. [The Soviet press] can't criticize him; they can't take potshots, write insulting stories about him when he takes a day off to go swimming [as Reagan did in the Caribbean recently] ... On the other hand, there's something to be said for a controlled press ... No, I don't mean that. You [journalists] just keep on seeking the truth and I'll keep on telling it, even though you don't recognize it ... [But] the White House press corps is part of the family. Like family members, you're aggravating at times, but you're never unloved.

At White House Correspondents'
Association dinner, Washington, April 24/
The Washington Post, 4-26:(C)1,4;
Chicago Tribune, 4-26:(1)9.

Gene Roberts
Executive editor,
"Philadelphia Inquirer"

2

[On the use of unnamed sources in newspaper articles]: To be an absolute purist, to say we will never permit anyone to say anything ... without having his name attached to it would so restrict the flow of information that we would fail in our basic mission, which is to ... keep people informed ... One very important role a newspaper performs is being a conduit for [internal] government policy debates ... and we wouldn't be able to do that if we refused to print all anonymous quotes.

Los Angeles Times, 11-17:(I)17.

A. M. Rosenthal
Executive editor, "The New York Times"

3

[On reporters secretly taping interviewees]: Any time you don't want to do something, you can rationalize your way out of it. I generally believe in [doing] what sits well in the stomach ... It doesn't sit well in the stomach to tape someone and not tell them you're doing it. It's not honest. It's not fair. Period.

Los Angeles Times, 4-14:(I)30.

Van Gordon Sauter
President, CBS News

4

Critics take a certain glee in saying that the use of graphics and charts [on TV news programs] represents "show business." Well, that's not it at all. For us, it's a way of better conveying information. I don't call it show business; I call it television. We have a different relationship with viewers than newspapers do. We're more visual and more intimate.

Interview/The New York Times, 10-17:(2)33.

Jessica Savitch
Anchorwoman, NBC News

5

[For TV newscasters,] looks are part of it, for both men and women. Television is a visual industry. Your looks can't be distracting. You can't be so knockout gorgeous that everybody says, "Oh my goodness! Who's that gorgeous man? What a particularly attractive woman!"— and then they don't listen to you. On the other hand, you can't be so physically unattractive that somebody says, "Wow, she looks really terrible."

Interview, Los Angeles/Los Angeles
Herald Examiner, 10-25:(D)8.

George Seldes
Author, Journalist

6

The honor roll of good newspapers has increased impressively ... [There is] an almost revolutionary change that has resulted in the nation's having a fairer and more honest press than ever before.

Interview, New York/The
Washington Post, 5-19:(B)13.

William French Smith
Attorney General of the United States

1

I can personally attest to the accuracy of what is called Knoll's Law of Media Accuracy: "Everything you read in the newspapers is absolutely true except for the rare story of which you happen to have first-hand knowledge."

Before American Bar Association
House of Delegates, Chicago, Jan. 25/
The New York Times, 1-26:8.

Arthur Ochs Sulzberger
Publisher, "The New York Times"

2

[Calling for an end to the broadcast Fairness Doctrine]: It is time for print publishers to join with their electronic brethren to close this First Amendment gap . . . The line between print and electronic journalism is thin at best and getting thinner. Any oversight of free speech is not the role of government.

Upon receiving Alexander Hamilton
Medal, Columbia University, Nov. 17/
The New York Times, 11-18:18.

Grant Tinker
Chairman, National Broadcasting Company

3

[Saying the news media should reduce coverage of negative news and accent more positive stories]: I don't mean [limit] news about Poland or Lebanon—or, closer to home, unemployment and the struggling economy. Those are world and domestic problems, to be considered and addressed and, hopefully, solved. [Rather, I refer to the current fascination with] stealing, cheating, embezzling, divorcing, ailing, even dying. We have learned far too well the axiom that good news isn't news at all. We specialize, even revel, in bad news, whether nightly on television, in the daily newspaper or, perhaps worst of all, over the backyard fence. [The] ultimate, awful, lasting effect is that the people we are communicating with or to . . . can finally only think and feel and act negatively.

Upon receiving Humanitarian Award
of Entertainment Industries Division,
National Conference of Christians and
Jews, Sept. 29/Daily Variety, 10-1:39.

Chris Wallace
Co-anchorman, "Today" show, NBC-TV

4

There was a time on TV when all [newsmen] had to do was be good. Now you have to be good and have a 30 share [in the ratings]. Not that there is anything wrong with being popular—after all, we are a mass medium concerned with reaching as many people as possible. But there are now certain pressures on newsmen that aren't always healthy pressures—to look good and to be entertaining.

Interview, New York/The
Christian Science Monitor, 4-20:19.

Av Westin
Executive in charge,
"20/20" program, ABC-TV

5

In television [news], stardom is born of credibility, and that comes not only from being able to elicit information from reluctant sources, but also from being able to communicate an idea clearly. Credibility in television is translatable into stardom, which translates into ratings, and ratings are not unimportant, even to broadcast journalists.

Interview/The New York Times, 6-23:18.

Theodore H. White
Author, Historian

6

The over-simplification of American politics is due largely to the [TV] evening news. It's not that the medium is the message; it's that technology takes over from the best people in television. Technology makes them think in terms of 90-second or 2-minute segments. The medium itself and the competition among correspondents for air time enforce a capsulization of problems that are too complicated to lend themselves to capsulization.

Interview/U.S. News & World Report, 7-5:60.

Charles Z. Wick
Director, International
Communication Agency
of the United States

7

[On the selection of material presented on the Voice of America, which his agency oversees]: The principles for selection go through

313

(CHARLES Z. WICK)

the same editorial judgments that any journalistic enterprise has. Very frankly, in the past a lot of those people down there [in the Voice of America newsroom] have thought they had First Amendment rights. What you had was 32 or 34 people . . . exercising their own interpretation of what the news is. We said, no, there's only one editor-in-chief, and that's the director. He delegates the authority . . . As in any other journalistic enterprise, whether the people who work there [are] on the [political] left or right, they must leave their preferences at home.

Interview, Washington/
Los Angeles Times,
6-17:(I-B)6.

George F. Will
Political columnist

1

When was the last time the press admitted anything wrong? That's one reason journalism can't be called a profession. It doesn't have professional standards. Lawyers get disbarred, but what discipline is there in journalism?

Interview, Washington/"W":
a Fairchild publication, 4-9:12.

Don Wright
Political cartoonist, "Miami News"

2

I don't see too many cartoonists taking strong stands on anything. We have too many younger cartoonists who've lost sight of what should be motivating an editorial cartoonist and that is issues. They look at it primarily as an opportunity for a gag of the day, dimly related to some issue.

Interview/Los Angeles Times, 3-17:(I)1.

Bill Young
United States Representative,
R–Florida

3

I'm concerned that the media have been used. Because we are such an open society, because we enjoy the freedom of the press, *any*thing can be reported. But I think it's the obligation of an anchorman or a reporter—if he has an inkling that the sources he's using may be suspect, or a "front"—to determine his report's accuracy, or at the least to add some qualifiers. The viewing audience would appreciate that. You know, you hear all these things on television and I sometimes get to the point where I don't know what to believe any more.

TV Guide, 6-12:6.

Literature

Mortimer J. Adler
Author; Former professor of
philosophy, University of Chicago   *1*

I don't think children in school are taught to read any more. I'm not talking about functional literacy; I'm talking about real reading. The worst thing is this: You can go to any college in the country, as I have, get all the seniors together in one room, and ask what books all of them have read in common. I doubt there will be more than one or two books. It all stems from the fact that we've lost the sense of what general culture is.
Interview, New York/The
Christian Science Monitor, 12-22:15.

John Barth
Author; Professor of English
and creative writing,
Johns Hopkins University   *2*

Surely one of the reasons I've been fascinated by [the fictional literary character] Sheherazade is that stories in which the characters tell other stories is very much a part of the way all of us lead our lives. I will meet my wife in 45 minutes, and I will say, "What have you been doing?" And she will say, "How did the interview go?" And we'll be telling two stories. That's how we live. We like to imagine that our lives make sense, and storytelling is one way of ordering events. Of course, Sheherazade literally has to keep telling stories or she's *kaput.* In a less dramatic way, that's true of every writer in the world—you're only as good as your next story.
Interview/The New York Times, 6-28:18.

Saul Bellow
Author   *3*

[On writing novels]: I don't know how it's done. I suffer through it. It's not just suffering. I am deeply moved. I am up and around at night when I am writing a novel. I'm just recovering, really, from writing this last one. [The work of some popular novelists is] apparently delivered by truck to the publishers and, unedited and uncorrected, immediately set into print. I work over my manuscript many times until I feel that there is nothing more that I can change to improve it. I've thrown away many books, books that were almost finished, books that might have enriched me . . . I am deeply moved when I write. I get turned on by it. I've never used any drugs for stimulation. I don't use words loosely. When I'm working and the right word comes, there is an answering resonance within me. There is also a hardness of intention that goes with it. There is no idleness in it.
Interview, Chicago/Chicago
Tribune, 1-10:(Book World)7.

Gwendolyn Brooks
Pulitzer Prize-winning poet   *4*

It is *never* easy writing poetry. The interest is in getting down on paper what you *really* feel. That's very difficult to do—to be honest and to see to it that your vision is honest. A thousand things might try to influence you otherwise, but that's your duty. That's your obligation. To see honestly and to report honestly what you have seen honestly. You keep at it until you say, "Hey! *That* approx-i-mates what I had inside."
Interview/Chicago Tribune Magazine, 3-28:18.

Sylvia Burack
Editor, "The Writer" magazine   *5*

. . . if I were a young new writer I'd be very discouraged. I'm very down on publishers who will not read the material of new writers—and

(SYLVIA BURACK)

very few of them will. I think that is a travesty. It is also very shortsighted, because somewhere along the line some of these [current] luminaries are going to die out. Quite honestly, a lot of the trouble publishers are in is of their own doing. They all got so carried away that they kept giving all their money to a few people. Another problem is what publishers think of as marketable. There is great controversy now as to whether or not the marketing people have superseded the literary people, so that the judgment is made in advance as to what is salable, and if it's good or bad doesn't interest them. It is a very cynical vulgarization of the literary world.

*Interview, Boston/The
Christian Science Monitor, 12-1:(B)10.*

Ron Busch
*President, Pocket Books,
publishers*

1

The Harvard Business School says that 80 per cent of all new products fail. Eighty per cent of all new books fail. I can go through a list with you, month after month, of books we're putting out, and I can pretty much say to you, failure, failure, failure, failure—I mean financial failure. Good books. Public doesn't want them. The fact of the matter is, if you were manufacturing soap—and we're in the package-goods business, the product happens to be books—but if the public told you over a period of 20 years that they didn't like 80 per cent of the scents you were manufacturing, you'd stop and try to give them what they want.

Interview/Chicago Tribune, 1-15:(1)15.

John Cheever
Author

2

[On being a writer]: For me it's never been anything but a wish to communicate with sympathetic, presumably mature and intelligent men and women. I find that part of it thrilling. It dispels loneliness; it breaks the confinement that I feel is sometimes our lot. I can't think of

316

anything more exciting than to feel you've reached out and touched someone. Sometimes I really feel I have succeeded at doing that with my books and short stories.

*Interview, New York/The
Christian Science Monitor, 1-11:15.*

Norman Cousins
*Adjunct professor of psychiatry and
behavioral sciences, University of
California, Los Angeles; Former
editor, "Saturday Review"*

3

Writers are an amplifying system. And there is no better way of establishing communication between the nations than through the works of their writers . . . Writers give people beliefs, and giving people beliefs helps change history. Writers work with words, and words are the basic energy of civilization.

*At conference of Chinese and
American writers, Los Angeles, September/
Los Angeles Times, 9-29:(V)1.*

E. L. Doctorow
Author

4

[Saying he doesn't teach writing at colleges any more]: Universities were very good to writers after the Second World War, but in the long run it's not right. The writers stop being writers and become academic politicians. You get the phenomenon of writer-teachers turning out other writer-teachers. That's why I'm not doing it any more.

*Interview, Washington/The
Washington Post, 1-17:(K)7.*

John Gregory Dunne
Author

5

I think a writer basically only has one character. What I mean is, I have one character or sensibility which I project into situations that I, as a 49-year-old writer living in Los Angeles, normally would not see. A number of writers just end up writing about themselves; but by just using the details of your life, you feed off yourself and you can end up a kind of husk . . . I think you write to find out what you think, though that's hardly an original thought. Writers basically work by instinct—I think you

(JOHN GREGORY DUNNE)

have only an inchoate sense of what you're doing. For now, I just want to get through the next book—that's all you can hope to do.

Interview/The New York Times, 5-3:22.

John Fowles
British author

1

[Saying he dislikes revisions]: You sit over yourself like a schoolmaster . . . First-draft and revision writing are so different they hardly seem to belong to the same activity. I never do any "research" until the first draft is finished. All that matters to begin with is the flow, the story . . . [It is] an intuitive thing . . . Follow the accident, fear the fixed plan . . . A lot of revision is really a form of masochism . . . Research . . . is like swimming in a strait-jacket . . . I don't take kindly to [revisions]. I think there is something to be said even for mistakes . . . I have always liked in novels a fluctuating quality. I find it attractive. I think that sometimes boring passages are quite important.

Interview, Lyme Regis, England/
Esquire, October:92.

2

Writers usually want to talk about royalties, agents and things like that, and I have quite enough of that in my own life. It hasn't made me too popular in this country [the U.S.]—it's better to be a part of the literary establishment—but you can't, I think, explore inward if you lead a busy public life. Writers are basically egotists. You *must* be narcissistic because the things that happen in fiction—you can't look at them as an outside observer; they're all going on inside you.

Interview/The New York Times, 10-5:24.

Max Frisch
Author, Playwright

3

[On the difference between writing plays and novels]: My novels deal with personal relationships, especially between men and women. Theatre makes a social statement. Unlike readers of a novel, members of an audience go to the theatre together, confronting one another. I came to prose writing not as a novelist but from the theatre. I write my plays and novels alternately. When I write a play I embark on a kind of dialogue with a problem. If I go on to another play, it also is shaped by that dialogue. But if I turn to writing a novel, I forget the dialogue and am forced to create something new.

Interview/World Press Review, November:58.

Carlos Fuentes
Author

4

When I was a young man, I wrote to live. Now, at 54, I write not to die. Like Sheherazade in the *Arabian Nights*, I'll live as long as I have another story to tell.

Interview, Cambridge, Mass./
The New York Times, 6-6:(2)1.

Jack Geoghegan
Editor, William Morrow &
Company, publishers

5

There was a time, not too many years ago, when a publisher's pride was involved in two things: one, that he was surviving and making a profit, and, second, he had a balanced list. There was commerce, there were commercial novels, but also the effort to continue to publish significant biographies, *belles lettres.* A good publisher felt a certain obligation to do more than just try to make a buck . . . [But now,] there's a tendency to say, "We don't want to be fooling with this [smaller stuff]. Sure it's a nice novel and it might sell 10,000 or 15,000 copies, but so what? It's just small change."

Interview/Chicago Tribune, 1-15:(1)15.

Robert Giroux
Chairman, Farrar,
Straus & Giroux, publishers

6

[Saying many editors today are more concerned with deals than with books]: Editors used to be known by their authors; now some of them are known by their restaurants.

Time, 1-18:73.

317

WHAT THEY SAID IN 1982

(ROBERT GIROUX)

1

Publishing is merely a mirror of what's going on in writing. What good are publishers without writers? Publishers play a supportive role. We don't establish trends—writers do. There's a lot of talent around. There's not always public acceptance of it. We look back on the era of Fitzgerald and Hemingway as a golden age, but a lot of their books were not best sellers and a lot of books that were are not better than best sellers now.

Interview/"W": a Fairchild publication, 6-4:22.

Graham Greene
Author

2

The more I think of it, the more I worry about the division of literature into the great, because hard to read, and the not so great—or certainly the ignorable by scholars—because of the desire to divert, be readable, keep it plain. You don't find Conan Doyle dealt with at length in the literary histories. Yet he was a great writer.

Interview/Saturday Review, May:46.

Russell Hoban
Author

3

[On how he writes] : I never have an outline; I never have a plan of attack. In all the novels I've written, something I see gets me started. Usually that starting element is a nucleus that gathers other things to itself . . . My function as a writer is to offer what I hope will be a fruitful confusion. All kinds of stupid people are offering sterile clarity. What needs to be recognized is the confusion.

Interview/San Francisco Examiner & Chronicle, 1-3:(Review)9.

John Jakes
Author

4

I feel a real responsibility to my readers. I began to realize about two or three books into the Kent series [of historical novels] that I was the only source of history that some of these people had ever had! Maybe they'll never read a Barbara Tuchman book—but down at the K-mart, they'll pick up one of mine.

Interview, Washington/The Washington Post, 2-28:(L)1.

Elia Kazan
Author; Motion-picture director

5

To write a novel is tough work, just going over and over it, insisting that every page be good. I think I'm slowly getting better at it. I make a living out of it. Not a big living. I used to make three or four times in films what I make now. But the nice thing about writing is that you don't have to please anybody but yourself.

Interview, New York/ San Francisco Examiner & Chronicle, 7-18:(Scene)2.

Michael Korda
Editor-in-chief, Simon & Schuster, publishers

6

I'm a great believer in apprenticeship. With the exception of the rare genius, the best novels tend to be written by people who have had varied and strong writing apprenticeships before tackling novels. The problem is that so many people want to step full-blown into the pages of *People* magazine without an apprenticeship. It just isn't that easy. When I buy novels I ask whether it has a story that keeps you turning the pages. If it does, you can fix anything else. If it doesn't, nothing else matters.

Interview/The New York Times, 3-19:23.

Milan Kundera
Exiled Czech author

7

At the beginning of the century, Central Europe was the crucible of Western culture. [Now] traditional theatre no longer exists. Any Czech literature of value circulates underground in typewritten pages. We've been pushed back to the pre-Gutenberg galaxy.

World Press Review, June:47.

Arthur Miller
Author, Playwright

8

The public library is the foundation of our freedom and cannot be diminished without diminishing the essence of what we are and have to become.

The New York Times, 1-30:15.

Robert Nathan
Author

1

Writing was once a valid profession. We had publishers who would publish for the love of books and for what they thought was good and effective writing ... [Today] books are marketed like every other produce. They're on the shelves, and if they are not sold, they are taken off the shelves. There is no market today among publishers just for its literary value.

Interview/Los Angeles Times, 9-16:(IV)2.

Laurence Olivier
Actor

2

If you're going to write an autobiography, your duty is clear. You've got to open up them golden gates and let all the filth out, the full horror.

Interview, Los Angeles/Los Angeles Times, 11-7:(Calendar)5.

Frederik Pohl
Author

3

The library has been valuable not only to me but to the government. I've returned several hundred thousand dollars in taxes, and I can't believe that I would have had the sort of income to require that without the help the library gave me in the 1930s. The library was a major part of my education. I dropped out of high school, but it hasn't handicapped me very seriously—I've published more than 100 books and been translated into 40-odd languages. But most of what I've learned came from reading books; and in the formative years from 12 to 20, most of the books came from the Brooklyn Public Library.

The New York Times, 1-30:15.

Maurice Sendak
Author of children's books

4

It's becoming harder not only for the crazy, fun [children's] books, but, even more important, for the more serious [children's] books to

get published. Publishers are much less willing to take chances. There are a few publishers who are still interested in literature for children. But they are becoming fewer and fewer. There's a trend toward big books and big bucks.

At forum sponsored by San Diego Museum of Art and University of California-Extension, San Diego, Dec. 8/ Los Angeles Times, 12-10:(V)1.

Leonard Shatzkin
Publishing consultant

5

Any publisher will tell you that, in relation to any trade title he publishes, he's only sold a fraction of what the people out there would buy if they could get to them—if there was a bookstore handy, or if the bookstore that was handy had the book in it, or if, in the confusion of so many books coming out, he could make people aware that the book existed.

Interview/The Christian Science Monitor, 11-3:17.

Irwin Shaw
Author

6

As in the case of almost all American writers, my real education and the first hope that I might be a writer myself came to me in a public library ... It is painful to think that now, so many years later, our public libraries, those founts of culture and inspiration, are being neglected, their services curtailed, their eager young readers turned away. [Rich cities] cannot afford to risk [their] great heritage by putting books in the profit and loss column.

The New York Times, 1-30:15.

Sidney Sheldon
Author

7

I'm expected to deliver Big Books. I'm expected now to reach Number 1. And yes, I'm terrified about that. Because nobody reaches Number 1 every time at bat. So I will slip, and it terrifies me. This fall I have competition like James Michener, Stephen King, Harold Robbins—and they worry me. The only ones who don't worry me are my friends: Irving Wallace, Steve Shagan, Judy Krantz. I just wish them well.

Interview, Los Angeles/ Los Angeles Times, 10-3:(Calendar)5.

Isaac Bashevis Singer
Author   1

When I was young, the study house was the important place in my life. Now the library has taken over. When I come to a new place, my first question is, "Is there a library here?" I cannot imagine myself living in a town or a village without a library. The book and the library are as important in my life as bread and love. Sometimes I envy the people who lived in prehistoric time, and when I think about the fact that they had no library, I immediately exchange my fantasies for some beautiful library with valuable books in the future.

The New York Times, 1-30:15.

Susan Sontag
Author   2

I've written an enormous amount. I always thought I was going to write, and the only question was how well would I do it. Certainly I never felt consciously or unconsciously that there was any conflict between my vocation and being a woman. Writing is the one art, perhaps, where there are a great many first-rate women. So that's the only activity where one would probably have, even in the benighted bygone days, the least problem.

Interview, New York/
The New York Times Book Review, 10-24:11.

George Steiner
Author   3

I believe that a work of art [such as a novel], like metaphors in language, can ask the most serious, difficult questions in a way which really makes the readers answer for themselves; that the work of art [novel], far more than an essay or a tract, involves the reader, challenges him directly and brings him into the argument.

Interview, Cambridge, England/
The New York Times Book Review, 5-2:13.

William Styron
Author   4

I've always felt that the ultimate source of the writer's quality has finally less to do with the exterior of his life than with what he is. We tend to think romantically in America of writers as projecting a horribly tumultuous

image, that a writer has to be a victim of his own neuroses to the point that he is half mad or a total alcoholic. However, I can think of significant exceptions. One of them would be someone like Faulkner, who, though an alcoholic no doubt, nonetheless controlled it and lived a remarkably uneventful life.

Interview, New York/Esquire, January:90.

5

I think I've realized I've achieved a voice. It may not be as striking as that of some of my predecessors, but who cares? I think that every writer who is serious, who grew up in my generation, has wanted to say, "Okay, look here, we cannot be epigones for the rest of our lives. We are now grown men. *Don't* compare us with our predecessors. Read us because we are whoever we are—Styron, Mailer, Updike, Roth or whoever, and judge us on our own achievement." And I think we have finally achieved that. I don't think there's been any successor to Faulkner in terms of sheer protean genius and energy, but I think there have been a significant number of writers of the generation after Faulkner who have written beautifully and well about their times. The point is that in our own way we are as good, and I don't think that's a vainglorious statement. I think the post-war writers have achieved a rather remarkable body of work.

Interview/The New York
Times Magazine, 12-12:26.

Studs Terkel
Author   6

The trouble with censorship is that once it starts it is hard to stop. Do you ban the Bible, or *Hamlet*? Just about every book contains something that someone objects to.

At town meeting, Girard, Pa./
U.S. News & World Report, 3-8:66.

D. M. Thomas
Poet, Novelist   7

I certainly don't feel that I've got the ready-made techniques of a novelist. I don't feel that I *am* a novelist in any traditional sense. In this phase of my work, I've translated my poetry into novel form because I'm interested in narrative at this stage, in work which will

(D. M. THOMAS)

allow me to interrelate images in a wider sense than a poem does, and to bring in human characters. But I feel that the poetry is there all the time, though at the moment it's under the surface, mainly—an underground stream . . . I have no idea where I'm going to go next, after this novel. I have no idea whether it will be another novel or whether I'll go back to poems or what. It's a bit unnerving at times. On the other hand, perhaps that's good. It means that there's still discovery.

Interview, Hereford, England/
Esquire, November:100.

John Updike
Author   *1*

. . . writing any book seems, in a way, silly and probably less good than it should be because what you write down is so less brilliant than the glimpses in your mind of the world. It's sort of like painting. The attempts to paint what's in front of you are always so grossly inadequate. It's only when you actually get it away from the bowl of apples that you can appreciate your own painting. So it is with writing fiction.

Interview/Chicago Tribune, 4-29:(1)12.

Mario Vargas Llosa
Peruvian author   *2*

In Western countries, societies are quite free and have many instruments for self-criticism. In countries where there is no political freedom, no free press, I think writers are much more privileged than other people. They know how to write and read while many people don't know how to do either. Writers have an audience and have the possibility of reaching people. In these societies, I think writers *must* do something to fight barbarism, illiteracy, social injustice, economic inequality, dictatorship. In Latin America a writer becomes a public figure whom people respect, very naively sometimes. A writer is considered a kind of social conscience. The problem is how to use this power in a constructive way, no?

Interview, New York/The New York
Times Book Review, 8-1:15.

Gore Vidal
Author   *3*

The kind of writer who tries to use the novel to change the world is incredibly naive. You can't do it through the novel—that only produces bad work. You must maintain the separation between the artist and the citizen. As an artist, you write novels; as a citizen, you make speeches and write essays.

Interview, Los Angeles, Jan. 25/
Los Angeles Herald Examiner, 1-27:(C)5.

Kurt Vonnegut, Jr.
Author   *4*

Here in America, for 200 years we [writers] have been allowed to say whatever we want to, as loud as we want—and the politicians are wholly unafraid of us. So I would say that any society is foolish to fear its writers. It might as well fear its bakers.

At conference of Chinese and American
writers, Los Angeles, September/
Los Angeles Times, 9-29:(V)8.

Irving Wallace
Author   *5*

I would tend to favor a writers union because one out of 10 writers don't make it only because they have no one to hold their hand and offer support. But I don't think [collective union action] can work. The problem starts with the very nature of writers, who are individualistic and insecure. How would you withhold stories for a year or more? How could you ask writers not to write?

The New York Times, 5-27:22.

Robert Penn Warren
Poet   *6*

What can take the place of art in life? [Poetry] is one of the arts. Why does it survive? Because there are people who make their profession at it, or want to. [Why?] Because it's the only thing that makes life comprehensible. If you read a decent poem by someone you've never heard of, you're establishing a relationship with him through the medium. It's part of the human community, it reaffirms the human community . . . Human beings, it seems to me—now, this is hip-shooting—are trying to

WHAT THEY SAID IN 1982

make sense of the world. But the whole business of any art is to put order, to express an order on the world of some kind. Everybody yearns [for order]. How stupid, you could almost say, to find somebody who doesn't want order in the world.

Interview, Fairfield, Conn./
The Christian Science Monitor, 3-4:(B)4.

1

The problem in reading poetry is in reaching beyond our own moment. So I don't think we should throw anything away—not yet. Poetry involves persuasion to see things differently from the way you normally do.

At "The Arts and Politics" symposium,
Claremont (Calif.) College Graduate School,
May 14/Los Angeles Times, 5-18:(VI)9.

Theodore H. White
Author, Historian 2

Political novels are all hyperbolic. The actual scene in Washington is so crazy that to dramatize it is to exaggerate it. Wilbur Mills, Fanne Fox—you cannot do more with reality than reality offers you in fact. I guess Robert Penn Warren's *All the King's Men* is the best example of a political book. Allen Drury's *Advise and Consent* was a good political novel. But basically, it's almost a hopeless enterprise . . . You know, one of the greatest novels of American life could be written about [the late Chicago Mayor] Richard Daley. But nobody—like Saul Bellow—has tackled him yet. If you have a vivid

character at the heart of it, then perhaps you can write a good political novel.

Interview, New York/
Chicago Tribune, 5-16:(7)7.

3

[On authors traveling around the country promoting their books] : What you're trying to do is the hootchy-kootchy to get them [the people] into the tent. It's demeaning and degrading. You have to strip yourself threadbare like a piece of fabric. But it's necessary because we are living through a period of cultural discontinuity in the United States— look at the arcades with Atari guns and the "E.T." mores . . . In a way, [promoting your own books] makes you feel slimy. You want your book to be discovered for itself, and instead you find yourself pleading for it. And you're competing for air time with "Jane Fonda's Workout Book" or "No Bad Dogs" or "Thin Thighs in 30 Days" and others publicizing their books, as well as entertainers and people selling products or viewpoints, sometimes on the same [TV] show. So you swallow your pride and say to yourself, "I have 20 years of my professional life invested in this book; I can't let it go down the drain." You wake up early, polish your anecdotes, catch the planes, sleep in the Atlanta hotel that doesn't have room service when you get there, not even a glass of milk, and start out all over again the next day.

Interview, New York/
The New York Times, 7-24:15.

Medicine and Health

Christiaan Barnard
Former heart-transplant surgeon

1

[On his notoriety when he was a pioneering surgeon]: Operating used to be the most exciting thing in the world to me. But the world kept looking over my shoulder. It's human to be tense when you're on display all the time. You know headlines will result if you do well, but that much bigger headlines will come if you don't.

Interview/
Chicago Tribune,
1-5:(1)13.

2

I can't describe the feeling of uselessness that sweeps over you when a [heart-transplant] patient dies. The only way I could cope was by going back and doing it again—showing myself and everyone else that I could. I knew transplantation could work. Why should these patients die because the central pump of their existence was failing them? It would have been immoral, even unethical, to wait around until the immunological problems had been worked out. I went straight back with the remaining confidence I had and did it again . . . The public misunderstood transplantation from the beginning. None of us . . . thought of the procedure as a cure. It is palliative; it eases without curing. How long you live is not as important as *how* you live. [Transplant patient] Phillip Blaiberg was asked when he realized the operation was worthwhile. Blaiberg said he realized it when he came round from anesthesia and found he could breathe again.

Interview/
San Francisco Examiner & Chronicle,
1-10:(A)12.

Karl D. Bays
Chairman, American
Hospital Supply Corporation

3

With the pressure on to contain costs, we are seeing a continuing consolidation of hospitals. This is an effort to be responsive to the cost-containment problem. Hospitals are forming multi-hospital systems to try to get economies of scale, to share expensive equipment and services, to allocate resources better and to make better use of their personnel . . . Critics of the consolidation trend contend that we run the risk of losing local community involvement and personal service. The concern is that the business aspects are overcoming the medical aspects. My experience has been that you can provide compassionate care through a multi-hospital system and still be more efficient than a less financially stable, smaller hospital. The way that can be done is by centralizing the financial and business aspects of various hospitals at the system headquarters. The interaction with the patient and with the local community remains decentralized and very much in the hands of the local medical staff and local management.

Interview/
The New York Times,
11-9:30.

John C. Bedrosian
President, Federation of
American Hospitals

4

The insatiable quest for immortality makes patients demand the latest in high-technology treatment and other therapy promising to lengthen life. Very simply, that is why hospital costs can only continue to go up.

Chicago Tribune, 3-26:(1)1.

WHAT THEY SAID IN 1982

Norman Cousins
Adjunct professor of psychiatry and behavioral science, University of California, Los Angeles; Former editor, "Saturday Review"   *I*

Many patients have a growing sense of impersonalization and fragmentation. They go to their doctors' offices seeking refuge from their fears and loneliness and do not adjust easily to new encounters, either with those who preside over separate domains in medical science or with highly sophisticated marvels of diagnostic technology. The conclusion is clear: Doctors who spend more time with their patients may have to spend less money on malpractice insurance policies.

At Tulane School of Medicine commencement/Time, 6-21:83.

Dennis Driscoll
Meteorologist, Texas A&M University   *2*

[Saying people use weather as a scapegoat for health problems]: Where do you draw the line? If you catch a cold during winter weather, is it really weather or because you didn't dress warm enough, or went to work when everyone was getting a cold? ... The classic example of this kind of thinking is what happened with polio. For many years polio was thought to be caused by summer weather until scientists discovered the organism responsible lived in water and was picked up by people who went swimming outdoors. Very few people go swimming outdoors during winter, so few if any cases were reported during that time. Now, is that weather?

College Station, Texas/ Los Angeles Times, 4-15:(I-B)7.

Arthur Hull Hayes, Jr.
Commissioner, Food and Drug Administration of the United States   *3*

The [food-safety] laws are not always flexible enough. They currently mandate, for example, that if a food additive causes cancer at any dose in any species of animal, it may not be licensed. It doesn't matter that the incidence of cancer was minuscule or that it occurred only in mice and only at extremely large dosage levels. It doesn't matter that science has changed since 1938, when many of the food laws were passed, or the 1950s, when they were amended ... I want to make regulatory decisions based on the risk as we perceive it and as science determines it to be ... We take soap into the bathtub, yet we know how many people slip on soap and smash their heads. Still, people don't want to give up soap, which is the only way to reduce the "soap risk" to zero. In the case of saccharine, Congress said zero risk is not what people want and told this agency, in law, not to ban it.

Interview, Washington/ The New York Times, 1-25:(4)8.

John Bernard Henry
Dean, School of Medicine, Georgetown University   *4*

The laboratory seldom seems to beckon with the same drama and excitement as the hospital —but let me assure you it is there. The laboratory and the classroom are the parents of medicine. It could not have been born without them. All that this profession is and has become is based on investigation and research. Someone, somewhere, sometime had an inquiring mind and the intelligence and stick-to-it-iveness to labor long hours with one goal in mind: discovery! And it is their discoveries and their accomplishments that enable us to treat our patients and exercise our profession. We would have no knowledge to impart had someone not investigated. The clinician receives the gratitude, undying affection and applause of his patients; but his colleagues know all too well that he has, technically, put into "practice" the fruits of someone else's "labor." I like to think that makes good sense etymologically, for the words "practitioner" and "laboratory" imply practice and labor.

Before Georgetown University School of Medicine freshman class/ The Washington Post, 10-8:(A)14.

John Paul II
Pope   *5*

[Criticizing abortion]: I speak on the absolute respect for human life, which no person or

(JOHN PAUL II)

institution, private or public, can ignore. There-fore, whoever denies defense to the most innocent and frailest human person, to the human person conceived but not yet born, commits a most grave violation of moral order. Nothing can legitimize the death of an inno-cent. What sense can there be in speaking of the dignity of man, of his fundamental rights, if one does not protect the innocent, if one goes as far even as to facilitate means and services, private or public, to destroy defenseless human lives?

At mass, Madrid, Nov. 2/
The New York Times, 11-3:3.

C. Everett Koop
Surgeon General
of the United States   *1*

The crisis in health care is a crisis in the cost of health care, and there's no doubt that the cost crisis is very serious. In March, the cost of living dropped 0.3 per cent, whereas the cost of medical care went up 1 per cent. In April of this year, medical-care prices were up 12.1 per cent over April, 1981, compared to a 6.6 per cent increase for all consumer items over the same period. In this same period, hospital-room charges—the most expensive item within the total cost of medical care—rose 16.6 percentage points, which figures out to an alarming 10 percentage points above the over-all rate of inflation. The crisis in medical costs is easy to understand: When you and I are sick, we don't want second-rate treatment and we don't care what treatment costs as long as it can make us well. But from the point of view of what health care costs the nation—what it costs the govern-ment and ultimately the taxpayer—then this attitude of not caring about individual costs is a significant problem.

Interview/U.S. News & World Report, 6-28:35.

Bernard J. Lachner
Speaker of the house of delegates,
American Hospital Association   *2*

Every successful business has learned the economic concepts of supply and demand. In hospitals, too, we work with supply and demand. We have supply, which is the hospital, physician or other provider. We have demand—

the health-care consumer. But in some signifi-cant ways, supply and demand in health care differ from the traditional economic model. For one thing, the purchaser of the service rarely makes the decision to be hospitalized or decides which tests and treatment he needs or has an economic reason not to go to a hospital for the service. These decisions are made by the physician. And patients rarely pay directly for their hospital stays. Their costs are paid by insurance companies or Medicare and Medicaid with money from taxes or their employer. Ninety per cent of the hospital bills in this nation are paid by someone other than the patient.

Before American Hospital
Association Trustee Forum, Boston/
The Wall Street Journal, 7-9:14.

Alex McMahon
President, American
Hospital Association   *3*

Now hospitals are under the greatest finan-cial pressures there have ever been, and there will be an increase in the number of hospitals that close . . . Hospital people are greatly con-cerned. The pressures on hospitals to cut costs are now so great that we are going to have to do something about it. We have to listen to the message from the public, from Congress and from business to reduce the rate of increase [in health-care costs] .

Chicago Tribune, 4-18:(1)8.

Steven Muller
President, Johns Hopkins University   *4*

We believe there should be a decrease in the enormous pressure that is put on students in the medical schools. We are doing an excellent job in training clinical scientists. But there are some things they are not getting, in part because of the extraordinary dosage of science they receive . . . [Most medical students] can only get by [by] working roughly 18 hours a day. They don't do anything else. All they do is go through that curriculum . . . How much of it are they really going to use? . . . [This total immersion could lead to a] fascination with

325

(STEVEN MULLER)

technology that makes the device more important than the patient ... We should ... pay more attention to the promotion of values and attitudes that physicians must have to withstand the stress of their own careers and to serve patients in a humane manner.

To reporters, Washington, Oct. 19/
The Washington Post, 10-20:(A)2.

Robert Nimmo
Administrator, Veterans
Administration of the United States

1

[Saying veterans' medical benefits may have to be trimmed]: What has to be recognized, I think, by those people if they want to be realistic, is that there are more words in the dictionary than "more, more, more." At some point they're going to have to decide what benefits are most important to them and which can be cut back ... Recently I talked to an attorney of some substance who is 68 years old and a veteran, and he said, "Bob, is it true that I am now eligible for unlimited free medical care in a VA hospital?" I said, "Yes, it's true," and he said, "Then why have I been spending my money to get medical care?" ... The Congress, and the people through the Congress, are going to have to make some very serious decisions about who will be entitled to medical care and other benefits, what the eligibility standards will be and what their level will be.

Interview, Washington/
The New York Times, 1-11:15.

Bob O'Leary
President, Illinois Hospital
Association

2

I don't know how many [hospitals in the U.S.] will close [due to financial pressure], whether it will be 300, 500 or 1,000. The important thing is that we are going to see hospitals close at a rate that is unprecedented in this country. Because large numbers of hospitals have not closed in the past despite their financial problems, many people think it will not happen. But they are just fooling themselves.

Chicago Tribune, 4-18:(1)8.

Nancy Reagan
Wife of the President of the
United States, Ronald Reagan

3

[Criticizing media glamorization of drugs]: We've all seen the TV shows where the punch line is about getting high or getting good stuff. To those writers and comedians, let me say—it's not funny any more. Children are being destroyed and lives are being ruined, and that's not something to laugh about ... And in many dramas, the lead no sooner enters the room than he or she is at the bar pouring a drink ... The lyrics of modern songs—quite a few modern songs—shout at kids to get high and get stoned. And the drug-paraphernalia shops cater to kids as surely as candy stores once did.

Before Advertising Council,
Washington, April 23/The
Washington Post, 4-24:(C)4.

Ronald Reagan
President of the United States

4

[Arguing against abortion]: If you cannot determine when life begins, then doesn't simple morality dictate that you opt for the fact that it is alive until and unless someone can prove it dead? If we came upon a body in the street that was unconscious and we weren't sure whether it was unconscious or dead, we wouldn't say, "Let's bury it." We'd wait until someone assured us that it wasn't alive. And I think the same thing goes of the unborn child. I happen to believe the unborn child is a living human being. I think the fact that children have been prematurely born even down to the three-month stage and have lived to, the record shows, to grow up and be normal human beings, that ought to be enough for all of us.

To religious editors, Washington,
Sept. 14/The Washington Post, 9-15:(A)2.

Arnold Relman
Professor of medicine,
Harvard Medical School

1

It does violence to reality to imagine it is possible [for a doctor] to tell the whole truth and nothing but the truth to a patient and to believe that this is what the patient wants. The attitude that says the truth is the important thing, not the patient, allows for a lot of damage ... In my experience, patients do not want to hear about everything that could possibly go wrong or the limitations of their doctor's understanding of their case. The sicker the patient, the more readily he accepts the knowledge gap. Patients are often frightened, even terrorized, by information thrust on them by doctors who use a truth-at-all-costs paradigm.

At medical symposium, Columbia University,
April/The Washington Post, 5-2:(C)2.

William Rial
President-elect, American
Medical Association

2

[Saying the cost of a medical-school education is going up and fewer prospective students can afford it]: It's a very hazardous situation. You could see an era of elitist medical students, where those who could afford it are the only ones who get a medical education. Schools might be forced to accept students who have the money, even if they don't have the grades.

Before American Medical Association
House of Delegates, Chicago, June 13/
Chicago Tribune, 6-14:(1)9.

David Rothman
Professor of history, and director,
Center for the Study of Society
and Medicine, Columbia University

3

There is a growing recognition that a host of decisions that have to be made in the realm of medicine are no longer made exclusively under criteria understood as strictly medical. Medicine in all sorts of ways is capable of doing things we no longer want to do. We can keep brain-dead patients alive much longer than anyone would wish. In essence, technology is more powerful.

It forces patients, their proxy, physicians and medical centers to make decisions.

The New York Times, 12-12:(1)50.

Larry Sage
President, National Association
of Public Hospitals

4

[On financially troubled public hospitals' turning away of unemployed patients who have lost their health insurance]: We are not far from health riots. If public hospitals reach the point where they have to refuse to accept emergency patients, then it's fairly obvious what's going to happen. Once the first 10 patients show up at closed emergency-room doors and die, then something's got to blow.

Interview, Boston/
Los Angeles Herald Examiner, 5-17:(A)6.

Richard S. Schweiker
Secretary of Health and Human
Services of the United States

5

[Saying he will not reduce the government's role in assuring proper standards for nursing homes]: The existing health and safety requirements will remain untouched. I will not turn back the clock ... Contrary to recent reports in the press, I will not imperil senior citizens in nursing homes, our most vulnerable population, by removing essential Federal protections. I will not eliminate any staffing requirements for nursing homes such as medical directors, dieticians, social workers and other necessary health and safety consultants.

Washington, March 20/
The New York Times, 3-21:(1)1.

Ronald K. Siegel
Psychopharmacologist, School
of Medicine, University of
California, Los Angeles

6

[On cocaine]: It is a drug for the Protestant ethic and the spirit of capitalism, a drug for "producers."

U.S. News & World Report, 3-22:27.

B. F. Skinner
Psychologist

1

Leisure [for senior citizens] should be relaxing. Possibly you like complicated puzzles, or chess, or other demanding intellectual games. Give them up. If you want to continue to be intellectually productive you must risk the contempt of your younger acquaintances and freely admit that you read detective stories or watch Archie Bunker on TV.

Before American Psychological
Association, Washington, Aug. 23/
The New York Times, 8-24:19.

Peter Steinglass
Professor of psychiatry, School of
Medicine, George Washington University

2

Patients who are hooked to machines for the rest of their lives can develop a feeling of dependency, a love-hate relationship with the devices. Having a part of one's self that isn't one's self arouses complicated emotions . . . Everybody thought the dialysis machine was nirvana, but it proved to be very difficult for many people.

The New York Times, 12-12:(4)8.

Martin A. Swerdlow
Chief of pathology, Michael Reese
Hospital and Medical Center;
President, Chicago Pathology Society

3

Many physicians have the mistaken notion that autopsies work against them. It is important for them to realize that autopsies do not put them on the spot, that, in fact, they are important in verifying that a physician did practice good medicine.

Chicago Tribune, 5-2:(2)6.

William B. Walsh
President, Project Hope

4

National-health-insurance systems in other countries are shown to be less cost-effective than our own [U.S.] free-market system. Certainly this has been the case in Europe, where there are six different approaches to a national system of health care. In Great Britain, people have to wait three years to have a hernia operation, two years for gall-bladder surgery. That's a lot of discomfort to have for two years.

Interview/U.S. News & World Report, 3-8:67.

5

What is needed in the health-care industry is prospective reimbursement. Each hospital should determine a budget at the beginning of the year and then live within that budget—just like all other businesses operate. The way it is now, hospitals are reimbursed retrospectively for what they do, no matter what the cost. There is no incentive to perform efficiently. Government programs of Medicaid and Medicare should establish a lump sum for reimbursement at the beginning of the year and make hospitals live within that amount. If hospitals and nursing homes were required to provide services on a system of prospective reimbursement, health-care costs would be reduced.

Interview/U.S. News & World Report, 3-8:68.

The Performing Arts

MOTION PICTURES

Woody Allen
Actor, Director, Screenwriter

1

[On his favorite part of film-making] : The writing is the most pleasure. The idea exists only in your mind's eye, and consequently it's perfect. Everything works, and it's brilliant because you're months away from having to execute it on the screen. So, the writing is great. I get up in my apartment, eat my sandwiches when I'm not lying in my bed practicing my clarinet, and write. It's just a pleasure. When you got to get out and make the picture, that's tough. Then you have to get up at 6 in the morning every day and work all day long, then see dailies in the evening. There are meetings and the weather changes, and it's very tough. And then the editing becomes fun again. You go into the cutting room, order coffee and sandwiches, and you're relaxed. So the best part is writing, the second best is editing and the worst is filming.
Interview, New York/
Chicago Tribune, 7-11:(6)5.

Lindsay Anderson
Director

2

It's odd that my film work tends to be theatrical whereas my stage work is based on scrupulous naturalism. But why should the cinema tie itself down to naturalism? After all, the greatest living director is Luis Bunuel, who is a poetic anarchist. And the great commercial successes of the moment, like the *Star Wars* and *Superman* sequences, are all fantasies'. In fact, America is sweeping the screens of the world with essays in infantalism. But audiences like circuses; in an age of bland, conformist television, they hunger for extremism.
Interview, London/The
New York Times, 1-17:(4)26.

Richard Attenborough
Actor, Director

3

The prerequisite to be a movie director is energy—forget the talent. Talent you can get away without; energy you can't.
Interview, Beverly Hills, Calif./
Los Angeles Herald Examiner, 11-28:(E)8.

4

[On making biographical films about famous people] : Overriding all judgments must be, and always will be, the need to establish acceptability and credibility—the humanity—of the leading character. The great Paul Muni and Charles Laughton biographies worked, even if in a superficial way, because of the credibility of the central figure. And in Peter O'Toole's *Lawrence of Arabia,* however enormous the Arabic scale was, you were captivated by the person.
Interview/The New York Times, 11-28:(2)15.

Steven Bach
Former president of production,
United Artists Corporation

5

What really separates the great Hollywood moguls from the people running the [film] companies today is the moguls got into the movie business because they loved the movie business, they loved stars, they loved stories, they loved audiences, and that is not true today. Those people created the business. Everybody else has inherited, and it has been inherited by the ranks of agents and lawyers, people who are expert in making deals, rather than people who may or may not know anything at all about what is a good story.
Interview/Chicago Tribune, 1-13:(1)14.

WHAT THEY SAID IN 1982

Ingmar Bergman
Director

1

Directing a film, you always say we're one big family, we all love each other, we are together. And in a way that's true—but in another sense, you are totally isolated. There is the crew, over here the actors, and here stands the director. And he makes all the decisions. He makes about 10,000 decisions every day, and he knows that 50 per cent of those decisions will be bad ones. Only a very small percentage will be good decisions.

Interview, Stockholm/
Saturday Review, April:39.

2

[On his objectives in making a film]: It sounds crazy, but it must be alive. You must have the feeling that what you see on the screen is alive. Not necessarily that it represents reality, but that it's alive. I always try to create something with the actors that has its own nerves, emotions, voices, movements.

Interview, London/The New York
Times, 10-10:(2)26.

Tony Bill
Producer, Director

3

I'm not a believer in that widely held belief that great movies can only come out of a crucible of suffering where everyone on the set is tense and everyone is afraid to voice an opinion. Since I clearly lack the blessing of bi-location, I can't see everything that's going on; so if a crew member sees an extra picking his nose while the camera's rolling, I want to know about it before I see it in the dailies. This, the actual filming, is the only part of making a film that can actually be a collaboration, and, therefore, fun for everyone. The rest—the pre-production, the casting, the finding of locations, and the editing later—is rather solitary, hard work.

Interview, New York/
The New York Times, 1-3:(2)13.

4

I tend to think people overrate the expertise that movie directors are supposed to have. And

I disapprove of directors becoming stars in their own right. When that happens, their ability to accept input is threatened. We all make mistakes—you just hope that a producer or a grip will point yours out to you. But if you're a superstar director, they don't tell you and you wouldn't listen anyway.

Interview, Los Angeles/San Francisco
Examiner & Chronicle, 12-26:(Datebook)25.

Joseph Brooks
Producer

5

Making a movie is truly like running a war. There are all the contingency plans. If Plan A doesn't work, then we go to Plan B or Plan C. Plus all the equipment, all the trucks, all the people—it runs into the hundreds.

Interview, London/"W":
a Fairchild publication, 11-5:8.

Richard Brooks
Director, Screenwriter

6

Audiences aren't getting their money's worth [at movie theatres] and nobody cares. The managers don't care, the projectionists are so old they can't see, and everybody is ankle-high in soda-pop cans, popcorn butter and melted Hershey bars. The glass windows in the projection booths are covered with lint, dust, cigarette tar and chocolate ice cream. These people never heard of Windex. With the new sound coming from five speakers, you can't hear the dialogue half the time. Kids talk all the way through everything just like they do at home watching TV.

Interview/San Francisco Examiner &
Chronicle, 5-9:(Datebook)19.

Richard Burton
Actor

7

In almost every artistic career, at a certain period, there's an enormous burst of energy. Take Shakespeare—his early plays are relatively indifferent; the middle comedies begin to show his genius and then there's that tremendous burst of energy that produces the five great tragedies. Energy is so important to an actor. At first, my acting was physical. I charged into

(RICHARD BURTON)

parts like a bull. Now I don't use as much energy. Experience comes into play. That's why I'm not frightened of aging.

Interview, Venice, Italy/San Francisco Examiner & Chronicle, 4-18:(Datebook)35.

Michael Caine
Actor

1

One thing I always try to do in acting is listen. Perhaps that makes the acting seem more natural. When you hold a conversation in real life you always listen to what the other person is saying in order to formulate your reply. When you act, you've known for weeks what the other actor is going to say to you and what your reply will be, so it's not always easy to make it look as if it's the first time you've heard it. I work hard at that.

Interview, Beverly Hills, Calif./ Los Angeles Times, 3-21:(Calendar)27.

2

It takes brains to be an actor. Not clinical brains, but emotional brains. Great actors go beyond intelligence. They don't know what's happening, or why, but it's not necessarily true that the more you can theorize about something, the more you know.

Interview, Los Angeles/Mademoiselle, May:60.

3

[On a film he was recently making with Laurence Olivier]: His view seemed to be that since he was already a lord and had a couple of Academy Awards, the only thing he was going to get out of the picture was some money. And if that wasn't forthcoming [due to financial problems of the producers], then he wasn't going to be in the picture. Interesting, isn't it? If you're an actor you're always going to be asked if you're in the film for just the money. You're supposed to say no. But everyone around you is in it for the money—the assistant director, cameraman, the crew. Why do you have to be different?

Interview, Los Angeles/ Los Angeles Times, 7-15:(VI)1.

Frank Capra
Director

4

[On his advice to young film-makers]: Don't follow trends; start trends. Don't compromise. Believe in yourself. Only the daring should make films—the morally courageous speaking to their fellow man.

Upon receiving American Film Institute's Life Achievement Award, Beverly Hills, Calif., March 4/Los Angeles Times, 3-6:(V)1.

5

[On winning an "Oscar"]: What happens to you overnight is incredible. Suddenly, you're on the front page all over the world; people in the interior of Asia know who you are. It's pretty heady stuff and it can be a very shocking thing. It affects different people in different ways; it can affect your work, and you can go downhill afterward.

The New York Times, 3-28:(2)19.

John Cassavetes
Actor, Director

6

Everything here [in Hollywood] is dictated by profits and grosses. It's hard to find people who still want to make movies with no regard for that stuff. If the major people want to make money, let them make it. I just want to make movies. I want to be in them, direct them, have a good time with other talented people . . . It's just the stupidity of not allowing certain pictures to be made simply because they're not expensive enough. You have to kill yourself to make an expensive picture out of an inexpensive movie, in order to suit the economic standards everyone is used to. Why? It's a camera and some people—why should that cost more than a five-story building? It's dumb, and it's really frustrating.

Interview, Los Angeles/ Los Angeles Times, 8-12:(VI)1,4.

Francis Ford Coppola
Director, Screenwriter

7

I believe in a cinema of many possibilities. I want to work in different styles and be unpredictable, just to get interested again. I don't like going to the movies any more. Years ago, you

(FRANCIS FORD COPPOLA)

could choose from 20 kinds of films to see: swashbucklers, musicals, comedy, social drama, romance, Abbott and Costello. Now there's just three or four things you're allowed to make: screwball comedy, psychosocial stuff, and space opera. You don't have diversity any more. It's like a 55-m.p.h. speed limit. But what if you want to go 2,000 m.p.h.? There are plenty of areas in life where you have to stick by the rules. In this field, it shouldn't be that way.

Interview, New York/The Christian Science Monitor, 2-18:18.

1

In Hollywood, creative people are dealt with in a very simple way. Management understands that we are, by nature, a very insecure and nutty lot or we wouldn't have developed these unique talents. It is very difficult for creative people, with their vanities and peculiarities, to sit around a table and agree on anything. Artists have a hard time congregating in a way that gives them some clout because each is thinking about his particular and peculiar dream. So the managers rule things. They lavish and cultivate talent and provide superficial benefits. They, in effect, say to the artist class, "Hey, *you* take a lollipop, and *you* have a girl, and *you* have an estate."

Interview/U.S. News & World Report, 4-5:68.

Tony Curtis
Actor
2

I'm Bernie [his real name], I'm Tony—both screwed up. But I have a third person I can go into to get rid of both of the others. Myself, the Actor. Ah, that's the fun of it—getting rid of those two phony grabbers when I'm doing a show. Ha, ha, ha, ha, leave them in some dim past, behind. Ditch them. I become the actor. No name; just the actor. In a dressing-room I put on the makeup, clothes. I begin to put on the mannerisms and the posture, the carriage, the walk. Then I go toward the lights and the camera and I become less and less of me and more and more of who I am. Closer and closer, farther and farther; and when those lights go on, and the camera rolls, and I hear "Action!" I don't even know who I am or where. I'm

332

transported, euphoria; and I don't come out of it until "Cut!" and long after.

Interview/San Francisco Examiner & Chronicle, 5-2:(Datebook)27.

Bette Davis
Actress
3

People look back on those early days of film and it is as if every film was the greatest. That's nonsense. If there were five good films in one year it was a bonanza year. Some old films stand up to close scrutiny today, others are interesting only as artifacts ... The "golden years" were just hard-working years as far as I am concerned. One year I made five in a row; I had to rest when it was over ... Now [actors] do one film and wait and wait and wait. If it isn't a blockbuster, you don't get hired again.

Interview, New York/The Christian Science Monitor, 2-2:19.

Richard Dreyfuss
Actor
4

The theory many people have that an actor is someone who was denied love as a child and is consequently seeking love from other people through acting strikes me as a lot of absolute rubbish. I had a great deal of love as a child. The reason I act, I promise you, is because I love doing it. My theory is that an actor is someone who was smart enough to know a good thing when he saw it.

Interview, Los Angeles/Los Angeles Times, 1-3:(Calendar)16.

Clint Eastwood
Actor, Director
5

Casting is one of the most important aspects in making a film. A film can live or die on it. The cast has to bring those characters to life. If you miscast a character, or one stands out wrong, you can throw the whole picture out of whack. It's like having a pebble in your tire.

Daily Variety, 9-3:23.

Federico Fellini
Director
6

We have made too many movies. This disproportionate, emphatic production of pic-

(FEDERICO FELLINI)

tures has taken away the power of movies. They have lost their authority and seductiveness. We have been submerged in images. It is as if all the streets and squares, all the walls of the homes, were full of paintings. So you need no more go to museums to see paintings of great artists. It is the same with cinema. Our eyes are bursting. We have been bombarded with images.
Interview, Rome/San Francisco Examiner & Chronicle, 5-30:(Datebook)19.

Sally Field
Actress
1

My feeling is that it's very important for actors to try to get a blend in their wanting to do a role and in recognizing that movies need an audience. You can't just act by yourself in a closet. You can, but it's not as much fun. You have to try, your whole career long, never to lose each side of your wants—wanting to act, and wanting to be in films that people want to see.
Interview/Daily Variety, 1-13:38.

Freddie Fields
President, motion-picture division, Metro-Goldwyn-Mayer Film Co.
2

This has become a director's medium, and not all for the good. There was a time when it was a producer's medium, and I think all directors should work with a good producer to keep a step ahead of him, to help him plan. You go back to the days of Selznick and Spiegel. They knew what they were doing. The producer is forgotten now a lot of the time. The director is trying to run the whole show, and it's taken away the director's support system. I don't think it's good. This is a collaborative art form.
Interview/The New York Times, 2-14:(2)16.

Jane Fonda
Actress
3

As actors analyzing a character, we're so conditioned to think Freudianly in this country, to think in terms of the Oedipal influences

and things like that—the very personal, individual psychological framework that made that person what they are. But when you begin, as I have since 1968 through my political activism, to understand people on a different level, understand society on a different level—the degree to which we are affected by what's happening, the social forces around us—it makes your ability to act, to sense what needs to be included in the development of a character, much, much richer ... I'm actually aware all the time when I'm acting of the degree to which I'm a better actress because I'm an activist.
Interview, San Francisco/San Francisco Examiner & Chronicle, 1-17:(Datebook)22,23.

4

Sitting at the major studios lately, you feel like you're riding on a dinosaur. Clearly, the way that movies have been made since I've been in the business—for 25 years—isn't going to be in existence for very much longer. I don't mean that there won't be movies *made* any more, but there certainly will be much fewer of them made. And unless the whole economics of movie-making changes, it's going to become more and more difficult to make decent things for a reasonable amount of money.
Interview/The Hollywood Reporter, 4-13:6.

John Frankenheimer
Director
5

I've never really understood why the press is so interested in the problems of movie-making, particularly the feuds and things. It seems to me it's really nobody's business what goes on while a picture is being made—as long as it's not going wildly over-budget or anything like that. Who cares if this actor and that actress don't get along? Why isn't there the same interest in television? There must be some good feuds going on there. Wouldn't you think? But nobody cares.
Interview/Los Angeles Times, 9-26:(Calendar)28.

Carlos Fuentes
Author, Playwright
6

Movies are bearers of the collective unconscious, the warehouse of modern myths. It

333

(CARLOS FUENTES)

would be difficult to overestimate the impact of movies. Hollywood manufactures the archetypes we need to understand our collective life. Marilyn Monroe is one of the great totems of the tribe. She arose from the same realm of the imagination as Venus. She fulfills the same need. American pop archetypes have permeated the world from the mountains of Tibet to the jungles of Brazil.

Interview, Cambridge, Mass./
San Francisco Examiner & Chronicle,
7-18:(Datebook)32.

James Garner
Actor

1

It's usually business things that get me upset. Dealing with networks, studios and so on. You say, "Good morning" in this business and they say, "What did he mean by that?" So many people simply do not understand the direct approach. Power is probably the reason. This is big business today. Many people—not all, but many—are clawing their way to the top. They will do anything to get where they are going, no matter what happens to anybody else along the way. It's a power drive and I don't have it. I don't understand it. I've never been ambitious, and I think that's why they don't understand me. I tell them exactly what I think. I don't lie to them or lay any phony stories on them. I tell them the truth, and only a few people in the business know how to handle that.

Interview, Burbank, Calif./
American Way, January:55.

Jean-Luc Godard
Director

2

I would like to make people laugh, but I am not very good at it. The silent cinema comedians who managed to get laughs with just pictures fill me with admiration. Strangely enough, they did so with mechanical objects, whereas nowadays people play on the senses or on literary allusions. [Charles] Chaplin always produced a laugh by showing a character who could not find his money or change a tire on a car.

Interview/World Press Review, October:59.

334

William Goldman
Screenwriter

3

I hate that attribution billing, the [director] *auteur* thing of "A Film By . . ." The director would have been nowhere without his scenic designer, his cameraman, his lighting man, his film editor, not to mention his screenwriter. Any concept of movies which emphasizes individual contributions is false. Movies are a group endeavor, and everybody has to do a good job to make one work.

Interview, New York/
Los Angeles Herald Examiner, 5-19:(B)4.

Cary Grant
Actor

4

I had a theme in most of my movies—in the comedies and later in the Hitchcock comedy-mysteries: to take a fellow who seemed to dress rather well, who was moderately well-educated and sophisticated and should know his way around, and put him in a series of ridiculous and untenable situations. How is he going to get out of that? *To Catch a Thief* and *North by Northwest* come quickest to mind. The attraction then to the audience is this: "If it can happen to him, it can happen to me." And the fact that it's happening to me and not to them is their relief.

Interview, New York, May/
Los Angeles Herald Examiner, 5-20:(B)6.

Gene Hackman
Actor

5

[Winning an "Oscar" causes] a lot of actors to price themselves out of the market or expect too much. I seem to have been lucky; I've been working pretty steadily, although not as much as I would like. There is a loss of privacy, but that kind of thing I guess is crying poor mouth. Acting is exciting. You pay for it in many ways and in many ways it pays you.

The New York Times, 3-28:(2)19.

Dustin Hoffman
Actor

6

I guess I'm getting top salary. I don't set it—it's there if I'm worth it, and I deliver. They

(DUSTIN HOFFMAN)

don't give it to me because they think I'm a good actor or because they like me. They give it to me because statistically they think I'm going to deliver [the audience]. Box-office has nothing to do with acting ability. I could be a lousy actor and still get the money. It's strictly an investment.

Interview, Malibu, Calif./
Los Angeles Times, 12-16:(VI)5.

John Huston
Director
1

I "direct" as little as possible. I try to get to the heart of the matter and understand the spirit of an endeavor or an occasion.

At tribute to him by
Directors Guild of America,
Los Angeles/Daily Variety, 5-25:9.

Sam Jaffe
Actor
2

[On acting]: In movies, you learn to be economical, to hold in. I don't believe in tearing a passion to tatters. At my age, you have your knowledge of people, your cumulative knowledge, to use as you dig. A good director leaves you alone. John Huston chooses the right person and leaves you alone. Frank Capra looks into your eyes to make sure you understand and are not just a record talking.

Interview, Beverly Hills, Calif./
The New York Times, 6-9:23.

Norman Jewison
Director
3

... if you've got a good idea, the chances are you can make a good picture. If all you've got is a mediocre idea, then no matter how hard you try or who you put in the film, it won't work.

Interview, Los Angeles/
Los Angeles Times, 12-2:(VI)4.

Nastassia Kinski
Actress
4

Actors ... dream. They don't live in the real world. It's like peeling off your skin. You go somewhere else and become someone else. It's true what people say—that actors are the closest thing there is to children. They play. You play a part, and as soon as a movie is over and the camera stops, you go home and you're not really responsible for what you've done.

Interview/Cosmopolitan, January:58.

Jack Lemmon
Actor
5

[Acting in] film is a bitch, with the stop-start, in and out of sequence. Suddenly it's magic time! You're supposed to be hysterical in two seconds. It's harder to do without building to it [as on the stage]. The real reward [in acting] ... what you're really there for, is that acceptance, and you get it. But to a great extent in film, it's in the laps of your director and God.

Interview, Washington/
The Washington Post, 3-7:(G)4.

Sidney Lumet
Director
6

The nature of this work is very intimate. You're dealing with feelings all the time. On each picture I break down the touching barrier very quickly. But I don't push it on them [the actors]. I treat actors with respect, and I also know a lot of ways of turning their motors on. I'm not an intellectual who can recite ideas. I can actually deal with them on an emotional level. The bigger name the actor, the less afraid they become. They're not afraid to make their own suggestions, which are [very often] wonderful.

Interview/San Francisco Examiner &
Chronicle, 12-12:(Datebook)33.

Dusan Makavejev
Yugoslavian director
7

I have always been happy that the dogmatists—the little radical groups—have never seen my films as political. I use politics as raw material, but the essence of movies is escapism. You cannot begin a revolution in the theatre.

Interview/World Press Review, June:60.

WHAT THEY SAID IN 1982

Marcello Mastroianni
Actor

1

You must not suppose that an actor always chooses a film because it is a good one. Often it is because he must find money to support his mistress or build a new swimming pool. Always it is a compromise. Sometimes, of course, you are offered a film which pays the bills and is worth doing too—like the Fellini films. But they do not happen often.

Interview, Los Angeles/Los Angeles Times, 7-25:(Calendar)25.

Walter Matthau
Actor

2

My childhood was tough. We lived in the ghetto, and I was painfully shy. An insecure childhood makes many people want to become actors. Show me any successful actor, and I'll show you a person who was insecure as a child. People from unhappy or insecure childhoods want some way to express themselves. Acting usually gives them that chance, because you want to be recognized as someone who has something to say. After all, no one pays attention to the kid from the ghetto. The essence of acting is having someone pay attention to you.

Interview/Los Angeles Herald Examiner, 2-26:(A)6.

Paul Mazursky
Director, Writer

3

The greatest time for me is making the movie. That's the holiday. Writing it is a powerful experience but sometimes frightening. But if you're making the movie, it means you've already got the deal. It means you're being paid for your fantasy. You're with all these people. You're on vacation. There's no judgment. You're the benevolent dictator. It's quite wonderful. You know, you have coffee and a chair and a drink, and at the end of the day you go into a dark room and see movies. Cars pick you up. You take rides in helicopters to see what the location is. It's fantastic.

Interview/The New York Times, 8-8:(2)13.

Robert Mitchum
Actor

4

I played a lot of detective roles . . . Once you get typecast, it's hard to get the studios to change their minds. The one thing I learned out here is that when you do well you don't get better roles—you get more.

Interview, Montecito, Calif./"W": a Fairchild publication, 12-31:16.

Burton I. Monasch
Executive vice president, 20th Century-Fox Film Corporation

5

There's such a small amount of success to be had in Hollywood. Even the most successful people have one failing or aborted project after another. In sports, one athlete revels in another's success. Here [in Hollywood] everybody's happy when a new picture is rumored to be terrible. Everybody wants to believe the worst because the failure of somebody else lets you know you're not alone.

Interview, Los Angeles/ The New York Times, 12-12:(2)32.

Dudley Moore
Actor

6

. . . I play my character just as I'm talking to you. I don't believe in sitting in a bucket of ice water for six months to soak up the traits of a character. An actor is most convincing when he injects himself into his role.

Interview, New York/ The New York Times, 1-3:(2)17.

Jeanne Moreau
Actress

7

When you start filming, you're in a dangerous zone—for the actress, for the director, for everyone. It's like being on a raft in the middle of the ocean. You feel that the person in charge has tremendous power, and can order many things that would not be possible on dry land.

Interview, New York/ The New York Times, 10-3:(4)23.

Jack Nicholson
Actor

1

The main goal of most actors is to get variety into their work. And if there's conflict with every director you work with, then your work is going to have a sameness about it. I always say what's on my mind but—unlike in real life—if there's any conflict I do tend to give in. Because in the long run most of what gets on the screen doesn't have as much to do with concept, which is what you're usually arguing about, as with execution.

Interview, Beverly Hills, Calif./
Los Angeles Times, 2-21:(Calendar)34.

Nick Nolte
Actor

2

With scripts, I like to go story first, character second. I mean, a story line strong enough to carry the characters—the audience, too—to some kind of catharsis. Brilliant character studies without a narrative through-line are an invitation to narcissism; and if acting isn't narcissistic to begin with, it constantly runs the danger of becoming so.

Interview/Horizon, Jan.-Feb.:52.

Laurence Olivier
Actor

3

[On actors]: When anyone is frankly in the business of showing off—of self-presentation—with each appearance you are bound to take a leap in the dark.

Interview, New York/
The New York Times, 12-22:25.

Roman Polanski
Actor, Director

4

I have no problem directing myself because I am a very obedient actor. It's much easier to direct while acting than to act while directing. Directing is extremely difficult because you have to pay attention to everything and everyone at once. But acting is like sports. One does not know until the performance is over whether one has won or lost.

Time, 1-18:73.

Sydney Pollack
Director

5

There are lots of jobs the director has. But the primary job is . . . the director is the only one whose responsibility essentially is to imagine the complete film, and make judgments based on what he imagines to be the complete film. It's what, in a more pretentious way, people call vision. They say the director has a vision. Well, that's a very high-fallutin way of putting it. You have a fantasy of a film in your head, and you imagine how it would look completed. You try now to get all the clay you need to sculpt that into this imaginary picture you have in your head. Sometimes that's a question of what point of view are you seeing it from which dictates a camera setup, a lens choice, or a way in which it's lit. Sometimes it's the degree of anger necessary for a character to have at a certain moment. And that becomes, then, working with the actor. Sometimes it's hearing it happen to music, and that is work with a composer. Sometimes it's visualizing a gray day with a gray sky and having to take a blue, sunny day and turn it into a gray one . . . with some sort of technical expertise. It's such a mosaic kind of work, very much like impressionist painting in a way. You do something that upon close scrutiny doesn't seem to have any relationship to a finished product. You paint this little dot in, you know, then pretty soon you combine all these hundreds and hundreds of little dots. And if it works well, there's a "vision" that happens. It's a difficult job to define precisely.

Interview, Washington/The
Christian Science Monitor, 1-21:(B)13.

Vincent Price
Actor

6

Heroes have no character, really. Once they get a few wrinkles or a paunch, they're washed up. But villains last. The more wrinkly and creviced they get, the more an audience loves to hate them.

Tucson, Ariz./Los Angeles
Times, 2-17:(I)2.

WHAT THEY SAID IN 1982

(VINCENT PRICE)

1

[Comparing today's horror films with those he made in the earlier days of the film industry]: These days they've gone too far toward the shock-horror cult, showing all the lurid details, the blood and gore. It has a bad effect on people, especially on the unbalanced in society. Our films never sent anyone out to kill anybody. What we did was fantasy. There was always an element of the fairy story about it—and good always triumphed in the end.

Interview, Hampshire, England/
Los Angeles Times, 12-26:(Calendar)5.

Ronald Reagan
President of the United States

2

[On motion pictures]: They don't make them any more like we made them then [when he was an actor]. We used to fret a little bit under the strict production code—rules, morality and so forth. [But] it made for great writing. Today they can turn to obscenities or profanity. The oldest rule is that you can't do anything onstage that's as good as the audience's imagination. Today they don't leave anything to the imagination.

Interview/Time, 8-23:9.

Debbie Reynolds
Entertainer

3

I'm afraid I'm from the romantic era and don't go for the near-pornography in some movies today. I can sing and dance and act, and I don't have to do films for a living any more. Actress friends of mine say, "That's part of being an actress," and I say, "NO, that's part of being a stripper—or another profession." But they're working in films, and I'm not.

Interview, Seattle/
Chicago Tribune, 3-30:(1)2.

Ralph Richardson
Actor

4

[On how he prepares for a role]: Dig, dig, dig, dig. Find out more and more about the character. What does he eat? What trousers does he wear? What does he do? What does he drink?

What is he afraid of? All these things and more you've got to know. And you add to that rags and tags, chance conversations you hear, people you see walking down the street, anything that might fit the part. Dreams, especially dreams. I dream a lot.

Interview, London/
The New York Times, 12-19:(2)5.

Mickey Rooney
Actor

5

[Saying he helped Bing Crosby begin the Crosby golf tournament]: ... I started that with Bing when I was on top [in films]. When my career went to the bottom of the basement floor, I was never invited any more ... No aspersions on Bing, but I guess that's just the way the game is played [in the film business]. Everyone is afraid in Hollywood that someone will find out they all go to the bathroom.

Interview/Los Angeles Times, 10-26:(III)2.

Francesco Rosi
Italian director

6

Every person sees a scene differently. But if you work honestly and sincerely, and deal with basic human themes—life, death, time, loneliness, solidarity among all people—your message will be felt. The basic emotions are the same all over the world, and sincerity will always communicate. Sincerity is the key.

Interview/The Christian Science Monitor, 3-4:18.

7

[Film] is a good medium with which to inject personal [beliefs] into some aspect of life in one's country. American films, during the 1930s and '40s, didn't bring about any changes, but they were the cinema of American public life. After the end of the war, the neo-realistic films of Italy were influential in depicting the way things were with us. My films correspond to an intention to testify the evolution of the social and political events of the time. In this way, I think one can participate.

Interview, New York/Daily Variety, 3-11:10.

Gena Rowlands
Actress

1

I have a little secret for you. It's about how to handle critics. You must know what they say. To not read them takes a superhuman lack of curiosity. And once in a while they will say something helpful . . . . if you're a young actor without your sea legs, I have a secret for you. Have your best friend read the review to you. You will hear it with a normal, reasonable detachment. That won't be true if it's in front of your face. We've been taught to worship the written word. [But] it can murder you. If it's a screaming rave, have it blown up. Put it up on the wall. Then . . . put on your glasses.

At symposium sponsored by Academy of
Motion Picture Arts and Sciences, Beverly Hills,
Calif., June/Los Angeles Times, 6-5:(V)4.

Budd Schulberg
Screenwriter

2

Ever since I basically left Hollywood 40 years ago, I still feel, as I did then, that the writer is the forgotten man in the whole operation . . . I don't believe at all in the old Hollywood cliche, which ran, "If you want to send a message, call Western Union." Every so often, I think, you can fight to get your message on the screen and both shock people and entertain them. You've got to do both.

Interview/The New York Times, 4-25:(2)29.

Ettore Scola
Italian director

3

In life, the tragic and the comic often coincide. Even in Shakespeare, there's always a lot of laughter. I think these comic instances underline the tragedy and make its essence stand out. The *real* Italian comedy resembles life. [Directors Dino] Risi, [Mario] Monicelli and I show the comic, but the tragic is never far behind. Italian comedy is the offspring of neo-realism, which showed the true face of Italy after World War II. Cesare Zavattini said that a film should follow a character—in his gestures, actions and feelings—not unlike a policeman who follows a thief.

Interview, New York/Los Angeles
Times, 5-30:(Calendar)28.

George C. Scott
Actor

4

[Being an actor is] a horse race—sometimes you're successful and sometimes you're not. You try to find something that you feel you can make a contribution with, but material is limited—like gold. You have to go and dig for it or get lucky. I doubt if the average person knows how many things you turn down. It runs into the hundreds and hundreds. Partly it's a question of availability and timing—those rules govern your life, and they're one of the reasons this is such a capricious profession. You'll sit around with nothing to do for months and then have three things you want to do at the same time. You just have to be mature enough to let go of the other two and pick the one and hope to God you've made the right choice.

Interview, New York/
The New York Times, 7-11:(2)22.

Sid Sheinberg
President, MCA, Inc.
(Universal Pictures)

5

The challenge [in making a film] is not to creativity, but to controlling costs. The solution, in many cases, is eliminating waste, eliminating folly, eliminating the absurdity of the director who needs to do something 40 times to get it right. I mean, if it takes him 40 times to get it right, he shouldn't be doing it.

Interview/Chicago Tribune, 1-15:(1)15.

Don Simpson
President of production,
Paramount Pictures Corporation

6

[On criticism that the film industry is not creative or original enough in its product] : I don't think the *world* encourages originality. Forget the movie business; go back to Copernicus and Ptolemy. Originality is not something easily found or brought to the fore. Go try and be different; watch them hit you on the head with a stick. It's called show biz. I don't think it's fair to saddle [the] motion-picture business with that onus. If anything, the entertainment world is more adventurous than most other areas. God, give me an original idea. I mean, I

WHAT THEY SAID IN 1982

(DON SIMPSON)

don't want an idea about two transsexual short people on roller skates; that's original, but who cares?

Interview/Chicago Tribune, 1-15:(1)15.

Sam Spiegel
Producer

1

The amount of greed about today dismays me. When I made *On the Waterfront* with Marlon Brando and all those other stars, I brought the film in for just $750,000. And everyone, including Marlon, got his full salary. I think Marlon got $150,000 and he was a happy actor. Today, he gets $4-million material he holds in contempt and is no longer happy. The trouble, of course, is that today most producers can only raise money by putting such stars in their pictures. They cannot raise the money because they are good producers with an interesting film to make. A pity.

*Interview, London/Los Angeles
Times, 6-20:(Calendar)35.*

Steven Spielberg
Director

2

I have a real chemical imbalance between what's real and what's not. I tend to side with what isn't real in picking a subject, more than I do with what's really happening out there in the street—enough directors make movies that reflect life as we see it every day. There's no proof UFOs exist or that ghosts exist, but it's always nice to imagine what you think could be there, and the best movies I've ever seen are movies that are slightly above one's normal eye level—something you have to reach up to and suspend your disbelief.

Interview/The New York Times, 5-30:(2)30.

Peter Straub
Author

3

[On his experience having a book of his made into a film]: I have a feeling that directors poison a lot of films. What they bring to a film isn't intellectual in any way. Their depth of involvement is limited by three months, whereas the book itself represents a year or two of solid concentration. So when they begin to talk about their "visions" [for the film], my stomach begins to turn. Just whose vision is it?

Interview/Chicago Tribune, 1-15:(1)15.

William Styron
Author

4

. . . I've often been baffled by the schism between Hollywood and literature. I've tried to figure out how many good novels have been turned into good movies, and I don't come up with too many . . . One would think, for instance—because of its great simplicity of story and richness—that a book like *Huckleberry Finn* would make one of the fine movies of all time. And it has been tried over and over and every version is ridiculous. Yet here is this magnificent and glorious story with humor, horror and the anguish of slavery, and it just somehow eludes Hollywood. I just don't think you can duplicate the same emotions on the screen and on paper. You can approximate them, not duplicate them.

Interview, New York/Esquire, January:87.

Francois Truffaut
Director

5

They have machines now [home video-cassette and videodisc players] on which you can skip past all the scenes [in a film] that might be boring. That frightens me. I'm worried that we're entering a subliterate age, in which nobody will ever read *War and Peace* unless he's in a sanatorium. All these cassettes, video-discs . . . the complete works of any artist in 153 minutes. Like those volumes I see in American bookstores—"Portable Tolstoy"! I'm afraid this will happen to film-makers, too.

Interview/The Wall Street Journal, 2-19:27.

Peter Ustinov
Actor, Director, Writer

6

Acting is probably much safer than directing or writing. You're like a chameleon, adapting yourself to various circumstances and to what other people are writing. A movie, for example,

(PETER USTINOV)

is a cocktail of artistic manifestations. The only person who sees the whole thing at the time it's done is the cameraman. Acting is intrinsically easy.

Interview/The New York Times, 3-7:(2)28.

Brenda Vaccaro
Actress

1

Hollywood is a closed, tight marketplace, without much productivity. The recession and the actors' and writers' strikes have afflicted and depressed our industry. The opportunities go to those few who've appeared in movies that were huge box-office successes—people who are known entities, such as Goldie Hawn and Jane Fonda. Those people are in a position to buy a script, have it written and induce a major studio to co-produce it, with them in the starring role. So if there were parts I could or should be playing these days, they'd probably go to people like that.

*Interview, Los Angeles/
Los Angeles Times, 5-21:(Fashion82)1.*

Jon Voight
Actor

2

My feeling is that most scripts today are much too complicated, so I try to simplify stories. My first feeling about a script is, does it tell a good tale? Tell me a story, that's my attitude—don't complicate it. Sometimes, when I'm telling my son a story I'll add something like—"it's just like when you do . . ." putting in a bit of moralizing—and he'll say: "Daddy, get on with the story." There's not nearly enough simple storytelling these days.

*Interview, Los Angeles/San Francisco
Examiner & Chronicle, 10-10:(Datebook)33.*

Lina Wertmuller
Director

3

. . . it is really playtime making a film. So I shoot a lot of film. It should be this way. Like a magic circle. Be careful when it is not a magic circle; I mean, the joy must be there. I may not fall in love with people on a set right away. There may be terror, but that ends. When I leave, there's love. Not when I come, maybe, but definitely when I leave. It's love, baby—it has to be!

*Interview, Beverly Hills, Calif./
Los Angeles Times, 7-4:(Calendar)28.*

Gene Wilder
Actor

4

I don't read reviews. If you can realize that what they're praising you for they're probably wrong about, and what they're blaming you for you probably didn't do, then it's silly to leave yourself open for that kind of hurt.

*Interview, New York/
The New York Times, 6-4:20.*

Fred Zinnemann
Director

5

I owe [Hollywood] an enormous debt of gratitude, and I think there are a great number of very talented people there now. But perhaps making films has become too much of a business, too little of a passion. In the old days people talked about the picture itself; now they talk about deals, working conditions, salaries. They are much saner than they were, but also much cooler. And I worry that films that don't look like making a lot of money, that aren't in the mainstream of whatever the trend is, may get lost.

*Interview, London/The
New York Times, 11-7:(2)16.*

MUSIC

Janet Baker
Recital singer

1

A singer needs a 16-inch gun to serve a composer best—he [the composer] comes first, ego trips [for the singer] come second. So, even though I get tired of playing second-fiddle, which is the mezzo's usual lot, I stay with it, hoping my voice can beautify the role, not glorify myself.

Interview/The New York Times, 7-12:15.

Tony Bennett
Singer

2

Originally, a record was supposed to go into your collection, like stamps. A work of art was supposed to be a joy forever. But today, instead of being silver, records are like lead. All the business is interested in is the break [money], and it's become like the car companies in Detroit. The integrity is no longer there. They've forgotten about the quality of music. My friend Percy Faith used to say, "Either music is good, or it isn't." No in-between. If something gives you those goose bumps, you say, "Yeah, there it is again." I just know I'm on the right side because I've never let the people down. My music has been about quality, and I've never been out of focus or away from the scene. And quality lasts.

*Interview, Los Angeles/Los Angeles
Herald Examiner, 9-10:(D)23.*

Jorge Bolet
Pianist

3

A young person trying out for a [piano] competition today has to make sure of one thing, and that's that he doesn't do anything that can be considered personal, individual or original. He must stick absolutely to every detail a composer has written, regardless of whether he is convinced it should be that way or not; because the minute he plays something that is not quite kosher, according to the academicians and the jury, he's out of the running ... [Conversely,] once my students come to me with a score they have studied and learned very carefully, I tell them, "Fine, you know the score, you know every indication and every note, and you have it well memorized. Now throw the score away, and from now on forget what's written and use your imagination, your musical insight and your musical taste when you play" ... After all, music is the most emotional of the arts—you can move more people with music than with any other artistic medium. Well, perhaps drama, in performance, is equally as moving. But I can't think of too many paintings that can make people cry, the way a great piece of music can.

Interview/The New York Times, 4-25:(2)22.

Alfred Brendel
Pianist

4

When you examine prejudices [in music], you discover that they are to a large degree unfounded, or maybe based on some little thing blown out of proportion. Like the [scurrilous] aspect of Mozart that is made absolute in *Amadeus*. It tells you nothing about Mozart. Same thing about Haydn being "predictable." Actually his works are filled with humor and wit. Sometimes he imitates the sound of laughter with a short staccato that the people in his day would have known represented laughter. We've lost that knowledge. I think romanticism has made people think that fun in music is not allowed, that music should be solemn. That's another item in my prejudice book.

*Interview, New York/The
Wall Street Journal, 2-26:27.*

Renato Bruson
Opera singer

1

All the major [opera] theatres use the same singers, who rush from one end of the world to the other, and it is like a closed circle. Recently there was one who sang a leading role in Paris one night, another at La Scala the following night and a third in Rome the next. Is this art, seriousness, dedication? If you want to work, it does become a rat race; and once you are in, it's difficult to get out. The system is wrong, but how to undo all the mechanism that has come into motion? I haven't found the answer. I won't sing in three cities on three consecutive nights, and I do limit the number of performances a year. They've waited for me this long—they can wait a little longer.

Interview/Opera News, 4-17:11.

Joe Bushkin
Jazz pianist

2

If you're a classical pianist you have to practice, because everything has to be precise. In jazz, if you've been playing as long as I've been playing . . . it's like riding a bike . . . When I haven't played for a while, my ideas are very fresh. If I'm playing every night—well, even a train stops, you know. I get a little bored . . . [An interviewer once asked how a jazz musician improvises.] I said, "No one has ever asked me that, so this may take a minute or two while I order room service, while I decide how I improvise!" So the interviewer started to improvise what he wanted to eat, and I started to improvise what I wanted. See, there you go, we were improvising! So I said, "You see, before I mentioned lunch, you weren't thinking of lunch, were you?" He said, "No," and I said, "Well, that's the idea—blank your mind out so you can put something in it—that's improvising."

Interview, New York/
The Christian Science Monitor, 12-15:14.

Ray Charles
Singer, Pianist

3

. . . I don't hear anything now that's up to the standards of the music I heard when I was coming up—Charlie Parker and Art Tatum, people like that. Why? Well, when I was coming up, you had places you could go, clubs where you could go and sit in with guys who were really great, who could make you realize that what you thought you could play wasn't nothing . . . I got a chance to get a feel of greatness next to me, but kids today are not exposed to situations where they can listen to great music and then, if they have any talent, they can sit in with the cats. When I came up, they'd let you do that . . . *if* you could play. And if you couldn't play, you'd find out in the first song and you'd become embarrassed. That would be it. You'd wag your tail and go home and study some more. Whereas all they have now is the records they buy, which they take home and play as loud as they can. But you can't learn much that way. Even if the music is good, you're always going to hear more when you're there in person than you will on record. Besides, the kind of music the kids listen to today, I have to tell you that I could play that when I was 7 or 8 years old. For me there ain't much to learn from what's out there now.

Interview/Chicago Tribune, 5-16:(6)17.

James Conlon
Conductor

4

"Knowledge" is I think a misleading word. Auden wrote a wonderful essay on Othello in which he talks about the corruption of the word. It used to be—in Biblical times—that knowledge and love were the same word, the same idea. Then through a gradual evolution—in his view corruption—it became separate. Knowledge took on an objective, scientific connotation. And Auden presents Iago, the man who knows but does not love, as an exemplar of corruption in our time. It's important for any artist to recognize that knowledge and love are not separate things. There are conductors and pianists who know all the facts, know the right tempo and so on, but they still bore. You have to love the theatre and have an empathy for humanity.

Interview, New York/
The Wall Street Journal, 2-12:25.

Aaron Copland
Composer, Conductor

1

... if you write music with harmonies and rhythms that some people may not like, and that was always the way, you have to expect not to be liked. Even by the critics. But you know, the ultimate fate of a piece of music does not depend on whether either the politicians or *The New York Times* likes it.

Interview, Washington, May 30/
The Washington Post, 5-31:(D)4.

Andrew Davis
Conductor

2

I don't like to lecture an orchestra. I don't think of the conductor primarily as a teacher. It's part of the job, I suppose, but it's more a question of gathering musical talents into one unit. Obviously I have to talk to the musicians about balance and mood and phrasing, but I can never talk about the essence of music.

Interview, New York/Opera News, 3-13:16.

Neil Diamond
Singer, Composer

3

When I'm on stage, I do feel confident. That's *my* audience out there, that's *my* music. I should know how to perform it ... But it's more difficult to live your own private life—to be a husband, a father, or a friend—than to be a performer. Here [on stage] the ground rules are set: I'm here to do one thing, the audience is there to accept whatever it is that I'm doing, and it's pretty straightforward. Real life is not quite that simple.

Interview, Washington/
The Washington Post, 9-14:(B)4.

Placido Domingo
Opera singer

4

Let's face it: I have a tremendous advantage being a real musician because I never have to think about the music. It flows. The only moments I feel awkward are when I've just learned something and am still relying on the prompter and conductor. I realize then how

difficult it must be for people who aren't musical, who must always be looking for the attack of the conductor.

Newsweek, 3-8:58.

5

Singers can be musicians but not know music. Conductors can know all the music in the world but have no feeling for music, because they are intellectual, analytical. Yes, it is good and necessary to know music—all the facts, rules, the deep things of harmony and counterpoint, all the keys of what instruments play, and be able to read scores. *But,* the moment you are on the podium it is essential to be a musician by nature, despite all you know. With a singer too, I do not like to hear a musically well-trained one who makes me feel they are singing a dotted note. It's the *line* of singing with the dots and legato and staccato, but not making me feel these things are there. To make music, you have to go beyond all these things. Music is like painting, in terms of technique. The colors are there, but the painter doesn't tell you about the blue and yellow and brown used in a certain way to create the feeling of gold. You see it or you don't. It is there or it is not.

Interview/Opera News, 3-27:40.

Philippe Entremont
Music director, New Orleans
Symphony Orchestra; Pianist

6

The fact is, the piano is the closest thing to an orchestra. Because a pianist has 10 fingers which can play at the same time, it already means that we have 10 instruments at our command, and we can produce all kinds of sounds, shadings, accents, colors. And so, when a pianist is also a conductor, that intuitive sense of color and nuance spills into leading an orchestra. As for learning to be a conductor, my feeling is that one is born with the gift. You either have it or you don't. If you don't have the "natural arm," and if you don't know how to communicate with an orchestra, all is lost! As for myself, I have had the privilege of performing with almost all the great conductors of the world, and I have always watched them like a hawk. It was, and still is, the greatest conductorial training imaginable; because I do

(PHILIPPE ENTREMONT)

not just play my concerto and leave, but stick around to hear the rest of the concert—staying for the full rehearsal in order to listen and learn.

Interview/The New York Times, 1-3:(2)15.

Ernest Fleischmann
Executive director, Los Angeles
Philharmonic Orchestra
1

[On the lessening of government funds for the arts, including orchestras]: The idea of doing more with less is not a philosophy, but empty rhetoric. We've still got to pay the musicians, the utilities, the rent, the music rental fees, the publishers. No, we're not going to do better with less. We can cut services up to a point. But we can't play louder and faster.

Interview/Los Angeles Times, 1-18:(I)12.

Henry Fogel
Executive director, National
Symphony Orchestra (Washington)
2

Statistics are not as clear for orchestras as for baseball teams. The wins, the losses and the strikeouts are not as clearly defined. It is more a matter of conjecture, opinion and public perception.

Interview, Washington/
The New York Times, 3-31:14.

Nicolai Gedda
Opera singer, Metropolitan
Opera, New York
3

In my opinion, many young [opera] singers today limit themselves by failing to study language as hard as they study music. It's not just a matter of learning the meaning of words, but of learning a cultural heritage, a tradition. When I go to hear Verdi, for example, I prefer to hear Placido [Domingo] or Luciano [Pavarotti] or another Latin singer who will give an authentic, idiomatic presentation. It's the same with Russian or German pieces. I'm made uncomfortable, even irritated, by singers who know how to sing very well but don't know the languages. Recently I went to hear Fischer-Dieskau in an all-Schumann program. He sang with absolute authority, and that's what I want.

Otherwise, I don't enjoy it—it doesn't give me anything.

Interview/Opera News, November:13 .

Michael Gielen
General music director,
Frankfurt Opera
4

In Frankfurt we call it "music theatre," not opera. We consider all the elements—scenic, dramatic, vocal, the contents of the piece, what it means to an audience today—on the same level. In big theatres like the Met or La Scala it is, generally speaking, 90 per cent singing, 6 per cent music and 4 per cent the stage. This is a wrong attitude to this complex art form.

Interview, New York/Opera News, May:26.

Carlo Maria Giulini
Music director, Los Angeles
Philharmonic Orchestra
5

When I hear the phrase, "The orchestra is an instrument," I get mad. It's a group of human beings who play instruments. They have problems, like all people, but everybody in the world has to work, and what a privilege it is for a musician to play beautiful music with beautiful instruments in a beautiful hall . . . The first thing I said to the Philharmonic at our first rehearsal was that I don't come as a "conductor" or "music director" but as a human being who is making music with other human beings. It is much better to do something when you are convinced, not obliged.

Interview/The New York
Times Magazine, 11-21:76.

Jerry Goldsmith
Film-music composer
6

Music gets somehow deeper inside you than anything else does, stirring emotions nothing else touches. It's the most emotional of the arts. We have emotions that cannot be expressed in words, pictures, painting—only in music. A spoken line moves you because you connect it with something, some loss you've experienced, for example. You're emphatic. But with music, you're just struck by the music.

Interview/Los Angeles Times,
2-7:(Calendar)30.

Lena Horne
Singer

1

I had to be strong because success wasn't that easy to get, and I had to work harder for it. I find that young people today don't have the sticking power that they need to have, and a lot of the media eats them up so fast and chews them up and spits them out. I mean, you have a hit record last year and if you don't come up with another one, they're already pushing the next one with a hit record. So the young talent is burned out before they even got started. I think it's easier for them to make it, but not as easy to hold onto it.

*Interview, Denver/San Francisco
Examiner & Chronicle, 9-5:(Datebook)18.*

Vladimir Horowitz
Pianist

2

I feel I am the composer himself when I am playing. I play differently each time. That's why I never listen to my records—they're like photographs. Music is alive.

London/Los Angeles Times, 5-13:(I)2.

Herbert von Karajan
*Conductor, Berlin
Philharmonic Orchestra*

3

If I exert control, it is in rehearsal. When I rehearse, I am like a man with a microscope. I hear everything, every sound. But in the performance, I let them [the orchestra] be free. At least, they feel they are free though they remember the work that has gone on before. When I was young and taking riding lessons, I can remember being afraid of a jump. How, I thought, will I get this huge animal over the fence? My instructor said to me, "You must put the horse in the right frame of mind. Then it will carry you over." This is what I do in conducting.

*Interview, New York, Oct. 21/
The New York Times, 10-22:20.*

4

At first you must concentrate on how the music is played rather than its content. Is it properly phrased? Is the rhythm right? Is the length of the notes right? It's as if I'm using a

microscope; I turn it and turn it until every detail is magnified just so. I cut out every feeling. Only then, when you have no more concerns with the actual music-making, can you enter into the spirit of the music.

Interview/Newsweek, 10-25:98.

5

I can see the birds flying past, especially this time of year. And I can endlessly watch them, what they do, and think about what is the soul of what moves them. Nobody collides with the other. And that is exactly what you do with music.

*Interview, New York/
The Washington Post, 10-27:(D)1.*

Cyprien Katsaris
Pianist

6

I believe in music as a spiritual erotic act in which the spirit of the composer is expressed according to the culture of the interpreter. The result is a child. The interpreter must have enough knowledge and intuition to figure out what the composer is suggesting, but should add something of his own personality as well ... I doubt that any composer is ever 100 per cent satisfied by a work. That's what I call the compositional option. And if the composer had options, we have the right to exercise an interpretive option.

Interview/The New York Times, 6-13:(2)42.

Lorin Maazel
*Artistic director and general
manager, Vienna State Opera; Former
conductor, Cleveland Orchestra*

7

[Criticizing flamboyant conductors] : You're not up there to *choreograph*. Everything you do should be functional. These histrionic gestures, this floating through the air—they don't mean a thing to the orchestra. The art of conducting most basically consists in being able to communicate everything you feel about a piece of music through the baton.

Interview/Esquire, September:204.

Henry Mancini
Composer

8

[On what he, as a composer of film music, sees when he watches a film] : When I look at a

(HENRY MANCINI)

movie, it's like a painter looking at a picture. He sees every stroke. He sees every color variation. There are times when I'm wondering, "What the hell is he [the film's composer] doing?" Then, of course, there are times when people say that about what *I* do. It's just so personal. There are things we composers see that we like, things that we don't like and things that break new ground.

Interview/Los Angeles
Herald Examiner, 10-20:(B)5.

Terence A. McEwen
General manager,
San Francisco Opera

1

... [opera] people are not willing to develop, to stay in one place long enough to develop a really deep conception. I'm talking about conductors, stage directors, singers, everybody. They're too busy rushing to get somewhere else ... The economic pressures on all of us are much heavier than they were before, and they force people into this kind of thing. It's like famous conductors—I've asked every famous conductor in the world to come to San Francisco, and some will come and regularly. But one had promised to come and do something important for me this fall. Then he called and said, "Terry, you know, I've been thinking it over, and if I come to you, with all the rehearsals you have, it's seven weeks, and eight performances, and I get eight fees—whereas I can get four fees a week guest-conducting [elsewhere]. So I can't do it." It has nothing to do with art. You're a boring singer if you don't know about coloring and shading of words and nuance and so on. But how can you learn that if you're singing every three days in a different town? You don't have time to settle in with a part.

Interview, San Francisco/
Opera News, October:12.

Ethel Merman
Actress, Singer

2

I've introduced wonderful songs through the years, but there was a melody to them.

[Today] I can't come out of the theatre humming anything any more. Where are those songs? Where are those composers? I don't like what I hear. I don't like what I don't hear. I don't understand the lyrics. Nobody seems to have any enunciation. And the lines aren't commercial. The bottom seems to have fallen out somehow.

Interview, New York/The
New York Times, 5-9:(2)22.

Jonathan Miller
Producer, Director, Writer

3

[On transferring classic operas to a modern setting]: Every now and then you can play provocative games with the classics, but I don't think it ought to be a consistent policy in the effort to be "relevant" or more engaging to an audience. After all, one of the purposes of doing works from the past is to have the privilege of visiting the past, whereas if the past is merely ransacked for the purpose of reinforcing your views about what things are like today, there's no point in really producing these works at all. It's like going to Spain on holiday and insisting on having fish and chips.

Interview/Opera News, June:12.

Seiji Ozawa
Music director, Boston
Symphony Orchestra

4

You know, conducting is very strange. With a bad orchestra, good conducting doesn't matter all that much. With a good orchestra, it does matter. There's this very private language between the conductor and his orchestra. You have to establish this conversation in the first 15 minutes or you don't do it at all. You know Danny Kaye? He conducted the Toronto Symphony once. In 15 minutes they knew what he wanted. It works, or it doesn't.

Interview, Lenox, Mass./"W":
a Fairchild publication, 12-3:12.

Andre Previn
Composer; Music director,
Pittsburgh Symphony Orchestra

5

Some observers say that the composers of today are not of the same stature as those of a

(ANDRE PREVIN)

century ago. It is tempting to ask, "Where are the Brahmses, the Mahlers and the Mozarts of today?" But 100 years ago people were voicing the same complaints about composers of that time. Unfortunately, hindsight is really the only proof of who the great composers in a century are. I think that there are some composers in the 20th century who will be just as revered in the 21st century as the 19th-century giants are now. Benjamin Britten, Dmitri Shostakovich, Bela Bartok, Aaron Copland—to name just a few—are all on that plane.

Interview/U.S. News & World Report, 1-11:59.

Leontyne Price
Opera singer

1

People [today] are less afraid of this grandiose form we call opera. TV helped bring opera into the home, and to dispel the aloof attitude which used to keep many away. The availability of recordings has been a fantastic help, thanks to pioneer efforts. And I hope that I helped a little. It has become like a popular club-cult, almost like baseball.

Interview, San Francisco/San Francisco Examiner & Chronicle, 11-14:(Datebook)35.

Johnnie Ray
Singer

2

[On today's method of studio recording]: I know it's all stop and go these days, but I try to make every recording an actual performance. That's the way we always did it when I started out. I think you're cheating the listener if you record in bits and pieces and go back and put a note in here, four bars there. It's not real to me. I don't think there's any great sin in hitting a bad note—it makes it human.

Interview, New York/The Christian Science Monitor, 2-23:19.

Nelson Riddle
Conductor

3

[Saying pre-rock popular music was not always as good as it is remembered]: Garden of

Eden? I don't think that for a moment. I always have respect for good music and good singing, of whatever era. But I have no respect at all for the people in my era who came up with calculating, money-making junk. A lot of terrible songs were written and recorded before rock-and-roll came along . . . I'm very proud of my best arrangements from the past eras, but you can't live in the past. I read an article by [critic] Charles Champlin recently that put it very well. "All oldies are not goodies or golden or capable of bringing back our lost youth."

Interview/The New York Times, 9-10:18.

Smokey Robinson
Singer, Songwriter

4

I guess at heart I'm a romanticist. I do write songs of love. I've found that is everlasting, forever, always; love is never *passe*. You can never look ahead and say there won't be love in the world. It's not like a dance or something political that's here today and gone tomorrow. Take *I'm In the Mood for Love*. That probably came out at the same time as the Charleston. The song is *still* going strong, it's been great all those years, making plenty of money for whoever wrote it. The Charleston is dead; no one is talking about *it*.

Interview/The Washington Post, 7-17:(C)3.

Aaron Rosand
Violinist

5

[On whether he wishes to dispel his image as a romantic]: Not in the least. If performing "romantically" means projecting yourself into the period in which the music was written, and then injecting your own personality to show what that music means to you, then romanticism is for me. Basically, every piece that I play is a very personal experience. What I give to a piece of music is what I have lived, what I have seen, what I have felt. It's my life which I project into every note that I play.

Interview/The New York Times, 4-11:(2)32.

Leonard Rosenman
Composer

6

Film and concert music entail entirely different processes. With film one is given an *a priori*

(LEONARD ROSENMAN)

construct. It is a very sophisticated version of seeing an array of numbers from one to 100, connecting them and winding up with a picture of George Washington. The point is to fill up space, and the work is dictated by literary considerations. With concert music—even in opera, the most literary form—the composer's task is to shape the text into a fundamentally musical work.

Interview, New York/
The New York Times, 8-29:(2)15.

Gerard Schwarz
Conductor

1

If one has the ability to guide one's colleagues, as a conductor must, and if you have good ideas and are reasonably intelligent, it can be very fulfilling to be a conductor. It's like preparing a great meal, and whether you're the dessert chef or the chef of the whole meal. In my life and my personality, I prefer the whole meal to just the dessert. Yet, being the dessert chef is wonderful too.

Interview/The New York Times, 7-11:(2)19.

George Shearing
Pianist

2

If I were to record today's music, I'd be kidding myself. It would be hanging onto someone's current marquee value. Producers will sometimes do that to you; they'll give you a title like *Here and Now* that will supposedly sell more records, but it won't. I've done Beatle things I've loved and there are songwriters like Sondheim that I enjoy, but I'm grateful for my era. I'm glad that I don't have to start my career today with the terrible economy and the fickleness of the public. Meanwhile, some radio executive decrees that people can only listen to "these 40 songs." God bless the jazz and MOR stations that can buck this mentality.

Interview, San Francisco/San Francisco
Examiner & Chronicle, 8-8:(Datebook)28.

Beverly Sills
General director, New York City
Opera; Former opera singer

3

Right now, my company is 99 per cent American. It's terribly important that we look at the American artists as part of our national heritage. They have to know that they can have a dream that can come true just the way mine did. And in order to make that dream a little bit more real for them, they have to have a home to come to; and I want to turn the New York City Opera into [that home]. My plan at some point is to turn that company into the American National Opera. We are called the New York City Opera because our theatre happens to be in New York. But we have singers from almost every state in the Union. I'd like some kid in Peoria one day to wake up and tell her mother she'd like to be an opera star and the mother will be able to say to her, you work, honey, and maybe some day you'll go to New York and sign with the American National Opera.

Lecture, National Museum of Natural History,
Washington/The Washington Post, 1-5:(A)15.

4

What I'm trying to do is pull away from the idea of lavish, lavish productions and try to concentrate on other values. We will try to have one or two lavish productions, but I really think the company ought to turn into much more of an experimental theatre—which will bring on many more boos [from the critics]. ["Experimental" means] less scenery, perhaps moving the time period of the opera, bringing in directors who are not so wedded to the traditional concept of the traditional works, that kind of thing.

Interview, New York/
The Washington Post, 5-1:(C)9.

Carly Simon
Singer

5

[On her new album which includes songs from the 1940s]: What with today's pressures and the fast-moving pace, people want to relax a bit. They want to romanticize, and they want to feel that there's some sort of peace and harmony in music. With new-wave and rock-

349

(CARLY SIMON)

and-roll and disco, there's a tenseness to the music. With the old songs, the changes are more predictable. You feel like you're coming home when you sing them. The music makes you feel more secure.

Interview/Chicago Tribune, 3-7:(6)5.

Rod Stewart
Singer   *1*

[Rock music] didn't change the world because of its lyrical or social comment. It changed the world because teen-agers wanted something to grasp hold of, and it came along at the right time. It wasn't a revolution in that we all go out in the streets and overthrow the government, and I don't think any of the writers have managed to do that. Bob Dylan's probably the only one. Bruce Springsteen, maybe a little bit, and a few others. But they haven't changed anything. They've just made us aware of what's going on around us. What rock-and-roll can do is comment on what's going on and hope it will change.

*Interview/San Francisco Examiner &
Chronicle, 4-18:(Datebook)21.*

Jule Styne
Songwriter   *2*

If I had to write eight songs for someone by tonight, I'd say, "Give me my pencil and my manuscript paper, and I promise you in about four hours I'll have written eight professional songs." Look, you either know how to compose or you don't. I studied classical music and I coached people and I played in bands so I know what sounds good, and all that registers in your brain like a computer. You feed it the information, and when you sit down, the brain executes it for you and something wonderful comes out.

*Interview, Chicago, December/
Chicago Tribune, 12-15:(1)14.*

Mel Torme
Singer   *3*

... when people ask me whether jazz is coming back, I always have the same answer:

350

The big bands, and jazz, never went away. The audience, to some extent, went away; now they're coming back, and there's so much good music to be heard, it's incredible.

*Interview, Los Angeles/San Francisco
Examiner & Chronicle, 4-4:(Datebook)25.*

Joan Tower
*Composer; Winner,
Koussevitsky Prize*

                                                            4

The composer isn't visible. There's no one to identify with ... Unlike writing, to make music two people are always involved—the composer and the performer. What's happened is the performer has taken over. People go to concerts to hear Horowitz, not Rachmaninoff.

*Interview/"W": a
Fairchild publication, 12-3:20.*

Pete Townshend
Musician, the Who

                                                            5

Out on a stage you get affirmation of what you've done. You can see it, you can sense it, whether one song worked, whether people understand it, whether it's touched the spot that you originally intended to touch. Most writers live in a vacuum and they're just names on book jackets. But rock 'n' roll isn't like that; it's reality, not fiction. If you meet somebody like [Bob] Dylan, you know the man better than he knows himself, because rock-and-roll is open-heart surgery.

*Interview/San Francisco Examiner &
Chronicle, 10-17:(Datebook)17.*

Conway Twitty
Singer

                                                            6

First I make sure I've got a song a woman will like, because they realize the sincerity in a song, and they're the ones that mostly buy the records. Then I want to make the same song say things that most men find hard to say. Like "Hello, Darling"—most men are too macho for that; they'd say "Hi, baby." But all they've got to do is drop a quarter in the jukebox and play this Conway Twitty song, and at the right point in the song, where it says whatever he's wanting to say, he just kind of squeezes her—and you've said it for him.

Interview/Newsweek, 3-1:76.

Robert Ward
Opera composer

1

The most difficult part about writing a new opera is composing the first few pages. The first notes have to be just like the stage set. Once the lights go up, both the set and the music have to give you a feeling of the opera's aura, a sense of what's to come. So in every opera I do, I try to find a musical ambience that is right for the time and place. In that sense, one of the greatest tools an opera composer has is eclecticism. Some might find that disturbing, but I find it is the best way to define the situation, sharply and immediately.

Interview, New York/Opera News, June:24.

Joe Williams
Singer

2

"Blues singer" just means "colored," that's all. Some writers still refer to Ella Fitzgerald as a blues singer, or Sarah Vaughan as a blues singer. It just means you're black, honey, that's all.

*Interview, New York/The
Christian Science Monitor, 5-17:15.*

John Williams
*Composer; Conductor,
Boston Pops Orchestra*

3

American popular music—the music of George Gershwin, Cole Porter, Jerome Kern, Johnny Mercer, Harold Arlen, Duke Ellington —is a great creative legacy. It has been one of our greatest exports over the last 60 years. There was a tremendous vitality then, a cultural energy in American music especially between the 1920s and 1950s. I don't mean to suggest

that what is written today is not good and that the future isn't going to be better. We all hope it will be better. But if our grandchildren want to hear Cole Porter or Jerome Kern, where will they hear it and in what form? Most of that music was written for little pit orchestras as accompaniment. What must be done is that music must be put in a performable form so that orchestras like the Boston Pops and others like it can offer it to our grandchildren 30 years from now. That's what a symphony orchestra can do: enlighten, educate and entertain.

Interview/American Way, January:18.

4

What is inspiring is this whole art of music which is the product of the whole civilization that we're given. It's like language. We didn't invent any of this. We perceive it, practice it, use it—use it as kind of a tool. Music is that way. It's all there. I get the feeling ultimately that the music is doing you, not you doing the music. We are just sort of messengers. It's a commanding thing, music. It's this reverence or awe for the art of music that I feel. It is so awesome that it affords a life-time of fascination.

*Interview, Los Angeles/San Francisco
Examiner & Chronicle, 7-18:(Datebook)40.*

Franco Zeffirelli
Director

5

I'm not a [opera] director who worries only about the stage. The music is an essential part of the package, and I'm stunned by the shortage of first-rate singers. I can always find solutions for great singers who are not gifted actors, but there's nothing to be done about those who have a sense of theatre and no voices. While acting is important in opera, the voice comes first, in no uncertain terms. Pathos or comedy is just as much vocal as visual.

Interview, Rome/Opera News, 1-16:11.

THE STAGE

Edward Albee
Playwright

1

It is very dangerous, whenever you sit down to write a new play, to think how it is going to relate to what you have already done. So I try not to dwell on continuity, progression. Oh, I re-read my plays. Not a lot, though. I look at them with a kind of . . . mild . . . curiosity. I possess them, but they no longer possess me.

Interview, New York/
San Francisco Examiner
& Chronicle,
3-28:(Datebook)33.

2

I lament the fact that the middlebrow is now what passes for excellence in the theatre. It's conceivable that in 10 years no straight play of any real worth will be done in New York commercial theatre . . . I write only when I think I have something to say. Judging from the plays that are successful these days, maybe I should write only when I have nothing to say.

Interview, New York/
San Francisco Examiner
& Chronicle,
3-28:(Datebook)33,34.

3

If you have a hit, I suppose you make a lot of money, but very few playwrights even make a living off of the playwriting craft. Most playwrights teach, or write television scripts, or do other things to survive. It goes back to the old saw, "You can't make a living in the theatre, but you can make a killing." And I certainly don't think playwrights are the cause of the economic dilemma of the theatre.

The New York Times, 8-21:14.

Emanuel Azenberg
Producer

4

[On the financial crisis in the Broadway theatre]: Commercial theatre as everybody knew it for 40 years has had its last hurrah . . . In the long run, the combination of problems is going to make the "fabulous invalid" less fabulous and more invalid. There's no law that says Broadway has to go on forever.

U.S. News & World Report, 12-13:85,86.

Mikhail Baryshnikov
Ballet dancer; Artistic director,
American Ballet Theatre

5

A real choreographer must understand theatre, not just dance. He must be born there. He must see so much, so early. The fact that I grew up in Russia limited my vision. My imagination is blocked because when I was young I couldn't see enough. Maybe when I stop dancing I will be able to see more. Maybe then I will choreograph. A real choreographer listens to music alone in his apartment, closes his eyes and sees movements, people, patterns. I close my eyes and see nothing. A blank. I fall on cliches. I hate cliches more than anything else. A cliche is the worst thing that can happen. I'll give others a chance.

Interview, Los Angeles/
Los Angeles Times, 3-7:(Calendar)55.

Michael Bennett
Director, Choreographer

6

My musicals are very different. They're very tough—very real. They address themselves directly to an audience. They're not elitist in the old-fashioned sense where one went to the theatre and pretended one wasn't there, suspending disbelief. I want an audience to be a

(MICHAEL BENNETT)

part of what I'm saying—my mirrors in *Chorus Line* did that. So, the audience was part of the experience, along with all the associating and relating they did with the characters. Basically, I've tried to change the idea of what a musical is supposed to do. I mean, the form used to be that there's the book, and it takes over for a while, then someone sings a song, then it's time to bring on the dancers. Well, I've mixed up the notion of what the score is supposed to do, and what the dancing is supposed to do, and what the book is supposed to do. *Chorus Line* was that kind of show . . .

*Interview, New York/
After Dark, Jan.-Feb.:52.*

Ingmar Bergman
Director   *1*

At the theatre you have your security, you can relax, you're surrounded by friends. That's why working in the theatre is, for me, a way of living—that's the best of all. It's not the result that matters most; it's the atmosphere that matters—the time we had together when we worked on the play. And if you are together with actors who share the same way of thinking, the same attitude toward their job, it's wonderful.

*Interview, Stockholm/
Saturday Review, April:39.*

Hume Cronyn
Actor   *2*

[Saying he always looks forward to performing on Broadway]: I've learned that to be "out of town" with a production is to be in trouble. Even if you're satisfied with a given play, everyone knows that you are trying to make it better. As a result, you are always either seeking out advice or fending it off. It can be quite bewildering.

*Interview, Boston/The
New York Times, 11-7:(2)4.*

Hugh Cruttwell
*Principal, Royal Academy
of Dramatic Arts, London*
                                                      3

[On his choosing would-be actors for the Academy]: I am not interested in competence. I want a blank sheet on which they can write something. I can't be more precise than to say I'm looking for a capacity to transfix an audience. A dull actor's no good to anybody, no matter how accomplished. If an applicant makes me sit up and take notice, that's what I want. They will acquire the technique . . . You can easily fill an academy with able people who do efficient work. A great pitfall of auditions is that you can be dazzled by mere competence. But I believe one ought to be able to discover a person's potential, even if a candidate becomes unstuck during an audition. There's certainly no objective way to measure acting talent.

Interview/The New York Times, 8-15:(4)3.

Colleen Dewhurst
Actress   *4*

Theatre should be a revelation. I don't care if it's farce or a musical. If it's perfect, it brings out a unity between actors and audience. We live in a society so tense, so hidden from one another, so unable to express our fears and passions, that we wake up feeling like robots. We hide from ourselves. But the theatre, at its best, makes those people in the dark, in the seats, reach out, feel, go with it. We should have a great respect for the theatre. It's an effort to coordinate a group of people—actors and audience—into a living experience.

*Interview, New York/
The New York Times, 9-26:(2)4.*

Richard Dreyfuss
Actor   *5*

I don't believe there's such a person as an intelligent critic. I really don't. So I wonder why I care so much about what they say. But once it's down there in print it seems to carry such a lot of weight. The odd thing is that I read all their reviews and care desperately what they say. And I get hurt often because most of

(RICHARD DREYFUSS)

the reviews I get, particularly in the theatre, are bad. But I could no more not read them than jump off the Brooklyn Bridge. I know a lot of my [actor] friends never read reviews . . . And sometimes when I'm in a play I'll come crawling in on the second night, bleeding and wounded from some critical barb, and there will be the rest of the cast laughing and happy. And I'll know it's because they didn't read the papers. But I just have to.

Interview, Los Angeles/
Los Angeles Times, 1-3:(Calendar)16.

Faye Dunaway
Actress   *1*

For all the hard work in film, there is a cushion if something doesn't work. You can cut and do it again. But in the theatre, you have to rely on your own skill, your own technique, your own wits, your own intelligence. Sure, it's frightening.

Interview, New York/
The New York Times, 1-24:(2)4.

Jules Feiffer
Playwright   *2*

There simply is no longer a tradition of serious American plays having a place on Broadway. The ones that make it are few and far between, and they are usually about a terminal illness that an audience can distance itself from. I don't believe in neat plays or neat art. I think that one of the things that makes theatre boring is that rather than represent life as it is, it represents a nice, neatly contained lie.

Interview/The Washington Post, 1-31:(K)5.

Margot Fonteyn
Ballet dancer   *3*

[Some writers] make so much about how difficult dancing is, the ones who keep fussing over aches and pains and broken bones. Is dancing difficult? I don't know. In a sense, every job is difficult. I know I couldn't sit behind a typewriter all day. I'd find that very difficult, indeed! But I think that dancers who sincerely desire to be artists always give wholly of themselves and don't stop to worry about

whether what they do is difficult. Sometimes, you know, what you say is difficult is either what you don't want to do or what you can't do at all. And no matter what hardships you may encounter as a dancer, I think you should never lose sight of the real elan of dancing.

Interview, New York/
The New York Times, 10-24:(2)28.

4

I think dance has always been a natural part of people's lives. It has always been a part of any society. But dance in the theatre is something different. It is comparatively recently that theatrical dance has become an important part of cultural entertainment. I hope it is very important in people's lives today, because it is essential to form links between people, links that are not political. Dance and music have a universal quality that transcends verbal language. Dance and music and painting are the kind of non-political links between people which the world needs.

Interview, New York/The Christian
Science Monitor, 10-29:19.

Carlos Fuentes
Author, Playwright
5

[On his becoming a playwright as well as being an author]: The theatre is a public art. I wanted to communicate with others beyond the printed word. I had something to say which could be said only if my words were given faces and voices. I wanted to give my language a body. The stage is a vacuum which I want to fill up physically with my language . . . Language comes alive on the stage as nowhere else. You have a living, human voice interfacing with other voices. No experience can replace this verbal presence. The word incarnate cannot be filmed or taped or canned. I love movies as well, but the theatre is the real thing, a living, breathing organism made up of author, actors, audience. The audience actually finishes writing the play for me. They recreate it in their own mind.

Interview, Cambridge, Mass./San Francisco
Examiner & Chronicle, 7-18:(Datebook)33.

John Gielgud
Actor
1

One is very cold about acting in films. When they come out, it's been two or three years since you've done them and you've forgotten them. In the theatre, one is worred about the immediate reaction, the reviews the very next day. It is more urgent, more fresh.

*Interview, London /"W":
a Fairchild publication, 11-5:8.*

Louis Gossett, Jr.
Actor
2

[Saying he prefers acting on stage to acting in films]: There's really nothing like a live audience right there. When you're in a bad show, you can hear the creaks in the chairs.

*Interview, New York/
The New York Times, 7-25:(2)13.*

Martha Graham
Modern-dance choreographer
3

I don't use the term "creation." I think there is only one creation, and that has to do with inner life. Choreographers are an instrument of that power, whatever it is. You don't know what it is, but one day you wake up with an idea ... Everyone is doing something in dance all over the world today. There has been a step up in the world's dance consciousness. That has always happened in history when there is political disturbance. People are so eager for physical experience. They want to live life to the fullest, as though they had some premonition. Everyone now seems to be seized.

Interview/The New York Times, 3-7:24.

4

I'm interested in sound, not just organized sound. Sounds, such as gongs, that are evocative of things may mean more to me than a very complicated manipulative score. Nature is very close to me. When I first did things, I wanted the sound and the dance to be a whole, not an interpretation of a period. If the immediacy is gone, you go back to interpreting music, which is what I didn't want to do. I always felt the music and the dance had to be a unit, rather than one subservient to the other.

Interview/The New York Times, 5-30:(2)22.

Edward Herrmann
Actor
5

I don't read my reviews ... If a review is good, it is never good enough. If a review is bad, it really hurts. It makes it difficult to work. It doesn't matter if it was written by an idiot.

Interview, New York/The New York Times, 11-5:21.

Pat Hingle
Actor
6

The stage is my favorite [medium]; it's the actor's medium. The curtain goes up and it's us and the audience; we're like mother and child, still connected with the umbilical cord. Film wears me out. And in television, the first usable take is the one people are going to see.

*Interview, Washington/
The Washington Post, 9-14:(B)2.*

Lincoln Kirstein
Director, New York City Ballet
7

My whole life has been trying to learn how things are done. What I love about the ballet is not that it looks pretty. It's the method in it. Ballet is about how to behave.

The New York Times Magazine, 6-20:24.

David Mamet
Playwright
8

We don't have a regular theatre-going public any more. There's a very small coterie of people who go to Off Broadway and Off Off Broadway, but a large, knowledgeable theatre public doesn't exist. The producers have, in a certain sense, done themselves in by advertising on television, by miking, by putting television actors on stage. Rather than building an audience, they're destroying the audience, so they have to go farther and farther afield. They have to appeal to a lower and lower common denominator of theatrical knowledge.

*Interview, New York/
The New York Times, 10-24:(2)4.*

Arthur Miller
Playwright

1

A playwright is different from other people who write in that he is an actor who doesn't know how to act. Novel-writers are on the whole people who can't dance and sing. Play-wrights are either people who can, or who think they can.

At conference of Chinese and American writers, Los Angeles, September/Los Angeles Times, 9-29:(V)8.

Jonathan Miller
Producer, Director, Writer

2

I've always thought that directing is about two things: reminding people of what they know already but have forgotten, and persuad-ing them to forget what they should never have known.

Interview, St. Louis/The New York Times Magazine, 8-1:37.

John Mortimer
Playwright

3

Comedy is the only thing worth writing. The essence of life is comedy. I think comedy reflects the truth about human existence—which is essentially absurd. And it's much harder to write. Anyone can toss off a tragedy. Actually, comedy—or farce—is really tragedy speeded up—played at 45 rpm. Take *Othello:* That silliness about the lost handkerchief is the very plot of Feydeau's farce, *A Flea in Her Ear.* Of course, to be good, comedy must have serious meanings underneath, something sub-stantial. I suppose Chekhov is the ideal—he's pure fun, but we never play him that way.

Interview, Los Angeles/ Los Angeles Times, 7-15:(VI)4.

Anthony Newley
Singer, Composer

4

[On performing on-stage]: There is nothing that compares with pleasing 500 strangers. It's an incredible gift. Sometimes I feel like a king . . . People who walk out on a stage are not like other people. They wouldn't be up there if they were well-balanced.

Interview, San Francisco/San Francisco Examiner & Chronicle, 3-7:(Datebook)41.

Rudolf Nureyev
Ballet dancer

5

Dancing gives me the most extraordinary pleasure, although I am in pain because I started to dance professionally so late—I was 17 instead of 8—and I worked so hard the muscles in my body are deformed. When I look at myself in the mirror I say, "How can he dance?" I perform on my second wind, always, because I am like a runner who has to break through the stitch to give him the stamina to go on, and ballet dancing is stamina. Immediately before I perform, I rehearse on stage until I am exhausted. Then there is the complete conquest of the body and you have the ability to do the impossible.

Interview/The New York Times, 8-22:(2)15.

Laurence Olivier
Actor

6

[As an actor,] you must contrive to make an audience believe. My own childish belief would have them think that what was going on on-stage was really happening. When I was 17, I saw John Barrymore's *Hamlet* in London, and I thought that it was burningly real. I believed he was Hamlet, and I believed in the situations through which he was going. The actor's ambi-tion is to put an audience in the position in which they are lost in you, in what you are doing.

Interview, London/Time, 11-15:80.

Milo O'Shea
Actor

7

[Actors must make the audience laugh,] stop them laughing, touch them very deeply, move them to tears and then bring them back to laughter. An actor is almost a shepherd, and he has this herd of goats—I don't mean that to be insulting at all—and sometimes there are a few strays that wander, and you put them in this pen, and then take them out and put them

(MILO O'SHEA)

in another pen. You're getting them all to laugh at the same time, to get a sense of your rhythm of delivery. After a while it's almost like hypnotism.

Interview, New York/
The New York Times, 4-6:24.

Lester Osterman
Producer; Former theatre-owner

1

The structure of ticket prices is the structure of the theatre, and there's no one culprit. It's all along the line. To roll back prices, you'd have to start with the impossible task of getting everyone to change.

The New York Times, 3-7:(2)28.

Geraldine Page
Actress

2

Critics affect me because they can take away my livelihood. If they could be fired from their paper the next morning because three actors who have never written anything in their lives besides a laundry list said, "I don't know, I don't like the syntax. I thought he used too many adjectives"—that would be something. But then if not only were they fired but all the other newspapers and magazines were afraid to hire them because one actor didn't like them, they would have some idea about how we [actors] feel when they don't like what we do.

Interview, New York/San Francisco
Examiner & Chronicle, 8-15:(Datebook)35.

Joseph Papp
Producer

3

The theatre is supposed to be a living force which absorbs in some way what is happening in the world, and in some way expresses it. There have been times when the historical circumstances of everyday life were closer to what was being done in the theatre than they are today. During the 1960s, for example, the theatre here reflected the Vietnam war and the civil-rights movement. Writers were writing plays that reflected what was happening in the world on a major scale . . . [But today, film and

television] give me much greater satisfaction—the subject matter is more interesting than the subject matter on the stage.

Interview, New York/
The New York Times, 5-2:(2)1,10.

Hildy Parks
Producer

4

[On the TV broadcast of the Tony Awards]: In the theatre, we have an identity problem that the [motion-picture] Academy Awards don't have and, God knows, the Emmys don't have. Every now and then you get a [Broadway] season where you have an Ellen Burstyn, Liv Ullmann and Lauren Bacall up for the big awards. But that doesn't happen often. This year I can hardly think of anybody, in any category, that anyone outside the theatre has ever heard of. In Iowa, they don't really know who Raul Julia is, and they certainly don't know who Karen Akers is. And the names of Michael Bennett and Tommy Tune, great as they are, do not mean anything to that great television audience.

Interview, New York/The
New York Times, 6-6:(2)4.

Christopher Plummer
Actor

5

I really do feel I'm slightly out of epoch. I don't think I'm a particularly contemporary fellow. I got in on the end of an era of gentleman theatre, but the theatre is very different now. I've always missed my time, because I never knew what the hell it was. I think I would have done much better as a movie actor, for example, in the 1930s.

Interview, New York/
The New York Times, 3-9:20.

Murray Schisgal
Playwright

6

The business of a playwright is to hold an audience by its lapels and not lose its attention. I am interested in having a life take place on-stage. That theatrical moment where I feel a sense of relationship between the actor and the audience—that's all I want.

Interview, Washington/The
Washington Post, 8-28:(C)2.

WHAT THEY SAID IN 1982

George C. Scott
Actor

1

[On acting on the stage]: You really can't spend such an extended period of years doing something without having an affinity for it and appreciation for its finer points. There's that wonderful feeling in the theatre, which is really irreplaceable—that feeling of getting that instantaneous, hopefully pleasant, reaction from someone [the audience] who doesn't know the next line. To me, that's still a wonderful thing.

Interview, New York/
The New York Times, 7-11:(2)22.

Neil Simon
Playwright, Screenwriter

2

For the next three or four years, I will be working exclusively in the theatre. After 17 or 18 movies, I hate walking onto a soundstage. I love walking into a theatre. It's infinitely more satisfying. Over-all, my plays generally come out to be more of what I intended than my films. You have more control in the theatre. It's my first love.

Interview/The New York Times, 10-1:21.

3

I'm never surprised at what I see on stage. When I see a film, what a surprise *that* is sometimes. The editor tones a film, gives it its rhythm. But the rhythm of a play is completely in the hands of the cast, the director and myself. I always think of the analogy of a test in school. If you fail it, you can usually make it up or take it over again. If you fail a movie, that's it.

Interview, Beverly Hills, Calif./
Los Angeles Times, 12-5:(Calendar)55.

Jean Stapleton
Actress

4

I'm not as pessimistic as some people about the entertainment business. It seems to me that this great cable [TV] revolution that they're all saying will make the home the center of everything is going to wind up sending a lot of us stir-crazy. We'll be looking to find reasons to go out to enjoy a live experience in the theatre.

Interview, Los Angeles/
Los Angeles Times, 5-6:(VI)12.

Tom Stoppard
Playwright

5

I've never actually directed a play of mine, [but] ...I am in more or less constant attendance [during rehearsals]. When you write a play, your page is making a certain kind of noise, and rehearsals have to make the actors reproduce this noise, and simply uttering the right words in the right order won't do that for you.

Interview, Boston/
The Christian Science Monitor,
7-8:(B)4.

Paul Taylor
Dancer

6

I did choose modern dance and I could have been a ballet dancer ... I think modern dance is a kind of make-do operation. And I don't mean to sound like I'm putting it down, but we Americans—whether we're dancers or choreographers—do the best we can with what we've got around. I actually enjoy ...not to throw anything away, and make something out of a discard. I think modern dance is sometimes like that. To use what's available and to create something out of nothing almost.

Interview/The New York Times,
11-7:(2)6.

Elena Tchernicheva
Ballet mistress,
American Ballet Theatre

7

The younger dancer has no advantages or disadvantages over the more experienced performer. They're just different. The gifted younger dancer can project an image that is so strong and touching that you are moved by its freshness. With the more mature dancer, the pleasure is in nuance and detail. In terms of pure ballet execution, the young tend to serve the technique and choreography, and part of the pleasure lies in seeing their pleasure in presenting a step or executing a combination. With the more mature dancer, the pleasure lies in *how* the step is done.

Interview/The New York Times, 2-14:(2)36.

Liv Ullmann
Actress
1

...I believe in no makeup on-stage. I can't understand why actors put on all this makeup. People's faces change all the time. You get the flush, you get the pale—it's what happens in life. When you start certain emotions and you control them, your bodily fluids will follow. It's a good effect. [Director] Ingmar [Bergman] has used it a lot in his films because we don't have makeup there either.

Interview, Washington/
The New York Times, 8-29:(2)4.

Peter Ustinov
Actor, Director, Writer
2

...writing for theatre is the most difficult of all. In a novel, it's enough to know what to write; in theatre, it's essential to know what *not* to write, and a lot of famous novelists have come croppers when they tried to write plays. As an actor you're not dealing entirely with the unknown. Writing is much more mysterious, and more personal. Sitting in front of a white piece of paper and filling it, and then doing that four or five hundred times—it's like a miracle. When writing comes off, it's absolutely thrilling.

Interview/The New York Times, 3-7:(2)28.

Mario Vargas Llosa
Author, Playwright
3

A novel develops slowly. You have all the time and space you need. There are no limitations. But a play is like a poem in that you must respect time, and it should be spoken. The first time I wrote a play, I had a hard time stopping myself from writing lengthy description.

Interview, New York/
The New York Times, 7-31:13.

Sam Waterston
Actor
4

For a long time I had this misunderstanding that there was this "good" theatre that addressed itself to fine material, and then there was this "crummy" stuff people did "for a living" and stupid people watched. But there's so much to get out of doing things directly aimed at entertaining. It takes away an awful lot of phony self-important stuff that wraps itself around the classics.

Interview/"W":
a Fairchild publication, 5-21:24.

George White
President, Eugene O'Neill Theatre
Center, Waterford, Conn.
5

In five to 10 years, motion pictures and television won't be as we know them at all. Our houses will be electronic marvels linked by fiber optics. We won't need to go out to the movies—we'll simply go to the telephone and dial a number that'll be announced in the newspaper and have it charged to our phone bills. So the reason to go out will be to go to the theatre. And because of the artistic freedoms achieved in the '60s, the theatre has become the true medium for writers to express what they really want to say about themselves and about society. It's still the only place going.

Interview/The New York Times, 7-25:(2)20.

359

TELEVISION

Mortimer J. Adler

Author; Former professor of
philosophy, University of Chicago

1

[Saying television is no worse than the book-publishing industry]: I think nine-tenths of the 40,000 books published every year are crap. They shouldn't be published. Television hasn't got a worse record than that. Quite seriously, the publishing industry makes a social, educational contribution by the relatively few good books a year published. Well, there are a few good television programs a year, too. I don't see any difference. Sure, most of the stuff is tawdry, vulgar, trivial. So? Think of the paperbacks in the grocery store, the drugstore. Lousy! They're just as much mind-killing as the bad TV is mind-killing. What's the difference?

Interview/The Washington Post, 10-25:(C)3.

James M. Collins

United States Representative,
R—Texas

2

Public television can take on controversial subjects only if they show both sides fairly. Documentaries are a field they perhaps shouldn't be involved in, particularly if they take a point of view. Public television is not a medium for taking an advocacy position.

The New York Times, 4-26:22.

Bette Davis

Actress

3

... I manage to make about one movie a year for TV, which makes good pictures these days. Oh, I know some stars are snobbish about TV. But people like Katharine Hepburn and I will work in TV, movies, anywhere. There used to be the same snobbery, on the part of stage actors, against those of us who worked in the movies; but we wound up saving the theatre.

New York, Jan. 21/The New York Times, 1-22:10.

Jane Fonda

Actress

4

Most of television is extremely disturbing. Clearly, the only interest of most of the people who do it is profits, and they play to the lowest common denominator. And I don't see *any* effort toward stimulating thought or deepening the public's perception of society—except shows like *M*A*S*H* and *Lou Grant* and sometimes *Hill Street Blues.* But don't get me wrong. That doesn't mean that it can't be better. One of the problems has been that it's been unchallenged for quite a long time. Too many people who are *really* creative and not so much interested in just making a buck have said, "Ugh! Television. Why even get into it?"

Interview/The Hollywood Reporter, 4-13:6.

Mark S. Fowler

Chairman, Federal
Communications Commission

5

The biggest change we need is to eliminate Federal regulations on [TV] program content. This agency should be no more than a technical traffic cop when it comes to broadcasting. That means we make sure that the stations are operating on the proper frequencies, with the proper power and so on. But I believe that it is totally improper, because of the First Amendment, for government, through the FCC, to determine what people see and hear over the airwaves. That is very unwise and, I think, un-Constitutional ... In broadcasting, consumers, through the marketplace, subject the broadcaster every hour to a national plebiscite. When you turn that dial, advertisers and broadcasters get the message. Those programs that most people will want to watch will be supported by advertising; those they don't want to watch will generally not be. It's not always perfect. Some-

(MARK S. FOWLER)

times programs that people would say are very meritorious don't make it. But, by and large, the ones that people want to watch survive.

Interview/U.S. News &
World Report, 4-12:43.

1

[Calling for broad deregulation of the broadcast industry]: The broadcaster should be as free from [government] regulation as the newspaper you share the press table with and compete with for advertisers. No [license] renewal filings, no ascertainment exercises, no content regulation, no ownership restrictions beyond those that apply to media generally, free resale of properties, no petitions to deny, no Brownie points for doing this right, no finger-wagging for doing that wrong.

Before North Carolina Association
of Broadcasters, Oct. 25/
The Hollywood Reporter, 10-26:1.

Milton Friedman
Economist; Senior fellow, Hoover
Institution, Stanford University

2

[On the *Free to Choose* series he did for television]: Television is an extraordinarily powerful medium, but it has no intellectual depth–it lacks persuasive power. I've said before that I've often thought of the television series as simply a large-scale advertisement for my book. Television is good for getting people interested enough to read books.

Interview/The New York Times, 10-24:(2)27.

Edward O. Fritts
President, National Association
of Broadcasters

3

[Criticizing a court ruling negating the NAB's self-imposed limits on the frequency, length and placement of TV commercials]: This is a sad day for the American public. Pure and simple, today's action means that the government does not want television broadcasters to attempt to govern themselves by voluntarily limiting the amount of advertising broad-cast into the public's homes. Broadcasting as a guest in the home is unlike any other business in the nation. Thus, television broadcasters feel a unique responsibility to maintain a balance of programming and advertising. We are dismayed.

Nov. 23/The Washington Post, 11-24:(A)6.

John Kenneth Galbraith
Professor emeritus of economics,
Harvard University

4

[On *The Age of Uncertainty* series he did for television]: From the point of view of my own enjoyment, I haven't done anything in my life that I liked better. But I was not impressed with the enduring value of the television program. A television series, particularly one on economics, is a fairly transient experience. Anything that is intellectually durable has to be looked at carefully and reviewed constantly. A reader can reflect and turn the pages back to trace an argument; on television, the timing is out of your control. You glimpse something once and it's gone forever.

Interview/The New York Times, 10-24:(2)27.

David Gerber
Producer

5

[Television] is a gigantic need with 300 hours to fill every week. Our biggest weakness right now, and maybe I shouldn't be saying this since I'm producing one, is the weekly series. It's repetitious, its point of view is one-dimensional, and mediocrity and apathy are bound to set in. There's timidity on the part of the networks. People are being turned off by series and going to other stations showing the oldies-but-goodies. And there's cable, ever growing ... TV must be improved or it s going to lose out. It won't die overnight, but the next 10 years will tell the tale. We could see the last hurrah. On the other hand, I hope to see molds and standards broken, and I hope I'm one of the guys breaking them.

Interview/San Francisco Examiner &
Chronicle, 9-19:(Datebook)47.

WHAT THEY SAID IN 1982

Lawrence K. Grossman
President, Public
Broadcasting Service

1

[On Federal funding cuts for PBS]: If ever there was a domino theory this is it. Fewer programs will mean fewer viewers, and this will mean fewer [corporate] underwriters. Public TV as we know it today will be destroyed . . . When the day comes that all specialized programming is provided on other channels, PBS should fade away. But this hasn't happened yet, and I don't think it will happen. Why replace a reality with a hope? But let me make clear that I've not the slightest doubt that the pendulum will swing back and that people will wake up to the fact that the diversity of PBS programming is now too pervasive and too important to this society to be decimated.

New York, March 10/
Los Angeles Times, 3-12:(VI)23.

2

As vigorously as I can say it, I am against advertising on public television. If the programming were supportable by advertising it would be on commercial television. Public television was set up with a different mission. I have nothing ideological against advertising. I spent most of my working life in it. But it doesn't belong on PBS.

Interview/The Christian Science
Monitor, 10-20:(B)2.

Gustave M. Hauser
Chairman, Warner Amex
Cable Communications

3

Studies show that the availability of cable television channels, which in major markets usually number more than 50 channels, does divert the viewership of mass-appeal network TV. However, I believe cable will co-exist with network TV. As you will recall, the advent of broadcast television affected the radio and motion-picture industries, but both continued to prosper . . . Cable is already beginning to provide educational services, home security, information retrieval and "narrow-casting" programming for specific professions, such as doctors, lawyers and businessmen. Home interactive services, coupled with the vast array of

video programming currently available, should result in a cultural change in which a high percentage of homes will ultimately find it convenient and desirable to be connected to the cable.

Interview/The New York Times, 1-19:28.

Joel Heller
Director of children's
programs, CBS News

4

[On violence in children's programming]: I hate to say it, but I think kids have the same bad taste as a mass audience as adults. They love it [violence]. There's no way to keep the kids away from violence.

Los Angeles Times, 5-7:(VI)17.

Neil Hickey
New York bureau chief,
"TV Guide" magazine

5

[On the effect on television of cable and other new technologies]: We are entering the time when we might begin to think of television as an extension of the human mind. Television as an unpredicted evolutionary leap in this century—expanding our awareness, raising our consciousness. Television as external circuitry of the mind. The thing we now call television—a one-way purveyor of over-the-air entertainment, news and sports—is about to become a thing of the past.

TWA Ambassador, March:52.

Gene F. Jankowski
President, CBS/Broadcast Group

6

Entirely too much time and space have been devoted to the gee-whiz magic of technological development [in the video business] and not enough attention has been given to the importance of the message. The medium is not the message. The message is the message just as it always has been and always will be . . . Shakespeare reaches out to us across 300 years, not because his plays have appeared on television and radio, movies and on stage. His words live because of what they say, not because of the way they happened to be delivered.

Before CBS-TV affiliates, San Francisco,
May 26/Daily Variety, 5-27:1,
The Hollywood Reporter, 5-27:1.

(GENE F. JANKOWSKI)

1

[Denying that TV contributes to violence in society]: I am not a sociologist; we've got a lot of them around CBS, however, and they help us maintain the highest standards in what we broadcast over the air . . . We take our responsibility very seriously. And much of the problem is a matter of definition. As we look at our 22 hours of scheduled prime-time shows, exactly *what* is violence and *which* acts to take out is open to interpretation. We go out of our way to make certain that our 22 hours are the best. And our standards now are higher than they were five years ago. Of all the media, television is the most conservative.

News conference, Phoenix/
The Hollywood Reporter, 6-14:6.

Mary Ann Leveridge
President, National
Parent-Teachers Association

2

[Television] saturates kids with things beyond the norm. Murder, violence, explicit sex, family life-styles. It gets so that the child begins to think that his family's life-style is out of step with the norm of that seen on TV. That is why we are promoting the development of critical viewing skills in the schools. Feed a steady diet of fiction and soon the child has trouble sorting fact from fiction and gets to believing the make-believe is the norm.

Interview/Los Angeles Times, 6-10:(V)2.

Frank Mankiewicz
President, National Public Radio

3

[Comparing Public Radio with television]: Radio is live. People know that when they listen to the radio that a live voice is going to be there. It's a link to the world. It's flesh and blood. Television is not. You can watch TV for three hours and not know for sure that anyone's alive . . . If you watched public television all day, you'd know how to make a terrific quiche; you'd know how to strip the veneer off your furniture; you'd know a lot about Edwardian England. [Violinists] Pinchas Zuker-

man and Isaac Stern and the other one, Itzhak Perlman, would be like neighbors. But you wouldn't know if there were a war on in El Salvador.

Interview, Washington/
The New York Times, 3-4:14.

Delbert Mann
Director

4

[On whether the "golden age" of television was really golden]: I think of it that way now, in a nostalgic sense. It was a wonderful period of experimentation, and some very good things came out of it. At the time, however, it seemed to be just a job to get on with. The production values were terrible—the lighting, the sets, all the technical aspects wouldn't stand up by today's standards. But even the poorest of shows had the energy that is the nature of live television.

Interview, Los Angeles/
The New York Times, 12-19:(2)40.

Stan Margulies
Producer

5

There is a famous quote from Napoleon which I keep up on my wall: "A general's reward is not a bigger tent, but command." In television, the networks look to the producer rather than to the director. All of that is sauce for the ego. But I don't do this because it's an ego-building business. There are many days when it's an ego-destroying business. Whether it's for theatrical release or commercial television, for cassette or cable, making the movie basically stays the same. And the work is its own reward.

Interview, Burbank, Calif./
The New York Times, 7-11:(2)28.

Bill Moyers
Commentator, CBS News

6

[Television] is the most wonderful medium, next to the printing press, that God ever allowed to be invented. Television has an endless horizon. You can sail it as far as your imagination will take you and into as many different ports as you care to go. You can do

WHAT THEY SAID IN 1982

(BILL MOYERS)

commentary, documentary, drama, comedy, Shakespeare, conversations with George Steiner and Saul Bellow ... It sounds trite, but I think television is like life. I think that we will discover one day that television is so much like life, that perhaps it *is* life. Television is everything—one experience one day, another the next. How many sensations bombard you in the course of one day? We have been thinking too narrowly of news and public affairs—TV must include family, thinking, ideas, education, entertainment, everything. It is the human experience.

Interview/
The Christian Science Monitor,
1-8:19.

1

I maintain that there is now more good television available than there is time to watch. But if you looked at it all, you'd be a passive spectator of life, not a participant. I'm not sure I want to make a case that there ought to be more good television because I am afraid that we'd stop being participating citizens. But the trick is to be selective. Choose carefully from among what is available. Good television does what a good book does—spurs the imagination and creates images in your mind that compel you, the individual, to cross boundaries that have psychological "no trespassing" signs on them. That happens when you have good television.

Interview/
The Christian Science Monitor,
1-8:19.

2

Television is to be damned for its omission rather than its commission, for not devoting more time to the issues, for not allotting opportunities for debate. [Its failure] is in limiting itself on the Evening News to only 22 minutes of information [and] overdosing us on banal entertainment at the expense of rigorous discourse.

Interview/Chicago Tribune, 4-17:(1)6.

Edward J. Pfister
President, Corporation for
Public Broadcasting

3

Congress recognized that PBS has a great and powerful constituency. They themselves are part of it—Congressmen are men with families who know the impact of television. They know that the issue of whether we will have a public broadcasting entity is a crucial societal issue that goes beyond just the pressure of the stations back home. In Britain the government remits a billion and a half dollars a year for BBC. In Japan the government commits up to $1.2-billion per year. Is our own society really ready to admit that it cannot afford $250- to $300-million a year for public broadcasting? ... It would be a sad day for our society— and for future generations of Americans—if we ever have to admit that we cannot afford to support non-commercial, non-profit public institutions like PBS and NPR. They have already become an integral part of our cultural and educational heritage. I believe they will survive this period of uncertainty—and future generations of Americans will be grateful.

Interview, New York/
The Christian Science Monitor,
8-6:14.

4

[Arguing against advertising on PBS]: Advertising could be the death knell for PBS. It would certainly be a step backward. Once the camel gets its nose under the tent, the nature of what we do will necessarily change.

Interview/
The Christian Science Monitor,
10-20:(B)2.

5

If commercial broadcasters, in time, are able to do what we [in public broadcasting] do now, then bless them. I'll be the first one to lead the charge out of here, because we ought not put this burden [of supporting public broadcasting] on the American taxpayer if it can be done another way. But I just don't see it happening.

TV Guide, 12-11:14.

THE PERFORMING ARTS—TELEVISION

Robert Preston
Actor   1

Years ago, Ralph Bellamy was doing a live TV show called *Man Against Crime,* playing a fellow called Mike Barnett. One day he came to me and said, "Come on the show with me. I'll introduce you as my young brother Pat and you can take over for six weeks while I take a break. I've done 82 shows without a week off and I'm going crazy." So I did. And after a while, where people had once called out "Hi, Bob," as I walked to the theatre, they now began saying, "Hi, Pat." And I thought: "My God, if it takes that short a time to lose my identity I'd better be careful." After that I... never did much television again. You've got to keep yourself fresh for the public. That way, every three years or so I'm a new face.

Interview, Los Angeles/
Los Angeles Times,
3-16:(VI)6.

James H. Quello
Commissioner, Federal
Communications Commission
                                                                       2

There is nothing immediate to replace Federal funding [of public broadcasting]. But if we are not going to have Federal funding for PBS in the future, there are practical means we must start applying to reduce and possibly eliminate the need for indefinitely continuing Federal funding... The most viable alternatives would be 1) a tax credit for contributions to public broadcasting and 2) an excise tax on the sale of new television and radio receivers... Whatever the means of raising revenue for PBS, and I suspect it may be several simultaneous methods, the most important thing is that the character of public broadcasting not be altered. It is the people's only alternative to the mass-appeal programming of commercial television. Americans deserve the quality programming provided by PBS. All of us in government owe it to the public to make certain public broadcasting survives intact.

Interview, Washington/
The Christian Science Monitor,
10-20:(B)4.

William Reed
Senior vice president
for educational programming,
Public Broadcasting Service
                                                                       3

For far too long we have acquiesced to the charge that public television does not provide educational program services beyond our children's programming. Yet some of public television's most memorable programs are clearly educational: *Nova, National Geographic* and others... Public television has worked hard to bury the myth that opera, symphonic music and dance only appeal to the so-called up-scale audience. It is time now for public television to put aside the myth that educational programming is dull and pedantic. It is time now to acknowledge that our finest efforts in stimulating and creative programming are also educational.

Los Angeles Times, 6-30:(VI)1,10.

Carl Reiner
Director, Writer
                                                                       4

[On TV networks canceling "quality" programs because of low ratings]: Those network executives should be ashamed of themselves. When they go to a party and somebody says, "What did you do today, you big executive?" they have to say, "I canceled a show written by a major talent who cares about quality." Those guys should have their heads examined. And the reason I can say this, and so clearly, is because first of all I've got a [film] career going that doesn't seem to need them at the moment and, by the time I'm ready to go back to television, if I ever am, they'll be gone. Because they make mistakes like that, and they'll get kicked out... In any field, whether its comedy, sciences, physics, music, whatever it is, the level of excellence is, like, 1 per cent. And in television, there's always 1 per cent of the stuff that's good. There's so much volume now, but if you measured what was great and what was terrible and what was mediocre, I bet the percentage remains the same.

Interview, Washington/
Los Angeles Times, 5-27:(VI)13.

365

Carl Sagan
Director, Laboratory for Planetary
Studies, Cornell University   *1*

Television has outstanding outreach, which should be used by academics and scientists to increase people's understanding of science and technology—something that is extremely important in an increasingly technological society . . . Human beings are hereditary scientists. Knowledge is what we're good at. When human beings understand more about the world, they feel *better*. People are hungry to learn, and television is the mechanism by which learning can be done most effectively.

Interview/The New York Times, 10-24:(2)28.

John Schmul
General manager, Qube
(two-way cable TV system)
    2

We're not banking all this investment [in Qube] just on entertainment. Today, entertainment pays the bills. But the payoff to building these two-way interactive plants isn't simply from entertainment. Some people go so far as to say the entertainment's going to be free in the future. You'll give that away in exchange for the right to enter a home, so you can offer a diverse menu of services—everything from home security to shopping to banking and all kinds of non-entertainment and ancillary services.

TWA Ambassador, March:54.

Eric Sevareid
Former commentator, CBS News
    3

On balance, TV is better for us than bad for us. When Gutenberg printed the Bible, people thought that invention would put bad ideas in people's heads. They thought the typewriter would destroy the muse, that movies would destroy legitimate theatre, that radio would destroy newspapers, and that TV would destroy everything. But it doesn't happen that way.

U.S. News & World Report, 8-2:28.

John C. Severino
President, ABC-TV
    4

Competition is a fact of life in television; it always has been. Competition from the new

technologies [cable, pay-TV, etc.] and independent stations doesn't change what we all know so well about broadcasting: Advertisers pay our bills . . . And I'm confident that network television will remain the predominant mass advertising medium throughout the decade and beyond.

At ABC-TV affiliates meeting, Los Angeles,
May/Los Angeles Times, 5-17:(VI)1.

Jerome L. Singer
Professor of psychology,
Yale University   *5*

[On the effects of TV on children] : Unfortunately, the focus in the media has been almost exclusively on the findings with respect of violence. [Of importance also is] the potential of television to teach behaviors like sharing, cooperating and taking turns. Television can be extremely effective in these constructive directions. It can also portray positive héalth attitudes, like not smoking. Unfortunately, television programming is not constructed so these capabilities are fully utilized.

The New York Times, 8-2:18.

Michael Sullivan
Director of comedy
development, ABC-TV   *6*

Innovation [in TV programming] is a matter of degree. I mean, we are all here today as derivatives of other successful human beings; plants are derivatives of other plants; and all TV shows come from other shows. There is no such thing as total originality or innovation. What you hope to get is a *degree* of innovation that will give you success.

At television seminar, University
of California, Los Angeles/
Los Angeles Times, 3-15:(VI)4.

Brandon Tartikoff
President, NBC Entertainment
    7

The adage that operates in television is that the hits are the flukes. You really don't know where the next hit is going to be. If you talk about shows that have gone on to be hits, they haven't been part of trends. They're the ones that have started trends.

At television seminar, University
of California, Los Angeles/
Los Angeles Times, 3-15:(VI)4.

(BRANDON TARTIKOFF)

1

[The problem with TV programming is] television creating new television by writers sitting in bungalows watching old television shows.

Broadcast interview/"Don't Touch
That Dial," CBS-TV, 12-23.

Arthur Taylor
President, Entertainment Channel;
Former president, CBS, Inc.

2

Let's not be confused. Network (TV) programming is not designed to entertain people. It's designed to sell products and services. Our goal here [at the Entertainment Channel pay-TV service] is much simpler: We want to entertain people. We want to put stuff on that we believe in, shows that are compelling, that have a beginning, middle and end, with plots and characters we care about. We can't be esoteric; we can't be cultural; we have to be popular—and we have to have quality.

Interview/Chicago Tribune, 9-15:(1)14.

Grant Tinker
Chairman, National
Broadcasting Company

3

[On criticism of TV sex and violence by Rev. Donald Wildmon's Coalition for Better Television]: My feeling is that maybe here and there you'll find patches of violence and gratuitous sex, but that isn't really the big sin. The big sin is that so much of it is not good enough, either forgettable or, in some cases, downright witless. We should address that, and if we did, the air would go out of all of Reverend Wildmon's complaints.
Interview, Burbank, Calif./
Los Angeles Times, 5-17:(VI)4.

4

[Saying he emphasizes quality in his network's TV programming]: It's not that we want only Pulitzer Prize-winning material. This is a mass medium, and you can't be quite so precious. But you hope you can elevate it some. Bad shows, the ones that are like Muzak humming or a light bulb burning, really offend me.
Interview, Los Angeles/The
Wall Street Journal, 12-16:1.

Jack Valenti
President, Motion Picture
Association of America

5

[Saying producers are not compensated for material taped off the air by home video recorders]: The video recorder is the real villain here. Its only mission is to record other peoples' copyrighted material. The new technology has outstripped copyright law all over the world.
The New York Times, 10-23:19.

William C. Westmoreland
General, United States Army (Ret);
Former Commander,
U.S. forces in Vietnam

6

Vietnam was the first war ever fought without any censorship [of the news media]. Without censorship, things can get terribly confused in the public mind. Television is an instrument that can paralyze this country.
At Fort Lewis College, March 17/
The New York Times, 3-21:(1)13.

Timothy E. Wirth
United States Representative,
D—Colorado

7

[On Reagan Administration cuts in funding for public broadcasting]: There is a compelling need for a modest [government] investment in public broadcasting—a service that brings the world to a country so misunderstood abroad, that brings an understanding of our society closer to the millions who care about it and want to make it work better, that brings a knowledge of the sometimes Byzantine workings of government to a people who are increasingly alienated from it and cynical about it. To say this is a non-essential service is patent nonsense . . . Our society depends on the gathering, processing and delivery of information . . . For only a handful of dollars we can ensure the survival of the finest news and information and arts-performance programming in America.
At Public Radio Conference, Washington/
The Washington Post, 4-21:(A)24.

Philosophy

Cleveland Amory
Author

1

I think anybody who thinks he or she has "arrived" probably hasn't ... Anyone with a sense of perspective or humor, which really is perspective, would, I think, feel that compared to what they once, when starting out, dreamed success to be, whatever success they have actually achieved is far from it.

Interview/American Way, October:99.

Saul Bellow
Author

2

We've lost the penumbra of private inviolability and mystery that used to surround people. We are sort of ciphers under a 200-watt bulb ... In modern times ... everything is done brutally and in haste and processed quickly. We are divested of the deeper human meaning that has traditionally been attached to human life. So it becomes possible to send people to extermination camps because their lives don't have any meaning. There's no sacred space around human beings any more. It's not necessary to approach them with the tentativeness and respect that civilization always accorded them. People now are out there in the open: They're fair game. This is true in many spheres, including our sexual life and the education of our children. We are turning the kids over to the computers to be taught. This is proof that the teacher with her or his penumbra doesn't matter any more. You learn everything you need to know from a box.

Interview/U.S. News & World Report, 6-28:50.

Daniel J. Boorstin
Historian; Librarian of Congress of the United States

3

Man is a problem inventor, not a problem solver. Man's humanity is measured by his ability to invent problems not authorized by government or approved by professors.

Time, 1-11:21.

Barbara Cartland
Author

4

... part of my philosophy of life is never to admit that you've been beaten or done down. Quite early on I learned that the best way to survive is to pretend that anything unpleasant simply hasn't happened.

Interview, Camfield Place, England/ McCall's, March:105.

Morris E. Chafetz
Psychiatrist; Former Director, National Institute on Alcohol Abuse and Alcoholism of the United States

5

Holding power is an aphrodisiac. Men who do not look attractive before they achieve power suddenly have great attractiveness to women, an appeal they lose the moment they leave power ... Unless someone can know how it feels to slip instantaneously from *Who's Who* to "Who's he?", he doesn't understand the transient nature of power. When I was in power [in the Federal government], if people were able to talk to me for three minutes on the telephone, it made their week. After I left power, they didn't even bother to return my calls. I was the same person; they were the same. But the power relationship had changed.

Interview/The New York Times, 11-9:19.

Kenneth E. Clark
Professor of psychology, University of Rochester; Former president, American Psychological Association

6

[Society] now lacks universal values and beliefs—so that one person's hero is another's

(KENNETH E. CLARK)

villain. Heroes stand for what is right. If someone is your hero, it's because that person does what you would like to see accomplished. But there is a prevailing attitude today that there are no *right* answers, which is a way of saying that there is no *right* and *wrong*. Our young people are unable to talk about right and wrong; they don't know the language of ethics and religion. If there is no agreement on what is right, then a consensus on what is heroic can apply only to a limited type of hero—the rock stars, the athletes.

Interview/U.S. News & World Report, 6-7:68.

Arthur C. Clarke
Author

1

[On what is real civilization] : Not having to commute is one of the first requirements; not having to travel unless you want to, not breathing carbon monoxide and traveling an average speed of 15.5 miles an hour. One definition of a civilized country is that police don't carry guns. In a really civilized society, of course, there aren't any police either. I mean, there are no civilized societies; there never have been any.

Interview, Los Angeles/
Los Angeles Times, 12-1:(V)15.

Harlan Cleveland
Director, Hubert H. Humphrey
Institute of Public Affairs,
University of Minnesota

2

The idea used to be that the purpose of making a living was to stop working when you had it made. According to this philosophy, you would retire as early as possible, pull up stakes and head south to spend the golden years fishing in the sun, snoozing in a hammock, watching the surfers, playing cards in glorious idleness, and happily awaiting the Grim Reaper in bovine indifference to the world about you. But once a whole population decides to be prosperous, the traditional forms of leisure are somehow not so attractive any more. The lakes and coastlines are crowded, the country lanes become clogged highways, the fishing streams

get polluted. The need for TV talent runs hopelessly ahead of the talent supply. The theatres and courts and courses and pools and beaches and restaurants are congested with people who have just as much right to be there as you do. Because playtime is available to all, it comes back into perspective. As a by-product of a busy, productive, relevant life, leisure is a boon and a balm. As the purpose of life, it is a bust.

At Harvard Medical School bicentennial
celebration, Minneapolis/The Christian
Science Monitor, 12-15:23.

Henry Steele-Commager
Historian

3

There's been a disappearance of "fame" and an emergence of "celebrities." Little [John] McEnroe [the tennis player] earns 10 times as much as the Chief Justice of the United States, and will be forgotten as soon as he stops playing. You hear an announcer saying at a tennis match, "On this serve rests $40,000." Imagine saying that about a sonata performed by Serkin.

The New York Times, 10-26:28.

Archibald Cox
Professor of law, Harvard University;
Chairman, Common Cause

4

Some may think it odd to describe the immediate future as bright and exciting. Even a sanguine disposition might characterize the present in Charles Dickens' ambivalent words: "It was the best of times, it was the worst of times." Granting all this and more, granting— nay, emphasizing—that all times are a mixed bag, still I would emphasize the best of times. Let me put it to you directly as a colleague put it to me when I asked him what I should say in a commencement address. He replied, "Can you think of a better time to be alive?" Can you?

At Vassar College commencement/Time, 6-21:83.

Hume Cronyn
Actor

5

I don't understand life, but I think the key, if not the answer, to it is affirmation. We can't

(HUME CRONYN)

figure it out, any of us, but if we can embrace the mystery, it can be quite wonderful.

Interview, New York/The
New York Times Magazine, 12-26:40.

Alan M. Dershowitz
Lawyer; Professor of law,
Harvard University

1

The key to success in anybody's life is to find out what you really are and pick a profession that suits you rather than trying to suit yourself to a profession.

Interview/Chicago Tribune, 6-14:(1)14.

Thomas J. Downey
United States Representative,
D–New York

2

Protest is a legitimate part of the operation of a democracy. It is the steam valve for a boiler that has built up too much pressure.

U.S. News & World Report, 3-1:66.

Ralph Ellison
Author

3

We try to inspire the young with daring, we entice them with ads and jingles and with every damn thing else; but somehow along the way we forgot to teach them—and we forgot ourselves—that certain restraints placed upon the human instincts are not simply there because there were some bluenoses who lived a few years ago, but because we deal with powerful instincts which, if not given some sort of order, make for social chaos.

Interview, New York/The
Washington Post, 4-21:(B)15.

Millicent H. Fenwick
United States Representative,
R–New Jersey

4

I think being old is liberating . . . It's terrible to be young. You see, the other side of opportunity is insecurity. Suppose I do lose [the election for the U.S. Senate]? It isn't the same for a young person who has the mortgage still

to pay, the children's dentist bills still to pay. It's far freer; you travel lighter. You don't carry the burden of choice.

Interview, Bernardsville, N.J./
Los Angeles Times, 4-23:(V)12.

Joao Baptista de Oliveira Figueiredo
President of Brazil

5

Democracy, even one in trouble, is worth far more than any progressive dictatorship.

The Christian Science Monitor, 11-29:13.

R. Buckminster Fuller
Engineer, Author, Designer

6

I'm not an optimist or a pessimist. Optimists and pessimists are unbalanced people, although you don't have to know anything to be negative and you have to know a hell of a lot to be positive.

Washington/The Washington Post, 7-19:(C)3.

Gerald Goodman
Associate professor of psychology,
University of California, Los Angeles

7

I would argue that there never was a "golden age of conversation" in the U.S. Even in the days before radio and television, good conversation probably was not all that common. Despite the visions we have of colonial times when people supposedly sat around parlors and exchanged ideas, my guess is that most people then were just too busy surviving to have much time for free-flowing talk . . . In many ways, conversation should be of higher quality today because the range of experience is broader and because we can hear others converse on television, radio and in the movies. Those very things that keep us from spending more time in conversation, such as TV, are the things that can enrich our conversation. It's a paradox.

Interview/U.S. News & World Report, 11-8:57.

Cary Grant
Actor

8

There are such awful things going on in the world today. There's such stupidity in mankind's progress. What's the nuclear threat that

(CARY GRANT)

we have upon us if it's not the result of, I suppose, avarice on both sides? I can see why some don't try to get ahead: They're going to blow the blessed joint up anyway ... The world's going in a direction I deplore, but I think it has to. You cannot destroy something without creating something.

Interview, New York, May/
Los Angeles Herald Examiner, 5-20:(B)7.

Helen Hayes
Actress
1

I know too many young women today who are desperately searching for themselves, and who have tossed a lot aside to do so. I suppose this business of being in search of yourself is all right, but not to the exclusion of other things, of your duty or your obligations to other people—like spouses and children. I think you can be a free spirit and still be a giving one, and marriage is one long giving on both sides. I don't think there's enough of that today.

Interview, Nyack, N.Y./The
Christian Science Monitor, 11-9:18.

Jesse A. Helms
United States Senator,
R—South Carolina
2

We live in a time when the characteristic values of the West are collapsing, disintegrating, decomposing. This is hardly surprising, because these values have fallen victims to neglect and indifference on the part of those who have most benefited from them, and of assault and battery on the part of those who should be their staunchest defenders.

At Grove City (Pa.) College
commencement/Time, 6-21:82.

Katharine Hepburn
Actress
3

[On what makes a marriage work]: There has to be, between the male and the female who are going to stay together, some mysterious attraction. And it can't just be sexual. It

has to be a respect, an admiration, as women, as men, as *something.* It's enormously difficult and getting even more so, now that the ladies are bored ... There's a wonderful remark by Dorothy Dix, the advice-to-the-lovelorn columnist. Someone wrote to her and said: Should she get married? And she wrote back and told them: "If you want to sacrifice the admiration of many for the criticism of one, get married." It's the most terrible, terrible truth, isn't it?

Interview, New York/Chicago Tribune, 5-2:(12)4.

Soichiro Honda
Founder, Honda Motor Co. (Japan)
4

One good thing always has an adverse impact on society, and we're convinced that we must utilize our wisdom to resolve these problems. God seems to give humans good things and, proportionately, the same degree of bad things to go with it. We humans must develop means to eliminate those bad aspects.

At symposium, Ohio State University/
The Wall Street Journal, 5-28:16.

Thomas P. F. Hoving
Editor-in-chief, "Conoisseur"
magazine; Former executive director,
Metropolitan Museum of Art, New York
5

Most terrors in history were perpetrated by academics. The studious, the mean, the quiet person—he's the one you've got to watch out for. Politicians are a great deal more straightforward and honest than academics.

Interview, New York/Los Angeles
Times, 12-22:(I-A)9.

Yoshihiro Inayama
President, Japan Federation
of Economic Organizations
6

Why [should businessmen] not be satisfied with what we have? Why should we want more, in terms of material goods? What we should really be emphasizing today is not growth but stability ... I don't decry work. Many people do find their joy in living in work. I think that's splendid. But even with such people, I don't think it's just the prospect of earning more and more money that motivates them. They find

(YOSHIHIRO INAYAMA)

their joy in the work itself—without it they would feel lost. What I decry is the idea that because we business people have been devoting all our energies for all these years to making more and more goods, and competing with each other for a larger and larger share of the market, we have to continue to do so ad infinitum. And I particularly disagree with the idea that, unless we do so, we will lose our vitality . . . I think the competitive spirit is a fine thing and keeps us on our toes. But competition over things can get out of hand. What people really want today is stability. Let's keep our competitive spirit, but do away with competition over things. It's time we started thinking, What is man? In the old days, thrift and endurance were almost a kind of religion. Today, people work and get paid a fair reward for their labor. Beyond that, why not enjoy life?

Interview, Tokyo/The
Christian Science Monitor, 12-29:10.

John Paul II
Pope

1

Man can become a slave in different ways. He can be a slave when his liberty is restricted, when he is deprived of objective human rights. But he can also become a slave through the abuse of the liberty that is his. Contemporary man is menaced by a constraint derived from products of his own thought, of his own will, products that can serve man or be turned against man.

Public homily, Vatican City, Jan. 1/
Los Angeles Times, 1-2:(I)7.

Henry A. Kissinger
Former Secretary of State
of the United States

2

[Saying he admires courage in people]: I don't mean physical courage—although that's also attractive—but moral courage to trust your judgment. That is much more important than intelligence. You can always hire intelligence. But intelligence alone isn't enough to see you through a crisis.

Interview, Washington/Chicago Tribune, 3-7:(2)2.

Edward I. Koch
Mayor of New York

3

It makes no difference whether you're a minority of one or a majority of a thousand. If you feel strongly on a matter of morality, you are required, as I perceive the disciplines of life, to speak out.

Interview/The New York Times, 8-12:18.

4

You know you have "arrived" professionally when you feel comfortable with what you are doing and you have the respect of others for the way you are doing it. Success is achieving the goals you have set for yourself. What is important is not to be a perfectionist but to know when the maximum closest to the ultimate goal has been achieved.

Interview/American Way, October:100.

Theodore R. Kulongoski
Oregon State Senator (D)

5

You can always tell a fellow who has done nothing. Nobody is mad at him.

The New York Times, 9-28:10.

Milan Kundera
Exiled Czech author

6

Totalitarianism is not only hell, but also the dream of paradise—the age-old dream of a world where everybody would live in harmony, united by a single common will and faith, without secrets from one another. Andre Breton, too, dreamed of this paradise when he talked about the glass house in which he longed to live. If totalitarianism did not exploit these archetypes, which are deep inside us all and rooted deep in all religions, it could never attract so many people, especially during the early phases of its existence. Once the dream of paradise starts to turn into reality, however, here and there people begin to crop up who stand in its way, and so the rulers of paradise must build a little gulag on the side of Eden. In the course of time this gulag grows ever bigger and more perfect, while the adjoining paradise gets ever smaller and poorer.

Interview/The Wall Street Journal, 10-29:22.

Christopher Lasch
Professor of history,
University of Rochester

1

It is very difficult for people to reach beyond themselves and make commitments to family life and work when they are concerned with survival in a world they perceive as extremely dangerous and threatening. Instead of making commitments, people feel it is important to stay loose and maximize their options. They feel they have to be prepared to get into the lifeboats ahead of anyone else—or to keep people away from their bomb shelters. Contributing to this mentality is the feeling of living in a world dominated by total systems of power absolutely unamenable to any kind of control or understanding. Some individuals see the achievement of a state of emotional anesthesia as the only hope of dealing with such a world. And what I fear might happen is that not only will people begin to think of themselves as living in a world where change is no longer possible, but they will also learn to like it.

Interview/U.S. News & World Report, 5-17:59.

William G. Milliken
Governor of Michigan (R)

2

The personal task of making a living, as crucial as it is right now, will not be the sole purpose, nor should it be, of what your education has given you. If your occupation becomes your sole preoccupation throughout your lifetime, or if your only interest beyond making a living is in shallow, passive entertainment before a television set or in a stadium, then both you and the society of which you are a part will fall far short of your potential. Both you and society eventually will lose the essence of your freedom, which lies in wisdom, compassion, integrity and responsibility.

At University of Michigan commencement/
The Christian Science Monitor, 6-11:16.

Ralph Nader
Lawyer; Consumer-rights advocate

3

I've always been interested in humor. It's often a way of communicating that allows things to be said that couldn't be said other-

wise. I wanted to see whether you can intellectualize the process and still enjoy it. If you can do that, you have the ability to deprofessionalize humor, to decentralize it and make it part of an ongoing community culture. My hope is that if we take humor more seriously, we'll be able to enjoy it more frequently.

At International Conference on Humor,
Washington/The Wall Street Journal, 9-10:26.

Robert Nathan
Author

4

The world changed completely after World War II. Things that were important to us, the values that we lived by, the American dream, the family, our ideas of beauty, love and harmonious life have completely changed. My generation has vanished. The world I knew doesn't exist any more.

Interview/Los Angeles Times, 9-16:(IX)2.

Peter O'Toole
Actor

5

There isn't a day of my life, not one day, not one, that I don't wake up in the morning with such a sense of futility. Every single day. It lasts for about 10 minutes, that's all. I think it's a little like immunization. It's built-in. I'm immune to the great failures and defeats; I think one should keep one's expectations low.

Interview/San Francisco Examiner &
Chronicle, 11-28:(Datebook)19.

Ronald Reagan
President of the United States

6

Totalitarian rule has caused in mankind an uprising of the intellect and will. Any system is inherently unstable that has no peaceful means to legitimize its leaders.

Before Parliament, London, June 8/
The Christian Science Monitor, 6-9:6.

Carl Reiner
Humorist

7

In times of depression and repression people need laughter more than ever to release their pent-up energies and relieve the fear and

(CARL REINER)

neuroses that are growing within them. Just look around—there are Comedy Stores and Improvs North, West, East and South. They're popping up all over the place. And where people used to go to variety shows, they're now sitting in a room listening to one stand-up comedian after another . . . There's no doubt about it. As life gets more complex and people get more frustrated with the mechanized society, we all really need someone to tell us, "Hey, it's all right. You're not crazy. The world—that's crazy."

Interview/American Way, October: 96.

Ralph Richardson
Actor

1

[I] can't afford to retire. I don't know enough. The older you get, the more you realize how little you know. No, I can't afford it, not for my inner self. It's like pottery—the more you make it, the more you see you're not very good. You're like a bull in a field, chasing after a cow, trying to get it, and you never quite catch it. Never quite learn how to act. Yes, I'm very anxious to learn more in the short time before I get my ticket, before it all ends. Which might, of course, be very soon.

*Interview, London/The
New York Times, 12-19:(2)5.*

Mickey Rooney
Entertainer

2

I have this insatiable desire to create. It's like manure. If you leave it all in one place, it stinks. If you spread it around, something grows.

Interview, New York/TV Guide, 3-20:34.

Carl Sagan
*Director, Laboratory for Planetary
Studies, Cornell University*

3

I think nature is a continuum, and for convenience people do things, put things into separate pigeonholes, and they forget that those pigeonholes are entirely made by humans. And because there are a whole lot of things to know,

people tend to specialize, concentrate on one thing and figure the other things are for someone else. I think that's very dangerous. I think it's dangerous, for example, for politicians not to know science, and for scientists not to know politics.

*Interview, Washington/The
Christian Science Monitor, 7-1:(B)14.*

John Paul Schaefer
President, University of Arizona

4

We are going to have to recognize that equal opportunity cannot guarantee equal results. When a society refuses to distinguish between achievement and non-achievement, its standards are reduced to the least common denominator. Not only does no one win . . . everyone loses.

*At University of Arizona commencement/
The Christian Science Monitor, 6-11:15.*

Jackie Sherrill
*Football coach,
Texas A&M University*

5

One of the things that upsets me is the people who have made millions saying how to get rich quick, how to get where you want to go. I don't think anyone knows where they're going; if they do, they die. It's the difference between being ripe and rotten, and green and growing. But what these people don't understand is, you have to experience failure in order to understand success.

Interview/The Washington Post, 9-15:(D)4.

Roger B. Smith
*Chairman, General
Motors Corporation*

6

The world needs specialists and highly trained people with advanced degrees, no question about it. But the world also needs diversity and versatility. It needs people who know as much about our value system as they do about our solar system.

*At Albion (Mich.) College commencement/
U.S. News & World Report, 6-7:66.*

Sylvester Stallone
Actor

1

I learned the real meaning of love. Love is absolute loyalty. People fade, looks fade, but loyalty never fades. You can depend so much on certain people, you can set your watch by them. And that's love, even if it doesn't seem very exciting. Let me put it on a real crass level. Love is like a new car. The leather smells great for a while, and it's so exciting to drive it around and show it off to your people. You keep it shined and polished. You make love to it, you might say. Eventually it gets old. But you know what? As long as it keeps running and is reliable, you hang onto it. You change the tires, keep it tuned up, and it's reliable and loyal. Okay, that's love.

Interview, Pacific Palisades, Calif./
Chicago Tribune Magazine, 5-30:13.

William Styron
Author

2

. . . it seems to me that human beings are a hair's breadth away from catastrophe at all times—both personally and on a larger historical level, and this, perhaps, is why I've written the sort of books I have. I mean, I was never a slave nor was I at Auschwitz, but somehow these two modes of existence sort of grabbed me and became a kind of metaphor for what I believe a great deal of life is about. This theme has really found me. Why, I don't know. Perhaps it's the result of being in World War II— being a fairly sensitive boy of 18 and finding myself in a war which, however just it might have been, nonetheless threatened to kill me. I think something like that, which affected many men of my generation, caused me to wonder about human domination, about the forces in history that simply wipe you out. You're suddenly a cipher—you find yourself on some hideous atoll in the Pacific, and if you're unlucky you get a bullet through your head. And within the microcosm of the Marine Corps itself you're just a mound of dust in terms of free will, and I think this fact of being utterly helpless enlarges one's sensitivity to the idea of evil.

Interview/The New York Times
Book Review, 12-12:3.

I. F. Sunia
Delegate to the United States
House of Representatives
from American Samoa

3

I've accepted the notion that progress has its price. The price of progress I guess everywhere is losing something of what you had yesterday. Somebody once said "it's best to hang on to what you had before because you know what it is, whereas you don't know what you're going to get." But no ventures, no gains.

Interview, Washington/The
Washington Post, 4-26:(C)11.

James Taylor
Singer

4

Publicity and celebrity is something that some people handle better than others, and I handle it particularly poorly. It confuses me. There's a real cycle to it: When they discover you, you're the best thing since canned tomatoes; then when you don't turn out to be the savior of the Western World, they write about what a disappointment you are.

Interview, Washington/The
Washington Post, 7-15:(D)10.

Mother Teresa
Roman Catholic missionary;
Nobel Peace Prize winner

5

[On her winning the Nobel Prize]: The Nobel Prize has created in the world an awareness of the presence of the poor. And a tremendous concern for the poor. And I think now people less and less are talking *about* the poor and they are trying to talk more *to* the poor. That's a great step.

News conference, Santa Paula, Calif./
Los Angeles Times,
6-9:(V)3.

Margaret Thatcher
Prime Minister of the United Kingdom

6

Look at a day when you are supremely satisfied just at the end of the day. It's not a day when you lounge around doing nothing. It's when you've had everything to do, a real chal-

WHAT THEY SAID IN 1982

(MARGARET THATCHER)

lenge, and you've done it. Life really isn't just an existence. It's using all the talents with which you were born.

Interview,
London, June 2/
The Washington Post,
6-4:(A)26.

Stephen J. Trachtenberg
President, University of Hartford

1

A central quality of leadership, as far as I can see, is [a] difficult combination of receptivity and outgoingness—the ability at one and the same time to take in and to give out. In general, I think, this fact is good news. It means that leadership roles are open to sensitive people, some of whom might conclude—after watching the latest war movie—that they have no chance of ever making the grade. It means, too, that the most effective leaders, and the ones who endure over the long run, may not necessarily be the tough macho types who look impressive on first acquaintance but soon come to sound like broken records. There is a time for toughness, but there are also times when toughness should definitely be turned off.

At Hartford Student Leadership
Awards Banquet/
The Wall Street Journal,
4-20:30.

2

One of the efforts we make here at the University of Hartford—the effort that is closest to my heart—is to demonstrate that *decency* and *survival* are not antitheses, and that we are surviving in a relatively fine style because we have not forgotten the need to be human.

Fall convocation, University of Hartford,
Aug. 31/The Wall Street Journal, 9-10:26.

Desmond M. Tutu
General secretary, South African
Council of Churches

3

The truth the church cannot compromise is that human beings are freely created by God for freedom. An unfree human being is in a profound sense a contradiction in terms, for freedom is the irreducible prerequisite for moral responsibility. God, who alone has the perfect right to be a totalitarian, has such a profound respect for our freedom that He had much rather see us go to Hell freely than compel us to go to Heaven.

At University of Witwatersrand, South
Africa, Aug. 3/The New York Times, 8-4:2.

Richard Warch
President, Lawrence University

4

We often find that in university discourse the ultimate put-down, the true mark of erudition, is to look in the eye someone who has just commented on the worthiness or unworthiness of an idea and say, with just a hint of a sneer, "That's just a value judgment." There is a classic illustration of treating values as simply personal preference, as merely matters of opinion ... Whether confronting hard ethical choices in public policy, or issues of personal identity in psychology, or questions about beauty in art or literature, or problems of environmental consequences in the sciences, we need to admit questions of values to the arena of discussion and debate. The moral arguments of a poem, the social implications of a political system, the ethical consequences of a scientific technique, and the human significance of our responses should have a place in classrooms and dormitory rooms. To deny that place is to relinquish any claim or attempt to link thought and action, knowing and doing.

Convocation address/The Christian
Science Monitor, 12-28:23.

Religion

Charles V. Bergstrom
Executive director, Office for
Governmental Affairs, Lutheran
Council in the U.S.A. 1

I support the [U.S.] Supreme Court's decisions that removed from public schools mandated prayer by groups but not voluntary prayer by individuals. Nobody can stop an individual from praying. As an evangelical Christian, I believe that mandated prayer can distort what prayer really is—a personal communion with God. It is a religious experience and therefore belongs in the home or church. We need to protect the family. Also involved are social-justice issues. Every child has a right to go to public school without any pressure on his or her religious faith or, if he or she has no faith, any efforts to bring religion into that experience, or make this a Christian nation.

Interview/U.S. News & World Report, 11-15:73.

Joseph Louis Bernardin
Roman Catholic Archbishop
of Chicago 2

Some people say we [in the church] shouldn't talk politics and that we should address ourselves to truly religious issues. Well, it's not as simple as all that. It's our responsibility to address the moral dimension of the social issues we face. These issues, of course, do have a political dimension as well as a moral dimension. I don't deny that, but that doesn't mean we're not permitted to talk about them. But our perspective must always be from the moral or ethical dimension. I reject out of hand that we have taken a leftward swing. What we are trying to do is focus on the teaching of the Gospel as we understand it, and to apply that teaching to the various social issues of the day. Our central theme is our respect for God's gift of life, our insistence that the human person has inherent value and dignity.

Time, 11-29:77.

George Bush
Vice President of the United States 3

[Saying it is wrong to fear that the "religious right" wants to impose its moral values on the rest of America]: [The movement] has been a healthy development in our politics. I think wisdom counsels us not to fear it or condemn it but to welcome it, and I embrace the constructive contributions it can make to strengthen the United States as one nation under God.

At Southern Baptist convention, New Orleans,
June 13/Los Angeles Times, 6-14:(I)2.

Edward J. Ciuba
President, Immaculate Conception
Seminary, Mahwah, N.J. 4

[On the decline in the number of men entering the priesthood]: Priests used to come out of a family atmosphere of strength and stability. Now the entire family structure is weaker. Also, in a secularistic age, priesthood as a way of life doesn't have the attraction of other professions. Finally, there's celibacy. With a culture so given to sexual freedom, celibacy to many people doesn't appear to be a vital and a viable way of life.

Interview/The New York Times, 4-8:16.

Maurice Dingman
Roman Catholic Bishop
of Des Moines, Iowa 5

We have gone from being a fortress church to a lighthouse church. When we were an immigrant church, we put a wall around the people, and we did a good job of protecting them. We maintained their faith. But we could no longer stay in our shelter. We let down the drawbridge and crossed the moat, and we're out in the mainstream of America.

Time, 11-29:71.

WHAT THEY SAID IN 1982

A. Bartlett Giamatti
President, Yale University

1

[Arguing against a U.S. Constitutional amendment permitting voluntary prayer by students in public schools]: The public school is not the arena to teach children how to pray or what or whom to pray to. The church or synagogue or house of worship is the place ... The family is the forum for that teaching and practice. A public school is not a family or a house of worship. Any American government concerned with the integrity of the family and viability of places of worship must recognize that its obligation is to keep some things separate, like church and state, and that it has no role sustaining particular religious values. Its role is to preserve and protect a pluralistic environment.

Baccalaureate address, May 23/
The Washington Post, 5-25:(A)16.

Billy Graham
American evangelist

2

We may not fully understand why God—who is all-powerful and loving—permits evil in this world. But whatever else we may say, it must be stressed that man, not God, is guilty for the evil of the world. It is man that bears the responsibility, because man was given the ability to make free moral choices, and he chose deliberately to disobey God. The world as it now exists is not the way God intended it to be.

At religious conference, Moscow, May/
Los Angeles Times, 10-19:(I)15.

3

[On his visit to Moscow]: I go back to the United States with my head full of new thoughts and ideas [about the Soviet Union], and with my heart also—in some respects, as John Wesley said two centuries ago—strangely warm ... There are differences, of course, between religion as it is practiced here and, let's say, in the United States. But that doesn't mean there is no [religious] freedom [in the Soviet Union] ... I have experienced total liberty in what I wanted to say. So from my personal

experience I have had liberty. It seems to me that [Soviet] churches that are open, of which there are thousands, have the liberty to hold worship services.

News conference, Moscow, May 12/
Los Angeles Times, 5-13:(I)1.

John Paul II
Pope

4

[Calling for improved relations between Christians and Jews]: The terrible persecutions suffered by the Jews in various periods of history have finally opened many eyes and wrought up many hearts. Christians are on the right path, that of justice and fraternity, in trying, with respect and perseverance, to join with their Semitic brothers around the common heritage, so rich for all ... We must reach the point at which ... teaching, at different levels of religious education, in the catechism taught to children and adolescents, presents the Jews and Judaism not only in an honest and objective manner, without any prejudice and without offending anyone, but even more with an active consciousness of the heritage that we have broadly outlined.

Before commission studying relations
between Christians and Jews, Rome,
March 6/The New York Times, 3-7:3.

5

Never before as in recent years has the teaching of the Catholic Church been so extensively reformulated, precisely with the issues that trouble the modern conscience and mind. I assure you that we are acutely aware of the problems you have to face in life and of the anxiety which so often fills your hearts.

At mass, Glasgow, Scotland, June 1/
The New York Times, 6-2:6.

Dean M. Kelley
Authority on church-state relations,
National Council of Churches

6

[Arguing against prayer in public schools]: Prayer in public schools is a custom characteristic of a homogeneous community and nation, but ours is no longer such ... For better or worse, it is pluralistic, and the decisions of the

(DEAN M. KELLEY)

Supreme Court [against school prayer] were belated recognition of the fact ... It is sometimes claimed that some children would never hear the name of God if they did not have the benefit of public-school prayer; but that is precisely the kind of intrusion that some parents, if they are intentionally bringing up their children in a non-theistic approach to life—as is their right—may wish to avoid.

Before Senate Judiciary Committee, Washington/
The Washington Post, 8-14:(C)10.

George A. Kelly
Catholic priest and scholar

1

[Criticizing many bishops for not taking a stand against "radical" theologians]: American bishops are reflective of American society. We don't have great Presidents any more, and we don't have great bishops. To use the pulpit or the classroom to deny the teachings of the church is a scandal, but most of the bishops just look the other way.

Interview, Chicago/Chicago Tribune, 3-28:(2)3.

Bill Moyers
Commentator, CBS News

2

I learned about democracy in a Baptist church. I learned about the freedom of an individual there, about the inviolability of the conscience. I learned how to scheme, how to compromise, how to negotiate, and how to speak, in a Baptist church. And I learned about caring.

Interview/Chicago Tribune, 4-17:(1)6.

Edward O'Rourke
Roman Catholic Bishop
of Peoria, Ill.

3

[On the church becoming involved in political issues]: I'm not confident we bishops have the ability to tell the President of the U.S. how to get the world out of the dangerous position in which it finds itself. If I were that wise, I wouldn't be sitting here in Peoria.

Time, 11-29:74.

Albert C. Outler
Professor emeritus, Perkins
School of Theology, Southern
Methodist University

4

There has been a subtle redefinition of the Pope and the teaching of the magisterium. It is no longer a question of whether or not the Pope is in charge. Actually, I see John Paul II as having accepted this role of doing what he can but not supposing he can do everything he sees as right and fitting. A whole new dynamic is in process. Namely, that issues are not to be settled by fiat or order from the papacy, or other authority sources, but by ferment and the shaping of a whole new consensus by the whole church. It is now a matter of having a Pope who is responsible for integration of the teachings of the church, but not to shape them solo.

The New York Times Magazine, 10-10:102.

Ronald Reagan
President of the United States

5

... it would be a good thing for the soul of this country to encourage people to get involved and accept more direct responsibility for one another's health, happiness and well-being, rather than leaving it up to the bureaucracy. There is, for example, expertise in America's churches that could be put to use teaching the unemployed skills that would change their lives. We have problems in our country and many people are praying and waiting for God to do something. I just wonder if maybe God isn't waiting for us to do something ... For some time now I've been convinced that there is a great hunger on the part of our people for a spiritual revival in this land. There is a role for churches and temples, just as there has been throughout our history. They were once the center of community activity, the primary source of help for the less fortunate ... As late as 1935, at the depth of the Great Depression, a substantial portion of all charity was sponsored by religious institutions. And today, as we all know, the field seems to have been co-opted by government.

At luncheon for religious leaders, Washington,
April 13/Los Angeles Times, 4-14:(I)11.

WHAT THEY SAID IN 1982

(RONALD REAGAN)

1

[Calling for a Constitutional amendment to permit voluntary prayer in schools]: No one must ever be forced or coerced or pressured to take part in any religious exercise, but neither should the government forbid religious practice ... No one will ever convince me that a moment of voluntary prayer will harm a child or threaten a school or state.

At National Prayer Day observance, Washington, May 6/Los Angeles Times, 5-7:(I)1.

2

Today prayer is still a powerful force in America, and our faith in God is a mighty source of strength. Our pledge of allegiance states that we are one nation under God, and our currency bears the motto "In God we trust." The morality and values such faith implies are deeply embedded in our national character. Our country embraces those principles by design, and we abandon them at our peril.

At National Prayer Day observance, Washington, May 6/The New York Times, 5-7:12.

3

More and more of us are beginning to sense that we cannot have it both ways. We cannot expect God to protect us in a crisis but turn away from Him too often in our day-to-day living. I wonder if He isn't waiting for us to wake up, and if He isn't starting to run out of patience.

At Kansas State University, Sept. 9/ Los Angeles Times, 9-10:(I)11.

John R. Roach
Roman Catholic Archbishop of Minnesota

4

It is essential that we initiate an explicit, public, systematic dialogue about the relationship of religious communities and the political process in the U.S. Whether we like it or not, a whole range of public policy issues are permeated at the very heart and core by moral or religious themes. From the debate on abortion to decisions about nuclear armaments, from care of the terminally ill to the fairness of [government] budget cuts, the direction our society takes must include an assessment of how moral and religious convictions relate to the technical dimensions of policy. And so long as we are true to our competence, so long as we are true to our responsibility, then I would submit that we as church have an important and essential role to play in that public debate.

At College of St. Thomas commencement/Time, 6-21:83.

Robert Runcie
Archbishop of Canterbury

5

[On Pope John Paul II's current visit to Canterbury to take part in services together with Anglican Archbishop Runcie]: I rejoice that the successors of Gregory and Augustine stand here today in the church which is built on their partnership in the gospel. If we can lift our eyes beyond the historic quarrels [between Catholics and Anglicans] which have tragically disfigured Christ's church and wasted so much Christian energy, then we shall indeed enter a faith worthy of celebration, because it is able to remake the world.

At Canterbury Cathedral, England, May 29/The Washington Post, 5-30:(A)30.

Alexander M. Schindler
President, Union of American Hebrew Congregations

6

[Criticizing President Reagan's call for allowing voluntary prayer in public schools]: "Voluntary" school prayer is a misnomer. There is nothing voluntary in the school setting, where pupils are taught, and rightly, to obey the teacher and cooperate in class.

The Washington Post, 5-7:(A)10.

Science and Technology

David Baltimore
Nobel Prize-winning biologist,
Massachusetts Institute of Technology

1

The last few years have seen a waning of the American commitment to science. Our institutions are poorly maintained and chronically at the margin of survival, we are training fewer scientists and to lower levels of competence, our laboratories have out-dated equipment, and fewer grants are available, at lower levels of funding.

Before House Energy and Commerce
subcommittee, Washington, March 15/
Chicago Tribune, 3-16:(1)4.

James M. Beggs
Administrator, National Aeronautics
and Space Administration
of the United States

2

[On the main motivation of the U.S. space program]: It's the knowledge—the human knowledge. With the space telescope in operation, we'll be able to peer out close to the edges of the universe, and we'll be able to find answers to some of the questions that astronomers have been asking for a long time. We will better understand the way our solar system operates: why it came into being the way it is; whether we are alone in the universe or not. We will begin to understand some of the processes that have taken place in the creation of the universe. And all of that, I think, is a very strong motivation, particularly for young people.

Interview/Chicago Tribune, 3-28:(2)5.

James Botkin
Consultant on technology

3

. . . there needs to be a rethinking of the role of the social sciences and humanities in the general education of college students to insure that they have both technological training and grounding in values and ethics. If they do not have both, we could end up with either technological illiteracy or a technocracy. The consequences of people not being well-grounded in technology can be seen in legislative policy. It is estimated that something like half of all bills before Congress have a strong technological component, but 2 out of 535 Congressmen have engineering training. I'd hate to give a quiz to the other 533 Congressmen and ask them what a semiconductor is.

Interview/U.S. News & World Report, 11-1:61.

D. Allan Bromley
Physicist, Yale University;
Chairman, American Association
for the Advancement of Science

4

[On U.S. Federal budget cuts in scientific research]: At a time when internal activities in science and technology are perhaps more exciting than they have been in decades, we face some of the most serious external problems ever encountered by the science and technology enterprise in this century. Following a year marked by change, confusion and great alarm concerning Federal support of research . . . the fraction of our resources now being invested in long-term research and development is at a low ebb. It is now less than at any time since World War II. Investment by U.S. industries in research as a percentage of U.S. sales has decreased by one-third between 1968 and 1980. These, too, are matters of serious concern.

At meeting of American Association
for the Advancement of Science, Washington/
The Christian Science Monitor, 1-5:1.

WHAT THEY SAID IN 1982

(D. ALLAN BROMLEY)

1

[On U.S. government attempts to prevent the leakage of sensitive scientific information to potential enemies]: What worries me is a kind of knee-jerk reaction on the part of the scientific community that, by God, nobody's going to infringe on my publication rights, and the same knee-jerk reaction on the military side that, by God, nobody's going to publish anything that I don't approve of. That kind of thing will lead to major loss both to the military and to the scientific community.

Interview/Los Angeles Times, 2-1:(I)3.

Edmund G. Brown, Jr.
Governor of California (D)

2

Electronics, computers, satellites, biotechnology, robots—these new technologies are fundamentally changing our communications, agriculture, environment, schooling, financial institutions, family life and our national security ... Our schools must augment the 3 R's with the 3 C's—computing, calculating and communicating through technology—or succeeding generations will inherit a society stagnating in the aftershocks of massive foreign imports and obsolete industry. Japan, with half the population of America, graduates more electrical engineers each year. In California, 15 years ago, we graduated about 1,500 lawyers and electrical engineers a year. Now we graduate three times as many lawyers as electrical engineers. In the Soviet Union, five million Soviet students study calculus in high school, compared to 500,000 American students. We must act.

State of the State address/
The New York Times, 3-7:(4)3.

William J. Casey
Director of Central Intelligence
of the United States

3

We have determined that the Soviet strategic advances depend on Western technology to a far greater degree than anybody ever dreamed of. It just doesn't make any sense for us to spend additional billions of dollars to protect

ourselves against the capabilities that the Soviets have developed largely by virtue of having pretty much of a free ride on our R&D. They use every method you can imagine—purchase, legal and illegal; theft; bribery; espionage; scientific exchange; study of trade press; and invoking the Freedom of Information Act—to get this information. We found that scientific exchange is a big hole. We send scholars or young people to the Soviet Union to study Pushkin poetry; they send a 45-year-old man out of their KGB or defense establishment to exactly the schools and the professors who are working on sensitive technologies.

Interview/U.S. News & World Report, 3-8:25.

Edward E. David, Jr.
President, Exxon Research and
Engineering Company

4

... new technology is not the answer to everything. We are all aware that new technologies create their own set of problems. I am not just talking about the threat of nuclear war or environmental pollution. New technologies like the auto, the telephone, television and the computer have changed the way we are human. They have changed the way we perceive and think about the world. They create ethical challenges so simple and personal as whether we Americans should spend a large fraction of our leisure watching network programming or playing Pac-Man [a video game]. And they create profound problems of public policy ... [There must be] competence in regard to science and technology, those most powerful instruments of our will .... much depends upon how knowledgeably and wisely they are used.

At University of Florida commencement/
The Christian Science Monitor, 6-11:15.

Val L. Fitch
Professor of physics,
Princeton University

5

The public, which has learned to live in a highly technological society, tends to take many marvelous machines for granted without ever attempting to understand them. Business managers tend to dismiss technical achieve-

(VAL. L. FITCH)

ments because they don't grasp how they work. Even non-scientists in a university refer to rather elegant technical achievements that are on the market as "just widgets." Somehow in our culture it is quite acceptable not to know anything about science, but it's not acceptable to be ignorant about Beethoven or Shakespeare. I enjoy and appreciate great music and literature, but my friends in the humanities don't show a corresponding interest in and appreciation for the scientific. I resent the negative attitude on the part of those who have given up trying to understand what is going on in science. This attitude is a phenomenon of our culture that is incubated and developed in the school system. It may be part of the general lack of emphasis on reading, writing and arithmetic. I see signs that things are turning around, however. The rash of new magazines devoted to science is one example of a renewal of interest. These shifts in attitude toward science illustrate that the country tends to operate in gigantic oscillations—cycles of enthusiasm followed by cycles of disillusionment. Somehow it averages out all right, but in the peaks and valleys it certainly gives one pause.

Interview/U.S. News & World Report, 6-21:56.

Newt Gingrich
United States Representative,
R—Georgia
1

I think we need a much more aggressive planetary science program. I think we want as many efforts as possible to create jobs in space. And I think we want a much more aggressive program for national security in space. All of those things, it seems to me, would make for a safer, more prosperous America. When you cut the [Federal] budget, don't cut out the things that would make your life better in the future.

Interview/Los Angeles Herald
Examiner, 4-13:(A)7.

Stephen Jay Gould
Evolutionary biologist,
Harvard University
2

I wish scientists scrutinized more rigidly the sources of justification for their beliefs. If they

did, they might realize that some of their findings do not derive from a direct investigation of nature but are rooted in assumptions growing out of experience and beliefs. But don't draw from what I have said the negative implication that science is a pack of lies, that it's merely social prejudice. On the one hand, science is embedded in society, and scientists reflect the social prejudices of their own lives and those of their class and culture. On the other hand, I believe that there are correct answers to questions, and science, in its own bumbling, socially conditioned manner, stumbles toward those answers.

Interview/U.S. News & World Report, 3-1:62.

Roald Hoffmann
Nobel Prize-winning scientist
3

[Saying U.S. and Soviet scientists should continue to communicate with each other]: Scientists have a responsibility, based on the rational and open tradition of their activities, to keep talking to each other, even when the rest of the society is disposed to get angry. It is not that we are better people. Perhaps it is that we have a base of "small talk, shop talk"—namely, the facts and excitements of science—by which an angry discourse is turned into polite, friendly conversation. If we are to achieve a rational and secure plan to put an end to the horrible prospect of nuclear war, we need to keep in touch. Be firm with the Soviets on the level of governmental relations, but let the scientists talk to each other.

Before House Science and Technology
Committee, Washington/The
Christian Science Monitor, 5-19:16.

Paul DeHart Hurd
Professor emeritus of science
education, Stanford University
4

A majority of our high-school graduates are becoming members of the fastest growing minority group in the United States—the scientifically and technologically illiterate.

At convocation sponsored by
National Academy of Sciences,
May 12/The Washington Post, 5-13:(A)4.

WHAT THEY SAID IN 1982

Bobby R. Inman
Former Deputy Director of Central Intelligence of the United States

1

[On whether scientists should be restricted in their exchange of technological information with their foreign counterparts]: I have finally come down to taking the position that it's neither feasible nor probably even desirable to try to restrict dialogue and exchange on basic research. It may be necessary in some very narrow fields—nuclear power, cryptanalysis— but these are exceptions. One can more easily try to draw the line if you look at advanced technology. There is where another country has the potential for bringing something to bear in a shorter time-frame that could have a direct impact on our own defense capabilities or needs. And there I think we are going to have to have constraints in the foreign dialogue. It should be voluntary. We clearly should try a voluntary mechanism rather than one of regulation or legislative constraint. But we will never solve this problem completely—not if we want to remain an open society.

Interview/U.S. News & World Report, 12-20:38.

David T. Kearns
President, Xerox Corporation

2

Let's face it. Automation does eliminate jobs. But automation does not put people out of work. That's an important distinction. The jobs automation eliminates are old jobs in old sectors. Automation creates new jobs—and more of them—in new sectors of the economy. It's true that the automobile, textile and steel industries have lost thousands of jobs—at least in part because of a shift to computer-based manufacturing. But it's also true that thousands of other jobs in data processing, accounting and word processing are going unfilled for lack of trained people. Those jobs are in new industries using new technologies—not old ones.

Before American Business Press, Boca Raton, Fla./The Christian Science Monitor, 7-20:23.

George A. Keyworth II
Director, Federal Office of Science and Technology Policy

3

Technology transfer [from the U.S.] to the Soviet Union is a clear national-security risk. We are not talking about choking off academic freedom in American universities; the implications are grossly over-inflated by academics. Nobody is talking about putting a wrench on the nut of academic freedom. But there is a real hemorrhage of technology flowing to the Soviet Union . . . The dominant source is not universities, but the flow from universities is a substantial one, and the more I learn about it the more amazed I am about how large it is.

To reporters, February/ The New York Times, 2-16:21.

Jonathan King
Professor of molecular biology, Massachusetts Institute of Technology

4

I think most scientists and engineers would still like to pursue their research and not be bothered by value issues or what the community wants. But the public has come to realize that the scientific and technological decisions that are really major social decisions are not to be left in the hands of scientists. You have people saying, "No, we don't trust the decisions of the nuclear engineers on this." We have to fight for a basic value: that the reason for developing science and technology is to advance human welfare and human possibilities. While we're continuously trying to more deeply understand and modify the world to make it more suitable for life, we must maintain a deep humility about how partial this knowledge always must be and how careful we should be in putting it to use.

Interview/U.S. News & World Report, 7-5:49.

Christopher Kraft
Director, Lyndon B. Johnson Space Center, Houston

5

People don't understand it when I say the Apollo 11 moon landing [in 1969] was not as exciting as Apollo 8. On Apollo 11, we knew exactly what we were doing; but on Apollo 8,

(CHRISTOPHER KRAFT)

there were a lot of unknowns. We moved to a new generation of flight that we hadn't even planned to do, and we did it very quickly. It was the first time we had left earth orbit, the first time we had navigated to the moon, the first time in orbit around another planet, the first time we had put men on the Saturn 5 launch vehicle, the first time we had depended upon one engine to get us out of orbit and around another planet. It took a hell of a lot of guts to undertake all of that, and people still don't understand the magnitude of it.

Interview/Los Angeles Times, 6-25:(I)14.

Christopher Kraft
Former director, Lyndon B.
Johnson Space Center, Houston
1

The response of this country [the U.S.] to the Sputnik challenge [in 1957] is something I think the Russians have reflected on many times since. It woke us up. It was the spawning of the technological explosion ... I would guess the Russians probably rue the day they woke us up. That's probably the reason they're not making more strides than they are today. They're probably afraid to wake us up again.

Chicago Tribune, 9-26:(2)8.

Harry Lustig
Dean for science, College of
Liberal Arts and Science,
City College of New York
2

At the highest level—scientists, doctors, research engineers and so on—we [in the U.S.] have for a long time been ahead of the rest of the world. But the signs are that this is no longer true. More and more of the basic research, more and more of the basic inventions are already being done in other countries. There are not enough people [in the U.S.] with Ph.D.s in engineering to even teach engineering ... I see us becoming industrially a second-rate power. I see us losing our lead in health research and basic science, in military strength. But most of all I see a population that I really don't want to be a part of. Most of our population knows no more about nature, about their surroundings than the aborigines did. And

that at a time when technology has added so much complexity. Most people don't have the vaguest notion even why they stand on the ground—why they don't fly up. They don't understand where life comes from; they don't understand about plants growing. They don't understand anything fundamental, much less technology. In addition—and here I'm on dangerous ground—I think science adds another dimension to human life. And that is one of absolute beauty. Science to me is very much like poetry. It's like writing poetry or music.

Interview/The New York Times, 4-6:22.

S. M. Miller
Sociologist, Boston University
3

Computers are one of our great disasters. If you multiply data at an enormous clip, you have very few ways of analyzing it. A famous study a few years ago came up with the most meaningless results you could imagine. Why? They threw every variable into the computer and cross-tabulated it. Fifty thousand correlations overwhelmed them—they had no sense of what was going on.

U.S. News & World Report, 5-31:71.

Bruce Murray
Director, Jet Propulsion
Laboratory, Pasadena, Calif.
4

The big question is, will [the U.S.] invest in [new planetary space missions] for the '90s during the '80s. If we don't, we won't be a significant player in planetary exploration. Other countries will. The decision to be made is do we care about the future. It's the same decision we blew in the '70s ... The future is under our control if we choose to influence it.

At California Institute of Technology/
The Christian Science Monitor, 1-26:5.

Michel Poniatowski
Member, European Parliament; Former
Minister of the Interior of France
5

All the technological discoveries of the scientific era, from nuclear power to robotics, derive from the insights of Albert Einstein— from the theory of relativity and the quantum

(MICHEL PONIATOWSKI)

physics of 1930-35. Today's major strides in non-logical physics take the theory of relativity a step further. Einstein defined the relativity of time and space; non-logical physics defines the relativity of objects. Everything becomes relative, not only time and space but the object contemplated in relation to time and space. That means that two plus two no longer equal four but always more than four, something more than the truth.

Interview/World Press Review, October:24.

Ronald Reagan
President of the United States   1

The fourth landing of the [space shuttle] *Columbia* is the historical equivalent to the driving of the golden spike which completed the first transcontinental railroad. It marks our entrance into a new era. The test flights are over; the groundwork has been laid. Now we will move forward to capitalize on the tremendous potential offered by the ultimate frontier of space.

At landing of "Columbia" space shuttle, Edwards Air Force Base, Calif., July 4/ The Christian Science Monitor, 7-6:3.

Hyman G. Rickover
Admiral, United States Navy (Ret.)   2

It troubles me that we are pressured by technology to alter our lives, without attempting to control it, as if technology were an irrepressible force of nature to which we must submit. Not everything hailed as progress contributes to happiness; the new is not always better, nor the old always outdated.

At Virginia Polytechnic Institute, April 1/The Washington Post, 4-5:(C)1.

Herbert A. Simon
Professor of computer science and psychology, Carnegie-Mellon University   3

The basic set of abilities that we call "thinking" is something humans share a little bit with their cats and dogs and a lot more with their computers. When appropriately programmed computers solve a problem, they make the

same kind of highly selective search among possibilities and the same kind of inferences I see my friends making. Computers have the capacity to build up a very large assembly of recognized patterns, and the information associated with them, in the same selective way that humans do. So I see no reason to use the word "thinking" in the case of humans unless I'm also willing to apply it to computers. Viewing computers in this light can be fairly upsetting if your life is made worthwhile by the thought that humans are different. But maybe uniqueness is a poor way to look for one's values in life. Maybe we ought to look at the world in terms of what we share with the rest of nature rather than looking for that uniqueness.

Interview/U.S. News & World Report, 9-27:50.

William E. Spicer
Professor of engineering, Stanford University   4

One of the real problems we face today is the schism between pure science and applied science. The end result is that there is one group of people who think of themselves as pure scientists, with little contact with the applied world. On the applied side, I can give you many examples of hundreds of millions of dollars which are lost by groups taking empirical approaches—Edisonian approaches—rather than trying to understand scientifically what is going on, and building from there . . . This is an area in which one has to tread very lightly, because you don't want to destroy the ability of science to find new, unexpected things. On the other hand, our scientific establishment is getting rather large to justify, and is in financial difficulties because of this.

Interview/The Wall Street Journal, 5-26:28.

Ronald H. Stivers
Assistant Deputy Under Secretary of Defense of the United States for Policy Review   5

[On the possible military uses of space]: Whoever has the ability to control and dominate space will likewise possess the capability to exert control on the surface of the earth. This is a fact we cannot overlook.

U.S. News & World Report, 6-28:34.

Alvin Toffler
Futurist

1

When I talk about the "electronic cottage," I mean basically the use of the home for cottage industries . . . the use of electronics for production rather than consumption. The big change will come soon, when the electronics introduced into the average American home become a work tool rather than just an entertainment or consumer tool. There are millions of workers out there typing, filing memos, writing out invoices, who will no longer need to be in central locations like offices. They can do their work from their homes, sometimes with the aid of the rest of the family. And they can start new cottage industries with the electronic information and services available to them within arm's reach. All of this may sound Utopian now, but the logic of declining energy and improved telecommunications at favorable cost definitely points in that direction.

TWA Ambassador, March:53.

Clifton von Kann
Executive director, National Aeronautic Association

2

Despite our [the U.S.'] success with the space shuttle, we have no national space policy. We are uncertain of our objectives in space. By contrast, the Soviets are moving into space with a steady, well-funded program which will give them a permanent manned presence in space.

U.S. News & World Report, 3-15:9.

Joseph Weizenbaum
Computer scientist, Massachusetts Institute of Technology

3

Technology will not only allow you to enjoy luxuries, it may become a membership-card required to function at all in society. What happens to those who don't participate? The difference between those "out" and those "in" will be much sharper in the future, and migrating from one group to the other will be more difficult. It is possible that we will have a society split apart, in a permanent state of civil war.

San Francisco Examiner & Chronicle, 1-3:(This World)26.

Sports

Henry Aaron
Former baseball player,
Atlanta "Braves"

1

If I had to pay to go see somebody play for one game, I wouldn't pay to see Hank Aaron. I wasn't flashy. I didn't start fights. I didn't rush out ·to the mound every time a pitch came near me. I didn't hustle after fly balls that were 20 rows back in the seats. But if I had to pay to see someone play a three-game series, I'd rather see myself.

Interview, New York, April 21/
The New York Times, 4-22:26.

2

. . . baseball is structured differently today than when I played. It used to be that a player's salary was based on what he did the previous season and rarely was anyone offered more than a one-year contract . . . But now, at least where the stars are concerned, salaries are predicated on what you might do over the next four or five years. Most owners are willing to pay that kind of money so as not to upset the balance of their teams. Only there are a lot of young guys who can't handle that much security and end up giving you only part of their talent. There is no reason for a player to stand around and punish himself physically any more, because even if he retires early, his pension years are not only big but not that far away. There are also a lot of high-paying jobs outside of baseball. available to name players that weren't that plentiful years ago.

Interview, Beverly Hills, Calif./
The Christian Science Monitor, 6-1:10.

Roger I. Abrams
Professor of labor law,
Case Western Reserve University

3

[On the current NFL player strike]: This is a battle over a pot of gold [club revenues].

388

There is a bonanza, and the question is how to allocate it . . . By demanding a wage scale, the players' association is trying to establish itself as a traditional union—the exclusive bargaining representative for wages and conditions of employment. That has not happened in any other sport, and it's only happening here because of the tremendous largess.

U.S. News & World Report, 10-4:57,58.

Sparky Anderson
Baseball manager, Detroit "Tigers"

4.

Ideally, you would like every guy in your lineup to hit 35 homers and run the 100 in 9.4. But if you have to choose between power and speed—and it often turns out you have to make that choice—you've got to go for speed. In today's baseball, pitching is getting so special that a team at bat doesn't dare consider the big inning. You have to score piecemeal with your legs. You must go for the guys who steal and who take the extra base on a hit. Over a season of 162 games, a Rickey Henderson, a Willie Wilson and a Tim Raines will win more games on the bases than a man who belts 30 home runs.

Interview/TV Guide, 4-3:13.

Mario Andretti
Auto-racing driver

5

[On last year's Indianapolis 500 race, when he was awarded the victory because of an alleged foul by Bobby Unser, only to have that ruling reversed and the victory given to Unser]: I respect Indy less, and I'm going to enjoy it 80 per cent less. Indianapolis used to really stand up and mean something to me because of the tradition. Now it's almost just a duty. There is no way I'll ever enjoy coming here again the way I used to. Time will not heal what happened, because it's something that was too important and too strong. The way it was

(MARIO ANDRETTI)

handled was totally unacceptable to any fair-minded person. It demonstrated incompetency and lack of courage. I think they [the U.S. Auto Club] made a mockery of their own officials. I hope they never have to deal with this again, but the precedent they set invites a repetition, and they are the ones who set the precedent, not me.

Indianapolis, May/
Chicago Tribune, 5-16:(4)2.

Roger Angell
Sports writer; Senior fiction editor,
"The New Yorker" magazine

1

The thing that frightens me the most about baseball is that it may turn into a television production and lose its appeal as a competitive game. There's a heavy trend in that direction. And something like the All-Star Game adds to the trend. It's an exhibition. It's a big television program. But I don't think the public senses this. The fans have changed, too. So many of them have grown up with the changes since World War II, and their ideas have been shaped by things like TV. They're saturated with baseball and celebrities of all kinds, but they go along with it. Everybody gets hyped up.

The New York Times, 7-12:26.

2

... the fans have come to some degree both to envy and despise [baseball] players for their money and celebrity. Baseball used to be a blue-collar sport. It wasn't much of an effort [for a fan] to say: "That's me; he represents me; he's one of us; he's on *our* team." Now it's very hard to say "our team" with much conviction if we know that the average pay on a team is around $300,000 and that there are [players] out there earning more than $1,000,000 a year ... Most owners have an intense feeling of envy, a need to patronize these athletes because they are young ... I think a lot of sportswriters tend to feel this way, too. Sportswriters get older but athletes are always the same age. They're always at some peak of success and physical beauty and

achievement. Added to this is the fact that they make enormous sums of money. This seems almost insufferable. It's against the American work ethic: You're not supposed to make so much money when you're young. Going along with this, of course, is the sexual success. These athletes lead lives of great sexual freedom. Writers don't write about it—it's part of the code—but we know it's there. We envy this, too.

Interview/Los Angeles
Herald Examiner, 11-30:(A)2.

Nate Archibald
Basketball player, Boston "Celtics"

3

[On today's city-bred high-school basketball players]: A lot of these kids learn to do the difficult before they learn to do the easy. They'll try to do something beyond the norm, something extraordinary, just to show how good they are. I always say that it's best to learn the basics first, then to go to what we call "the freak bag," but some kids will want to put that into their game first. It's what is noticed.
The Christian Science Monitor, 1-13:10.

Red Auerbach
General manager, Boston
"Celtics" basketball team

4

[On "holding" and other maneuvers that slow the game in basketball]: I go and scout a kid nowadays, and the game doesn't have enough movement for me to even tell if a kid's quick. How can you find the next Julius Erving when a kid grabs a rebound and looks to break downcourt, and the coach says, "HOLD IT ... Slow it up, right there"? Certain talents are going to deteriorate if this keeps up.
The Washington Post, 2-27:(D)2.

Joe Axelson
President and general manager,
Kansas City "Kings" basketball team

5

[On his contract with the *Kings*]: It's a typical NBA contract ... paying me about four times what I'm worth.
San Francisco Examiner &
Chronicle, 5-9:(C)1.

WHAT THEY SAID IN 1982

Johnny Bench
Baseball player, Cincinnati "Reds"

1

You can say this for [player] free agency. There are some teams that people will just not go out and see. I think of the Houston *Astros* of a few years back. Now with a Nolan Ryan or a Don Sutton [whom they acquired through free agency], somebody people identify with, people will go out and watch them. Then they might see one or two other players who interest them and that may bring them back. So free agency has created a little bit more for the game in some ways. There has also been so much written about it. Everybody's got an opinion about [free agency] now. The fan is much quicker to voice his opinion. It's not just, "I love to come out, have a hot dog, and watch the game." Rather it's, "The players make too much money; the owners are crazy." We've made the public more aware of things. They are getting more involved.

Interview, New York, May 18/
The New York Times, 5-19:26.

Mike Blanchard
Tennis referee

2

[On the complaints and other negative behavior of pro players against referees]: Twenty, thirty years ago, tennis was played mostly by college guys competing for a pewter mug. Today it's big business. Make a questionable call and a guy thinks you're taking money away from him. He gets a lot madder.

The New York Times, 10-27:46.

Vida Blue
Baseball pitcher

3

[On success]: It's a weird scene. You win a few baseball games and all of a sudden you're surrounded by reporters and TV men with cameras asking you about Vietnam and race relations.

Los Angeles Times, 4-14:(III)2.

Bjorn Borg
Tennis player

4

[There are] too many tournaments. People who follow tennis, they pick up a newspaper, they see different tournaments all [over] the world, they have no idea what's going on. The only thing they can follow is the really big tournaments. They have to cut down the tournaments.

Interview, Las Vegas, Nev./
The New York Times, 4-25:(1)27.

Gil Brandt
Director of personnel, Dallas "Cowboys" football team

5

It's easy for any trained scout to distinguish the top pro prospects, and those who have no chance of making it. But there's another bunch of players caught in the middle, and the key to keeping your team competitive is finding enough of these guys to fill in the holes.

Interview/San Francisco Examiner &
Chronicle, 1-10:(C)4.

Jim Breech
Football player, Cincinnati "Bengals"

6

Being a kicker is a very tenuous position. It's mostly because of impatience on the part of the coaches. In most positions, they'll stick with a guy, but with kickers they can't afford to put up with you if you're not kicking well. And there's always other kickers waiting around for a job. The coaches kind of throw you into a hat and pull out a name.

Interview, Pontiac, Mich./
Los Angeles Times, 1-21:(III)3.

Jim Brown
Former football player, Cleveland "Browns"

7

There's a general feeling in the air that I was a bruising fullback. I wasn't a bruising fullback. I was fast, quick. But I know very few people can analyze my performance; they just don't have the time. If they did, they'd say, "He was big and fast, but other people have been big and fast." All of a sudden you've got to come up with something more ... There's a trillion factors that go into a performance. You'd think if you played me one-on-one in basketball, I'd post you and muscle you. But my greatest attribute is my shooting eye. In golf, it's my

(JIM BROWN)

putting touch. In tennis, it's angles and finesse. I'm not trying to play opposite of what I am, but what I am is finesse first, not brute force first.

Interview, Los Angeles/
Los Angeles Times, 12-21:(III)3.

Lou Carnesecca
Basketball coach, St. John's
University; Former coach,
New York "Jets"

1

[On changes in college basketball rules, such as adoption of shot clocks and three-point baskets] : If this keeps up, pretty soon we will be playing with a red-white-and-blue ball. They laughed at us when the ABA started the three-point basket; now it's a big part of the game. Let's face it. We're in the entertainment business. The days when players played the game for themselves are gone. With television and the admission prices we charge, we've got to give the people more excitement. This season we had people starting to hold the ball in the first half.

Springfield, Mass./San Francisco
Examiner & Chronicle, 7-25:(C)4.

Frank Cashen
General manager, New York
"Mets" baseball club

2

You always dream of trading for the pluperfect player. But you can't, because if an excellent player isn't scarred in some way, you don't get a chance to trade for them.

Interview, St. Petersburg, Fla./
The Washington Post, 3-17:(D)1.

Chris Collinsworth
Football player, Cincinnati "Bengals"

3

NFL players have become very polished at coming across as God-fearing, humble-pie kind of guys. But you have to be deranged, deep down, to play this game. All of us are able to call upon that sickness when the whistle blows.

Interview, Pontiac, Mich./
Los Angeles Times, 1-22:(III)1.

Jimmy Connors
Tennis player

4

. . . now I don't think about my matches until it's time to play. I used to start some matches one quart low on tennis because of all the energy I spent thinking about them. Now I have a full tank. It's what happens away from the court that sometimes permits you to play the best tennis. Now I just come and shoot the tennis balls, that's all.

Interview, New York/The
Christian Science Monitor, 9-14:14.

Jack Kent Cooke
Owner, Washington "Redskins"
football team

5

[Criticizing a court decision that the NFL violated antitrust laws by trying to block the move by the Oakland *Raiders* to Los Angeles] : If the decision stands, it is a threat to the stability of the League and, more important, the stability of professional sports . . . It means the nefarious type of sports owner, the greedy sports owner, could play a few years in a town, skim the cream off that city, make unreasonable demands of the city and, if the city is unable to meet those demands, could simply say good-bye, I'm now going off to another city which is eager to have me and which will give me everything I'm asking for. You then could have—apart from the larger cities in America, the Los Angeleses, the Chicagos, the New Yorks—almost a gypsy caravan of sports leagues.

Interview/The Washington Post, 5-9:(F)3.

Lee Corso
Football coach, Indiana University

6

Coaching is not a job; it's a privilege. Coaching is like being a sculptor. You can create something no one else has created. It's yours; it's from your soul, your work. It's like a painting. That's the thrill of coaching. You don't get bored doing it.

Interview, Dallas/
Los Angeles Times, 7-13:(III)9.

391

Howard Cosell
Sports commentator, ABC-TV

1

[Saying he will no longer do broadcasts of professional boxing] : I love amateur boxing, and if the company wants me to, I would do Olympic boxing. But professional, no. I have walked away from it. I am past the point where I want to be a part of it. I don't want to be a party to the hypocrisy, the sleaziness . . . If I were the [TV] networks, I would declare a moratorium on boxing until some form of legislation was passed to, one, protect the men who fight with the strictest rules for safety and medical examination; two, create an honest system of ratings and records; and three, create one Federal government group to administer boxing.

Interview/Chicago Tribune, 12-3:(4)2.

Ben Crenshaw
American golfer

2

[On playing golf on courses in Scotland compared with courses in the U.S.] : To me, this is playing golf in its ancestral fashion, playing golf the way it should be played. Back home [in the U.S.], our courses are built with bulldozers, with smooth fairways and sculptured contours. Here [in Scotland] the links courses were created by the interaction of rain, wind, snow, tides, erosion, even sheep and burrowing animals. Here, it's man against the elements, golf in its natural state. Back home, we demand good lies. Here you take lies as they come; you take the bad bounces with the good ones.

Interview, Troon, Scotland/
The New York Times, 7-14:25.

Harry Dalton
Executive vice president, Milwaukee
"Brewers" baseball club

3

Clubs go through strange cycles. For a while, they get heated up on speed, then they shift back to power. But the truth is, there is no formula that can be applied to producing a winning team. That's because the amount of talent available is limited. You have to go for the best players. Sometimes they have power,

392

sometimes they have speed. But if a good property becomes available and he's got power—and you reject him because you want speed—you're going to get into trouble.

Interview/TV Guide, 4-3:14.

Al Davis
Owner, Oakland "Raiders"
football team

4

[On the court ruling permitting him to move his team to Los Angeles despite an NFL rule that would have prevented it] : It won't hurt the NFL one bit if we bring this rule—as we brought the draft and we brought the compensation rule—in conformity with the rules of this country. I thought we won it overwhelmingly in terms of credibility and the integrity aspect and the true facts. For 15 years we've been told the rules were illegal.

San Francisco Examiner &
Chronicle, 5-9:(C)5.

Doug DeCinces
Baseball player, California "Angels"

5

Good defense in baseball is like good umpiring: It's there, you expect it, but you don't really appreciate it. But when it isn't there, then you notice it.

Interview/Chicago Tribune, 9-16:(3)1.

Edwin Diamond
Director, New Study Group,
department of political science,
Massachusetts Institute of Technology

6

In the pre-television days, football used to be a compact, dense game of 3 yards and a cloud of dust. Now the game has opened up to meet the interests of television—to make it more visual so the guy at home can follow it easier. It's become highly visual . . . The changes in costumes and rules came, I'm convinced, to meet the needs of television.

The New York Times, 10-30:16.

John M. Donlan
Executive director, National
Football League Management Council

7

[On the current player strike in which the players demand a 55 per cent share of all team

(JOHN M. DONLAN)

revenues]: The percentage-of-the-gross concept is alien to American business. It would turn over control of the business to the players. The owners believe pro football is the most successful of all the sports-entertainment businesses because of the business decisions made by the owners over the years, and the owners don't want to give up the right to make those decisions ... The owners have said that they are willing to increase further the wages of their players and improve the benefits. But they're unalterably opposed to the percentage-of-the-gross concept. We had hoped that the players would move away from this idea and propose some specifics such as high minimum salaries or something like that. But they didn't.

Interview/U.S. News & World Report, 9-6:59.

Lefty Driesell
Basketball coach,
University of Maryland

1

Teams aren't running like they used to. Everybody is slowing the thing down and making every possession important. Look at the box scores. There used to be scores in the 80s and 90s every night. But people have become adept at holding the ball. And they want to win. Now a lot of the scores are in the 40s and 50s ... I'm violently opposed to slower play. I don't like to coach that way ... But nowadays, it's the way everybody else is going to. I think the passing game started it. It's almost impossible to take the ball away ... people picking and screening, and moving all over the place.

To reporters, Jan. 14/The
Washington Post, 1-15:(D)1,3.

Ken Dryden
Former hockey goalie,
Montreal "Canadiens"

2

As a goalie, you perform a highly critical, responsible task. You have the feeling your position has an enormous effect on the outcome of the game. Only a very special player in another position could feel the same. I suppose we have a heroic view of the position. When

you're the last margin for error, you become more serious, more intense and individualistic. Like surgeons, we have little margin for mistakes. In the record book only a goalie has the wins and losses next to his name. This, I suppose, gives us the feeling of utter control, utter command. When the other team scores, you tell yourself, "I must put a halt to that—there will be no more." It is a position of considerable satisfaction.

The New York Times, 3-8:32.

Wayne Duke
Commissioner, Big Ten College
Football Conference

3

...if the truth be known, the officials of the Rose Bowl would just as soon we send a different Big Ten champion here each year. That's a bit idealistic, of course ... But it is better for the Conference, better for college sports all over, to have competition. The games are more meaningful. What more could you ask than what we had in the Big Ten this season? Every week, it seemed, the leader got knocked off. There is much more involvement everywhere ... There is another area where balance will help, too. An important area. I'm a firm believer that there has to be a winner and a loser to every game. In some place accustomed to winning, there is an awful lot of pressure to keep winning. Too much. But as balance spreads, maybe fans in those places will understand that one team can't win every game and every title any more. That may reduce pressure, and a lot of things that go with it.

Pasadena, Calif./Chicago Tribune, 1-2:(4)1.

Ray Eisenhardt
Owner, Oakland "Athletics"
baseball club

4

[On the high and steadily increasing player salaries]: We are watching ... inflationary psychology in action. We rush to buy players on the assumption that if you don't buy today, it'll cost even more tomorrow ... We are forced, out of a fear of failure, to do things that, in the long run, insure failure. I sense an

WHAT THEY SAID IN 1982

instinct for constraint [among owners], but we seem incapable of executing it.

Los Angeles Times, 2-18:(III)9.

Cliff Ellis
Basketball coach, University
of South Alabama

1

[On the shot clock in basketball, designed to speed up the game]: ...I'm in favor of it. From a coaching standpoint, it takes away some of the strategy. But if a family spends 25 bucks to see a game, they should see basketball. We've got to entertain, and it's not entertainment when the fans have to come and see teams sit and hold and wait for the final two minutes to see what happens.

The Washington Post, 2-27:(D)2.

Julius Erving
Basketball player, Philadelphia "76ers"

2

I really resent people associating my game with being a hotdog or hamming it up, because I approach basketball very seriously. The power I use on a slam-dunk or the finesse I use on a move is what was available to me ... The result of the play was more important than the effect on the crowd. People started labeling me the most exciting player. In 10 out of 10 instances, I'd rather be labeled the *best* player.

Interview/Los Angeles Times, 6-3:(III)12.

Carlton Fisk
Baseball player, Chicago "White Sox"

3

If the human body recognized agony and frustration, people would never run marathons, have babies or play baseball.

Los Angeles Times, 3-22:(III)2.

Larry Fleisher
Executive director, National Basketball
Association Players Association

4

There are two critical times in the marital life of a professional basketball player—the first year in the league and right after the player retires. There are problems at first because the player has more money all of a sudden and he's idolized on the road; women chase him and he

sees the freedom others have and thinks that's what he wants, too. Retirement is just as bad because the player and his wife often find out that they aren't used to each other and their life-styles are so different they can't get along. The player suffers withdrawal pangs, but the wife's life is going on as usual.

Interview/The Washington Post, 3-22:(D)2.

George Foster
Baseball player, New York "Mets"

5

A hitter who is ball-shy literally has two strikes against him. I believe that my faith gives me a spiritual or divine protection. I've been hit, but not hurt. I believe that though I may be hit, I'm not going to be *penetrated.* You believe that, no matter how close, you'll get away.

Interview, St. Petersburg, Fla./
The Washington Post, 3-17:(D)5.

A. J. Foyt
Auto-racing driver

6

[On why he is still racing at age 47]: It's my life—just like Harry James still plays the trumpet at the age of God-knows-what because that's what he does .... some people think racing is just a business to me. But it's more than a business. I wouldn't feel natural, not racing. And anytime I race, I want to win. I'm not here to run second ... I don't care if it's a heat race, a helmet dash—I want to win whatever I'm in. If it's a go-kart race, I still want to win.

Interview, Indianapolis/
Chicago Tribune, 5-16:(4)1.

Ed Garvey
Executive director, National
Football League Players Association

7

[On the current player strike and the players' demand for 55 per cent of all NFL revenues]: The NFL owners decided many years ago that they would share all revenues with one another equally. That has brought economic stability, but it eliminates any economic reward for winning or signing star players. A team that never has a winning season makes as much money from the playoffs as

(ED GARVEY)

teams that are in the playoffs every year. The system is pure socialism ... We want 55 per cent of all revenues put into a fund from which all players would be paid. Of that fund, 70 per cent would go to base wages. You'd start with about a $90,000 base for rookies and work on up, on a basis of seniority, to about $450,000 base pay for a player with, say, 14 years of experience ... We are fighting socialism with socialism. What else can we do?

Interview/U.S. News & World Report, 9-6:59.

Bill Giles
President, Philadelphia
"Phillies" baseball club

1

I do have confidence in baseball's future. Baseball definitely has problems, most of them financial, a lot of them labor related. The battles that we have had over the past four or five years with the players' association bother me. And the salary structure is, without question, the biggest over-all problem we have. But I believe that these problems are going to be solved over a period of time. I think that the game itself is so appealing to the American public that, eventually, the problems will work themselves out and we will have a very viable commodity ... The players are getting the message that the free-agency route is not as lucrative as they might have expected it to be. The new compensation rule is going to have a deterring effect—I don't think players are going to be as anxious to become free agents as they have in the past. I also think that it's going to slow down the bidding war for free agents. Club owners ponder a lot harder now about signing a Class A player that requires compensation in the form of an established player.

Interview/U.S. News & World Report, 4-12:55.

Tom Glassic
Football player, Denver "Broncos"

2

Football is a military operation. Football is war. You take an end sweep. What is it but a flanking maneuver? What is football but an attempt to take the high ground from the other fellow? What is a 4-3 or a 3-4 defense but a deployment to hold back reserves to rush them into battle at the critical moment? Football is a war game. You have your chain of command. Your army is broken up into corps—the defensive line, defensive secondary, special teams, your offensive line or your assault troops. You have infantry and you have conscription—the draft ... Napoleon revised the art of war. He was not only noted for massed artillery but he was the master at choosing the best terrain, picking the time and place for his attack. What else is that but field position?

Los Angeles Times, 12-9:(III)6.

Harold (Red) Grange
Former football player, University
of Illinois and Chicago "Bears"

3

The players today are good, but I don't think they're any better than in my day. They're bigger, that's all. When I joined the *Bears* in 1925, the linemen averaged 235 pounds. Now they go at least 260 or 270. People seem to try to make the game more complicated than it is. The team that blocks better and tackles better still wins.

Interview/The New York Times, 1-19:23.

Jerry Grant
Racing series coordinator,
Champion Spark Plug Co.;
Former auto-racing driver

4

The driver's role has become less significant. It's possible now for someone who has never been at the [Indianapolis] Speedway to buy a ride in a new car and go fast. A lot of very inexperienced drivers are posting very fast times. I'm not sure that's the way it ought to be. Technical superiority of the car makes that possible ... I've carried many a car, bad-handling cars, but those days are gone. Today it's like trying to feather a light switch—either it's on or off. Mike Mosley, whom I consider one of the bravest and best drivers out there, has told me these cars can't be carried by the driver; they have to be set up perfectly to work, and if they're not, no one can drive them successfully.

Interview, Indianapolis/
Los Angeles Times, 5-17:(III)6.

Calvin Griffith
President, Minnesota
"Twins" baseball club

1

[On high-salary player contracts and teams bidding for free agents] : Years ago, ballplayers had to accomplish something to get paid. These days, they don't have to do too much ... In anything in life, you've got to have incentives to work for. Every day should be a battle. But if you've got a big, fat contract, you're not going to work as hard. What security do they give us that they're going to play their hearts out every day? ... I'd rather win a pennant with home-grown boys. Then you could take pride in them and know you accomplished something. Winning a pennant with players you buy, I don't think you accomplished anything.

Interview, Minneapolis/The
Wall Street Journal, 7-22:1,13.

Robert Gurland
Professor of philosophy specializing
in sports, New York University

2

We've created a system [in sports] that makes cheating viable, and in the end rewards cheaters. The ethic in this country is one of expedience and gratification. People are willing to pay the price long-term to enjoy short-term pleasures. My students think that [former baseball manager] Leo Durocher was the real philosopher [when he said,] "Nice guys finish last." Well, I tell them that Durocher finished last, too.

The New York Times, 10-27:45.

Howie Haak
Chief scout, Pittsburgh
"Pirates" baseball club

3

The people won't come out if you have too many blacks on a team, not if you have nine. We're going to have to trade for some whites. I'd say you'd have to have about four whites starting ... To me personally, nine blacks would be acceptable. I'd go to a game if there were all blacks out on the field. But I've been hearing people talk and I don't think you can in Pittsburgh.

Interview, Oregon/Los Angeles
Times, 5-18:(III)1.

Red Holzman
Basketball coach, New York "Knicks"

4

When you're dealing with players whose prime interest is offense, and we've got a lot of that on the *Knicks*, it's hard to sell them on the idea that *defense* is what wins most games. Now, I'm not talking about some exotic defense that requires a lot of practice and a lot of thinking. What I'm talking about is going out and using your body to stop the man you're guarding, denying him the ball, forcing him to make his pass before he wants to, and blocking him off from the boards. You know, hard work. Everything in pro basketball is predicated on your defense. With defense, you're in every game. With defense, you can still win on nights when your offense isn't up to par. With defense, you're forced to learn to play as a team. Basically, a good defense creates extra opportunities for your offense and will get you a lot of easy baskets.

Interview/The Christian Science
Monitor, 2-11:14.

Ralph Houk
Baseball manager, Boston "Red Sox"

5

I'm not a strong believer in [the theory that] the manager has that much to do with the ballclub. The players are the ones that do the job and do the winning and make the manager.

Interview, Boston/Los Angeles
Times, 7-4:(III)1.

Jack Lambert
Football player, Pittsburgh "Steelers"

6

[On charges that some players are involved with illegal drugs] : [Some professional football players] are spoiled little brats who have never grown up, live in a sort of dream world. They're given special privileges, treated like royalty since the first day they ran for four touchdowns. It's the fans, television, [the press'] fault. We just keep hearing what great guys they are and some start to believe it. That, in conjunction with so much money, guys get swelled up and full of self-importance .... so many of the types you're dealing with think they're above everybody, even the law ... What

(JACK LAMBERT)

should be done? As far as I'm concerned, if you've got a [drug] problem, you should get yourself treated and be given a second chance. If some of the stories are true, and guys are actually selling, they ought to be treated like the criminals they are. They should get the hell out of the league because they are detrimental to the league and to society.

The Washington Post, 7-4:(E)1.

Tom Lasorda
Baseball manager, Los Angeles "Dodgers"

1

There is no way you'll get me to knock good base running. But if God were to say to me, "Tom, you can have your choice of power or speed," I'd take power. The reason is simple. If a guy beats out a hit and steals second, you've got no assurance he's going to score. But when a man hits one out of the park, you've got a guaranteed run.

Interview/TV Guide, 4-3:13.

2

I motivate players through communication, being honest with them, having them respect and appreciate your ability and your help. I started in the minor leagues. I used to hug my players when they did something well. That's my enthusiasm. That's my personality. I jump with joy when we win. I try to be on a close basis with my players. People say you can't go out and eat with your players. I say, why not?

The New York Times, 5-17:39.

Ron Luciano
Former baseball umpire,
American League

3

A lot of the calls [by an umpire] are guesses. They have to be. How can you really tell, for example, when a ball is trapped [rather than caught] by an outfielder? The gloves today are so big they can cover the side of a building. So you make the call and hope they don't show you up on the instant replay. With balls and strikes, it's impossible to get them right all the time. I mean, every major-league pitch moves some way or other. None go straight, not even

the fastballs. And the batters often can't do any better than the umpires.

Interview/Chicago Tribune, 3-28:(4)2.

Greg Luzinski
Baseball player, Chicago "White Sox"

4

Baseball's a routine. You're doing the same thing day in, day out. You try to reach a certain level and once you're there you try to maintain it. If you don't do it one day there's always the next, and it always comes in a hurry. You can be headlines as a hero one day and a goat the next.

Interview/Chicago Tribune, 5-2:(4)3.

John Madden
Former football coach,
Oakland "Raiders"

5

[Saying everybody in pro football works full time, except the officials]: It's time for those guys [the officials] to come join the party. The players work six days a week, the coaches work seven days a week, the commissioner works all week, and so do I [as a sports commentator]. It doesn't make any sense for the officials to just show up on weekends ... Under the circumstances, the officials do a good job. But they'd do it much better if they had training camps in the summer and worked all week in the fall like the players do. This is a business you have to get your mind into. During the week you build up to the big weekend game. It's just plain wrong for the officials to breeze in the day before the game and maybe work it with jet lag.

Los Angeles Times, 9-8:(III)9.

Leo Madow
Consultant, Institute of the
Pennsylvania Hospital,
Philadelphia; Former chairman,
department of psychiatry,
Medical College of Pennsylvania

6

One of the great outlets for anger is through vicarious entertainment. Take hockey. People go to the game and enjoy the expert skating and the good playing. But when do they get to their feet? When the fight breaks out. They are ecstatic. It is the same way with football and

(LEO MADOW)

boxing. Despite criticism that such sports may be too violent, I believe that, for spectators, they are a tremendous outlet for hostility, because sports are viewed as not quite real. Players are not really out to kill each other. People go to a wrestling match and see what appears to be one person breaking another person's arm, and they enjoy it because they believe it is phony. It is a wonderful outlet for them because it isn't genuine. Now, if those same people walked outside and saw two people fighting and drawing blood, it would not be entertaining, because it would be real.

Interview/U.S. News & World Report, 4-26:75.

Billy Martin
Baseball manager, Oakland "Athletics" 1

I get fired because I'm not a yes-man. The world's full of yes-men. The first year that I became a manager, 1969, with the *Twins,* I won a division championship. And got fired. The *Tigers* hired me. I had made $35,000 and the *Tigers* gave me a big raise. I won another division title and got fired again. Texas hired me, and with a bigger raise. I came in second, and got fired. The *Yankees* hired me, and tripled my salary. When I got fired there, and Oakland hired me—they gave me an unbelievable raise. I've got a long-term contract now, but if I get fired again, I might run for President.

Interview, Montreal, July 13/
The New York Times, 7-15:25.

Al McGuire
Former basketball coach,
Marquette University 2

What it takes to be a great player, beyond raw talent, is self-centeredness and a certain numbness to the crowd. Super-intelligent people can't be superb athletes. They're too aware.

Los Angeles Times, 10-26:(III)1.

Tom McMillen
Basketball player, Atlanta
"Hawks"; Member, 1972
United States Olympic team 3

The [Olympic] Games are idealistic in theory, but not in practice. There were so many

problems [during the 1972 Munich Olympics] —refereeing disputes, drug disputes, all the political activity in the pristine Olympic village, and then the massacre [the attack on Israeli athletes]. I'm not knocking the Olympic ideal, though. It's a noble attempt, and I don't in any way want to demean it. In a lot of ways it parallels the United Nations. There are many problems, but if we don't try these things, we'll certainly never approach the ideal. Surely it's better than not having it. Sports is an international language—a great medium. The majority of the world's population is under 25, and young people are sports-oriented. The Russians understand this. They're always building factories in satellite countries and in places like the Persian Gulf. When they give a gym to a thousand East German kids, it's a big propaganda bonanza. We've [the U.S.] never seemed to fully understand this.

Interview/The Christian Science Monitor, 1-29:16.

Marvin Miller
Executive director, Major League
(baseball) Players Association 4

[On the effect on fans of player salary demands and strikes]: There are two groups of fans. The first type understand the economic battle between the employee and employer. The second group are the know-nothings. They are the hard-hat mentality who think these [players] are lazy, spoiled bums playing a boy's game for a fabulous salary. And there are some who see what blacks in sports are making and they say, "Look at me." Don't think it doesn't bother them. So the fans are the customers and the players should have a certain concern. But should the fans' views affect the careers of players? Absolutely not. Just because they [the fans] can't have their ballgame when they want [during a player strike] doesn't mean we have to sell the players down the river.

The New York Times, 9-26:(1)26.

Paul Mulvey
Hockey player 5

[On his being removed from the roster of the Los Angeles *Kings* because he refused to leave the bench and participate in a fight with

(PAUL MULVEY)

the other team]: I'm not going to be a designated assassin who just comes off the bench and fights. I'm a human being and I stuck up for my rights as a person. I was being shoved out there as if I was nothing, with no respect for my hockey ability at all. I like to consider myself a hockey player, that I can play in this league, and I think I've proven that.

Interview/The Christian Science Monitor, 2-5:14.

Terry O'Reilly
Hockey player, Boston "Bruins"

1

[On game violence]: The league's showing signs of change, but it won't happen overnight. If you're going to have a sophisticated game, the fans are going to have to be educated. In Montreal, they are. If a guy can't skate, handle the puck and shoot, he gets the rap. But I've come off the ice sometimes after scoring a goal or two and playing a real solid game and some fan shouts, "Hey, O'Reilly, how come you didn't deck someone out there?" The mentality will have to change along with the game.

The Christian Science Monitor, 2-5:14.

Alan Page
Former football player, Minnesota "Vikings" and Chicago "Bears"

2

Baseball players are tougher than football players. I don't mean this in a disparaging way—we have plenty of courage in football—but there's a tremendous difference in the background of baseball and football players. They're two different types of Americans ... The average guy in baseball is more self-reliant. He's more used to thinking for himself and fending for himself. He's tougher-skinned—and more of an individualist ... You have to examine where major-league athletes come from. In high school and especially college, football players are pampered and idolized all the way. At the same time—the very time when football players are having it so easy in college—baseball players are having it very tough in the minor leagues. You have to fend for yourself on farm teams or you don't survive. The [baseball] minor leagues are the pits compared to campus life at USC or Notre Dame. When you bat

0-for-10 you're booed. But who knows when a defensive tackle goes 0-for-10? He remains a hero for as long as he's in the lineup ... In baseball, a guy matures into an individualist. He's forced to mature. In football, a "good team player" is one who does as he's told, and football teams search out that type. Baseball clubs just look for guys who can hit and throw.

Interview, Minneapolis/
Los Angeles Times, 6-10:(III)3.

Jacques Plante
Former hockey goalie

3

[On being a goalie]: How would you like it if you were sitting in your office and you made one little mistake. Suddenly, a big red light went on and 18,000 people jumped up and started screaming at you, calling you a bum and an imbecile and throwing garbage at you. That's what it's like when you play goal in the NHL.

Los Angeles Times, 7-20:(III)2.

George Plimpton
Author

4

I have a theory: The larger the ball, the less the writing about the sport. There are superb books about golf, very good books about baseball, not many good books about football, and very few good books about basketball. There are no books about beachballs.

Los Angeles Times, 3-9:(III)2.

Dan Quisenberry
Baseball pitcher, Kansas City "Royals"

5

It really helps to be stupid if you're a relief pitcher. You can't be thinking about too many things. You can't be on the mound worrying about a 35-inning streak where you haven't given up a double to a left-handed batter or something. Relief pitchers have to get into a zone of their own. I just hope I'm stupid enough.

Interview/Los Angeles
Times, 6-26:(III)8.

WHAT THEY SAID IN 1982

Pete Rozelle
Commissioner, National
Football League

1

Professional sports leagues are at a point where—because of the novel business form of a sports league—every league action, every league business judgment and every league decision can be characterized as an "antitrust" issue. This serves no one's interest. On the playing field, the teams are clearly competitors, but in producing and marketing the NFL product, the clubs are co-producers and co-sellers, not competitors. They are partners acting together in a common enterprise. About 95 per cent of all league revenues are shared among the clubs on one basis or another.

Congressional testimony, Washington/
The New York Times, 1-23:17.

2

[On the court ruling permitting Oakland *Raiders* owner Al Davis to move his team to Los Angeles despite an NFL rule that would have prevented him from doing so]: If the jury's verdict and related rulings of the court are sustained, sports leagues will have been told that league objectives and community commitments are of no legal consequence in antitrust cases. The long-range effects could include a serious erosion of the competitive balance that makes sports entertaining.

San Francisco Examiner & Chronicle, 5-9:(C)5.

Bo Schembechler
Football coach,
University of Michigan

3

[Opposing adding a national playoff to an already long college football season]: I can remember when I started coaching. We had nine games. We went to 10 because we wanted more money. We went to 11 because we wanted more money. We play in a bowl game, that's 12. And now you want us to compete for a national championship. I don't think that's practical. We can do it, but we're going to lose a lot of kids on the way. You can't just continu-

ally compete in football and expect these [student-players] to get a viable degree.

The Christian Science Monitor, 1-13:10.

Tom Seaver
Baseball pitcher, Cincinnati "Reds"

4

What a pitcher tries to do is work on a batter step by step . . . I'm thinking even before he steps to the plate what I want to do. Of course, it depends on the situation—how many outs, how many runners on, what I did against him the last time, and so on. This is the fascinating part of pitching; this is what I love about it. You're challenged and making an important decision every 20 minutes.

Interview, Greenwich, Conn./
The New York Times, 12-13:32.

Jackie Sherrill
Football coach, Texas
A&M University

5

I discipline players harder than other people discipline them, but it's like raising a kid. Every kid does things wrong; it doesn't mean you abandon them. But if they did something wrong and felt they couldn't tell me, then I'd know I'd failed. If a player does not want to have the discipline, the respect and the compassion, then this is the wrong place for him. I don't want anyone around me that isn't willing to pay the same price as I do.

Interview/The Washington Post, 9-15:(D)4.

Sam Snead
Golfer

6

[Golf pro tours were] a lot more fun when I was playing then [in the 1930s]. At night, it was who could get the drunkest. Now, at nine, they're all in bed. I don't blame them. But it's like watching robots.

Los Angeles Times, 5-26:(III)2.

Dave Stalls
Football player,
Tampa Bay "Buccaneers"

7

[On the current NFL players strike]: People have said that we really don't know what we're

(DAVE STALLS)

doing, and that we're following [Players Association head] Ed Garvey like lemmings to the sea. But I believe the players for the most part have a very good grasp of the issues. We also want to maintain our dignity. Owners for the most part think they can bully us or trick us into making a dumb deal. We're not going to. And, sure, the players are being hurt financially by this right now. Probably more so than the owners, because they might be hurt from a corporate standpoint but not individually, like us. But I think they're surprised that we've been so solid—I mean, this has been going on for nearly seven weeks. What I don't think they understand about us is that we have tremendous pride, and that's one of the reasons we've become the best at what we do.

The New York Times,
11-7:(1)26.

Peter Stearns
Professor of history,
Carnegie-Mellon University

1

One of the reasons we [men] are so clearly interested in spectator sports is that they demonstrate virtues that we think men used to have but that most men can no longer utilize in their work or family lives. I do not want to be construed as attacking sports. I am simply concerned about the way in which contemporary adult males have gone overboard in the extent to which they prove their masculinity vicariously by association with spectator sports and by identification with people who perform heroic athletic feats that men, including myself, really enjoy so much. There is a danger in saying, "Okay, we know we are men because we watch real men perform every Saturday or Sunday." Reliance on symbols of masculinity that have become partially outdated creates problems in defining the male role.

Interview/
U.S. News & World Report,
11-22:86.

George Steinbrenner
Owner, New York
"Yankees" baseball club

2

What many people—including many in baseball—don't realize is that the game has changed. Players are making more money than the managers and the coaches. This requires more involvement from the owner to reinforce discipline and team direction. I try to study the psychological aspects of any situation before I get involved in it. Managers don't hold the sway they once did. They need some help. I'm willing to take the heat for unpopular moves I may make. I am certainly not an easy guy to satisfy. Everyone knows that. But I'm down here [at the *Yankee* training field] in Florida trying to put together a winning team. I'm not here to get a suntan.

The New York Times, 3-29:37.

3

[Saying some players don't give enough back to baseball]: You bet it bothers me, and I'm not going to put up with it much longer from some of them. I'm telling you that right now. I've had a belly full. When I look at some of those construction workers in New York, climbing around 20 stories high, working for their bucks the way they do, as hard as they do, and a cab driver eight or ten hours a day . . . and I see how hard these guys work, and then they come out here [to the ballpark], and they pay their good money to see what happened last night, when we [the *Yankees*] got wiped out 14-2, in a lackadaisical performance, that gets to me. I'm tired of the complaining. [Baseball players] should be the happiest guys in the world; they're being paid megabucks for playing a kids' game.

Broadcast interview/"CBS
Morning News," CBS-TV, 8-5.

Chuck Stobart
Football coach, University of Utah

4

Coaching is not a job, it's a great challenge, a different game every week. Freshmen leave as

(CHUCK STOBART)

mature college people and I enjoy seeing the success they have. It's an exciting life. Have you ever stood on the sidelines with 58 seconds left to play, fourth and three inches to go and say, "I know we can make that"? Not many people have had excitement like that.

Interview, Dallas/Los Angeles
Times, 7-13:(III)9.

Chuck Tanner
Baseball manager, Pittsburgh "Pirates"

1

People never look at it that way, but a 162-game season is actually made up of three parts, consisting of 54 games each. While it's nice to get away well during those first 54 games, it isn't absolutely necessary. Mostly it's what a team does during that second 54-game stretch that determines where it is going to finish at the end of the season. If a manager has his pitching and his defense set by then and he's also getting consistency from his hitters, then he can generally count on being a pennant contender for the rest of the year. What you have to remember is that baseball isn't a week or a month but a season—and a season is a long time.

Interview/The Christian
Science Monitor, 6-3:18.

Lee Trevino
Golfer

2

[Saying professional sports players should get paid according to their performance, as in golf]: [Now,] if a baseball player strikes out, he still gets paid. He just goes back to the dugout. I think if a football player doesn't score a touchdown, it should come out of his pocket. If a baseball player strikes out, it should cost him. He should get so much for a single, a double and a home run. And if he makes an error, that costs him $1,000.

Los Angeles Times, 6-9:(III)2.

Ted Turner
Chairman, Turner Broadcasting System

3

[Arguing against baseball commissioner Bowie Kuhn's proposal to impose a 50-mile

blackout on cable-TV telecasts of games in order to protect the financial position of the teams]: [Sports franchises] in general are owned by the wealthiest individuals and corporations in America ... These men need no government handout. That this group needs a government-mandated monopoly is like saying the Arabs need more oil. For the government to further support this industry at the expense of the average fan, by denying the public the availability of cable retransmissions of broadcast games, would be a perversion of the public interest.

Before Congressional subcommittee/
Chicago Tribune, 4-30:(4)6.

Gene Upshaw
President, National Football
League Players Association

4

[Saying football is more of a team sport than baseball or basketball]: I don't care how good the quarterback can throw, a receiver can catch, a line can block. They all have to do it at the same time. It has to work like a Swiss watch.

Los Angeles Times, 10-25:(I)1.

Bill Walsh
Football coach, San Francisco "49ers"

5

[On how to pick a coach]: If you have followed the history of pro football, you have found that owners go through cycles. In one wave, they recycle head coaches fired by their rivals. In another, they elevate chief assistants. And in still another, they go for coaches from the college ranks. The truth is, it's mostly a gamble ... Obviously, you start looking for basic intelligence. Then, in my judgment, you look for a technician. Leadership ability is grossly over-rated. You keep hearing about guys who are great motivators and great organizers. But what you need are great technicians—people who understand what is happening on the field once the game begins and who can react to the circumstances.

Interview/TV Guide, 9-4:15.

Tom Watson
Golfer

1

Kids grow up playing team sports. Baseball, football, basketball—there's always somebody else to help you win. But in golf, you have to learn to win by yourself. That's why golf is the greatest game. You win by yourself. And you win *for* yourself. You hear that winning breeds winning. But no; winners are bred from losing. They learn that they don't like it.

Interview/The New York Times, 7-25:(1)23.

2

I learned how to win by losing and not liking it. You hate to lose and you don't want it to happen again.

The New York Times, 12-26:(1)27.

Dick Williams
Baseball manager, San Diego "Padres"

3

[On "communication" between players and manager]: It's the most over-used word in baseball. When my teams have gone well, it has been said I'm a good communicator. When they have gone bad, it has been said I've lost the ability to communicate. But the truth is, through all of it, I have been my same obnoxious self. People confuse communication with execution. Once a team has been taught to play, it starts losing only because it stops executing.

Interview/Los Angeles Herald Examiner, 7-4:(D)1.

4

My philosophy as a manager has always been pitching and defense, and let the offense take care of itself. Basically I care everything about fundamentals and nothing about individual statistics ... I also don't think you can play this game and win without being aggressive—offensively, defensively, and especially on the bases. Any team that runs as often as we do is occasionally going to take itself out of an inning. But over-all you benefit more by running than you do by always playing things safe.

Interview, Los Angeles/The Christian Science Monitor, 9-20:14.

Dave Winfield
Baseball player,
New York "Yankees"

5

Everyone [in baseball] has a breaking point, turning point, stress point. The game is permeated with it. The fans don't see it because we make it look so efficient. But internally, for a guy to be successful, you have to be like a clockspring—wound but loose at the same time.

Interview, New York, July 18/ The New York Times, 7-19:29.

Dave Wohl
Assistant basketball coach,
Milwaukee "Bucks"; Former
player, New York "Nets"

6

Pro basketball really is a five-man game with much room for variation on the part of the players. But the difficulty has been that the [TV] camera and the announcers tend to overlook the beauty and the skill and the importance of a player setting up either himself or his teammate. Despite what most people think, there is a great deal of coaching and preparation done in the NBA. Some teams are executing intricate offensive patterns, and yet all the camera focuses on is the sacred basket—which is like seeing a halfback race into the end zone without seeing the play or the players that helped make the run possible. Color men ... have not broken down the game enough, have not given enough insight into the role of each player within the team concept.

Interview/TV Guide, 2-6:14.

The Indexes

Index To Speakers

A

Aaron, Henry, 388
Abbot, William W., 166
Abdel-Fattah, Mahmoud, 199
Abourezk, James, 266
Abrams, Elliott, 117, 204
Abrams, Richard I., 388
Adams, Pete, 42
Adler, Mortimer J., 315, 360
Aitken, Jonathan, 266
Albee, Edward, 352
Alexander, Benjamin M., 110
Alibrandi, Joseph F., 27
Allen, Richard V., 302
Allen, Woody, 329
Allen, Zachariah, 110
Alvarez Martinez, Gustavo, 204
Aly, Kamal Hassan, 266
Amadon, Dean, 110
Amaya, Naohiro, 27
Amin, Mustafa, 266
Amory, Cleveland, 368
Anderson, John B., 49
Anderson, Lindsay, 329
Anderson, Martin, 140
Anderson, Sparky, 388
Anderson, William S., 297
Andretti, Mario, 388
Andropov, Yuri V., 49, 117, 239
Angell, Roger, 389
Arafat, Yasir, 266-267
Araskog, Rand V., 27
Arbatov, Georgi A., 117
Arcand, Theodore, 267
Archibald, Nate, 389
Arens, Moshe, 267
Arias Stella, Javier, 204
Armstrong, William L., 140
Arthurs, Alberta, 99
Asner, Ed, 166
Aspin, Les, 49, 75
Assad, Hafez al-, 268
Atkins, Thomas I., 15
Attenborough, Richard, 329
Atwood, Margaret, 15
Auchter, Thorne O., 140
Auerbach, Red, 389
Avnery, Uri, 268

Axelson, Joe, 389
Azenberg, Emanuel, 352

B

Babbitt, Bruce, 99, 178
Bach, Steven, 329
Baker, Howard H., Jr., 140, 156
Baker, James A., III, 141
Baker, Janet, 342
Baker, John, 15
Baker, Russell, 302
Baldrige, Malcolm, 27, 75
Ball, George W., 268
Ball, Robert M., 178
Ball, William Bentley, 99
Baltimore, David, 381
Banowsky, William S., 99
Bar-Lev, Haim, 268
Barnard, Christiaan, 323
Barone, Michael, 117
Barth, John, 315
Baryshnikov, Mikhail, 352
Barzini, Luigi, 11, 239
Batten, William M., 75
Baumol, William J., 75
Baxter, William, 28, 156
Bays, Karl D., 323
Bazelon, David L., 42
Beals, Alan, 193
Beatrix, 117
Becton, Julius, 15
Bedrosian, John C., 323
Beggs, James M., 381
Begin, Menachem, 49, 268-270
Beilenson, Anthony C., 50, 118
Bell, Daniel, 11, 16
Bellamy, Carol, 193
Belli, Melvin, 156
Bellow, Saul, 315, 368
Ben-Elissar, Eliahu, 270
Bench, Johnny, 390
Benn, Tony, 204
Bennett, Michael, 352
Bennett, Tony, 342
Benton, Philip E., Jr., 190
Berendzen, Richard E., 99
Bergland, Bob, 28
Bergman, Ingmar, 297, 330, 353

407

C

Index to Subjects

A

Abbott, Lou, 331:7
Abortion—*see* Medicine
Abscam—*see* Politics: ethics
Academics, 371:5
Acheson, Dean, 119:4
Achievement, 374:4
Acting/actors, 332:3, 333:1, 335:2, 337:4,
   340:6, 353:2, 357:5
  attention paid to, 336:2
  audience, 353:4, 355:2, 355:6, 356:6,
   356:7, 358:1
  auditions, 353:3
  becoming someone else, 332:2, 335:4
  capricious profession, 339:4
  childhood, 332:4, 336:2
  choice of material, 336:1, 339:4
  competence, 353:3
  critics/reviews, 339:1, 341:4, 353:5, 355:1,
   355:5, 357:2
  director, conflict with, 337:1
  emotion, 331:2
  energy, 330:7
  experience, 330:7
  film vs. stage, 335:5, 354:1, 355:1, 355:2,
   355:6, 360:3
  intelligence, 331:2
  listening, 331:1
  makeup, 359:1
  money/salary, 331:3, 334:6, 336:1, 340:1
  narcissism, 337:2
  oneself in role, 336:6
  in opera, 351:5
  "Oscar" award, 334:5
  politics, 166:2, 168:1, 170:1, 333:3
  potential, 353:3
  preparing for role, 338:4
  real world, 335:4
  respect, treatment with, 335:6
  schools, 353:3
  self, presentation of, 337:3
  television, 360:3, 365:1
  typecasting, 336:4
  variety, 337:1
  villains/heroes, 337:6
Advertising—*see* Commerce; Television

Afghanistan, 72:5, 119:3, 123:3, 126:2, 132:1,
  133:2, 136:4, 229:1, 229:6, 234:6, 234:7,
  237:6, 253:4, 262:6, 265:3
Africa, pp. 199-203
  Cape of Good Hope, 231:5
  foreign affairs:
    Eastern Europe, 200:3
    Middle East, 277:1
      Egypt, 277:5
      Iran-Iraq war, 127:6
    Soviet Union, 118:1, 133:2, 203:1
    U.S., 119:1, 121:1, 132:1, 199:4, 200:3,
     203:1
  socialism, 203:1
  See also specific countries
Age, 370:4, 374:1
Agriculture/farming:
  Agriculture Dept., U.S., 28:5
  air pollution, 110:4
  grain sales/embargoes, 130:6, 131:5, 133:5,
   251:1
Air transportation—*see* Transportation
Akers, Karen, 357:4
Algeria, 201:1
America/U.S., pp. 11-14
  challenges, 13:1
  community, national, 13:5
  crisis to crisis, 11:3
  democracy, making world safe for, 11:1
  ethnic heritage/diversity, 13:3, 128:6, 129:1,
   151:5
  expediency/gratification, 396:2
  hope, last best, 13:3
  humor, 12:4
  individualism, 11:5
  limits, 13:4
  melting pot, 102:6
  opportunity in, 11:2, 11:4, 13:4
  progress, 14:1
  renewal, national, 13:1
  sex and money, 12:2
  "upper Americans," 11:6
  values/principles, 12:1
  voluntarism, 13:2
  weakness, exaggeration of, 12:3
American Telephone & Telegraph Corp.
  (AT&T), 28:1

Americas/Latin America/Central America/Caribbean, pp. 204-227
Communism / Marxism / socialism, 222:6, 224:1, 226:2
cooperation of nations, 218:5
democracy, 209:3
dictators, 217:1, 217:3, 217:4
economy, 205:2, 205:3, 211:4
foreign affairs:
Cuba, 200:2, 205:5, 209:1, 209:2, 211:3, 211:4, 217:4, 221:3, 222:6, 223:2, 223:4, 224:1
France, 217:3, 217:4
Nicaragua, 205:5, 211:3
Soviet Union, 133:2, 209:1, 211:3, 211:4, 212:5, 217:2, 217:4, 221:3, 223:2
U.S., 119:1, 121:1, 204:2, 210:2, 211:4, 212:5, 217:2, 217:4, 218:1, 218:4, 219:2, 219:4, 221:3, 221:5, 223:2, 223:3
Monroe Doctrine, 217:1
immigration, 211:4
independence of states, 120:1
individual countries, 222:3
literature, 321:2
nationalism, 210:2
peace/war, 223:5
press, 307:5, 309:4
See also specific countries
Andropov, Yuri V., 120:3
Angola:
foreign affairs:
Cuba, 200:1, 200:2, 200:4, 201:2, 209:2
Namibia, 200:2, 200:4, 202:2
South Africa, 200:2, 200:4
U.S., 199:4, 200:1, 201:2
Antitrust—see Commerce
Antony, Marc, 170:1
Arafat, Yasir, 269:2, 274:5, 279:3
Architecture—see Arts
Argentina:
defense/military:
nuclear weapons, 207:1
U.S. arms sales, 215:3
foreign affairs:
Falkland Islands (Malvinas)—see Falkland Islands
Spain, 205:1, 220:3

Argentina (continued)
foreign affairs (continued)
United Kingdom—see Falkland Islands
U.S., 129:5, 215:3, 217:2
See also Falkland Islands
human rights, 215:3
Arlen, Harold, 351:3
Arnold, Thurman, 39:2
Arts, the, pp. 297-301
agents/marketing people, 298:2
architecture, 298:6
artists as nation's headlights, 298:2
audience, 298:5
avant-garde, 298:3
challenge ideas, 299:2
change, agents of, 297:2
criticism/critics, 300:2
culture, general, 315:1
dissatisfaction of artist, 299:3
fulfillment, essential for, 298:1
germinates by itself, 299:4
government support, 297:3, 300:1, 301:1
National Endowments (U.S.), 297:4, 299:1
greatness, 297:4
iconography, 298:3
immortality of, 300:6
impossible, notion of, 298:4
meaning of, 300:2
national cultural policy, 297:4
neglect of, 300:5
order on world, 321:6
painting/painters, 321:1, 342:3, 344:5, 346:8, 354:4
photography, 299:5
private/corporate aspect, 297:1, 300:1, 301:1
quality of life, 300:1, 301:1
technology, 298:5
transcends transient events, 300:4
what is worth thinking, 300:3
See also Performing arts
Asia/Pacific, pp. 228-238
foreign affairs:
Europe, 232:2
Middle East, 232:2
Soviet Union, 133:2, 229:5, 231:5
U.S., 119:1, 121:1, 232:2, 233:1
Malacca, Strait of, 231:5
See also specific countries
Auden, W. H., 11:5, 343:4
Austria, 132:4
Auto racing, 388:5, 395:4
winning/losing, 394:6
Automobiles—see Transportation

B

Bacall, Lauren, 357:4
Bahrain, 275:3, 279:2
Ballet—*see* Dance
Banking—*see* Commerce
Barrymore, John, 356:6
Bartok, Bela, 347:5
Baseball:
  aggressiveness, 403:4
  All-Star Game, 389:1
  agony, player, 394:3
  black players, 396:3
  Canada, 225:5
  compensation, 395:1
  defense, 392:5
  execution/fundamentals, 403:3, 403:4
  fans, 389:1, 389:2, 390:1, 398:4, 402:3
  flashy players, 388:1
  football compared with, 399:2, 402:4
  free agency, player, 390:1, 395:1, 396:1
  future, 395:1
  hitting/power/home runs, 388:4, 392:3, 397:1
  hurt, players getting, 394:5
  individualist players, 399:2
  managing/managers, 396:5, 397:2, 398:1, 401:2, 403:3
  minor leagues, 399:2
  motivation, player, 397:2
  owners, 389:2, 393:4, 401:2
  pitching/pitchers, 388:4, 399:5, 400:4
  player performance, 401:3, 402:2
  routine, 397:4
  salary, player, 388:2, 389:2, 393:4, 395:1, 396:1, 398:4, 401:2, 401:3
  season length, 402:1
  speed/running, 388:4, 392:3, 397:1, 403:4
  stress, player, 403:5
  strike, player, 398:4
  success, player, 390:2
  team sport, 403:1
  television, 389:1, 402:3
  trading, player, 391:2
  umpiring/umpires, 392:5, 397:3
  clubs:
    Detroit *Tigers,* 398:1
    Houston *Astros,* 390:1
    Minnesota *Twins,* 398:1
    New York *Yankees,* 398:1, 401:2, 401:3
    Oakland *Athletics,* 398:1
    Texas *Rangers,* 398:1
Basketball:
  basics, 389:3
  coaching/coaches, 394:1

Basketball *(continued)*
  college 391:1
  football, compared with, 402:4
  great player, 398:2
  hamming it up, player, 394:2
  high-school, 389:3
  "holding," 389:4, 391:1, 393:1, 394:1
  and marriage, 394:4
  offense/defense, 396:4
  salary, player, 389:5
  shot clock, 391:1, 394:1
  slow game, 389:4, 393:1
  team sport, 403:1, 403:6
  television, 391:1
  three-point basket, 391:1
  teams:
    Kansas City *Kings,* 389:5
    New York *Knicks,* 396:4
Baxter, William, 39:2
Beatles, the, 349:2
Beethoven, Ludwig van, 382:5
Bellamy, Ralph, 365:1
Begin, Menachem, 267:3, 271:4, 272:4, 275:4, 276:1, 278:2, 282:1
Bellow, Saul, 322:2, 363:6
Bennett, Michael, 357:4
Bergman, Ingmar, 359:1
Berlin, Germany, 245:5, 257:4
Bernstein, Leonard, 100:5
Bill of Rights—*see* Constitution, U.S.
Bismarck, Otto von, 252:1
Blacks—*see* Civil rights
Blaiberg, Phillip, 323:2
Bob Jones University, 20:3, 20:6
Bolivia, 223:6
Bonaparte, Napoleon, 363:5, 395:2
Books—*see* Literature
Boston, Mass., 191:6
Boxing, 392:1, 397:6
Bradley, Tom, 18:5
Brahms, Johannes, 347:5
Brazil, 217:2
Breton, Andre, 372:6
Brezhnev, Leonid I., 132:5, 135:7, 136:5, 263:3, 312:1
Britain—*see* United Kingdom
British Broadcasting Corp. (BBC), 364:3
Britten, Benjamin, 347:5
Bunuel, Luis, 329:2
Burger, Warren E., 159:3
Burke, Edmund, 113:1
Burstyn, Ellen, 357:4
Business—*see* Commerce
Busing—*see* Civil rights: education

C

D

Europe *(continued)*
   Eastern Europe, 120:3, 200:3, 250:2, 259:4,
      262:6
      economy, 245:4
   economy, 97:3, 245:4, 261:2
   foreign affairs:
      Africa, 200:3
      Asia/Pacific, 232:2
         Japan, 231:6, 237:1
      Cuba, 222:6
      Egypt, 277:5
      Falkland Islands, 127:6
      Libya, 202:5
      Soviet Union, 120:3, 131:2, 133:2, 262:6
         See also Europe: gas pipeline
      United Kingdom, 254:1
      U.S., 97:3, 121:1, 239:2, 239:3, 242:2,
         243:3, 248:5, 250:3, 254:1, 259:6,
         261:2, 263:4
         See also Europe: defense; Europe: gas
            pipeline
   gas pipeline from Soviet Union, 251:6,
      257:3, 261:5, 265:2
      U.S. aspect, 225:4, 240:2, 242:4, 242:5,
         247:5, 251:1, 252:5, 253:2, 254:4,
         256:3, 256:5, 258:1, 260:2, 260:4,
         262:2, 263:2.
   importance of, 262:5
   medicine/health, 328:4
   socialism, 222:6, 230:2, 240:1
   See also specific countries
Evil, 375:2, 378:2

F

Faith, Percy, 342:2
Falkland Islands/Malvinas:
   Argentine-U.K. conflict, 56:4, 60:1, 60:2,
      60:3, 61:6, 206:3, 206:4, 206:6, 207:1,
      208:5, 210:1, 210:3, 210:4, 210:5,
      210:6, 210:7, 213:1, 215:1, 218:3,
      220:4, 221:4, 224:3, 224:4, 225:1,
      227:1, 254:3, 261:4, 268:5
   Europe, 127:6
   Spain, 205:1, 220:3
   U.S., 204:3, 204:4, 206:5, 212:5, 213:2,
      215:3, 218:2, 219:3, 222:1, 223:3,
      225:2
Family, the, 182:5, 377:1, 377:4, 378:1
Farming—*see* Agriculture
Fame/celebrity, 369:3, 375:4
Fascism, 136:2
Faulkner, William, 320:4, 320:5
Federal Aviation Administration (FAA), U.S.—
   see Transportation: air

Federal Bureau of Investigation (FBI), U.S.—
   see Crime
Federal Communications Commission (FCC),
   U.S.—*see* Television: government
Federal Trade Commission (FTC), U.S.—*see*
   Commerce: government
Fellini, Federico 336:1
Feydeau, Georges, 356:3
Films—*see* Motion pictures
Finland, 240:4
Fischer-Dieskau, Dietrich, 345:3
Fitzgerald, Ella, 351:2
Fitzgerald, F. Scott, 318:1
Florida, 112:3, 159:1
Fonda, Jane, 341:1
Football:
   antitrust, 391:5, 400:1, 400:2
   baseball compared with, 399:2, 402:4
   basketball compared with, 402:4
   Big Ten, 393:3
   coaching/coaches, 390:6, 391:6, 401:4,
      402:5
   college, 393:3, 399:2, 401:4
      national playoff, 400:3
   deranged players, 391:3
   discipline, player, 400:5
   drugs, illegal, 396:6
   kickers, 390:6
   military operation, 395:2
   moving franchises, 391:5, 392:4, 400:2
   officials, 397:5
   owners, 391:5, 392:7, 394:7, 400:7, 402:5
   player performance, 390:7, 402:2
   player quality, 395:3
   players, spoiled, 396:6
   Rose Bowl, 393:3
   salary, player, 388:3, 392:7, 394:7
   scouting, 390:5
   strike, player, 388:3, 392:7, 394:7, 400:7
   team sport, 399:2, 402:4, 403:1
   television, 392:6
   violence, 397:6
   winning/losing, 393:3, 395:3
   teams:
      Chicago *Bears,* 395:3
      Oakland *Raiders,* 391:5, 392:4, 400:2
Ford, Gerald R., 119:4
Ford Motor Co., 29:4
Foreign affairs/policy, pp. 117-139
   aid, foreign, 121:6, 131:4
   adventurism, 118:5, 119:1
   alliances/commitments/obligations, 123:4,
      138:5
   Ambassadors, 122:2, 123:1, 137:2
   assertive policy, 117:5
   asylum, political, 122:5

H

M